Intercultural Rhetoric and Professional Communication:

Technological Advances and Organizational Behavior

Barry Thatcher
New Mexico State University, USA

Information Science
REFERENCE

Managing Director:	Lindsay Johnston
Senior Editorial Director:	Heather Probst
Book Production Manager:	Sean Woznicki
Development Manager:	Joel Gamon
Development Editor:	Julia Mosemann
Acquisitions Editor:	Erika Gallagher
Typesetters:	Jennifer Romanchak
Print Coordinator:	Jamie Snavely
Cover Design:	Nick Newcomer, Greg Snader

Published in the United States of America by
Information Science Reference (an imprint of IGI Global)
701 E. Chocolate Avenue
Hershey PA 17033
Tel: 717-533-8845
Fax: 717-533-8661
E-mail: cust@igi-global.com
Web site: http://www.igi-global.com

Library of Congress Cataloging-in-Publication Data

Thatcher, Barry, 1964-
Intercultural rhetoric and professional communication: technological advances and organizational behavior / by Barry Thatcher.
p. cm.
Includes bibliographical references and index.
Summary: "This book explores the theory and practice of rhetoric and professional communication in intercultural contexts, providing a framework for translating, localizing, and internationalizing communications and information products around the world"--Provided by publisher.
ISBN 978-1-61350-450-5 (hardcover) -- ISBN 978-1-61350-451-2 (ebook) -- ISBN 978-1-61350-452-9 (print & perpetual access) 1. Business communication. 2. Organizational behavior. 3. Intercultural communication. 4. Communication and culture. I. Title.
HF5718.T453 2012
658.4'501--dc23

2011038330

British Cataloguing in Publication Data
A Cataloguing in Publication record for this book is available from the British Library.

All work contributed to this book is new, previously-unpublished material. The views expressed in this book are those of the authors, but not necessarily of the publisher.

I owe much to many colleagues, friends, and families. First, my colleagues, research participants, and friends in Ecuador, Mexico, and the border area have helped immensely, especially those friends who are experienced and adept at dealing with cross border issues. They have demonstrated both cultural sensitivity and culturally appropriate strategies, a balance that is difficult to achieve. And finally, this book is especially dedicated to my colleagues in Ciudad Juárez: may they continue to develop peace, justice, and prosperity for themselves, their families, and their communities.

Barry Thatcher
New Mexico State University, USA
November 2011

Table of Contents

Detailed Table of Contents

Preface

APPROACHING INTERCULTURAL RHETORIC/ABORDAR LA RETÓRICA INTERCULTURAL

This book is a culmination of almost 25 years experience teaching, researching, consulting, and living in intercultural contexts. The writing itself has taken almost three years, and as I write this preface as the last piece of the book (but the first thing the reader encounters), I find myself reflecting upon my bilingual and intercultural situation, and in many ways, wishing the readers could understand this situation better as a way to approach this book. Like many academics, I keep myself busy teaching, researching, and consulting, but this semester has been a bit different. As a "Profesor Asociado" at the Colegio de Chihuahua, a new graduate research university in Ciudad Juárez, Mexico, I have been teaching a ten-week empirical research methods course to the first group of 19 doctoral students. Helping 19 doctoral students design their research methods for their dissertations has been invigoratingly challenging, to say the least. However, my feelings have been rather poignant at this juncture for two reasons. First, I have been working with El Colegio de Chihuahua and the Autonomous University of Ciudad Juárez for nearly eleven years, teaching a variety of methods and pedagogy courses. This cross-border experience has been combined with my four years living and teaching in Ecuador, both of which have greatly enriched and impacted my perspectives on intercultural communication, something that the reader will witness throughout this entire book. Much of this book combines lots of theory with relevant research, and my reflexive, concrete, and lived experience.

However, for the past two years (2009-2011), I have not been able to travel into Ciudad Juárez because of its extreme levels of narco violence, which has earned this city the dubious honor of being the most violent in the world. At the same time, El Paso, Texas, which is right across the border from Ciudad Juárez, had been earning recognition as being the safest city in the United States. Feeling grateful for my relative safety on the El Paso side of the border, but wanting to participate somehow in the reconstruction of Ciudad Juárez, I accepted the invitation to teach this methods class. In September 2011, I nervously crossed the border and traveled to El Colegio de Chihuahua. I was grateful to learn that the violence had really been subsiding to more "tolerable" levels, which I had noticed in the Juárez papers but was anxious to confirm. There, while I was reuniting with colleagues and friends whom I had not physically seen for two years, I noticed two things: that my friends look spent but the same time strong. Then my colleagues began to relate their stories of the narco violence in Juárez. All of them had either witnessed or heard a murder; all of them have known people who had been shot; most of them had been repeatedly extorted; and all of their children or family members know of innocent friends being killed. Many showed physical signs of the emotional, interpersonal, cultural, and social costs of the violence.

But all were totally committed to making Ciudad Juárez a better place to live and not caving into the desperation; they were also very angry and tired of their situation; and most of their dissertations and research address these issues. I felt an amazing strength in them that I will continue to admire and emulate. I am not relating these stories to sensationalize the violence, or awkwardly romanticize Ciudad Juárez, or somehow place this book in a more privileged context. It is simply my situation along the U.S.-Mexico border.

At the same time, however, I think it is illustrative to view this U.S.-Mexico border context as an important introduction or *abordamiento* to the intercultural rhetoric of this book. Although this book does not discuss narcotics trafficking, border law enforcement, and drug related issues (perhaps my next book), it does discuss the great complexities and roles of rhetoric and professional communication in intercultural, global, and border contexts. For example, one of the reasons that the violence in Ciudad Juárez has been subsiding is that Mexican law enforcement has improved their ability to find, arrest, and prosecute narco criminals. (Another reason is that one of the cartels, the Juárez Cartel, has actually won the drug-turf war). One of the main reasons for this improvement in law enforcement is that U.S. and Mexican law enforcement and other agencies have been able to see the narco violence as a cross-border, regional issue, requiring close collaboration in ways not previously carried out. In other words, it's not just a Mexican or U.S. problem, but a joint problem, shared by two closely related countries. There have been significant amounts of cross-border collaboration, training, and intelligence sharing among Mexican and U.S. Federal, State, and local agencies, producing tangible results. It has been a successful example of intercultural communication and collaboration on this issue, not only in the ways the issues are framed, but how the work is carried out. Thus, in spite of all the angry rhetoric among politicians, law enforcement, academics, and community activists, a growing number of border residents are quietly finding ways to improve their communities, especially on the Mexican side. It is the quiet, often subtle, but highly effective intercultural work that I value and hope is exemplified in this book. As I mention frequently, the theory and approaches in this book do not have the fancy heat of most critical theory, but they are surprisingly effective in their reach and application.

This obvious example of the narco wars in Ciudad Juárez, however, has not been a life-changing event for me regarding intercultural inquiry; it is simply a demonstrative but poignant and current life experience that contextualizes me and this book. In my 25 years of intercultural experience, I have approached intercultural inquiry with the same need to balance the sophistication and complexity of intercultural rhetorical theories and methods with the need to make them work on the ground. And if making the theories and methods work better requires revising or even throwing out privileged and predominant approaches in rhetoric and professional communication, then so be it. Thus, achieving this balance is very important for developing theories and methods that are successful at explaining, researching, and intervening appropriately in intercultural rhetorical situations. In other words, praxis is critical to the approach to this book. For example, more than half of the book examines the concrete practices of intercultural rhetoric and professional communication, including policies and procedures documents, distance education course designs, and teaching intercultural and global writing.

Second, like the border situation, an important ramification for this praxis approach is situating ethics in the intercultural situation. As this book delineates, far too many academic theories of intercultural rhetoric and culture are developed by ivory-tower academics who have neither the courage to get meaningfully involved, nor the theories, methods, and experience to understand how they might work towards a more just and peaceful society. This is demonstrated rather strongly in one point of the book when I describe the event of U.S. academics erecting pink crosses at New Mexico State University to protest the problems of female murder in Juárez. From the perspective of my Ciudad Juárez colleagues, it was very easy for U.S. academics to erect an abstract symbol by people who are safely away from the violence; it's much more difficult to develop meaningful interventions in the political, judicial, police, and transportation agencies. Likewise, just as I was reading an article on the postmodern conceptions of ethics in our field on one day, and then the next day, while returning home after teaching the methods course at El Colegio de Chihuahua, I began discussing with my colleague about the nature of evil. This wonderful colleague is designing her dissertation to research the ways that Ciudad Juárez youth are re-configuring and re-constructing symbols of violence. Although steeped in all the critical theories of myth, symbolism, postmodern culture, and violence, this colleague has no trouble delineating the nature and structure of evil in our border area, which cannot be reduced to a hermeneutical textual interpretation. Similarly, this book, following the work in human rights and intercultural relations, argues for the need to see the ethical dimensions of intercultural situations. In other words, like my cross-border experience, this book demonstrates a strong exigency for placing ethics in conjunction with tangible and workable approaches for intercultural inquiry. For example, Chapter Eight explicitly draws connections among legal traditions, ethics, and rhetoric, showing how the UN's *Declaration of Human Rights* is a viable model for discussing intercultural rights, despite its 60-year age. It then extends this discussion to new communication technologies such as Google Earth.

Finally, one of the joys and frustrations about working across two languages and cultures is the desire to use a word in one language that does not have an equivalency in the other. In writing this preface, I am facing the problem with finding the English equivalent of the Spanish verb *Abordar*, which has two meanings: to board a plane/train and to begin addressing an issue. One of the most pleasurable parts of teaching the methods course in Ciudad Juárez is that most of the students have enough knowledge of English to aid in translations problems. I teach the course entirely in Spanish, but often, when I try to teach difficult concepts, I will use English words and syntax; then, together, we begin comparing and constructing the meanings in both English and Spanish. This rich bilingual approach is very effective in many ways. Outside this bilingual context, however, it is not as easy. Thus, I would love for my readers to approach the reading of this book using the Spanish *abordar*, that is, your reading is both an introduction to and ride with its theme, intercultural rhetoric and professional communication. It is my attempt to present intercultural inquiries, but it is fraught with problems of translation—translating my experience into something you can understand well. Often, I use binaries or oppositions to explain cultural differences and similarities, but these are meant to demonstrate predominant, bell-curve approaches, which become a translation problem for many steeped in derridian poststructuralism. However, if the reader can grant me the patience of my Ciudad Juárez students and try get beyond the cultural attributions that are presented in bell-curve opposition and focus on understanding this approach as a frame, then perhaps we can see the benefits of the approach. This ride should be constructive (I hope), filled with surprises, chaos, challenges, and probably annoyances. I am hoping, however, you enjoy the overall trip.

In giving this translation metaphor as an entrée into the book, however, I want the readers to rest assured that intercultural rhetoric and professional communication cannot be reduced to translation issues; in fact, often when my Juárez doctoral students and I wrestle with important concepts of empirical methodology, we conclude that it does not matter whether we are discussing the concepts in English or Spanish; it's much more complicated than that. Translation is an issue in intercultural professional communication, but there's a whole more to it than that. Thus, this the scope of this book ranges from problems of violence and ethics to word-to-word translation, a very large scope indeed. For example, it looks at the structure and presentation of a simple set of instruction but connects that set to very large legal, economic, social, and industrial values. In many ways, the presentation of the different documents, web, or curriculum designs demonstrate that language is just one of the many variable connected to intercultural rhetoric and professional communication.

LAYOUT AND APPROACH TO THE BOOK

This book is organized into three basic parts. Chapter One lays out a comprehensive framework for approaching intercultural rhetoric and professional communication, carefully defining culture, rhetoric, and intercultural rhetoric. Chapter One also explores the ethical dimensions of intercultural rhetoric and the need to revise many contemporary theories and methodologies in rhetoric, professional communication, and cultural studies. Chapter Two grounds that comprehensive framework of theories and methodologies in a discussion of eight common variables for intercultural rhetorical research. It first provides the metaphor of the border as an example of these variables and then explores the relation of these variables to patterns of intercultural rhetoric, drawing on the wealth of intercultural research in organizational behavior, linguistics, and international relations. This chapter then exemplifies the intercultural approach by evaluating Anzaldúa's *The Borderlands*.

Chapter Three further grounds this intercultural approach, connecting it to theories of linguistic relativity from contrastive rhetoric, showing how many differences in culture have strong connections to languages. It also discusses the relevance of English and Chinese as world-dominating languages. Chapter Four is parallel to Chapter Three because it argues for the influence of a very important intercultural medium, but instead of connecting the intercultural variables to language, it connects them to technologies. It constructs the theories of fit, reciprocity, and kairos in intercultural contexts, showing how some communication media fit better cultures with certain predominant values, that this fit corresponds to distinct reciprocal relations of culture and rhetoric, and that the timing of discourse events needs to be grounded in the predominant values of the context.

Chapters Five through Ten apply these comprehensive theories to six specific intercultural professional contexts: website design and analysis (Five); organizational behavior (Six); distance education and e-training (Seven); law and legal traditions (Eight); health literacy and communications (Nine); and instructions and manuals (Ten). Chapters 11 and 12 connect the theory, methods, and applications discussed in Chapters One-Ten to the classroom and research. Chapter 11 lays out a set of core competences and criteria for designing and conducting intercultural education and research.

Chapter 12 demonstrates my approach to intercultural education, detailing an intercultural writing class I routinely teach at New Mexico State University; and it explores the cultural approaches to three predominant U.S. textbooks in writing and professional communication, showing educators how to denaturalize their approaches to intercultural and global writing. Finally, the Conclusion discusses issues of translation, globalization, and localization, showing how to use the book to carry out these important services for intercultural contexts.

CHALLENGES AND CONTRIBUTIONS

As will be evident, the challenges to writing this book have been many. First, the methodological and theoretical challenges are unique, from my perspective. Despite the rich, detailed, and rigorous approaches of intercultural research in organizational behavior, anthropology, law, and intercultural communications, many scholars in rhetoric and professional communication are usually not familiar with this history or their familiarity is obtained through superficial and uninformed, often second-hand critiques of that very research and history. Thus, much of the current intercultural research in rhetoric and professional communication either ignores this body of research and rather superficially examines intercultural issues such as translation of currency, numbers, and symbols or issues of technology access and use. Or even worse, some research examines intercultural situations without the benefit and experience of this long history, committing serious and often ethnocentric errors in theories and methodologies. In other words, the academic community in rhetoric and professional communication seems not prepared to work across cultures. Hopefully, this book will provide some starting points and useful contributions. Regardless of whether the reader agrees with my approaches, I hope he or she at least can engage the issues that I believe are worth engaging. These issues seem to revolve around the nature of culture, language, social constructions, and all the institutions involving intercultural encounters, globalization, and intercultural relations.

Secondly, another re-occurring issue throughout the book is my argument that many U.S. scholars in rhetoric and professional communication relentlessly denaturalize approaches to culture, writing, and communication, while their foundations for doing so are based on U.S. cultural values of individualism, universalism, low-context communications, specificity orientation, and other U.S. values. In other words, these scholars do not denaturalize the very methods and assumptions they use to denaturalize rhetoric and culture. Consequently, many of the current approaches in rhetoric and professional communication presuppose basic rhetorical assumptions such as author-audience relations, need for information, document or communication organizational strategies, and stylistic preferences that are based on U.S. cultural values and are at best unworkable in other cultural contexts. This ethnocentrism extends to the valuing in U.S. theories, methods, and curriculum of certain rhetorical objectives (such as U.S. democratic purposes), rhetorical processes (co-constructive of meaning), and rhetorical relations in the context (U.S. organizational behavior). This ethnocentrism is perhaps ok in U.S. contexts, but across cultures, it causes all sorts of problems. These critiques will seem to most unduly broad, but perhaps in the light of this book are not too much of a stretch.

One of the most significant problems of this U.S-centric approach, which this book soundly engages with, is the penchant for much current theory to valorize the local-only approaches to culture and communication. Based on U.S. versions of poststructuralism and postcolonial theory, many of these local approaches are finding their ways into intercultural theory, which present problems of ethnocentrism and poorly developed methods and inquires. Thus, as I explain elsewhere (Thatcher, 2010), despite a strongly emerging and complexly formed globalization, much research and theory in rhetoric and professional communication still rely on outdated critical and cultural studies models that are based on local approaches. Not surprisingly, using local approaches for global inquiries presents serious problems, including ethnocentrism, methodological aporia, poorly theorized global-local relations, ignoring large-scale variables (such as global markets, outsourced manufacturing, and law), and unworkable ethics. Thus consequently, professional communication scholars need to carefully re-develop these theories and methodologies to work successfully in global and intercultural professional contexts. This book provides a framework for doing so.

Finally, this book is both detailed and exhaustive on the other hand, and sketchy and abstract on the other. The first four chapters concretely and comprehensively lay out the theories and methodologies of intercultural inquiry for professional communication, based on extensive research, theory, and experiences. Chapters Five through Ten, however, sketch a broad framework for understanding how rhetoric works in the specific intercultural rhetorical contexts such as website designs and health communications. Thus, while Chapters One-Four are carefully crafted theoretical and methodological pieces, the application pieces in Chapters Five-Ten are much more exploratory, trying to bring together rather disparate bodies of theories and methodologies and make some coherence places and points for further inquiry. Unfortunately, many of these application chapters are based on my analysis of intercultural rhetorical contexts without the benefit of a more developed body of research. Chapters Eleven and Twelve are based on some theory and research but mostly my long experience teaching intercultural rhetoric and writing. But that's where the theory and research in intercultural professional communication are. Thus, the frame of the book models the state of inquiry of our field of intercultural rhetoric and professional communication. Ojalá que el libro sea el medio para avanzar este estado de investigación.

Barry Thatcher
New Mexico State University, USA

Chapter 1
Approaching Intercultural Rhetoric and Professional Communication

ABSTRACT

This chapter defines professional communication in intercultural contexts. It presents a workable model of culture, connects that model to rhetoric, and provides a method to analyze rhetorics and cultures in intercultural contexts. It also contextualizes the model of intercultural rhetorical research in prevailing paradigms of rhetoric and professional communication, strongly criticizing the local-only and ethnocentric modes that are so in fashion. It then presents a global model of rhetorical inquiry.

INTRODUCTION TO INTERCULTURAL RHETORIC AND PROFESSIONAL COMMUNICATION

As most major intercultural scholars and theorists have argued, the purpose of an intercultural inquiry is to understand relevant cultural similarities and differences across groups of people (Hofstede, 2010; House, et al, 2005; Hampden-Turner & Trompenaars, 2000; Stewart & Bennett, 1991). This argument is fairly simple in principle, yet profoundly complex in practice, especially for professional communication, the topic of this book. First, what does it mean to *understand* cultural differences and similarities? Is knowing superficial cultural differences such as those explained in lists of cultural taboos (see for example, McGraw Hill's series Kissbowshakehands.com) a sufficient understanding of a target culture? As this book explains, approaching an intercultural situation with a list of do's and don'ts probably does more damage than good. Rather, it is much more effective to understand how deeply held, but hidden values structure a variety of activities, essentially explaining the *why* and *what* of social behavior. Second, what are *relevant* cultural differences? For example, some cultural scholars like to focus on unique fragments of pottery, weapons, and clothing that are often part of museum displays (Bakhtin, 1990), while others focus on popular culture or consumerism and transnational organizations (Hall, 1997). However, as this book explains, the most relevant cultural differences and similarities for intercultural professional

DOI: 10.4018/978-1-61350-450-5.ch001

communication are those generalized or bell curve patterns of everyday activities (Bourdieu, 1999), such as lining up at a bank, giving instructions about a new technology, negotiating a business transaction, or enforcing policies and procedures in an organization.

The next question focuses on how we define and operationalize the relations between *culture* and *rhetoric.* Does rhetoric simply reflect cultural values, or does it refract them based on mutually constructive relations? Or can rhetoric have the power to reconstitute cultural patterns or vice versa? In other words, how do rhetoric and culture influence or act upon each other? These questions are critical for intercultural inquiry because they directly assess human agency, rhetorical purpose, and corresponding ethics. As this book explains, *culture* is a group of people that share a common sense of humanity, epistemology, ideology, and rhetorical patterns (Berlin, 1987). This shared definition of humanity creates a distinct epistemology, both of which imply an ideology or appropriate social behaviors; and all three encourage corresponding rhetorical patterns. The rhetorical patterns then mutually influence and inscribe themselves upon the previous three categories.

This view does not assume that individuals within a culture share a unified relation to their values or that cultures are monolithic and static, two attributions that some in rhetoric and professional communication (Hunsinger, 2006) level at intercultural research based on their innumeracy or inability to distinguish a cultural generalization from a cultural trait (Pinker, 2003). Rather, it assumes a bell-curve distribution of these values, that is, a group of people are distinguished as a culture, because a majority in that group shares the same values, but there are always exceptions on both sides of the bell curve. This is precisely the approach of most intercultural researchers such as Hofstede (2010), Hampden-Turner and Trompenaars (2000), House, et al (2005), and many others. Further, this sharing of values can happen at many levels and is not necessarily at the nation-state level such as Mexico and the United States, which is the focus of many researchers and this book. However, the approach articulated in this book can easily be operationalized at a variety of smaller levels such as institutional, disciplinary, regional or even local. In fact, this intercultural approach is highly effective at the personal and local level because it shows how an individual draws on a variety of rhetorical strategies for daily sense-making activities.

Next, how do we compare *similarities and differences* across groups of people? Do we compare the groups at the personal, local, regional, ethnic, linguistic, or global level? This is the problem of the one and many or of the level of analysis that we use to categorize people according to cultural constructions. As this book explains, most contemporary rhetorical and professional communication approaches (Scott, Longo, and Willis, 2007; Herndl & Nahrwold, 2000; Sullivan & Porter, 1998) are unreflexively entrenched in the local and individualistic theories. Using the individual or local, however, as a unit of analysis for cross-cultural comparison presents many significant problems, including ethnocentrism, invalid gathering and analysis of data, poorly theorized global-local relations, ignoring large-scale variables (such as global markets, outsourced manufacturing, and law), and unworkable ethics (see Thatcher, 2010a). Instead of looking at the uniqueness of one group and then moving to another, intercultural researchers need to recognize similarities of groups of people (at a variety of levels) based on shared contexts and then consider differences within the framework of these similarities (see Thatcher, 2010a; Thatcher, 2001; Jarvis & Pavlenko, 2008; Hofstede, 2010; Lucy, 1996; Bhawuk & Triandis, 1996). This process works against analyzing a second culture using the cultural constructs of the first culture (Bhawuk & Triandis, 1996) because it establishes a common ground in which to operationalize and compare the variables of both cultures in the intercultural context (Lucy, 1996).

And finally, what does *professional communication* across cultures mean? Professional communication is a broad term that includes:

- Technical communication such as proposals and technical specifications
- Management and business communication such as reports and feasibility studies
- Internet, email, video, distance education, Web 2.0, social media, and other "new media" communications for professional contexts
- Legal communications such as intellectual property, joint ventures, and policies and procedures
- Instructional materials such as how-to manuals, on-line tutorials, and technology literacy
- Medical, environmental, health, and other forms of electronic, print, and oral communications
- And many other communications in government, industry, and non-profit organizations.

This is the scope of this book. What is not included in this book is the reason for examining professional communication across culture and technologies. Perhaps the author is presumptuous and simple minded in believing that the need for understanding and improving intercultural communication in professional contexts is painfully obvious. If the reader needs further justification, he or she may simply contemplate how global our world has become and how important effective and ethical cross-cultural professional communications are for continued sustainable and peaceful development of our world.

The rest of this chapter follows the original inquiry articulated in the introduction. It first develops a theory of intercultural rhetoric and professional communication. Next, it explores the historical nature of the local approach and its corresponding problems for intercultural inquiry. Finally, the chapter presents nine needed developments for theory, practice, and methodology in intercultural professional communication contexts.

DEVELOPING A MODEL OF INTERCULTURAL RHETORIC

This section lays out a model of intercultural rhetoric, which will be operationalized in professional contexts in Chapters 3-12 in this book. It answers the questions of what it means to understand culture, what are relevant definitions of culture for professional contexts, and how to connect culture to communication patterns. It also provides the etic or universal frame for comparing rhetorics across cultures. This section develops the intercultural rhetorical model drawing on four related bodies of work: (1) rhetoric, writing, and cultural studies, most notably James Berlin (1987); (2) intercultural organizational theorists such as Hofstede (2010) and Hampden-Turner and Trompenaars (2000); (3) discourse theorists such as Bakhtin and Bourdieu; and (4) theories and methodologies from English as a second language studies (ESL).

First, Berlin (1987), a U.S. rhetorical scholar grounded in Neo-Marxism, cultural studies, and poststructuralism, shows how deeply rooted cultural, social, historical, political, and economic values correspond to a distinct rhetoric or communicative expectations and patterns. Unlike many theorists, however, who simply assume the close correspondences between culture and rhetoric, Berlin analytically frames the rhetoric-cultural relations using a four-part model. The first part is the definition or conception that a culture develops of the self or human being. This conception of the self, in turn, constructs or reinforces distinct thinking or cognitive patterns, and these cognitive patterns construct appropriate social behavior. All three of these categories—conception of the self, thinking patterns, and social behaviors—correspond to distinct rhetorical patterns. And finally, the rhetorical patterns themselves simultaneously reinforce or re-create the previous three categories. Table 1 demonstrates this process and relationship:

For example, as explained in Chapter Two, two critical differences surface from defining the self as essentially independent from others, or as interdependent and collective. Cultures that see the self as essentially independent usually valorize analytical and objective epistemologies and competitive and individualistic social behaviors. This sense of self, thinking patterns, and social behaviors correspond to communication patterns that are direct, overtly argumentative, personal, analytical, and objective. Cultures that see their self as inextricably connected to others and interdependent tend to valorize particular or more contextual and relationship-based thinking patterns; consequently, their social behaviors reflect their collective sense of self and thinking patterns. Finally, the collective sense of self thinking patterns and social behaviors strongly correlate and reinforce a rhetoric that is more holistic than analytical, indirect, hierarchically structured rather than agonistic, interpersonal rather than personal, and more overtly political than objective.

This rhetoric-culture model can then be integrated into an intercultural layered or onion model, which was first explained by Trompenaars (1994), but I have revised and expanded using Berlin's four categories. As shown in Figure 1, the center of intercultural rhetorical theory is the definition of the self.

The second layer moving outward is the epistemology; the third layer is the ideology; and the fourth layer is the rhetoric. As one strength, this onion model shows that only the outer two layers (social behaviors and rhetorical patterns) are empirically observable while the inner two layers are implicit. In addition, each inner layer structures the outer layers, while the outer layers continuously restructure the inner layers in a mutually constructive process much as described by Bourdieu (1999) and Bakhtin (1990). In other words, the same logic or pattern appears across all four layers. As a result, we can observe the social behaviors and the rhetorical patterns, and from most patterns we can infer the epistemologies and definitions of the self. In other words, as explored by many ESL theorists and in Chapter Three, the writing patterns are a surface manifestation of deep but implicit cultural values (Connor, Nagelhout, & Rozycki, 2008).

This model is particularly relevant and valid for intercultural rhetorical theory. First, as will be shown later in this chapter, each one of the four parts forms a nice "etic" or universal frame for comparing cultures, drawing on the large body of existing intercultural research. Second, the onion model becomes an effective way to link current research in intercultural studies to intercultural rhetorical patterns. For example, as shown in Chapter Two, much intercultural research has already assessed comparative definitions of the self (I/other), thinking patterns (universal-particular, specific-diffuse, and time frames), and

Table 1. Model of Culture and Rhetoric

Model of Culture & Rhetoric Relationships						
Sense of Self	→	**Thinking Patterns**	→	**Social Behaviors**	→	**Rhetorical Patterns**
Definition of a human being.		The appropriate lens to the world		Valuing of distinct social behaviors.		Patterns that logically link people with thinking and social behavior.
View of the self in relation to others.		How to divide up and categorize phenomena such as cause and effect.		Relative worth of and way of social structure.		Patterns that seem natural to and reflect self, thinking, and social behavior.
Evaluation of the worth of a self		Persuasive logic.				

Figure 1. Onion Model of Rhetoric and Culture

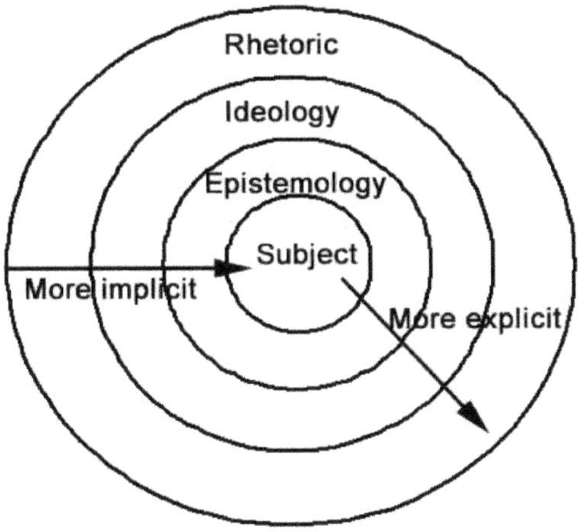

social behaviors (achievement-ascription, context in communication, and power distance). Thus, intercultural rhetorical researchers can connect these first three elements to rhetorical and communication patterns, which I have demonstrated in Chapters 3-12 of this book.

Third, this model is particularly effective for intercultural rhetoric because it shows how tacit or unconscious values systems are related, and how and why they surface in communication patterns. This is what many intercultural scholars have labeled as the iceberg theory (Hoft, 1995): Only 10% of an iceberg shows above the water, with the remaining 90% below the surface. Likewise, the communication patterns are usually the only tangible manifestation of deeply rooted, yet hidden conceptions of the self, thinking patterns, and social behavior, and thus, a miscommunication is not simply an improper transfer of information. A miscommunication implies a deviation from the target audience's conception of humanity, of thinking, and of appropriate social behavior. For example, as I have often experienced in Latin America, a person coming from an individualistic culture (such as the United States) will most likely draw upon direct, more objective and analytical, and openly agonistic communication patterns, which are not only misunderstood by those from more collective cultures, but are deeply offensive because they contradict the interdependent and collective self, thinking patterns, and social relations. Thus, a miscommunication can strike a discordant chord at the very essence of the deeply embedded cultural values of the target audience.

For intercultural rhetoric researchers, this connection among the four layers is important because we can observe the social behaviors and the rhetorical patterns, and from these patterns, we can infer the epistemologies and definitions of the self. Consequently, we can infer the implicit inside layers from the explicit outside layers of social behaviors and rhetorical patterns. For example, we can understand the conception of the self or epistemology based on the observable social or rhetorical behaviors. This inference, connecting the explicit to the implicit values, is critical in developing intercultural competence. However, the rhetorical patterns are much like genres—oversimplified patterns that belie the complexity of the cultures that create them. Thus, we must not equate the generalized patterns with the behavior of the culture that is responsible for those patterns, a deductive stereotype that is discussed in Chapter Two.

Now that this basic model is in place, I want to define and operationalize each of the four elements of the model carefully as they are central to the overall approach of the book.

THEORIES OF SUBJECTIVITY AND HUMANITY

As a foundation of an intercultural rhetorical theory, this book defines the self from a variety of cultural and sociological theories. Although a number of cognitive studies have shown strong evidence for human universals (Pinker, 2003), this book will focus on the social and cultural definitions of the self, or, as the intercultural model articulates, the definition of the self is a product–and reproducer– of the culture's prevailing epistemology, ideology, and rhetoric. This definition of the self rejects the view that the self is the autonomous, independent product of its own rational or natural thinking and consciousness. Instead, the self is intimately connected to the social context, including its relation to the economic system and cultural system, as explored by wide variety of discourse theorists such as Bakhtin (1990; 1993), Bourdieu (1999), Foucault (1972; 1979), and others. This argument also ties the subject or the self to formations of power and domination, articulated by many in the critical studies movement such as those coming from the Frankfurt school. It is critical to view the self as tied to the social context, because if the self is autonomous, culture would indeed be reduced to McDonald's, or Hollywood, or fragments of pottery.

Although this social definition of the self is critical to intercultural rhetoric, it is important to point out that the evolution of this social theory from the poststructuralist camp is problematic for many reasons. As seen in the latter works of Barthes (1972), Baudrillard (1983), Derrida (1998), Jameson (1990), Foucault (1972; 1979), and Deleuze & Guattari (1987), the self in poststructuralist and postmodernism is thoroughly social, yet it is also defined is a chaotic, fragmented, pastiche of social forces with little integrity and coherence and little or no agency. The first problem with this fragmented subject is actually a theoretical problem: if history, discourse patterns, and social formations are the key components of the self or subject, then people who share the same language, discourse patterns and history share the same subject formation and hence a certain coherency or integrity across many people. Further, as explained in Chapter Three, if language encourages or predisposes thinking patterns, an argument known as a Sapir Whorf hypothesis, then there is a significant amount of consistency and coherence across groups of people who share the same language, despite the vehement arguments to the contrary by many postmodern theorists.

As I thoroughly interrogate later in this chapter, another critical problem of this fragmented postmodern self is that is has become so entrenched in the local view that it does not enable the comparison of cultures. Further, and paradoxically, the postmodern view of humanity closely resembles the independence of individualistic cultures; and perhaps, because of its extremism, the postmodern view of the self has now become a romantic or platonic view because it strongly encourages a unique view of each human being or the snowflake view of humanity. Thus, I situate much of western/U.S. postmodernism in U.S. individualism. Finally, if all humans are incoherent fragments of rationality, there can be no discussion of agency and ethics across culture, and very problematic issue for human rights discussions, and a point that deserves careful attention.

Consequently, a key component of this definition of the self is a sense of agency, albeit complicated and contextualized. If we merge the human agent so completely into social context, we cannot explain the accountability, or as Bakhtin (1990) explains, the *answerability* of the discourse agent. As many theorists have argued (see Bourdieu, 1999; Tamanaha, 2006, McCormick, 2005; Twining, 2000), the critical error of the local and individual approach is its inability to articulate the difference between the human agent and the social context. Thus, there is no mechanism for social change or ethics. However, a theory of agency is critical, especially in the global context. This book will draw on the theory of culture and agency articulated by Bakhtin who clearly rejects both the idea of a mechanical or deterministic cultural unity and the postructuralist fixation on difference because both extremes work against individuality, creativity, and "answerability" (see, for e.g. Bakhtin, 1990).

To reconcile unity, diversity, and agency, Bakhtin theorizes (1990) that verbal art (or rhetoric) takes place in three related dimensions: the material/physical, cognitive/ethical, and emotional/volitional. To exemplify this approach,

I will setup a cross-cultural comparison of résumés. According to Bakhtin, the material/physical dimension comprises not only the material and economic conditions that surround, for example, the writing of a résumé, but also the physical conditions in which the document is read—at a busy workplace with thousands of applications landing on the desk of the human resource manager. In addition, global, national, local, and organizational economic situations significantly influence the résumé's rhetorical situation. This physical dimension includes both the availability and structures of technology, especially information technology. These physical and material conditions structure the cognitive/ethical possibilities. For Bakhtin, cognitive simply means decision-making patterns and processes and ethics means how people relate to each other, structured by these processes. In other words, the categories of the résumé (i.e. education, work experience, extra-curricular) are the decision-making criteria for evaluating candidates in the job search. This category should include how information technologies encode cognitive and ethical structures. These previous two dimensions—physical/material and cognitive/ethical—provide certain rhetorical spaces and structures for the third dimension, the emotional-volitional. In this dimension, rhetors can understand the structures and space for their own agency and voice, including technologies, writing genres, expression, and a rhetor's ability to carry out change. In other words, job candidates have a certain degree of space within the résumé genre to express themselves and their will concerning that specific job or position.

In an interesting move, Bakhtin argues that discourse plays an important role in all three dimensions and especially agency or answerability. He argues that discourse structures thinking processes, mirrors corresponding cultural patterns, and provides space for agency and expression (Bakhtin, "Content" 1990). Thus, a group of people that shares certain discourses also shares the cultural patterns of those discourses, despite their other differences. For example, the categories or contents of résumés in the United States are strikingly standardized, despite the great heterogeneity in the United States. According to Bakhtin, this sharing of discourse features creates a rhythm or unity, a dialogized configuration of agreed-upon cognitive processes and accompanying ethical actions (see "Content" 1990). This unity is situated in a physical context and is constantly being dialogized (emotionally and volitionally) and subjected to change by the human agent because it is the meeting point of authoritative and persuasive discourses and centripetal and centrifugal forces; however, such dialogism is permitted precisely because of the dialogic unity—not the heterogeneity. In other words, the categories on the résumé (education, work experience, extra-curricular) are the very necessary starting points or "unity" needed for dialogism. And only through this dialogized unity can people meaningfully participate in and be answerable for the events in their lives (Bakhtin, 1990: "Art;" "Content;" "Author"). In other words, the fragmented, totally localized pastiche does not provide the consistent unity from which a rhetorician can draw to make sense of everyday activities.

This dialogized, ever-changing, and culturally produced unity then becomes the point of comparison with the "unity" of another culture as well as the repertoire of strategies that individual human agent use in their everyday sense making activities. For example résumés in Ecuador tend to share the same categories as résumés in the United States except—among other small differences—there is a strong tendency to have a personal section that communicates age, gender, personal features, and social and family relations, including space for a photograph of the job candidate. These differences (deemed "illegal in the U.S.) are not surprising, given the collective and interpersonal values of Ecuadorian rhetorical traditions (Thatcher, 1999). However, it is only because there are dialogized unities of U.S. and Ecuadorian résumés that this comparison can take place. As such, the unity is not naturalized or essentialized behavior, nor is it autonomous; it is by definition, in flux and contextual, but it is identifiable and comparable, two key attributes of intercultural comparison.

A fourth weakness of the postmodern view of the self or subject, however, is that it is essentially based on 50-year-old environmental or behaviorist theories of social formation, ignoring a great body of research in a variety of fields such as cognitive psychology, linguistics biology, neurology, and others that show with compelling data that some, if not many, cognitive functions of the brain are not culturally or environmentally determined (see, for example, Pinker, 2003). The metaphor for this rejection of the behavioral model is that the brain is hard-wired for certain functions that continuously adapt and evolve. Lately, as explained in Chapter Three, researchers have argued for a synthesis of the nature-nurture dilemma of the brain and society and instead argue for a concept called neural plasticity (see, for example, Pinaud, Tremere, & De Weerd, 2006). Some evolutionary psychologists have developed adaptations of neural plasticity that are highly appropriate for intercultural rhetoric because generally they argue that many human patterns of behavior are simply psychological adaptations that formed to solve recurrent problems in common human contexts (see, for example, Buss, 2005). Pinker (2003), for example, argues that humans have inherited through evolution special mental capacities for acquiring language, making it nearly automatic, while inheriting no capacity specifically for reading and writing, which takes considerable effort to develop. Following this model, this book defines the self as socially composed, yet, as explained in Chapter Two, there are most likely a variety of universal cognitive functions that are general in nature yet get operationalized uniquely across cultures. This approach draws on the behavioral or environmental definitions of the self, yet it retains the concept of neural plasticity.

As explained later in this chapter, this social yet universal approach is critical because the basis of comparison across culture is a series of etics–common human thresholds that all cultures share, and therefore, have to develop reoccurring responses to those thresholds, some of which might be a universal adaptation from evolution. For example, all cultures have to deal with nature, time, relation of the self to others, rules, reputation and achievement, and many others. Thus, the definition of the self that structures intercultural rhetoric is a social self that is intimately tied to the context, including a wide variety of social and cultural patterns; yet this self is not an incoherent mass of irrationality; rather, this self participates in and gets meaning from the reoccurring patterns that are common in that culture (Bakhtin, 1990; Bourdieu, 1999).

Epistemology and Thinking Patterns

Following Berlin's general framework (1987), the definition of the self or humanity closely corresponds to each culture's working definition of epistemology or thinking patterns. Epistemology simply means what counts as knowledge, how that knowledge is acquired, how people ascertain that they have that knowledge, and how people evaluate that knowledge. Closely following the previous definitions of the self, the thinking or epistemological patterns of a culture resemble that culture's economic and social structure, languages and discourse patterns, and reoccurring, typified human contexts. For example, as a variety of Marxist scholars have argued, the economic structure of a culture strongly influences day-to-day decision-making patterns. In addition, many of the decision-making criteria and "logic" of a given culture are contained within—and exemplified by—their discourse patterns (see, for example, Foucault, 1972). Many critical theorists such as Bhabha (1994) argue about the power differentials contained in certain discourse structures especially in the context of postcolonialism. Finally, the geographic, political, ethnic, and linguistic contexts of many cultures or groups of people predispose them to certain reoccurring types of interaction, all of which encourages predominant thinking patterns (Diamond, 2005).

Social Behaviors and Ideologies

Following Berlin's connections (1987), the predominant conception of the self and epistemology of a culture implies appropriate social behaviors or, as loosely defined, ideology. In this book, the term *ideology* does not usually imply the more Marxist or critical definition; rather it simply means the appropriateness of certain behaviors in a given cultural system. Since ideologies are tied to conceptions of the self and thinking patterns, the variety of ideologies is endless, ranging from large social, religious, and educational institutions, to behavior within a family, or on the street, or in any place. The key is that the appropriateness of the social behavior is based on its connections to the definition of the self and thinking behaviors. For example, in an individualistic culture, it is perfectly acceptable behavior to think for one's self and to act independently. However, in a collective culture, this thinking for oneself and acting independently is antithetical to that culture's sense of self and epistemology. In addition, drawing on the onion model of culture, ideologies are usually the first explicit manifestation of the thinking patterns and definitions of the self.

Rhetoric and Communication Patterns

The definition of the self, the thinking patterns, and the social behaviors closely correspond to communication patterns or a rhetoric. These communication patterns can be oral, written, visual, electronic, or corporal. The key is that the pattern of communication matches the pattern of the definition of the self, thinking patterns, and social behaviors. As compared to epistemology and ideology, defining rhetoric is a little more complicated and needs further explanation. As commonly described by Aristotle, Plato, and others, rhetoric can best be exemplified in what is called the rhetorical triangle. (See Figure 2.)

The rhetorical triangle has four elements: the author or originator of the message; the audience or the recipient; the medium such as the book, the e-mail, or the oral conversation; and the topic of the conversation or message. The three sides of

Figure 2. The rhetorical triangle

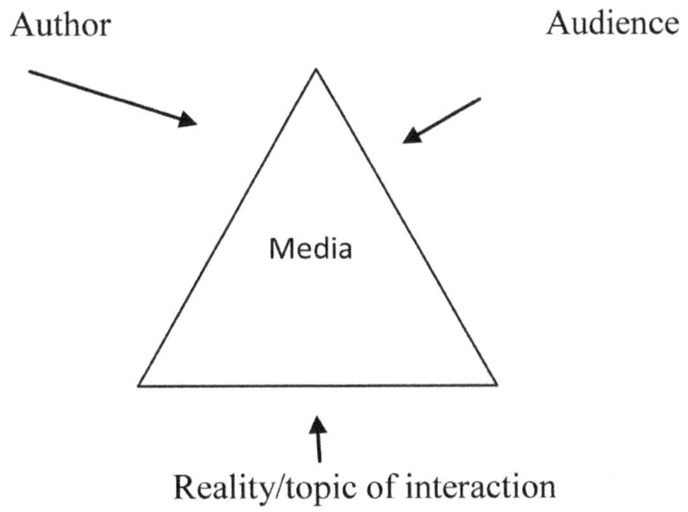

the triangle are mediated by the medium such as the e-mail. As many composition and rhetorical theorists have explained, the four elements of the triangle are discursively developed and shift positions constantly in dialogic interactions, with the author becoming the audience. Further, as Berlin (1987) explains, the rhetoric of a distinct culture both defines the elements of the rhetorical triangle as well as the relationships among the four elements. The definitions and relations of the rhetoric derived from that culture's definition of the self, thinking patterns, and social behaviors.

For example, an individualistic culture where analytical and objective thoughts and social behaviors are valorized develops a rhetoric that is distinct from the rhetoric of a collective culture. In the more individualistic culture, the author is more of the objective and impersonal observer; the audience is more on equal footing with the author and is independent to critically evaluate the information; the topic is rarely connected politically to either the author or audience because of the independence fostered by individualism; and the medium is more or less of an independent mirror that does not interfere with the independence of the author and audience. A collective rhetoric usually defines the author and audience in a political, interpersonal, and social hierarchy where the author is usually in more powerful position, and the audience is in a subordinate position. The topics are usually connected to the group's social and political patterns, and the medium is usually a political choice.

Understanding these close correspondences between the definition of the self, thinking patterns, ideologies, and rhetorics demonstrates what it means to actually *understand* cultural differences and similarities. That is, the rhetorical patterns are surface or explicit manifestations of underlying implicit patterns that run deep and are difficult to change and cultures.

APPROACHING INTERCULTURAL RESEARCH: THE PROBLEM OF THE ONE AND MANY

The previous section lays out a theory of intercultural rhetoric, explaining the intimate connections between culture and rhetoric, which is a necessary foundation for moving beyond the taboo approach or believing that appropriate intercultural adaptations are simply translating surface features of communications. This intercultural rhetorical theory also forms an integral part of the next section, of how to approach intercultural inquiry, which I can best describe as the problem of the one and many (Miller, 1993). That is, how can we appropriately discuss differences and similarities across cultures in ways that acknowledge both cultural consistency as well as personal differences?

This is a tough question, and I have thought about, researched, and experienced it for more than 25 years, including four years in Ecuador and 11 years on the U.S.-Mexico border. In these 25 years, I have also become accustomed to the questions from colleagues, family, and friends about my interest in Latin America and intercultural rhetoric and professional communication. Usually, these inquiries take two forms: Those who have spent a fair amount of time living in other countries usually ask me how I can frame an intercultural inquiry that makes sense of cultural differences while not engaging in ethnocentric or colonialist strategies. These inquiries are formed by rich and extensive experience across cultures yet demonstrate a thorough sense of the uniqueness of the human experience. This is a viable, challenging inquiry, indeed.

The second inquiry is less informed interculturally and more disturbing because of its ethnocentrism. It usually comes from those who have not experienced cultural differences other than the regional and ethnic multiculturalism of the United States or as a tourist in another country. These "tourist" questions usually take the form of "how can you compare rhetorical or communication differences across cultures when everyone is different? A similar question consists of "aren't cultures too complex for comparison?" And finally, though seemingly different, this inquiry usually takes the form of "intercultural differences are not that important; and from my experience, it takes just *a little* getting used to other's cultural patterns." Although seeming distinct, these three questions are grounded in a subjectivity of deep-down similarities accompanied by superficial individual differences, a sign of what Stewart and Bennett (1991) call a deeply developed, naïve, and ethnocentric individualism.

When I first began my intercultural experience and research, these questions surfaced regularly, but I was content to respond to them in light of my interest in Latin America. Now, however, I would like to respond to them because the news has made it very obvious that our current models for understanding international issues are poor at best. This inadequacy must change, and the challenge I articulate in this book is that if we, as rhetoricians, want to take an active part in using our discipline to shape global relations, we have to develop global rhetorical models that work effectively and ethically across cultures.

To exemplify the difficulty in exploring the problem of the one and the many, I will present an example of intercultural professional communication, which is based on a car registration and taxation issue in the South American country of Ecuador that occurred in the mid 1990s (and I actually faced when living there). Like many countries in development at this time, Ecuador imported many of their cars, which made their price almost double compared to prices in the United States or other more developed countries. Further, the salaries in Ecuador were usually much less, making the ownership of cars relatively much more expensive. As I explain more fully elsewhere in this case study (Thatcher, 2001; 1997), cars registered in Ecuador at this time were taxed based on purchase price, and it had been unclear as to when to levy the tax and to whom the money should be paid. As shown below in Figure 3, Letter O (Original version) is a close English translation of an actual letter that was published in 1993 in Guayaquil, Ecuador's daily newspaper, *El Universo*. Letter R (Figure 4: rhetorical revision) is my rhetorical reworking of Letter O to make it fit the cultural and rhetorical values of U.S. audiences (based on my knowledge as a U.S.-born expert in professional communication). As part of my research in U.S/South American professional communication (1997), I surveyed 200 Ecuadorians and 200 US-Americans about their rhetorical preferences, asking them which letter they preferred and why. The surveys carried out in Ecuador were in Spanish and those in the United States were in English.

I present these letters here not to essentialize or reify Ecuadorian or U.S.-American writing patterns but to demonstrate how we can approach the intercultural situation systematically and fairly. Although US researchers might not be surprised to learn that all 200 U.S-Americans preferred Letter R, they might be surprised that 67% of Ecuadorians preferred Letter O, 21% were undecided, and 12% preferred Letter R. After this initial research, I have given this survey to more than 1000 U.S.-Americans and Latin Americans, including many Mexicans in Mexico City and along the U.S.-Mexico border. Never has any U.S.-American preferred Letter O. However, most Latin Americans are split in preferring Letter O or Letter R, and the closer I get to the United States, the more Latin Americans and Mexicans prefer Letter R. (These border patterns are very interesting, but cannot be developed here.)

The goal of an intercultural inquiry is to understand why, in this case, the U.S.-Americans, Ecuadorians, and Latin Americans presented in many ways a unified response to these two letters without discounting the infinite variety of people, regions, and cultures. In other words, if there is so much diversity in the United States, why is there 100% consistency in the response of U.S.-Americans to this survey? And if Latin America

Figure 3. Original Ecuadorian Letter (my translation)

TRANSIT COMMISSION
OF THE GUAYAS PROVINCE

[O]

TO THE PUBLIC

In response to the publication made by the Bureau of Industrial Development on April 15, 1993, the Transit Commission of the Guayas Province unanimously resolved to publish a clarification and/or answer through the means of communication about the assessments and negotiations that this body adopted against the methods of **REGISTRATION** and **TAXATION** of new and imported cars. That in a terse and clear way it was determined that this Directorate which began to function since August of 1992 has been against those procedures that have been utilized for more than twenty years and began to carry out negotiations so that this system did not continue, as is evident in the deliberative nature of the resolution adopted by this organization in an ordinary session on February 15, 1993, in which it was unanimously resolved to solicit the most distinguished Constitutional President of the Republic, Sixto Durán-Ballén to reform by executive decree, according to the Art. 78, Letter A) of the Constitution, the Art. 14 of the General Rule of Tax Law of Motorized Vehicles of Land Transportation, published in the Official Register N. 127 on February 13, 1989, in the sense of which: "The owners of new vehicles will pay the tax within 30 days from the date of acquisition, according to that which is established in the Art. 8 Law 004 and the Art. 52 of the political constitution of the state, that is, paying the annual portion determined from the first day of the month following the month of acquisition of the new vehicle, until the 31 of December of that year, or giving up ownership of the vehicle, this last applicable in the case of residents or naturalized persons that are not dedicated to the selling of automotive vehicles."

What is needed is to respect the proportionality that the constitution mandates without having an answer for the moment to the legal requirements from the Ministry of Finances that was sent in a correspondence dated February 9, 1993. In light of that we are doing the respective consultations to the Attorney General and Inspector General of the government to avoid possible future clarifications, since the civil servants of this Ministry in multiple occasions have verbally indicated to our civil servants to levy taxes for the complete year, notwithstanding the date in which the vehicle was registered.

Clarifying that the Transit Commission of the Guayas Province does not receive not even five percent (5%) of the total value that the owner of the vehicle pays.

The problem first presented itself to our institution from the moment we were converted to an agency for withholding monies which corresponds to the Treasurer and we hope the Finance Ministry will receive tax payments through the province administrators and that as requirement for registering the vehicle, the owner will have to present the receipt for having fulfilled the payment of this obligation to the Treasurer.

José Plaza Luque
President
TRANSIT COMMISSION
OF THE GUAYAS PROVINCE

is so diverse, what can account for the kinds of consistency and variation in the Ecuadorian and Mexican responses to this survey? This is a very complex inquiry indeed, especially in light of the predominant modes of inquiry in rhetoric and professional communication.

When I present this survey to many of my colleagues in rhetoric and professional communication, their responses usually reflect the earlier characterizations of intercultural work. Those who have actually lived outside the United States and speak a second language are usually interested in

Figure 4. Rhetorical Revision of Original Letter

TRANSIT COMMISSION
OF THE GUAYAS PROVINCE

[R]

TO THE PUBLIC

The Transit Commission of the Guayas Province proposes to reform the terms and administration of new car registration and taxation.

The terms of taxation are unfair. The Attorney and Inspector General insist that taxes are to be levied for the whole year, notwithstanding the date the car was registered. As a result, one car owner pays the same tax for a car acquired on December 31 that another owner pays for the same vehicle that he acquired on January 1st of the same year. Because of this inequity, we resolved to solicit President Durán-Ballén to reform the terms of taxation by executive decree.

To be more fair to the owners, we suggest changing the terms to a monthly basis, or as follows: "The owners of new vehicles will pay the tax within 30 days from the date of acquisition, according to that which is established in the Art. 8 Law 004 and the Art. 52 of the political constitution of the state, that is, paying the annual portion determined from the first day of the month following the month of acquisition of the new vehicle, until the 31 of December of that year, or giving up ownership of the vehicle, this last applicable in the case of residents or naturalized persons that are not dedicated to the selling of automotive vehicles."

In addition to these terms, the methods of charging and withholding taxes need clarification. Although the Attorney and Inspector General want our Commission to administer the transaction, they have not given us the legal guidelines. Thus, we suggest for the time being that the Finance Ministry receive tax payments through the provincial administrators.

José Plaza Luque
President
TRANSIT COMMISSION
OF THE GUAYAS PROVINCE

the methodologies and specific patterns, discussing ethical issues of intercultural research and connecting culture to writing patterns. Those who have only experienced the multiculturalism in the United States and are mostly monolingual simply do not understand the research, with most trying to reduce the differences to government bureaucracies, the specific car-taxation context, or the personal style of Jose Plaza Luque, the author of Letter O. Those who are less politically correct comment about the "awful" writing patterns of Letter O and the crisp patterns of Letter R, not understanding the connections between culture and writing. Those who are thoroughly schooled in postmodern and postcolonial thought actually shudder at the comparison because it involves dirty, empirical work and "objectively" comparing cultures. But generally, most of my colleagues are baffled. Thus, I have learned (often by sad experience) that most in rhetoric and professional communication are ill-equipped to think about intercultural research.

There are many reasons for this lack of preparation, including U.S. ethnocentrism, mono-lingualism, and monoculturalism; but others include a very inadequate theoretical and methodological orientation that works against reconciling similarities and differences across cultures. In the rest of this chapter, I explore the problems with this predominant approach in rhetoric and professional communication and then explain nine needed developments, based on this approach, for effective intercultural inquiry. This section draws on my introduction to the new journal *Rhetoric,*

Professional Communication, and Globalization (Thatcher, 2010a), but here, I expand and carefully integrate it into the context of this book.

NEEDED DEVELOPMENTS FOR GLOBAL CONTEXTS: MOVING FROM LOCAL TO GLOBAL

As shown by the often weird responses to the Letters O and R, and despite a strongly emerging and complexly formed globalization, scholars in rhetoric and professional communication still lack viable and productive models for exploring intercultural rhetoric in professional contexts. Among the many reasons are the difficulties in defining globalization (Grewel, 2008) and assessing the roles of intercultural professional communication in its development (Starke-Meyerring & Wilson, 2008). However, the main reason is that much research and theory in rhetoric and professional communication still rely on outdated critical and cultural studies models that are based on local approaches (Scott, Longo, and Willis, 2007; Herndl & Nahrwold, 2000; Sullivan & Porter, 1998). Not surprisingly, local approaches are not well suited for global inquiry.

The reliance on local approaches has a long history and perhaps first initiated as a response to the hegemonic narratives of modernism, including Marxism, capitalism, Darwinism, and others. Lyotard (1984), for example, severely criticize these grand narratives, denaturalizing their social composition and, instead, arguing for local approaches. Deleuze & Guattari (1987) similarly argue against organic narratives of singular cause and effect, especially of late capitalism; and denying any larger global and social patterns, they argue that the best metaphor for the human as a subject and corresponding cultural patterns is the rhizome, which is a stem of the plant that shoots off roots in multiple nonhierarchical and nondualistic patterns. Their example of the rhizome precisely exemplifies this move to the difference and unique and the postmodern penchant for anything but regularity and uniformity.

Derrida (1998) focused attention on the binaries that most western thinking relied on and developed deconstructive methods that rejected binary thinking, and instead, privileged processes of knowledge grafting and textual dissemination, which are fleeting, momentary performances that greatly privileged local approaches but are not sustainable beyond the local situation. His deconstructive methods have been enormously influential. For example, Butler (2006) argues that gender constructions are based on derridian-like local performance, eschewing larger than local narratives for personal gender orientations. Again, the derridian approaches favor slippery identities and cultural constructions based on ephemeral, fleeting performatives.

From a broader sociological perspective, Foucault's (1972; 1979) reverses common cause and effect constructions of identity, institution, knowledge and power, showing how the subject does not create, but is created by, these discourses. This approach opens up space for the larger, global views of discourse and culture, which are highly relevant to globalization and intercultural inquiry, but not surprisingly, most U.S. scholars draw on Foucault to advocate for local approaches (Scott, Longo, and Willis, 2007; Herndl & Nahrwold, 2000; Sullivan & Porter, 1998). Baudrillard's (1983) concept of simulacrum followed Foucault's reversing subject formation, which argued for the pervasive power of media and popular culture to displace stable notions of stable identity and reality and in its place he argues for a local epistemology. Barthes (1972) later rejected his earlier structural inclinations and integrated a more Derridian rejection of binaries and Foucaultian reversal of cause and effect in the context of authorship.

Later, perhaps in the early 1990s, as globalization began to become an issue, many theorists used the turn to the local as a strategy to resist growing globalization of world economies (see, for example, Burbach, Nunez, & Kagarlitsky,

1996). When the former Soviet Union collapsed, it seemed that capitalism had won and nothing could stop the global economy. Thus, without state sanctioned resistance, the only viable forms to resist the problems of global capitalism occurred at the very local level—the Zapatistas in southern Mexico, labor unions in France, students in Britain, and local environmentalists (Tokar, 2009). This turn to the local seemed a necessity since all forms of larger, institutionalized movements were either ineffective or politically suspect.

Postcolonial theory seems appropriate for global inquiry, but it is also prone to grounding itself in local approaches. Perhaps the groundbreaking work for postcolonial theory—although this word was not used—was Edward Said's *Orientalism* (1979) which drew heavily on Derrida (1998) and Foucault (1972) to deconstruct the Euro-centric lenses that were used to describe eastern cultures. Said's influence is remarkably profound, setting the stage for almost every intercultural inquiry after. As explained later, however, the problem with this stage is that no one dares do an intercultural study because he or she will be labeled as carrying out an act of colonialization or Orientalism. Many other significant works similarly drew upon postmodern local approaches to denaturalize views of colonized cultures and bring to light issues of power, race, ethnicity, hegemony, and economic, social, and cultural domination between the colonizer and colonized. More recently, scholars like Bhabha (1994) and Garcia-Canclini (1992) draw on Derridian poststructuralism to deconstruct binary oppositions in postcolonial theory, arguing for complex theories of hybridity across and among cultural formations based on performatives in local contexts.

From a potentially useful approach, scholars in the late 1980s and 1990s begin developing the mode of inquiry known as the New Literacy Studies (Street, 2001), which appropriately rejects the "autonomous model" of literacy (universal-decontextual) and situates literacy in prevailing social and ideological contexts, much of which had a global focus. The following excerpt explains the approach of New Literacy Studies and New London Group:

The multiplicity of communication channels and increasing cultural and linguistic diversity in the world today call for a much broader view of literacy than portrayed by traditional language-based approaches. Multiliteracies, according to the authors, overcomes the limitations of traditional approaches by emphasizing how negotiating the multiple linguistic and cultural differences in our society is central to the pragmatics of the working, civic, and private lives of students. The authors maintain that the use of multiliteracies approaches to pedagogy will enable students to achieve the authors' twin goals for literacy learning: creating access to the evolving language of work, power, and community, and fostering the critical engagement necessary for them to design their social futures and achieve success through fulfilling employment. (p. 60)

On the surface, New Literacy Studies seems perfect for the global approach, for they look at a variety of literacy skills in the broad social and cultural context. In practice, however, it has fallen back on situating literacy at the local and individualistic level. For example, Brian Street's collection *Literacy and Development* (2001) uses only ethnographic studies to explore local literacies around the world, never addressing development issues beyond the specific local conditions. Likewise, Hawisher & Selfe's (2000) collection *Global literacies* explores ten local situations of web use around the world, explicitly drawing on New Literacy Studies. However, despite their goal of theorizing global web literacies, Hawisher & Selfe (2000) cannot connect any person in the ten sites to anything larger than the local situation, which not only fails to define a global web literacy, but is also a validity error because the local is not contextualized in the regional, national, or international web context (Thatcher, 2010b).

Thus, like the postmodern approach, New Literacy Studies is prone to unreflexively embracing the local-only approach, a weakness that Brandt & Clinton (2002) have been criticizing for almost a decade.

In the later 1980s and early 1990s scholars in rhetoric and writing began to draw on these local approaches. Porter's widely influential 1986 article "Intertextuality and the discourse community" drew on most of these local theorists. Berlin's social theories and the social approaches of composition (1987) (Bizzell, 1982) and professional communication (Blyer & Thralls, 1993) similarly moved the field of rhetoric and writing to the postmodern local. Faigley's *Fragments of Rationality* (1992) serves as a nice summary and baseline for the field in this movement. Currently, the New Literacy Studies approaches significantly influence rhetoric and writing, especially literacy studies (Goggin, 2008). Now, most cursory reviews of works cited lists in recent articles or dissertations show a significant portion of the field is founded on these postmodern approaches to the local and difference.

Not surprisingly, the local approach is so predominant that is has become hegemonic, implicitly and deeply structuring many approaches to rhetoric and professional communication and thus, to think otherwise is to not be part of the community (Brandt & Clinton, 2002; Thatcher, 2001). For example, in Johnson-Eiloa & Selber's edited collection *Central Works in Technical Communication* (2004) only four or five of the 32 works do not explicitly draw on local theories and methodologies. Further, even work that attempts to look at intercultural professional communication (Ding, 2007; Hunsinger, 2006) explores intercultural relations using these local, deconstructive approaches.

All these local approaches (whose great complexity is beyond this chapter) strongly reject decontextual, stable, and rational knowledge, subjectivity, and social institutions, which fits perfectly with the intercultural rhetorical model. However, they replace the modernist, rational models with localized rationality, fragmented subjectivities, and local differences, and this replacement has as many–if not more–flaws than the original model, not only for global contexts, but for rhetoric and writing in general. Regardless of whether the inquiry is global or local (but especially for the local), using the local approach presents serious problems of ethnocentrism, methodological consistency, theorized global-local relations, assessing large-scale variables (such as global markets, outsourced manufacturing, and law), and ethics. Thus, professional communication scholars need to carefully re-develop these theories and methodologies to work successfully in global and intercultural professional contexts. The rest of this chapter explores nine critical developments for doing just that.

DEVELOPMENT ONE: MOVING FROM LOCAL TO GLOBAL USING ETIC FRAMES

First, the local approach is not designed to assess cultural and rhetorical interactions beyond the local level and across groups of people, two critical needs for global and intercultural inquiry (Lucy, 1996; Bhawuk & Triandis, 1996; Thatcher, 2001; Jarvis & Pavlenko, 2008; Hofstede, 2010). For example, in advocating their postmodern methodologies, Sullivan & Porter (1998) argue for the local approach, using the analogy of an NCAA basketball game. In this analogy, Sullivan & Porter carefully lay out the details of one women's game at Purdue University and how each of the nine members of their two families perceived and documented the game differently. The rest of their book outlines the localized methodologies based on this one-game approach. This analogy hits home for me because my oldest daughter played NCAA Division I women's basketball, and from many years of experience, I have never seen–nor do I expect to see–the same basketball game. All are highly unique. This is the fact of difference.

This unique, one-game approach, however, also belies or masks the consistency across basketball games or other sports. When I watched my daughter play Division I basketball, I recognized the incredible amount of consistency in her game as compared to my old high school days, the NBA, my son's 8th-grade team, or a pick-up game at our city park. In addition, basketball games are so consistent that distinguishing them from a soccer or football game is remarkably easy, something Sullivan & Porter (1998) never discuss. This internal consistency of basketball as compared to soccer or football is obvious even though all three sports are team-based, use a similar sized ball, have a field that is not that different, and score goals. This consistency is also not grounded in positivism, but rather a constructed methodology such as articulated by Bourdieu (1992; 1999). Bourdieu (1992,) for example, uses the sports metaphors as an analogy for sociological inquiry and argues that the sports *field*[1] is remarkably the same; and the same kinds of *habitus*[2] (abilities, weaknesses, struggles, plays, strategies, and triumphs) occur over and over again. The teams always have different players, coaches, or contexts, but the sport is extremely easy to identify across town, nations, genders, and ethnic groups. This regularity is simply impossible to dismiss, but it is almost never discussed in most current research in rhetoric and professional communication.

Bourdieu's sports analogy reconciles the two facts of sports and society—regularity and difference. Although a sport such as basketball may have remarkable regularity in its field and habitus, each player's cognitive and physical makeup interact with that field in highly unique ways. For example, my oldest daughter is too tall and strong to play as a guard or small forward, but she is not heavy or big enough to be a power center. Thus, she has developed a unique approach, moving back and forth between center and forward positions depending on the play the team is running and who is guarding her. Each game is unique, and my daughter is unique, but the game, its field, and habitus are the same, and basketball is remarkably similar across the globe.

However, since local methodologies rely on the one-game approach, ignoring the comparable consistencies across the games or sports themselves, they cannot situate the sports globally. For example, if I were to compare the sports of basketball and soccer in a global context using the one-game approach, I would examine the details of *a* basketball game, compare these details with *a* soccer game, and then I would try to assess fairly the similarities and differences, but these methods would fail quickly. First, because I started with the basketball game, the details of the soccer game would be seen in light of the basketball game, a perfect example of orientalism. Second, since I did not set up beforehand variables that both sports share, I would face a methodological impasse due to the highly disparate and unique types and amount of data for both games. Third, because I compared only two games, I would not be able to assess ethical issues in performance (maybe I thought that all basketball–instead of soccer–games ended in brawls). Fourth, because I compared only two games, I would not be able to adequately understand performance of the players in light of the sports (Since player X scored only two soccer goals, and player Y scored 22 basketball points, player X is much worse than player Y). Fifth, since I saw only two games, I would not understand how the performance in these games compares to other games at local, regional, national, and international levels. Sixth, since I cannot assess performance beyond the local level, I would not be able to understand how large economic, political, and social structures affect both sports. In other words, the local approach is almost completely inadequate for global inquiries.

Likewise, it is utterly impossible to use the one-game approach to understand Letters O and R. First, using the local approach would mean that I would start, for example, with Letter O;

and thus, the details of Letter R would always be seen in light of Letter O. Second, without comparative variables, I would face a methodological impasse because the amount of highly localized characteristics of one letter would be very hard to compare to the second letter. Third, since I am only comparing two letters, not larger legal and economic issues, especially for developing countries, I would not be able to assess ethical issues. Fourth, because I compared only two Letters, I would not be able to adequately understand how Letter O is situated in the actual local Ecuadorian situation and Letter R in the local U.S.-American situation. Fifth, since I reviewed two Letters, I would not understand how these letters compare to the cultural and rhetorical patterns beyond the local, including regional, national, and international levels. Sixth, since I cannot assess beyond the local level, I would not be able to understand how large economic, political, and social structures affect both contexts.

Instead of the one-game approach, viable global inquires are like comparing the sports of basketball and soccer because global inquiries focus on how different cultures, groups of people, or regions relate to each other, based on sustained interactions and formations (Bourdieu, 1999; 1991). Generally, for this method, researchers need to create and assess variables that the cultures share and then integrate these variables into the local cultures, which, as explained next, is the Etic-then-Emic approach. This is precisely the reason for the intercultural rhetorical model, which uses variables common to all humanity. For example, when comparing basketball to soccer, I could compare the field/court, ball, scoring, typical offensive movements and defensive responses, objective of the games, and rules of engagement. Next, I could examine these variables across of number of games, teams, and leagues. Third, I could integrate this analysis into a global comparison of other sports, including their relations to market structures, politics, finance, and other cultural phenomena. Finally, I could integrate these comparisons into the local cultures. For many reasons, this comparative frame provides not only a valid, ethical, and balanced approach to global inquiry, but it also helps us understand better the local situation. For example, this global framework would greatly help in situating any specific basketball game, showing how the game and its players draw not only from larger, global habitus, but also the local situation and their specific talents.

EMICS AND ETICS AS BASIS FOR INTERCULTURAL INQUIRY

Using the sports analogies highlights the need for a comparative frame for intercultural work, which linguists and anthropologists have developed over the last 60 years, using the etic-then-emic approach. Etic and emic are terms first developed by the linguist Kenneth Pike (1967). Emic derives from the term phonemic and etic from phonetic. A phoneme is the smallest linguistic unit of meaningful sound, depending on language and culture. Phonetic is the smallest unit of language sound that can be made by humans across all languages. For example, English and Spanish speakers (not writers) have different phonemes for the same letters in the alphabet. For many Spanish speakers, the consonants S and C or B and V often sound the same and are used more or less the same in spoken, but not written language. Thus, it is common, for example, to see Spanish signs in stores that have mixed these pairs up, using "serrado" (closed) for the correct "cerrado" or "avierto" (open) for the correct "abierto." Since most Spanish speakers cannot tell a difference between these two consonant pairs, each pair is usually a single phoneme, in other words indistinguishable in spoken language. However, English speakers distinguish between C and S and B and V, so each of the pairs is a separate phoneme forming four phonemes instead of two. This difference between Spanish and English phonemes is a culturally specific difference, or an emic difference, based not on universals but on cultural evolution and use of the two languages.

This "emic" approach has been operationalized in anthropology as "the intrinsic cultural distinctions that are meaningful to only the members of a given society in the same way that phonemic analysis focuses on the intrinsic phonological distinctions that are meaningful to speakers of a given language" (Lett, 2010; see also Lucy, 1996). Thus, only members of a given culture can judge the emic descriptions of their culture or language because this knowledge is insider-based, or only available to those from that culture. In other words, a Spanish speaker would have to learn that the English pairs B and V and C and S are separate phonemes—mean something different as compared to Spanish.

As mentioned, the etic approach derives from the term phonetics, which is an area of linguistics that studies the physical elements of speech sounds and their processes of production, reception, and perception. A phone is a specific speech sound made by a distinct working of the mouth, tongue, throat, and air. Unlike phonemes, phones are not language or culture specific; in fact, any normal speaker of a given language can physically articulate all of the phones available to the human species. Thus, phonetics is not cultural specific; rather it is universal and often explores how different languages utilize phones to form phonemes, exemplifying the etic-then-emic approach.

These emic and etic distinctions developed into competing paradigms. The emic approach argues for the intrinsic incomparability of one culture to another culture, while the etic camp argues for the need to provide neutral frameworks or approaches for comparing cultures. This division focuses squarely on epistemology. Emics argue that knowledge is fundamentally local based and culture specific, while Etics argue that just like possible speech sounds, in the human race, there are similar universals of knowledge and behavior across cultures (see Morris, et al., 1999 for a better discussion of this distinction). Despite these often stark differences, most anthropologists and linguists agree that researchers should use both emic and etic approaches (Lett, 2010; Lucy, 1996; Bhawuk & Triandis, 1996; Morris, et al, 1999). Emic gets at the intuitive and empathic elements of culture and is critical for carrying out ethnographic fieldwork. In addition, emic often produces important variables for later etic hypotheses. Etic approaches, on the other hand, are essential for cross-cultural comparison but need to be qualified with emic details. For example, the intercultural rhetorical model is a nice etic frame that can be contextualized well in emic circumstances. All cultures develop a conception of the self, with accompanying epistemological, ideological, and rhetorical patterns. However, these conceptions vary, often radically, and need to be contextualized in order to understand how they work inside and outside that culture.

Using Etic-then-Emic to Assess the Global

Using the etic-then-emic frame for understanding—and then reconciling—this fact of difference with regularity across cultures is essential to developing an intercultural or global competence. First, this reconciliation allows us to understand the regularities across a specific culture, giving us the ability to anticipate cultural and rhetorical patterns. Second, it also makes us aware of intercultural differences within the culture so that we understand the highly unique behaviors of each individual. Third, it is the large cultural patterns that structure the general rhetorical and communication patterns of a culture. In other words, even though cultures exhibit a wide variety behavior within that culture, that wider variety of behavior is homogenized into the larger rhetorical patterns. In other words, the communication patterns are the much more generalized brodes behavior of the people within that culture. Finally, understanding the broad cultural patterns helps us better understand the meaning of local behavior. For example, if we did not understand the generalized rules and patterns of basketball, we would not know how to distinguish a great play from a dumb play. The larger patterns help us evaluate the local behavior.

Resisting Global Approaches

Unfortunately, looking at the broad cultural and rhetorical differences is a difficult competence to develop, especially for those living in a highly individualistic culture such as the United States, a point explained later. Adding to the difficulty of entrenched U.S. ethnocentrism and local focus, intercultural inquiry requires comparing groups, a method that forces a greater focus on the regularities in a culture rather than uniqueness and differences. Thus, intercultural inquiry focuses on the composition of the *field* and the patterns of the *habitus* of the culture, knowing full well that individual differences and cultural uniqueness do exist; but that cultures—like sports—share values across people and nations. In other words, if we were to compare the sports of basketball and soccer, we could not really focus on individual players, teams, memorable games, etc. Rather, we would look the broad regularities of the field and habitus that are cultural, social, economic, aesthetic, and physical constructs (see Bourdieu, 1991, 1999). This kind of inquiry would allow us to see what the two sports share and do not share, but most importantly, why. Why, for example, do basketball and football share a similar economic "field" in the United States, in distinction to soccer, which draws many fewer fans with much smaller operating budgets and salaries?

Despite these advantages, however, many cultural-critical studies scholars resist the comparative frames. First, it draws on somewhat of an empirical epistemology, that is, of deciding what is comparable before doing the research. As is extensively documented, the cultural studies model inherits a strong distrust of empirical designs, which it defines as "inextricably linked to European imperialism and colonialism" (Denzin, Lincoln, & Smith, 2008, p. 4; see also, Herndl & Nahrwold, 2000). Second, the comparative frame probably hints at objectivity and universality (albeit constructed), which are two attributes that cultural and critical studies scholars historically distrust and are the main reason for their favoring the local approach. Not surprisingly, when I have presented Letters O and R at conferences, I have experienced strong negative reactions from these types of scholars who continually accuse me of gringo imperialism, without knowing my background or experience, by the way.

Rarely, however, do these scholars reflect upon the disadvantages of this local thinking, but when they do, they often revise their positions. When the critical studies scholars Denzin, Lincoln, & Smith (2008) moved from local to global inquiries, they began urging scholars to think that empirical research "does not have to be a dirty word" (Denzin, Lincoln, & Smith (2008, p. ix). Rather, empirical work is essential in the comparative context of "merging critical and indigenous methodologies," but only if done with an appropriate comparative framework, or it can easily "perpetuate neocolonial sentiments" (p. 4). Similarly, as explained later, key critical theorists including Bhabha (2003) and Latour (2003) argue for moving beyond local methodologies in order to understand our global context.

DEVELOPMENT TWO: MOVING BEYOND WESTERN, MONOCULTURAL METHODS

The second development for valid intercultural inquiry is to draw on methods that are designed for intercultural/global inquiry and by more than U.S. and western scholars, a very difficult development given the history of theory and methodology in this area, which privileges the local. Not surprisingly, the great majority of cultural-studies scholars in U.S. rhetoric and professional communication (Scott, Longo, and Willis, 2007; Herndl & Nahrwold, 2000; Sullivan & Porter, 1998) draw upon western approaches to culture and rhetoric, privileging derridian deconstruction and Foucaultain analysis. Further, although postcolonial scholars such as Said (1979) and Bhabba (1994) are contextualized in non-western areas, they are significantly influenced by western scholars such as Derrida and Foucault.

This monocultural genesis combined with the lack of a global framework and a penchant for local views perfectly exemplifies *neocolonialism* (Denzin, Lincoln, & Smith, 2008), *orientalism* (Said, 1979), or *ethnocentrism* (Thatcher, 2001; Lucy, 1996; Bhawuk & Triandis, 1996; Stewart & Bennett, 1991), all of which mean viewing other cultures in light of the first or predominant culture or not appropriately unmasking the lenses of inquiry, thus favoring one culture over the other. The intercultural research literature is replete with examples of this type of U.S. colonialism (Stewart & Bennett, 1991).

For example, when viewed from the context of U.S. universalism, individualism, and level of economic development, the solution to the car tax problem in Ecuador is to equally enforce the law, regardless of circumstances. But this oriental approach, for example, does not consider the different levels of legal infrastructure and development and social and economic inequalities in Ecuador as compared to the United States. Or a similarly neocolonial approach would assume that Letter O is simply the local Ecuadorian context, reflecting Jose Plaza Luque's unique writing style, which blatantly disregards the larger cultural and rhetorical situation of Ecuador.

From another perspective, one of the key ethnocentric approaches of these U.S. and western theorists it to privilege a textual, written view of the world, including ethics, something that is being challenged by the new media (see Chapter Four) but is still significantly in place. For example, as explained later, the predominant view of ethics from the local approach is based on a textualized, derridian hermeneutic (Sutch, 2001, p. 20), which is not applied well in cultures that do not presuppose the same roles for writing. For example, as I learned quickly in my research in Ecuador (Thatcher, 2000), the textual or written view of the world is based on western and U.S. cultural and legal values, mainly, common law legal systems and cultural values of individualism, universalism, specific orientation, and low context communications. Letters O and R speak very clearly of this orientalism because Letter O is written to be heard, based on the predominance of orality in Ecuador, while Letter R is written to be read, based on the predominance of writing in U.S. cultures. This difference will not be detected by those entrenched in the textual view of the world. Finally, as I explain in Chapter Four, many rhetorical theories of information and communication technologies are based on this same textual view, with its accompanying cultural values. Thus, these researchers universalize a U.S. view of email, hypertext, and social media, which will demonstrate ethnocentrism and orientalism in non-U.S. contexts (Thatcher, 2010b "Reading and writing new media across cultures"). Many U.S. researchers and practitioners in rhetoric and professional communication assume the U.S. textual view of the world, a perfect example of orientalism if that view is transplanted to global and intercultural contexts.

Thus, the great advantage of using the etic approach in global professional communication research and then qualifying it with emic details is that this method works against analyzing one culture in light of the other culture (Lucy, 1996; Bhawuk & Triandis, 1996). For example, in previous research (Thatcher, et al, 2007), I teamed with nine other scholars to examine 27 public university websites in nine countries. However, before we selected the sites, we setup criteria for comparability of the universities (public, mid size, comprehensive curriculum); we selected universal features of the websites for analysis (language, layout, colors, links, html programs, etc); and then we analyzed the cultural values of the website using the common human thresholds of interaction or etic frames. We set up all three etic layers (site comparability; web units of analysis; and thresholds) beforehand as a way to ensure validity. For example, had we compared private, religious, or very large websites to these public universities, we would most likely have conflated a difference in the university culture with the website design. Finally, we integrated the etic data into the local universities themselves. From this integration, we could view commonalities among all the Latin American websites, for example, but we were also able to complicate these commonalities with more emic differences.

DEVELOPMENT THREE: METHODS AND COURAGE TO ACT IN GLOBAL CONTEXTS

Global and intercultural researchers must move beyond the methodological aporia and fear involved with comparing cultures. Because most postmodern and postcolonial scholars so intensely focus on the local nature of cultures (see, Scott, Longo, and Willis, 2007; Herndl & Nahrwold, 2000), these theorists often advocate for the *incommensurability* or incomparability of cultures. As exemplified by Harris (2005), incommensurability is the snowflake theory of culture, meaning that cultures are so unique that comparing one snowflake (or culture) to another is simply not possible; in fact, it's an absurdity.

This snowflake approaches produces many significant logistical problems for intercultural work. For example, if a researcher looked at all of the emic characteristics of Letter O and then compared them to emic characteristics of Letter R, that researcher would be inundated with so many different details and variables that it would be extremely difficult to connect or compare them equally across the first two letters. For instance, the syntax in Letter O is remarkably different, and so are the word choice, tone, author-audience relations, persuasive strategies, and length. In addition, the context for these letters is the coastal area of Ecuador, which differs from the *sierra*, the Andean plateau of Ecuador. Also, the relationships between the various government entities continuously evolve in the Guayas Province and often crisscross in their responsibilities with the other provincial and federal entities. José Plaza Luque has a unique and emerging relationship with this topic and with the other people and institutions involved. In fact, José tends to change his mind every day on how to address this difficult situation. Thus, the emic details in Letter O are virtually endless, so comparing the emic details of Letter O to Letter R is logistically impossible.

In addition to the emic details being endless, researchers espousing the emic approach also maintain that if the researcher is not thoroughly aware of the emic cultural patterns of Letter O, that researcher simply cannot adequately understand the letter. In other words, from an emic perspective, only an Ecuadorian from the Guayas province who is thoroughly familiar with the car taxation issue can understand the rhetorical patterns of Letter O. This demand for insider information makes cross-cultural research very difficult to carry out, because there are very few people who are actually bi-cultural. Consequently, just as phonemes do not across cultures, the unique characteristics of Letters O and R are very difficult to compare.

In addition to the methodological aporia, many local researchers believe that any act of cultural comparison is an act of colonizing because it represents the instantiation of the "always already" power-laden relations, producing a great deal of fear among scholars from "privileged" cultures (Denzin, Lincoln, & Smith, 2008). However, as I learned quickly from my Ecuadorian colleagues, I cannot simply believe that the taxation problem was just a manifestation of Ecuadorian culture that was too sacred to be analyzed or interrogated; rather, it was for most Ecuadorians an unjust system that needed reworked. However, the only way to argue for this reworking is to compare the two systems. Regardless, most postmodern and postcolonial scholars lack the courage, theory, and methods to carry out viable and ethical intercultural or global inquiries.

Although some critical and cultural-studies scholars acutely sense this fear, they maintain that the need to understand global discourse and culture is more important than fear and methodological aporia (Denzin, Lincoln, & Smith, 2008, p. 14). In addition, many leading scholars now acknowledge that our current globalized world demands courage to reflect upon methods and seriously engage in intercultural and global inquiry. This change was especially evident in discussions of the September 11th attacks. In a 2003 Symposium hosted by the Journal *Critical Inquiry*, prominent scholars openly questioned the relevance of postmodern and postcolonial theories, perhaps for the first time. Bruno Latour, an influential postmodern theorist of the epistemologies of science, asks a simple question:

What has critique become when a French general, no, a marshal of critique, namely, Jean Baudrillard, claims in a published book that the World Trade Towers destroyed themselves under their own weight, so to speak, undermined by the utter nihilism inherent in capitalism itself–as if the terrorist planes were pulled to suicide by the powerful attraction of this black hole of nothingness? What has become of critique when a book can be a best-seller that claims that no plane ever crashed into the Pentagon? I am ashamed to say that the author was French too.

Throughout this symposium, key critical, postmodern, and postcolonial theorists began to revise their local-only, power-relations emphasis to better assess global inquiry, including revisions for comparative frameworks involving the environment, outsourcing, government, and markets.

Likewise, one goal of this book is to draw on current postmodern and postcolonial methods but adapt them with the appropriate cross-cultural methods, a combination that will allow for the kind of cross-cultural theorizing and research methods necessary to understand the relations of rhetoric and culture at truly a global level (see Lett, 2010; Denzin, Lincoln, & Smith, 2008; Lucy, 1996; Bhawuk & Triandis 1996; Thatcher, 2006; Thatcher, 2010a "Introduction").

DEVELOPMENT FOUR: MOVING FROM LOCAL INDIVIDUALISM TO GLOBAL STRUCTURES

Global and intercultural scholars must avoid using approaches that implicitly espouse U.S. or western cultural values, most notably individualism. As explained earlier, this problem of ethnocentrism is well documented in intercultural research (Stewart & Bennett, 1991), but, in rhetoric and professional communication, it is still readily apparent (Thatcher, 2001). The problem has many roots, especially that of drawing on monocultural methods, as discussed earlier. However, one main cause is that U.S. and western individualism correlates strongly with the local views of postmodernism and postcolonialism. Put simply, the snowflake or incommensurable approach to cultures strongly correlates to seeing people as incommensurable or unique and, as a consequence, not grounded in anything other than the local situation. These features perfectly exemplify U.S. individualism (Hampden-Turner & Trompenaars, 2000; Hofstede, 2010; Stewart & Bennett, 1991), which is not surprising, given the U.S. foundation for these theories.

U.S. and western individualism has many problems for intercultural research, but as exemplified in the sports analogy, the most damaging is that the highly localized approaches simply cannot account for discourse influences beyond the local level, such as organizational, regional, national, or international (Brandt & Clinton, 2002; Thatcher, 2001). In other words, this approach cannot assess how people share discourses at many levels, forming a flat rhetoric. This conflation of personal with other levels also strongly works against understanding global rhetorical strategies such as purpose, audience, information and organizational needs, and style.

For example, as I show elsewhere (Thatcher, 2000), South Americans in a multinational organization drew on collective, particular, and high-context communication patterns, which their U.S. counterparts never connected to South American culture. Consequently, the U.S. personnel perceived their S.A. colleagues as bound in group-think, too context sensitive, and illusive. However, the S.A. personnel perceived themselves as building consensus, contextualizing well the issues, and being sensitive to the intelligences of their U.S. counterparts. These rhetorical assumptions were grounded in the U.S. and South Americans' broad–not local–cultural patterns.

Further, this flat rhetoric also prohibited these same U.S. employees from understanding the difference among local, personal, discipline specific (such as accounting) or organizational patterns of South American discourse as well. All were lumped into one incoherent category. Thus, rhetorical strategies are understood only in the light of the variously structured cultural background from which the communicators are drawing them, and thus, a viable global rhetorical inquiry must assess a variety of levels of discourse working in a local situation, including personal, organizational, discipline, regional, language (such as English or Spanish), and international (Thatcher, 2000).

As mentioned, some current critical studies scholars are moving beyond the flat rhetoric and trying to situate various levels of culture and discourse in the context of globalization. In the same 2003 symposium, Bhabha backs off his deconstruction of binaries and individual identities formed in hybrid spaces and focuses on global influences:

The discourses of cultural globalization have become a major intertextual and interdisciplinary highway between the humanities and the social sciences; and the traffic of ideas and methods that passes between them shapes much of our thinking in the arts and the humanities. And it is to this junction of ideas that I now want to turn. The global influence of world markets—their cunning commodifications—must not be underestimated; nor, however, must the world's trade zones be celebrated as a bricolage of borderless bazaars... It would be more accurate to suggest that the "national" system is being reinvented and hybridized to deal with the governance of globalizations—its formal institutions and informal arrangements that strive for sovereignty in a world economy that is still substantially "national." Culturalist globalization often works by analogy, mapping an equivalence between the conceptual language of cultural studies and selective aspects of the political economy—financial flows, capital transfers, outsourcing, flexible accumulation.

This concept of analogy as a mapping strategy of cultures relations to the global economy is a significant shift to the larger, broader approach needed for global rhetorical research. At this symposium, Gilman, an important contemporary theorist, similarly argues for taking the global turn:

Environmental criticism, globalization theory, the study of alternative modes of transmission of knowledge (such as the World Wide Web) generate and absorb theoretical models. They are often highly theoretical and use case studies to present complex theoretical issues, applicable to a wider range of topics, in the pursuit of any given specific study. Often the best theory today is found in these contexts.

Although these theorists advocate for taking the global turn and hint at possible approaches, they have yet to articulate specific and comprehensive approaches. They offer critiques mostly along the lines of Said (1979) showing us exactly how not to engage in ill-conceived and unethical intercultural inquiries, but not showing the opposite—how to actually theorize globally.

However, as explained by other contemporary theorists, this global turn must move beyond four privileged postmodern concepts that undergird U.S.-like individualism: difference, anti-binary, local-particularist, and incommensurability or cultural comparison. The problems of these four concepts were observed most prominently in the collaborative work of Zizek, Laclau, & Butler'*Contingency, hegemony, and universality: contemporary dialogues on the left* (2011). In this text, which is a series of interactive essays, these prominent theorists argue that in order to understand the cultural and social implications of capitalisms, critical theorists must shake off the particularist, local views and reconcile them with universalist approaches; reduce the fixation on anti-binary thinking; and develop some sense of shared but contingent universalism in order to theorize the impacts of capitalism around the world. This shared sense of universalism would allow the theorizing of identities and social and cultural formations across different groups, identities, and cultures.

This move towards a post-Hegelian universalist approach to social and cultural issues is becoming an important element in current critical thinking. One of the strongest advocates of this universalist approach is Alain Badiou, who argues, that in terms of ethics, postmodernism has been a political and social disaster because of its localized focus on identity and its accompanying inability to theorize relations of human beings to events in the social and cultural processes. Drawing on mathematics and set theory, Badiou argues for taking advantage of situations in profoundly transformative ways, developing in the process a reconciliation of the "indifferent multiplicities" of being with "external truths" through events (Badiou & Feltham, 2007). These external truths are not foundational, platonic truths; rather, they are contingent upon events.

In many ways, Badiou's approach is similar to many current discussions of human rights, which are designed to be as free as possible of ethnocentrism, a concept that is fully developed in Chapter Eight. In 1997, celebrating the 50th anniversary of the U.N.'s *Universal Declaration of Human Rights*, a large number of human rights activists, politicians, and scholars symbolically re-ratified the *Universal Declaration*, not as a demonstration of agreed upon universal truths that transcend humanity; rather, as a need to construct some universals ideas upon which human rights can be discussed fruitfully as a way to solve common human rights problems around the globe. Later, the United Nations developed the Universal Ethics Project, which has the following goals:

- **Analyze** the social, economic and environmental challenges and consequences of globalization;
- **Determine** the resulting problems and their ethical implications;
- **Identify** basic ethical principles for the emerging global society of the 21st century, by putting together a set of ideas, values and norms that would help humanity to deal with these problems;
- **Articulate** the wide array of trans-cultural "overlapping" values;
- **Forge new understandings of universality itself**, in the context of cultural diversity. (www.unesco.org/opi2/philosophyandethics/intro.htm)

Although not couched in critical theory, these objectives correlate strongly with the global turn outlined by the theorists: understand the local in light of the global; argue for ethical implications of local-global relations; and forge contingent understandings of a human universality.

DEVELOPMENT FIVE: QUANTITATIVE LITERACY AND HUMAN AGENCY

Next, global and intercultural researchers need a modest amount of quantitative literacy, something that is increasingly uncommon in rhetoric and professional communication (Charney, 1996). Concerning Letters O and R, one of the things that most puzzles many of my colleagues is that the 100% consistency in the U.S. responses to the Letter O does not mean that all U.S.-Americans are the same; rather, in spite of our great diversity, we have developed very homogenized approaches to these kinds of situations. Frequently, however, the hegemony of the local approach is made worse by the scholars who simplistically conflate a cultural generalization with a stereotype or static, monolithic culture, demonstrating what Pinker calls "innumeracy" (2003, pp.197-218). However, this is a misperception based on flawed views of generalizations, the relations between the human agent, the social context, and communication patterns.

A cultural generalization has a bell-curve logic, which means focusing on the predominant behavior of the group but also expecting exceptions to both sides of the bell curve. For example, I will present a bell curve distribution, comparing Spanish versus English speakers in the United States and Mexico. In my local context, Las Cruces, New Mexico, the bell curve distribution of Spanish versus English speakers would show the bell curve as being centered about in the middle, demonstrating an almost equal distribution of Spanish native speakers versus English native speakers. See Figure 5 as an example of this bell curve distribution.

However, if we were to travel 40 miles to the south to Ciudad Juárez, Mexico the bell curve distribution would be different, as shown in Figure 6.

There would be a shift of the bell curve to the Spanish side, but they are still would be a significant number of English speakers. If we were to move further south into Mexico, the bell curve which shift even more to the Spanish side, while if we were to move north of Las Cruces, such as the state of Idaho, depending on where we went, there would be a dramatic shift to the English side of the bell curve.

It is the shift or differences in the bell curve distribution that are of most interest to intercultural researchers. As explained in Chapter Two, cultures can be examined for their variations in the bell curve distribution of a great variety of cultural values. And most of the key intercultural researchers such as Hofstede (2010), Trompenaars & Hampden-Turner (2000), and House, et al (2005) use quantitative descriptive methods to explore bell-curve values or norms across cultures, looking for predominant patterns as well as the ranges and types of exceptions. However, the cultural

Figure 5. Bell curve graph of Spanish versus English speakers in Las Cruces, New Mexico

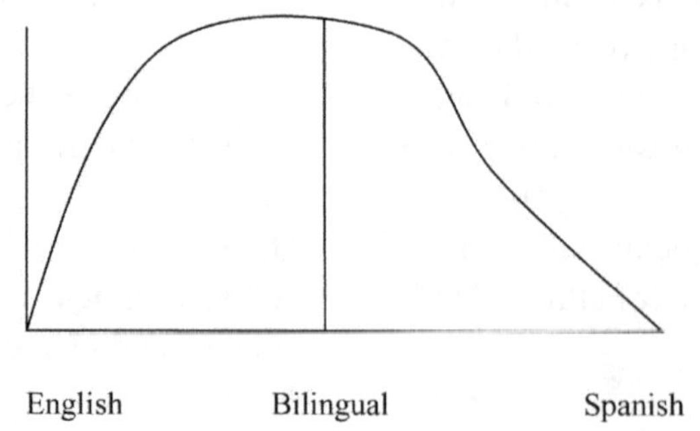

Figure 6. Bell curve of Spanish and English speakers in Ciudad Juárez, Mexico

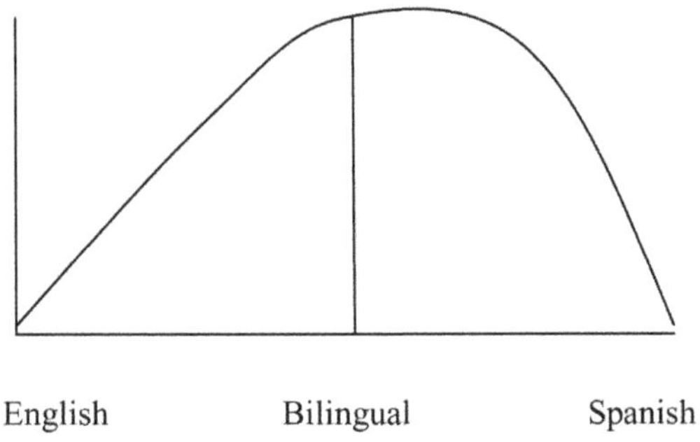

patterns that are presented as bell-curve statistics are often read erroneously as monolithic traits (see Hunsinger, 2007) perhaps as a result of the flat rhetoric tendencies and innumeracy. In other words, just because I say there are more English speakers in Las Cruces, NM as compared to Cd. Juárez, Mexico does not imply that all Las Crucens speak English and not Spanish. The problem is compounded even more because frequently these same critics of intercultural research have never read the primary texts and make claims based on the textbooks or secondary sources (see Hunsinger, 2007).

Understanding that the cultural generalizations are based on bell-curve values works against stereotyping. As Bennett (1998) explains, there are two kinds of stereotype in cross-cultural analysis: inductive and deductive. For example, when I was a professor of organizational communication in Ecuador, my Ecuadorian students loved the American television series, *The Simpsons*. In a teasing manner, some of the students would ask me if I were like Homer Simpson, the father on the show. This question presents both kinds of stereotypes: first, it is an inductive stereotype, because it is based on an insufficient amount of data. The Ecuadorian students did not have enough experience with fathers in the United States to understand how Homer might be an exception to the bell curve distribution of values. It could also be a deductive stereotype in assuming that all fathers fit the same pattern in the United States. A valid intercultural approach for my Ecuadorian students would need to gather as much data as possible about fathers in United States, situate Homer Simpson in that data, and then finally situate me in the data to understand how I relate to Homer Simpson.

As Pinker (2003) explains, many cultural and social scholars from the poststructuralist tradition simply cannot draw the distinctions between an inductive and deductive stereotype and a cultural generalization. Perhaps one reason that many poststructuralist theorists conflate stereotypes with cultural generalizations is because they have not developed or do not assume agency for the human actors. Whenever a researcher explores and operationalizes a cultural value in a given culture, the poststructuralist researcher will often cry *essentialization* or *overgeneralization* because the poststructuralist researcher assumes that any description always implies that all in that cultural tradition must act that way. This is simply deductive stereotype. Or one of the most famous claims of many poststructuralist as well as other armchair cultural theorists is the "I know a person who is different" argument. Just because there is an exception to all the generalizations does not mean that the generalization does not hold. In fact as many researchers have argued, the exception proves the generalization. Thus, the larger cultural patterns are not viewed as internally driven, determined rhetorical patterns of each individual communicator. Rather, the approach in this book shows how rhetorical patterns originate in larger cultural-historical contexts but serve as a repertoire of strategies that writers and communities appropriate and individualize to make sense of every-day rhetorical situations (Thatcher, 2000).

Consequently, in many ways, this repertoire and bell-curve approach highlight the agency of the human communicator, showing why it is critically important to understand and distinguish among an author's rhetorical approach with the general cultural patterns of the audience's culture, and the localized rhetorical patterns of the organization or context, which have been developed in response to typified rhetorical situations (Thatcher, 1999; 2001). All three variables (and many more) interact in complex ways to construct meaning in rhetorical situations. For example, some larger rhetorical patterns might be more easily "personalizable" by individual authors or communities, while others could depend more on the context rather than individual intentions to structure their meanings.

DEVELOPMENT SIX: USING BELL-CURVE APPROACHES RATHER THAN RACE, GENDER, AND ETHNICITY

One of the hallmark approaches of the critical tradition (Richter, 2006) and diversity work in the United States is their use of race, gender and ethnicity as the unit of analysis (see, for example, Butler, 2006). In other words, what is counted and analyzed are the race, gender, and ethnicities rather than the behaviors or patterns of people. Drawing on the sports analogy from Bourdieu, this approach looks at a sport such as basketball or soccer to define and categorize people, rather than looking at the person in the context of a sport or multiple sports. This approach has a significant number of fatal weaknesses. First, it presupposes that race, gender, ethnicity correlate with behavioral patterns, an assumption that is not only statistically incomprehensible but pragmatically impossible to carry out. In other words, it will assume that an athlete has certain characteristics based on the sport he or she plays. Sometimes this correlation holds but more often than not it fails. In addition, it presents serious problems of agency, stereotypes, and ethics.

For example, in my U.S.-Mexico border region, it is utterly impossible to connect someone's racial features or ethnicity with cultural patterns. The U.S. side of border is composed of roughly 75% Latino or Hispanic heritage and 15-25% anglo or white, while the Mexican side is overwhelmingly Latino/Mexican; but there is a small anglo/white population in Mennonite and Mormon colonies in the Mexican state of Chihuahua. Thus, when I am in Cd. Juárez, most Juarenses wonder if I am Mexico (from the Mormon colonies) or American; they simply cannot tell by my racial features. Further, some Latinos have lived on the U.S. side of the border for many generations and are landed aristocracy from old colonial times, while others are first generation Americans whose parents recently emigrated from Mexico or other Latin American countries. There are many types and ranges. Thus, it is extremely difficult to connect the racial features to cultural patterns because the cultural patterns of Latinos who have lived in the United States for many generations are significantly different than those who just emigrated from Mexico. In addition, many people in the border region travel back and forth between Cd. Juárez and El Paso, TX, forming a bicultural populations; but one cannot tell a bicultural, U.S.-American or Mexican national from racial features. Put simply, the ethnicity of a person in the US-Mexico border region will have very little–or nothing–to do with the cultural and rhetorical traditions that that person connects to.

Instead of race or ethnicity, is much more productive to understand the bell curve or predominant cultural and rhetorical traditions of Mexico and the United States and then explore how residents of the border region connect complexly to these rhetorical traditions. For example, when I am teaching writing courses at New Mexico State University, about 70% of my students are defined as Hispanic. However, of the 25 or so students in my class, usually three or four self identify as connecting strongly but complexly connected to Mexican rhetorical and cultural traditions. Usually half or more of my Hispanic students strongly identify with US cultural and rhetorical traditions, while four to six can be identified as "G1.5 students." G1.5 is a term developed in ESL to designate a speaker as not fully Spanish-English bilingual, nor is English their first language, nor their second. Most were born in the U.S. but from immigrant parents. Very often their parents speak Spanish in the home, yet they have learned English all their lives outside the home. You cannot observe this self identification through racial or ethnic features.

Thus, it is much more fruitful to define and operationalize the U.S. and Mexican rhetorical and cultural traditions and then explore how all of us connect to these traditions uniquely. Some students understand explicitly the US and Mexican traditions and can articulate precisely how their families reject, reconstruct, or simply accept and integrate parts or the whole from each of these traditions. This includes the minority Anglo students at New Mexico State who understand their complex minority status there. This approach eliminates the reductive and absurd connection between ethnicity and cultural and rhetorical patterns, but it does not reduce people's subjectivities to the local or individual level. It also highlights how the rhetorical and cultural traditions are strategies that are more or less effective in a certain, structured rhetorical situation. For example, many of the Latino students have grandparents and family in Mexico, usually in the state of Chihuahua. Those who routinely cross borders are usually bi-cultural, a concept synonymous with bilingualism in that they can use the Mexican rhetorical and cultural traditions while in Mexico and use a mix of the US and Mexican traditions while in the United States, depending on the rhetorical context.

DEVELOPMENT SEVEN: HUMILITY, REFLEXIVITY, AND FLEXIBILITY

Global rhetoric researchers need humility, reflexivity, and flexibility, attributes that greatly facilitate intercultural inquiry (Bennett, 1998). Some critical and cultural studies scholars, however, reveal a smug insularity as they advocate for their own methods. For example, the term "always already" is commonly used in critical and cultural studies arguments, usually pertaining to the connection among methods, culture, and power. However, the level of surety in the "always already" construct is rarely, if ever, seen in other disciplines. For example, a recent Google Scholar search for the phrase "always already" yielded 46,300 results, and while I did not check all of them, the first 100 results were all based upon critical and cultural studies theories and textual methodologies. This seems to be the only discipline that has a100% level of surety, which is amazing, given the complexities of culture, rhetoric, and power relations.

Because of the surety and simplicity of this one-to-one correspondence between method and culture (innumeracy and using race instead of behavior), these critical and cultural studies theorists can simply critique the results of any work as simply hegemonic, racist, reductionist, or binary, not understanding the constructed framework from which many intercultural studies are housed and the epistemologies that are used to report the results. For example, Zhang (2008) criticizes the intercultural field of contrastive rhetoric (discussed in Chapter Three) as developing hegemonic powers for speakers of English in developing areas such as India, China, and other parts of Asia. Zhang also claims:

> *Furthermore, the overemphasis on cultural difference in contrastive rhetoric can lead to regressive, limiting, and even blinding stereotypes and unwarranted categorical distinctions among groups. For example, the categorical distinctions to which contrastive rhetoric seems to be prone may have a distancing and exoticizing effect, leading to native English speakers to experiencing themselves as the norm, as straight-line, direct writers, and constructing cross-cultural students as the exotic Other and as irrelevant, though perhaps also quaint and thus appealing. (p.18)*

Drawing on Foucaultian and postcolonial methods of textual criticism, Zhang makes these large claims of "social control" without any evidence other than textual interpretations of research reports. She does not theorize or explain the cultural connections between the rhetorical patterns and cultural backgrounds; she never engages contrastive rhetoric methodology; she never argues why her methods are better, more valid, or more accurate; and she never feels it necessary to qualify the very strong language of her claims. She derives all her results from textual interpretation. Her thinking grossly oversimplifies the connections between culture and writing, becoming more problematic than the contrastive rhetoric patterns she seeks to critique. As Bennett (1998) so aptly explains, this approach provides "little light and much heat" (p. 11).

Finally, in addition to the "always already" surety, the tone in many of these approaches seems like proselytizing. For example, in the introduction to their collection *Critical Power Tools*, Scott, Longo, and Willis (2007) say that "This collection testifies and responds to our field's needs for more teaching and research approaches that historicizes technical communication's roles in hegemonic power relations" (p. 1). The word "testify" hints of the rhetoric researcher as missionary, which is problematic in a single culture (Segal, et, 1998), but could be disastrous in cross-cultural research, which needs significant flexibility and tolerance, not missionary zeal.

DEVELOPMENT EIGHT: EFFECTIVE THEORY AND PRACTICE

Effective global and intercultural inquiry seeks a balance between theory and practice or praxis; consequently, it needs to work against the privileging of cultural theory in much rhetoric and professional communication. To demonstrate this need for global praxis, I will narrate one of my many U.S.-Mexico border experiences.

In spring 2006, I was working on an interdisciplinary study of U.S.-Mexico border health and found myself (as usual) in Ciudad Juárez, Mexico (adjacent to El Paso, TX) talking to a director of the Chihuahuan State Women's Hospital. That same week, New Mexico State University held its J. Paul Taylor Symposium on Social Justice, which that year, focused on promoting justice for the more than 500 women and girls murdered in Ciudad Juárez and Chihuahua City since 1993. The crowning event for this symposium was to place hundreds of small pink crosses covered with the personal data and photos of murdered women on a beautiful, cemetery-like lawn at NMSU. This scene garnered much media attention, especially in Mexico. Although I strongly agreed with the cause, I was embarrassed by the approach and worried it would be problematic for my Mexican colleagues. I thought of sharing my worries with the symposium directors, but I felt it would be useless.

At this large state hospital dedicated entirely to women's issues, after I conducted my scheduled interview with the Director, I simply asked for her thoughts of the pink crosses. In her role as Director, she was intimately involved in the treatment of many female victims of violence in Cd. Juárez and was acutely aware of the femicide problem. At first, she was hesitant to speak because she knew I was an NMSU professor, but when I hinted that I was embarrassed by it, she unloaded: She was deeply offended by the approach. First, it was done by sanctimonious Americans who had little more than newspaper knowledge of the events. Second, it was cowardly because it was carried out in a safe place with the supporters risking nothing. Third, the publicity did nothing to improve the situation; in fact, it probably emboldened the perpetrators. Fourth, as naïve academic symbols, the crosses were too weak to make any real statement. Fifth, of course people in Cd. Juárez were aware of and deeply missed these young women and did not need Americans to remind them. I was stunned, not because of her anger and frustration, but because of the clarity and cogency of her response. Based on much experience and like many of my Mexican colleagues, she clearly perceived it as another U.S. neo-colonial approach to Mexican situations.

I asked her what she would have our NMSU faculty and students do. She said: support women's shelters concretely with resources; work through well established venues of public outreach against female violence; work through Cd. Juárez non-profit agencies that investigate and ameliorate judicial and police incompetence in Cd. Juárez; and perhaps work towards improving the safety of public transportation to and from the manufacturing plants (maquilas) where most of the murdered women worked. I agreed.

After the symposium, the pink crosses were discussed just a few more times in the media, and the incident was reported in one academic article. That's it. Thus, as Stuart Hall explains, when working in cultural studies, scholars must honestly problematize their methods if they are not producing grounded, tangible, and effective results; otherwise, theory is letting them off the hook:

At that point, I think anybody who is into cultural studies seriously as an intellectual practice, must feel, on their pulse, its ephemerality, its insubstantiality, how little it registers, how little we've been able to change anything or get anybody to do anything. If you don't feel one tension in the work that you are doing, theory has let you off the hook. (p. 285)

Frequently, theory lets many cultural studies scholars off the hook because they do not have to offer alternative methods or ground their conclusions in anything other than a theoretical interpretation of the local situation. This is very easy, safe research that while offering some considerations, does not have the courage to ground itself sufficiently in methods and qualified conclusions, which then serve as something with which others can engage meaningfully beyond the local situation. The pink crosses seem to be such an approach: abstract yet personal, safe but useless, and seemingly politically correct, yet strongly ethnocentric.

Furthermore, as Bhabha (2003) states earlier and explored throughout this chapter, this local-only approach is further weakened when connected to issues of power and domination at a larger than local level. In other words, despite all of the grandiose claims of examining power relations (Scott, Longo, and Willis, 2007), cultural studies and critical theory seems poorly situated to observe power relations beyond the local-level. It simply presents pink crosses ornamented with personal pictures and data on a lawn, safely away from the problem, instead of aggressively interrogating the judicial, police, industrial, cultural, and transportation powers tied to the unresolved murders.

DEVELOPMENT NINE: A WORKABLE ETHICS FOR GLOBAL CONTEXTS

The ninth development is perhaps the most important: constructing a workable ethics for global contexts, which is difficult in the postmodern framework. Although the work in postmodern ethics is complicated (Porter, 1998; Dombrowski, 1999), three key concepts can be traced. First, as Scott, Longo, and Willis (2007) explain, critical and postmodern discourse often views humanity as fragmented and often just as much "the object of discourse" as the producer of discourse (p. 4).

In addition, much postmodernism situates ethics in the dialogic relations of the local context (Porter, 1998; Sullivan & Porter, 1998), reducing ethics to local choices. And third, since these two concepts combine to situate the application of ethics to the local context, outside views of ethics are not allowed to interfere. From the postmodern perspective, the car taxation problem in Ecuador was simply a local problem in their discursive situation. However, it is my belief that it was perhaps a human rights problem. Because of corruption, the elite and rich usually did not pay any kind of tax, while those of lower classes did not have the connections to avoid the tax. Thus, the lower-income Ecuadorians were forced to pay a higher percentage of their wages on a more regular basis than the rich elite. This human rights issue is only understood outside the postmodern framework.

Thus, as most human rights scholars maintain, the local, postmodern ethics might seem palatable theoretically, but it is a disaster for dealing with human rights (see, for example, Sutch, 2001, p. 20. Also see McCormick, 2009; Twining, 2000; Higgins, 1999; Glendon, 1999). First, "the postmodern agent (the liberal ironist of Rorty or the itinerate condottiere of Ashley) struggles against orthodoxy of any kind" (Sutch, 2001, p. 20). In other words, because the human agent is both the object and subject of discourse and culture, the agent has little ability to effect change against a strong cultural formation. This weakness emphasizes the need for human agency in intercultural contexts, a point discussed earlier. Second, the postmodern approach avoids the search for human rights in the "larger community" or "human solidarity" and replaces it with "post-philosophical hermeneutic textualism and thereafter with postmodern pragmatism" (Sutch, 2001, p. 20).

From this perspective, the "postmodernist attempts to engage the political and ethical are schizophrenic" (Sutch, 2001, p. 22). This is because reducing the definition of ethics to textual interpretation (usually resulting in derridian nihilism) and reducing practice to local dialogue are both universal in an abstract and ephemeral form and concretely local in application, much like the pink crosses. Because of its schizophrenic disjuncture between an abstract nihilism and local practice, postmodernism is very ill-equipped to connect ethics to anything beyond the local situation, including politics, larger-than-local cultural forms, and nation-states (Sutch, 2001; Higgins, 1999; Glendon, 1999; McCormick, 2009).

The third problem is that because of its textual hermeneutics and disjuncture with other-than-local situations, postmodern ethics has to assume that whatever local cultures and situations (such as female circumcision) have deemed correct (in their dialogic relations) is not subject to intervention from outside forces (McCormick, 2009; Twining, 2000; Higgins, 1999; Glendon, 1999). From this view, activists and scholars have almost no hope for changing some of the most abominable treatment of human beings.

Consequently, scholars and activists have **not** been able to use difference-based, postructuralist discourse to argue against female circumcision or authoritative regimes because the supposed human rights violators argue that the "violation" is just a "cultural difference" in the myriad of different cultures; thus, no argument can be made against it (Otto, 1997; Higgins, 1999; Glendon, 1999). Thus, even the most thoroughly postmodern human rights scholars and activists are now openly constructing what they believe all humanity should share, regardless of the cultural differences (Otto, 1997; Higgins, 1999). These constructed universals then become the benchmark for evaluating local human rights violations, such as the case of the United Nation's *Universal Declaration of Human Rights*, which is discussed in Chapter Eight. Likewise, rhetoric scholars might consider developing essentialized "universal" rhetorics to facilitate effective and ethical intercultural communications in a variety of international academic, governmental, and business situations. Much like the earlier discussion of fear and aporia, most human rights scholars acknowledge the inevitability of postmodern critiques (Higgins, 1999), but they simply "put their helmets on" and believe that addressing human rights is more important.

CONCLUSION

As articulated, the predominant local approaches present serious challenges to overcome with global inquiry in rhetoric and professional communication, including ethnocentrism, validity of constructs, conceptualization of global-local dynamics, balance and fairness for cultures being examined, and ethics (Morris, et al, 1999; Lett, 1996; Lucy, 1996; Bhawuk & Triandis, 1996; Hussein, 2000; Muntarbhorn, 2000; Thatcher, 2001; Thatcher, 2006; Thatcher, 2010; Jarvis & Pavlenko, 2008; Pinker, 2003; Higgins, 1999; Twining, 2000; Tamanaha, 2006; and McCormick, 2009). The proposed intercultural rhetorical theory, combined with the etic-then-emic frame, becomes a useful tool for overcoming these challenges.

In addition to validity, using the etic approach to frame cross-cultural research and then qualifying it with emic details works against analyzing one culture in light of the other culture; it provides for a viable comparative methodology that is not lost in the aporia of details; it highlights differences among levels of discourse and human agency; and it provides a basis for effective practice and ethical discussions (Morris, et al, 1999; Lucy, 1996; Bhawuk & Triandis, 1996; Thatcher, 2011). This is why Hofstede (2010), Hampden-Turner and Trompenaars (2000), House, et, al, (2005), and many others use the dimensions, value sets or intercultural traits, for these serve as etic frames for understanding cross-cultural differences.

Thus, we have a large task ahead of us: to develop and operationalize models of intercultural rhetoric and professional communication in the context of globalization. From my perspective, the challenge is to fruitfully reconcile emic and etic approaches, drawing on models of existing intercultural research, but also integrating those models with many other compelling theories and methods of intercultural inquiry. This book attempts to accomplish this purpose. Chapter Two carefully explores the etic frames, as developed in cross-cultural research, but especially applying them to rhetorical patterns. Chapter Three specifically examines the effects of language on writing patterns, drawing on research from ESL, neurobiology, and evolutionary psychology. Chapter Four explains the relations of communication media to the etic value sets as a way to situate discussions of communication media across cultures. And the rest of the chapters focus on practice: Chapter Five examines website designs across cultures; Chapter Six explores intercultural organizational communication; Chapter Seven examines intercultural distance education; Chapter Eight explores global legal communications; Chapter Nine describes intercultural health communications; Chapter Ten lays out parameters of intercultural instructions; Chapter Eleven examines curriculum and research; and Chapter Twelve articulates the need to internationalize rhetoric and writing textbooks.

REFERENCES

Badiou, A., & Feltham, O. (2007). *Being and event.* Continuum.

Bakhtin, M. M. (1990). Art and answerability. In Holquist, M., & Liapunov, V. (Eds.), *Art and answerability: Early philosophical essays* (Liapunov, V., Trans.). Austin, TX: University of Texas Press.

Bakhtin, M. M. (1993). *Toward a philosophy of the act* (Holquist, M., & Liapunov, V., Eds.). (Liapunov, V., Trans.). Austin, TX: University of Texas Press.

Barthes, R. (1972). *Mythologies* (Lavers, A., Trans.). New York, NY: Noonday Press.

Baudrillard, J. (1983). *Simulations. Semiotext(e)*. Press.

Bennett, M. J. (Ed.). (1998). *Basic concepts of intercultural communication*. Yarmouth, ME: Intercultural Press.

Berlin, J. (1987). *Rhetoric and reality: Writing instruction in the American colleges, 1900-1985*. Carbondale, IL: Southern Illinois University Press.

Bhabha, H. (1994). *The location of culture*. Routledge.

Bhabha, H. (2003). Statement for the *Critical Inquiry* Board. *Critical Inquiry, 30*(2). Retrieved from http://criticalinquiry.uchicago.edu/issues/v30/30n2.Bhabha.html.

Bhawuk, D., & Triandis, H. (1996). The role of culture theory in the study of culture and intercultural training. In Landis, D., & Bhagat, R. (Eds.), *Handbook of intercultural training* (2nd ed., pp. 17–34). Thousand Oaks, CA: Sage.

Blyler, N., & Thralls, C. (Eds.). (1993). *Professional communication: The social perspective*. Newbury Park, CA: Sage Publications.

Bosley, D. (2000). (Ed.) *Global documentation: Case studies in international technical communication*. Boston, MA: Allyn & Bacon.

Bourdieu, P. (1999). *Language and symbolic power*. Boston, MA: Harvard University Press.

Bourdieu, P., & Wacquant, L. (1992). *An invitation to reflexive sociology*. Chicago, IL: University of Chicago Press.

Brandt, D., & Clinton, K. (2002). Limits of the local: Expanding perspectives on literacy as a social practice. *Journal of Literacy Research, 34*(3), 337–356. doi:10.1207/s15548430jlr3403_4

Burbach, K., Nunez, O., & Kagarlitsky, B. (1996). *Globalization and its discontents: The rise of postmodern socialisms*. Pluto Press.

Buss, D. (Ed.). (2005). *Handbook of evolutionary psychology*. New York, NY: John Wiley & Sons.

Butler, J. (2006). *Gender trouble: Feminism and the subversion of identity*. Routledge.

Charney, D. (1996). Empiricism is not a four-letter word. *College Composition and Communication, 47*(4), 567–593. doi:10.2307/358602

Connor, U. (1996). *Contrastive rhetoric: Cross-cultural aspects of second-language writing*. Cambridge, UK: Cambridge U Press.

Connor, U., Nagelhout, E., & Rozycki, W. V. (Eds.). (2008). *Contrastive rhetoric: Reaching to intercultural rhetoric*. Amsterdam, The Netherlands: John Benjamins Publishing Company.

Deleuze, G., & Guattari, F. (1987). *Thousand plateaus: Capitalism and schizophrenia*. Minneapolis, MN: University of Minnesota Press.

Denzin, N. K., Lincoln, Y. S., & Smith, L. T. (Eds.). (2008). *Handbook of critical and indigenous methodologies*. Thousand Oaks, CA: Sage Publications.

Derrida, J., & Spivak, G. (1998). *Of grammatology*. Baltimore, MD: The Johns Hopkins University Press.

Ding, H. (2007). *Rhetoric of a global epidemic: Intercultural and intracultural professional communication about SARS*. Unpublished Doctoral Dissertation, Purdue University.

Dombrowski, P. (2000). *Ethics in technical communication*. New York, NY: Allyn & Bacon.

Donnelly, J. (2003). *Universal human rights in theory and practice*. Ithaca, NY: Cornell University Press.

Faigley, L. (1992). *Fragments of rationality: Postmodernity and the subject of composition*. Pittsburgh, PA: University of Pittsburgh Press.

Foucault, M. (1972). *The archaeology of knowledge* (Sheridan Smith, A. M., Trans.). New York, NY: Harper Colophon.

Foucault, M. (1979). *Discipline and punish: The birth of a prison* (Sheridan Smith, A. M., Trans.). New York, NY: Vintage/Random House.

García-Canclini, N. (1992). Cultural reconversion In Yudice, G., France, J., & Flores, J. (Eds.), *On the edge: The crisis of contemporary Latin American culture* (pp. 29–44). Minneapolis, MN: University of Minnesota Press.

Glendon, M. A. (1999). Foundations of human rights: The unfinished business. *The American Journal of Jurisprudence*, *44*, 1–14.

Gumperz, J., & Levinson, S. (Eds.). (1996). *Rethinking linguistic relativity*. Cambridge, UK: Cambridge University Press.

Hall, S. (1997). *Representation: Cultural representations and signifying practices*. New York, NY: Sage.

Hampden-Turner, C., & Trompenaars, A. (2000). *Building cross-cultural competence*. New York, NY: Wiley.

Harris, R. A. (2005). *Rhetoric and incommensurability*. West Lafayette, IN: Parlour Press.

Hawisher, G., & Selfe, C. (2000). *Global literacies and the world-wide web*. London, UK: Routledge.

Herndl, C., & Nahrwold, C. (2000). Research as social practice: A case study of research on technical and professional communication. *Written Communication*, *17*(20), 258–296. doi:10.1177/0741088300017002004

Higgins, T. E. (1999). Regarding rights: An essay honoring the fiftieth anniversary of the *Universal Declaration of Human Rights*. *Columbia Human Rights Law Review*, *30*, 225–247.

Hofstede, G. (2010). *Cultures and organizations, software of the mind* (3rd ed.). New York, NY: McGraw Hill.

Hoft, N. (1995). *International technical communication*. New York, NY: John Wiley & Sons.

House, R. J., Hanges, P. J., Javidan, M., Dorfman, P. R., & Gupta, V. (Eds.). (2005). *Culture, leadership, and organizations: The GLOBE study of 62 societies*. New York, NY: Sage Publications.

Hunsinger, R. P. (2006). Culture and cultural identity in intercultural technical communication. *Technical Communication Quarterly*, *15*(1). Retrieved from http://www.informaworld.com/smpp/content~content=a785834024~db=all. doi:10.1207/s15427625tcq1501_4

Jameson, F. (1990). *Postmodernism, or, the cultural logic of late capitalism*. Durham, NC: Duke University Press.

Jarvis, S., & Pavlenko, A. (2008). *Crosslinguistic influence in language and cognition*. New York, NY: Routledge.

Johnson-Eilola, J., & Selber, S. (Eds.). (2004). *Central works in technical communication*. Oxford, UK: Oxford University Press.

Latour, B. (2003). Why has critique run out of steam? From matters of fact to matters of concern. *Critical Inquiry*, *30*(2). Retrieved from http://criticalinquiry.uchicago.edu/issues/v30/30n2.Latour.html.

Lett, J. (1996). Emic/Etic distinctions. In Levinson, D., & Ember, M. (Eds.), *Encyclopedia of cultural anthropology* (pp. 382–383). New York, NY: Henry Holt and Company.

Lett, J. (2010). *Emic/Etic distinctions*. Retrieved from http://faculty.ircc.cc.fl.us/faculty/jlett/Article%20on%20Emics%20and%20Etics.htm

Lucy, J. (1996). The scope of linguistic relativity: An analysis and review of empirical research. In Gumperz, J. J., & Levinson, S. C. (Eds.), *Rethinking linguistic relativity* (pp. 37–69). Cambridge, UK: Cambridge University Press.

Lyotard, J. F. (1984). *The postmodern condition: A report on knowledge*. Minneapolis, MN: University of Minnesota Press.

Marcus, J. (1992). *Mesoamerican writing systems: Propaganda, myth, and history in four ancient civilizations*. Princeton, NJ: Princeton University Press.

Martín Barbero, J. (1988). Communication from culture: The crisis of the national and the emergence of the popular. (P. Schlesinger, Trans.). *Media Culture & Society*, *10*, 447–465. doi:10.1177/016344388010004004

Miller, C. R. (1993). Rhetoric and the community: The problem of the one and many. In Enos, T., & Brown, S. C. (Eds.), *Defining the new rhetorics* (pp. 79–94). Newbury Park, CA: Sage.

Morris, M., Leung, K., Ames, D., & Lickel, B. (1999). From inside and outside: Integrating emic and etic insights about culture and justice judgments. *Academy of Management Review*, *24*, 781–796.

New London Group. (1996). A pedagogy of multiliteracies: Designing social futures. *Harvard Educational Review*, *66*(1), 60–92.

Pike, K. (1967). *Language in relation to a unified theory of the structure of human behavior*. de Gruyter Mouton.

Pinker, S. (2003). *The blank slate*. New York, NY: Penguin Books.

Plato,. (1956). *Phaedrus*. New York, NY: Macmillan Publishing.

Porter, J. E. (1986). Intertextuality and the discourse community. *Rhetoric Review*, *5*, 34–47. doi:10.1080/07350198609359131

Porter, J. E. (1998). *Rhetorical ethics and internetworked writing*. Greenwich, CT: Ablex Publishing.

Said, E. (1979). *Orientalism*. New York, NY: Vintage Books.

Scott, J. B., Longo, B., & Wills, K. V. (Eds.). (2006). *Critical power tools: Technical communication and cultural studies*. SUNY Series, Studies in Scientific and Technical Communication.

St.Amant, K. (Ed.). (2007). *Linguistic and cultural online communication issues in the global age*. Hershey, PA: IGI Global. doi:10.4018/978-1-59904-213-8

Starke-Meyerring, D., & Wilson, M. (Eds.). (2008). *Designing globally networked learning environments: Visionary partnerships, policies, and pedagogies*. Rotterdam, The Netherlands: Sense Publishers.

Stewart, E., & Bennett, M. (1991). *American cultural patterns: A cross-cultural perspective* (Rev. ed.). Yarmouth, ME: Intercultural Press, Inc.

Street, B. (Ed.). (2001). *Literacy and development: Ethnographic perspectives*. London, UK: Routledge. doi:10.4324/9780203468418

Sullivan, P., & Porter, J. E. (1998). *Opening spaces: Writing technologies and critical research practices*. Greenwich, CT: Ablex.

Sutch, P. (2001). *Ethics, justice, and international relations: Constructing an international community*. New York, NY: Routledge.

Tamanaha, B. Z. (2006). *Law as a means to an end: Threat to the rule of law*. Cambridge, UK: Cambridge University Press. doi:10.1017/CBO9780511511073

Thatcher, B. (1997). *Orality and writing in Latin American and USA professional communication*. Unpublished doctoral dissertation, Purdue University.

Thatcher, B. (2001). Issues of validity in intercultural professional communication research. *Journal of Business and Technical Communication, 15*(4), 458–489. doi:10.1177/105065190101500403

Thatcher, B. (2006). Intercultural rhetoric, technology, and writing in Mexican maquilas. *Special Technology Transfer Edition of Technical Communication Quarterly, 15*(3), 383–405.

Thatcher, B. (2007a). Online education in an age of globalization: Foundational perspectives and practices for technical communication instructors and trainers. *Technical Communication Quarterly, 16*, 13–30.

Thatcher, B. L. (1999). Cultural and rhetorical adaptations for South American audiences. *Technical Communication, 46*(2), 177–195.

Thatcher, B. L. (2000). Writing policies and procedures in a U.S. and South American context. *Technical Communication Quarterly, 94*, 365–400. doi:10.1080/10572250009364706

Thatcher, B. L. (2009). Understanding digital literacy across cultures. In Spilka, R. (Ed.), *Digital literacy for technical communication: 21st Century theory and practice* (pp. 169–198). Routledge.

Thatcher, B. L. (2010a). Introduction. In *Rhetoric, Professional Communication, and Globalization, 1*, 1-34.

Thatcher, B. L. (2010b). Reading and writing new media across cultures: Issues of fit, reciprocity, and cultural change. In Kalmbach, J., & Ball, C. (Eds.), *Reading and writing new media*. Hampton Press Series New Dimensions in Computers and Composition.

Timmerman, C. E. (2002). The moderating effect of mindlessness/mindfulness upon media richness and social influence explanations of organizational media use. *Communication Monographs, 69*, 111–131. doi:10.1080/714041708

Tokar, B. (2009). *Social ecology: Resistance and reconstruction*. Retrieved from http://news.infoshop.org/article.php?story=20090506123901 70. December, 2010.

Trompenaars, F. (1994). *Riding the waves of culture: Understanding diversity in global business*. New York, NY: McGraw Hill.

Twining, W. (2000). *Globalisation and legal theory*. Cambridge, UK: Cambridge University Press.

Zhang, Y. (2008). Social science or social control: Qualitative researchers' dilemma in contrastive rhetoric. *Small Cities Imprint, 1*(1), 15–20.

Zizek, S., Laclau, E., & Butler, J. (2011). *Contingency, hegemony, and universality: Contemporary dialogues on the left* (2nd ed.). Verso.

ENDNOTES

1 Drawing on the sports metaphor of a court or field, Bourdieu defines field as a structured system of social relations and positions that allow for—or facilitate—play or struggle to score, or in social terms, to appropriate social, cultural, or symbolic capital. The field provides the physical and cognitive arena that allows social agents to "play" the game. The architecture of a field derives from underlying vision of variously related stakeholders, economic forces, material realities, aesthetic values, and cultural capital.

2 Bourdieu (1999, 1992) defines habitus as a system of tendencies or dispositions that

are acquired through structured perception, thought, and action. Like a basketball player, the individual learns these habitus in more or less objective conditions of the game—the field and game do not respond or change according to individual players. Thus, players must internalize the cognitive, physical, and social structures of the game to play successfully. Consequently, since each player personally internalizes the very structures of the game, each player embodies these structures' social, cognitive, cultural, economic, ethical, and personal values. Finally, the habitus that are developed in a game then become naturalized, the self-evident universals thought to belong to everyone involved in the game. Consequently, cognition and action become unconsciously objective and explicitly reproducible.

Chapter 2
Borders and Etics as Units of Analysis for Intercultural Rhetoric and Professional Communication

ABSTRACT

This chapter lays out the methodological frame for intercultural inquiry, based on a quasi-structuralist approaching using common human thresholds of interaction. It then explains in detail eight of these common human thresholds of interaction and showing how all eight surface in rhetorical patterns and strategies. The chapter then exemplifies this frame by examining Anzaldúa's Borderlands.

INTRODUCTION

The purpose of this chapter is to lay out and demonstrate the variables or units of analysis that will be used for intercultural comparison for the rest of the chapters in this book. These variables are founded on four critical characteristics of intercultural research that are carefully explained in Chapter One. These include:

- Focusing primarily on the regularities in cultures while acknowledging differences, using a bell curve logic to demonstrate this variation. This is the etic-then-emic approach.
- Drawing on deep and often implicit variables that underlie everyday sense-making activities, which works against using race, gender, and ethnicity variables for cross-cultural comparison but highlights a situated agency.
- Connecting variables to intercultural rhetoric and communication patterns.
- Using variables that are fair and equitable for the cultures being compared so as to avoid biases and orientalism.

As introduced in Chapter One, the type of variable that meets these four criteria is the etic, which I define as a common human threshold of

DOI: 10.4018/978-1-61350-450-5.ch002

behavior. These thresholds are boundaries or borders that all cultures share, and therefore, have to develop reoccurring responses to; and using these thresholds places the cultures for comparison in a valid, reliable, and balanced framework.

This chapter first explores the need for using common human thresholds by presenting an analogy of the U.S.-Mexico border. Second, this chapter summarizes eight common human thresholds and the cultural variation to these thresholds in a multitude of intercultural studies around the world. Finally, this chapter exemplifies the border-etic approach by evaluating Anzaldúa's (2007) influential work *Borderlands/La Frontera* on the U.S.-Mexico border.

BORDER AS ANALOGY OF COMMON HUMAN THRESHOLDS

As explained in Chapter One, the most fruitful, valid, and fair approach to intercultural inquiry is using an etic frame that then integrates emic details. This chapter examines more closely the dynamic of the etic frame itself. To explain this dynamic, I will draw an analogy between geopolitical borders and the etic frames. Below, I present three Google images of my U.S.-Mexico border region (the El Paso, TX-Ciudad Juárez, Mexico region). Figure 1 is a large overview of the entire border, with the border highlighted in yellow. Figure 2 is a middle class neighborhood in El Paso, and Figure 3 is a middle class neighborhood in Ciudad Juárez.

From these images, it is easy to identify the two sides of the border, which means that geopolitical border, in this case, the Rio Grande/Rio Bravo, is significant in many ways, despite all the arguments that the border is essentially meaningless. First, on the El Paso side there is more space between the buildings, whereas on the Ciudad Juárez size things are more compact, except for the large park shown on the east side. In fact, the cost per square-foot on the Ciudad Juárez side is two to three times the cost compared to El Paso, but the cost of labor is about one third of that in El Paso; and water and electricity are more expensive in Ciudad Juárez. Not surprisingly, you will also observe many more swimming pools

Figure 1. Google image of El Paso, Texas and Ciudad Juárez, Mexico

Figure 2. Middle class area of El Paso

and warehousing and storage in El Paso but more manufacturing in Ciudad Juárez.

In addition, is it is easy to see that the architecture and city blocks are significantly different between the two areas. Homes and businesses in Ciudad Juárez are almost always bound together in small city blocks, often with the home attached physically to the business; and the blocks almost always have high and secure fences surrounding the outside perimeter of the space and are self-contained units. In distinction, in El Paso Texas, there is a much clearer separation of homes from businesses; and there is very little perimeter security; in fact, it is very easy to walk up to the front door in any neighborhood in El Paso Texas. Although it is difficult to see from these images,

Figure 3. Middle class area of Ciudad Juárez

it has also interesting to point out that homes and businesses in Ciudad Juárez have a much greater variety of paint colors, while El Paso has a handful of muted desert colors. What cannot be seen in the images but is relevant is that Ciudad Juárez exhibits many more buses on the road and many more people walking.

These are some of the differences between the two cities, but the Google Earth perspective will show almost an exact match in terms of terrain and plant life. In addition, as explained in Chapter One, it is virtually impossible distinguish by sight residents of Ciudad Juárez and El Paso, Texas, and there is so much flow across the border on a daily basis that this effort would also be futile. Further, the food, dress, and many cultural characteristics are likewise similar. Finally, researchers could view from Google Earth any US-Mexico border region and see the same kind of picture: similarities in terms of terrain and plant life, but significant differences in many other ways.

These three images demonstrate three crucial points in valid intercultural research: that borders such as the geo-political one between Mexico and the United States are significant; borders that serve as etic comparisons are a good mechanism for revealing or unmasking this significance; and some differences and similarities matter, while others are irrelevant. As mentioned in Chapter One, the key to intercultural research is to understand the similarities and differences between two cultures and then evaluate which of these similarities and differences are relevant and why (see Hofstede, 2010). And perhaps the best way to make these distinctions is to use an etic frame such as a border.

This need for the etic or border frame becomes obvious when examining cultural research that does not use it. For example, despite the ease in which one can see the Mexican or U.S. side of the border, it is surprising that most U.S.-Mexico border theorists actually discount the relevance of the geo-political border and argue instead for continual fluidity and hybridity of cultural and rhetorical patterns. The U.S.-Mexico border region according to the U.S. scholar Anzaldúa (2007) and the Mexican scholar Garcia-Canclini (1992) is one of great fluidity, hybridity, and uniqueness based on the local situation with the border having little or no relevance. Further, many current globalization theories would have us believe that globalization means a significant amount of cultural blending, hybrization, glocalization, and cross-border flow of rhetorical and cultural patterns with geopolitical borders relatively meaningless, and as such, an out-dated mode of inquiry.

After eleven years of systematically working on both sides of the border, that's not my picture. In other words, this emic-only, totally fluid and hybrid approach is simply not compelling. In addition to the obvious differences displayed in the three Google snapshots, there are many others. For example, in 2010, El Paso, Texas was the safest city in the United States (for cities over 500,000 inhabitants) with a murder rate of three or four a year. However, Ciudad Juárez, Mexico (1.5 million) was the most dangerous city in the world, with an average of 12 murders a day. So much for the free flow of cultural practices across borders. Ghemawat (2007) similarly argues

Globalization has bound people, countries, and markets closer than ever, rendering national borders relics of a bygone era–or so we're told. But a close look at the data reveals a world that's just a fraction as integrated as the one we thought we knew. In fact, more than 90 percent of all phone calls, Web traffic, and investment is local. What's more, even this small level of globalization could still slip away.

A more viable, compelling globalization theory would examine the relevance of the border for rhetorical and cultural patterns.

The geo-political border significantly mediates the relationships between the two nations, allowing some patterns to flow freely while prohibiting others and reconstructing or reconstituting still more values. For example, many cultural values and practices move back and forth across the U.S.-Mexico border rather seamlessly such as food and language, while others are refracted or reconstituted differently on the other side (such as time or collective relations), and still some, such as violence, have not crossed at all. Thus, much like my colleague, Pablo Vila (2000), the postcolonial and postmodern views of the U.S.-Mexico border that argue for free-flowing hybridity and localization are very un-compelling in light of my experience.

As such, the border as a model of the etic frame for looking at cultures in the context of globalization provides a much more compelling view of intercultural research, as already articulated by Bhabha in Chapter One. It does not fall back on the previous modernist narratives that postmodern and postcolonial scholars have worked so hard to disavow; however, it does not use the local approach as a replacement; instead, it looks at the etic frames as complexly constructed borders that complexly mediate groups of people. Thus, it provides for an etic frame to situate fairly the comparison, but within this frame it allows for the integration of emic details. Like my U.S.-Mexico border area, many intercultural and border researchers are most interested in question that assess which values cross and do not cross fluidly across the border. It is also important to understand how different kinds of borders influence the cross-cultural relations of a variety of groups of people. For example, in other cross-border areas such as the U.S.-Canadian border where the two populations share a similar level of development and infrastructure, the architecture might be remarkably similar but other cultural values could be different. In other words, not only does the border matter, but using the border as a lens to understand the cultural differences remarkably highlights the differences and similarities.

As I explain at the end of this Chapter, this is precisely the approach that would have helped Anzaldúa ground better her depictions of U.S.-Mexico border cultures. However, Anzaldúa does not look across the border to Mexico, and, therefore, simply does not understand the significant influence of a variety of cultural and social institutions such as the law, education, economic system, political system, history, and societal foundation and how the different US and Mexico systems all come together and are refracted, reconstituted, and magnified at the border. Further, because Anzaldúa does not understand the border as the mediator between two cultural, geopolitical, and rhetorical systems, she unconsciously draws on U.S. cultural values to paradoxically make an argument for mestizaje or borderlands. Rather her version of the "border" simply means Tejano or the U.S.-Texas side of the border. This is ethnocentrism. Consequently, she commits the fatal flaw of not recognizing the differences as well as similarities in a cross-cultural work. This flaw severely weakens her understanding of all three cultural systems in the US-Mexico border region: the United States, the border region, and Mexico; and it severely weakens her understanding of her overall personal situation on the border because she doesn't not understand how all three of these cultural systems structure or encourage her own cultural identity and composition.

Consequently, the most effective etic-then-emic approach for cross-cultural research uses the border analogy. However, this constructed universal framework, though necessary for the comparison, is not neutral and will mediate the two cultures dynamically, often intertwined in a Ying/Yang dynamic (see Yuan, 1997). In this ying/yang dynamic, the two values are strongly complementary; that is, cultures never have only one or the other; rather they are defined by their relation to the other; and each position on a value set has a complimentary opposite position. Likewise, the US-Mexico border region tends to define itself in the light of the other, in both sides of the border are intimately connected to each other.

In addition to the Ying/Yang complementarity, the border analogy exemplifies a very important point about the common human thresholds, what

Hampden-Turner and Trompenaars (2000) label as virtues and vices. Each cultural orientation such as collectivism or individualism has both a positive and negative side. In a structured situation, collectivism has both positive effects for the people involved, such as teamwork ability, but collectivism can also encourage nepotism and corruption. Similarly, individualism can inspire an entrepreneurial work ethic, but at the same time can breed selfishness and isolation. Likewise, there are many virtues and vices to both Mexican and U.S. cultural rhetorical patterns on both sides of the border. For example, the Northern parts of Mexico are some of the most dynamic and innovative regions of Mexico. Delphi, the GM-based manufacturing plants in Ciudad Juárez has the most patents of any company in Mexico. Among many reasons for this dynamism is perhaps the close proximity to the more individualistic, and, therefore, historically innovative, United States. Likewise, on the U.S. side of the Mexican border, it is easy to observe many of the strong collective and family values from Mexico.

THRESHOLDS OF HUMAN INTERACTION AND RHETORICAL PATTERNS

The US-Mexico geo-political border is easy to observe and operationalize for cross-cultural comparisons. However, it is not as easy to construct and operationalize other kinds of borders, especially for cross-cultural rhetoric and professional communication. As explained in Chapter One, the "border" that is used to compare values across cultures is the etic or what I have labeled the common human threshold of interaction. These are borders that all human beings share regardless of other orientations or values, much like phonetics or the total available speech sounds for human. For example, all cultures on this planet deal with time: yearly, daily, and seasonally, and past present and future. Thus, time is a border or a common human threshold that is useful for cross-cultural comparisons because it is first a commonality that the cultures share, and upon his commonality, we can analyze differences and similarities. Similarly, all cultures share the I/other relation, which simply means how one person relates to others and to the group. Other common human thresholds or borders include roles of context and communication, rules or norms, status and achievement, source of virtues and truth, relation to nature, division between public and private, and handling inequality or equality in communications.

As explained in Chapter One, most intercultural researchers either explicitly label or assume some kind of common human threshold of interaction as their units of comparison across cultures. Hofstede (2010) doesn't explicitly call it a common human threshold; rather he simply argues for setting comparable units of analysis. This is the reason he chose to use IBM middle management as participants in his research—to make everything as equal as possible so as not to conflate a cultural value with an organizational value. Hampden-Turner and Trompenaars (2000) label their units of analysis as common dilemmas, which is reasonable given their context is organizational behavior. House (2005) generally follows Hofstede (2010) in developing cultural dimensions. None of these researchers, however, contextualize their work as common human thresholds or borders, describing how each constructed border or unit of analysis mediates the cultural system in dynamic ways. For example, Hofstede (2010) and Hampden-Turner and Trompenaars (2000) assume that both universal and particular cultures are mediated the same way the common human threshold of rulemaking. But they are not.

This section lays out eight common human thresholds of interaction as described by a variety of intercultural researchers. All of the researchers present cultural differences and similarities from a bell curve perspective, showing how many nation-states compare in these values or thresholds across the world. This chapter relies on much of this research to lay out the foundation for the cross-cultural research and subsequent chapters. However, it adds to the intercultural discussion by complicating the unit of comparison as a border, showing how each construction of a border might mediate differently the two compared groups. In addition, it connects these common human thresholds to corresponding rhetorical patterns.

I have chosen these eight common human thresholds based on 25 years of experience researching, practicing, and teaching intercultural professional communication. These seem to be the most important in professional communication contexts. There are many other common human thresholds that need to be researched, including the very important common human threshold of gender. Hofstede (2010) and House, et. al (2005) both look at gender as a variable for cross-cultural research. However, I am not persuaded by their methods or findings with gender. For example, Hofstede (2010) correlates gender with aggressive or passive behavior, while House, et. al (2005) looks at egalitarianism and gender. Neither one of these approaches matches my experience with gender in cross-cultural interactions. I think it is best to look at gender relations in the total context of the other common human thresholds. For example, in collective, diffuse, and high power distance cultures, gender relations are very different than in individual, specific, and low power distance cultures. My hunch is, which needs a significant amount of research to verify, is that there are very few if none feminine or masculine traits across cultures.

Another cultural dimension that both Hofstede (2010) and House, et. al (2005) utilize but I do not in this book is *uncertainty avoidance*. This dimension assesses how cultures deal with ambiguous situations, with both of these authors arguing that some cultures avoid uncertainty more than others. However, in my experience as a researcher, teacher, and practitioner, all cultures exhibit great uncertainty avoidance concerning a specific constellation of cultural values, much like gender. For example, Hofstede (2010) and House, et. al (2005) both argue that Germany is a high uncertainty avoidance culture, while Latin American countries exhibit low uncertainty avoidance. However, from my experience, Latin Americans can exhibit high degrees of anxiety about ambiguous situations that deal with interpersonal relationships and social hierarchies, and they take great pains to develop formal rules and procedures for dealing with these. This kind of Latin American uncertainty avoidance seems opposite of the German uncertainty avoidance. Consequently, rather than being a common human threshold, uncertainty avoidance seems to be the explicit manifestation of anxiety about specific underlying cultural values. For me, uncertainty avoidance is more of an emic value, not useful for cross-cultural comparison.

EIGHT ETIC BORDERS INTEGRATED INTO INTERCULTURAL RHETORICAL MODEL

This section integrates the research of prominent intercultural scholars into my etic framework of common human thresholds of interaction, using the intercultural rhetorical model as a frame. First, it defines and operationalizes the following etic borders or eight common human thresholds:

- **I/Other:** Measures the boundaries between human beings, often operationalized as levels of independence or interdependence among groups of people.
- **Rules orientation:** All cultures develop and enforce rules, but how they do that, and to what extent they acknowledge the context and the relationship of the rule varies.
- **Public/Private:** All cultures create boundaries to define what is public and what is private; however, the definitions and methods for crossing these boundaries vary greatly.

- **Source of virtue or guidance:** All cultures look to a variety of sources to guide their behavior. Some cultures look to nature and the outside world as patterns of virtue, while other cultures tend to trust each person's individual or inner direction.
- **Status and accomplishment:** All cultures grant status to different types of individuals, and this status relates to accomplishments, however broadly construed.
- **Context in communication:** All cultures communicate in contexts, but the relevance of the context to the communication purpose and style varies greatly.
- **Time:** All cultures deal with time, both the linearity or simultaneity of time, and past, present, or future orientations
- **Power Distance:** All cultures deal with inequality, however defined, but how they deal with it varies significantly, especially when a subordinate and superior are communicating.

These eight are then integrated into the intercultural rhetorical model. As described in Chapter One, the model centers on the definition of the self, which implies an epistemology, both of which correspond to distinct ideologies, and all three correspond to a rhetoric. The following Figure 4 presents the etic borders situated within three layers of the circle: definition of the self, epistemology, and ideologies. I did not include the fourth layer, rhetoric, because rhetorical patterns are evident with all the value sets. This is entirely my application, showing where I think each of the etic borders best fits the intercultural rhetorical model. It's not a perfect model because the logic or patterns replicate themselves across the layers, but at least it will guide the readers as to where I think each etic border manifests itself most clearly.

As shown in this circle, the most important etic borders for the definition of the self are the I/Other, Virtues, rules orientation, and public/

Figure 4. Three Inner layers of intercultural rhetorical model

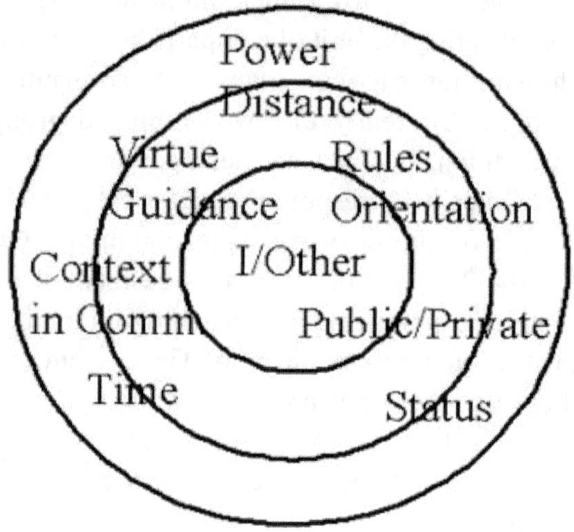

private, although the latter three are probably best seen in epistemology. Context in communication, time, and status are best seen in the epistemology and ideology layer. Each one of these eight common human thresholds is a boundary, either physical, analogical, or behavioral. Thus, each threshold both places the cultures in comparison on a fair and equitable playing field, while acknowledging the dynamic nature of the border or boundary itself.

I/Other

All cultures share the I-other threshold of human interaction, that is, how a single person relates to others or to the group. Essentially, this value assesses the levels of dependence or independence among people. For some cultures, the most likely approach to the "I" relating to the group is individualistic, while in others it is collective. Individualism exists when people see themselves as primarily independent of others and define themselves, see the world through, and negotiate life based on individual identities and efforts. Most intercultural researchers agree that individualism is the strong default approach in the United States, Australia, South Africa, and other western European-Protestant countries (Stewart & Bennett, 1991; Hamden-Turner & Trompenaars, 2000; House, et al, 2005; Hofstede, 2010). One very common touchstone for individualism-collectivism is the use of senior citizen or retirement homes, with individualistic cultures having a much higher ratio of use than collective cultures where older people simply stay with their children or relatives. For example, Las Cruces, New Mexico with a population of about 100,000 inhabitants has more retirement homes than Ciudad Juárez, Chihuahua just 40 miles south of the border into Mexico, which has a population of about two million inhabitants.

The communication patterns of individualism include a focus on the "I" rather than on the group, with the individual as the unit of analysis; a strong bifurcation between personal and objective communication strategies, which resolve interpersonal conflicts by going back to the uniqueness of the individual rather than to that person's political or social context (Stewart & Bennett, 1991); a dumbed-down readership level so as to un-complicate the interpersonal dependence of communicators (Kras, 1991); and an emphasis of personal achievement, self-creation, and reader-friendly document design patterns (Hinds, 1987). As shown in Chapter One, these individualistic tendencies are easily observable in Letter R, including the individual as a unit of reference, the ease in which the author articulates the problem, and the focus on action.

On the other hand, a very common approach to the I-Other threshold is collectivism, which predominates when people view themselves as highly dependent upon others and define themselves, see the world, and negotiate life based on social or family groups. Most intercultural researchers argue that collectivism is the most likely approach in Central and northern South America, Asia, and the Middle East (Stewart & Bennett, 1991; Hampden-Turner & Trompenaars, 2000; Hofstede, 2004). Some researchers have distinguished between a more horizontal or vertical collective values (Triandis, 1995), with Latin America usually exhibiting a vertical collective orientation, while countries in Asia usually reflect a more horizontal collectivity. House et al (2005) distinguishes between institutional collectivism and in-group collectivism. Like Triandis (1995), institutional collectivism predominates in Asian cultures, while in group collectivism predominates in Latin America and Arab cultures.

Collective communication patterns emphasize interpersonal relationships, social hierarchy, social leveraging, group identities, close personal space, and writer-friendly writing patterns (Hinds, 1987).[1] Collective communication patterns do not have a strong bifurcation between personal and objective strategies because they see the person in light of their social context, effectively combining the personal and social political. Thus, instead of resorting to the uniqueness of the individual to resolve interpersonal conflicts, collective communicators usually say something like "we don't get along because we come from very different social or political grounds." Instead of a dumbed-down readership level, collective communicators tend to complicate their interpersonal dependence as a way of stating the purpose of the communication and their involvement; this creates writer-friendly document design patterns Hinds, 1987). Letter O is a perfect example of a collective writing pattern because it is very group oriented, focusing on interpersonal relationships and especially on authority.

Using the analogy of the border, the common human threshold of I/Other mediates collective and individual cultures paradoxically. In short, this threshold seems to imply that individualism means uniqueness while collectivism means harmonious group thinking. This correlation is simply not true. As Stewart and Bennett (1991) explain, individualism does not mean it uniqueness and collectivism does not mean harmony. They explain the difference between individualism and uniqueness and argue that collectivism actually breeds uniqueness and individualism breeds the sameness. I have sensed that this is true but I don't have empirical data to back it up. However, the analogy of the U.S.-Mexico perhaps represents this paradox. If I go into middle-class neighborhoods in El Paso, Texas or Las Cruces, New Mexico, I can only observe a handful of colors for their homes in those neighborhoods. Most of these are earth colors, but some are white. However, if I go into middle-class neighborhoods into Ciudad Juárez, Mexico, I see an infinite variety of colors, and most of these colors are not muted earth tones; rather they are vibrant and flashy colors. This difference in the amount of house colors represents the paradox of individual and collective cultures. For some reason, individualism tends to cultivate the sameness; perhaps all individuals are unique the same way, much like house colors. As Stewart & Bennett (1999) and Hamden-Turner and Trompenaars (2000) explain, collective cultures tend to breed strong and idiosyncratic personalities, which might be a check on the power of dependency in collective cultures. As a result, vibrant, distinct house colors are collectively-sanctioned manifestations of uniqueness.

Norms/Rules

All cultures establish norms or rules, but their approaches and applications greatly vary. The two most common approaches are universal and particular. In universalist cultures, the default approach is to establish rules that define what is good and right regardless of the social standing of the individual. The ideal of a "level playing field" is an apt analogy for universalist cultures. In these cultures, many of which share a common law legal traditions, laws are based on precedence and should have equal application from the one case to everybody. Not surprisingly, "family businesses" are possible, but not the norm, in universalist cultures because a family business cannot treat its employees "fairly" or hire according to universalist protocols. Universal communication patterns include strategies of fairness, justice, equality, and parallelism, and strong use of templates or branding. In addition, in universalist cultures, addressing a person in light of that person's background or ethnicity is often defined as stereotyping because in universalist cultures, this background information is irrelevant to the equal treatment of everybody. For example, in the United States it is illegal to ask for certain kinds of information in a job interview, such as ethnicity, social background, age or gender.

In particularist cultures, the default approach is to apply rules and decisions depending on relations and context. Instead of "the level playing field," the particularist playing field is overtly structured, and thus, there is a specifically tailored set of rules for each social relationship. For example, in many particulars cultures such as those in China or Ecuador, resumes frequently require a picture and commonly have space for marital, political, ethnic, and other personal information usually deemed illegal to include in the universalist cultures such as the United States but in particular cultures, are often the most critical decision-making criteria for hiring. In addition, hiring employees from within the family or close social groups is frequently the default approach especially at the small and mid level because the rules for treating each other are established by familial roles, so structure and trust are built-in.

Particular communication patterns include uniqueness in document design; emphasis of context and particular relationships; attention to exceptional circumstances; and consideration of social prestige and power relations. According to most intercultural researchers, universalism is the default approach in many western European countries, the United States, Canada, and South Africa, while Latin American, Arab, and Asian cultures show the strongest particular approaches (Hamden-Turner & Trompenaars, 2000; Hofstede, 2010).

The universal/particular difference can easily be seen in Letters O and R. Both of these letters are making an argument for fairness, but they do it using entirely different strategies. The particular strategy in Letter O focuses on how the situation has strained and created awkward relationships among the different groups, which strongly implies that the law needs to be changed. Letter R simply makes the argument that the law is unfair because it is treating people differently based solely on the fact of when one person buys a car, not on the value of the vehicle itself.

Using the analogy of the border and ying/yang complimentarity, the common human threshold of rules mediates universal and particular cultures in unexpected ways. When I teach this threshold to my U.S. students, they automatically think that particular cultures have a strong sense of relativity with few laws, while universal cultures tend to have a strong sense of law. The opposite is actually true. Particular cultures have many more laws to regulate human behavior because each law is context- and relationship- based. Thus, instead of one law regulating the behavior of a specific topic, there must be many laws depending on the nature of the relationship. For example, in a family business, employees are not treated equally, but according to their particular relations, with men and older staff often receiving "preferential" treatment. In fact, contrary to what many of my American students at New Mexico State University believe, Mexico actually has more laws on the book than the United States. Some of this difference is because Mexico has a civil law system while the United States has a common law. However, much of it has to do with their particular orientation, which demands more precision in laws because laws are based on relations and context, which is more complicated than simple precedence.

Another paradox of the rules orientation is that universalists tend to think the universal system is fairer while particularism is another word for corruption. This is also simply not true. I often give this example to my students: let's suppose that it is final exam time and then you are driving to the final exam and get a flat tire and miss the final exam. A universalists would say "too bad." A particularsist would have two approaches: first, if this student had never missed a class and was on time for everything, a particular teacher would most likely let the student take the exam late. However, if this student were "always getting flat tires" and late for class, then too bad for that student. This example also demonstrates the more complex rule system of particularism. The question here is what is fairer? Hampden-Turner and Trompenaars (2000) describe compellingly how both systems need to be in place to ensure fair treatment of individuals and organizations.

Public/Private Degree of Involvement and Holistic/Atomistic

A third common threshold of human interaction is degree of involvement across different spheres of life, usually involving a public/private divide and trust. Researchers (Hampden-Turner & Trompenaars, 2000) have defined the two most likely approaches as diffuse or specific. The following Figure 5 shows public/private relationship circles (adapted from Trompenaars, 1994) that best demonstrate these different approaches.

The specific orientation is characterized by the ease in which a person can enter the relationship from a public sphere, which is shown by the dashed line, but once in, that relationship is usually sphere based and rarely crosses over. For example, in the specific model, friends made at school do not have automatic access to your fridge or to your friendships in other places. Further, it is very difficult to enter the small, private world signaled by the small center circle. The diffuse circle shows that it is very difficult to pass from the public into a relationship, signaled by the thick line of the outer circle. And there is a small public/private mixture area between the two circles,

Figure 5. Specific and Diffuse Relations Models

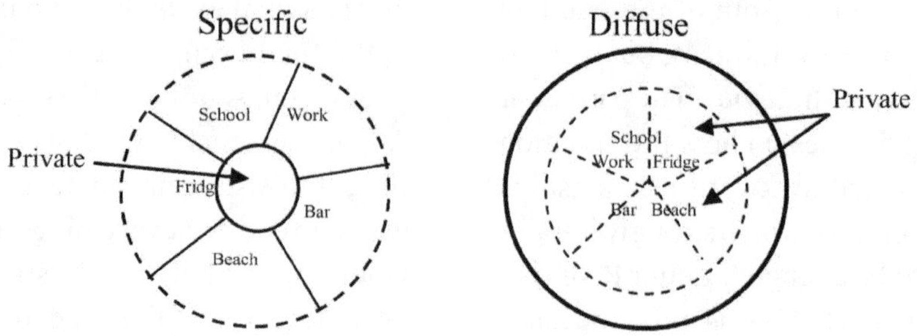

but once inside the larger private sphere (signaled by dashed smaller circle), the relationship crosses boundaries, and there is no distinguishable private self.

As shown by these circles, diffuse cultures are usually collective cultures; as a result, involvement in friendships, social relations, and work environments often crosses boundaries—you work with your friends and close social acquaintances, thus sharing the relationship across these spheres. These acquaintances usually also cross over into your more private life, including religion, family, recreation, and business. Also, the hierarchy of the relationship may also cross over into other spheres. And so, the boss at work may also be the boss on the tennis court, at school, and so forth. At the university, a student's professor, for example, is an authority not only on composition, but also on all aspects of life, and assumes the role of a holistic mentor. In addition, it takes a very long time for students to make friends in class, because with the making of a friendship, there is an expectation that the friendship will move beyond the classroom and into different areas, such as the same social, work, or recreational activities. Consequently, in diffuse cultures, there are high levels of mistrust between people of different social groups or families, making work or collaboration in a public sphere fraught with many conflicts. This is why some researchers have argued that democracy is difficult to develop in more particular cultures such as Mexico and Latin America (see Thatcher, 2005).

On the other hand, specific cultures are based on the ease and public trust that individualism and universalism give people in separate spheres of life, with friendship belonging to one or two spheres only, with little or no cross-over of authority. For example, university professors are only authorities on particular topics; outside those topics, they are just other people. Specific orientation also relies on the reliable social structure of the level playing field, which allows them to quickly work or make friends with people in all kinds of spheres. Consequently, the specific orientation favors more public collaboration, something that is much more difficult in diffuse cultures. It is not surprising, therefore, that democracy has been relatively simpler to establish in specific cultures. In specific cultures, the hierarchies that are in place in business or education, for example, do not transfer as easily to the political realm, or vice versa. Thus, there is an easier transition to more democratic or egalitarian forums.

NMSU University students, for example, can often quickly make friends in the classroom so as to facilitate effective learning and group projects, but outside or beyond the classroom, these relationships rarely continue. One of my favorite examples of this diffuse/specific orientation is when I happen to meet a student outside of the classroom such as at the grocery store. In Ecuador and Mexico, it does not matter where I am, for I am always that student's professor. For example, about four years ago, I taught a qualitative research methods course to beginning professors at the Autonomous University of Ciudad Juárez. I still meet and work with these people occasionally in new contexts, but today they still treat me as their professor. In the United States, my experience is different, although U.S. universities, as a whole, probably tend to be more diffuse than is common in other U.S. business and organizational contexts. Thus, when I meet a U.S. student at Wal-Mart, for example, that student is often torn between addressing me as his professor at Wal-Mart (diffuse) or just another acquaintance (specific). Regardless, the quickness in making friends is possible in specific cultures because of the strong correlation between specificity and individualism and universalism. Individualism provides the personal freedom and universalism the security for quickly making and then disposing of friendships, especially in business relations. This quickness, though, is impossible in diffuse and collective cultures, which use interpersonal relations to structure the crossing over of boundaries, rather than the laws and policies of universalism.

Consequently, in specific cultures, there is little transfer of authority or social hierarchy across spheres. You have a boss at work, but she is your boss only at work; at the beach, she is just another acquaintance. Thus, you have school friends, work friends, beach friends, and bar friends, with little crossover. As I have documented elsewhere (Thatcher, 2006), this specific and diffuse dilemma created difficulties for some of my Ecuadorian students when they first begin using email because they did not understand how the diffuse relations could be communicated in that medium. As I will explain later in this book, in this more "decontextual" medium, the diffuse symbols of authority and status were not transferring as quickly as in other media, thus frustrating my Ecuadorian students.

In very interesting ways first described by Hall (19976), this value set is clearly reflected in architecture. For example, this difference is why the businesses and homes in Ciudad Juárez are both joined together and have high security walls; the architecture perfectly exemplifies the cultural value. In other words, we can place the architectural designs of middle class El Paso, Texas and Ciudad Juárez, Mexico precisely in the same frame as the specific and diffuse circles. It's easy to walk right up to the front door in almost all neighbors in El Paso, but passing from the front door into other areas is usually quite difficult. However, in Ciudad Juárez, the blocks are more self-contained units with perimeter fencing around; visitors have to face this strong perimeter and request entry; but once inside, they have access to most of the homes in the self-contained block.

Currently, I am working on a project in El Paso where we are developing septic and water sanitation training materials for recent Mexican immigrants. One of the most difficult issues for housing in El Paso is that many recent immigrants want to follow the diffuse model and join their houses and businesses together, something which is almost always restricted by U.S. zoning laws. For example, in Latin America, it is very common to have the business or store front on the bottom floor and the dwellings up above, thereby combining them. Further, following the collective and diffuse values, many recent immigrants in El Paso are very accustomed to having the father simply give a piece of his current property to his children to build houses one. This also causes great zoning issues in El Paso, first for septic systems, because a single septic system is not designed for multiple dwellings; but also because of zoning for single-family homes. Zoning laws strongly correlate with the diffuse and specific orientations, much to the difficult adjustment of many recent Mexican immigrants.

As many intercultural researchers have argued, the specific approach is most likely in the United States, Canada, and Western Europe, while the diffuse approach predominates in Asian, Latin American, and Arab countries (Stewart & Bennett, 1991; Hampden-Turner & Trompenaars, 2000). Diffuse communication patterns emphasize approaches that address the whole person in all aspects and dimensions, including social hierarchies. As a result, persuasion does not require salesmanship, but rather a long-term establishment of interconnected, interpersonal values. Consequently, diffuse patterns seem (to specific people) very indirect and to circle around the point, because diffuse communicators need to understand the whole person before getting to the point. Consequently, to critique one part of a person or a communication is to critique the whole thing. It is precisely the circularity in Letter O that that causes much of the difficulty for US-American readers. Specific communication patterns easily section off people into different groups: students, faculty, staff, alumni, parents, and so on. Specific communications are also direct and inductive, stating the main point quickly and then supporting it. They also can more easily de-personalize communications to facilitate critique and development, separating "professional" or specific attributes that are open to objective critique from other attributes that should not be touched. And it is precisely the directness and focus in Letter R that make it so clear to US-American readers.

Using the analogy of the border and ying/yang complimentarity, the common human threshold of public/private mediates specific and diffuse cultures in unexpected ways. This has significant relevance to public places. As is obvious, diffuse cultures tend to correlate strongly with collective, high context, particular, and outer directed values. Because of this, it would seem that diffuse cultures would develop harmonious and long-lasting patterns of relationships in public spheres. On the other hand, specific cultures strongly correlate with individual, universal, and inner directed values. Thus, it would seem that specific cultures would be at a great disadvantage when developing communities or public places for discussion. However, the opposite is true. In public places, diffuse cultures are at best arrogant and standoffish, at worst mean and uncaring. On the other hand, almost all of the specific cultures have developed very effective mechanisms for community building. Something that needs much more research but also seems anecdotally true is that the rates of community centers and community activism are almost always significantly higher in specific-individualistic cultures as compared to diffuse-collective cultures.

I will give my favorite example of this public/private divide in Quito, Ecuador. One of my Latin American colleagues, who was born and raised in Bolivia, but educated in the United States, lived in a 10-story apartment building. Each of the occupants owned one of the 10 stories. One day the phone routing box that directed the telephone lines from the street to the individual departments broke. My friend tried to gather all of the owners together and have them all agree on paying 1/10 of the purchase price for a new router. His efforts failed miserably because no one trusted each other to carry out this public work. This friend, a professor of management and development, linked this *desconfianza* (mistrust) to a lack of development in Ecuador. Another great example of this public-private paradox is in public places such as Wal-Mart. If I were walking down the aisle in Wal-Mart and observed two friends talking and blocking the aisle, it is much more common for diffuse people to simply not recognize or ignore my need to pass by, while it is a hallmark of specific cultures to recognize much more quickly my need in a public place to get by them in the aisle. As Rosenn (1988) explains, this great lack of mistrust in the public sphere has significantly worked against the development of viable democracies in Latin America. On the other hand, United States has a long history of bringing strangers together to develop public works to benefit all involved. Thus, the specific and diffuse orientations strongly correlate with contradictory public contexts.

Sources of Virtue and Guidance

The next common human threshold assesses the source or origin of virtue, guidance, or method of aligning oneself appropriately. In other words, all cultures look to different sources to understand if they are heading in the right direction, so to speak. This dimension was developed by Hampden-Turner and Trompenaars (2000), although House, et. al. (2005) assesses at some of it with his distinction between human and nonhuman orientation of cultures. Hampden-Turner and Trompenaars (2000) explain that there are generally two sources of virtue: the inner-directed source that "conceives of virtue as inside each of us–in our souls, wills, convictions, principles," or believes–in the triumph of conscious purpose. Outer direction conceives of virtue as our site each of us in natural rhythms, in the beauties and powers of nature, in aesthetic environments and relationships" (p.234). Hampden-Turner and Trompenaars (2000) explained how Martin Luther exemplified this inner direction because he withstood tremendous outside pressure to do with something deep down inside of him told him was correct. Not surprisingly, inner-directed cultures are mostly Protestant and believe that inside of each person is a spirit or conscience that tells the person the path to truth or virtuous behavior. Japanese haiku poetry is a great example of our direction because it looks at to the rhythms, patterns, and relationships of a natural setting as a source of virtue to guide all kinds of human relationships. Not surprisingly, outer-directed cultures tend to come from Asian and Catholic countries.

Although a seeming anachronism in the era of postmodernism, this dimension has very important ramifications for intercultural rhetoric and professional communication because they are clearly connected to persuasive strategies and communication. In rhetoric and professional communication, three types of persuasive strategies are common: ethos, pathos, and logos. These are classical Greek and Roman rhetorical constructions. Ethos has a dual meaning, focusing on both the credibility and morality of the speaker or author as critical to believing in the communication. Logos, as the name implies, focuses on the logic or reason of the communication. Pathos basically means emotions. As Aristotle explains, all three are commonly used to convince an audience of one's communication purposes or objectives. Each of the strategies differs significantly depending on whether the culture is inner or outer direct.

In outer-directed cultures, reason or logic is usually not analytical or vertical, universally breaking down of the parts into its whole. Rather it is what Stewart and Bennett (1991) label as horizontal and relational, focusing on the *what* and its relations rather than the *why*. For example, if I walk out my office door and looked at the NMSU campus using an outer-directed lens, I am more interested in how the buildings, the trees, the sidewalks, the students, and the faculty are all interacting as I gaze upon them. Thus, what is defined as logic focuses on the pattern-like correlations between one behavior and a natural setting. From this perspective, one looks to harmonize himself or herself with the natural world. This harmonizing logic is very powerful and often uses analogies and metaphors of the natural world as logical patterns to replicate, which, not surprisingly, often show up in communications.

On the other hand, logos and inner directed culture focuses on the vertical *why*, which is often analytical and universal. Instead of using a natural haiku poem, the inner directed person focuses on rational and universal principles of behavior that supposedly derive from the inner will or conscious. The analogy of deep thinking is an important characteristic of inner direction (Stewart & Bennett, 1991). Consequently, if I walk out my office door and look at my campus from an inner directed lands, I contemplate why the students are there, why the building are there, and what universal principles structure this context.

Ethos is defined and operationalized very differently in inner and outer directed communications. One of the clearest examples of this difference occurs in beginning writing courses in the United States. Very often, U.S. composition instructors tell their students that clichés are sign of stupid and unoriginal thinking. The best ethos from the U.S. instructors' perspective is to find your inner voice and help it come out in its unique and original form. However, much to the chagrin of U.S. composition instructors, many students from Asia directly draw on famous sayings from important people from their culture to add credibility to their papers. Or they use traditional analogies or references to natural imagery. The inner and outer distinction explains clearly a different ethos approaches between the U.S. instructor and Asian students. The U.S. instructor believes that the most credible and moral author is one that draws that credibility from the down inside aligns the paper accordingly. The outer directed perspective believes that what is most credible and moral is that author aligns himself or herself to the great ones that have come before. This outer directed alignment gives great strength and credibility to the ethos of the author. Not surprisingly, many Chinese scholars of second language writing argue that Chinese students have to dramatically change the sense of who they are when they are writing composition papers in US university classes.

Pathos also differs significantly between inner and outer directed cultures. Inner directed cultures tend to see emotions as unique to the individual and difficult to share, while outer directed cultures tend to see emotions as a way of connecting to others in a common way. Bennett (1998) sees this as a distinction between empathy and sympathy. He argues that communicators from individualistic and inner directed cultures have a hard time showing empathy because they literally cannot see life from the other's viewpoint; rather they can only sympathize with the emotions of the other human being. Collective and outer directed cultures, however, are naturally inclined to be empathetic because they can adapt or connect their emotions to the emotions of others much more easily.

Hampden-Turner and Trompenaars (2000) connect these three differences with common communication approaches and, interestingly, marketing. The inner directed approach is the "hard sell" (p. 263) and adversarial because the inner directed person has to change his or her inner voice to be convinced all on his own of the path communicator is trying to sell. Not surprisingly, one of the most common rhetorical textbooks in the United States is titled *Everything is an Argument*, a textbook that I analyze in Chapter Twelve. The marketing strategies in inner directed cultures emphasize creativity and uniqueness of the product, that is, the product is so unique that it will create its own market. The outer directed approach is more of a "soft sell" because change means harmonizing values and approaches between the communicator and audience. Not surprisingly, as Hampden-Turner & Trompenaars (2000) theorize, outer directed cultures are not as good at creating new products, but are fantastic at realigning or harmonizing these products with local markets. For example, the automobile, television, computer or many other electronic devices are all original inventions of Western and inner directed cultures; however, the outer directed cultures have significantly surpassed many of the inner directed cultures in their consistent re-development and redesigning of these original innovations for the market. Another common characteristic of inner directed cultures is that the audience tends be the detached and objective observer who needs to be surveyed or questioned about his or her unique attitudes (Hampden-Turner & Trompenaars, 2000), while the outer directed communicator seeks to harmonize the communications in more of a conversation rather than a survey.

A border analogy of this difference between inner and outer directed communicators shows the paradoxical differences in strength and resiliency.

For example, Trompenaars narrates his experience of an automobile accident between his Volvo and a Mitsubishi sedan (Hampden-Turner & Trompenaars, 2000). The cars collided head-on, and the Mitsubishi sedan suffered significant damage to the front part of the car, while the Volvo sustained very little damage. However, Trompenaars, the driver of the Volvo, received real damage to his body, while the driver of the Mitsubishi received very little damage to his body because his automobile received the impact of the crash. This analogy is important because it shows that outer directed cultures are much better equipped to handle the outside forces and can adjust accordingly, while inner directed cultures have a unique inner strength, but this inner strength can crash dangerously against outside forces. This is a border paradox that will most likely mediate comparisons differently.

Another great border analogy of this difference is in the development of the Sony Walkman. According to Trompenaars (1994), Mr. Sony developed the Walkman idea while he was riding on the noisy subways in Japan. Coming from his outer directed orientation, Mr. Sony believed that the Walkman would provide music to the individual without offending those in the subway by forcing them to listen to his music. A typical inner directed approach would be that the Walkman allows me to shut out the noise of the subway and allow me to be alone with myself and my music.

These differences can easily be seen in Letters O and R. Jose Plaza Luque, the author of Letter O, is significantly concerned with aligning or harmonizing himself with all of the other agencies. Letter R is much less concerned about harmony and much more concerned about the fairness and application of the law. It is interesting to note that this difference surfaces in tone. Often unobserved by my American students is the fact that tone of Letter R is quite negative and pushy for many Latin American readers, while the tone of Letter O is respectful and diplomatic.

Status

The fourth common threshold of human interaction is status—how it is developed and communicated. The two most common approaches are ascription and achievement. Ascriptive-oriented cultures derive status from their social group, race, gender, age, ethnicity, and language. These variables provide the communicator with the power to get things done in complicated social structures. Ascription orientation says: I am great because of my ascribed background; therefore, I can do. In organizational communication, ascription is often operationalized through overt signs of ascribed status, power through people, and importance of context and history to the university. Ascriptive communicators highlight social attributes that enable work to get done through power structures, and they tend to emphasize latent versus observed potential.

In achievement-oriented cultures, it does not matter where you come from, who your family is, your age, language, etc, as long as you can achieve your goals. Achievement orientation says: I have achieved many things; therefore, I am great. In organizational communication, achievement orientation is often operationalized by emphasizing accomplishments such as concrete business goals, number of clients, market share, and CEO honors. Achievement communicators emphasize action, change, statistics, and other observable and verifiable demonstrations of accomplishment. Hofstede (2010) and Hampden-Turner and Trompenaars (2000) argue achievement is the most likely approach in the United States, Canada, Australia, and the United Kingdom, while ascription is the most likely approach in Asian, former communist countries, and Mexico and Central America and Andean south American countries.

It is easy to notice the difference between ascription and achievement orientation in Letters O and R. Letter O is trying to use this strategy of the lever, or as we say in Latin America, "La

Palanca," which is a Spanish term meaning a lever. To accomplish something in ascription cultures, one must get the appropriately authorized person to make that change, or in other words using palanca. Letter O artfully tries to draw on the president of Ecuador or other authorized people to implement the change, demonstrating that power works through people. Letter R simply states that a change needs to be done and the focus is on the action. As demonstrated later in Chapter Ten, this difference significantly influences the approaches to instructional writing, with achievement oriented cultures focusing on a-personal process and ascriptive cultures emphasizing power through people.

An easy touchstone for the ascription versus achievement orientation is to look at resumes. A typical US resume emphasizes achievements. Figure 6 is a U.S. resume found on www.avisto/rob/portfolio, which is shown in the lower left hand corner.

Much of the language is focused on doing or accomplishing with relatively fewer connections to power structures or other ascriptive values. In contrast, Figure 7 is a resume template taken from the website www.resumel.com, which demonstrates a typical approach in China.

When my US students see the typical Chinese resume, they are dumbfounded by the significance of the ascriptive values such as gender, age, region of the country, and others. At the same time, my U.S. students typically comment about what the writer of that Chinese resume has actually accomplished. These seemingly indistinct differences surface quite easily in resumes and other professional documents and can profoundly influence the reader's perceptions of these documents depending on their cultural background.

One of the ying/yang and border paradoxes of this value set is accomplishment. Many people who come from achievement oriented cultures simply believe that ascriptive people do little or nothing, resting on the work on their ascriptive predecessors. This is simply not true. As Melton (2008) describes in his cross-cultural work in Asia, much of the "work" in ascriptive cultures happens behind the scenes through powerful people. And once this work is carefully planned, the plan is put into action. On the other hand, ascriptive cultures often emphasis the work itself and getting things going (Stewart & Bennett, 1991), which appears, on the surface, to be doing more, but in reality, it is probably not.

Context

The next cultural value is the role of the context in the communicative interaction. All cultures communicate in contexts, but how they rely on these contexts for the meaning of their communications differs. Hall (1976) originally developed the distinctions of high- and low-context to study these roles. Low context means that the meaning of the communication resides primarily in the explicitly coded part of the communication, not in the surrounding context. Thus, there is a focus on information that is specific to individuals at hand, increasing involvement of a few select people. There is greater focus on the accuracy of the explicitly coded text. Low context communicators strongly adhere to and require clearly written protocols. There is a high attention to detail and low attention to intention. In addition, low context communicators try to program into the communication all of the verbal signs and cues to carefully guide the reader through the message. Consequently, low context communicators use parallel lists as a common organizing strategy. Connor (1996) and Hinds (1987) similarly labels this type of writing as "reader friendly," writing that assumes a reduced reliance on the reader to bring in contextual cues and create transitions to understand the writing. In other words, there is an overt emphasis of organizational and transitional strategies to guide readers through the writing. From this view, good writing is focused on the accuracy and interpretation of the explicitly coded text.

Figure 6. Typical U.S. resume

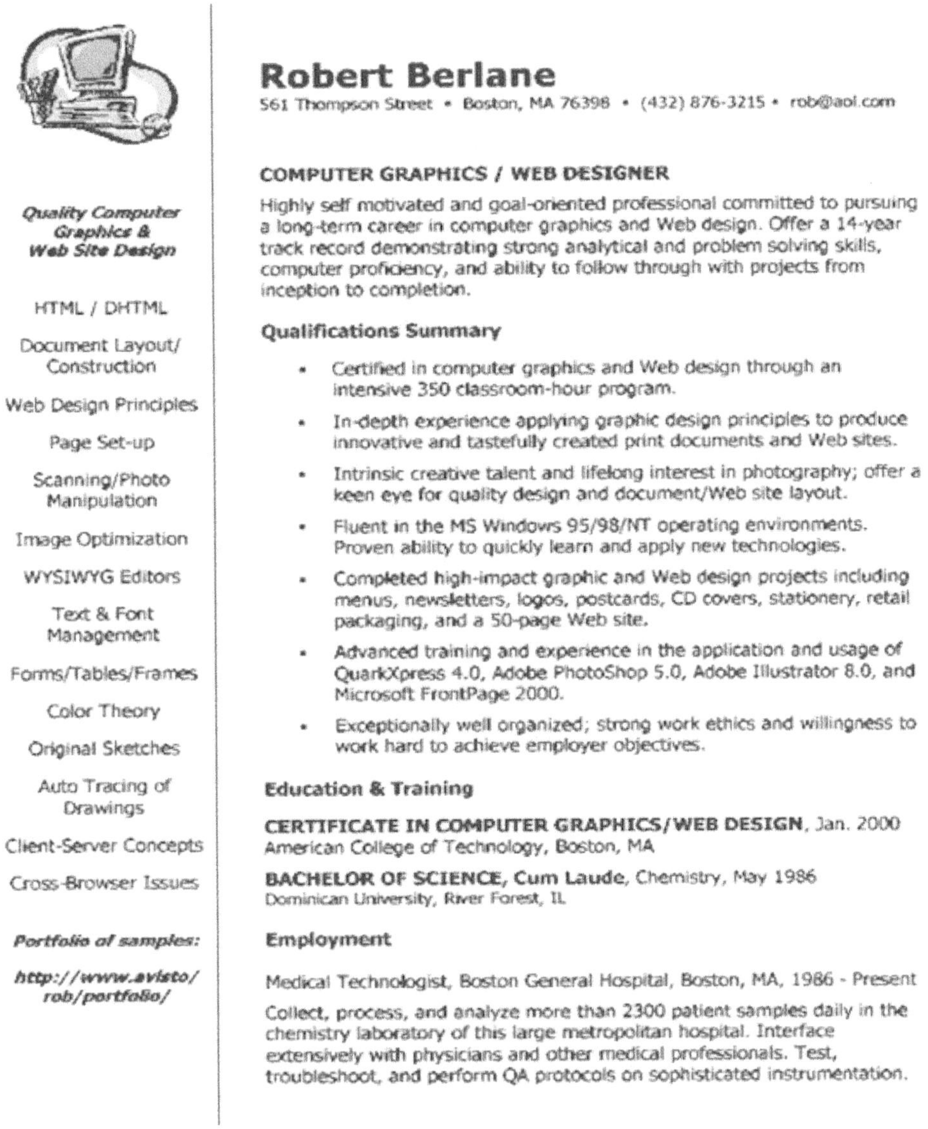

Quality Computer Graphics & Web Site Design

HTML / DHTML

Document Layout/ Construction

Web Design Principles

Page Set-up

Scanning/Photo Manipulation

Image Optimization

WYSIWYG Editors

Text & Font Management

Forms/Tables/Frames

Color Theory

Original Sketches

Auto Tracing of Drawings

Client-Server Concepts

Cross-Browser Issues

Portfolio of samples:

http://www.avisto/rob/portfolio/

Robert Berlane

561 Thompson Street • Boston, MA 76398 • (432) 876-3215 • rob@aol.com

COMPUTER GRAPHICS / WEB DESIGNER

Highly self motivated and goal-oriented professional committed to pursuing a long-term career in computer graphics and Web design. Offer a 14-year track record demonstrating strong analytical and problem solving skills, computer proficiency, and ability to follow through with projects from inception to completion.

Qualifications Summary

- Certified in computer graphics and Web design through an intensive 350 classroom-hour program.
- In-depth experience applying graphic design principles to produce innovative and tastefully created print documents and Web sites.
- Intrinsic creative talent and lifelong interest in photography; offer a keen eye for quality design and document/Web site layout.
- Fluent in the MS Windows 95/98/NT operating environments. Proven ability to quickly learn and apply new technologies.
- Completed high-impact graphic and Web design projects including menus, newsletters, logos, postcards, CD covers, stationery, retail packaging, and a 50-page Web site.
- Advanced training and experience in the application and usage of QuarkXpress 4.0, Adobe PhotoShop 5.0, Adobe Illustrator 8.0, and Microsoft FrontPage 2000.
- Exceptionally well organized; strong work ethics and willingness to work hard to achieve employer objectives.

Education & Training

CERTIFICATE IN COMPUTER GRAPHICS/WEB DESIGN, Jan. 2000
American College of Technology, Boston, MA

BACHELOR OF SCIENCE, Cum Laude, Chemistry, May 1986
Dominican University, River Forest, IL

Employment

Medical Technologist, Boston General Hospital, Boston, MA, 1986 - Present

Collect, process, and analyze more than 2300 patient samples daily in the chemistry laboratory of this large metropolitan hospital. Interface extensively with physicians and other medical professionals. Test, troubleshoot, and perform QA protocols on sophisticated instrumentation.

On the other end, high context communication assumes a strong reliance on the contextual and social cues for the meanings of communications. Here, good writing focuses on information that elucidates the influence of the social context on meaning of the communications. High context communicator's generally focus on adhering to interpersonal relationships instead of fixed guidelines. There is low attention to detail and high attention to intention. Instead of parallelism, high context communicators prefer novelty so as to match the uniqueness of the evolving relationship in the specific context. Parallelism is boring and artificial. Connor (1996) and Hinds (1987) label this type of writing as a "reader-responsible" (Connor 1996, p. 42) or writing in which the reader is expected to fill in the information and create the transitions. In high context communications, there also tends to be more non-verbal, indirect forms of communication and complex overtures

Figure 7. Typical Chinese resume

My Resume				
Name		Sex		Photograph
birthday		Height		
native place		nationality		
membership		School		
curriculum vitae		Major		
Tel		Email		
Postal Code		Address		
self intro				
hobbies				
demonstrate work experience				

and concrete sensory stimuli to evoke the physical, social, and interpersonal contexts that add meaning to the discourse.

In addition to the greater reliance on the context, the organization and development of high context communication also varies much more based on prior knowledge of the context. As Hall (1976) explains, when high context communicators understand the context, their communications can be very quick and agile, often needing no more than one word or a glance. However, when the communication context is not understood, high context communicators tend to painstakingly articulate or evoke into the coded text all the fine nuances of the context before communicating the main message. Victor (1992) explains that many Asian, Latin American, and Middle Eastern countries tend to value high context communications, while Germany and Germany Swiss cultures tend to value low context communications. The U.S.

tends to be mid- to low-context. Although this variable has been in existence for more than 30 years, there is still a lack of research on different countries and cultures.

The differences in context are easily apparent in Letters O and R. Letter O is full of contextual information such as dates, places, relationships, and events. In fact, the first phrase of Letter of is a contextual phrase: "in response to," which is a very high context way to start the letter. The high level of contextual information demonstrates that the author, José Plaza Luque, felt that his audience would be unfamiliar with the circumstances, so he had to contextualize the topic so that his high context readers would understand it. Letter R has deleted most of the contextual markers so as to facilitate the more low-context readers.

Like other common human thresholds or cultural dimensions, high and low context present contradictory relationships. Because high context communicators strongly correlate with collective and diffuse values, low context communicators often believe that high context communicators are always going to "beat the around the bush," while high context communicators often believe the low context communicators are often too direct and get to the point to quickly. The example of Kaplan's doodles in Chapter Three demonstrates this assumption, with low context and specific communicators writing in a line, while high context and diffuse communicators communicating in circles, starting from the outside and moving in.

Again these are mistaken assumptions. As explained earlier, high context communicators can be exceedingly direct when the communicator and the audience are in common or well-known contexts. However, in unknown contexts, high context communicators are laborious and careful in their communications. Low context communicators are simply much more homogenized in their communications strategies because they are often writing to universalist cultures, which means that their strategies vary much less than those of high context communicators.

TIME: MONOCHRONIC OR POLYCHRONIC, AND PAST, PRESENT, AND FUTURE

Many researchers have explored the different ways that cultures view and use time. Hall (1976; 1983) first articulated a very useful distinction between linear and nonlinear time. Hall defines linear time as monochronic and nonlinear time as polychronic. Hampden-Turner and Trompenaars (2000) offer similar definitions of synchronous (polychronic) and sequential (monochronic). Polychronic or synchronous time frames mean simultaneity, multiple tasks managed at the same time, and apparent disorganization, focusing on the importance of place, and involvement of people rather than adherence to present schedules. On the other hand, monochronic or sequential time frames mean linked linear structures of cause and effect with an organized flow of events (Hall, 1976, 1983). This monochronic time "seals off one or two people from the group and intensifies relationships with one other person, or at most, two or three people. .. [and] it alienates people from the context and experience of social relations" (Hall, 1976, pp. 19-20). Polychronic time frames enhance the relationships of a variety of people in rich contextual detail. Written discourse in monochronic cultures emphasize linear structures of topics, a direct topic sentence to situate discourse, and given/new discourse structure. On the other hand, polychronic communicators favor the artful orchestration of events, people, places, and issues in discourse. Often, writing in polychronic cultures exemplifies complex syntax and paragraph structures, with many narrative structures in polychronic or multiple timeframes.

This difference in polychronic or monochronic time frames can easily be identified in a variety of everyday activities, such as lines at a bank or store or waiting to meet people. In monochronic cultures, lines are very important, and people are herded much like cattle, one by one in a precise order. In polychronic cultures, lines basically don't exist; usually, it is a first come first serve and whoever has the strongest elbow or quickest feet is the first in line. This difference was brought home to me in a powerful way is some of my first encounters with polychronic culture in Ecuador. About my second day on the job at a private university in Ecuador, I was invited to meet the president of the University. I walked into the receptionist area, and she told me to go into his office. However, when I entered his office, I noticed that there were already six other people in the office, and the president was talking to those six people, while he was on the phone with another person, and he was taking notes about a third party at the same time. As I peeked my head around the corner in apparent fright, the university president, sensing my uneasiness, told me to come in. He laughed a little bit because he, having been educated in the United States but also an Ecuadorian, understood my dilemma. I soon joined the conversation and realized that as a group we began to learn a lot about each other and a lot about how the president made decisions. It was my first polychronic experience, which was duplicated many times over in other scenarios in Ecuador. This kind of simultaneity is rare in the United States, Western Europe, and other more universal and individualistic cultures.

The differences in time orientation for Letters O and are exemplify dramatically how time connects to communication. Letter O is multi-time framed; in the first paragraph there are probably four to five things going on at the same time. This simultaneous, narrative approach is actually an important literary genre in Latin America called magical realism. Letter O also focuses much more on the past and present and very little on the future. Letter R reduces significantly the simultaneity and instead develops a more linear approach and explains step-by-step what happened and what needs to be done. There is a strong correlation between polychronic cultures and more narrative and complexly written communications, while there is a strong correlation between monochronic cultures and very analytical and signposted types of communications. Signposted simply means clear intros, clear transitions, and the conclusion that backs up what is said.

The border dynamic of the polychronic and monochronic time frames are often paradoxes. Monochronic people usually panic at apparent chaos of the simultaneity in polychronic cultures, thinking it is inefficient chaos. I will never forget the first time that I took my mother in law, an American of German descent, for a drive in the polychronic driving situation of Ecuador. In Ecuador, driving is in flux, that is I will have someone to my left, someone to my right, a bicycle, a motorcycle, a pedestrian, a chicken, a bus, all flowing down the road in apparent chaos. I thought my mother law was going to have a heart attack when she experienced this. But, in reality, it was very efficient. Another example of polychronic driving is the use of roundabouts or circles at intersections, which are common in Latin America and Europe but not so in the United States. In a roundabout intersection, each driver enters the intersection with a requirement to yield to if there is a car coming from the left going clockwise in the roundabout. However, if no cars are coming, the driver can immediately enter the intersection. One of the difficulties for monochronic drivers is to time the entrance into the intersection, for some drivers coming from the left might appear to be making it all the way around to that drivers quadrant in the intersection but actually turn right at a 90° angle to the driver wanting to enter the intersection. Indeed, it took me a couple of years to become used to the polychronic driving, especially with roundabouts. However one of the contradictions or paradox is that this apparent chaos of simultaneity actually can be very efficient, like the roundabouts while monochronic driving can be very inefficient: after experiencing the efficiency of roundabouts, I cannot stand to sit at a red light knowing that no cars are using the green light coming from the 90° directions.

Another important component of time orientation is past, present, and future. All major intercultural researchers have assessed this variable, and all argue for significant variation of it around the world (Hofstede, 2010; Hampden-Turner & Trompenaars, 2000; House, et.al, 2005). This is actually an easy variable to assess, and Trompenaars' (1994) visual analogy of three circles is perhaps the best way to do that. Trompenaars draws three circles representing past, present, and future orientations for a given culture (1994, p.130). The size of the circle and its connection to the others to circles represents how important and how connected are the time frames for that culture. Figure 8 represents a culture that equally values past, present, and future, but the time dimensions do not influence each other.

An alternative to this would be a culture that equally values past, present, and future but also sees them as connected to, as exemplified in Figure 9.

Another variation shows some orientations having more significant influence, whether they are connected or not to each other. For example, Figure 10 shows the present having more significant influence, with the first version showing the present connected well to the past and future in the second example showing disconnection.

The first circle diagram means that the present is very important while the past and future are equally less important. The second diagram shows the same importance but also shows that the present is significantly influenced by the past and will significantly influence the future.

Although Trompenaars' circle analogies are very useful for demonstrating time orientations, his research in this chapter seems to present many flaws because it is not correlated with the other value sets or common human thresholds. The later research of House, et. al. (2005) demonstrates significant variation in future orientation, but this research does not connect future with past or present nor demonstrate their mutual influence. Much more research is needed for this portion of the time dimension.

The circle diagrams, however, are very useful as a diagnostic tool for professional communication. For example, it is easy to note in Letter O of a strong past orientation that significantly connects to the present but has little relevance to the future. If I were to render the past, present, and future orientation of Letter O compared to Letter R, I would render it this way, as exemplified in Figure 11.

These two differences in time frames (monochromic/polychromic and past, present, and future) are easily identifiable and operationalized in professional communication. The typical US and Chinese resume, which were exemplified

Figure 8. Rendition of equal but disconnected past, present, and future orientations

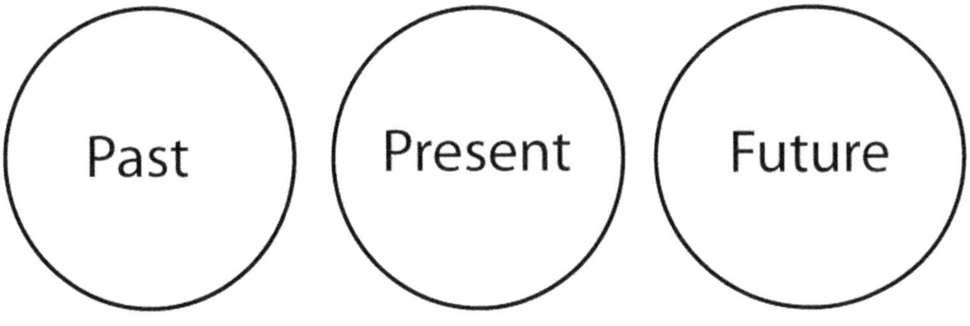

Figure 9. Circle rendition of equal and connected time orientations

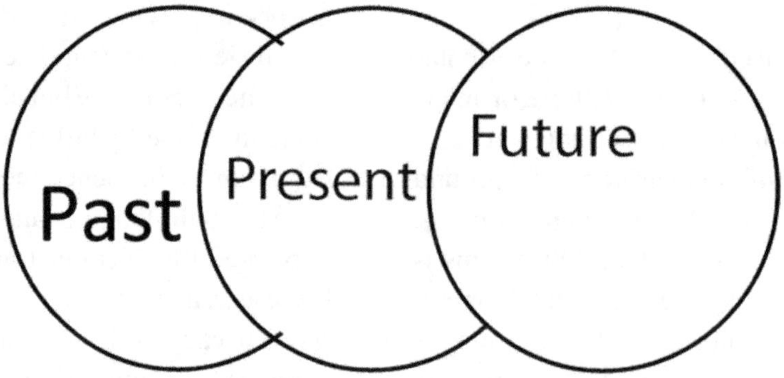

earlier demonstrate significant differences in time orientation. The US resume is strongly oriented to the present with some connection to the future, while the Chinese resume as a strong past orientation which significantly influences both the present and future.

Power Distance

Power Distance is Hofstede's (2010) concept, and it measures how inequality is handled in communications. In high power distances cultures, there is unequal, centralized distribution of power, acceptance of authority, high levels of overseeing, and top-down communication styles. Further, in high power distance cultures, subordinates are afraid to just disagree with their superiors; and there is a high level of overseeing of subordinate activities. In short, high power distance cultures use communications to reinforce and exemplify the hierarchy. For example, teachers in high power distance cultures will always have the answers to their students' questions regardless of whether they know the answers are correct or not. Hofstede's (2010) research labels as high power distance cultures Japan, Mexico, Andean South America, many Arab nations, Korea, and China. House, et.al.'s (2005) work basically reinforces Hofstede's concept and cultural variation around the world. The communication patterns connected to high power distance include top-down communication patterns, strict lines of authority and subordination, and formalities and titles that show social hierarchy; in addition, high power distance communicators are very careful with lines of authority, showing respect and deference.

Low power distance cultures use communications to downplay inequalities among people. As Hofstede (2010) explains, low power distance cultures expect more mutual interdependence

Figure 10. Strong present orientation

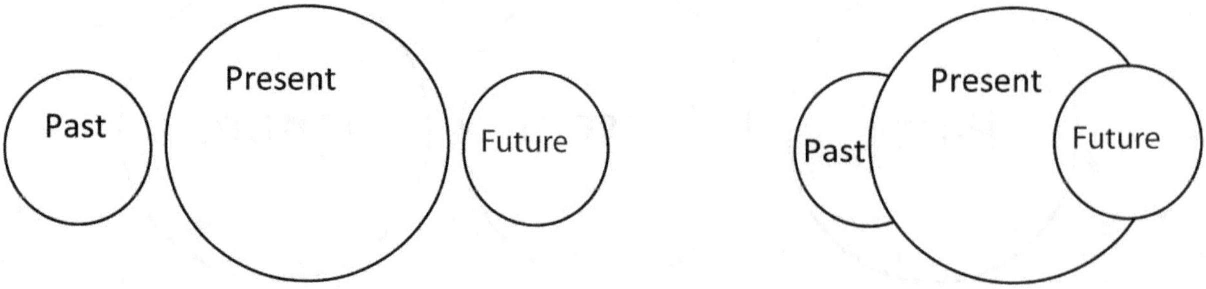

Figure 11.Circle analogy for Letters O and R

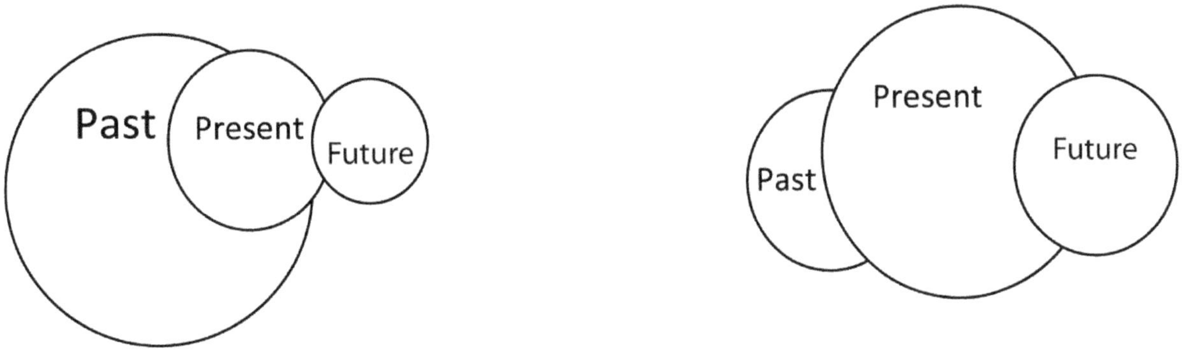

between subordinate and authority. For example, parents tend to treat children as more or less equals; children treat their parents as equals; teachers expect initiative from students; and teachers are content-area experts who should not go beyond their individual expertise. Hierarchies in organizations are established for convenience; the ideal boss is a resourceful diplomat who seeks subordinate input. Communications between superior and subordinate tend to be more consultative, with the superior acting as perhaps someone with more knowledge, but not in reality being in a higher position. Authority is something to be used only as more of a last resort rather than the explicit framework for the communication situation. Subordinates are not afraid to disagree with superiors; in fact subordinates are often a source of good feedback for decisions is that the superiors need to take. Hofstede (2010) argues that the Northern European countries such as Denmark and Finland and Israel are low power distance cultures. The United States is ranked by Hofstede as mid-to low power distance. House, et.al. (2005) generally confirms Hofstede's rankings.

In low power distance cultures, communicators tend to make the communications less formal as a way to ease the feelings of inequality in the communication situation. Condon (1997), for example, explains how the then president of the United States Jimmy Carter failed in his communications with the Mexican president. Carter, hoping to ease the feelings of inequality between Mexico and the United States, treated the Mexican president as more of a friend rather than the constitutional president of the United States or Mexico. Carter even put his feet up on the desk as a symbol of informality, hoping to ease the tension. His lack of understanding the high power distance culture of Mexico actually exacerbated the feelings of inequality because the Mexican president felt that Carter was not treating his authority with the respect and deference.

I have a personal example that is just as revelatory concerning high and low power distance cultures (Thatcher, 2006). I was doing some research for the U.S. Environmental Protection Association along the US-Mexico border. We were trying to help the Mexican manufacturing plants or maquilas develop ISO 14000 Certifications, which is the environmental management certification. I had been studying the role of the user manuals in the manufacturing processes of the maquilas. At the same time, the maquilas were experiencing a high rate of turnover and were frustrated because they had to continually re-train new employees; in addition, management felt that employees were too afraid to take calculated risks, and that employees have a hard time solving basic problems. I learned that the maquilas used the instructional manuals not to guide the individual operating machinery; rather, the instructional manuals were used to legitimize the engineering processes; writing served more like a notary than a guide to behavior. The new employees were shown the instruction materials in their introductory training but were not allowed access to materials after that training. Coming more from a low power distance, U.S. perspective, I asked the engineers why they would not give their employees access to the instruction materials. I actually asked this question in a large focus group of 15 engineers from a variety of Ciudad Juárez maquilas. Of the 15 engineers only two were women; the rest were men. All of the male engineers simply and emphatically replied that they would not give their employees access to the instruction materials because they would lose their power in that context. The two female engineers and I then argued extensively about the connections between accessibility to instruction materials, ability to take risks in that context, and problem-solving. But this was to no avail.

The differences in low and high power distance are clear in Letters O and R. Letter O shows significant care and deference in the use of titles, hierarchy, and other formalities that signal the social hierarchy surrounded this issue. Letter R shows much less care and gets right to the point.

This common human threshold mediates power differently between the two orientations. For example, low power distance people tend to think that high power distance patterns are abusive, while low power distance patterns are conducive to more harmonious relations. It is usually the exact opposite. High power communicators favor formality and rigid guidelines of high-power communication guidelines, much like the military, in order to establish clear lines of authority and communication so that abuses cannot take place; and it is in ambiguous situations where lines of authority are not clear that are ripe for abuse. Further, low power distance communicators might feel that the relationship is equal based on the low power distance communication patterns, when in fact there is much hierarchy built-in. Researchers need to understand clearly these border-like contradictions of power distance.

SUMMARY OF EIGHT COMMON THRESHOLDS

In summary, these eight cultural dimensions or common human thresholds provide the units of analysis to analyze and understand cross-cultural rhetoric and professional communication. The subsequent chapters in this book draw on these eight dimensions as they explain professional communication in the variety of contexts. As a concise guide, the following Table 1 outlines the major units of analysis and their connections to the four elements of the intercultural rhetorical model.

Table 1 helps researchers and students focus on the most valid units of analysis to assess a cultural and rhetorical pattern. For example, is a formal, hierarchical communication an example of collectivism, high power distance or diffuse orientation? It is probably all three, but to assess collectivism, the communicator or researcher needs to look at how the formality and hierarchy create interdependence; to assess high power distance, the communicator looks at the flow of communication and power relations; and to assess diffuseness, the communicator examines how authority crosses spheres of activity in public and private contexts. Thus, an example of communication can exhibit a great variety of values, but students, researchers, and communicators must focus on the actual units of analysis to make valid assessments.

Consequently, as the intercultural rhetorical model implies, there is much repetition of the logic or patterns across the eight value sets. For example a collective culture is most likely particular, diffuse, ascriptive, high context, polychronic, outer-directed, and high-power distance; and an individualistic culture is most likely the opposite. These correlations present two problems for students, researchers, and communicators: First, it is easy mix up the value sets, describing "a behavior" or rhetorical patterns as collective when in fact the researcher is analyzing public-private interactions, which is a unit of analysis

Table 1. Summary of etic borders and units of analysis for intercultural rhetorical model

Etic Border/ Thres-hold	Unit of analysis	Subjectivity	Epistemology	Ideology	Rhetorical patterns
I/Other	Dependence or independence among people	How separate or con-nected are people's identities?	Are decision-making criteria and processes group or individual?	How strongly does the group or individual define appropriate social behavior?	Effective rhetoric is bringing to the surface uniqueness or connect-ing to social traditions?
Rules	Universal versus particular rules.	Are humans inherently equal or unequal?	Transparent, universal process or relation- and context- sensitive?	Are exceptions to rules acceptable for powerful people?	Appeals to fairness based on equality or relations and circum-stances?
Specific/Dif-fuse	Crossing between public and private domains	Are human relations connected by common sphere of activity or holistic grounding?	Objectivity possible by separating personal attri-butes from professional behavior?	How much does authority cross-over into different spheres of activity?	Circular/holistic grounding or direct, thesis driven state-ment?
Virtue	Source of virtue or alignment	Virtue resides deep down inside or in aligning oneself with outside forces.	How much do outside or inside forces become models for criteria and processes?	Is appropriate be-havior aligned with–or in opposition to–outside forces?	Direct statements from the inner self or ana-logical alignments with outside forces
Status/ accomplish-ment	Status → ac-compli-shment or accomplish-ment→status	Self-concept built by doing or by inherited attributes?	Tangible and measurable performance or power through people?	Are social levers required or trans-parent, universal processes?	Appeals to tangible performance or lever-aging power through people?
Context	Role and rel-evance of con-text in personal interactions	How separable are humans from their context?	How much does the context frame decision-making criteria and processes?	How relevant is the context to social interactions?	Does the context or the codified language provide most of the meaning?
Time	Conception and relevance of time	Humans connected to natural rhythms or creators of mono-chronicity?	Is the process made explicit, counted, and rationalized or based on simultaneity?	Are interactions based on the sched-ules or social needs and circumstances?	Narratives and stories versus analytical and sign-posted descrip-tions
Power Dis-tance	Handling inequality in relations	Assumption of equality or inequality in humans	How connected are the criteria and processes to personal power?	Are power differ-ences reinforced or downplayed?	Formalities that reinforce power or informalities that downplay it?

for the specific and diffuse value set. This table shows how to operationalize the value sets very carefully without mixing them up.

Second, students, researchers, and communicators must be very careful not to correlate together too strongly the eight etic borders. For example, the United States almost always ranks as the most individualistic culture, yet they consistently rank in the middle area of power distance. Or Germany consistently ranks in the middle area of individualism/collectivism and very highly for universalism, but it also ranks as mostly diffuse and fairly ascriptive. These inconsistencies among the value sets are the source of many problems and contradictions, a topic that is far beyond this chapter. However, as a side note, it is highly likely that when one or two value sets value sets seem inconsistent with the other value sets, this inconsistency often becomes areas of much controversy and discussion for a given culture.

For example, as explained earlier in this chapter, one of the value sets that Hofstede (2010) developed and operationalizes is *uncertainty avoidance.* He defines this value set as the level of anxiety–and the overt efforts and procedures to combat that anxiety–in a given culture. However,

I do not use this value set in this book because I think Hofstede does not operationalize it universally. For example, he ranks some cultures as showing high levels of avoiding uncertainty, while other cultures showing low levels of uncertainty avoidance. He assessed Latin America as showing very low levels of uncertainty avoidance, an attribution that I cannot understand, because in Latin America there is strong anxiety about power relations and other cultural values. I would certainly argue that in the United States there is strong anxiety about authority and discrimination. Thus, my reassessment of uncertainty avoidance is that it is connected to the value sets; that is, each culture has anxiety about perhaps the virtues and vices of their predominant values sets. For example, the United States is strongly universal, a value that does not correspond to its mid-ranking in power distance. Thus, the mid-ranking in power distance produces great anxiety. We see, perhaps, the same anxieties with the contradictions in the predominant values among all cultures. In other words, uncertainty avoidance is a useful tool for assessing rankings in a value set for a group of people that do not correlate positively with the logic of the other value sets for the same group of people.

APPLYING INTERCULTURAL THEORY TO ANZALDÚA'S THE BORDERLANDS

This section demonstrates how to apply five of the eight etic borders or common human thresholds analyzing Gloria Anzaldúa's *The Borderlands* (2007) from intercultural perspective. It demonstrates why the etic then emic framework is so important, and why researchers must draw from the common human thresholds to understand the differences between people, organizations, regions, and broad cultural rhetorical patterns.

The Borderlands has always been one of my favorite contemporary texts, so rich in cultural and linguistic theory. And as one who has dedicated years to develop Spanish-English bilingualism, I learned to love its nuanced Spanglish. In addition, I relished Anzaldúa's admonition about the need for Anglos and Mexican-Americans to understand each other and work together effectively (the goals of much of my research). However, as an example of intercultural inquiry, it has two serious flaws, ones that are continually duplicated in much current cultural and rhetorical theory. First, even though she titles it the *Borderlands*, Anzaldúa's focus is clearly on the Mexican-American experience on the U.S.-side of the border, and thus, she fails to analyze the three border cultures—Mexican, Anglo-American, and Mexican-American—from a comparative frame. Thus, her conceptions of mestizaje or feminisms, for example, commit a kind of orientalism because she views these concepts from a Mexican-American experience in the United States but does not explore their Mexican roots or the influence of Anglo-American legal, economic, or cultural values on her definition. This is seen in Anzaldúa's great disparagement and fascination of stereotypes, a common rhetorical strategy in an individualistic culture. Instead, in a typical poststructuralist move, she argues for the great need for the fluidity of boundaries and corresponding uniqueness for her own local Mexican-American situation only.

As someone with very different border experience, I quickly noted this flaw. I grew up in an almost entirely Anglo-American context; then I lived four years in South American, in an entirely Latin American context; and then I moved to the U.S.-Mexico border and worked with Mexican-Americans in New Mexico, but I have spent a significant amount of time in Mexico, researching border technical communications and teaching courses as an adjunct professor at two Mexican Universities. I understand all three worlds that make up the U.S.-Mexico border area.

Because of this lack of a comparative frame, Anzaldúa praises the great fluidity and uniqueness of Mexican-Americans, showing herself as an example of this uniqueness. But all Anglo-Americans are lumped into a basic, stereotypical, uncomplicated category. And rarely does she address or acknowledge *that* country on the other side of the river—Mexico. Her lack of knowledge of Mexico in the *Borderlands* is actually astonishing, something she acknowledged and tried to remedy in the latter part of her career. Further, as explained in Chapter One in the section on humility and reflexivity, this privileging of Mexican-American culture by showing its great richness and complexity, while at the same time denying that same complexity to Anglo and Mexican culture is, paradoxically, one of the results of the local approach. Anzaldua's approach also impoverishes our understanding of how Anglo-Americans, Mexican-Americans, and Mexicans might live and work together. As Bhawuk &Triandis (1996) explain, it is impossible to set up a comparative framework when the scholar starts with—and is fixated upon—the emic characteristics of one population.

An intercultural inquiry into the U.S.-Mexico borderlands would welcome Anzaldúa's kind of complexity and richness, but it needs to place that complexity in a framework that allows for equal comparison and a self-reflexivity in understanding the sources of often conflicting values. This next section does just that as it explores *Borderlands* from the comparative frame of five common human thresholds in the United States and Mexico. Space prohibits using the final three thresholds, but the five are sufficient for this demonstration.

From the I/Other threshold, it is clear that Anzaldúa is caught between the Mexican collective orientation and U.S. individualism, and most of the book narrates the struggle between these values. However, it is also apparent that U.S. individualism is not only her default approach, but it is one that she does not explicitly reveal as her foundation. In arguing for her unique identity from multiple perspectives (linguistic, ethnic, generational, and sexual orientation), she consistently references her own struggles to create her identity as a way to get through life, an identity that fits who she is deep down inside and one that is based on the identity-constructing processes of language, a very common practice in individualistic and universalist cultures (Trompenaars & Hampden-Turner, 2000). Her language is almost always referencing her unique experience and her own methods of getting through life. She does discuss the tension that this uniqueness creates for her family and community, but she does not tie that uniqueness and tension back to Mexico's collective orientation. In about every case, Anzaldúa herself is the unit of reference, not the group, a hallmark of individualism (Stewart & Bennett, 1991). In other words, she is a self-made woman. Perhaps as multiple scholars have argued, she simply does not understand Mexico. Perhaps, she is simply manifesting a version of U.S. individualism. Regardless, she simply explains her growing sense of identity using herself, the individual, as the benchmark or unit of analysis.

As demonstrated throughout this book in multiple genres such as websites, instructions, law, and health communications, the unit of reference for discussion in collective cultures is the group first, individual second. A collectivist would understand how one's identity is significantly dependent upon the group; and changes in personal identity means significant changes in group identity. This difference might seem insignificant in Anzaldúa's case, for she does explore extensively her background; however, in the end, she relies on individualism. This difference is often represented in contradictory views of clichés in personal writing. In individualistic cultures, clichés are a bad thing because these worn out phrase deny the unique creativity of the author. However, in collective cultures, clichés are necessary because they ground the author in his or her appropriate context and speak for the author. Anzaldúa is the opposite: she focuses almost all her energy on creating highly unique and personal renditions of her background and avoids any cliché as representations of detrimental binary, fixed thinking.

Ironically, because Anzaldúa does not understand the tension between individual and collective approaches, she also cannot understand why her strong, Anglo-like individualism is misunderstood by many family members and friends who come from a more collective, Mexican tradition. Nor does she understand the true strength and richness of these collective traditions such as roles in family and community because she does not understand their Mexican origins and is assuming a U.S.-like individualism where these values can be changed rather quickly. A truly denaturalized approach to the I/other threshold would draw from both the strengths and weaknesses from both approaches and strategically argue for combinations of both, given the specific structured situation (Stewart & Bennett, 1991; Hampden-Turner & Trompenaars, 2000). For example, in my work with cross-border, U.S.-Mexican manufacturing plants, or maquilas, I have observed that almost all human resource managers are Mexicans but are trained in U.S. systems. These resources managers understand the great collective and interpersonal traditions when managing their Mexican workers, but they also draw on U.S.-like traditions for training and promotion, in effect combining the best of both traditions.

From the rules threshold perspective, Anzaldúa is likewise caught between the borders of U.S. universalism and Mexican particularism. And just as in the case of the I/other, Anzaldúa un-reflexively draws on the "level playing field" assumption of U.S. universalism, without highlighting the pros and cons of this American approach. The tension between universalism and particularism manifests itself with the way people choose to apply rules. As many intercultural and Mexican researchers (Castañeda, 1995) have argued, Mexicans have a strong tradition of applying rules to people according to that person's group affiliation, while Mexican-Americans having assimilated the strong U.S. universalist value of avoiding group labels (which is decried as stereotyping) and judging people based on other references such as "actions" or education and economic status (Vila, 2000). For example, "racial profiling" is strongly discouraged in the United States because it attaches a certain kind of behavior to ethnicity, something anathema to universalist thinking, and as explained in Chapter Two very problematic and inaccurate. Another example of this difference is the use of photographs and other "personal" attributes on résumés. Surprising to many Americans is that in much of Latin America, Asia, and Africa (and France, for that matter) jobs ads routinely asked for personal photographs, age, family background, and marital status to be placed on the résumés. In the United States, this information is irrelevant and illegal because in a universalist, level-playing field context, this information is not relevant. All job candidates should be judged by their ability to do the job. In particularist cultures, however, the ability to do the job—get things done—has much to do with the candidate's background such as family name, gender, and age.

This universal-particular difference clearly manifests itself in the use of group stereotypes, something Anzaldúa seems obsessed with. From the U.S.-universalist perspective, stereotypes are like racial profiling or placing a photograph and personal information on a resume—they are a very negative thing, a sign of poor education. Thus, in a universalist cultures such as the United States, people usually avoid being labeled as a Latino, Hispanic, Anglo, etc because that unfairly places them in a group, and no group can account for their uniqueness; again, everyone is different. In Mexico and other particular cultures, the communicator needs to understand the group affiliations of the person he or she is talking to in order to actually talk to that person. For example, Pablo Vila explains that one of the greatest communication differences between Mexicans in Cd. Juárez and Mexican-Americans right across the border in El Paso is that the Juarenses use the group affiliation to ground communications, while the Mexican-Americans use economic status, a more individualistic approach (See Vila, 2000). In other words, in particular cultures, group affiliation—often labeled as stereotyping—lays the conversational groundwork for productive communications. Consequently, the very communication patterns used to lay the groundwork in Mexican communicative traditions are avoided or severely criticized from Anglo-American traditions. One indicator of growing enculturation into American culture by Mexican-Americans is the preoccupation with—and avoidance of—stereotypes.

Like many current U.S. academic theories of people, groups, and cultures, Anzaldúa reacts strongly against labels and stereotypes. In fact, most of this work argues for the fluidity of identity in names, labels, attributes, anything associated or connected to the judging of people in particular circumstances. In many ways she has "Americanized" Derrida by using his fixation on–and critique of–binaries to produce a corresponding fixation and critique of stereotypes. Anzaldúa's definition of fluidity is also a wonderful analogy for U.S. universalism because it implies any "fixed" attribute is bad because "fixed" necessarily implies unequal treatment. Unfixed or fluid means you have to be treated equally. From a particularist culture, however, fixed means being treated more fairly because it recognizes the cultural background for behaviors and adapts the application of rules to it.

However, Anzaldúa seems unaware that she is exemplifying basic U.S. individualism and universalism because she never ties the anti-stereotyping thinking to U.S. individualism-universalism and particular thinking to Mexican culture, which are strong correlations throughout all the intercultural research. And not surprisingly, poor communication is a result. She relates many examples of others routinely misunderstanding her fluidity and routinely stereotyping her because of labels. An intercultural framework would have helped her understand why her strong, Anglo-like universalism would not harmonize well with many of her family and Mexican-American friends who come from more of a particular orientation. In addition, a more reflexive view of her universalist foundation would have revealed the strength of universalism—a mechanism against corruption—but also its weaknesses—the absurdity of a level playing field in the more structured societies.

From the perspective of the status threshold, Anzaldúa is stuck between U.S. achievement and Mexican ascriptive orientations, but she favors the American approach. Put simply, her "status" as a person is not based on her ethnicity, gender, or socio-economic group; rather, her status is self-made as a unique, personal creation of that background. Closing following many behavioral theories of the construction of the subject, Anzaldúa presupposes that the person—subject—is mostly an empty, blank slate that is continuously constructing herself through linguistic and other cultural processes but one in which she is—or should be—in charge of her own construction. Clearly, there are social structures that impinge upon the construction of the person; but again, there is an emphasis on how she negotiates this self construction. Further as demonstrated in Chapter Ten Instructions and Chapter Eight Legal Orientations, achievement oriented cultures strongly assert the importance of process, rather than the power players associated with the situation. Also, in interestingly contradictory ways, she asserts an achievement orientation of the self-made person by drawing on Derridian and Foucaultian views of subject formation, which imply that the subject is often the product of social structures, not the author of them (which more closely resembles the French version of ascription). A more ascriptive, Mexican-like approach would have grounded her status and power through the group and presupposes a framework of social networks that often implicitly structure the process and must be competently handled.

Not surprisingly, Anzaldúa relates many significant communication problems when she uses her "constructive, fluid" approach to argue for change with people from more ascriptive orientations who disagree, often vehemently, with the supposed ease of this constructive, fluid version of subject formation. An intercultural perspective based on etic borders would have helped her understand the pros and cons of both ascriptive and achievement orientation and strategically use both for her desired means. For example, the ascriptive orientation would have helped her understand better the significant strength of ascribed Mexican values of machismo and marianismo; thus, simply "writing these values away" through self creation does not mean that they will go away. This is similar to the critique of Baudrillard who argues that the events of September 11 were discursive creations and therefore, they can be done away with discursively. Rather, the ascriptive strength of machismo and marianismo is so profound in Mexico that changing it means changing many of the other gender, legal, cultural, religious, and social values in Mexico. However, other values along the U.S.-Mexico border are much more likely to fit with achievement orientation, such as performance in the workplace which has as much to do with bottom-line achievement in many places as opposed to more ascribed variables such as social groups.

The fourth common threshold of human interaction is the public/private degree of involvement across different spheres of life; and Anzaldúa exemplifies very clearly by her form of presentation the default U.S. approach. In specific cultures, there is an enhanced ability to reveal oneself and one's interpersonal attributes in very public forums, while in diffuse cultures, public forums are shunned. Perhaps an example from the internet will help explain this difference. As described in Chapter Five, university websites from specific cultures displayed pictures of people much more frequently than in diffuse cultures. In addition, the pictures displayed in specific cultures almost always had friendly postures with open, inviting smiles. This tendency perfectly exemplifies that quickness to break down the public-private divide, as shown earlier by the specific and diffuse circles. In highly diffuse cultures, rarely do people smile in public photographs; and usually, they simply show clear emotional and social barriers, which is represented by the thick outer line of the diffuse circle.

Put simply, Anzaldúa's *Borderlands* is like the U.S. university websites that show very personal information quickly. It is an intimate, personal, diary-like account of her life presented to the public to view. There are very few, if no barriers (other than Spanish-English). And we learn about all facets of her life: family, relationships, age, and sexual orientation. It could easily be classified as the stereotypical, friendly and smiling American approach to communication based on specific orientation (see, Stewart & Bennett, 1991). This kind of approach simply does not happen in diffuse cultures when the venue is so public. Rather, in diffuse cultures, this level of intimacy is reserved for the in-group, and it is shared much more guardedly in public. Thus, it is not surprising that many of Anzaldúa's friends and family were shocked and dismayed at her intimate revelations in this public forum. It is also interesting to note that this kind of personal narrative has become an important strategy for many contemporary scholars, who, in their attempt to resist positivistic paradigms, turn to U.S. specific orientation.

However, it is important to view the pros and cons of specific and diffuse orientation in a structured situation. For example, it is very easy to be specific in a public forum for a U.S. academic with tenure who wants to reveal personal information that might shock friends and colleagues. However, in a more vulnerable situation such as in the workplace, such specificity can be highly risky; and thus, careful lines between public and private must be maintained. It is also not surprising that Anzaldúa's public rendition of her own unique personal journey into her subject formation has been almost universally endorsed by U.S. academics but almost entirely ignored by Mexican scholars.

The final common human threshold for this analysis addresses power distance, the handling of inequality in interpersonal communication.

As with many of these variables, power distance correlates with the other variables. High power distance cultures are usually collective, particular, ascriptive, and diffuse, and low power is the opposite. Anzaldúa's *Borderlands*, put simply, presupposes a low power distance context. Although her language is academic and presupposes grounding in academic jargon and theory, she does not use the formalities, status markers, and other power symbols that structure high power communications. She talks to readers as if we were somewhat equals, trying to understand her points of view. Very little inequality or social hierarchy is assumed between the writer and reader. It is like the classic example of Jimmy Carter's experience working with Mexicans (Condon, 1997). For those in high power distance cultures, these intimate, low power distance approaches might significantly reduce Anzaldúa's credibility as an authority in the areas for discussion, something that Anzaldúa clearly does not want to portray but in actuality might be portraying.

In summary, if I were to display Anzaldúa's cultural orientation in the rhetorical model, it would look something like Figure 12.

As shown in this circle, the major foundation of her orientation is her individualistic construction of the self, which has critical ramifications for her universal and process-heavy epistemology and her low power distance and specific public orientations.

As evidenced by this discussion, despite the great richness of the *Borderlands*, from an intercultural perspective, the approach is based on—and reinforces—predominant American values. On the one hand, does this matter? It is written by an American. On the other hand, it does matter. First, this U.S. bias and associated problems of orientalism beg the question of diversity. Very often, U.S. diversity means bringing other types of view into the organization, but the values of the organization do not change, and these diversity people have to give up parts of their values in order work within that context. This reminds me of the "diversity" pictures that are often on the homepage of New Mexico State University, showing a multiplicity of ethnicities on the homepage, but this multiplicity in no way represents the actual student populations at New Mexico State University, and these same students need to adapt to U.S. values or they do not survive. Not really diversity.

In another example, I was recently invited to discuss ways to increase diversity in the Council on Programs in Technical and Scientific Communication. My desire was to internationalize the curriculum, understanding how U.S. theory and practice of technical communication might work in other cultures, and then recruit international students to fully participate in a global curriculum. However, I was quickly outvoted by those who wanted to bring in more "diverse" student populations, such as Latino, Asian, etc, into the programs but not address the curriculum. I strongly argued that bringing in diverse students into programs that un-reflexively reflect U.S. American cultural values is simply Americanizing them because they almost overwhelming begin to mimic these values. Likewise, for Anzaldúa, diversity seems to show how each individual is unique; that stereotypes should not be used; and that the construction of the

Figure 12. Anzaldúa's cultural and rhetorical model

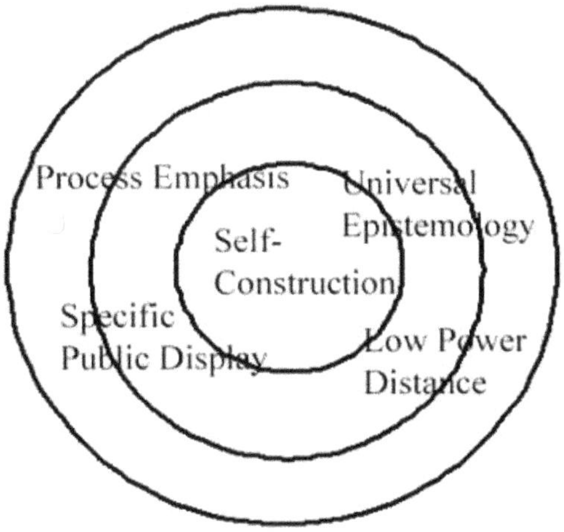

subject is a continuous and fluid process based on a blank slate. However, both versions of diversity are based on predominant U.S. cultural values. It becomes, from an intercultural perspective, an *ethnocentric diversity*. What are other types of diversity? True diversity is understood when the sources of those competing values are denaturalized and understood in their context and origins; and thus, the approaches used in context are given their fullest meaning. A viable intercultural framework provides such a method.

CONCLUSION

This chapter provides the necessary variables for examining intercultural professional communication in a variety of contexts and media. For example, it shows how the conception of contrastive rhetoric, as explained in Chapter Three, cannot be based solely on the language but must have the additional elements of the eight common human threshold of interaction. Chapter Four contextualizes the use of communication media (orality, writing, hypertext, and e-mail) in concrete rhetorical situations, showing how these eight dimensions or thresholds influence the purpose, audience author interaction, information organization and style of each one of these medium based on different cultural systems. Chapters Five through Twelve similarly draw on this etic border frame to explore intercultural professional communication.

REFERENCES

Anzaldua, G. (2007). *Borderlands/La frontera: The new Mestiza* (3rd ed.). Aunt Lute Books.

Badiou, A., & Feltham, O. (2007). *Being and event*. Continuum.

Bennett, M. J. (Ed.). (1998). *Basic concepts of intercultural communication*. Yarmouth, ME: Intercultural Press.

Bhabha, H. (1994). *The location of culture*. Routledge.

Bhabha, H. (2003). Statement for the *Critical Inquiry* Board. *Critical Inquiry, 30*(2). Retrieved from http://criticalinquiry.uchicago.edu/issues/v30/30n2.Bhabha.html.

Bhawuk, D., & Triandis, H. (1996). The role of culture theory in the study of culture and intercultural training. In Landis, D., & Bhagat, R. (Eds.), *Handbook of intercultural training* (2nd ed., pp. 17–34). Thousand Oaks, CA: Sage.

Castañeda, J. G. (1995). *The Mexican shock: Its meaning for the U.S.* New York, NY: The New Press.

Condon, J. C. (1997). *Communicating with the Mexicans* (2nd ed.). Yarmouth, ME: Intercultural Press, Inc.

Derrida, J., & Spivak, G. (1998). *Of grammatology*. Baltimore, MD: The Johns Hopkins University Press.

Foucault, M. (1972). *The archaeology of knowledge* (Sheridan Smith, A. M., Trans.). New York, NY: Harper Colophon.

García-Canclini, N. (1992). Cultural reconversion. In Yudice, G., France, J., & Flores, J. (Eds.), *On the edge: The crisis of contemporary Latin American culture* (pp. 29–44). Minneapolis, MN: University of Minnesota Press.

Hall, E. T. (1976). *Beyond culture*. New York, NY: Doubleday.

Hall, E. T. (1981). *The silent language*. New York, NY: Doubleday.

Hall, E. T. (1983). *The dance of life*. New York, NY: Doubleday.

Hampden-Turner, C., & Trompenaars, A. (2000). *Building cross-cultural competence*. New York, NY: Wiley.

Hinds, J. (1987). Reader versus writer responsibility: A new typology. In Connor, U., & Kaplan, R. (Eds.), *Writing across languages: Analysis of L2 text* (pp. 141–152). Reading, MA: Addison-Wesley.

Hofstede, G. (2010). *Cultures and organizations, software of the mind* (3rd ed.). New York, NY: McGraw Hill.

Hoft, N. (1995). *International technical communication*. New York, NY: John Wiley & Sons.

House, R. J., Hanges, P. J., Javidan, M., Dorfman, P. R., & Gupta, V. (Eds.). (2005). *Culture, leadership, and organizations: The GLOBE study of 62 societies*. Newbury Park, CA: Sage Publications.

Kras, E. (1991). *Management in two cultures*. Yarmouth, ME: Intercultural Press, Inc.

Melton, J. (2009). Going global: A case study of rhetorical invention, packaging, delivery, and feedback collection. *IEEE Transactions on Professional Communication*, *52*(3), 229–242. doi:10.1109/TPC.2009.2025305

Osland, J. S., De Franco, S., & Osland, A. (1999). Organizational implications of Latin American culture. *Journal of Management Inquiry*, *8*(2), 219–234. doi:10.1177/105649269982018

Paz, O. (1985). *Labyrinth of solitude* (Kemp, L., Trans.). New York, NY: Grove Press.

Said, E. (1979). *Orientalism*. New York, NY: Vintage Books.

Stewart, E., & Bennett, M. (1991). *American cultural patterns: A cross-cultural perspective* (Rev. ed). Yarmouth, ME: Intercultural Press, Inc.

Thatcher, B. L. (1997). *Orality and writing in Latin American and USA professional communication*. Unpublished doctoral dissertation, Purdue University.

Thatcher, B. L. (1999). Cultural and rhetorical adaptations for South American audiences. *Technical Communication*, *46*(2), 177–195.

Thatcher, B. L. (2000). Writing policies and procedures in a U.S. and South American context. *Technical Communication Quarterly*, *94*, 365–400. doi:10.1080/10572250009364706

Thatcher, B. L. (2001). Issues of validity in intercultural professional communication research. *Journal of Business and Technical Communication*, *15*(4), 458–489. doi:10.1177/105065190101500403

Thatcher, B. L. (2006). Intercultural rhetoric, technology, and writing in Mexican maquilas. *Special Technology Transfer Edition of Technical Communication Quarterly*, *15*(3), 383–405.

Thatcher, B. L. (2009). Understanding digital literacy across cultures. In Spilka, R. (Ed.), *Digital literacy for technical communication: 21st Century theory and practice* (pp. 169–198). Routledge.

Thatcher, B.L. (2010a). Introduction. *Rhetoric, professional communication, and globalization*, 1, 1-34.

Thatcher, B. L. (2010b). Reading and writing new media across cultures: Issues of fit, reciprocity, and cultural change. In Kalmbach, J., & Ball, C. (Eds.), *Reading and writing new media*. Hampton Press Series New Dimensions in Computers and Composition.

Triandis, H. C. (1995). *Individualism and collectivism*. Westview Press.

Trompenaars, F. (1994). *Riding the waves of culture: Understanding diversity in global business*. New York, NY: McGraw Hill.

Victor, D. (1992). *International business communication*. New York, NY: HarperCollins Publishers.

Vila, P. (2000). *Crossing borders, reinforcing borders: Social categories, metaphors and narrative identities on the U.S.-Mexico frontier*. Austin, TX: University of Texas Press.

ENDNOTE

1 Writer-friendly patterns, according to Hinds, means writing that reflects the complexity of the author's thoughts with little effort to revise the writing to accommodate different levels of audience knowledge and attitudes.

Chapter 3
Contrastive Rhetorics and World Englishes

ABSTRACT

This chapter provides the linguistic base to intercultural rhetorical research, exploring theories of linguistic relativity and contrastive rhetoric. It contextualizes much of this work into a broader social and cultural framework, showing how intercultural rhetorical patterns are not solely based on language, but also on other values, such as the eight common human thresholds of interaction. It also hypothesizes about the cultural and rhetorical relevance of English as a world language

INTRODUCTION

This chapter explores how distinct features of human languages might encourage correspondingly distinct cultural and rhetorical patterns, generally connecting specific languages such as English or Chinese to the eight common human thresholds. This body of research is known as the theory of linguistic relativity (for speech) and contrastive rhetoric (for writing), and for many reasons, it is critical to intercultural rhetoric and professional communication. First, because human language is the medium of most intercultural communication, it is important to understand how one language might predispose communicators to naturally draw on the common human thresholds differently than speakers of a different language. This language-rhetoric connection can significantly influence how communications are developed, translated, and used in cross-cultural contexts. Further, as demonstrated by the work in contrastive rhetoric, the language-rhetoric connection can remarkably influence writing pedagogy, especially for second language writers. And third, if specific languages correspond differently to the eight etic thresholds, then language domination might lead to cultural domination, a line of research that is very critical because of the spread of English as a second language and Chinese, two world dominating languages.

This Chapter first explores linguistic relativity and contrastive rhetoric, connecting this work to the eight common human thresholds articulated in Chapter Two. This chapter concludes with a brief discussion about globalization and the role of English as the defacto language for globalization.

DOI: 10.4018/978-1-61350-450-5.ch003

THEORY OF LINGUISTIC RELATIVITY AND SAPIR WHORF HYPOTHESIS

An important line of inquiry for professional communicators working across cultures is the connection between the native language and corresponding rhetorical and cultural patterns. Known as the theory of linguistic relativity or the Sapir-Whorf hypothesis, this theory examines how the differences in the ways languages encode cultural, rhetorical, and cognitive categories influence the way people speak, write, and reason. In 1956, Benjamin Whorf describes the theory this way:

We dissect nature along lines laid down by our native language. The categories and types that we isolate from the world of phenomena we do not find there because they stare every observer in the face; on the contrary, the world is presented in a kaleidoscope flux of impressions which has to be organized by our minds—and this means largely by the linguistic systems of our minds. We cut nature up, organize it into concepts, and ascribe significances as we do, largely because we are parties to an agreement to organize it in this way—an agreement that holds throughout our speech community and is codified in the patterns of our language [...] all observers are not led by the same physical evidence to the same picture of the universe, unless their linguistic backgrounds are similar, or can in some way be calibrated (pp.134-5).

Eventually, Whorf and others embraced two versions of the hypothesis: The strong version maintains that one's native language determines thought and linguistic categories, while the weak version simply argues that a language encourages certain usage and perceptions. In other words, a speaker's native language is much like a computer's operating system, influencing what is inputted, what and how something is processed, and the output. Even though Sapir and Whorf reinvigorated the discussion in the 1940s through the 1960s, this connection between language and the brain has been strongly debated for more than 200 years or perhaps even as far back as St. Augustine or the Sophists.

Most early 20th century research in linguistic relativity examined the correlation between the availability of words in a certain language and how speakers of that language perceived color or time, with corresponding argument that if a speaker of the language did not have a word for it specific color, that speaker would not recognize (strong version) or leave in the background (weak version) the recognition of the color. For example, if we view the light spectrum as shown in Figure 1, we note that there are no clear separations of colors in the spectrum:

Because there are no clear separations of colors, according to most theorists of linguistic relativity, language is the vehicle for carving up the light spectrum. In other words, because English has the words of red, or blue or yellow, English speakers are predisposed to categorize the spectrum this way, while other languages that have words for colors such as blue-green or orange-yellow will predispose their speakers to categorize or carve up the light spectrum a different way. Thus, English speakers are more likely to categorize the spectrum with their words, as shown in the Figure 2:

Figure 1. Light spectrum

Figure 2. English categories for light spectrum

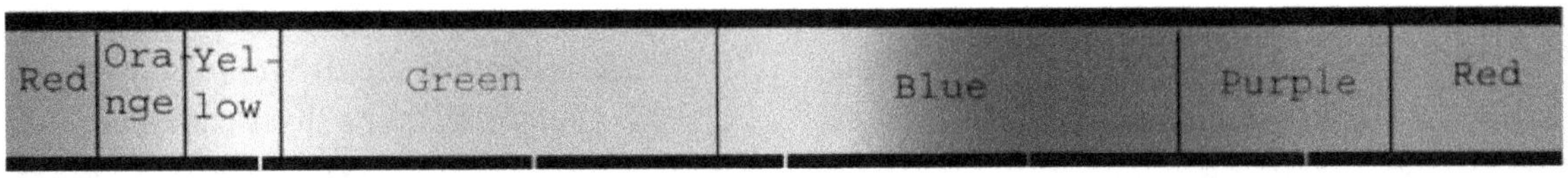

Thus, according to this theory, speakers of English would most likely naturalize these categories, not even realizing that Figure 2 is a linguistic construction. For example, when I present this theory to my English-speaking students at New Mexico State University, sometimes I present it with these categories and word already in place and asked them if anything seems unnatural or foreign. And very rarely do they realize that the designations and corresponding words are not part of the original color spectrum. From a similar perspective, Whorf conducted experiments with the Hopi Native Americans, showing that their perception, cognition, and operationalizing of time strongly correlated with the lexicon and syntax of the Hopi language. And just as a language predisposes its speakers to categorize the light spectrum or time, a language will predispose its speakers to categorize an infinite variety of reality based on the vocabulary, syntax, and other linguistic structures.

This theory of linguistic relativity has been hotly debated, and a significant body of scholars fundamentally disagrees on its relevance. In 1969, Berlin and Kay argued that terminology for colors was universal or crossed all cultures, and, therefore, the theory of linguistic relativity was either untrue or useless. Most linguists who followed or advanced the idea of universal grammar and Chomskyan linguistics similarly argued that all languages share color terminology, and that language is independent of thought. Other critics rejected linguistic relativity because of its causality problem; that is, it is difficult prove that a language causes of perceptual or cognitive behavior, despite the strong correlations between language and thought. From the onset of Chomskyan linguists in the 1960s until the present, the theory of linguistic relativity was mostly discredited.

However, despite these critiques, new language scholars begin working on the power of language to shape thought. Most notable are Lakoff's 1980s theory of metaphoric language; and later, a large number of cognitive psychologists, social linguists, and then finally, poststructuralists (discussed next) with their "linguistic turn" refocused their attention on the role of language in predisposing cognition. Beginning in the 1990s, researchers began to embrace the idea of linguistic relativity, drawing on qualified versions of the weak hypothesis. For example, John Lucy has conducted a significant body of research documenting linguistic relativity (1992). Likwise, Pütz, Martin & Marjolyn Verspoor (2000), Gumperz & Levinson (1996), and Dedre & Goldin-Meadow (2003) have published edited collections on this topic. The latter one is particularly comprehensive, having these three sections:

1. **Language as Lens:** Does the Language We Acquire Influence How We See the World?
2. **Languages as Tool Kit:** Does the Language We Acquire Augment Our Capacity for Higher-Order Representation and Learning? and
3. **Language as Category Maker:** Does the Language We Acquire Influence Where We Make Our Category Distinctions?

Each of these three sections contains 5-6 essays, each one affirming the distinct influence of the native language on thought patterns. Further, some recent studies have shown that color perception is particularly prone to linguistic relativity when processed in the left brain hemisphere, suggesting that this brain half relies more on language than the right one (Drivonikou et al. 2007, Gilbert et al. 2008). And as explained later, recent work in MRI (magnetic resonance imaging) and "cross linguistic influence" show very interesting correlations between a specific language and brain activity. Thus, this work in linguistic relativity and the Sapir-Whorf hypothesis has sufficient evidence to soften or soundly reject its harshest critiques.

LINGUISTIC RELATIVITY AND WRITING PATTERNS

Despite the early critiques from the 1960s and onward, the theory of linguistic relativity caught the attention of researchers, teachers, and scholars of English as a second language (ESL) and second language writing. After teaching ESL writing for a number of years, the American scholar Robert Kaplan noticed distinct paragraph organizational patterns in his students based on their native language. He set up a simple (and perhaps non-rigorous) study examining nearly 600 essays written in English by non-native speakers of English. He argued for a strong correlation between the native language of the ESL writer and paragraph organization.

In his famous 1966 article "Cultural thought patterns in intercultural education," Kaplan attempted to capture the differences in paragraph organization of students from with simple drawings, now infamously known as his "doodles," which are shown in Figure 3:

Kaplan explicitly drew upon the Sapir-Whorf hypothesis to argue for the differences among the paragraph organization of these five groups of ESL writers. He then named his study or theory "contrastive rhetoric." His methods lack transparency and rigor because he did not describe how he came to build these visual depictions of language, and many times after, he argued that these doodles are theoretical representations of what he found, not exclusive categories or generalizations.

Kaplan's work has been significant, because it opened up avenues of inquiry for both his supporters and critics. First, he has been widely criticized as being reductive, simplistic, ethnocentric, and behavioral, which it probably is. This critique is especially dominant with poststructuralist, postcolonial, and romantic theorists. For example, Ryuko Kubota (1999) who specifically draws on Foucault's theory of language and power criticizes contrastive rhetoric for its tendency to essentialize and reify cultures, rhetorics, and writers, freeze them in time, and implicitly create hierarchies. Kubota (1999), however, provides only textual or interpretive evidence for these conclusions,

Figure 3. Kaplan's visual depiction of paragraph organization of ESL writers

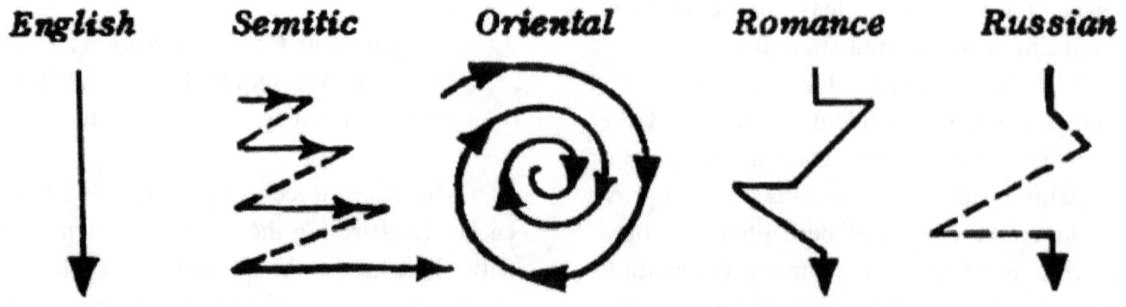

never makes transparent or interrogates her own methods for coming to these conclusions, and never evaluates the methods contrastive rhetoric researchers use. She simply critiques the research much like a work of literature or fiction. Similarly, as explained in Chapter One, Zhang (2008) criticizes contrastive rhetoric as developing hegemonic powers for speakers of English in developing, postcolonial areas such as India and in China and other parts of Asia. Drawing on specific postcolonial methods of textual criticism, Zhang makes these large claims without any empirical evidence other than textual interpretations. It is ironic that her article focuses on the qualitative methodology of contrastive rhetoric, but she does not theorize or explain the cultural connections between the rhetorical patterns and cultural backgrounds; she never engages contrastive rhetoric methodology; she never argues why her methods are better, more valid, or more accurate; and she never feels it necessary to qualify some of the very strong language of her claims. This thinking grossly oversimplifies the connections between culture and writing, becoming just as–or even more–overgeneralized than the contrastive rhetoric patterns they seek to critique.

Because Kubota and Zhang do not interrogate their own methods in light of contrastive rhetoric methods, and because they generalize without qualification or sufficient evidence, their critiques are weak, demonstrating, among other things, the innumeracy that I argue in Chapter One is so compellingly entrenched in postmodernism and deconstruction. Just because Kaplan presents patterns developed inductively from 600 ESL students does not mean that Kaplan argued or assumed that all the population is that way. In many ways, this difference is one of methodology, with the postmodern and postcolonial approach demonstrating a wholesale, but uninformed rejection of empirical methodology, and in its place a textual methodology, which might have advantages, but because they don't reflexively argue for their methodologies, the advantages are unclear.

Perhaps even worse for contrastive rhetoric research, this unreflexive postcolonial and postmodern approach is very seductive for researchers, journal editorial boards, and program developers who are trained in textual interpretation and have little foundation in empirical research but who are eager to work in intercultural and global rhetorical studies. Currently, in the United States, Departments of English continually produce more PhD graduates specializing in literature and literary theory than the market can accommodate. However, because academic positions in business and technical writing are more plentiful than qualified applicants, many PhD literature graduates take jobs in business and technical writing. And because they are required to publish, they bring the only methodologies to the research inquiry at hand: textual interpretation with the research report as an example of discourse to critique, not understanding the epistemologies implied in the different methodologies. Thus, while many of these researchers are using a singular and mostly unreflexive methodology, contrastive rhetoric researchers use a great variety, including textual, quantitative, qualitative, multi-modal, rhetorical, action-participatory, and others (See collection of Connor, Nagelhout, & Rozycki, 2008). In addition, many PhD programs in rhetoric and professional communication openly embrace the theories and methodologies of postmodernism and postcolonialism. For example, my PhD program at New Mexico State University has one of its four core areas as critical and cultural studies, requiring all PhD students to take courses in this area. Other methods and types of inquiry about culture and rhetoric are not allowed to count for this area. Consequently, it is not surprising–nor is it particularly relevant–that these scholars who simply rely on methods of textual interpretation find serious problems with contrastive rhetoric.

From an ironically similar perspective, there is strong resistance to contrastive rhetoric among a number of ESL writing researchers in the United States. Spack (1997), for example, critiques the overgeneralizing of contrastive rhetoric, including the many "harms" it perpetrates against ESL writers and teachers. Instead, she offers a model in which all students are unique and independent from their cultural background, drawing on a romantic theory of rhetoric. Like the postcolonial critiques, however, Spack (1998) offers no evidence for their approaches other than anecdotal experiences with their students; they never really engage contrastive rhetoric research methodologies; they never make transparent or explain their own approaches, showing how they are more accurate or more ethical; and the never engage the wide body of research showing some correspondences between culture and rhetorical patterns. Coming from their emic, romantic perspectives, they simply dismiss contrastive rhetoric based on their intuitive experiences.

Despite these critiques, there is a significant body of growing research examining the rhetorical strategies of second language writers, most of which generally confirms Kaplan's original arguments. This work is housed mostly in the area of second language learning and linguistics. Kaplan continued to publish work after this 1966 watershed article. Other contrastive rhetoric scholars include Connor (1996), Moder & Martinovic-Zic (2005), Panetta (2001), and many other ESL and second language writing scholars who examine the different rhetorical patterns in prose organization across languages. Most of this work examines academic, and not professional, writing, except for Reppen, Fitzmaurice, & Biber (2002) who look at newspapers across cultures; and my work examining Spanish-English business and technical writing (Thatcher, 2000; 2006). Connor, Nagelhout, & Rozycki's 2008 collection *Contrastive Rhetoric: Reaching to intercultural rhetoric* is the latest attempt to move contrastive rhetoric outside the strict ESL and linguistic area and into intercultural work. This book has four sections: the first tries to ground contrastive rhetoric in intercultural rhetoric, moving away from the simplistic connection between language and culture; the second section contains six articles that explore contrastive rhetoric across multiple genres of writing; the third section examines the relevance of contrastive rhetoric to the teaching of second language writing; and the four section focuses on the future of contrastive rhetoric. A good portion of this work now connects the contrastive rhetorical patterns to basic rhetorical concepts of context, purpose, and audience, which are important connections. All of these articles draw on explicit and generally transparent methodologies to report their findings and suggestions about the relevance of contrastive rhetoric. Although most of the articles are appropriately qualified, they all argue for the influence of culture and language in cross-cultural encounters.

In conclusion, much of the critique of contrastive rhetoric is more of field difference, with most of the strongest critiques coming from fields that use textual interpretation and anecdotal experience and intuition as predominant methods. Thus, just like the resurgence of the theory of linguistic relativity across a wide variety of fields, there is a strong interest in contrastive rhetoric, of how writing patterns vary across cultures.

LINGUISTIC TURN AND POSTSTRUCTURALIST THEORY OF SUBJECTIVITY

The linguistic turn in the humanities and social sciences closely parallels the same developments–and problems–of the theory of linguistic relativity. As stated earlier, the idea that language was an important vehicle for structuring both thought and human subjectivity is one of the most important developments for the humanities and social sciences in the 20th century. Rejecting the concept that the human subject was rational and thought was not connected to language, language philosophers began focusing on the relations between language, thought, and subjectivity. Like linguistic relativity, the idea that language is not transparent, but in fact, a structuring device has its origins as far back as the Greek sophists; however, in modern times, the late 18th century philosophers Johann Georg Hamann and Wilhelm von Humboldt began forwarding this idea, mostly as a rejection of the enlightenment conception of the subject and rationality. Later in the mid 20th century, Ludwig Wittgenstein continued this line of inquiry, and he was followed by Richard Rorty, and then a whole group of structuralists (Ferdinand de Saussure; Levi Strauss) and then poststructuralist scholars, including Jacques Derrida, Michel Foucault, Luce Irigaray, Julia Kristeva, and Judith Butler. Although vastly different in their specific approaches and fields of inquiry, these scholars generally shared the same argument that language was central to rationality (and therefore, cognition) and subjectivity. Thus, as Derrida so forcefully articulated, "there is nothing outside the text" (*Of Grammatology*). In other words, reality, subjectivity, reason, and communication are all constituted by the conventions of language.

In conjunction with these scholars who focused on language, a strong cohort of theorists similarly called into question the rationality of the human subject, which also opened space for understanding how language could structure thought, cognition, and communication. The most notable, of course, are Freud and Marx who are then followed by theorists such as Heidegger, Lacan, Foucault, Althusser, and Bourdieu. Marx and Freud provided much evidence against the autonomous, rational subject, and instead argued for economic and social constructions of the self (Marx) or the unconscious mind (Freud). Heidegger's concept of being and being there rejected the autonomous, pre-linguistic subject, while Lacan drew on Heidegger and Saussure to argue for a split subject grounded in an imaginary separation of the other. Althusser, Foucault, and Bourdieu focus more on the social construction of the self through institutions, power, disciplines, and routine daily acts of discourse.

Thus, in principle, these structuralist and then postrustructualist theorists have much in common with linguistic relativity and the definition of intercultural rhetoric developed throughout this book because they all argue that language and thought patterns are closely connected. For example, the onion model of intercultural rhetoric and culture assumes a combination of Marxian, structuralist, and linguistic relativity approaches. As seen in Figure 4, this model draws on the poststructuralist concept that the subject and language (rhetoric) mutually construct themselves; and because of this, the epistemologies and ideologies are deeply connected to–and replicate the logic of–a culture's implicit epistemologies and ideologies.

However, although these four approaches (linguistic relativity, intercultural rhetoric, structuralism, and poststructuralism) maintain that the self is constructed through language, and as a result, the corresponding epistemologies and ideologies are deeply connected through language, they differ remarkably, especially with the extension of structuralism to poststructuralism. As described in Chapter One, this difference resides in four areas: First, poststructuralism radically critiqued the notion of meaning, arguing instead for a continuous slippage of meaning because of the indeterminacy of language. For example, the

Figure 4. Onion model of culture and rhetoric

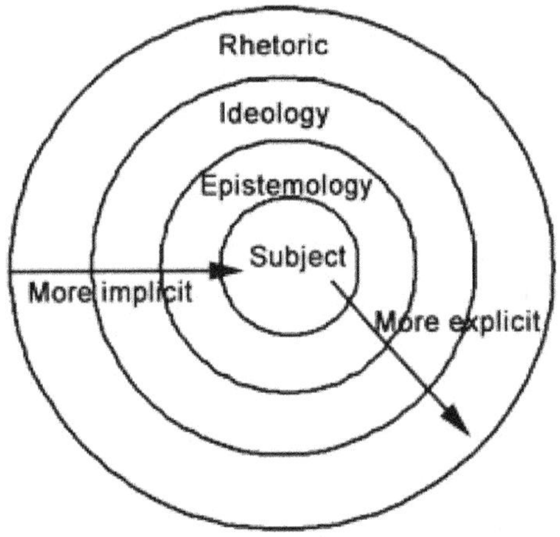

word "tree" in English has no iconic or symbolic connection to the actual object in my backyard. The only reason I know that "tree" refers to that object in my backyard is because I learned that word and reference from my parents and those before me, who learned it from those before them, in an endless chain for which we have no originary connection. Poststructuralism cannot let this slippage go even though there's much evidence for effective communication.

This slippage concept opened up the idea of authorship and interpretation, focusing on the multilayered and often chaotic, contradictory levels of meaning. For example, Barthes (1972) argues for the death of the author, or in other words, the death of understanding the author's will and intentionality because the author's discourse is not his or hers, but the author is a vehicle through which social discourses pass. In other words, Barthes argued that a text is not the author's original creation. This also makes interpreting the text difficult because the interpreter is bringing his or her own discourse to bear on the interpretation of a text that is not whole the authors.

Third, almost all poststructuralist (and postcolonial) theory argues that the subject is similarly fragmented and chaotic because it is constructed from multiple, contradictory discourses. Although versions of this fragmentation greatly vary among theorists, most center on the idea of the subject losing its center and agency because it is subjected to the multitude of competing discourses, making the subject itself the site of contestation (see Chapter One). In other words, the war of competing discourse grounds or exemplifies itself in the subject.

The theory of linguistic relativity and intercultural rhetoric simply assume much less chaos and fragmentation in the discourse and subjectivity, but linguistic relativity does not address the concept of meaning, a severe weakness to be discussed in the latter part of this chapter. As explained in Chapter One, perhaps the strongest reason why poststructuralist approaches focuses on the chaotic and fragmented sense of subjectivity and discourse is because they implicitly espouse the local, emic approaches, which strongly correlates to individualism. And not surprisingly, almost all of these critiques are based in the United States, a country that consistently ranks very high in individualism indices. Thus, poststructuralism is best for describing local languages and local situations, showing the uniqueness of each person's subjectivity, but it does not account for how a large level of discourse such as English versus Spanish might co-construct one's subjectivity. Contrastive rhetoric simply (but compellingly) assumes that because native Spanish speakers share the general structures and features of Spanish that these speakers also share similar conceptions of the self, epistemologies, and ideologies of these features, regardless of the local discourses. As explained in Chapter One (and explained very thoroughly by Pinker, 2003), this inability to see the larger patterns originates with an innumeracy, a lack of understanding numbers or statistics at a larger level.

Fourth, most poststructuralist theory is thoroughly, deeply, unrelentingly, and unreflexively enamored with deconstructing stable meaning as a construction based on binaries and the endless indeterminacy of language. And in so doing, poststructuralism rarely interrogates its own methods (even though they almost always argue that they do), and as a result, many poststructuralist arguments have very deterministic and inflexible approaches to cross-cultural inquiry, a point that I described earlier with Kubota and Zhang. For example, as explained in Chapter One, the term "always already" is a common term used in poststructuralist and postcolonial articles, and it usually pertains to the connection between methods and culture (subjectivity, epistemology, and ideology), much like the onion model. However, instead of arguing for more tentative connections between methods and culture, many postcolonial theorists simply say that the connection is "always already" there.

This very unusual surety of concept or construction that relies on the chaotic subjectivity and indeterminacy of language is also highly ironic and contradictory. How can a concept or construction that so strongly argues against any fixed meaning can depend on perhaps the most fixed concept in all fields of inquiry? My first guess, based on 25 years of experience with this epistemology, is perhaps much as I describe in Chapter One, theory is letting these scholars off the hook. Theory lets Kubota and Zhang off the hook because they do not have to offer alternative methods or ground their conclusions in anything other than a theoretical interpretation. To me, this is very easy, safe research that while offering some considerations, does not have the courage to ground itself sufficiently in methods and qualified conclusions, which then serve as something with which others can engage meaningfully.

Neural Plasticity, Evolution of Language, and Contrastive Rhetoric

Although Chomskyan and universal linguistics have critiqued contrastive rhetoric and the theory of linguistic relativity for a long time, and postructuralism emphasizes the emic-like uniqueness of each person, there is some resurging interest in the idea that the brain is perhaps not as hard-wired and fixed as previously thought, opening up room for the idea that language might have some role in influencing thought and reasoning patterns at more etic or larger levels. The usual starting point for this research is the obvious fact that humans have linguistic and communicative abilities far beyond any other species on our planet, and because of that difference, the brain must have evolved in light of evolutionary exigencies. The question is why and how? Why and how did humans develop this capacity? To answer this question, researchers draw on methods of inquiry and research in anthropology, biology, psychology, neural science, information theory, evolution, and others. This research, at least for me, reconciles many of the problems of the universal grammarians and theories of contrastive rhetoric and linguistic relativity.

The research on language evolution is too large to survey in this chapter (see Botha, 2003 for an excellent overview and critique), but we can sketch some simple frameworks. Chomsky originally argued for the innate language ability in humans, that is, humans have a language device that is so structured and generative that all natural languages have similar grammatical and lexical possibilities, and all humans have similar generative capacities for language. Chomsky bases most of his argument on the fact that a set number of language capacities in human can generate an infinite variety of language combinations, and that children can master this capacity so quickly that the language capacities must be innate. Chomsky does not really articulate well where this language device came from, opening him up to critiques from evolutionists. Some evolutionists, such as Stephen Jay Gould, argued that language was perhaps an adaptive advantage, and because of this advantage, humans with language capacity self selected and language became a human feature.

Steven Pinker (2003) builds on Chomsky's argument that there is an innate cerebral capacity or structure for language, but Pinker explains more carefully how this feature might have evolved. Pinker argues that the principal evolutionary mechanism for language was the Baldwin effect, which is essentially the theory that natural selection occurred because offspring have an enhanced capacity to learn (perhaps from the mistakes of the parents), and can pass on that learning in growing capacities to their offspring, rather than confining themselves to relatively fixed genetic abilities. In other words, the Baldwin effect emphasizes how the sustained behavior of a species or group can shape the evolution of that species. As a result, learning can make evolutionary change more likely because it enables greater flexibility in responding to typical human situations, thereby reducing the costs of genetic variability within populations. From this perspective, Pinker adds a key component to evolutionary theory, much as espoused by Gould, that is, humans have some sort of agency or will and can "learn" to adapt, much like my definition of human agency in Chapter One. Thus, language provided an enhanced ability to learn to adapt, making language learners more likely to survive, which in turn, genetically altered the brain of the human population to include what Pinker calls the "Language Acquisition Device." The evidence for this language device is because humans learn language in very similar patterns, processes, and milestones, it must be universal.

Both Chomsky and Pinker, however, focus their attention on the grammatical elements, but as many rhetoricians and professional communicators understand, language is more than grammar. Terrance Deacon argues that instead of grammar, the *symbolic power* of language was an important evolutionary advantage. As described in his 1998 book *The Symbolic Species*, Deacon argues that human linguistic ability perhaps resulted from a need to develop symbolic skills to handle increasingly complex social relations. Deacon argues that kinship and marriage was perhaps the strongest impetus for this adaptive capacity; that is, the need to distinguish between relatives forced a need to develop communicative abilities beyond iconic representation. Thus, this need required symbolic or arbitrary systems of representation. This argument resembles Pinker's argument that grammar evolved because of the evolutionary advantage, but instead of grammar was symbolic power. Deacon explains that symbols or arbitrary reference systems are uniquely human, closely following Saussure and eventually Derrida. Arbitrary simply means, for example, the word "tree" in English has not iconic reference to the physical object that grows in my back yard. The English word "meow" is not arbitrary or symbolic because it sounds like the actual sound of a cat. Deacon then shows that linguistic abilities in chimpanzees are usually indexical, and therefore, not really symbolic. He compellingly demonstrates that a chimpanzee's "word" is always indexed to the object the word represents in a specific context (the referent). Humans, on the other hand, develop complex relations of symbols to symbols in interlocking relationships, not symbols to referents. Deacon models this complex symbol-to-symbol interlocking relations to kinship, and argues for their co-development throughout evolutionary time.

Consequently, Deacon follows much of the work in poststructuralism that argues for the separation of the signifier ("tree") from its reference (actual physical object). As a result, language did not evolve in the form of grammatical categories but in the relation of symbols. Thus, humans that were capable of developing complex symbol-making abilities could manage better their kinship relations (which were models of this symbol relations) and thus were selected through evolution to pass on that trait.

These evolutionary psychology models, especially Deacon, are particularly powerful for intercultural rhetoric and professional communication because they connect brain functions to concrete daily situations and dilemmas, in other words, to the intercultural common human thresholds. Deacon shows how language helped early human manage the very complex, yet routine tasks of kinship and community building. However, Deacon's model does not go "off the deep end" (Pinker, 2003) of postructuralism and deconstruction, arguing for continuous slippage of meaning, rejection of authorship and reading, and against any fixed meaning; rather, it shows the great power of symbolic language in the evolutionary processes.

Brain Plasticity and MRI

Adding evidence to the argument that the brain evolved in connection to evolutionary needs for language and symbolic power, a growing number of researchers explore the ability of the brain to change itself according to environmental influences. Instead of believing the brain is hard-wired form infancy, like many of Pinker's and

Chomsky's arguments, researchers working in the field of neuroplasticity argue for the capacity of the brain to re-align neural connections because of experience (Pinaud, Tremere, & De Weerd, 2006). Many of these studies look at the influence of language on brain malleability and ground these inquiries using MRI (magnetic resonance imaging). Many of the most relevant research for contrastive and intercultural rhetoric look at cognitive structures for bilinguals, showing some connection between cognitive patterns and native languages (see for example, Perani & Abutaleb, 2005). For example, one of the central issues in second language acquisition (L2) is the fact that if a person learns a second language roughly before puberty, that person generally develops native-like competency in many areas such as pronunciation, vocabulary, and syntax. If learned after puberty, there is a noticeable difference in this competency. This difference becomes a central issue for brain plasticity or malleability, for the brain seems to be more malleable early on and then hardens, but perhaps not entirely. There is a significant amount of research and debate of this fact in L2 acquisition research (see de Groot, *Language and Cognition in Bilinguals*, 2010).

Other L2 research examines the different cognitive structures and patterns based on the native language of the research subjects. For example, Li (2009) compared the lexical organizing patterns of Chinese-English bilinguals to native language learners and argued that bilinguals who learned both languages early on (before puberty) have a different organizing pattern for lexicon or vocabulary than those who learned later. The later learners seem to face cognitive competition for the lexicon ability with the L1 language. Li backed up that research by comparing the neural imaging results. In earlier research, Li et al. (2004) examined the representations of nouns and verbs in Chinese as compared to English using MRI. Li found that statistical differences between the mental images of Chinese versus English speakers for verbs and nouns. Li argues that

> *Unlike in English, nouns and verbs in Chinese activate a wide range of overlapping brain areas as distributed neural networks, in both the left and the right hemisphere. We attributed the cortical response differences between Chinese and English to the language user's experience with and their sensitivity to language-specific properties of the lexicon and grammar: In English and other Indo-European languages, nouns and verbs are explicitly marked by grammatical morphology in a sentence context, whereas in Chinese, most of these grammatical markers for nouns and verbs are absent. (2009, p. 18).*

In other words, Li argues that the neurons of the Chinese speakers were more widespread across the brain perhaps because of the linguistic structure of Chinese verbs and nouns as opposed to English. Li (2009) makes the same argument about bilinguals and their brains using MRI. Li's work is just a small sampling of MRI imaging among speakers of different languages, including bilinguals. There is an impressive body of research to document small but significant differences in neural patterns and specific languages, showing that the brain arranges some of its neural pathways and patterns based on the native language (for a review, see Grosjean, Li, Mu¨nte, and Rodriguez-Fornells, 2003).

One of the potential problems of this MRI research and others focusing on the distinct differences across language is the tendency (which I critique in Chapter Two) of seeing language and brain patterns as inherently unique, and consequently, literacy capacities are not "autonomous," that is, transferable from one context or language to another. As I explain in Chapter Two, this emic-only view has many problems, the foremost being that many cross-cultural competencies do cross languages and cultures. For example, it has been clear to me that the ability for Ecuadorians (2000) and Mexicans (2006) to write effective professional communications in Spanish directly correlates to their ability to understand these communications in English, even though their English is limited. Accordingly, a growing number of linguistics researchers examine the "transfer" or "cross-linguistic" abilities of second language speakers across languages. "Transfer" simply means the ability to use a language capacity developed in one language to another language. Some is positive transfer such as English speakers having familiarity with some Spanish words because their English equivalents have the same Latin derivation, while some transfer is negative. For, example, many Spanish speakers find pronunciation is difficult to learn in English because the English vowels and consonants are not the same or consistent across words, as they are in Spanish.

Consequently, an interesting Deacon-like body of research is occurring with the study of transfer across languages. Scott Jarvis & Aneta Pavlenko (2008) examine a wide variety of transfer issues. A key component to this work is their four layered, progressive model of research and theory, something that is well beyond the language-culture connection in other fields such as poststructuralism. According to the model, Phase One simply identifies the features of cross-language influence or transfer; Phase Two tries to operationalize dependent and independent variables in this process, developing models of cause and effect and directionality; Phase Three tries to ground these models empirically in social, mental, and linguistic contexts; and Phase Four attempts to correlate these causal models with corresponding physiological research such as MRI studies. Jarvis & Pavlenko then examine the current state of research in the context of these four phases. For example, this book argues that emotions might correlate with linguistic categories.

Although much of the work of Jarvis and Pavlenko is focused on more traditional linguistic categories such as syntax, lexicon, and phonology, it does address more rhetorical concepts such as personhood, gender, space, and time. For example, certain bilinguals have difficulty expressing emotions in their second language because the second language does not contain the adequate words for expression. Thus, these L2 speakers have to draw from more conceptual categories to make up the transfer problem and explain their emotions based on their first language, all of which is reflected in MRI studies. Thus, it intelligently models the idea of transfer, comparing various levels of similarities and differences across language and showing what this comparison means for transfer. Jarvis and Pavlenko (2008) conclude that there is significant evidence for transfer issues; that is, the first language significantly predisposes approaches in the second language, but that these L2 speakers or writers can also make up for–or correct–these predispositions. In other words, there is evidence for a weak theory of linguistic relativity that varies according to the ability of the L2 speaker or writer to recognize and address L1 predispositions.

These recent MRI and transfer studies bring us all the way back to the Sapir-Whorf hypothesis, showing that despite the strong critiques, there is *something* to that original hypothesis. However, this hypothesis and the current MRI-brain and transfer research suffer from one major problem for intercultural professional communicators: meaning. That is, why are the patterns different for each language, and what do those difference mean for communicators? Deacon scratches the surface on this issue when he connects language to symbolic power, but I develop it fully next.

CONNECTING CONTRASTIVE RHETORIC TO INTERCULTURAL RHETORIC AND WRITING PEDAGOGIES

What is missing from the research in contrastive rhetoric and the MRI research is the meaning and the cause of the patterns. In other words, the different patterns in Kaplan's doodles are visually very recognizable, but what does the linear line mean as opposed to the oriental circles or romance zig-zags and what is their cause? Early ESL and contrastive rhetoric research tried to connect the cause of the patterns to the native language, which, as I found out early in my research does not work. In my work in Ecuador (1997), I quickly found that knowledge of English had no bearing on the rhetorical strategies of Ecuadorian business professionals. Instead, I later learned that the rhetorical and cultural tradition (as operationalized in the eight common human thresholds) explained much more fully the preferred rhetorical approaches of Ecuadorian and U.S. professionals in Quito, Ecuador.

Thus, one of the major problems of Kaplan's contrastive rhetoric model is that it is offered much like a taboo approach to cultural norms, not having any connection to routine, everyday tasks, which are intimately connected to the common human thresholds. Consequently, ESL writing teachers and professional communicators do not have a model for contextualizing Kaplan's advice. And as linguists such as Chomsky and Pinker have pointed out, there are too many similarities across language to believe that different writing patterns can be based on different syntactical or other linguistic variables across languages. This simple connection does not allow us to understand the cause of the patterns either. These patterns are not solely caused by language, although language might have an influence.

These patterns gain their meaning by connecting their logic to the etic borders or common human thresholds. As explained in Chapter Two, the eight common human thresholds are patterned responses to re-occurring situations and as such, the rhetorical or ideological manifestations of these responses signal a deeper foundation in corresponding subjectivities, epistemologies, and ideologies. In other words, the zig-zag means nothing unless it is connected to a diffuse culture and high context communications, which would understand and welcome the deviations, or a specific culture, which would see the deviations as problematic, off topic, or out of focus. Thus, writing teachers can analyze the diffuse and specific elements of the writing situation to help students understand how and why diffuse or specific approaches are needed. This will help them become strategic in their rhetorical approaches, allowing them to be more diffuse, for example, when diffuseness is appropriate.

This section contextualizes Kaplan's doodles with the eight common human thresholds, showing how the different rhetorical strategies correspond to concrete decision-making activities.

I/Other

As discussed in Chapter Two, people in individualistic cultures tend to be more self-reliant, competitive, and act in their own self interest for personal growth (Hampden-Turner & Trompenaars, 2000). In collective societies, individuals are integrated into strong, cohesive in-groups, with which they are loyal (Hofstede, 2010). In the doodles, one of the most obvious differences is that the English line is isolated and linear, not to mention the fact that it looks like an English "I," all of which perfectly exemplifies the fact that the most individualistic countries on earth all speak English as a native language. Kaplan's oriental approach seems collective because there is no independence or isolation; everything is drawn together in a circle, exemplifying the interdependence of collectivism. Thus, it is not surprising that many ESL and L2 theorists connect English paragraph development in the United States as enacting a more of an individualistic self, which Chinese and other students from more collective cultures have a hard time engaging (Ramanathan & Atkinson, 1999). True to the Kaplan doodles, the romance, Russian, and Semitic writing patterns correspond to the mixed indices of individualism and collectivism that are attributed to these areas by most intercultural researchers.

It is also interesting to note that structurally, English is a very agent-based language (see Stewart & Bennett, 1991). That is, there is a strong tendency in English to include the subject of a sentence, a cause to most things. For example, when I want to say "It's raining" in Spanish, I say "está lloviendo" or "se llueve." Literarly translated, these mean: is raining or rains. English is so subject or head based that it requires an agent to carry out the action. Similarly, when I am playing baseball, and a ball comes to me and goes in then out of my glove, I say in English "I dropped the ball." The Spanish phrase is "se me cayó la pelota" which means the ball fell from me. Similarly, English syntax almost always requires the noun or personal pronoun to become the subject of a verb phrase. In English, I say, "I want to go," which in Spanish is "quiero irme." Spanish does not require the "I" in the subject because it is conjugated into the verb. So, yes, individualism in English-speaking countries is based more on language, but perhaps language has been a significant influence.

This connection between linearity and individualism and circularity and collectivism has been the source of many misunderstandings in intercultural professional communication. For example, as shown earlier in Chapter One and grounded in the etic borders in Chapter Two, my early research examined the different reception of Letter O and R in the Ecuadorian Transit Commission Case. I noted that naming all the groups involved with Letter O was a significant burden for U.S. readers, because, instead of stating upfront the need for a change in the law, the original Ecuadorian letters cites all of the groups involved with the process and how the current situation made their relations awkward and tense. As I explain in Chapter Five, university websites from collective cultures present many collective rhetorical patterns such as group pictures, strong adherence to social hierarchies, group navigation structures, while universities from individualistic cultures almost always present pictures of single, isolated people, an elimination of social hierarchies, and individualized navigation structures. I articulate similar comparisons in instructions, health literacy, organizational behavior, legal traditions, and teaching.

Despite these strong correspondences between individualism and collectivism, I am not implying "an always already" approach; instead, as I document in many places, (Thatcher, 1999; 2000; 2006), people in collective cultures can easily draw upon more individualistic approaches. The key is that this individualism is counter culture, adding a new layer of meaning. For example, as I document elsewhere (1997), Ecuadorian accountants usually used collective symbols of power in their introductions of concrete business letters. However, when working with Americans, they quickly adapted to more individualistic and linear forms because the cultural context asked for it. Similarly, as I document in Chapter Two, one of the signs that Anzaldúa, for example, was rejecting her collective, Mexican ancestry for American individualism was her drawing upon an individualistic creation of subjectivity, something (ironically) predominant in Anglo-American culture. And as I document in Chapter Two, it is only when we understand both the Mexican and American predominant values can we really understand the position–and eventual statement–that Anzaldúa makes.

Rules Orientation

As described in Chapter Two, rules orientation in cultures seems to revolve around either the particular or universal orientation. In particularist cultures, the default approach is to apply rules and decisions depending on relations and context, while universalist cultures emphasize equal treatment regardless of social relations. This idea of a unique human being is more of a particular value, which is the opposite of universal value of the universalism which seeks for standardization. The linear English organizational pattern corresponds rather strongly to universalism because it's one path with no deviations. On the other hand, the other orientations have different, almost chaotic paths, showing a penchant for deviation, a sign of particularism. The Semitic model seems to have both because it deviates, but those deviations are parallel and grow systematically. The Russian and Romance models start with a rule or major point but consistently deviate only to wind up at the same point. This exemplifies the particularist approach that is reconciled to a universalist impulse.

There is some correspondence between languages and this structure. For example, English has only one real second or third person pronoun, the "you," while Spanish has two and Japanese and Russian have many. When referring to another person, a Spanish speaker is forced to use one of the two forms of you: either *usted* (formal) or *tu* (informal); and deciding on one depends entirely on the situation and personal relation. I will use *tu* with my spouse, dog, students, close friends, and those who are beneath my social status, an entirely contradictory and weird mix. I will use the *usted* to show respect to people in authority, higher status, older, or strangers. Thus, Spanish speakers are forced into their daily routine the careful analysis of particular relations in order to speak, while English speakers easily use just one form for all, even though they can make up for it in tone or vocabulary. Not surprisingly, almost all Spanish speaking cultures are particular, while many of the most universal are English speaking.

Throughout this book, I articulate the careful connections between the culture and patterns of universalism and particularism. For example, in Chapter Nine, I explain how Latino health communications dramatize family situations as a way to ensure better compliance with health practices, while Anglo-American approaches emphasize universal standard and procedures that are intended for all. As articulated elsewhere (Thatcher, 1999; 2000; 2006), the need to always articulate concrete situations has its virtues and vices and is connected to communication media and technology. For example, many Ecuadorians in one of my studies (2000) preferred to work with oral, and therefore, unwritten organizational policies and procedures, because orality allowed them the flexibility to judge each situation on a case by case basis, a perfect example of particularism.

However, this preference for orality is changing in many particular countries because of the integration of ISO standards, which require written procedures, as explained in Chapter Six. Thus, in three manufacturing plants in Mexico, the personnel were just beginning to work from written protocols, a change that significantly rippled across all layers of organizational culture (Thatcher, 2005). In addition, Mexico's new transparency laws (2002), enacted to force access to public information, will further disrupt the preference for orality and its connection to particularism. This law openly argues for the use of transparency as a way to universalize public entities and their transactions. Further, the development of international transparency and global competitiveness will further disrupt particularism at local levels.

Sources of Virtue and Guidance

The third value focuses on the source or origin of virtue, guidance, or method of aligning oneself rightly. In other words, all cultures look to different sources to understand if they are heading in the right direction, so to speak. Hampden-Turner & Trompenaars (2000) explained that there are generally two sources of virtue: the inner-directed source that "conceives of virtue as inside each of us–in our souls, wills, convictions, principles," or believes–in the triumph of conscious purpose. Outer direction conceives of virtue as our site each of us in natural rhythms, in the beauties and powers of nature, in aesthetic environments and relationships" (p.234). Not surprisingly, the Oriental circle exemplifies rather compelling the outer approach, that is, of starting from the outside and working towards the inside. The straight line of the English approach exemplifies the inner direction that lays out a direct path to the goal. The Russian, Romance, and Semitic are interesting in this context. It seems clear that the linear path is too simplistic and that something is causing a deviation and then return to the original trajectory. Perhaps it is the outside forces or context. Something seems to cause the Semitic model to grow systematically with indirect topical connection to the main point. With many of the other values, there is some correspondence between languages and this value. Stewart & Bennett (1991) argue that English is a direct, and digital-like, which is either one or off, while other languages are more analog, showing gradations.

As explained throughout this book, the correspondences between inner and outer cultures and their rhetorical patterns are very compelling. For example, Chapter Ten discusses how U.S. instructional materials assume a very linear, inner-directed reader, one who knows where he/she should be going. Chapter Five similarly describes linear navigation paths in websites for inner directed cultures, and collective, circular paths for outer directed cultures. Chapter Five also hypothesizes, however, that the newer media such as email, websites, and Web 2.0 or interactive social spaces might be disrupting these traditional definitions of inner and outer directed. The web is a much better analogy for outer directedness, symbolizing how one should harmonize. Thus, this value might be changing at a global level.

Public/Private and Degree of Involvement

This value set or etic border assesses the degree of involvement across different spheres of life, usually involving a public/private divide and trust. Diffuse cultures are usually collective, particular, and outer-directed; thus, involvement in friendships, social relations, and work environments often crosses boundaries, thus sharing the relationship across these spheres. On the other hand, specific cultures are based on the ease and public trust that individualism and universalism give people in separate spheres of life, with friendship belonging to one or two spheres only, with little or no cross-over of authority. Specific orientation also relies on the reliable social structure of the level playing field, which allows them to quickly work or make friends with people in all kinds of spheres. Consequently, the specific orientation favors more public collaboration, something that is much more difficult in diffuse cultures.

Perhaps this value set best describes the doodles. The English organization is very specific because it focuses on one direction only and moves only in that direction. The Oriental seems to clearly exemplify diffuse because it shows that coming to a single point requires circling around other points; there is nothing direct or specific about this model of organization. The Semitic is fascinating from this model because it has a strong parallelism that perhaps is based not on natural, but perhaps artificial rhythms because each deviation is systematically larger and connected only implicitly back to the original guiding idea. The Russian and Romance seem to combine specific and diffuse, starting with a major point but deviating considerably but ending up at the same point.

This difference is exemplified in language structures, especially those of conjugation. In short, Spanish speakers often do not have to use personal pronouns such as I, you, or we because these pronouns are integrated into the verbal conjugation. The English "I want" is simply translated into the Spanish conjugated verb "quiero." Thus, English speakers have to separate these linguistic categories much more than Spanish speakers.

This book makes significant connections between specific and diffuse patterns. Perhaps the best examples occur with the Ecuadorian Letters O and R in Chapters One and Two, and the instructions, health literacy, and website designs in their respective chapters. The more diffuse cultures strongly displayed holistic approaches to communication, encouraging a more circular approach, while the specific cultures easily sectioned people into their specific areas of activity, encouraging a very direct, and linear approach. And this value might be so entrenched that it might not be as susceptible to change as the other common human thresholds. For example, the newer media such as internet and Web 2.0 provide for a more diffuse approach because they are richer medium, yet at the same time, they are more distanced than usual specific approaches are used to.

Status

The next common human threshold assesses how status is grounded and communicated. The two most common approaches are ascription and achievement. Ascriptive-oriented cultures derive status from their social group, race, gender, age, ethnicity, and language. These variables provide the communicator with the power to get things done in complicated social structures. In achievement-oriented cultures, it does not matter where you come from, who your family is, your age, language, etc, as long as you can achieve your goals. Put simply, the English version is covering the most ground quickly, while the Oriental model is going nowhere. The Russian, Semitic, and Romance models cover ground but deviate as well, showing a combination of ascriptive and achievement orientations. In terms of linguistic structures, this point has already been discussed in the particular and universal section. Many languages have intricate ways of signaling status and power through their syntax.

With the development of globalization, this is perhaps the fastest value set to change, or the one prone to most change. Even though there is significant evidence for strong correlations between this common human thresholds and its rhetorical patterns, globalization requires a more achievement-oriented approach, simply because the ascriptive values tend to be local, not global. Thus, a market in Japan does not really care about the ascriptive values in Mexico where the produce is produced.

Context

This value set assesses the role of the context in the communicative interaction. All cultures communicate in contexts, but how they rely on these contexts for the meaning of their communications differs. Low context means that the meaning of the communication resides primarily in the explicitly coded part of the communication, not in the surrounding context. On the other end, high context communication assumes a strong reliance on the contextual and social cues for the meanings of communications. Here, good writing focuses on how information elucidates the influence of the social context on meaning of the communications. Low context cultures prefer parallelism, which helps the readers process the meaning without contextual influences, while for high context cultures, parallelism is boring and artificial. These doodles exemplify high and low in two ways: First, the dotted lines in the Semitic and Russian models might imply indirect connections between points, an indirection that is probably obvious based on the context. Further, the English and Semitic are the most parallel, while the Russian, Romance, and Oriental models are not parallel; rather, they are uniquely structured.

In terms of language structure, Chinese is the most interesting from a low and high context fashion. The Chinese writing systems is actually a little bit iconic in that the characters are brought together in unique ways to forms words, and understanding this connection requires well developed contextual knowledge.

This book provides plenty of examples of high context communication in high context cultures and vice versa, and it will be interesting to see how this value changes. For example, the newer media provide a richer context for their communications than the old media of writing, thus enhancing high context communication. But globalization requires more transparency and universalism in transactions, which correspond to low context communications.

Monochronic and Polychronic Time

As described in Chapter Two, cultures view and use time differently, especially in communications. Polychronic or synchronous time frames mean simultaneity, multiple tasks managed at the same time, and apparent disorganization, focusing on the importance of place, and involvement of people rather than adherence to present schedules. On the other hand, monochronic or sequential time frames mean linked linear structures of cause and effect with an organized flow of events (Hall, 1976, 1983). For the doodles, this is an easy connection: the English is strictly linear in its time frame, while the oriental is strictly polychronic. The Semitic has linked parallel forms that systematically grow, while the Russian and Romance are polychronic in the middle but start and end on the same point.

In terms of linguistic structures, it is well established that English is a relatively linear language, while Spanish, for example, has intricate time sequencing and gradations.

This book provides plenty of examples of polychronic and monochronic communications in specific contexts, and it will be interesting to see how this value changes. For example, the newer media provide a much less linear time frame than either orality or writing, which perhaps could encourage more polychronic communications. But globalization requires more synchronizations and universalism in transactions, which correspond to monochronic communications.

Power Distance

Power Distance is Hofstede's (2010) concept, and it measures how inequality is handled in communications. In high power distances cultures, there is unequal, centralized distribution of power, acceptance of authority, high levels of overseeing, and top-down communication styles. Low power distance cultures use communications to downplay inequalities among people. As Hofstede (2010) explains, low power distance cultures expect more mutual interdependence between subordinate and authority. Power distance is probably difficult to tell from the doodles. Perhaps the English model is low power distance because there are no sharp angles, while the Russian, Romance, and Semitic models are high power because the sharp angles of deviation and return to topic are sharply articulated. The Oriental model does not seem to correlate with the higher power distance values that are ascribed to Asian cultures. In terms of linguistic structures, this point has already been discussed in the particular and universal section. Many languages have intricate ways of signaling status and power through their syntax.

This book provides plenty of examples of high and low power distance communications across cultures, and it will be interesting to see how this value changes. But globalization requires more transparency and universalism in transactions, which correspond to low power distance communications.

U.S. AND ENGLISH DOMINANCE: SOME THOUGHTS ON CONNECTING WRITING PATTERNS TO GLOBAL CULTURES AND RHETORICAL PATTERNS

Now that there is some connection between languages and cultural patterns at a broad level, it is important to think about the effects of language at the global level. Given that English is the most spoken second language in the world, and that there are more Chinese ESL speakers than native English speakers, there is enough reason to think about the cultural ramifications of both English and Chinese. In 1997, John Swales simply argued that English was a "Tyrannosaurus Rex." Put simply, English has become the dominant language of science, business, academia, and information technologies and is trampling not only cultural and linguistic norms around the world. From Swales' analogy (1997), English is the t-rex of all languages. In the light of contrastive rhetoric and second-language studies, the cultural and rhetorical implications of this dominant language can be significant. Pennycook (1999) similarly argues that English is significantly influencing world cultural patterns, linking problems of development to this influence. In Figure 5, Pennycook traces the history of this connection between the English language and development.

Each one of these rows deserves a chapter itself, but all of them connect English to development in very interesting ways, which merits discussion. As stated in this chapter and throughout the book, one strong element of English is its connection to individualistic cultures such as that of the United States (Stewart & Bennett, 1991; Hamden-Turner & Trompenaars, 2000). The vice side of individualism has already been addressed, in terms of ethnocentrism and singular world views. However, the virtue of individualism is innovation and development (Hampden-Turner & Trompenaars, 2000), especially in technology, industry, and business. Theoretically, individualism provides the freedom to experiment and develop concepts and products without the constraints of community influence. Communitarian cultures, as argued by Hampden-Turner & Trompenaars (2000), have a smaller propensity for innovation but a much larger capacity to fine tune already-developed products into more marketable dimensions.

Thus, following the Sapir-Whorf hypothesis, the use of English would correlate to a similar acceptance or assimilation of individualism. The same could be said of universalism and its connection to development. As stated frequently, universalism means creating a level-playing field so that people are judged not on their relationships but on pre-determined rules; in essence, rule of law, rather than rule of will or relationship. This value is reflected in the strong push for anti-discrimination laws in the United States and other universalist countries. It is also reflected in the various international standards such as ISO, Global Competition Standards, and Global Transparency. Particularism is the counter to universalism, and it encourages context and relationship-based rules and exceptional thinking. The vice of universalism is using the level-playing field as a hypocritical and discriminatory excuse when exceptions to

Figure 5. Pennycook's history of spread of English and development

View of the global spread of English	**Implications for culture and development**	**Pedagogical implications**
Colonial celebratory	English an inherently useful language	Teach English to those who can appreciate it
Modernization	English a crucial tool for modernization	Teach English to modernize the world
Laissez-faire liberalism	English a functional tool for pragmatic purposes	Business as usual: give people what they want
Imperialism	Homogenization, destruction of other cultures and languages	Language rights, instruction in mother tongues; protectionism
Linguistic hybridity	Languages and cultures change and adapt	World Englishes, multiple standards; assume change
Postcolonial performativity	Cultural politics of change, language, knowledge and difference	Critical language education for struggle; appropriability

the rules are justified but not allowed. The vice of particularism is simply corruption—using a relationship to gain advantage. Almost all the international standards mentioned earlier rely on universalism for ranking de facto potential for development. Thus, is English a force for this internationalizing? Perhaps, but other languages might be international, too; we just do not have the data and theory to solidly interpret the connections.

The same could be said of the other six values: specific orientation, inner-directedness, monochronic, low power distance, low context communication, and achievement orientation. All of these values seem connected simultaneously to English speaking cultures and standards or mechanism of development. Thus, Pennycook's interrogation is apt. However, the connections between language and culture with Pennycook's models need to be questioned. As articulated very clearly in this book, especially in Chapters One and Two, local cultures do not readily assimilate languages and cultures; the process is much more complex and dynamic. Further, there is much evidence to the contrary as many chapters of this book show that the local cultures still dominate with website design (Chapter Five), organizational behavior (Chapter Six), distant education (Chapter Seven), legal traditions (Chapter Eight), health communications (Chapter Nine), instructional materials (Chapter Ten), and many others.

In addition, Pennycook's approach should already be familiar; he draws on postcolonial and postructuralism research methods of textual interpretation, not documenting results outside the appearances of textual patterns. Thus, I am slow to agree with his conclusions. Other work, such as Reppen, Fitzmaurice, & Biber (2002) who compare rhetorical patterns across languages in newspapers uses more appropriate and valid empirical models.

CONCLUSION

The theory of linguistic relativity, Sapir-Whorf hypothesis, and contrastive rhetoric have generated an enormous body of research and theory, most of which is critical for intercultural rhetoric and professional communication. In addition to their great evidence of cross-linguistic rhetorical patterns, their theories and methods offer much validity, generalizability, and reliability to cross-cultural professional communication research, theory, and teaching. For example, the accompanying L2 pedagogical and research methods, which will be discussed later in Chapters Eleven and Twelve, offer intercultural professional communication teachers and researchers important qualifiers or alternatives to the predominance of postructuralist and postcolonial modes of inquiry in English departments. In addition, researchers and scholars might consider broadening their methods to include MRI studies for focusing on the effects of different types of discourse structures across intercultural contexts.

REFERENCES

Berlin, B., & Kay, P. (1969). *Basic color terms: Their universality and evolution*. Berkeley, CA: University of California Press.

Buss, D. (2005). (Ed.). *Handbook of evolutionary psychology*. New York, NY: John Wiley & Sons.

Connor, U. (1996). *Contrastive rhetoric: Cross-cultural aspects of second-language writing*. Cambridge, UK: Cambridge U Press.

Connor, U., Nagelhout, E., & Rozycki, W. V. (Eds.). (2008). *Contrastive rhetoric: Reaching to intercultural rhetoric*. Amsterdam, The Netherlands: John Benjamins Publishing Company.

De Groot, A. B. (2010). *Language and cognition in bilinguals and multilinguals: An introduction*. New York, NY: Taylor & Francis.

Deacon, T. W. (1998). *The symbolic species: The co-evolution of language and the brain*. New York: W.W. Norton and Company.

Diamond, J. (2005). *Guns, germs, and steel: The fates of human societies*. New York, NY: W. W. Norton & Company.

Drivonikou, G. V., Kay, T., Regier, R. B., Ivry, A. L., Gilbert, A. F., & Davies, I. R. L. (2007). Further evidence that Whorfian effects are stronger in the right visual field than the left. *Proceedings of the National Academy of Sciences of the United States of America*, *104*(3), 1097–1102. doi:10.1073/pnas.0610132104

Gentner, D., & Goldin-Meadow, S. (Eds.). (2003). *Language in mind: Advances in the study of language and thought*. Cambridge, MA: The MIT Press.

Gilbert, A. L., Regier, T., Kay, P., & Ivry, R. B. (2008). Support for lateralization of the Whorf effect beyond the realm of color discrimination. *Brain and Language*, *105*(2), 91–98. doi:10.1016/j.bandl.2007.06.001

Grosjean, F., Li, P., Munte, Th., & Rodriguez-Fornells, A. (2003). Imaging bilinguals: When the neurosciences meet the language sciences. *Bilingualism: Language and Cognition*, *6*, 159–165. doi:10.1017/S136672890300110X

Gumperz, J., & Levinson, S. (Eds.). (1996). *Rethinking linguistic relativity*. Cambridge, MA: Cambridge University Press.

Hall, E. T. (1976). *Beyond culture*. New York, NY: Doubleday.

Hall, E. T. (1981). *The silent language*. New York, NY: Doubleday.

Hall, E. T. (1983). *The dance of life*. New York, NY: Doubleday.

Hofstede, G. (2010). *Cultures and organizations, software of the mind* (3rd ed.). New York, NY: McGraw Hill.

House, R. J., Hanges, P. J., Javidan, M., Dorfman, P. R., & Gupta, V. (Eds.). (2005). *Culture, leadership, and organizations: The GLOBE study of 62 societies*. New York, NY: Sage Publications.

Jarvis, S., & Pavlenko, A. (2008). *Crosslinguistic influence in language and cognition*. New York, NY: Routledge.

Kaplan, R. (1996). Cultural thought patterns in intercultural education. *Language Learning*, *16*(1-2), 1–20. doi:10.1111/j.1467-1770.1966.tb00804.x

Kubota, R. (1999). Japanese culture constructed by discourses: Implications for applied linguistics research and ELT. *TESOL Quarterly*, *33*(1), 9–35. doi:10.2307/3588189

Li, A. (1999). Agency: A cultural perspective implicit in language use. In Chu, M. (Ed.), *Mapping the course of the Chinese language field* (*Vol. III*, pp. 71–101). Kalamazoo, MI: Chinese Language Teachers Association Monograph Series.

Li, P. (2009). Lexical organization and competition in first and second languages: Computational and neural mechanisms. *Cognitive Science*, *33*, 629–664. doi:10.1111/j.1551-6709.2009.01028.x

Li, P., Jin, Z., & Tan, L. (2004b). Neural representations of nouns and verbs in Chinese: An fMRI study. *NeuroImage*, *21*, 1533–1541. doi:10.1016/j.neuroimage.2003.10.044

Lucy, J. (1996). The scope of linguistic relativity: An analysis and review of empirical research. In Gumperz, J. J., & Levinson, S. C. (Eds.), *Rethinking linguistic relativity* (pp. 37–69). Cambridge, MA: Cambridge University Press.

Moder, C. L., & Martinovic-Zic, A. (Eds.). (2004). *Discourse across languages and cultures*. Amsterdam, The Netherlands: John Benjamins Publishing Co.

Panetta, C. G. (Ed.). (2000). *Contrastive rhetoric revisited and redefined*. New York, NY: Routledge.

Pennycook, A. (1999). *Development, culture and language: Ethical concerns in a postcolonial world*. Retrieved from http://www.languages.ait.ac.th/hanoi_proceedings/contents.htm

Perani, D., & Abutaleb, J. (2005). The neural basis of first and second language processing. *Current Opinion in Neurobiology, 15*(2), 202–206. doi:10.1016/j.conb.2005.03.007

Pinaud, R., Tremere, L. A., & De Weerd, P. (Eds.). (2006). *Plasticity in the visual system: From genes to circuits*. New York, NY: Springer. doi:10.1007/0-387-28190-8

Pinker, S. (2003). *The blank slate*. New York, NY: Penguin Books.

Pütz, M., & Verspoor, M. (Eds.). (2000). *Explorations in linguistic relativity*. Amsterdam, The Netherlands: John Benjamins Publishing Company.

Ramathan, V., & Atkinson, D. (1999). Individualism, academic writing, and ESL writers. *Journal of Second Language Writing, 8*(1), 45–75. doi:10.1016/S1060-3743(99)80112-X

Reppen, R., Fitzmaurice, S. M., & Biber, D. (2002). *Using corpora to explore linguistic variation*. Philadelphia, PA: Johns Benjamin Publishing.

Spack, R. (1997). The rhetorical construction of multilingual students. *TESOL Quarterly, 31*(4), 765–774. doi:10.2307/3587759

Stewart, E., & Bennett, M. (1991). *American cultural patterns: A cross-cultural perspective* (Rev. ed). Yarmouth, ME: Intercultural Press, Inc.

Swales, J. (1997). English as Tyrannosaurus Rex. *World Englishes, 16*, 373–382. doi:10.1111/1467-971X.00071

Thatcher, B. L. (1997). *Orality and writing in Latin American and USA professional communication*. Unpublished doctoral dissertation, Purdue University.

Thatcher, B. L. (1999). Cultural and rhetorical adaptations for South American audiences. *Technical Communication, 46*(2), 177–195.

Thatcher, B. L. (2000). Writing policies and procedures in a U.S. and South American context. *Technical Communication Quarterly, 94*, 365–400. doi:10.1080/10572250009364706

Thatcher, B. L. (2001). Issues of validity in intercultural professional communication research. *Journal of Business and Technical Communication, 15*(4), 458–489. doi:10.1177/105065190101500403

Thatcher, B. L. (2006). Intercultural rhetoric, technology, and writing in Mexican maquilas. *Special Technology Transfer Edition of Technical Communication Quarterly, 15*(3), 383–405.

Thatcher, B. L. (2010a). Introduction. *Rhetoric, professional communication, and globalization*, 1, 1-34.

Whorf, B. L. (1956). The relation of habitual thought and behavior to language. In Carrol, J. B. (Ed.), *Language, thought, and reality: Selected writings of Benjamin Lee Whorf* (pp. 134–150). Cambridge, MA: Technology Press of Massachusetts Institute of Technology.

Chapter 4
Information and Communication Technologies and Intercultural Professional Communication

ABSTRACT

This chapter shows how definitions and assumptions about information and communication technology must be grounded in prevailing rhetorical and cultural traditions. It shows how much media research in the United States presupposes strong U.S. cultural values, including its legal traditions, the English language, and eight common human thresholds of interaction. It also show how each rhetoric and cultural tradition fit, remediate, and have distinct uses and timing for the information and communication technologies. Its purpose it to help professional communicators understand the use and forms of communication media appropriately around the world.

INTRODUCTION

As explained in Chapter Three, contrastive rhetoric examines the relations of L2 textual patterns and the rhetorical and cultural traditions of authors and audiences (see, for example, Kaplan 1966). This focus is based on the Sapir-Whorf hypothesis that one's native language determines (strong hypothesis) or encourages (weak hypothesis) one's thought—and therefore—writing patterns. Accordingly, as first argued by Kaplan (1966), many L2 students of English composition bring their textual organizing strategies from their L1 into their English compositions. As explored thoroughly in Chapter Three, contrastive rhetoric has moved beyond the simple one-to-one correspondences between writing patterns and culture. These developments look at a variety of cultural, linguistic, historical, and social factors that influence the complex acts of acquiring and demonstrating L2 writing competencies. In addition, other studies have demonstrated that L2 writing scholars and teachers need to understand not only the cultural background of their students, but also the specific context and audience-author relations to understand fully the textual patterns of the L2 writer (Thatcher 2000; 1999).

DOI: 10.4018/978-1-61350-450-5.ch004

These developments are important, but in this Chapter, I push contrastive rhetoric and the Sapir-Whorf hypothesis even further and suggest that the focus on the verbal medium as evidence for—and a reinforcer of—cultural and rhetorical patterns is too narrow and debilitating. In addition to language, a growing number of researchers (see, for example, Bolter & Grusin 1999) argue that communication media, such as orality, writing, e-mail, and hypertext, can similarly determine (strong hypothesis) or predispose (weak hypothesis) our mental and corresponding rhetorical patterns. Just like languages, communication media are not neutral devices that correspond equally and favorably to all rhetorical and cultural traditions. Instead, communication media restrain and reinforce certain communication possibilities and corresponding rhetorical and cultural patterns, thus developing complexly different relations to each cultural/rhetorical tradition across the globe. Consequently, each rhetorical tradition develops with each communication media a sense of purpose, audience-author relations, information needs, organizational patterns, and stylistic preferences. Researchers, practitioners, and teachers of intercultural rhetoric and professional communication, therefore, need to understand how professional communication is situated with communication media and cultures across the globe; otherwise, they might use one of these media assuming a rhetorical purpose that is not suited to the cultural context.

This connection between communication media and cultural patterns is a critical aspect of intercultural professional communication, but it is often ignored by many information and communication technology scholars. For example, in his *The World is Flat,* Friedman argues that newer information and communication media might be flattening hierarchies and democratizing relations. Friedman specifically identifies the role of the web in this influence, arguing that the web creates a triple convergence that will flatten the world: information access, more horizontal ways to collaborate, and opening up of new cultures (pp. 176-181). However, this triple convergence presupposes or is based on mostly U.S. and Western cultural values such as individualism, achievement orientation, low power distance communication patterns, and universalism, all of which are strongly rooted in the United States but not elsewhere. Similar arguments have been developed (and critiqued) about email and hypertext for a decade or so (see, for example, Hawisher & Selfe, 2000). However, a long history of media scholarship in Latin America shows how supposed democratizing media can actually strengthen status-quo oligarchies (Martin Barbero, 1993).

In other words, despite the huge movement towards situating new communication technologies rhetorically, most U.S. scholars fail situate how they situate their own theories. Consequently, many U.S. scholars commit the same kinds of ethnocentric theorizing about the new media that have occurred with other media-culture theories, especially those applied outside the United States. For example, in the early 19th-century, a large number scholars hypothesized that written constitutions would have a similar effect on Latin American countries as the U.S. Constitution did on the United States. And thus, there was a great push for developing written constitutions in Latin America. However, according to many comparative legal scholars (Rosenn, 1991), the signers of U.S. Declaration and Constitution were able to rely on a cultural and rhetorical context that encouraged or allowed such uses of written communication. In the U.S. tradition, writing correlated very strongly with the distance, isolation, and personal space of individualism and the backbone of the laws, rules, and regulations of universalism (Hampden-Turner & Trompenaars, 2000; Thatcher, 1999; Stewart & Bennett, 1991). In a collective culture such as Ecuador, writing will not have the same influence because orality is the preferred medium for regulating behavior (Thatcher, 2000). Thus, it is not surprising that documents like the U.S. Constitution have had significantly less influence in Latin American countries. Ecuador has developed about 34 constitutions since its independence with the newest one in 2008; but these written constitutions have not influenced Ecuadorian society the same way because Ecuadorian rhetorical traditions do not facilitate or encourage such uses of writing.

Political theorists now understand that the effect of media on a given cultural or political system has to be understood in light of the rhetorical tradition of that system, or they will unwittingly transplant a media-culture theory from one rhetorical tradition to another. This ethnocentric error is committed because scholars do not understand that communication media influence each rhetorical tradition differently, based on issues of fit, reciprocity, and kairos. Fit means the degree of correlation (positive or negative) between the rhetoric of the media itself and the rhetorical tradition of the population. Reciprocity means the mutually constitutive and remediative (Bolter & Grusin, 1999) relations of the media and the culture. Kairos means timing, that is, when and why to use each media according to the rhetorical situations. In other words, the U.S. cultural tradition fits the use of writing to regulate human behavior; and thus, the two—written constitution and U.S. rhetorical tradition—continue to evolve into mutually constituting relationships and continually remediate themselves.

These issues of fit and reciprocity between writing and orality and larger rhetorical traditions have been studied (see Kaufer & Carley, 1993), even though many U.S. scholars in rhetoric and professional communication still do not understand how the U.S. rhetorical tradition influences their theories about professional communication and culture (Thatcher, 1999; 2000). Kairos, or using each medium at different times, according to the rhetorical situation has not been addressed at all, except maybe in organizational communication, a point discussed later.

In addition to the traditional work on orality and writing, this Chapter focuses on the newer media, in this case, the worldwide web, including the interactive web sites and social media. Understanding how the worldwide web fits U.S. and other rhetorical traditions is critical now, for at least four reasons. First, this grounding denaturalizes the rhetorical foundation of web-cultural relations, further enhancing our understanding of how the web fits and influence specific rhetorical traditions around the world. Second, knowing the fit, reciprocity, and kairos of the web with a specific rhetorical tradition is essential for understanding how the web might influence cross-cultural communications between distinct rhetorical traditions. Third, scholars of the worldwide web must move into the global realm of inquiry because of the web's global reach and the changing global relationships encouraged by this greater reach (see a fuller definition of reach, see Kaufer & Carley, 1993). Fourth, as countries and cultures become much more inter-dependent, due in large measure to global economics, politics, environment, and immigration, they will rely much on the newer media such as the web to mediate these global relations.

This Chapter seeks to explore these issues. It first explores the culture-media relations of fit, reciprocity, and kairos; second, it explores the rhetorical aspects of communication media; and finally, it connects these media to broad cultural patterns around the world.

APPROACHING NEW MEDIA WITH FIT, RECIPROCITY, AND KAIROS

The concepts of fit, reciprocity, and kairos first must be situated in the history of media-culture relations. Plato originally argued that writing—the newest and most significant communication technology—would have damaging cultural and rhetorical effects because of its inherent weaknesses as compared to orality (*Phaedrus,* 1956). According to Plato, writing would deteriorate memory, wreak havoc on logical constructions, and create an artificial reality. As a result, argues Plato, cultures that embrace writing would become inferior mentally, socially, and logically. Later, Ong (1987) traces the evolution of oral to literate societies, arguing that the development of writing radically changed cultural and rhetorical patterns. Pre-literate societies developed cultural and communicative patterns based on the oral medium: repetition to increase memory and transference; logic based on narrative organizational patterns; and persuasion based on "presence," a development of concrete sensory language that evokes context, personal relationships, and events. Ong (1987) then argued that with the advent of literacy and writing, these cultural patterns changed: instead of repetition, concision; analytical organizational patterns instead of narrative; persuasion based on formal logic rather than presence. Ong labels this transformation of writing supplanting orality as perhaps the most significant cultural change in history. [1] In the 1960s, McLuhan (1967) offered similar deterministic accounts of communication media such as television and radio; in other words, the medium was the message in that the physical structure of the medium superimposed rhetorical and cultural patterns on its audiences.

In the mid 1980s and into the 1990s, many scholars, however, began to discount the simplicity of these deterministic and ethnocentric theories, arguing instead for mutually constitutive patterns. These relationships were based on the degree of commonality and difference between the broad socio-cultural patterns, the communication patterns the media reinforced, and the specific socio-historical context in which the media are associated. For example, Martín-Barbero (1993), a Colombian communication scholar, and Grossberg (1992), a U.S. scholar both argue that communication media such as movies, television, and print journalism do encourage or reinforce certain rhetorical and cultural patterns, but the effect of this influence varies greatly; and these scholars argue for exploring the ways local cultures appropriate, resist, and even reject cultural patterns associated with both the content and form of communication media. Kaufer & Carley (1993) similarly posit theories of mutually constitutive relationships among cultural patterns and writing and orality, and they explore the social and cultural dynamics reinforced—but not determined—by the print media. Rarely does one medium supplant another one, as Ong originally argued; rather, the rhetoric of one medium corresponds more closely to—and reinforces the rhetorical patterns of—a culture more than another medium. Kaufer and Carley (1993) did not extend this comparison to cross-cultural inquiries, but the connection is obvious. Some cultures feel more comfortable with some media over others because the patterns reinforced by these media correspond generally well with their overall cultural patterns. For example, as I document elsewhere (Thatcher 2000; 1999), the South Americans in one organization were more comfortable with orality to mediate organizational relationships because of their collective, particular, and interpersonal values, while their U.S. counterparts were more comfortable with writing because of their individual, universal, and analytical values.

Bolter and Grusin (1999) further explore this media-culture relationship in their conception of *remediation* and update the culture-media debate with discussions of email and hypertext. They argue that communication technology does not supplant older technology; it re-mediates it, influencing different types of mediations between communicators and older media than before. For example, writing did not replace orality; instead, writing changed the way people speak, in form, content, and speaker-listener relationships. Electronic discourses such as email and hypertext (exemplified by websites) have not replaced orality and writing, but they have changed the way people write and speak. Bolter and Grusin

(1999) demonstrate how early newspaper page designs, which were text based, are now significantly influenced by the more visual media, and some newspapers even are beginning to look like websites. In addition, television newscasts now integrate hypertext technologies such as buttons and flashing screens in their oral-visual reports, making some newscasts appear more like a webpage than a television screen. These later developments of Bolter and Grusin (1999) and Kaufer and Carley (1993) offer a much more compelling picture into the relationships of culture and communication media, showing how each rhetorical tradition fits and mutually constructs its relations to the media, including the web.

Kairos in the Context of Fit and Reciprocity

In addition to fit and reciprocity, the timing of when to use the media varies according to the value sets of the group. To exemplify this competency and its direct connection to research validity, I will highlight some recent work that I carried out for a U.S.-Mexico border environmental project, which I report on more fully elsewhere (Thatcher, 2009). For this project, we used e-mail, FTP, and web/Internet technologies to communicate with stakeholders. The main deliverable for this project was a collaborative test plan that I initially composed but submitted for review to a multitude of U.S. and Mexican stakeholders, including the U.S. Environmental Protection Agency (EPA) and its Mexican counterparts SERMANAT and PROFEPA. To help develop and review this test plan, the stakeholders needed to download the test plan document using FTP protocol over the internet, comment on it using Microsoft Word's review function, and send their comments back to our team via email. All of the stakeholders were required to be literate in these technologies, to have and appropriately use these media in order to participate in the design of the technology test plan. In addition, the test team needed to use the digital media in a cross-cultural situation, something that proved difficult for many to do.

This difficulty in cross-cultural communication occurred mostly because many of the Mexican and U.S. collaborators used the media according to ***their*** rhetorical and cultural traditions and sense of appropriate timing, not understanding how these traditions differed on the other side of the border, even though many have significant cross-border experience. Consequently, some collaborators used e-mail in situations or in certain stages of the document production that were appropriate for U.S. contexts but inappropriate for Mexican contexts and vice versa. Much of the difficulties centered on the fact that the EPA set up the document development cycle following U.S, not Mexican, cultural values. This cycle used e-mail and FTP for the initial planning stages, phone calls for the intermediate stages, and e-mail and FTP for the final stages of the document cycle. This review cycle works well in the United States because it corresponds with U.S. values of specificity, individualism, universalism, and monochronic time orientation. This cycle, however, did not work well in Mexico, which has a diffuse orientation, requiring much upfront time between the parties to develop a holistic, and therefore, trusting view of each other; a more collective orientation, which requires more attention to authority and roles; and a more polychronic orientation, which assumes more of a simultaneous, back and forth, process rather than the more linear process set up by the EPA. From this perspective, the Kairos or timing of when to use one medium versus another is a cultural construct.

Much research has documented the appropriate timing, for example, of e-mail, showing that e-mail is more appropriate to begin or end a discussion, depending on the circumstances (Sproull & Kiesler 1986, 1992). Verhulsdonck (2010) found that timing or kairos was somewhat altered or different in electronic and virtual environments, but that the same social cues that structure non-electronic environments most likely will structure the timing in electronic and virtual worlds.

Variables for Studying Culture and Communication Technologies

These concepts of fit, reciprocity, and kairos are connected to the value sets, but how? The rest of this chapter lays out the variables that communication media have and show how these variables connect to the common human thresholds or cultural values sets. In a helpful summary of the research in computer mediated communication, Durso (2009) outlines the critical variables and theories for researching the connections between communication technologies and cultures, which I draw on to present many of the basic theories. These include the following that are most salient for intercultural research:

- Social presence, critical mass, and social influence
- Media richness and naturalness
- Social information processing
- Social identity and deindividuation
- Hyperpersonal interaction
- Channel expansion, and
- Mindfulness/mindlessness

In addition to this list, scholars in rhetoric and professional communication have identified other critical components in the new media, which include the connections between the new media and knowledge management and information architecture.

Social Presence and Social Information Processing (SIP) Theories

Social presence theory was originally developed by Short, Williams, and Christie (1976) when computer-mediated communication was not a fully developed concept or theory, but it has influenced significantly much research since then. Social presence theory originally focused on telephone and face to face communications. Using a significant amount of empirical research, these researchers ranked communication media according to the degree of awareness one person has of the other person in a communication interaction. Higher awareness equaled social presence, while lower awareness did not. Social presence theory also argued that communicators need to adjust their communication media choices according to the degree of interpersonal involvement needed in the specific communication context. Social presence theory ranked face-to-face communication as having the highest social presence, while text-based communication had the lowest social presence. This research, however, did not connect the perceptions of social presence to intercultural values. For example, is this social presence defined in a specific or diffuse manner?

Social Information Processing (SIP) Theory extended social presence theory to the online environment (Walther, 1992). It theorized that electronic and online relations probably need more time to develop than face to face relations, but once established, these online relations maintained the same characteristics and relations as face-to-face communications. In addition, online media might facilitate interpersonal relations that were not possible with face-to-face, due to physical distance or social hierarchy or identity issues. Originally, much of this research focused on the negative aspects of online interactions, but more recently, research has focused on the positive, perhaps more egalitarian effects. The SIP theory argues that despite not having the traditional social and interpersonal cues from face-to-face communications, online media provide their own social cues, giving users ways to perceive, interpret, and interact with these cues in ways not possible with orality and writing. These include emoticons and other social information such as the user's signature. However, these online relations vary significantly across cultures, based on the value sets or common human thresholds. As I explain in earlier researcher, because of their high context, diffuse, and collective values, Ecuadorian students had considerable difficulty overcoming the lack of social cues when first introduced to online communications; but eventually, they re-introduced their social cues through careful use of titles, signatures, and other social information that placed them in the Ecuadorian hierarchy (Thatcher, 2006).

Media Richness and Media Naturalness Theories

Media richness theory is an extension of Social Presence Theory but taken to the newer communication media and operationalized more richly. Much like social presence, Daft and Engel (1986) rank the "richness" of the communication media based on capacity for immediate feedback, the type and number of cues and channels available (visual, corporal, verbal, audio), and how clearly speaker intentionality and purpose can be communicated. The richness also includes the ability of that medium to reproduce social cues such as tone of voice, interpersonal spacing, body language, and communication context. Richer media create greater immediacy and warmth of communication. This theory generally places face to face as the richest, with anonymous texts as the poorest (Daft & Engel, 1986). Consequently, communication media that most resemble face to face communications are richer (such as video conferencing), while those resembling anonymous texts are poorer (such as email). In addition, this theory postulates that the more ambiguous the communication situation is, the more the communicators need to use the richer medium so as to communicate more effectively the intended message. Thus, communicators need to understand clearly the rhetorical situation in order to select the most appropriate medium. However, communicators are often faced with rhetorical situations requiring richer media but only have the poorer media at their disposal.

Media naturalness theory is an extension and critique of media richness theory. It was first developed by Kock (2005) who drew upon evolutionary psychology as a way to model human-technological interactions. Kock (2005) argues that evolution predisposed humans to use face-to-face communications and that the more recent advancements of electronic communications have happened so quickly that the human brain has not had time to evolve. This lack of evolutionary adaptation produces cognitive obstacles to communication, especially in the context of complex tasks that are mediated over space and time. Like media richness theory, media naturalness theory ranks naturalness using face-to-face communication as the benchmark or baseline. This is because face to face communication permits communicators to be together physically, allowing them to hear and see each other; it also encourages enhanced levels of synchronicity, including the ability to convey and observe body language, facial gestures, tone of voice, and contextual information. Electronic communications present cognitive obstacles to the degree that they do not allow for the face-to-face cues and channels and are classified as unnatural. Frequently, the form of obstacles presented by electronic communications include information overload, the presenting of too much information too quickly.

Media naturalness theory predicts that the decrease in a medium's naturalness correlates with cognitive effort, communication ambiguity, and less physiological arousal. However, communicators using electronic media can adapt their behavior to overcome some of the limitations of these media (Kock, 2005).

Social Identity Model of De-individuation Effects (SIDE)

The Social Identity model of Deindividuation Effects (or SIDE model) explores the nature of anonymity and identifiability in computer-mediated communication (Spears & Lea, 1992). This theory extends Deindividuation theory, which was developed to explain why people in crowds act irrationally and often unethically. Deindividuation theory suggests that people in crowds become uninhibited and behave antisocially because of their reduced sense of self and lack of accountability. Online environments are simply like crowds where users experience the same lack of self awareness and accountability. The SIDE model, however, rejects the theory that lack of self awareness and anonymity encourage antisocial behavior. Instead it argues that online environments produce an enhanced ability to connect to the user's in-group and to segment off the out-group. This process depersonalizes the user himself and his or her audience, connecting the user more closely to his or her in-group and stereotyping more the out-group. Consequently, the user's self perception changes, from more individualistic to more interchangeable with the in-group. Likewise, individual norms are transformed into group norms; and as opposed to Deindividuation, depersonalization does not imply irrational or disinhibited behavior; rather, the individual behaves rationally because he regulates behavior according to in-group standards.

This process of depersonalization can only occur if social cues and social identity are available. If they are not available, however, and users interact anonymously, they will most likely produce an opposite response of highlighting the user's isolation from the group and obscuring group boundaries (e.g.,Spears & Lea, 1992). In other words, anonymity in the group either amplifies a shared social identity when social cues are already in place or individualism where this social identity is absent.

This dual function of anonymity affects individual and group power and identity in online environments (Spears & Lea, 1992). Individual users may downplay the level of social cues available so as to enhance their individualism, or they may emphasize the social cues so as to enhance the power of their in-group. If different groups are vying for power in online environments, users can chart their own identifiability with the groups based on the perceived or actual availability of social cues versus anonymity. In other words, more anonymity can be claimed as a way to oppose the out-group, which often manifests itself in personal expressions of individualism and identity. This personal expression, however, is not like the antisocial behavior of a person in crowds, as explained by Deindividuation theory; rather, SIDE proposes that this individual expression is often patterned and symbolic, based on the in-group's norms of behavior, rather than violent, irrational behavior (Reicher, Spears, & Postmes, 1995). As a corollary, this process of depersonalization might further isolate users from their groups where more anonymous or reduced social cues are present, further reducing the user's ability to counteract a more powerful out-group. A reduced social cue or anonymous online context might also work against the commitments of individuals to their in-group's norms.

Like the other theories previously described, these theories of online group relations presuppose western values of individualism, low context communication, universalism, a specific orientation, and an inner orientation. It is quite possible that the dynamics of online group relations change dramatically in a different cultural context. For example, in collective, particular, and diffuse cultures, the entrance into the group is much, much more difficult and time consuming; and the cues for admission into the group are based much less on the specific orientation of activity and more on the whole person. Much research needs to address this change across cultures.

Hyperpersonal Interaction

The Hyperpersonal Model is a theory first developed by Walther (1996) that suggests computer-mediated communication can be hyperpersonal because it provides communicators with more advantages over face-to-face interactions. Compared to orality or traditional writing, electronic communications offer a greater ability to strategically develop and edit self-presentation, enabling a selective and optimized presentation of one's self to others. Thus, in contradiction to media richness and naturalness theory, the Hyperpersonal Model suggests that in electronic communication environments, communicators can actually work alone or together to intensify the interpersonal element of the communication, often exceeding the dyadic norms of orality or even writing. Since the electronic channel lacks physical presence, receivers can maintain an idealized perspective, and senders can offer an optimized self-presentation. Further, the asynchronous quality may allow for less task/interpersonal interruptions elsewhere and promote a more focused, enjoyable experience. In addition, as the receiver-sender-channel-feedback cycle is played out over and over again, it should reinforce initial optimized impressions. However, just as in the previous SIDE theory, the Hyperpersonal model most likely works best in specific, universal, and individualistic cultures where the specific types of personal information is sufficient for group interactions.

Channel Expansion

Prefiguring much of intercultural rhetorical theory, the Channel Expansion theory argues that the richness of the communication media depends on the uses and experience of the groups using it (Carlson & Zmud, 1999). Experience of communicators with the media allow communicators to "develop associated knowledge bases that may be used to more effectively both encode and decode rich messages on a channel" (p. 155). As communicators adapt to the media, they can encode and decode messages better, a process that seems to make the media richer than it at first appears to be. Carlson and Zmud (1999) identify four media richness building experiences: familiarity with the media; familiarity with the topic of discussion; knowledge of the communication or organizational context; and experience with the other people involved with the communication. Because media richness is produced or structured by the social context, its richness will vary according to the local cultural values.

Mindfulness and Mindlessness

Another key attribute of communication technologies for intercultural contexts is the notion of mindfulness versus mindlessness. The concepts were first develop by Langer (1997) and connected to communication media by Timmerman (2002). As Langer explains, mindfulness means (a) openness to novelty; (b) alertness to distinction; (c) sensitivity to different contexts; (d) implicit, if not explicit, awareness of multiple perspectives; and (e) orientation in the present. In other words, mindfulness is the ability to continually see something as new or novel, something like a beginner's mind, which encourages a continual and active quest for novelty. Mindfulness is also closely connected to play. On the other hand, mindlessness is the tendency to operate on auto-pilot, either through sheer boredom and roteness or simply not paying attention. Instead of play, mindlessness is connected to work. As Langer explains, mindlessness often results from three types of thinking: categorical or stereotypical; acting from a single perspective; and repetition.

These two concepts are connected to communication media by choice and specific use of media (see, for example, Timmerman, 2002) and correlate nicely with intercultural awareness. First, categorical thinking clearly correlates with electronic mass media, which mostly likely encourages categorical thinking. In addition, communication media mediate authors, audiences, and reality, and therefore, become a type of routinized categorical thinking. In addition, media offer varied levels of sensory information, as explained earlier, thus facilitating a more rote approach to communication scenarios. Thus in organizations, tasks often require frequent and repetitive use of communication media, producing a primarily mindless scenario; however, when communicators are in the mindful condition, they were much more effective at selecting and using the most appropriate medium for the communication situation (Timmerman, 2002).

This concept of mindfulness is extremely rich for intercultural communication because what is deemed novel or interesting varies significantly across cultures. For example, in high context and polychronic cultures, websites are frequently full of movement, bright colors, and constantly changing templates. This approach continuously attracts the attention because of its novelty for high context and polychronic users but mostly confuses those from low context and monochronic cultures (See Thatcher, et. al., 2007). Thus, since novelty is a cultural construct, intercultural communicators must create electronic communications that keep the attention of the uses in the target culture.

Rhetorics of Orality, Writing, Internet, and Interactive Web 2.0

The media and culture theories provide the framework for understanding the rhetorical attributes of the media themselves and how each medium might fit with cultures around the world. This section highlights the rhetorics of the old and new media, in this case, orality, writing, and the newer media: email, the Internet, and interactive hypertext or Web 2.0. These two sections are combined in the last part of this chapter to explore how these media fit cultural traditions around the world.

Most scholars (see Kaufer & Carley, 1993) argue that orality is the richest medium, has the highest social presence, is the most natural, probably has the most mindfulness, and is most prone to deindividuation. This is most likely because this orality relies on the presence of both the speaker and listener in a concrete context where non-verbal, verbal, and contextual information is readily available. Orality is oriented to pre-existing group dynamics including observable social hierarchies, but group dynamics can quickly change; its topics are constantly changing with high levels of simultaneity; it easily draws on concrete details but in holistic approaches; and since it relies on the presence of speaker and hearer, there is also a heightened dependence on the communication context for meaning and a greater propensity for concrete and visual imagery, encouraging what Stewart and Bennett (1991) call "horizontal" or "perceptual" thinking rather than analytical thinking. These characteristics of orality correlate to communication patterns that are narrative in structure, emphasizing novelty and repetitive aids to enhance memory. These characteristics probably strongly correlate to enhanced mindfulness but probably negatively correlate to channel expansion and hyperpersonal interaction.

On the other hand, writing is one of the poorest medium for social information, has the lowest social presence, is the first widespread communication technology, and as such, is not that natural; it's probably the least prone to individuation; but it might foster channel expansion and hyperpersonal interaction in the appropriate contexts. It is also easy to ignore or not be mindful of. Because writing essentially severs the temporal, visual, and contextual ties to orality, it seemed to have encouraged different rhetorical patterns. Writing strongly correlates with the independence of individualism, but the development of writing is also correlated with "more developed" forms of communities (Kaufer & Carley, 1993, pp. 253-296). These "developed" communities are based on abstract, rule of law approaches for regulating interpersonal behavior and community relationships. Writing does not depend as much as orality on pre-existing group dynamics, and group dynamics associated with writing usually change much more slowly. Writing facilities a uniformity of topics in a more linear mode of development; and writing can be very concrete but this concreteness is not as easily connected to the writing context. Since writing relies on disconnecting author from audience, there is less dependence on the communication context for meaning and a greater propensity for abstract yet specific (versus diffuse) information and verbal imagery (versus visual). Consequently, writing been associated with more analytical thinking patterns, distanced interpretation skills, and abstract and more conceptual cognitive relationships (Ong, 1987; Kaufer and Carley, 1993), reinforcing what Stewart and Bennett (1991) call deep and analytical thinking (pp. 23-25).

The rhetorics of email and hypertext are more difficult to define perhaps because they are newer media and do not correlate as directly to rhetorical and cultural values. Both email and hypertext also have mixed indices of social presence, media richness, social information processing, Deindividuation, hyperpersonal interactions, channel expansion, and mindfulness. These mixed rankings develop a strong sense of rhetorical ambiguity in both email and hypertext in that these two media are able to take on characteristics of both orality and writing.

Most communication scholars agree that email has a complex mix of oral and written rhetorical patterns. According to Moran & Hawisher (1998) email tends to have a decided public/private duality. On the one hand, the communicator is isolated and alone when communicating, but the communications can be exceedingly public. Thus, email can favor oral rhetorical patterns such as orientation to pre-existing–but quickly changing–group dynamics; but email is also highly simultaneous with constantly changing topics, yet it cannot draw on the context nor non-verbal or visual imagery. Also, the technological issues of the ease of storage, retrievability, and speed encourage certain rhetorical characteristics. Moran & Hawisher (1998) argue that email fosters illusions of intimacy perhaps because of its immediacy and ostensible privacy. Email is a more decontextual medium because it doesn't offer the contextual cues that orality or other media offer. Email does not need the narrative structures, novelty, and repetitive aids to memory. However, email probably does not fosters the kind of rhetorical distance associated with writing, which facilities a more analytical, decontextual analysis. Email often is very mindful at times when important or critical communications are present, but mindless at other times (SPAM). Email can also facilitate hyperpersonal interactions, at times, but probably reduces personal cues at other times.

Hypertext is an electronic medium exemplified by Internet websites and has been distinguished from text communications by its lack of linearity—the interlinkings of information creates the web metaphors. A hypertext communication also contains many thousands of texts, pictures, sound bytes, files, documents, and other information all interrelated in complex, simultaneous ways. Kress (1998) argues that hypertext is more audience-driven than many communication media, that is, readers can create their own unique paths, offering some semblance of authorship to readers. Hypertext integrates written text with graphics and sounds in ways that are impossible for orality and writing. Hypertext is uniquely contextualized by its links to other websites, forming complex ideological and social relations with these sites (Kress 1998). Hypertext is perhaps the most explicitly global medium because of the World Wide Web and Internet.

From this perspective, hypertext and the web can have enormous social presence, critical mass, and influence. It is also a very rich medium with its ability to combine almost all elements of communication, including visual, audio, oral, written, color, and page design or layout. Further, the richness is also reflected in the actually structure of the website itself. Despite this richness, however, the web can also be quite anonymous, revealing little about the author, the rhetorical context, and purported readers. Accordingly, it might correlate positively with deindividuation and negatively with hyperpersonal interaction. Further, because of its richness, the web has great potential for channel expansion as well as mindfulness.

Interactive electronic media, commonly known as Web 2.0, combine elements of orality, writing, email, and hypertext in unique ways. As Carliner (2009) explains, these interactive technologies differ from both email and hypertext because they are a two-way medium for reading and writing. Further, these media are richer because they can seamlessly integrate all types of electronic information, such as database, PDF documents, login and user interfaces, and videos. Thus, users can browse a website for information, to buy something, or interact with other users. Web 2.0 is more microcontent oriented, that is, these websites are less holistic and more easily created with small bits of information and interactive technologies. For example, Facebook can "tell their contacts what they are currently doing, comment on what the contacts are doing, send messages, and post announcements, calls for help, and photos (among other things) within a single interface" (Carliner, 2009). These technologies are essential to knowledge management, of creating and using information online and across cultures. This includes re-using and revising documents and other kinds of information that are shared so quickly. The Web 2.0 also allows for a more consistent development and uniformity of documents and communications. Google Documents, for example, allows people to simultaneously write and critique the same document from a distance.

Another extension of the Web 2.0 includes the instant and public communication technologies such as Twitter. Clark (2009) summarizes the following three key characteristics of instant public communication technologies:

- Twitter is public. Unlike text messaging or Facebook status updates, by default "tweets" are publicly readable and searchable, making new connections possible.
- Twitter can be endlessly re-sorted and reorganized. Because Twitter allows for and encourages outside software developers, we have countless interfaces and points of entry. Unlike with most messaging systems, which are designed for short-lifespan messages, users can track popular current trends in lists, search via location or key word, or create historical snapshots or follow key topics with creative searching .
- Twitter is powerful in the aggregate. Because all tweets are public, Twitter offers new and interesting possibilities for searching, allowing users to find and track events too new to appear on Google.

The rhetorical connections to Web 2.0 are complicated, ambiguous, and not well understood. First, as Ong (1987) predicted two decades ago, these Web 2.0 media are probably more oral-like than any of the new communication technologies. The interactive element of Web 2.0 is much like the interactive dynamics of orality; but the context is online, not physical like orality. And the online context is not totally verbal like email; but it is highly mixed with many kinds of information, including verbal, visual, audio, and spatial. The simultaneity of Web 2.0 is probably even more pronounced than orality, perhaps encouraging an even more dynamic change in topics and communication purposes. Yet because of the indexing and search features, this dynamic simultaneity can be searched and analyzed like writing. Web 2.0 such as twitter is strongly oriented to pre-existing group dynamics, but these group dynamics are mediated by the online medium and total strangers are engaging in discussions. These discussions can be highly concrete and narrative but their context is not as immediate nor defined as orality. Consequently, Web 2.0 probably facilitates both horizontal and analytical thinking (Stewart & Bennett, 1991). Like email, Web 2.0 can probably be very mindful at times when important or critical communications are present, but mindlessness at other times. Web 2.0 can also facilitate hyperpersonal interactions, at times, but probably reduces personal cues at other times.

Fit, Reciprocity, and Kairos of Communication Media Across the Globe

Now that we have explored the basic rhetorics of the communication media, it is time to examine how the rhetorics of orality, writing, and hyptertext and Web 2.0 fit, remediate, and mutually constitute the default approaches to eight thresholds of human interaction. In Table 1, I summarize how the default rhetorical approaches of these communication media fit the eight values sets or common human thresholds of interaction. After this, summary, I explain in detail how this fit influences the uses of these technologies around the world. This discussion includes concrete analysis of contrastive websites as well as uses of the interactive Web 2.0 around the world.

Individual-Collective and Communication Media

As explained more thoroughly in Chapter Two, the individual-collective value set assesses the levels of dependence or independence among people. For some cultures, the most likely approach to the "I"

Table 1. Fit of New Media and Cultural Values

	Orality	Writing	Email	Hypertext	Interactive Web
Individual-Collective	Fits much more easily with collective approach	Fits better individualism, although writing can facilitate distance-based communities.	Mixed: isolation of individualism but immediacy and reach of collectivism.	Mixed: richness and reach encourage collectivity, but mass media and isolation encourages individualism.	Mixed, but the interactive qualities probably reinforces collectivism.
Universal-Particular	Strongly correlated with particularism.	Strongly correlated with universalism.	Immediacy of particularism but storage and dissemination of universalism.	Mixed: provides unique design of particularism but reach and permanence of universalism.	Mixed but storage and retrieval might encourage more universalism.
Specific-Diffuse	Strongly correlated with diffuse	Strongly correlated with specific	Probably fits specific because of isolation	Richness fits diffuse better	Interactive ability facilities public element of specific and private dimension of diffuse.
Achievement-Ascription	Presence allows strength of ascription but capable of achievement	Reach correlates with both	Reach correlates with both	Richness might favor ascription but reach favors both	Interactive elements exemplifies achievement
High and Low Context	Strongly correlates with high context	Correlates with low but high is also possible.	Mixed but not as rich as orality.	Richness favors high context	Richness favors high but acontextual interaction probably favors low context.
Power Distance	Strongly correlates with high power	Strongly correlates with low power	Mixed but probably favors low because it's not as a rich.	Richness allows for multiple power symbols, but dissemination probably encourages low power distance	Acontextual probably favors lower power distance unless power hierarchies are designed into the interactions.
Time	Strongly correlated with polychronic	Correlates with both but likely favors monochronic.	Probably favors polychronic.	Web is good metaphor for polychronic time but monochronic is also easy.	Mixed: architecture synchronous can be polychronic but asynchronous is monochronic. and
Inner-Outer	Strongly correlated to outer	Strongly correlated to inner	Probably favors inner but has strong reactive potential of outer	Allows for both.	Allows for both, depending on architecture.

relating to the group is individualistic, while in others it is collective. The communication patterns of individualism include a focus on the "I" rather than the group, with the individual as the unit of analysis; a strong bifurcation between personal and objective communication strategies, which resolves interpersonal conflicts by going back to the uniqueness of the individual rather than to that person's political or social context (Stewart & Bennett, 1991); a dumbed-down readership level so as to uncomplicate the interpersonal dependence of communicators (Kras, 1991); and an emphasis of personal achievement, self-creation, and reader-friendly document design patterns (Hinds, 1987).

On the other hand, collectivism predominates when people view themselves as highly dependent upon others and define themselves, see the world, and negotiate life based on social or family groups. Collective communication patterns emphasize interpersonal relationships, social hierarchy, social leveraging, group identities, close personal space, and writer-friendly writing patterns (Hinds, 1987).[2] Collective communication patterns do not have a strong bifurcation between personal and objective strategies because they see the person in light of their social context, effectively combining the personal and social political. Instead of a dumbed-down readership level, collective communicators tend to complicate their interpersonal dependence as a way of stating the purpose of the communication and their involvement; this creates writer-friendly document design patterns (Hinds, 1987).

These two variables seem to combine very differently with the four communication media, in terms of fit, reciprocity, and kairos. First, one of the traditional arguments about orality (Ong 1987) is that because of its richness, naturalness, and social information, it reinforces cultural collectivity. Orality tends to be the mechanism of sharing traditions and for maintaining face and relational solidarity. Orality comes first, while writing comes second in both timing and preference. Orality seems to have a much weaker role in individualist cultures, perhaps relegated to expressing personal opinions and beliefs, but certainly not the backbone of society, as orality in many collective cultures.

On the other hand, writing seems to correlate very strongly with individualistic cultures, most notably those with strong Protestant foundations (see Trompenaars, 1994). Writing is a predominant first in the time frame and represents the distance, isolation, and personal space of individualistic cultures. Often, writing and written communications become the backbone of the laws, rules, and regulations that allow individualistic cultures to flourish (Stewart & Bennett, 1991), and become the obligatory first step in laying out these laws, which can be discussed only after. But writing provides the first platform for all that follows. Writing does not have the same influence in collective cultures. Shared traditions, relational solidarity, and maintaining face can be accomplished through writing, but the preferred—and the most effective medium—is still orality.

Knowledge of these media is critical for cross-cultural communication research and teaching. For example, as explored in cross-cultural organizations in Ecuador (Thatcher, 1999), the communication patterns of many South Americans were more oral, contextual, particular, and narrative, while the patterns of U.S. personnel were more written, acontextual, universal, and analytical. But more significantly, these patterns corresponded to contrastive roles and purposes for writing and orality. Many of the U.S. communicators initiated discourse based on circumstances that they thought writing usually solved, further reinforcing their individualistic values. Thus, writing was the first medium to use in this context. Consequently, the audience-author interactions, information needs, document design, and content organization seemed to be developed from and for written literacies. On the other hand, many South American personnel initiated discourse based on situations that they thought orality should address, further reinforcing their collective and interpersonal approach to organizational behavior (Thatcher, 2000). Thus, orality was primary and first, and writing followed; and the South American personnel often assessed information needs, document design, and content organization based on this oral literacy. Only when the South American and U.S-American writers understood these contrastive relations to writing and orality were they able to carry out effective and ethical communications with each other. This kind of cross-cultural media and cultural literacy is critical for intercultural professional communication classrooms; for a student can develop a well written document, but unless that document corresponds to the rhetorical roles of writing in the target culture, it will most likely fail and offend the audience of that culture.

The relation of individual-collective variable to email, hypertext, and Web 2.0 seems not as clear-cut as with orality and writing, perhaps pointing to new cultural values that might be a product of these newer remediations (Bolter & Grusin, 1999). Email seems to have the distance and isolation of individualistic cultures, but the illusions of intimacy, dynamism, and sense of community that are more prevalent in collective cultures. Interestingly, the web metaphor for hypertext communication actually symbolizes the collective approach, the person at the center orchestrating relational solidarity. Hypertext is also more integrated with audio-visual elements, which are more characteristic of orality and collective cultures. Web 2.0 seems to mix even more radically, having strong oral elements but also retaining written features. The strong interactive features might correlate more strongly to collectivism. For example, Google Search shows that many of the current Web 2.0 technologies are very popular in Brazil, in social, business, and academic settings. Perhaps one reason is that the interactive technologies favorably map onto Brazil's collective culture.

While I was a professor in Quito, Ecuador, I carried out a study of how well my Ecuadorian students felt that email and hypertext fit their general rhetorical traditions and patterns. Most of their concern was over the lack of social cues available in these media and how this lack of cues made it more difficult to communicate with those in their collective, in-groups. One student mentioned that "I lose all the emotion on email and the internet...I cannot communicate all that I want to. It is really difficult." This student explained that several times she was engaged in "chat" (an electronic synchronous communication technology), but because she could not convey the emotions, the tones of voice, and other extra-linguistic factors, she ended up calling her friend instead. She explained that with the contextual cues of the telephone she "could be more herself" (*puedo ser más yo*).

It was interesting, however, to note that many of the Ecuadorians thought that one advantage to email and hypertext was that the lack of context actually permitted a more abstract approach to their discussions. In an on-line discussion group, the students began debating the use of the Ecuadorian military to help crack down on crime. After witnessing this debate, I asked the students about the effect of the lack of context on their argumentative strategies. Over half of the students thought that the lack of context encouraged a more "objective," "reasoned," and "productive" discussion of the issues. In other words, this lack of context worked against the strong tendency in collective cultures to focus on in-group and out-group distinctions when arguing points and more on the abstract principles and theories. This perfectly exemplifies the theory of hyperpersonal interaction. Further, perhaps, as Bolter & Grusin argue (1999), the use of email and Internet might be encouraging a less collective approach in other forms of Ecuadorian communications, including writing. Much more research needs to be carried out to address these relationships. If an intercultural communicator, for example, comes from an individualistic tradition that also has high uses of hypertext communications, what kinds of intercultural communication patterns would result? Do the intercultural patterns exhibit a complex mixture of individualistic and collective patterns based on the remediation of hypertext communications?

Universal-Particular and Communication Media

As discussed in Chapter Two, the Universal-Particular value set assesses the approaches to rules. In universalist cultures, the default approach is to establish rules that define what is good and right regardless of the social standing of the individual. The ideal of a "level playing field" is an apt analogy for universalist cultures. Universalist communication patterns emphasize uniformity, parallelism, and templating. Universal communication patterns also include strategies of fairness, justice, and equality.

In particularist cultures, the default approach is to apply rules and decisions depending on relations and context. Instead of "the level playing field," the particularist playing field is overtly structured, and thus, there is a specifically tailored set of rules for each social relationship. Particular communication patterns include uniqueness in document design; emphasis of context and particular relationships; mention of exceptional circumstances; and consideration of social prestige and power relations.

The relation of universalism and particularism to the communication media is a particularly important variable for intercultural professional communication. In my research in South America, many of the South American personnel preferred orality as the first and primary organizational communication medium because it facilitated a particular, case-by-case approach to the applications of norms and procedures (1999; 2000). This value was so entrenched that most of the South American personnel had never worked from written policies and procedures. If, for example, they were to write the policy first and then discuss orally, they would not have the ability to particularize the policy, that is, to adjust it according the context and relations. On the other hand, the U.S. personnel working in these South American contexts automatically correlated writing with universalism, and writing was the first medium in these communications cycles. Writing something down and accepting it meant universalizing it; it meant developing the distance to analyze and create objectivity and equal application. The U.S. personnel experienced great difficulties in developing oral policies first and procedures based on personal relations and a case-by-case scenario (see Thatcher 1999). The two media, however, were not deterministic. Many of the South American personnel brought their oral—and particular—rhetorics to the writing situation; and vice versa, many of the U.S.-American personnel brought their written—and universal—rhetorics to the oral situation. This lack of correspondence, however, between the medium and rhetorical purpose created even greater intercultural communication problems.

Intercultural professional communicators need to understand the roles of orality and writing in regulating interpersonal behavior across cultures. For example, U.S.-American communicators working with more particular-collective people need to understand that writing probably does not have the same constitutive, normalizing purpose in many of those cultures as it has been assigned in U.S. cultures.

The ways that email mediates the universal and particular cultural values is of significant importance to intercultural professional communicators. Since writing is so closely related to univeralist, precedence-setting values and orality to particular, case-by-case norms, instructors need to carefully consider the influence of the electronic media, which tend to be situated theoretically between writing and orality (Moran & Hawisher 1998; Kress 1999). In the area of law, for example, the debate about whether email is "writing" is becoming critical given the boom of Internet commerce

("Symposium"). Thus, intercultural communicators obviously cannot assume the same purposes, exigencies, and author-audience relationships with e-mail in the areas of policies, laws, and other standardizing efforts in intercultural contexts.

Furthermore, hypertext writing is considered as "soft" by many US legal scholars, not having the legal contractual ability of traditional print communications. For example, is a link to another corporation's website cause for copyright infringement? ("Symposium"). Or is linking to certain websites and avoiding others a reason for collusion? Thus, the US legal system is trying to articulate the logic of legal responsibility in Internet communications ("Symposium"). Many other countries are considering similar legislation to clarify the actual legal binding authority of internet/hypertext communications. Questions that need to be addressed include: What kinds of research designs can measure the universalizing or particularizing of media-participant relationships in hypertext and e-mail communications? Or are both of these electronic media creating new conceptions of universal and particular categories, essentially re-mediating these terms?

In the context of the interactive Web 2.0 technologies, the questions of universal and particular are fascinating. On the one hand, the interactive elements probably encourage very particular relations and circumstances. On the other hand, the ability to store and retrieve information correlates with universalism. Perhaps the different results are based on the strength of the context of use: in particular cultures, the particular seems to hold, while the opposite is true in universal culture. Much research needs to address these relations.

Specific and Diffuse and Communication Media

This value set assess the degree of involvement across different spheres of life, usually involving a public/private divide and trust. Researchers have defined the two most likely approaches as diffuse or specific. Diffuse cultures are usually collective cultures; thus, involvement in friendships, social relations, and work environments often crosses boundaries—you work with your friends and close social acquaintances, thus sharing the relationship across these spheres. Consequently, in diffuse cultures, there are high levels of mistrust between people of different social groups or families, making work or collaboration in a public sphere fraught with many conflicts.

On the other hand, specific cultures are based on the ease and public trust that individualism and universalism give people in separate spheres of life, with friendship belonging to one or two spheres only, with little or no cross-over of authority. Specific orientation also relies on the reliable social structure of the level playing field, which allows them to quickly work or make friends with people in all kinds of spheres. Consequently, the specific orientation favors more public collaboration, something that is much more difficult in diffuse cultures. It is not surprising, therefore, that democracy has been relatively simpler to establish in specific cultures. In specific cultures, the hierarchies that are in place in business or education, for example, do not transfer as easily to the political realm, or vice versa. Thus, there is an easier transition to more democratic or egalitarian forums.

Diffuse communication patterns emphasize approaches that address the whole person in all aspects and dimensions, including social hierarchies. As a result, persuasion does not require salesmanship, but rather a long-term establishment of interconnected, interpersonal values. Consequently, diffuse patterns seem (to specific people) very indirect and to circle around the point, because diffuse communicators need to understand the whole person before getting to the point. Specific communication patterns easily section off people into different groups: students, faculty, staff, alumni, parents, and so on. Specific communications are also direct and inductive, stating the main point quickly and then supporting it.

Diffuse cultures strongly correlate with orality, while specific correlates strongly with writing. Diffuse cultures seem to prefer orality as the first and primary medium in a continuous rhetorical situation because orality helps establish the holistic understanding much more quickly; and then writing can take place later as a secondary approach. Orality provides the richest social cues, social presence, and social information of all the media, which exemplifies a diffuse approach to communication. As much research has shown, writing is a significant mechanism for analytically breaking up the wholes of diffuse orality.

Because email has less context and is much poorer in social information and social presence, it is probably more specific than orality. In fact, an email conversation is a nice example of specific orientation because it is by default a selected medium and a specific relation. However, email can provide a certain online context, much like a hyperpersonal presence, which might encourage an online version of diffuse orientation. It will be interesting to see if the online presence relies on the same mechanisms of diffuseness, such as difficulty in engaging with strangers in a public place and poor public behavior and very attentive private behavior. As explained earlier, some of the research in hyperpersonal, social identity, and deindividuation might address these different mechanisms of online engagement.

Hypertext is a much richer medium than email and thus can correlate to diffuse values much better than email and writing. As mentioned, a hypertext communication can have words, sound, pictures, context, and movement, all of which is a more holistic approach to communication. As shown in Chapter Five, university websites displayed very easily diffuse information. However, I also found that specific cultures have no problem communicating specific information on websites. This strength probably originates from the ability to divide up webpages almost in an infinite amount of subpages, perfectly exemplifying a specific approach to communication.

Web 2.0 can facilitate both, depending on the boundaries and mechanisms of online relations. Certainly, an interactive website can set parameters for login and participation that carefully regulates admission and participation in group behavior. In addition, interactive design can also allow for carefully moderating of group behavior, a connection between diffuse and high power distance, collective, and particular orientations. On the other hand, some of the more public and instant technologies such as Twitter scream specific orientation because they are a very public display of often personal behavior will little to no mechanisms for regulating admission and participation. Further, tweets, though they might be about all aspects of life (diffuse), they are certainly low on the media richness scale, further connecting these instant public technologies to specific orientation. It is interesting to note that Google Search shows that public technologies are very popular across both specific and diffuse cultures. More research is needed to document how these technologies map on to the specific and diffuse orientations and how these evolving relations perhaps change the very nature of the specific/diffuse value sets.

Ascription-Achievement and Communication Media

This value set assess status—how it is developed and communicated. The two most common approaches are ascription and achievement. Ascriptive-oriented cultures derive status from their social group, race, gender, age, ethnicity, and language. These variables provide the communicator with the power to get things done in complicated social structures. Ascription orientation says: I am great because of my ascribed background; therefore, I can do. In organizational communication, ascription is often operationalized through overt signs of ascribed status, power through people, and importance of context and history to the university. Ascriptive communicators highlight social attributes that enable work to get done through power structures, and they tend to emphasize latent versus observed potential.

In achievement-oriented cultures, it does not matter where you come from, who your family is, your age, language, etc, as long as you can achieve your goals. Achievement orientation says: I have achieved many things; therefore, I am great. In organizational communication, achievement orientation is often operationalized by emphasizing accomplishments such as concrete business goals, number of clients, market share, and CEO honors. Achievement communicators emphasize action, change, statistics, and other observable and verifiable demonstrations of accomplishment.

This value set probably does not correlate as well with the media as the previous three value sets. For example, the personal presence and context of orality probably allows the ascriptive variables to be acknowledged, but these same variables can be communicated through writing. Orality is also a very "active" medium because its performance is live and can be documented. This active orientation correlates with achievement orientation. In addition, many of the achievements that are communicated as data, results, and concrete accomplishments are perhaps best documented in writing.

Email, hypertext, and Web 2.0 also correlate with both ascription and achievement. For example, in my study of Ecuadorians learning email, they learned to quickly use verbal signals of their ascriptive values in their emails such as degrees, family connections, and workplace affiliation. Hypertext is also quite adept at communicating ascriptive values such as graphics of coat of arms and traditional ascriptive icons. Because Web 2.0 has the same rich communicative potential and storage and retrieval abilities of both email and hypertext, it can also easily communicate ascriptive values. However, the interactive elements of Web 2.0, especially among relative strangers, probably encourages an approach that is less focused on ascriptive values of the participants and more on their actual performance or behavior, an achievement orientation.

High and Low Context and Communication Media

The next cultural value is the role of the context in the communicative interaction. Low context means that the meaning of the communication resides primarily in the explicitly coded part of the communication, not in the surrounding context. Thus, there is a focus on information that is specific to individuals at hand, increasing involvement of a few select people. Connor (1996) and Hinds (1987) similarly labels this type of writing as "reader friendly," writing that assumes a reduced reliance on the reader to bring in contextual cues and create transitions to understand the writing. In other words, there is an overt emphasis of organizational and transitional strategies to guide readers through the writing. From this view, good writing is focused on the accuracy and interpretation of the explicitly coded text.

On the other end, high context communication assumes a strong reliance on the contextual and social cues for the meanings of communications. Here, good writing focuses on information that elucidates the influence of the social context on meaning of the communications. Connor (1996) and Hinds (1987) label this type of writing as a "reader-responsible" (Connor 1996, p. 42) or writing in which the reader is expected to fill in the information and create the transitions. In high context communications, there also tends to be more non-verbal, indirect forms of communication and complex overtures and concrete sensory stimuli to evoke the physical, social, and interpersonal contexts that add meaning to the discourse. In addition to the greater reliance on the context, the organization and development of high context communication also varies much more based on prior knowledge of the context. As Hall (1976) explains, when high context communicators understand the context, their communications can be very quick and agile, often needing no more than one word or a glance. However, when the communication context is not understood, high context communicators tend to painstakingly articulate or evoke into the coded text all the fine nuances of the context before communicating the main message.

These two different approaches to the roles of communication and readers encourage different rhetorical patterns in the five communication technologies. High context communication correlates very closely with orality because, as is argued earlier in this Chapter, orality is a much richer medium. On the other hand, low context communication correlates closely with writing (see Victor 1992) because it does not provide the rich contextual details that orality can. Hinds (1987) makes a similar argument about Japanese ESL writers at U.S. universities who bring the higher context and reader-responsible strategies to their English compositions, approaches that directly contradict many traditional approaches to what good writing is in the U.S. U.S. researchers need to understand that the typical reader-friendly, decontextualized U.S. rhetorical approaches are culturally produced and, therefore, not transferable to many other cultural contexts. High context also functions more efficiently when orality is the primary medium regulating the kairos of the communication, that is, starting, pacing, and stopping a communication.

The roles of context for e-mail, hypertext, and Web 2.0 are critical rhetorical inquiries as well. Moran and Hawisher (1998) argue that e-mail is a decontextualized medium, maybe more so than written communications; therefore, many e-mail communicators have developed the use of emoticons, graphically codified symbols to represent emotions and context, a logical approach in a medium that is too decontextual for the communicators' needs. Further, hypertext incorporates audio-visual features such as color, photographs, graphics, voices, and sounds, which perhaps invoke the context better—and in different ways—than writing and orality. The interactions of Web 2.0 technologies are usually very low context as well.

As mentioned earlier, my Ecuadorian students who come from a high-context culture were frustrated mostly with the lack of context in their email and hypertext communications. It was interesting to note that although almost all of these students were from the same culture, and economic, social, and educational status, they all had a very difficult time contextualizing their email and hypertext discourse. Using the exact metaphor that Hall (1976) uses to describe how high-context communicators "context" a very low context medium, students marveled at how their attempts to "structure" their communication had become as fastidious as "the debates in their polemicized National Congress." Some members were offended by long messages, so they wanted to limit the lengths of messages. Others did not like messages about football, racing, and other sports, so they wanted to monitor those. Still others thought that jokes, songs, and recipes were great things to share, but some members wanted these types ruled and monitored. Still others suggested a complex system of subject-line abbreviations, including what city they are talking about, what topic, and how long the message was. In the end, however, they slowly began to feel more comfortable with the lower context medium; and as mentioned, some even began to prefer it.

From another perspective, a Chilean and a Mexican legal scholar argue that e-commerce is difficult in their countries because Chileños and Mexicans like the relational, social solidarity associated with normal commerce ("Symposium"). It could be argued, however, that because of its many communicative features, hypertext and Web 2.0 have has the potential to best represent the complexity of the sociality of Latin American commerce. In other words, the combination of pictures, contexts, sounds, images, graphics and the login interface and corresponding interactive parameters can more capably represent the social complexity of Latin American commercial relationships. Thus, an important question is how is the explosive use of hypertext and Web 2.0 influencing the more low-context communication styles of U.S. writers? Or might hypertext influence intercultural communicators from more collective cultures to maintain a more high-context style?

Power Distance and Communication Media

As explained in Chapter Two, Power Distance measures how inequality is handled in communications. In high power distances cultures, there is unequal, centralized distribution of power, acceptance of authority, high levels of overseeing, and top-down communication styles. High power distance cultures use communications to reinforce and exemplify the hierarchy. Low power distance cultures use communications to downplay inequalities among people. In low power distance cultures, communicators tend to make the communications less formal as a way to ease the feelings of inequality in the communication situation. Low power distance people tend to think that high power distance patterns are abusive, while low power distance patterns are conducive to more harmonious relations. However, high power communicators favor formality and rigid guidelines of high-power communication guidelines, much like the military, in order to establish clear lines of authority and communication so that abuses cannot take place; and it is in ambiguous situations where lines of authority are not clear that are ripe for abuse. Further, low power distance communicators might feel that the relationship is equal based on the low power distance communication patterns, when in fact there is much hierarchy built-in.

One of the traditional characteristics of high power distance communication is orality. Because orality provides the richest social presence and context, it is the best at communicating and maintaining authority. In addition, as I explain elsewhere (Thatcher, 2006), orality also allows those with information to use that information to maintain their power. In this study, Mexican engineers in border manufacturing plants chose not to disseminate instructions and specifications for their manufacturing process because this dissemination would reduce their power at the plant. Writing also obviously occurs in high power distance cultures, but once something has been written down and separated from that author, this is a loss of power, especially if that information is disseminated widely or democratically. As explained earlier, one of the reasons that the United States benefited so much from written constitutions is that the people were willing, to some degree, to share that power, and as a sign, they wrote and disseminated the documents as a democratizing force. Ecuador, despite its 34 constitutions, has not been able to wield much power away from the ruling oligarchy because this group of people has been capable of keeping their power way from the power in the constitution.

As a medium, email correlates rather oddly with power distance. Certainly, high power distance cultures can communicate their power symbols and control their power through email, but email has the dissemination, storage, retrievability, and thus, analyzability of writing, all of which probably encourages a more low power distance approach to communication. In fact, the distance and isolation of most email use means that people can simply ignore the power efforts in both high and low power distance cultures. Current literature on email has documented well how frustrated it is for some authoritarian (high power distance) people to exert their authority through email.

Hypertext has much more social and contextual richness of orality, which probably predisposes it to be a better medium for high power distance. In fact, as shown in Chapter Five, hypertext is great at communicating power symbols such as organizational charts, pictures in powerful places such as official offices, formal icons and symbols, and official decrees. Hypertext, however, has the same dissemination, storage, retrievability, and analyzability of writing, and as such might be a low power distance force, which is precisely the argument of Friedmann *In the World is Flat*. Like hypertext, Web 2.0 probably favors lower power distance especially because the interactions are usually not based on existing power structures in society. However, it is entirely possible for Web 2.0 creators to develop rigid power structures into the interactive interface, thus exemplifying perfectly high power distance relations.

Time and Communication Media

This value set assesses time orientation across cultures. Polychronic or synchronous time frames mean simultaneity, multiple tasks managed at the same time, and apparent disorganization, focusing on the importance of place, and involvement of people rather than adherence to present schedules. On the other hand, monochronic or sequential time frames mean linked linear structures of cause and effect with an organized flow of events (Hall, 1976, 1983). Polychronic time frames enhance the relationships of a variety of people in rich contextual detail. Written discourse in monochronic cultures emphasize linear structures of topics, a direct topic sentence to situate discourse, and given/new discourse structure. On the other hand, polychronic communicators favor the article orchestration of events, people, places, and issues in discourse. Often, writing in polychronic cultures exemplifies complex syntax and paragraph structures, with many narrative structures in polychronic or multiple timeframes.

Time orientation has an obvious correlation to the five communication media. Orality has built in polychronic time, that is, the simultaneity and flux, which is an original argument of scholars documenting the rhetorical effects of orality (see Kaufer and Carley, 1993). Because orality has a much more simultaneity, it can regulate the timing or kairos of the communication much more easily than writing. Writing, on the other hand, has a significant monochronic effect (see Kaufer and Carley, 1993). Obviously, written communications can be polychronic such as in the case of the Latin American genre of magical realism, which displays the multiplicity of times frames and narratives. And orality can be as linear. However, orality fits better polychronicity and writing with monochronicity.

Email has elements of both oral and written rhetoric in its time orientation. It has a strong simultaneity as multiple authors can be discussing the same issue at the same time. However, email also has storage ability of writing, which can encourage a linear analysis of the happenings. In addition, even though a person can email a huge variety of people at the same time, rarely do email users work with more than one email or topic at a time.

Hypertext and Web 2.0 correlate with and can accommodate both monochronic and polychronic time frames. However, these two media also fit very nicely with polychronic time frames. For examples, many websites in polychronic cultures such as South America consistently portray lots of movement and nonlinear displays of verbal, visual, and audio information. Hypertext as a system actually means multiple frames of reference at once, and the web as a metaphor is polychronic. Web 2.0 can also significantly encourage simultaneous interactions, especially with the instant public technologies such as twitter.

Inner and Outer Orientation and Communication Media

This value set assesses the source or origin of virtue, guidance, method of aligning oneself rightly. Inner-directed cultures "conceives of virtue as inside each of us--in our souls, wills, convictions, principles," or believes--in the triumph of conscious purpose. Outer direction conceives of virtue as our site each of us in natural rhythms, in the beauties and powers of nature, in aesthetic environments and relationships" (Hampden-Turner and Trompenaars, 2009, p.234). Hampden-Turner and Trompenaars (2000) connect these differences with common communication approaches and, interestingly, marketing. The inner directed approach is the "hard sell" (p. 263) an adversarial because the inner directed person has to change his or her inner voice to be convinced all on his own of the path communicator is trying to sell.

Another common characteristic of inner directed cultures is that the audience tends be the detached and objective observer who needs to be surveyed or questioned about his or her unique attitudes (Hampden-Turner and Trompenaars, 2000), while the outer directed communicator seeks to harmonize the communications in more of a conversation rather than a survey.

Like many of the other value sets, orality and writing strongly correlate with inner and outer directed. Orality exemplifies an outer orientation because it is highly contextual and focuses on managing the relations in this context. On the other hand, writing strongly correlates with inner directed, so much so, that most inner directed cultures derive from protestant-based countries where the written word (Bible) was the definitive source of direction and that outer forces were to be fought and controlled. Like writing, email probably is more comfortable with inner directed cultures where authors or audience can detach themselves from the communication context and ignore, fight, or accept the outside, contextual forces.

Hypertext and Web 2.0, unlike email, probably fit better outer direction. In fact, the web is a good metaphor for outer direction because its shows how all links and parts are harmonized into one whole. Even though the web is outer directed, much website design, especially in inner directed cultures such as the United States, focuses on the user's ability to create his or her own unique paths or control his path and processes. This is an outer-directed medium being designed for inner-directed users. The interactive features of Web 2.0 probably fit inner directed better than outer directed, unless those features significantly control the interactions, which is an outer-directed mentality.

CHANGING NATURE OF INFORMATION ARCHITECTURE ACROSS CULTURES

Because these communication media map onto the cultural values differently, technical and professional communicators must be able to either re-purpose the technologies to function in contexts the media are not most comfortable with or they must design information in these digital spaces according to the cultural value sets, a sort of intercultural information architecture. As Salvo & Rosinki (2009) explain in the U.S. context, professional communicators must make information findable, navegable, and retrievable; but these concepts as well as information architecture are cultural constructs. This section summarizes Salvo and Rosinki's (2009) eight key components of information architecture but connects these components to cross-cultural design.

The first of the eight components is *Granularity,* which refers to the size or level of information, starting from large websites, to documents, and to bits of information. The second is *Homogeneity and Heterogeneity*, which refers to levels of distinction given to information. Both of these components will vary significantly across the eight value sets or common human thresholds. Perhaps the most important is the specific-diffuse value set, which assesses how holistically or partially a culture prefers its communication patterns. In a specific culture, information is broken down analytically and concretely according to sphere of activity. For example, in university websites, specific cultures often design sections of websites according to students, faculty, alumni, visitors, staff, and other stakeholders (Thatcher, 2009). Diffuse university websites are broken down more holistically into content areas such as different colleges/schools, library, labs, etc. Thus, specific cultures are much more prone to concrete and more isolated information.

The third component is ***Mapping***, which means the visual design of the digital space such as sitemaps. And the fourth is ***Signposting***, which refers to helping users understand where they are in the context of the entire digital space. These two components vary according to the eight value sets. For example, as shown in Chapter Five, in low context and monochronic cultures, websites are designed in a very linear, box-like fashion, with many drop-down menus using verbal information and signposting. In high context and polychronic cultures, narratives and visual images are used much more. For example, in some high context cultures, instead of linear, drop-down menus as the predominant page design, pictures are used as visual analogies of the website design, with links coded into different parts of the picture. In addition, Mapping and Signposting will vary significantly in particular versus universal cultures. Universal cultures strongly correlate to templating, parallelism, overt signposting, and uniformity across the web page design, as an aid to users. On the other hand, particular cultures strongly focus on change, uniqueness, and novelty as motivation for reading webpages.

The fifth element is ***Metadata/Taxonomy***, which refers to the need to label information, that is, information about information. This includes routing and location information as well as file types. Sixth is ***Pattern language***, which refers to the use of official language structures, policies, and codes for hypertext and Web 2.0 technologies. These two components vary significantly across the value sets. For example, universal-low context and particular-high context cultures will vary in how much they design words or labels to categorize information. Universal and low-context cultures have a strong tendency to categorize and label information verbally and uniformly across websites (Thatcher, 2009). This is often due to the "dumbing down" of websites for the universal reader. Particular and high-context cultures are much more sensitive to the levels of audience knowledge and will categorize or label information only when necessary and will often use non-verbal or visual labels instead. Universal cultures also strongly emphasize the development and dissemination of official language structures, policies, and codes for hypertext and Web 2.0 technologies, while particular and high-context cultures assume this development and dissemination is part of the power structure and is not developed nor disseminated openly.

The seventh component is ***Ambience***, which refers to how the design of the communication technology allows the human agent to interact with it. This component is strongly influenced by the value sets, most particularly inner-outer and power distance. Inner and outer assesses the relation of the human agent to outside forces. Inner cultures assume human agency derives from the inner will, and thus, is in constant battle with outside forces to impose that will on them. Outer cultures assume human agency needs to be reconciled and harmonized with outside forces. Thus, websites in inner-directed cultures strongly emphasize designs that allow the user to impose an infinite variety of paths, while outer-directed cultures make that path more rigid, forcing users to follow much more rigid structures (Thatcher, 2009). The inner and outer orientation also strongly correlates to Power distance. In low power distance cultures, websites are like consultative peers, there to help in a more egalitarian manner, while in high power distance cultures, websites have a strong authority, often mandating use of the webpage.

The eighth component is ***Findability and Future***, which is an after effect of information design, that is, this term focuses on how the digital creation can be found and retrieved with search tools such as Google and Yahoo. Currently, little research has addressed the information logic of search engines such as Google and Yahoo. It can be easily supposed, however, that because they were conceived in individualistic, universal, specific, inner-directed, low context, and monochronic cultures, that the search logic correlates strongly with the logic of these cultural values. Much more research needs to address this connection between search logic and cultural patterns.

CONCLUSION OF FIT AND RECIPROCITY OF VALUE SETS AND COMMUNICATION MEDIA ACROSS CULTURES

What is clear from this chapter is that the newer media have a mixed fit for all the cultural values, while the old media (writing and orality) easily fit almost all the variables. This difference in correlation signifies a profound inquiry: if the older media strongly constitute—and are constituted by—the most common or default approaches to these five thresholds of human interaction, what are the newer media doing to the default approaches to these human thresholds? How, if at all, are the newer media re-articulating the I/Other relations, the development and applications of rules, degree of involvement, status, and power distance?

REFERENCES

Ball, C., & Kalmbach, J. (2010). (Eds.) *Reading and writing new media*. Creskill, NJ: Hampton

Bolter, J., & Grusin, R. (1999). *Remediation: Understanding new media*. Cambridge, MA: MIT Press.

Carliner, S. (2009). Computers and technical communication in the 21st century. In Spilka, R. (Ed.), *Digital literacy for technical communication: 21st Century theory and practice* (pp. 21–50). London, UK: Routledge.

Carlson, J. R., & Zmud, R. W. (1999). Channel expansion theory and the experimental nature of media richness perceptions. *Academy of Management Journal*, *42*, 153–170. doi:10.2307/257090

Clark, D. (2009). Shaped and shaping tools: The rhetorical nature of technical communication technologies. In Spilka, R. (Ed.), *Digital literacy for technical communication: 21st Century theory and practice* (pp. 85–102). London, UK: Routledge.

Connor, U. (1996). *Contrastive rhetoric: Cross-cultural aspects of second-language writing*. Cambridge, MA: Cambridge U Press.

Daft, R. L., & Lengel, R. H. (1986). Organizational information requirements, media richness, and structural determinants. *Management Science*, *32*, 554–571. doi:10.1287/mnsc.32.5.554

Durso, S. C. (2009). The past, present, and future of human communication and technology research: An introduction. *Journal of Computer-Mediated Communication*, *14*(3), 708–713. doi:10.1111/j.1083-6101.2009.01459.x

Friedman, T. (2005). *The world is flat*. New York, NY: Farrar, Straus and Giroux.

Ghemawat, P. (2007). Why the world isn't flat. *Foreign Policy.* Retrieved from www.Foreign-policy.com.

Hall, E. T. (1976). *Beyond culture*. New York, NY: Doubleday.

Hall, E. T. (1981). *The silent language*. New York, NY: Doubleday.

Hall, E. T. (1983). *The dance of life*. New York, NY: Doubleday.

Hawisher, G., & Selfe, C. (2000). *Global literacies and the World-Wide Web*. London, UK: Routledge.

Hinds, J. (1987). Reader versus writer responsibility: A new typology. In (eds.) U. Connor & R. Kaplan, *Writing across languages: Analysis of L2 text* (pp. 141-152). Reading, MA: Addison-Wesley.

Hofstede, G. (2010). *Cultures and organizations, software of the mind* (3rd ed.). New York, NY: McGraw Hill.

House, R. J., Hanges, P. J., Javidan, M., Dorfman, P. R., & Gupta, V. (Eds.). (2005). *Culture, leadership, and organizations: The GLOBE study of 62 societies*. New York, NY: Sage Publications.

Kaplan, R. (1996). Cultural thought patterns in intercultural education. *Language Learning, 16*(1-2), 1–20. doi:10.1111/j.1467-1770.1966.tb00804.x

Kaufer, D. S., & Carley, K. M. (1993). *Communication at a distance: The influence of print on sociocultural organization and change*. Hillsdale, NJ: Lawrence Erlbaum.

Kock, N. (2005). Media richness or media naturalness? The evolution of our biological communication apparatus and its influence on our behavior toward E-communication tools. *IEEE Transactions on Professional Communication, 48*(2), 117–130. doi:10.1109/TPC.2005.849649

Kress, G. (1998). Visual and verbal modes of representation in electronically mediated communication: The potentials of new forms of text. In Snyder, I. (Ed.), *Page to screen: Taking literacy into the electronic era* (pp. 53–79). New York, NY: Routledge. doi:10.4324/9780203201220_chapter_3

Langer, E. (1997). *The power of mindful learning*. Reading, MA: Addison Wesley Publishing Company, Inc.

Martín Barbero, J. (1988). Communication from culture: The crisis of the national and the emergence of the popular. (P. Schlesinger, Trans.). *Media Culture & Society, 10*, 447–465. doi:10.1177/016344388010004004

McLuhan, M. (1967). *The medium is the message*. New York, NY: Bantam Books.

Moran, C., & Hawisher, G. (1998). The rhetorics and languages of electronic mail. In Snyder, I. (Ed.), *Page to screen: Taking literacy into the electronic era* (pp. 80–101). New York, NY: Routledge. doi:10.4324/9780203201220_chapter_4

Olaniran, B. (2007). Culture and communication challenges in virtual workspaces. In St.Amant, K. (Ed.), *Linguistic and cultural online communication issues in the global age* (pp. 75–91). Hershey, PA: Idea Group. doi:10.4018/978-1-59904-213-8.ch006

Osland, J. S., De Franco, S., & Osland, A. (1999). Organizational implications of Latin American culture. *Journal of Management Inquiry, 8*(2), 219–234. doi:10.1177/105649269982018

Plato,. (1956). *Phaedrus*. New York, NY: Macmillan Publishing.

Press Series, New Dimensions in Computers and Composition.

Reicher, S. D., Spears, R., & Postmes, T. T. (1995). A social identity model of deindividuation phenomena. *European Review of Social Psychology, 6*(1), 161–198. doi:10.1080/14792779443000049

Salvo, M., & Rosinki, P. (2009). Information design: From authoring text to architecting virtual space. In Spilka, R. (Ed.), *Digital literacy for technical communication: 21st Century theory and practice* (pp. 103–127). London, UK: Routledge.

Short, J., Williams, E., & Christie, B. (1976). *The social psychology of telecommunication*. London, UK: John Wiley.

Spears, R., & Lea, M. (1992). Social influence and the influence of the "social" in computer-mediated communication. In Lea, M. (Ed.), *Contexts of computer-mediated communication* (pp. 30–65). London, UK: Harvester-Wheatsheaf.

Spilka, R. (Ed.). (2009). *Digital literacy for technical communication: 21st Century theory and practice*. London, UK: Routledge Press.

Stewart, E., & Bennett, M. (1991). *American cultural patterns: A cross-cultural perspective* (Rev. ed). Yarmouth, ME: Intercultural Press, Inc.

Swaak, M., de Jong, M., & de Vries, P. (2009). Effects of information usefulness, visual attractiveness, and usability on web visitors' trust and behavioral intentions. *IEEE International Professional Communication Conference*, (pp. 1-5).

Thatcher, B., Barrantes, E., Dalzell, A., Dong, Q., Ford, C., & Klein, S. … Ramirez, L. (2007). Website analysis across cultures. In K. St. Amant (Ed.), *Linguistic and cultural online communication issues in the global age* (pp.124-142). Hershey, PA: Idea Group.

Thatcher, B. L. (2006). Intercultural rhetoric, technology, and writing in Mexican maquilas. *Special Technology Transfer Edition of Technical Communication Quarterly*, *15*(3), 383–405.

Thatcher, B. L. (2009). Understanding digital literacy across cultures. In Spilka, R. (Ed.), *Digital literacy for technical communication: 21st Century theory and practice* (pp. 169–198). Routledge.

Thatcher, B. L. (2010). Reading and writing new media across cultures: Issues of fit, reciprocity, and cultural change. In Kalmbach, J., & Ball, C. (Eds.), *Reading and writing new media*. Hampton Press Series New Dimensions in Computers and Composition.

Timmerman, C. E. (2002). The moderating effect of mindlessness/mindfulness upon media richness and social influence explanations of organizational media use. *Communication Monographs*, *69*, 111–131. doi:10.1080/714041708

Verhulsdonck, G. (2010). *Virtual Chironomia: A multimodal study of verbal and non-verbal communications in a virtual world.* Unpublished dissertation, New Mexico State University.

Victor, D. (1992). *International business communication*. New York, NY: HarperCollins Publishers.

Walther, J. B. (1992). Interpersonal effects in computer-mediated interaction: A relational perspective. *Communication Research*, *19*, 52–90. doi:10.1177/009365092019001003

Walther, J. B. (1996). Computer-mediated communication: Impersonal, interpersonal, and hyperpersonal interaction. *Communication Research*, *23*, 3–43. doi:10.1177/009365096023001001

ENDNOTES

1 Ong later acknowledges the problems of this position in response to strong critiques of writing supplanting orality. See Kaufer and Carley (1993) for a detailed description of Ong's changing approaches and the ongoing debate of orality and writing.

2 Writer-friendly patterns, according to Hinds, means writing that reflects the complexity of the author's thoughts with little effort to revise the writing to accommodate different levels of audience knowledge and attitudes.

Chapter 5
Website Designs as an Indicator of Globalization

ABSTRACT

As the first application chapter, this chapter compares the cultural and rhetorical elements of websites around the world, showing strong correlation between website designs and the larger cultural values of the host culture. In this application, the chapter defines and operationalizes the units of analysis for website design, connecting websites to the common human thresholds of interaction.

INTRODUCTION: WEBSITE DESIGNS ACROSS CULTURES

For the last eleven years, I have had the privilege of living on the U.S.-Mexico border, witnessing, among many things, the blending, flux, and dynamics of two nations interacting. I also routinely return to Ecuador to visit friends and carry out research. But the border is a more interesting experience. I live only 45 minutes from three Mexican Universities and over 500 outsourced manufacturing plants or maquilas. Thus, I can be teaching or researching in Mexico in the morning and return to Las Cruces, New Mexico in the afternoon and do the same thing, but in a different language, culture, and educational, economic, social, and legal context. As explained in Chapter Two, the U.S.-Mexico border is a fantastic analogy and site of intercultural research, but the border area is much more complex than simply the merging of U.S. and Mexican culture. The border is significant and mediates complexly these two nations. Thus, the U.S. Mexico border is a great way to ground theories of globalization.

Globalization has many definitions (Grewel, 2008), but for me, the best is a growing interdependence among groups of people caused by a larger variety of factors, including international trade and manufacturing; global issues such as energy, environment health, and immigration; politics; education; information and communication technologies such as the internet; and a greater facility for world travel. Thus, it seems apparent that countries and cultures are becoming much more inter-dependent, due in large measure to these globalization forces. Not surprisingly, many current theories would have us believe that globalization means a significant amount of cultural

DOI: 10.4018/978-1-61350-450-5.ch005

blending, hybrization, glocalization, and cross-border flow of rhetorical and cultural patterns with geopolitical borders relatively meaningless, and as such, an out-dated mode of inquiry. However, as I explain in Chapter Two, these theories may be off. As mentioned, in 2010, El Paso, Texas was the safest city in the United States (for cities over 500,000 inhabitants) with a murder rate of three or four a year. Right across the border, Ciudad Juárez, Chihuahua, Mexico (1.5 million) was the most dangerous city in the world, with an average of 12 murders a day. This large difference calls into questions many simplistic theories of globalization. Ghemawat similarly argues that "more than 90 percent of all phone calls, Web traffic, and investment is local. What's more, even this small level of globalization could still slip away" (2007). In Chapter Two, I call for a more complex view of globalization, arguing that perhaps some cultural values (such as entertainment) might cross border rather easily, but others may not.

Consequently, the theories of globalization and communications technologies might be well served in light of culture and communication research, which maintains that enculturation and cultural change due to communication technologies are never straightforward (Grossberg, 1992). In other words, just because there is cross-cultural contact does not mean that the cultures in contact are simply blending or assimilating the influences. As Stuart Hall (1997) and Lawrence Grossberg (1992) have been arguing for decades, cultures adopt, resist, appropriate, refract, and reconstitute cultural and rhetorical patterns for a variety of social, economic, political, personal, and aesthetic reasons. Further, local cultures often not only reject assimilation, but re-trench themselves in their local values against cross-cultural influences (Adler, 2008).

As Chapter Four lays out, however, the new communication technologies might be encouraging cultural change because of their explicit global reach, perhaps both at the local and global level. It also seems obvious that the Worldwide Web has dramatically increased cross-cultural contact. This increase must be influencing the rhetorical and cultural patterns at the local, national, and international level, but researchers simply do not know how and what is happening. Consequently, this Chapter asks some simple but important questions: how much do website designs reflect local culture, or does there seem to be a more global approach to websites? Further, how is the web changing the rules of this intercultural dynamic of culture and communication technology? And if the web is influencing cultural change, what kinds of changes are occurring and why?

As explained in Chapter Four, website designs are a very rich medium, allowing for almost every kind of communication, including graphics, pictures, sound, movement, verbal, page layout, overarching web architecture, search features, input capacity, and so on. Thus, this richness seems well adapted to almost all of the cultural values. Further, websites are usually developed locally by the sponsoring organization but are available live around the world, so the website are a wonderful source of information about intercultural rhetorical and cultural values, and the results of intercultural web inquiry could point to some interesting qualifications of globalization.

To carry out this inquiry, this Chapter compares the website design and features around the world using three methods. First, I ground the connection between website design and cultural rhetorically analyzing the features of four public university websites, two on the U.S.-Mexico border and two outside border areas. After explaining the intercultural content of these four websites, I discuss a simple website analysis of eBay ads in five countries. I then integrate these two studies with research I previously carried out (Thatcher, 2010; Thatcher, et, al, 2007) that compares 27 public university websites around the world. With the results, I hypothesize not only about the connections between website designs and intercultural values, but also about globalization.

RESEARCH METHODS

The research methods for this analysis can best be described as a rhetorical analysis of websites using qualitative sampling (see Flicke, 2002) and intercultural empirical methods (Thatcher, 2000). For the first group of universities, I chose to analyze New Mexico State University (NMSU), which is located in New Mexico about 40 miles from Mexico. On the Mexican side, I chose the Autonomous University of Ciudad Juárez (UACJ), which is located right next to the U.S.-Mexico border (and 40 miles from NMSU). Both are public universities of about the same size, student population, and course offerings. The other university websites are Visvra-Bharati, a public regional university from India and the Autonomous Benito Juárez University of Oaxaca, which is a public regional university located in the southern part of Mexico. I chose the two border universities to explore issues of globalization and the other two for simple comparison.

For the international university website design across cultures, the researchers were nine graduate students in a graduate course in intercultural rhetoric that I taught at New Mexico State University, and as a group, we reported on this research elsewhere (see Thatcher, et al, 2007). These students first selected a target culture or country for their analysis, and each researcher needed to be either a native of that target culture or possess significant knowledge of its culture and language. Then the researchers selected public university websites from that culture, using New Mexico State University as a benchmark including university site, public, land-grant orientation, basic academic offerings, and website development. For the universities in China, South America, the United States, Canada, and Mexico, the researchers developed a list of public universities following these criteria, and then they randomly selected three universities for analysis. For Israel, Nepal, and Ireland, there were not sufficient universities to randomize effectively, so the researchers selected the universities that most closely followed these criteria. Table 1 displays the researchers and websites.

For the eBay advertisement research, I wanted to have a similar etic framework to ensure that what I was assessing was culture, not a product or venue. Thus, I selected the worldwide version of EBay as the venue, and I decided to analyze the same ads: computer memory (RAM or random access memory). For this approach, I simply selected the category of *Memory* under the major category of *Computers and Networking* and subcategory of *Computer Components*. Next, I searched the country of origin, using eBay's Advanced Search Function. I found all of the advertisements for computer memory and/or flash drivers from vendors from five countries: Germany, India, China, the United States, and Spain. Germany did not have a sufficient number for the memory category, so I added "flash drive" to obtain more than 30 ads. These five countries had a sufficient number of ads and sellers to ensure a nice, random selection of 30 ads for each country. As explained in Chapters One and Two, using eBay as a common context and the RAM memory as a common topic, I was able to examine the rhetorical characteristics of the ads and connect these characteristics to the intercultural values sets. All of these advertisements were sold from the individual country but marketed to the world, not just to the local context. Obviously, I did not have access to the sellers, nor could I decide how much they changed their rhetorical presentation for the world market. I simply analyzed what they presented according to the intercultural values sets. Table 2 summarizes the data from the EBay ads.

As outlined in Chapters One and Two, in order to be valid, intercultural empirical research needs to establish a comparative and etic approach to both data analysis and data collection and then ground the analysis to the common human thresholds. This is precisely the reason for the use of public universities and EBay.

Table 1. Researchers and Websites

Researcher and Country of Origin	Target Culture/ Nation	Websites Selected for Analysis
Edgar Barrantes-Costa Rica	Central and South America	· Universidad de Costa Rica (www.ucr.ac.cr) · Universidad Nacional de Colombia (www.unal.edu.co) · Universidad de Chile (www.uchile.cl)
Amy Dalzell-USA	Canada	· University of Calgary (www.ucalgary.ca) · University of Ottawa (www.uottawa.ca) · Concordia University (www.concordia.ca)
Qiumin Dong-China	China	· Hebei University (www.hbu.edu.cn) · Zhengzhou University (www.zzu.edu.cn) · Hunan University (www.hnu.cn)
Christopher Ford-USA-Ireland	Ireland	· University College Dublin (www.ucd.ie) · National University of Ireland Galway (www.ucg.ie) · National University of Ireland Cork (www.nui.ie)
Sipai Klein-Israel	Israel	· Hebrew University of Jerusalem (www.huji.ac.il) · Tel-Aviv University (www.tau.ac.il) · Ben Gurion University-Negev (www.bgu.ac.il)
Rachel Gallagher-USA	USA	· New Mexico State University (www.nmsu.edu) · Texas Tech University (www.ttu.edu) · Washington State University (www.wsu.edu)
Marohang Limbu-Nepal	Nepal	· Kathmandu University (www.ku.edu.np) · Tribhuvan University (www.tribhuvan-university.edu.np) · Mahendra Sanskrit University (www.msu.edu.np)
Lisa Ramirez-Belize	Mexico	· Benemérita Universidad de Puebla (www.buap.mx) · Universidad Autónoma de Campeche (www.uacam.mx) · Universidad Autónoma de San Luis Potosí (www.uaslp.mx)
Natalia Urbina-USA	Argentina	· Universidad Nacional del Cuyo (www.uncu.edu.ar) · Universidad Nacional de la Plata (www.unlp.edu.ar) · Universidad Nacional del Litoral (www.unl.edu.ar)

Next, for the international university website study, the research team decided that five intercultural variables or common human thresholds provided the comparative analysis and the criteria provided the universal framework for data collection. For the EBay study and my border university website comparison, I used all eight intercultural value sets or etic borders as described in Chapter Two. For all three studies, the units of analysis of the websites that were compared to the communication characteristics included: organization of text, screen layout, links, language style, graphics,

Table 2. Data on EBay RAM ads

Country	Number of Ads	How Ads Were Selected	Number and type of Sellers
Germany	30	Total number	12
India	30+	Random selection	30; half were dedicated RAM sellers; half were misc. sellers.
China	30+	Random selection	30; half were dedicated RAM sellers; half were misc. sellers.
United States	30+	Random Selection	30 different sellers; half were dedicated RAM sellers; half were misc. sellers.
Spain	30+	Selected by sellers	30. All were misc sellers; no companies.

artwork, use of flash and audio components, color, photographs, maps, icons, other html components. Table3 outlines the analytical connections between website features and the eight etic borders.

In distinction to the other tables, I present the data to be analyzed in the first column and coordinate the actual units of analysis for each of the major datasets and value sets.

To develop the results, the university website research team and I moved back and forth between inductive (open) coding to deductive (theoretical) coding (Flick, 2002, pp. 176-195). Moving back

Table 3. Units of analysis for web comparison

Units of Analysis for Comparing Cultural/Communication Patterns in Websites								
	Individual Collective	Universal Particular	Specific Diffuse	Achieve Ascribe	Inner Outer	Low - High Con-text	Poly & Mono-chronic	Power Distance
Photos of People	Alone vs groups	Equality of spacing, power symbols	▪ Smiles? ▪Categor-ized or holistic people?	Action vs. emphasis of traits.	Alignment with inner self or outer surround-dings	Person vs context ratio	Linear or simultan-eous flow	Inequal-ity empha-sized or hidden?
Photos-Build-ings and Nature	Tradition vs innovation	Roles in rule making and enforcement	In or out of context?	Performed actions or stability over time	Harmonize with nature or inner truth finding	Building vs context ratio	Linear or simultan-eous flow	Align with or downplay inequality
Menu Bars	Individual impatience vs group solidarity	Dumb vs specialized browsers	Categorized or holistic people?	Action vs. emphasis of traits.	Reader or organization driven?	Presence of context	Linear or simultan-eous flow	hierarchy or indepen-dence?
Graphics	Tradition vs innovation	Dumb vs specialized	Categorized or holistic?	Action vs. emphasis of traits.	Harmony with inner self or outer.	Presence of context	Linear or simultan-eous flow	Align or downplay inequality
Layout	▪ Individual impatience vs group solidarity ▪ User inter-activity	▪ Dumb vs specialized browsers ▪ Templates or uniqueness ▪ Parallel?	Amount of mixing of categories	Action vs. emphasis of traits.	Modeled after outer or inner patterns	Use of con-text models for layout	Linear or polychronic	Access to authority.
Links	Individual or group con-nection	Fairly linked?	Connections to greater good of community	Action vs. emphasis of traits.	Sources of information	Relevance of Context	Linear or polychronic	Name dropping/ power leverage
Words	We vs I	▪ Rules from words or relation-ships? ▪ General or concrete?	Alone or holis-tic words.	Action vs. emphasis of traits.	▪ Source of words? ▪ Clichés versus inner voice	General or contextual	Linear or polychronic	Authority or equality markers
Sentence syntax	▪ We vs I ▪ In- versus out-group	Parallelism vs uniqueness	Categorized or holistic?	Action vs. emphasis of traits.	Syntax of outer world or self-made harmony	Relevance of Context	Parallel or polychronic	Authority or equality markers
Paragraph organi-zation	Group relations or individual purpose.	Precedence vs uniqueness	Directness or Circum-locution	Action vs. emphasis of traits.	Syntax of outer world or self-made harmony	Relevance of Context	Narrative or abstract organi-zation	Authority or equality markers
Colors	Tradition versus in-novation	Parallelism vs uniqueness	Blending ver-sus distinctness	Active versus tradition	Natural or man-made colors	Relevance of Context	???	Tradition versus in-novation

and forth between open and theoretical coding ensures validity in the data analysis and construction of results. It is important to note that for a variety of reasons, we were not able to assess the influence of the individual web authors; rather the university website researchers and I simply assumed that the websites or eBay ads were duly reviewed and authorized by each university or seller and thus, reflected the values of each organization. Likewise, it was impossible to assess the influence of the web authoring tools on the website design, though this inquiry fascinated the research team and should be researched at a future time.

RESEARCH RESULTS OF WEBSITE DESIGNS ACROSS CULTURES

Generally, the university websites and eBay ads closely corresponded to the cultural and communication patterns connected to their countries by a great variety of researchers, and as discussed in Chapter Two. To begin this discussion of research results, I present screen captures of the four university homepages (See Figure 1, Figure 2, Figure 3, and Figure 4) used to demonstrate the intercultural differences in website design, starting with NMSU.

Individual-Collective Values across Websites

As explained in Chapter Four, the individual-collective values easily map onto website technologies. For example, the NMSU website shows strong individual tendencies. First, almost all of the photographs are of one person, or if a group were involved, most of the photographs highlight one person with the rest of the people faded into the background. The photograph on NMSU's homepage, exemplifies the individual value set because it shows the lone person highlighted with large space between herself and others. In addition to the pictures, the navigation of the web pages focuses on the individual. The homepage of NMSU is designed around the ease in which one person, whether that person is a student, faculty, or staff, can access quickly and easily information pertinent to that one person. For example, the design of the webpage (Figure 5) *Resources and Services for Current Students* (http://currentstu-

Figure 1. Homepage of New Mexico State University

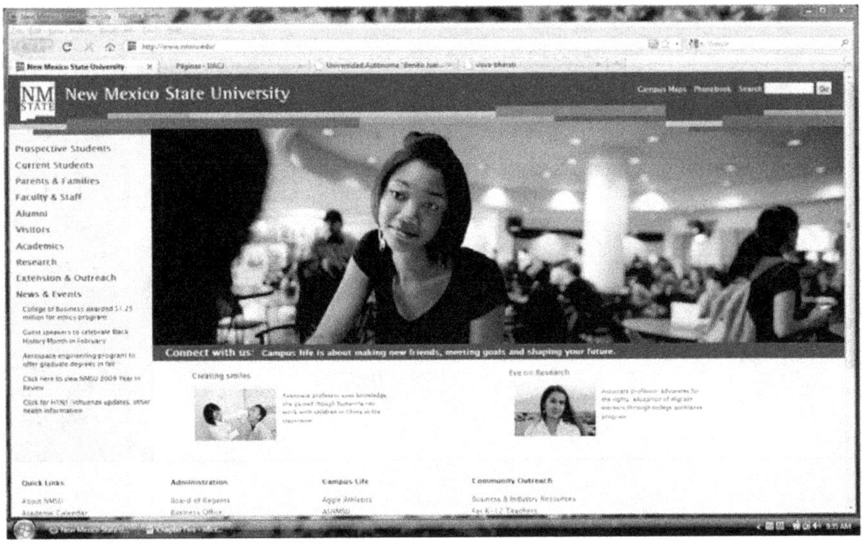

Figure 2. Homepage of Visvra-Bharati University

dents.nmsu.edu/) is based on the individual needs of the students, highlighting the choices that he student has in his or her education.

Like the pictures and the overall design, the language of the site is almost exclusively individual. Most sentences discuss a singular "you" or "I" and emphasize what individuals, rather than groups of people, have or can accomplish at NMSU.

The Visvra-Bharati has some elements of individualism, but its collectivism dominates in the visuals, overall design, and language. First, the only passage through the homepage to the other page is through the picture of the Founder, Tagore or through the University's icon or swastika, further reinforcing a common—not individual—path for all. In addition, Visvra-Bharati has very few photographs, compared to the other sites. And

Figure 3. Homepage of the Autonomous University of Ciudad Juárez

Figure 4. Homepage of the Autonomous Benito Juárez University of Oaxaca

when there are photographs of people, only the leaders and buildings are photographed. The small photographs on the home page show one person alone in a lab and two people in a classroom, but all the other photographs are people meaningfully grouped, meaning, that the purpose and hierarchy of the group are notable. Figure 6 captures exemplifies this collective orientation.

In addition to the group photograph, the language shows a strong collective and group orientation that is constantly reconciled with the rich context of joint celebration.

Figure 5. NMSU Resources & Services for Current Students

Figure 6. Way of life at Visvra-Bharati

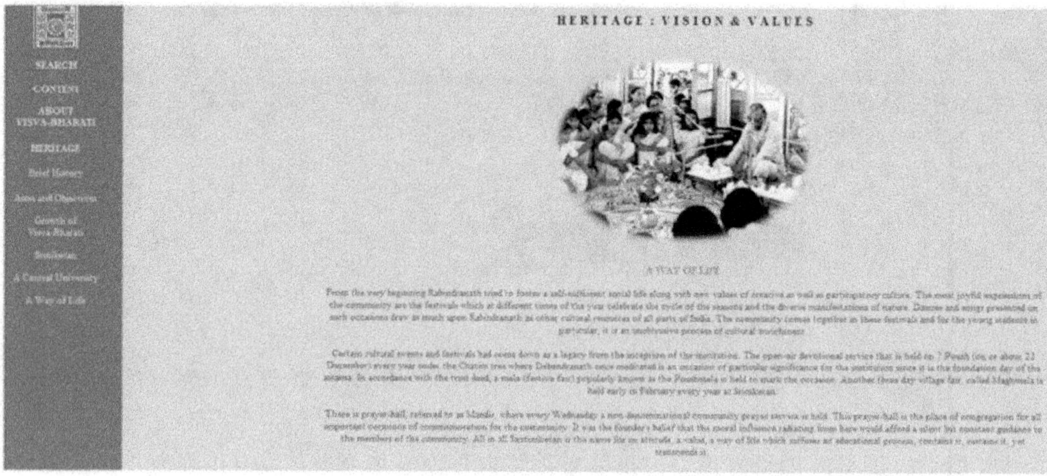

The two Mexican university websites show important intracultural differences in Mexico, concerning the collective-individual value set. The UACJ website rarely shows pictures of individuals, but most of the photographs are of small groups such as the masthead; in addition, most of its language has an individualistic approach, emphasizing what the individual student can accomplish there. For example, Figure 7 is the homepage from the Institute of Architecture, Design, and Art. It focuses on the excellence of the university as a key component of each individual's growth.

The first sentence in this page reads "Your admission to the Autonomous University of Ciudad Juárez is, by itself, a great achievement that was earned by each one of you due to your knowledge and abilities demonstrated during the entrance exam, for which, in the name of executives and professors, we extend to you congratulations

Figure 7. Homepage from UACJ's Institute of Architecture, Design, and Art

and recognition by forming part of the Institute of Architecture, Design and Art." This sentence shows almost equal values of individual and collective; it's individual because of the focus of the person gaining admission; it's collective because that person forms part of the great group.

In distinction to the UACJ, which is situated on the U.S.-Mexico Border, the UABJO from southern Mexico is strongly collective, much like Visvra-Bharati. The homepage only shows pictures of groups of people, and it also includes very traditional images of the founder, university coat of arms, and important dates. These differences in the Mexican websites simply demonstrate the intracultural differences in Mexico. Ciudad Juárez is so close to the United States that it's not surprising that it's more of a mixture of collective and individual.

From the worldwide research, the 27 websites generally followed the individual-collective values attributed to them by the intercultural scholars. Almost every picture in the U.S. and Canadian websites showed many more individualistic shots than group shots, and even the fewer group shots displayed large personal space, equal space distribution, and little evidence of social hierarchy. Further, the language in all U.S. and Canadian websites also emphasized the personal "you" and the "I" showing what each individual is capable of doing. For example, Figure 8 from Texas Tech shows a typical individualistic approach. It is full of individual "you" language and individual possibilities, aspirations, and journeys.

In addition, all six U.S. and Canadian websites were very reader-friendly, designed specifically for individual browsing according to individual needs. These characteristics set the individual, as opposed to the group, as the default user, emphasizing self-reliance and self-interest.

In distinction to the U.S. and Canadian sites, the universities in Mexico, Costa Rica, Colombia, Chile, Nepal, and China have a strong orientation towards collectivism. In these websites, the pictures generally portrayed students in tight-knit groups, working together to accomplish projects. For example, the Mexican websites rarely depict students in an individual setting, except on few occasions where students are involved in learning new technology or using lab equipment. But even in some of these settings, they are seen working in groups, with close personal space, and clear evidence of social hierarchy. Thus, although in

Figure 8. Homepage from Texas Tech University

the U.S. websites, the instructor and students often appeared in pictures together, the spacing of individuals and clothing made it difficult to distinguish instructors from students. But in these more collective websites, the group shots easily demarcated the social hierarchy with the instructor usually above or in front of the group, the students carefully paying attention to the instructor, and the instructor usually wore more formal clothing to distinguish him or her from the students. The language in the collective websites rarely focused on one individual and his or her needs; rather, the most common terminology was either the "we" or group names and affiliations. Further, even though many of the more collective websites were designed for individual users such as students, faculty, alumni seeking specific information, this content design was usually framed in terms of the group, rather than individual; that is, the "you" or "I" was used much less than the "you as students" or "you as faculty," terms that emphasized the connections to the groups.

In addition, these Mexican, Chinese, Nepalese, and Latin American universities are all seen as an integral part of the community in which they reside, emphasizing the total development of the student depends greatly on his or her ability to successfully cooperate in community projects. This evidence was clear with many links and pages devoted to the roles of the university in the local, regional, and national community. This approach is similar to the land grant approach of New Mexico State and Texas Tech, which were founded as community resources, but these U.S. universities emphasized the larger role of the university in the community such as research and development, while most of the websites in China, Nepal, and Latin America emphasized concrete examples of students involvement in the larger communities. From another angle, these more collective websites provide homepage links to national and even international news stories.

Figure 9, from the Nepalese Tribhuvan University shows the very clear collective orientation in the language of we.

In addition to the university websites, the individualism from the United States was clearly demonstrated in the assumed independence of the buyers in the EBay ads. Most of the 30 EBay ads from the United States assumed that the buyer was installing the memory him or herself and did not have available extra help, and thus, great pains were used to describe very clearly the compatibility of the memory and frequently, to help with

Figure 9. Page from Nepalese website

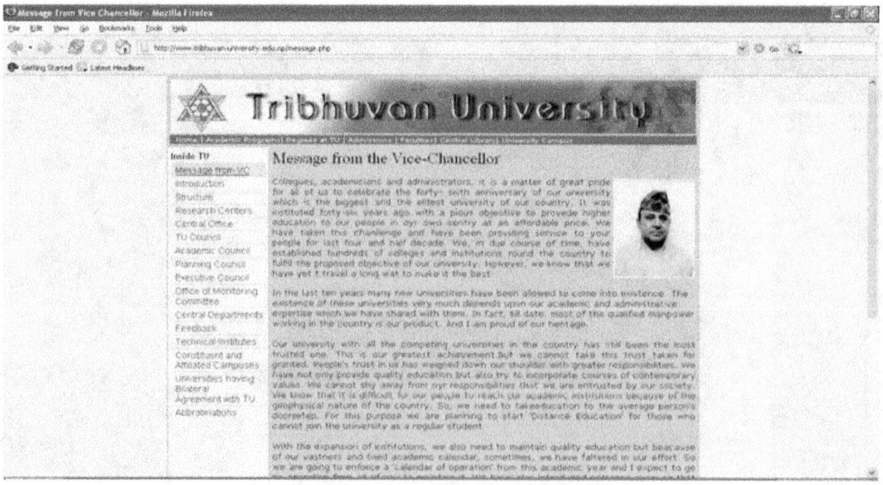

this installation, a feature common in U.S. instructions that I explore in Chapter Ten. Figure 10 exemplifies a typical U.S. EBay ad.

This EBay ad assumes that the U.S. buyer makes all the decisions him or herself such as explaining how not to be deceived; and it carefully explains compatibility with the drop down menu.

This independence and extra help with compatibility and assurance stands in stark contrast to the EBay ads from both China and India, which rarely explained compatibility or assumed a need for extra help. Ads from both these countries generally gave just the basic specifications of the memory, expecting the buyer to either know or find out from someone else the compatibility and installation, closely following the same patterns in Japanese auto repair manuals, which I discuss in Chapter Ten. Figure 11 is a typical EBay ad from India.

This ad shows a simple picture of the product in the standard EBay picture location and just these specifications. This kind of ad was typical not only for individual sellers, but also dedicated stores. They simply did not offer the compatibility assurance of U.S. ads.

Universal-Particular

The NMSU and Visvra-Bharat websites demonstrate clear differences in universal-particular orientation. First, in the NMSU site, almost all pictures of groups of people showed a variety of age, ethnicity, size, and gender, demonstrating the level playing field for all. In addition, NMSU explicitly states in their non-discrimination policies that all students, faculty, and staff can succeed regardless of age, religion, sex, etc. One of the strongest universal characteristics, however, is the use of templating or universalizing the web look regardless of the pages and including many linear lists so as to emphasize uniformity. New Mexico State's desire for this templating was so strong that at the time of the research, the approved template was found on the homepage itself and was presented as the authorized template for all webpages. Figure 12 is taken from NMSU's template page.

As a result, all pages on NMSU's website have a very similar feel; there is little uniqueness. In addition to the templating and non-discrimination, the NMSU website was designed for a universal audience: low reading level and little assumed

Figure 10. Typical U.S. EBay ad

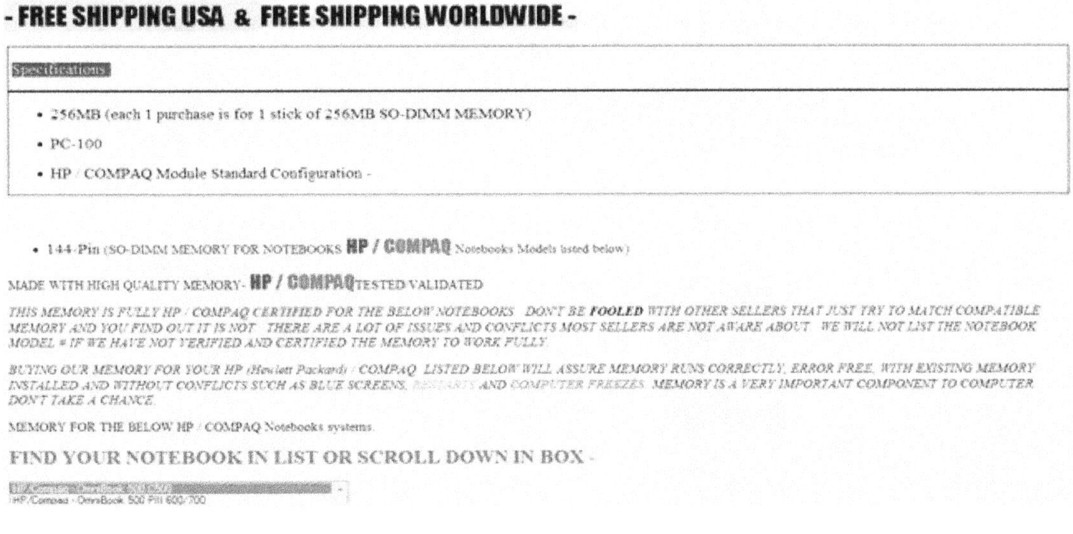

Figure 11. Typical EBay ad from India

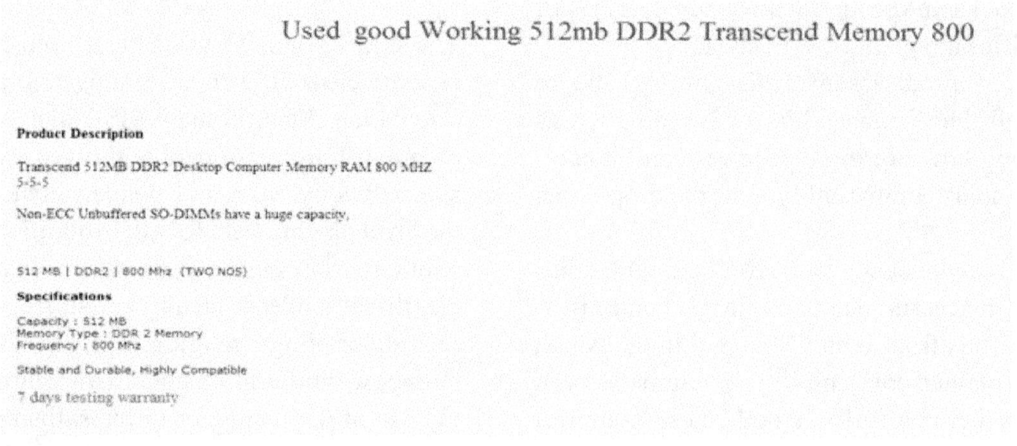

knowledge of Las Cruces and academia in general. And there are many lists of information in parallel fashion, further reinforcing uniformity and readability. In other words, almost any person could read and navigate through the NMSU website, a strong universalist feature.

In distinction to this strong templating, the Visvra-Bharati website is highly unique. Every major sub-category of homepage such as institutes and faculty contains an entirely different layout. For example, the "Heritage" page (Figure 13) looks entirely different from the homepage.

Figure 14, the General Information page, also has an entirely different organization, color, and iconography.

In addition, the few photographs of people include only those from India; and there are no anti-discrimination policies. Further, the language from Visvra-Bharati assumes a particular audience–one familiar with academic language and other Indian philosophies and approaches to learning and life. Only a select few can really navigate through this website, a great example of particularism.

Figure 12. Templating requirements

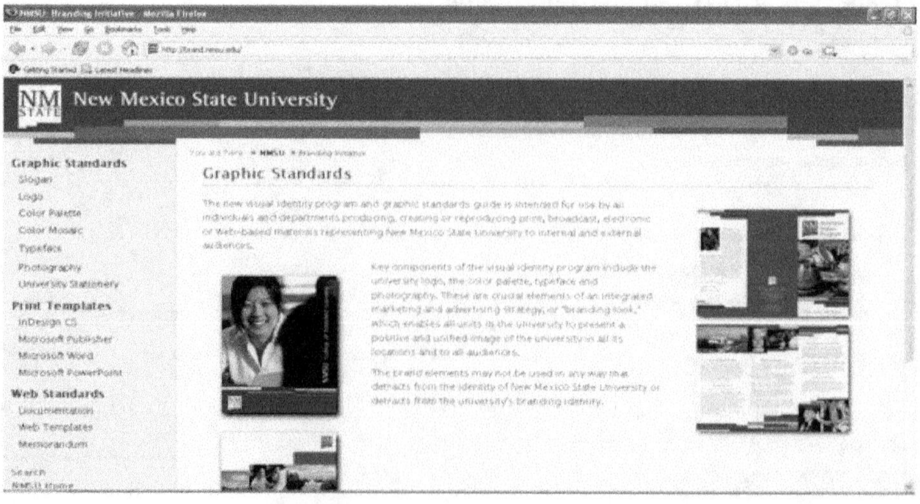

Figure 13. Heritage page of Visvra-Bharati

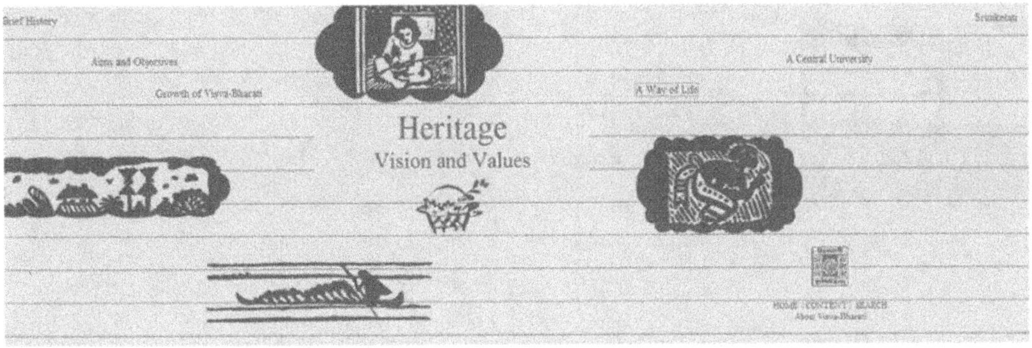

The websites from UACJ and UABJO showed mixed value sets. Both the UACJ and UABJO showed strong templating across most of their pages. However, they differed in assumed audiences. The audience in UACJ was more universal, and it consistently displayed information in lists, emphasizing uniformity and equality. Further, it has an important web section called "Transparency," which is devoted to making all processes and transactions transparent so as to combat the corruption problems of particularism.

In the UABJO, however, the audience is less universal. For example, the Figure 15 from the University President (rector) shows a more dignified and learned language:

The first sentence reads: "day by day, humanity constructs its legacy. Our daily activities go by occupying their place in history, which will be responsible for judging us by the decisions we make and the actions carried out." It has a more particular audience, one familiar with high academic language.

From the worldwide research, the 27 websites generally followed the universal-particular values attributed to them by the intercultural research. Much like NMSU, the Canadian and U.S. websites were strongly templated and contained explicit non-discrimination clauses and photographs of every possible variety of gender, age, ethnicity, etc. Further, these websites also catered to universal audience with their uniformity, parallelism, and universal audience strategies allow for the widest readership possible, further emphasizing universalist impulses (see Thatcher, et, al, 2007, for more information).

Figure 14. General Information Page from Visvra-Bharati

Figure 15. Page from UABJO President

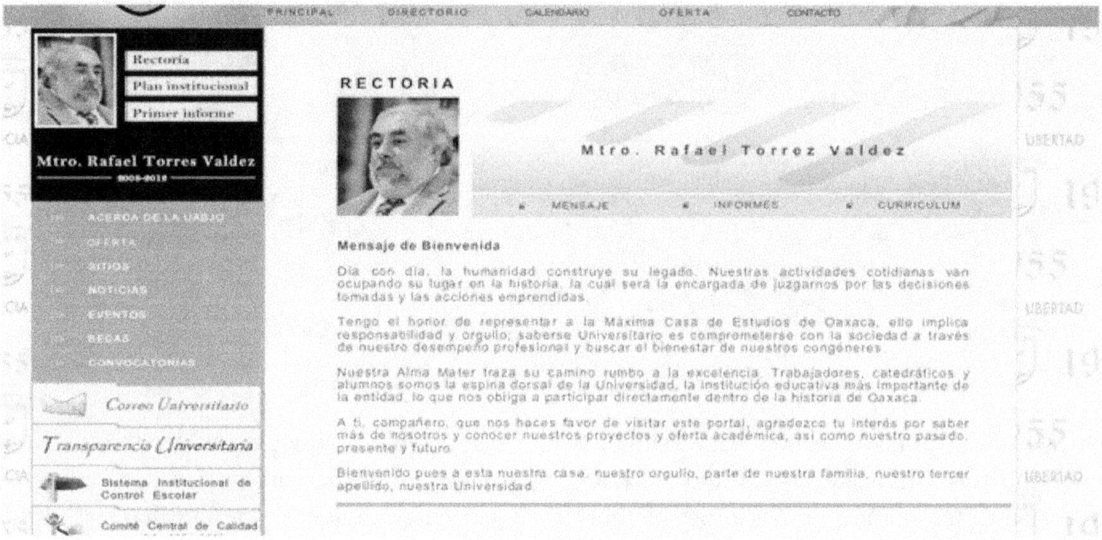

The universities in Latin America, Nepal, and China demonstrate a lot of uniqueness across each pages, making the pages feel particular, especially if the pages are links to the various academic departments. Whether they are structured differently, or use different degrees of animation, it is rare when the pages mirror each other exactly. Often, the format will remain, but some aesthetic feature is either added or altered in some way to preserve uniqueness. The universities in Latin America, in particular, also emphasized more aesthetic elements in their display of uniqueness, using art, symbols, or collages of scenes. Most departments in Latin American websites had its own unique logo and its own unique way of presenting its information, which is indicative of a particular environment. For example, Figure 16 displays Argentina's Universidad Nacional de Cuyo's homepage on the left and its College of Arts on the right. At this university, each college had a distinct web design.

As another particularist impulse, the Latin American, Nepalese, and Chinese universities displayed policies and procedures that are not uniform across groups. Rather, the rules were very specific to the roles, groups, and social structures

Figure 16. University of Cuyo

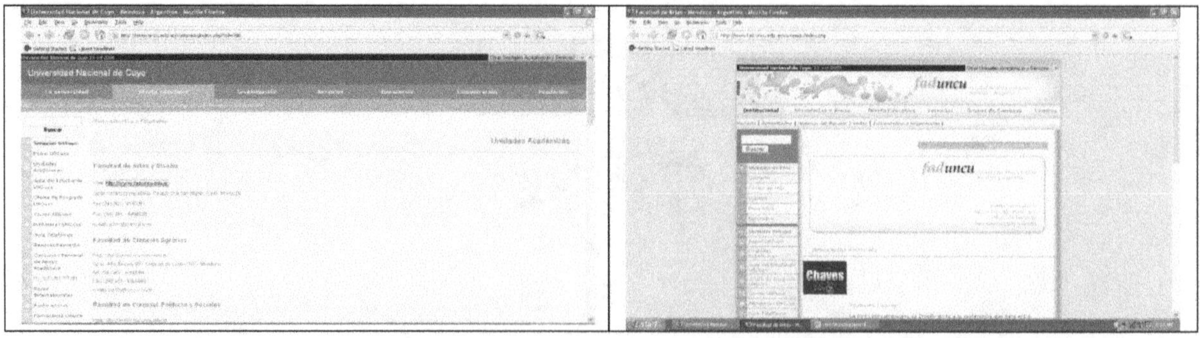

of the people involved, a classic sign of strong particularism. For example, while the U.S. and Canadian university would stress equality and uniformity of application across all groups in areas such as sexual harassment, academic honesty, self-governance, and use of university resources, the more particular universities would display code-like rules that were different for each group, with very little if no cross-over of policy and procedures among groups of different social hierarchy. Further, in distinction to the U.S. and Canadian universities, the rest of the universities did not display the diversity of their students. For example, Kathmandu University in Nepal has both male and female students from a variety of classes in Nepal, but the pictures only show males, and most often professors. There is no placing of men and women and people of different classes in the same picture, not to mention the same social positioning within that picture. Finally, the information on the more particular websites of China, Nepal, and Latin America is clearly not intended for the average individual, and the more specialized the faculties become, the more highly specialized the language, syntax, and knowledge becomes. Information is not written for a general audience, and the majority of it is written in very formal academic language.

The EBay ads also manifested different orientations towards rules. By far, the most explicitly rule orientated EBay ads came from Germany where long lists of information described buying, paying, shipping, and return procedures. Figure 17 from Germany demonstrates this strong universal orientation.

This screen capture only gets at only one half of the rules and procedures in this ad. It exemplifies the explicitness needed for this part of the EBay experience for German sellers and buyers. Similarly, almost every U.S. ad contained information about buying, paying, shipping, and returning the product, but the level of detail was generally about half that of the German ads. Most of the Indian and Chinese ads contained some information about these policies and procedures, but they contained even less information than the U.S. ads and focused more on ensuring the worldwide customers that they would receive quickly and

Figure 17. Typical EBay ad from Germany

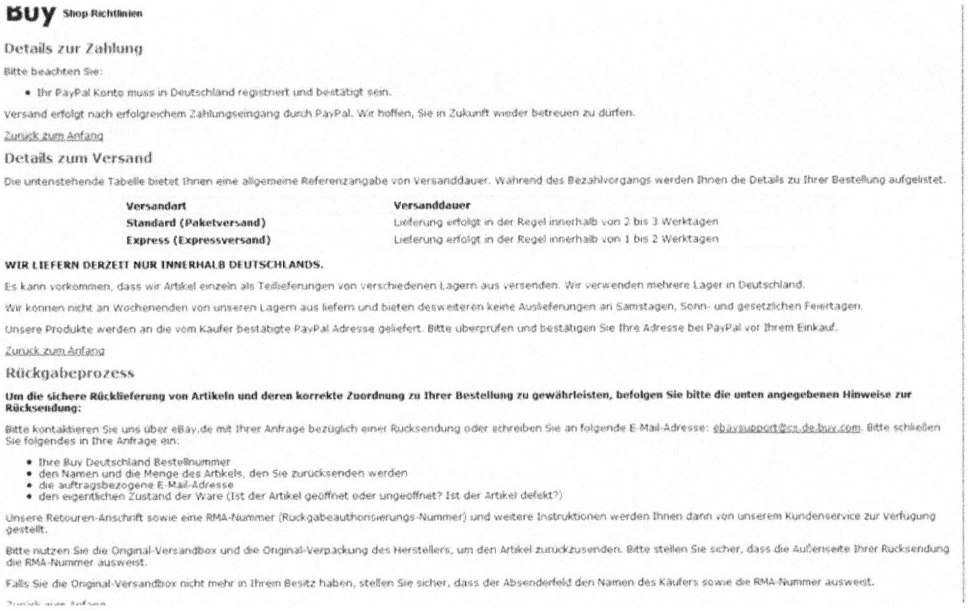

Buy Shop Richtlinien

Details zur Zahlung

Bitte beachten Sie:

- Ihr PayPal Konto muss in Deutschland registriert und bestätigt sein.

Versand erfolgt nach erfolgreichem Zahlungseingang durch PayPal. Wir hoffen, Sie in Zukunft wieder betreuen zu dürfen.

Zurück zum Anfang

Details zum Versand

Die untenstehende Tabelle bietet Ihnen eine allgemeine Referenzangabe von Versanddauer. Während des Bezahlvorgangs werden Ihnen die Details zu Ihrer Bestellung aufgelistet.

Versandart	Versanddauer
Standard (Paketversand)	Lieferung erfolgt in der Regel innerhalb von 2 bis 3 Werktagen
Express (Expressversand)	Lieferung erfolgt in der Regel innerhalb von 1 bis 2 Werktagen

WIR LIEFERN DERZEIT NUR INNERHALB DEUTSCHLANDS.

Es kann vorkommen, dass wir Artikel einzeln als Teillieferungen von verschiedenen Lagern aus versenden. Wir verwenden mehrere Lager in Deutschland.

Wir können nicht an Wochenenden von unseren Lagern aus liefern und bieten desweiteren keine Auslieferungen an Samstagen, Sonn- und gesetzlichen Feiertagen.

Unsere Produkte werden an die vom Käufer bestätigte PayPal Adresse geliefert. Bitte überprüfen und bestätigen Sie Ihre Adresse bei PayPal vor Ihrem Einkauf.

Zurück zum Anfang

Rückgabeprozess

Um die sichere Rücklieferung von Artikeln und deren korrekte Zuordnung zu Ihrer Bestellung zu gewährleisten, befolgen Sie bitte die unten angegebenen Hinweise zur Rücksendung:

Bitte kontaktieren Sie uns über eBay.de mit Ihrer Anfrage bezüglich einer Rücksendung oder schreiben Sie an folgende E-Mail-Adresse: ebaysupport@cs.de.buy.com. Bitte schließen Sie folgendes in Ihre Anfrage ein:

- Ihre Buy Deutschland Bestellnummer
- den Namen und die Menge des Artikels, den Sie zurücksenden werden
- die auftragsbezogene E-Mail-Adresse
- den eigentlichen Zustand der Ware (Ist der Artikel geöffnet oder ungeöffnet? Ist der Artikel defekt?)

Unsere Retouren-Anschrift sowie eine RMA-Nummer (Rückgabeauthorisierungs-Nummer) und weitere Instruktionen werden Ihnen dann von unserem Kundenservice zur Verfügung gestellt.

Bitte nutzen Sie die Original-Versandbox und die Original-Verpackung des Herstellers, um den Artikel zurückzusenden. Bitte stellen Sie sicher, dass die Außenseite Ihrer Rücksendung die RMA-Nummer ausweist.

Falls Sie die Original-Versandbox nicht mehr in Ihrem Besitz haben, stellen Sie sicher, dass der Absenderfeld den Namen des Käufers sowie die RMA-Nummer ausweist.

safely their products from China or India. Interestingly, none of the ads from Spain contained explicit policies and procedures for buying paying, shipping, and returning. Perhaps they assumed that these details could be worked out through negotiation, if needed. This could be a sign of particular orientation.

Specific-Diffuse

The websites from New Mexico State University and Visvra-Bharati exemplify the cultural differences of specific and diffuse. NMSU divided its homepage according to specific spheres of activities such as perspective students, current students, parents and family, faculty and staff, alumni, and visitors. This dividing of humans into their respective spheres of activity is a perfect example of specific orientation. On the other hand, Visvra-Bharati's homepage (Figure 18) has only two links: the picture of the founder and an icon, both of which link to the contents page. The homepage is as whole as it can be. Even its "Contents" page is divided mostly with non-human categories such as the campus, academics, institutes, and centers.

The only "human" division is for the leadership, a collective, particular, and high power distance trait.

In addition to the overall web design, NMSU and Visvra-Bharati differ in their focus on the human being. Almost all the pictures at NMSU are of people, and in these photographs, it's the people that take up most of the space, with relatively much less in the background, which represents a more specific view of humanity. For example, in the Current Student's page, shown earlier in Figure 5, all ten pictures are of people, and in eight of the ten, people entirely dominate the photo. In two pictures, the people and the context are about equal. In addition, almost every picture of person shows the person smiling, demonstrating the openness in public forums that is so important to specific cultures.

Visvra-Bharati shows very strong diffuse values in its pictures. When it has pictures of people, almost always there is a great amount of context to those pictures so that the viewer sees the human in his or her whole setting. However, there are many more pictures of the context such as buildings, facilities, and nature. And the pictures of people

Figure 18. Content Page of Visvra-Bharati

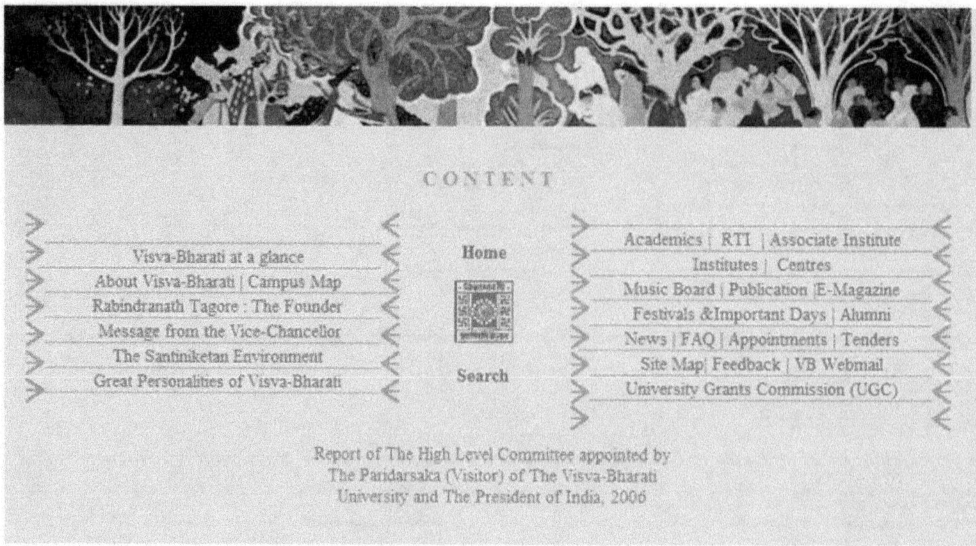

seldom show the openness of smiling; instead there is more of a reserved look. Almost every sub-section taken from the contents page shows a building, nature, or other non-person entity.

The UACJ and UABJO show mixed values, with the UACJ more like NMSU. Both these websites show a diffuse homepage design. UACJ's homepage only has one of the four major sections that divides "users" into categories such as students, alumni, teachers, and staff; the other three categories are more holistic divisions such as institutes, university structure, and services. UABJO is actually more similar to Visvra-Bharati because it has fewer links in its homepage than NMSU or UACJ, and none of the links are for specific kinds of people or spheres of activity. All links are holistic entities or institutions. In addition, like its homepage, the photographs of people at UACJ have a mixture of people and context, almost half and half. Thus, people are viewed in their context more than at NMSU. The pictures of UABJO are almost exclusively of buildings or the rector; very few if no pictures exist of people.

The worldwide research also showed these specific and diffuse differences. Texas Tech homepage divides the people up into very specific categories including types of students, sports fans, alumni, media, visitors, parents, and faculty and staff. This specific feature was very common at all three U.S. universities despite that the fact these universities are land-grant institutions dedicated to serving the citizens of each respective state, a diffuse attribute that the U.S. universities claim but seem not to emphasize. It is interesting to note that Tel Aviv University in Israel shares 15 of the 17 specific categories on their homepage with Texas Tech University. The websites in Ireland share almost all the same specific organizing categories as the U.S., Canadian, and Israeli websites (Thatcher, et al, 2007).

The Chinese and Nepalese websites show a mixture of specific and diffuse orientations. The Hebei and Zhengzhou (China) and Sanskrit University (Nepal) websites are strongly diffuse, while the Hunan University (China) and Tribhuwan University (Nepal) mix specific and diffuse, and the University of Kathmandu (Nepal) is specific. The Chinese and Nepalese websites that are more diffuse do not break down information according to the spheres of activity for the end user nearly as much as the U.S., Canadian, or Israeli sites; rather, they force all users through long introductions, descriptions, and common values and common navigation paths, highlighting the holistic and communal approach for the user. The Latin American websites were also a mixture of diffuse and specific categories. The websites in Argentina, Colombia, and Costa Rica, for example, showed a homepage design similar to the United States and Canada but with some key differences. Information is grouped by relationship or non-human entity such as institutions or areas of study, more than different kinds of people (such as students, faculty, etc). In order to see a list of faculties and degrees, the user needs to go to other menus, which in turn group information about the various campuses and faculties, and degrees. These differences mean that users are expected to possess a tacit knowledge that will make this sort of navigation possible and that will guide them to the appropriate places. The homepage of Argentina's Universidad Nacional de La Plata (Figure 19) is a good example of this more diffuse approach.

The categories or major links on the top for this homepage are institutional, academics, postgraduate, research, extension, and alumni. The links on the left are works in progress, administration and finances, newspaper, radio, culture, and opinion. The only specific link is alumni; all the rest are diffuse categories.

One interesting variable that emerged with the specific and diffuse threshold was the amount of pictures of people and their poses in the pictures. The Nepalese universities, for example, had very few pictures of people, because, according to Marohang Limbu, the graduate student researcher, this public space was not the appropriate medium

Figure 19. University of La Plata

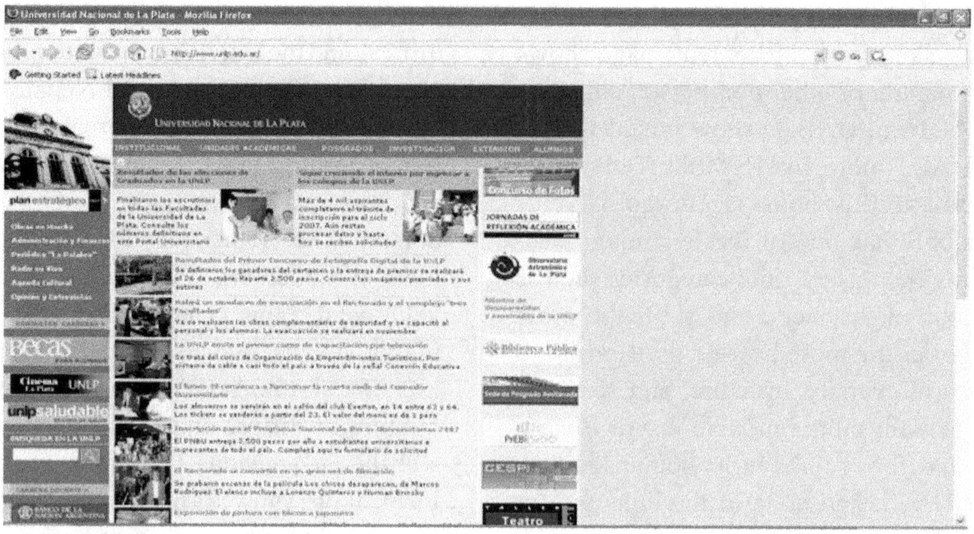

for something as private as a picture. Likewise, the more diffuse websites had relatively few pictures, and in almost no picture were the people smiling. On the other hand, the websites in the United States, Canada, Israel, and Ireland all had many pictures of people, and in most of the pictures, the people had big, bright, welcoming smiles. The websites in Latin America had few pictures than the U.S. or Canadian websites, but more than the Nepalese site, and about 1/3rd of the pictures of people displayed welcoming smiles. Figure 20, from Washington State University's page titled "World Class: Face to Face" features eight pictures of smiling and welcoming students. This very thin or non-existent boundary between public and private, which perfectly exemplifies

Figure 20. University of Washington Student Life page

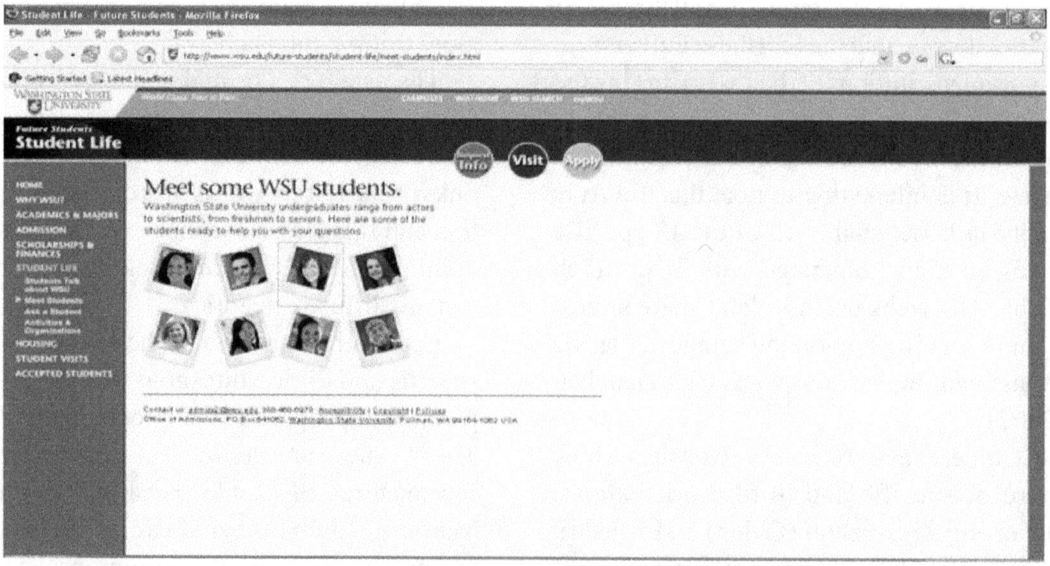

the specific circle described in Chapter Two, was common on the specific websites and was rarely apparent in the more diffuse pages.

This difference in smiles and public display perfectly exemplifies specific and diffuse. In diffuse cultures, the wide open public space is usually not comfortable or open because the public/private boundary is carefully guarded according to strict in- and out-group orientations that derive from their collective and particular orientations. On the other hand, in specific cultures, the wide open public space is the perfect place to welcome specific relationship building, a strategy that is particularly dominant in the United States since colonial times when developing good neighborly strategies was necessary for survival (Stewart & Bennett, 1991; Rosenn, 1991).

The EBay ads also demonstrate variance across cultures with the specific and diffuse variables. First, almost all of the U.S. ads addressed the buyer explicitly, often in the form of "you" such as you can be assured, you can believe. Figure 21 demonstrates this "you orientation."

In addition to explaining compatibility and assuring the reader, this ad exemplifies the lack of distance between the seller and buyer with the constant use of "you." Sometimes the Chinese ads addressed the buyer, but the ads from Spain, Germany, and India rarely, if ever, addressed the buyer as a "you" or a person. The tendency to address the buyer as a "you" exemplifies the specific orientation because the seller believes that he or she can connect to the buyer quickly across this very public domain.

One of the most salient strategies of the Chinese ads was to assure the buyer that the Chinese product was high quality, that the seller understood the EBay and world market, and that the buyer would indeed receive the product. In many ways, these are concrete strategies trying to overcome

Figure 21. You orientation in U.S. ad

Figure 22. Importance of seller and quality in China

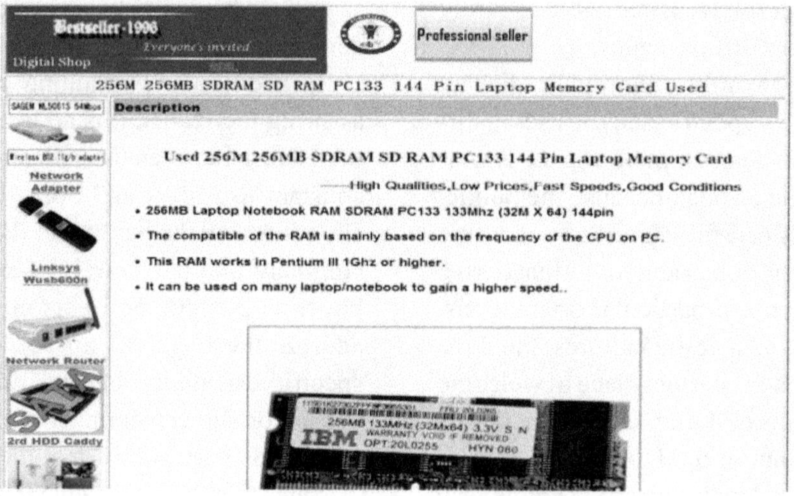

the lack of trust of a public venue such as EBay, which is so common in diffuse cultures. Figure 22 demonstrates the Chinese approach to ensuring trust across the public realm.

This ad emphasizes that the seller has been around for a long time, is a "BestSeller," "Professional Seller," and "Power Seller" on eBay. In addition, the RAM is "High qualities…fast speeds, good conditions." The references to the quality of the seller and product are traditional diffuse strategies for ensuring trust in a public realm. Rarely did the other EBay sellers use these diffuse approaches.

Ascription-Achievement

For this value set, the NMSU and Visvra-Bharati exemplify the different orientations. NMSU's website strongly demonstrates the achievement orientation. First, most of the pictures show people doing something. For example, Figure 23, the homepage of NMSU often portrays researchers or students in action, as the following demonstrates.

The three pictures in this homepage are of people doing something: the researcher in the lab preparing students for success; the associate professor creating smiles; and the associate professor

Figure 23. Homepage of NMSU

advocating rights. Further, four of the five news and events highlight achievements of the faculty members. The year in review highlights only achievements or events where prominent people participated. In addition, the "About NMSU" page is entirely dedicated to achievements, statistics, and other concrete data that emphasize a strong orientation to doing.

The Visvra-Bharati website does show some action, especially in the homepage; but most of it focuses on ascribed qualities and an orientation towards being, rather than doing. Figure 6, shown earlier, shows that Visvra-Bharati is focused on developing "a way of life" for all involved. This way does not self actualize through doing, but through being, through perceptions manifested in cheerful celebrations and social communion. Another very important ascribed quality of Visvra-Bharati is its celebration of great figures. The "Facts and Figures" page of Visvra-Bharati page (Figure 24) demonstrates that the university is great because of its great founders, councils, and institutes and because it was declared so by an act of Indian Parliament.

This university is great because its founders and current leadership are great, not because of

Figure 24. Facts and figures about Visvra-Bharati

its achievements. It is actually very difficult to find any concrete numbers about enrollment, types and numbers of degrees, or even famous alumni. Further, almost all of its pictures show the greatness of the buildings and facilities, arguing that the university is great because its facilities are great, not because students and faculty have achieved much. And the "About" pages is divided up into five categories with almost all of the information giving the history and context of the university to show its greatness. All this is greatness through ascription, not greatness through achievement.

The UACJ and UABJO show mixed values, with the UACJ more like NMSU. UACJ does show a strong achievement orientation because most of its pictures are of people in action. And many of the links on the homepage are of activities and events. However, it is also difficult or impossible to find lists of enrollment, number of graduates, famous achievements from faculty and alumni, and awards won by the university. UABJO is more like Visvra-Bharati in that it demonstrates its greatness by its president, leadership, and facilities. Further, the "About UABJO" page has five components, none of which emphasizes achievements, seen in Figure 25.

Much like Visvra-Bharati, this university is great because of its rich history, its coat of arms, hymn, and motto.

From the worldwide study, the U.S., Canadian, and Israeli websites clearly and strongly displayed the achievement orientation. This orientation was manifest in various ways. For example, the University of Calgary homepage shown below focuses on student, academic, and community achievement. The University of Calgary website (Figure 26) also displayed in prominent positions the achievement data of their university, including enrollment, graduation rates, placement of students, size of campus, building initiatives, and prominent graduates who achieved great things for Alberta and the society as a whole.

The other U.S. and Canadian websites similarly highlight the achievement of their faculty and students. This achievement orientation was also reflected in Israel. On the Hebrew University homepage there are both news of recent scientific discovery done at the university and a link to faculty member who recently became a

Figure 25. About UABJO page

Figure 26. University of Calgary website

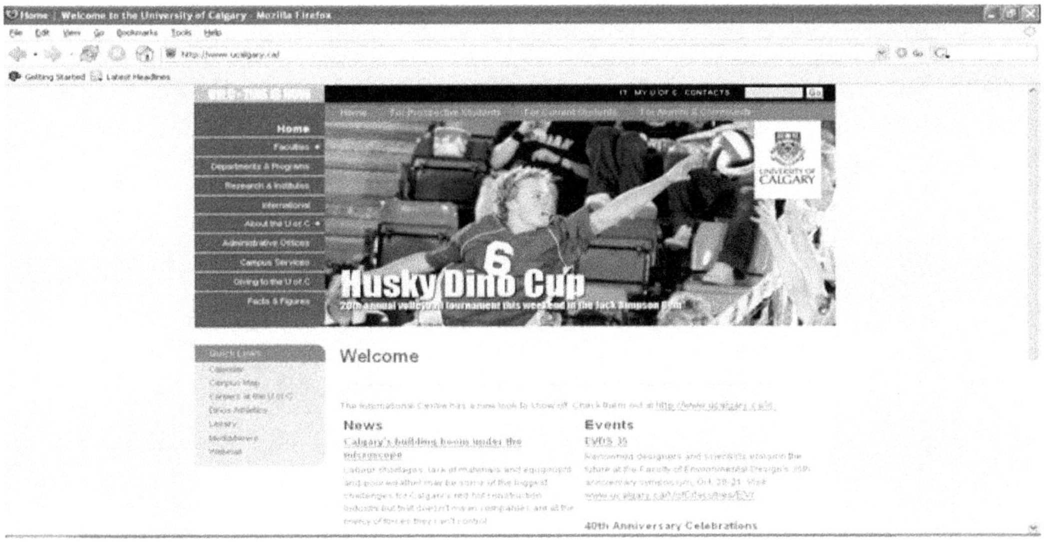

noble prize winner. On the Ben Gurion University homepage, there is a notice of a faculty member's recently earned award (Thatcher, et al, 2007).

The three Chinese websites display a complicated combination of both achievement and ascription, becoming more like an achievement-yielding-ascription. All three Chinese website devote much web space describing the success of their graduates in their specific field, listing and describing academy members and other prestigious professors, and announcing their achievements in research and teaching. All this indicates that individual achievement is highly valued. However, the introduction sections of the Chinese universities are long, consisting of information about the history, the presidents, prestigious alumni, and leaders of the country who visited campus, academy members, and well-known professors. Another example of the ascription orientation is reflected by the fact that all three Chinese websites quote from some historic and important figure and/or use his calligraphy as the school motto on the homepage. This historic person might be the first president of the university as evidenced by the motto of Hunan University, or a previous leader of the country, or a scholar who enjoyed high reputation. The calligraphy or quote of a well-known person, to the Chinese audience, increases the school's strength and raises its status. The English homepage of the Hunan University, shown in Figure 27, exemplifies this more ascriptive approach.

Like the Chinese websites, the Latin American and Nepalese websites showed combinations of achievement and ascription. These websites prominently displayed great achievements of faculty and students, but they also highlighted the history of great people who had been a part of the university, not in what they had contributed, rather, in that they were associated with it. In addition, these websites also prominently displayed social hierarchies in their websites, highlighting the titles and roles of the people filling those titles, a tendency that reflects, among many values, ascription orientation.

The eBay ads likewise demonstrate interesting variance with the ascribed versus achievement orientations. The most salient evidence for this was the brand name orientation and consumer

Figure 27. Hunan home page

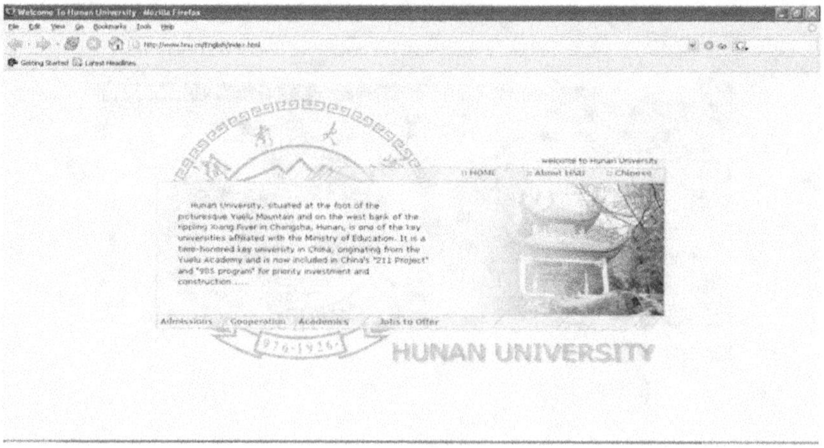

popularity among most of the Chinese ads and the performance orientation of the U.S. ads. For example, like Figure 28 demonstrates, most of the Chinese EBay ads included all of the important names and many times explained that it was "hot selling" or otherwise socially important.

This ad drops all the important names and terms: Plug and Play, Windows, Linux, Mac, and others. The other EBay ads usually gave just specifications or compatibility but never drew on key product names. In many ways, this name dropping is an ascription because it connects the products with the important names, not on how good the product actually is, which is a sign of achievement orientation.

Power Distance

The websites from NMSU, Visvra-Bharati, UACJ, and UABJO correspond closely to the power distance indices from their respective cultures. First, NMSU shows mostly a low power distance

Figure 28. Hot selling flash memory

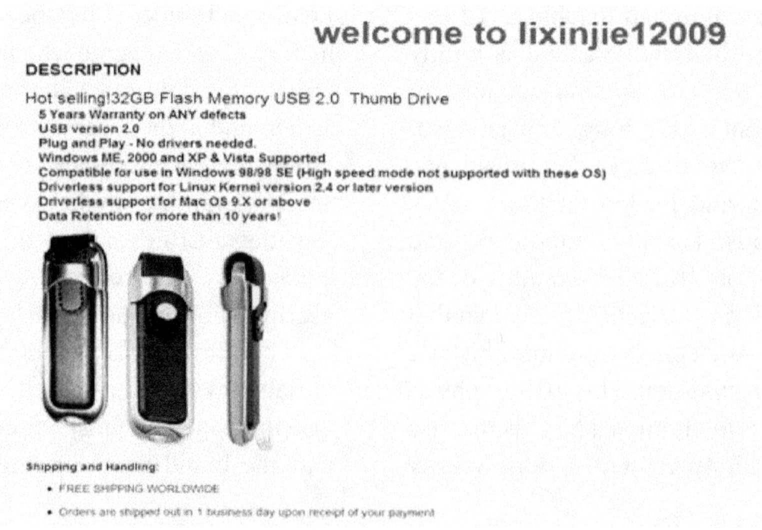

orientation. Most of the language–and especially language directed toward students–tries to reduce the distance between the students and the website. The "Prospective Students" webpage exemplifies this low power distance approach, as seen in Figure 29.

Following very closely low power distance assumptions, this page downplays the hierarchy between students and the university, especially with its language and colors; it also shows that students are in charge of their own lives and what they do on campus. The built-in search functions for where to start and how to apply lessens the distance between the students and university. In addition to this page, the photographs of students rarely show a professor or administrator alone in all his or her glory. Instead, most professors are shown mostly equal with students and showing them what to do, not telling or commanding. In many pictures, it is difficult to tell who the professor is and who the student is.

The power distance in Visvra-Bharati is somewhat different. The first power distance symbol is the large, prominently centered picture of the founder on the home page. In addition to this symbol, all web users have to enter the web page through a link on this picture or the icon, forcing all through the same path. In addition, in pictures of groups, it is almost always easy to distinguish who is in charge, the professors. However, despite these high power distance symbols, there low power distance symbols as well. This university stresses unity and harmony as one of its major goals.

The Mexican websites from UACJ and UABJO show strong indices of high power distance. First, both websites have as their first set of links the University's leadership and authority structure. And these links are well-developed and concrete displays of authority, of who is in charge. In addition, most of the pictures of professors or leaders show the leader in formal attire and at the center,

Figure 29. Prospective Students page

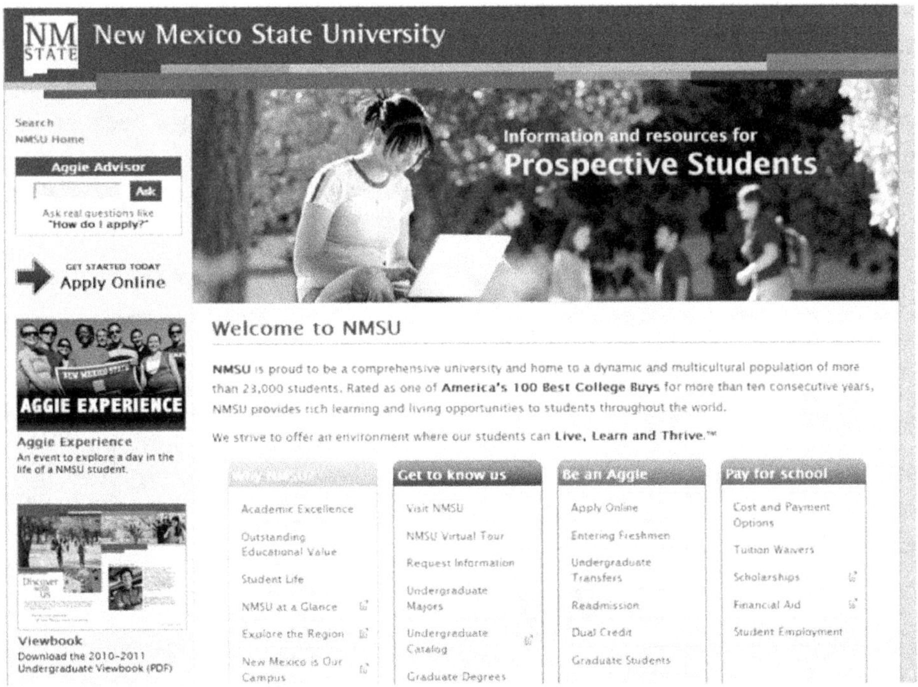

clearly in charge of what is going on. There is no mistake about authority.

From the worldwide study, the U.S. and Canadian websites rarely showed overt signs of power differences among groups of people, especially in instructional contexts, a sign of lower power distance. Instead, those in power usually welcomed students with a smile, more informal language, and seemed to try to lessen the power differences as a way to reach everybody the same way. This difference was evident in the pictures of the leaders of the U.S. and Canadian institutions who, even though they were clearly in charge, seemed to talk to the reader as somewhat of an equal. The U.S. and Canadian websites also did not overtly or prominently display organizational charts that delineate power differentials among the people. In fact, the Texas Tech, New Mexico State, and Washington State sites do not display any kind of organizational chart. While power differentials are certainly implied between graduate and under-graduate students, administration and faculty, the overall tone created on the sites is one of cooperative environment within which students can pursue their aspirations. The overt assumption is that everyone is on the same side and pursuing the same goals; nurturing independence brings success to all alike. There is little, if any, appeal to authority as a means of establishing influence over incoming students.

The websites in Mexico, Costa Rica, Colombia, and Chile show strong indices of high power distance in both the text organization and in pictures of university personalities. All six universities display organizational charts in prominent places; all show the people in authority in contexts where their power is clearly in effect, for example, in front of their offices with their leadership roles clearly delineated; and all show differences in dress—those in authority show it through their formal attire. In fact, the Colombian National University has its own URL for the organizational chart. In addition, even in the classroom settings depicted on these websites, high power distance is strongly evident. Teachers are depicted almost always in front of the class with more formal attire. Rarely, do the websites portray a teacher in a more egalitarian poses with students. A quick comparison of university president web pages exemplifies these power distance differences. Figure 30 displays two web pages, New Mexico State on the left and Benemérita Universidad Autónoma de Puebla on the right.

The Rector (President) of the Mexican University is shown in all his power context: the formal office, coat of arms, formal attire, and serious look, while NMSU's president has no power signals other than his suite, which still looks rather informal because his tie is loose.

Figure 30. Comparison of NMSU and Mexican University's President's pages

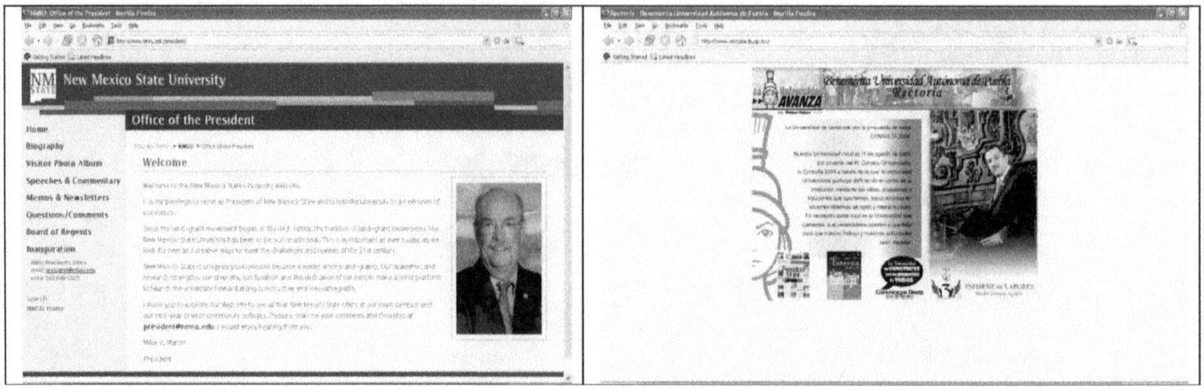

Furthermore, the NMSU's first word is welcome, a very low power distance approach.

The power distance variable in the EBay ads was not as easy to detect perhaps because the power between seller and buyer seemed not that important to the ad. It was clear that Germany's strong universal orientation tried to assure that no power struggles could happen between buyers and sellers. The ads from India and China generally gave just specifications with very little reference to the buyer or seller as a person. The U.S. ads, however, usually tried to lower the distance–or close the gap–between buyer and seller, using a variety of tactics. First, as described earlier, the U.S. ads tried to give as much information about compatibility and installation so that the buyer was free to make an informed choice. This is a low power distance approach. Also, the "you orientation" described in the specific and diffuse section demonstrates the desire to lessen the distance between buyers and sellers. Also, a good percentage of U.S. EBay ads used informal language and icons to make the buying experience seem less threatening or friendlier. For example, many U.S. ads wished their bidders "good luck" and "happy bidding." Almost all U.S. EBay ads explicitly explained how to ask questions and provided email links for doing that. Figure 31 demonstrates many of these low power distance approaches for the U.S. ads.

This ad tries to reduce the power distance by providing detailed compatibility information; an offer to assist in selecting the type of memory, and use of words like "please," "I'll get back to you asap," and "thanks for looking."

The friendly, low power distance approaches of the U.S. ads were in stark contrast to the ads from Spain. These ads were terse, the language was not friendly in any way, and no offers for help or questions were ever offered from the Spanish ads. Figure 32 is a typical ad from Spain.

This ad demonstrates a "take it or leave" attitude. It simply says that two memory stick are for sale, the brand is Extreme, and they are in perfect working order. No other details. Although some ads in the U.S. had a similar terse approach, none of the U.S. failed to address the reader as a person or imply that the seller was not a person. About half of the ads from Spain had a similar approach. The other ads from Spain did address

Figure 31. U.S. ad full of low power distance approaches

Figure 32. Typical ad from Spain

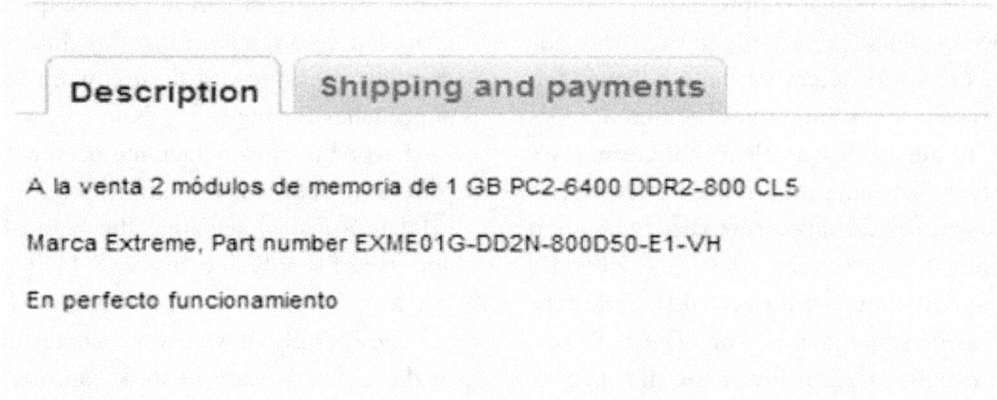

the buyer but usually as a "take advantage of this offer" approach. Rarely, if ever, did the Spanish ads volunteer to answer questions or help or try to lessen the distance. All of these characteristics correspond to more high power distance or perhaps diffusive strategies.

High and Low Context

This value demonstrates the relevance and role of the context for the universities. Closely following U.S. cultural values, NMSU's website is mid to low context; that is, the context has a reduced role in comparison to the people involved. This is seen through a variety of data. First, in the "About NMSU" page, very little description is given about the history of NMSU, southern New Mexico or Las Cruces; only a short paragraph is given about the history of NMSU; and very little is communicated about the climate, land, or area surrounding NMSU. As mentioned, in almost all the pictures of people, the people dominate the actual space or pixels with the context relegated to about 20% of the picture itself. In short, NMSU is not contextualized well.

This lack of contextualization stands in stark contrast to Visvra-Bharati where great effort is used to contextualize this university. First, the "About Visvra-Bharati" pages contextualize the university five ways: through its heritage, location, library, associate, and contacts. As exemplified earlier in Figure 11, Visvra-Bharati's Heritage Page has six subpages that uniquely contextualize the university. The facts and figures of Visvra-Bharati strongly focus on its history and development. In addition, Visvra-Bharati also has an environment page, which has a rolling documentary of the natural environment of the area of the university, a point that will be better documents in the next section. More than 3/4ths of the pictures in Visvra-Bharati are of the context, rather than people. And when people are shown in pictures, the environment takes about half of the space. In short, it is clear that in order to understand Visvra-Bharati, one must understand its full context.

The Autonomous University of Ciudad Juárez (UACJ) provides about as much context to its university as does NMSU: little. First, there is "Get to Know UACJ" page focuses exclusively on its leadership and organizational structure–that's what it means to "know" UACJ. And it's difficult to find the history of the university such as its foundation and growth. Its visitor's page only describes very briefly the City of Ciudad Juárez and basic transportation, eating, and other useful information. It is much more like NMSU. On the other hand, UABJO richly contextualizes itself, much like Visvra-Bharati. It has a long history element to the first part of "About UABJO." It also shows its role in the larger community where it resides. It also contextualizes its university more than NMSU but perhaps less so than Visvra-Bharati.

The eBay ads demonstrated an interesting variance for the high and low context. First, in perhaps a counter culture move, almost every ad from the United States explained the origin or context of the memory for sale. The memory was either "brand new," in an "unopened" or "opened" package or pulled from a working computer. Contrary to the lower context approaches in the university websites, it seems that U.S. buyers want to know the context of the product they are thinking about purchasing. Likewise, the Chinese ads emphasized their experience and reputation as EBay sellers to contextualize the buying processes, but rarely, if ever, did the Chinese explain the origin of the product. The ads from Spain, Germany, and India generally contextualized the product as new or coming from a working computer; but these three countries did not contextualize as much as the U.S. or China.

Virtues: Inner and Outer-Directed

This value assesses the source of direction or moral guidance of the person, whether it comes from a mechanism from within that gives the person the drive or whether the person seeks to draw guidance from the outside forces, often seen as harmonizing with nature. Because the outer-directed nature of Visvra-Bharati is so clear, it is useful to start there. The "Santiniketan Environment" page (Figure 33) shows how important it is to receive guidance through harmony with the environment.

This picture is the first of twelve pictures of nature and the Visvra-Bharati context showing how people become at one with their surroundings. The language of this first page also strongly demonstrates how important it is to have the environment "always present in one's consciousness. It becomes a part of one's being there." The other eleven pictures depict and explain how the university has harmonized itself with its surroundings, which has provided it great strength. Not only are there overt references to this harmoniz-

Figure 33. Visvra-Bharati Environment Page

ing, the Visvra-Bharati website design itself shows this source of outer direction. Although almost all of the web pages are unique, the colors on each page blend together almost seamlessly with the text, graphics, and pictures. For example, in the above Figure 19, the web page color is light green, which blends with the green trees and grass; the text color is light brown, which blends with the earth. The only real design consistency throughout this webpage is the blending and coordination of colors.

Visvra-Bharati's outer-directed orientation is also emphasized by not having the individual user's needs at the forefront for navigating the website. For example, it is difficult to find admissions information or other quick information needed by students, faculty, staff or visitors. Rather, the web design forces the user (by design or not) to navigate through many pages to find this information.

In terms of user-directed navigation, NMSU is directly the opposite. The major design features of the homepage provide quick access to the kinds of information that different kinds of users want. It even has a quick search function. This way, the site is user-friendly, exemplifying very clearly inner-directed orientation. As described in Chapter One, inner directed means that the person is responsible for his or her own path in life and that each person should be able to construct that unique path according to his or her own inner guide or needs. In addition to the inner-directed design, the NMSU website shows very little integration of people into their environment. As mentioned earlier, little or no context is shown in pictures, and most of the pictures of buildings shows just the building, not its context. Further, there is no explicit connection in the university's mission or philosophy about deriving direction and inspiration from harmonizing with its context. As a final element of inner direction, it is worth noting that the templated colors of NMSU's site are not harmonized but distinctive. The crimson red (school color), orange, blue, and green do not blend with the pictures; rather, they are set off in contrast to almost all the pictures. Further, white is used for the background in all the pages (per University requirement); thus, there is no blending.

The websites in Mexico are mixed. UACJ's demonstrates a mix of inner and outer virtues. Its homepage does not offer the huge array of quick, user-driven information that NMSU does, but it's much more user friendly than Visvra-Bharati. In addition, UACJ's colors are much like NMSU because they are contrastive, not blended. UABJO's website is much more like Visvra-Bharati's site. Although it does have pictures and text explicitly linking the source of guidance of the university to its context, it does not have the user-friendly design where users can create their own paths. Their paths are through the organization and leadership structure on the home page. In addition, UABJO's web colors blend much better than NMSU and UACJ, almost like Visvra-Bharati.

The EBay ads also demonstrated variance across the inner and outer-directed dimensions. First, as already explained, the U.S. ads assumed an independent U.S. buyer making a decision and installing the memory on his or her own. Thus, the U.S. ads, like the U.S. university websites, were very self-directed or driven, assuming the same level of independence. The ads from Spain and Germany also assumed a high level of independent decision making, but they generally did not provide the user-friendly designs and information to facilitate that.

One of the interesting units of analysis for this variable assessed whether the information contained in the ads was contained or boxed or simply given within the eBay parameters. About 1/3 of the EBay ads from India contained information that was boxed in, much like the website designs from Visvra-Bharati. Figure 34 is a good example of this boxing.

Using similar colors and approaches as the Visvra-Bharati site, this ad boxed in the information, demonstrating a more of an "outer moving to inner" approach. A few of the U.S., Germany, and Chinese ads boxed the information but none so consistently as India.

Figure 34. Boxing in information from India

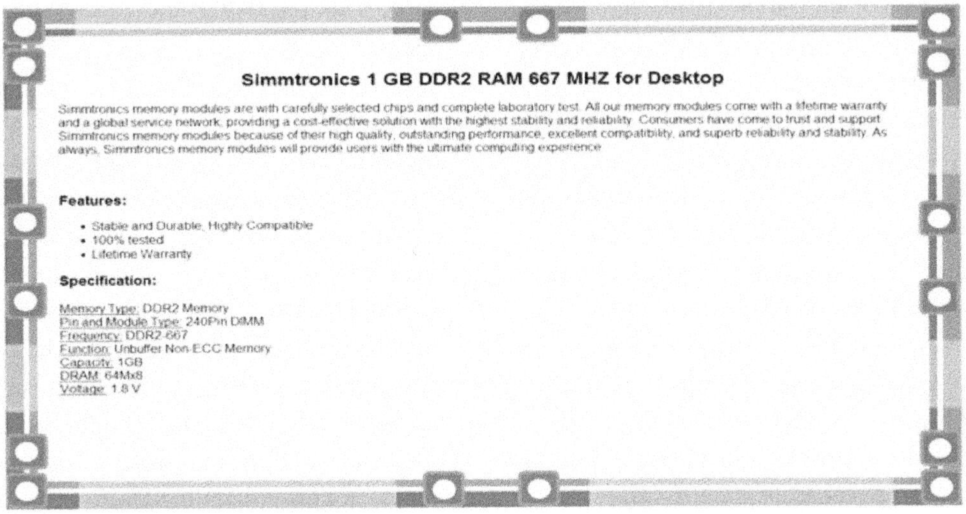

Polychronic and Monochronic Times

The final value looks at time frames and assesses their linearity or simultaneity. In short, all four university websites are fairly monochronic with Visvra-Bharati being mixed. First, all four have linear and parallel lists for menu bars and links; the difference is that Visvra-Bharati has only a few linear lists and has many other web pages that are non-linear. All four are relatively static, meaning that things do not change quickly. And most links on all four following a bread-crumb linear fashion, showing where you are, where you have been, and where you can go. This linearity is not universal however; to show how linear and static these websites are, we can compare them to a more polychronic website of EBay ads from China (See Figure 35), some of which were very polychronic.

Although difficult to tell from this screen shot, almost 90% of this website is in constant movement. All of the text at the top is constantly blinking; and the different font types and sizes emphasize the polychronic or nonlinear feel. The only thing that stays the same is the three small link bars on the side; everything else is in constant flux. I show this website only to demonstrate that the polychronic time frame can easily map onto website designs. Some of the U.S. and Indian ads were polychronic but never close to this level. None of the ads from Spain or Germany were polychronic.

DISCUSSION AND CONCLUSION

In short, the websites in this study almost overwhelmingly corresponded to the cultural values attributed to that culture or region by the intercultural research, as documented in Chapter Two. The only major exception was Mexico's Autonomous University of Ciudad Juárez. This border university reflected U.S. cultural values more consistently than Mexican values, except for the case of power distance, which is high, reflecting the Mexican value. Interestingly, although New Mexico State University is very close to the Mexican border, it rarely, if never, reflected cultural values from Mexico. In fact, it's almost impossible to tell from the website design that NMSU is anywhere near the border because it so closely paralleled the designs of Washington State or Texas Tech University.

Some interesting connections can be made from these results. First, although people have been arguing about the importance of globalization for a long time, only one website (UACJ) did not reflect its predominant cultural values. The other 30 websites as well as the five countries selling eBay memory reflected the local culture. My conclusion is much like Ghemawat (2007): globalization has not penetrated the local cultures nearly as much as many researchers would like us to believe. This closely corresponds to my U.S.-Mexico border experience. Of course, more research is needed to explore more fully this conclusion. It would be very helpful to enlist a much larger sample size with multiple researchers across the world.

Further, I think it is fascinating (but not at all surprising) that NMSU did not reflect the cultural and rhetorical patterns of its very close neighbor to the south (and NMSU does have many Mexican national students and faculty); yet, UACJ strongly reflected U.S. cultural patterns in all but one case. My next step is to analyze the University of El Paso-Texas website, which lies right on the U.S. side of the border. However, in non-systematic ways, I feel UTEP's site is much like NMSU: it draws on U.S. values almost exclusively. This is despite the fact that UTEP is strongly Mexican, with 90+ percent either Mexican-American or Mexican national. This might be very surprising to U.S.-Americans, but perhaps not to Mexican nationals who are very used to the great influence coming from the United States. I am also not surprised because many at NMSU seem to go to great lengths to ignore their border situation, a point that I would like to develop here but cannot, while UACJ and Ciudad Juárez are very international thinking, welcoming cultural influences, not only from the United States, but Asia, Europe, and many other parts of the world. Thus, globalization needs to look, as Bhabha (2003) explains, at the unequal flow of culture, goods, people, and capital.

This research also points to some interesting ramifications for technical communicators and web designers working in international contexts. How much should they re-design their websites

Figure 35. Polychronic Chinese ad

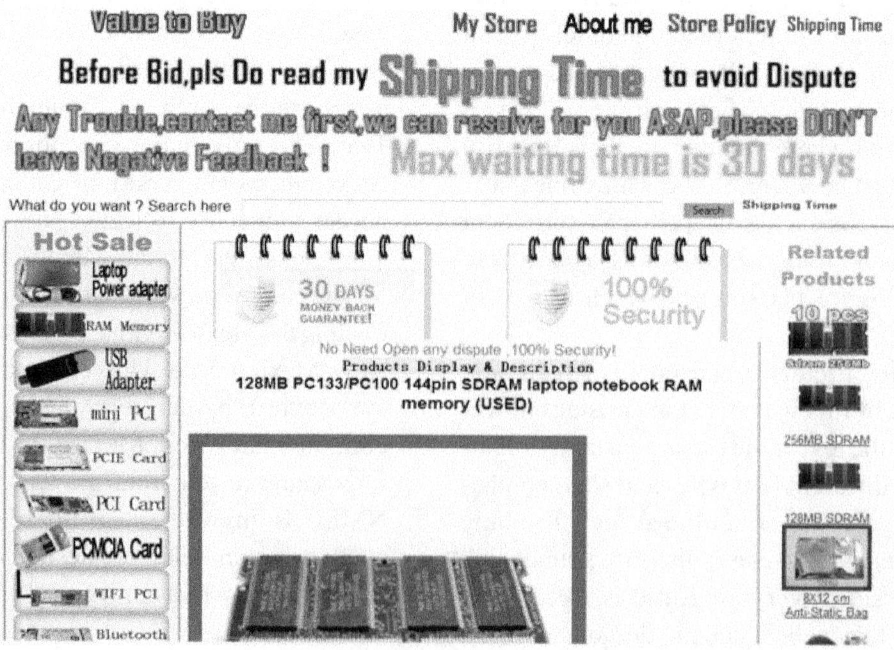

to fit the cultural patterns of the target audience? This is a tough question because the re-design could be total. In some contexts, such as the U.S.-Mexico border area, there is a high percentage of bilingual and bicultural people who function well across cultures and rhetorical systems. Thus, it does not really matter which system is used; and hybridity between systems is often used strategically (Hampden-Turner & Trompenaars 2000). For example, in many of my border meetings, some of my Mexican colleagues will speak English and draw from the more U.S. rhetorical system as a measure of goodwill; and not to be outdone, many of their U.S. counterparts will speak Spanish drawing on the Mexican cultural and rhetorical systems. However, outside the border area or with those unfamiliar with U.S. or Mexican cultural and rhetorical systems, serious misunderstandings occur on a daily basis. These misunderstandings do have ethical, cultural, economic, and often environmental impacts (Stewart & Bennett, 1991), which can be mitigated by cross-cultural adaptations.

REFERENCES

Adler, N. (2008). *International dimensions of organizational behavior*. Tampa, FL: Thomson Learning Center.

Alcalde, J. (1991). Differential impact of American political and economic institutions on Latin America. In Thompson, K. W. (Ed.), *The U.S. Constitution and the constitutions of Latin America* (pp. 97–126).

Bhabha, H. (2003). Statement for the *Critical Inquiry* Board. *Critical Inquiry*, *30*(2). Retrieved from http://criticalinquiry.uchicago.edu/issues/v30/30n2.Bhabha.html.

Flicke, U. (2002). *An introduction to qualitative research*. Thousand Oaks, CA: Sage Publications.

Grewal, D. S. (2008). *Network power: The social dynamics of globalization*. New Haven, CT: Yale University Press.

Grossberg, L. (1992). *We gotta get out of this place: Popular culture and postmodern culture*. New York, NY: Routledge.

Hall, E. T. (1976). *Beyond culture*. New York, NY: Doubleday.

Hall, E. T. (1981). *The silent language*. New York, NY: Doubleday.

Hall, E. T. (1983). *The dance of life*. New York, NY: Doubleday.

Hall, S. (1997). *Representation: Cultural representations and signifying practices*. New York, NY: Sage.

Hampden-Turner, C., & Trompenaars, A. (2000). *Building cross-cultural competence*. New York, NY: Wiley.

Hofstede, G. (2010). *Cultures and organizations, software of the mind* (3rd ed.). New York, NY: McGraw Hill.

House, R. J., Hanges, P. J., Javidan, M., Dorfman, P. R., & Gupta, V. (Eds.). (2005). *Culture, leadership, and organizations: The GLOBE study of 62 societies*. New York, NY: Sage Publications.

Kras, E. (1991). *Management in two cultures*. Yarmouth, ME: Intercultural Press, Inc.

Osland, J. S., De Franco, S., & Osland, A. (1999). Organizational implications of Latin American culture. *Journal of Management Inquiry*, *8*(2), 219–234. doi:10.1177/105649269982018

Participants, S. (2000). Responding to the legal obstacles to electronic commerce in Latin America: General Questionnaire. *Arizona Journal of International and Comparative Law*, *17*, 1–66.

Rosenn, K. (1988). A comparison of Latin American and North American legal traditions. In Tavis, L. (Ed.), *Multinational managers and host government interactions* (pp. 127–152). South Bend, IN: University of Notre Dame Press.

Stewart, E., & Bennett, M. (1991). *American cultural patterns: A cross-cultural perspective* (Rev. ed). Yarmouth, ME: Intercultural Press, Inc.

Sullivan, P., & Porter, J. E. (1998). *Opening spaces: Writing technologies and critical research practices*. Greenwich, CT: Ablex.

Sutch, P. (2001). *Ethics, justice, and international relations: Constructing an international community*. New York, NY: Routledge.

Swaak, M., de Jong, M., & de Vries, P. (2009). Effects of information usefulness, visual attractiveness, and usability on web visitors' trust and behavioral intentions. *IEEE International Professional Communication Conference*, (pp. 1-5_.

Swales, J. (1997). English as Tyrannosaurus Rex. *World Englishes, 16*, 373–382. doi:10.1111/1467-971X.00071

Tamanaha, B. Z. (2006). *Law as a means to an end: Threat to the rule of law*. Cambridge, UK: Cambridge University Press. doi:10.1017/CBO9780511511073

Tate, D. M. (2003). Cultural awareness: Bridging the gap between caregivers and Hispanic patients. *Journal of Continuing Education in Nursing, 34*(5), 213–217. Retrieved from http://www.jcenonline.com/view.asp?rID=4526.

Thatcher, B., Barrantes, E., Dalzell, A., Dong, Q., Ford, C., & Klein, S. Ramirez, L. (2007). Website analysis across cultures. In K. St.Amant (Ed.), *Linguistic and cultural online communication issues in the global age* (pp.124-142). Hershey, PA: Idea Group.

Thatcher, B. L. (2000). Writing policies and procedures in a U.S. and South American context. *Technical Communication Quarterly, 94*, 365–400. doi:10.1080/10572250009364706

Thatcher, B. L. (2010). Reading and writing new media across cultures: Issues of fit, reciprocity, and cultural change. In Kalmbach, J., & Ball, C. (Eds.), *Reading and writing new media*. Hampton Press Series New Dimensions in Computers and Composition.

Chapter 6
Organizational Theory and Communication across Cultures

ABSTRACT

This chapter analyzes organizational behavior and communication across cultures, using as a case study a cross-border project in hazmat transportation. It exemplifies the great complexity of global professional communications, equipping readers with both a model and application.

INTRODUCTION

This chapter explains the connections between organizational theory and intercultural professional communication. As much research has demonstrated (Adler, 2008), organizations vary significantly across cultures. In fact, most of the research about cross-cultural differences comes from the field of organizational behavior, including the significant studies of Hofstede (2010), Hampden-Turner and Trompenaars (2000), Adler (2008), and House, et. al. (2005). And most of these studies connect cultural differences in some fashion to communication. Consequently, discussing differences in organizational culture has the same breadth as discussing cultural differences, an endeavor that is well beyond this chapter. Further, much of the organizational theory developed by scholars for monocultural inquiry has become increasingly dependent on the local approaches (Weick, 2001) and has moved away from key intercultural variables such as structure, organization, and function and into more emic-heavy areas such as information flow, decision-making, and ecology. These latter models are too emic-based for the kinds of intercultural comparison I need to do in this chapter. Additionally, much work in intercultural professional communication is across organizations, not within organizations. Thus, most U.S. organizational theory is inadequate for this inquiry. Instead, this chapter lays out the complexities of intercultural professional communication across organizations in international contexts, looking at how the basic organizational structure, team work logic, and communication patterns influence intercultural professional communication. This approach is simple, but powerful, and can be used as a starting point for more sophisticated models of communication across organizations and cultures.

DOI: 10.4018/978-1-61350-450-5.ch006

To do this analysis and discussion, this chapter presents the case of a U.S.-Mexico cross-border Hazmat project that I directed for the EPA and which I reference in other chapters throughout this book. Next, the chapter grounds the organizational cultures of the agencies involved with the case using a simple organizational theory that was developed by the management expert Peter Drucker (1991). This theory exemplifies teamwork and organizational behavior using sports metaphors of baseball, football, and tennis doubles. Third, this chapter connects the organizational cultures and teamwork models with the eight value sets used throughout this book. This grounding and connection show intercultural professional communicators how to analyze the culture of organizations and their corresponding professional communication patterns in cross-cultural contexts. Finally, the chapter concludes by briefly discussing the roles of communication and information technology in facilitating change in organizational culture.

CASE OF US-MEXICO CROSS-BORDER HAZMAT PROJECT

In 2008, I directed a study funded by the EPA that evaluated the ability of Radio Frequency Identification (RFID) technologies to track the movement of hazardous materials between the manufacturing plants in Mexico and their disposal sites in the United States. According to NAFTA regulations, all hazardous materials used in the manufacturing of goods in maquiladoras (manufacturing plants) for sale in the United States must be returned to the point of their origin, which in most cases was United States. (This law has since changed, by the way.) Thus, the US-Mexico border region has some of the most concentrated flow of hazmat in the world, with raw chemicals moving from the United States into Mexico for the manufacturing processes, and the hazardous waste returning from Mexico to the United States for disposal. Unfortunately, due to a lack of regulation and oversight in the border region, some of the hazardous materials and waste ended up being dumped in clandestine sites, becoming a significant threat to the environment and health of border residents. In addition, because of the enhanced levels of hazmat flow, the chance of hazmat incident on the border is quite high.

The EPA hypothesized that RFID technologies could be used to track this flow. RFID technology is much like the barcode technology that we see in grocery stores only that instead of a barcode, there is a miniature radio transmitter (tag) that can send out a signal to a receiver when it is in a prescribed distance from that receiver. Many of these tags are smaller than a quarter, and, for example, some are placed in the ears of cows to track their movement. Some of the transmitters are self powered, while others receive their energy from the RFID receiver or transponder. The EPA believed that we could monitor the flow of hazmat if we placed RFID tags on the barrels and cartons of hazardous waste that were going/returning from the maquiladoras to their disposal sites in the United States. My job was to write the field test plan and then set up the technology field test of RFID for cross-border hazmat; I was charged with designing the study in life-like situations, tagging the cartons and drums as they left the maquiladoras and tracking them as they cross the border from Mexico into United States and eventually to their disposal.

For our discussion of organizational theory across cultures, the complexity of the project centered on the responsibility and roles of the U.S. and Mexican federal, state, and local authorities for hazmat transportation. Further, the transportation companies and maquiladoras were situated within this governmental complexity. There were at least seven federal and state agencies from the Mexican government and six from the US government that were responsible at some point and in some fashion for hazmat transportation. And in almost every case, the responsibilities and roles overlapped, often in ambiguous ways. Figure 1 is a Venn diagram of the organizations and their relations to each other.

This Venn diagram is perhaps rather ugly, but it compellingly demonstrates the multiplicity of roles and overlapping responsibilities, which is discussed next. This diagram also shows the need for communication between agencies, both across the border and between federal, state, and local agencies in either Mexico or the United States. All of these points demonstrate how both inter-organizational relations and cultures of organizations influence intercultural professional communication.

Perhaps the best way to explain these responsibilities and means of communication is to show the hazmat transportation route that was used for the technology field test, as shown in Figure 2.

Figure 2 shows, the test truck leaves a maquiladora in Ciudad Juárez's Bermuda Industrial Park area. It then travels south in Cd. Juárez until it picks up the Juárez-Casas Grande Highway where it travels west until it goes north on the Jeronimo Highway. It leaves Mexico and goes immediately into the U.S. Customs and Border Inspection Area. After that inspection, it drives 100 yards north into the joint FMCSA/NM State Police Inspection Station. (I define all these organizations next.) After that, it travels ½ mile to the disposal station. The return trip is the same except that the truck is inspected at the Mexican Port of Entry by Mexican Aduanas (Customs). Then it travels the same route as it returns to the maquiladoras in Cd. Juárez. The RFID systems' goal was to track the containers inside a semi-trailer for the entire round trip.

Throughout this round trip, there are multiple agencies responsible for the hazardous materials, truck, and trailer. At the maquiladora in Cd. Juárez, hazmat is regulated by Mexico's SERMANAT and PROFEPA. SERMANAT is Mexico's Secretaría de Medio Ambiente y Recursos Naturales or Secretary for the Environment and Natural Resources, which is roughly equivalent to the U.S.

Figure1. Venn diagram of cross-border hazmat relations

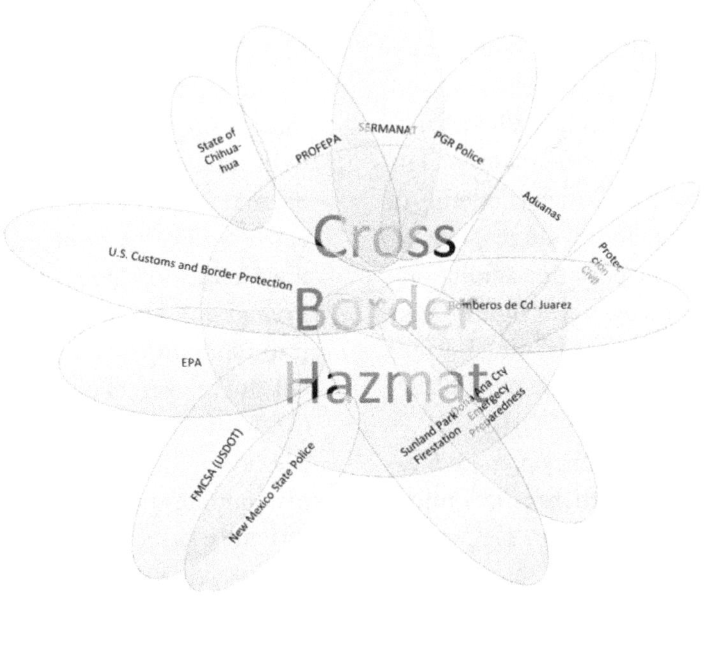

Figure 2. Map of hazmat route for RFID test

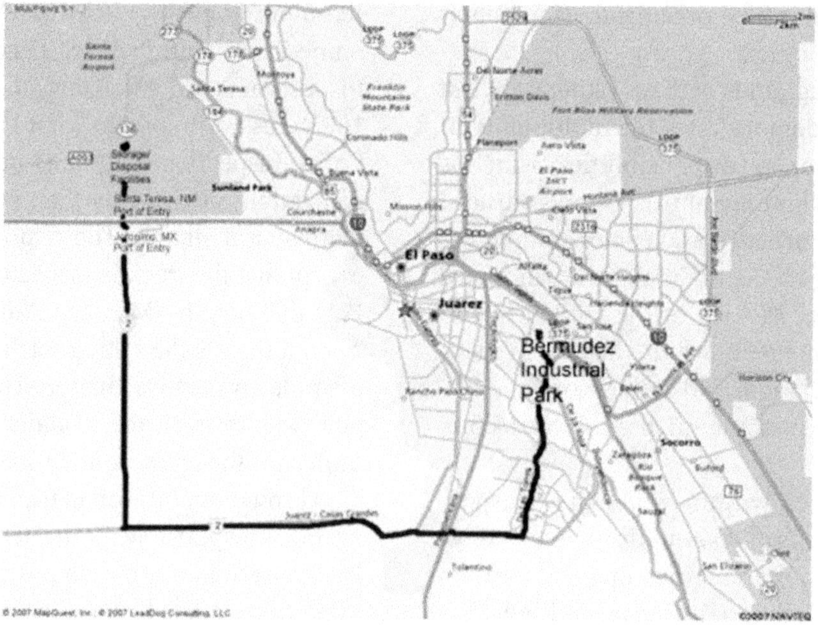

EPA. PROFEPA means the Procuraduría Federal de Protección al Ambiente or Attorney General for Environmental Protection. Essentially, Mexico splits the environmental responsibility into two agencies: SERMANAT, which sets up environmental laws and policies, while PROFEPA is charged with enforcing those laws. The EPA has both responsibilities. Thus, hazmat is regulated by both Mexican agencies while at the maquiladora. When traveling from the maquiladora to the U.S. border, hazmat is still regulated by SERMANAT and PROFEPA, but Mexico's Procuraduría General de La República and its Police (Federal Attorney General and Police force) are responsible for catching hazmat transportation violations. Thus, these three Mexican agencies significantly overlap with their hazmat responsibilities. Further, the Mexican state of Chihuahua is responsible for hazmat routes, while Protección Civil (Civil Protection) is responsible for emergency preparedness and the Cd. Juárez bomberos (Juárez Firestation) is responsible for hazmat cleanup. Regardless of these connections between the three federal agencies and Civil Protection and the fire station personnel, the three Mexican federal agencies rarely communicated with civil protection and fire station.

All of this Mexican responsibility changes when the truck-trailer passes into U.S. territory at the Santa Teresa, New Mexico Port of Entry. First, the truck driver must pass inspection at the U.S. Customs and Border Protection (CBP) Station. There officials are mostly worried about contraband and immigration status but have as their responsibility to enforce hazmat laws, as delineated by the EPA. However, in the case of a hazmat incidence or spill, the CBP officers will call the City of Sunland Park Fire Station and the County of Dona Ana Office of Emergency Preparedness who are charged with responding. If the spill impacts Mexico, CPB will also call the Cd. Juárez Fire station who will in turn call the Cd. Juárez Protección Civil. These phone calls to Mexico are "off the record" because there are no official lines but are a courtesy, worked about by "friendly neighbors." Once the truck leaves U.S. federal property, it is now regulated by State of New Mexico and Dona Ana county transportation policies. About ½ mile north of the CPB property, the truck has to undergo an inspection at the joint FMCSA/NM State Police Station. FMCSA is the U.S. DOT's Federal Motor Carrier Safety Association. This organization, as well as the NM State Police, inspects the drivers and his commercial driver's license, its insurance, and the truck, trailer, and containers for compliance to U.S. and New Mexico transportation laws, which have only minimal connection to the EPA. In a most unusual collaboration, this joint FMCSA/NM State Police Station is actually one building.

After leaving the FMCSA/NM State Police Station, the truck is under the regulations of the state of New Mexico, until it arrives at the disposal station where it then falls under the jurisdiction of the EPA, which has authority to dictate and enforce cradle-to-grave policies. Interestingly, however, the EPA and the FMCSA/NM Police Station do not exchange information about hazmat transportation policies and procedures.

As the truck leaves the disposal station, en route to Mexico, it must pass through Mexico's Aduanas or customs, where it is thoroughly inspected. However, unlike the U.S. CBP, Mexico's Aduanas has no policing power or authority. If inspection personnel note a violation on incoming or outgoing shipments, it does not have the power to stop, detain, and arrest. It can only issue citations, and then it has to call the Federal or municipal police, who could take a long time to respond.

In case of a hazmat incidence, the responsibilities are complicated but the same on both sides. On the U.S. side, the truck driver who has caused the hazmat incidence must call the EPA hotline, which in turn notifies the Dona Ana Call Center, which in turn, notifies the Sunland Park Fire Station, the Dona Ana County of Emergency Preparedness, and the New Mexico State Police. As mentioned, if the spill takes place in the Federal Port area, the CBP personnel will call the city fire station and county emergency preparedness team, but the CBP has sole responsibility for the port but does not have hazmat training or equipment. Thus, they "invite" the local personnel to help out. If the spill is outside the port, a citizen or local law enforcement must make the communication to the police or fire station. In this case, the county or city has responsibility for the hazmat incident and must "invite" appropriate personnel to help. At the incident, the New Mexico State Police are actually in charge, but the fire station personnel must contain the spill, while the Emergency Preparedness personnel secure the area.

Mexico is similarly organized according to federal, state, and municipality organizations, but a spill on the Mexican side that is close to the U.S. side invokes responses by both sides. Most border cities have Sister City agreements where fire station and emergency preparedness personnel are authorized to travel across the border to help. To be sure, a hazmat spill on the Rio Grande will affect both sides, regardless of where the original spill takes place. However, crossing the border complicates many things for both U.S. and Mexican personnel. First, many insurance companies and employers will not pay insurance or disability claims if problems take place on the other side of the border. Thus, visiting personnel from both sides risk their lives and livelihood to help the other side. Second, there are many problems of communication technologies, and third, there are often problems of language, training approaches, and culture.

Not surprisingly, maquiladoras and trucking companies have a very difficult time understanding and working with these thirteen organizations. Most of the problem results from overlapping responsibilities and problems of cross-agency communication in one nation, but this is doubly or triply compounded when not only crossing agencies but nation-states—between Mexico and the United States. In addition to the overlapping communication problems are the organizational structure and culture of each of the agencies. And there's a problem of working together, of how each agency assumes roles and types of collaboration. Finally, there is the problem of communication technologies—of the actual lack of electronic means for communicating. The next section describes these issues as it lays out simple theories of organizational culture, structure, collaboration, and communication and then connects those theories to the organizations using the eight etic borders or value sets.

MODELS OF ORGANIZATIONAL BEHAVIOR AND INTERCULTURAL PROFESSIONAL COMMUNICATION

This section lays out a simple framework of organizational behavior for analyzing the culture of these Mexican and US organizations. In the late 1980s to early 1990s, when it became apparent that many U.S. manufacturing organizations such as the automobile industries were not producing the quality demanded by consumers, and the Japanese organizations were exceeding consumer expectations, many management researchers began exploring the roles of collaborative work. Some researchers noted that perhaps one of the reasons for the much improved quality of Japanese products was due to their highly collaborative work. Consequently, many U.S. researchers and management specialists begin implementing collaboration at a level not seen before. Instead of the model of Ford Model T factory assembly line, which assumed little if no collaboration, many U.S. companies begin production in teams. Sensing that many of the researchers and practitioners drew on the Japanese models without considering the different models of teamwork and their connections to cultural values, Peter Drucker proposed researching the differences in teamwork models and collaboration. In a very terse column written in *the Wall Street Journal*, Drucker writes:

"Team building" has become a buzzword in American business. The results are not overly impressive. Ford Motor Co. began more than 10 years ago to build teams to design its new models. It now reports "serious problems," and the gap in development time between Ford and its Japanese competitors has hardly narrowed. General Motors' Saturn Division was going to replace the traditional assembly line with team work in its "factory of the future." But the plant has been steadily moving back toward the Detroit-style assembly line. Procter & Gamble launched a team-building campaign with great fanfare several years ago. Now P&G is moving back to individual accountability for developing and marketing new products.

One reason–perhaps the major one–for these near-failures is the all-but-universal belief among executives that there is just one kind of team. There actually are three–each different in its structure, in the behavior it demands from its members, in its strengths, its vulnerabilities, its limitations, its requirements, but above all, in what it can do and should be used for.

The first kind of team is the baseball team. The surgical team that performs an open-heart operation and Henry Ford's assembly line are both "baseball teams." So is the team Detroit traditionally sets up to design a new car.

The players play on the team; they do not play as a team. They have fixed positions they never leave. The second baseman never runs to assist the pitcher; the anesthesiologist never comes to the aid of the surgical nurse. "Up at bat, you are totally alone," is an old baseball saying. In the traditional Detroit design team, marketing people rarely saw designers and were never consulted by them. Designers did their work and passed it on to the development engineers, who in turn did their work and passed it on to manufacturing, which in turn did its work and passed it on to marketing.

The second kind of team is the football team. The symphony orchestra and the hospital unit that rallies round a patient who goes into shock at 3 a.m. are "football teams," as are Japanese auto makers' design teams. The players on the football team or in the symphony orchestra, like those on the baseball team, have fixed positions. The oboe never comes to the aid of the violas, however badly they might flounder. But on these teams players play as a team. The Japanese auto makers' design teams, which Detroit and P&G rushed to imitate, are football-type teams. To use an engineering term, the designers, engineers, manufacturing people and marketing people work "in parallel." The traditional Detroit team worked "in series."

Third, there is the tennis doubles team–the kind Saturn management hoped would replace the traditional assembly line. It is also the sort of team that plays in a jazz combo, the team of senior executives who form the "president's office" in big companies, or the team that is most likely to produce a genuine innovation like the personal computer 15 years ago.

On the doubles team, players have a primary rather than a fixed position. They are supposed to "cover" their team mates, adjusting to their teammates' strengths and weaknesses and to the changing demands of the "game."

Business executives and the management literature have little good to say these days about the baseball-style team, whether in the office or on the factory floor. There is even a failure to recognize such teams as teams at all. But this kind of team has enormous strengths. Each member can be evaluated separately, can have clear and specific goals, can be held accountable, can be measured–as witness the statistics a true aficionado reels off about every major-leaguer in baseball history. Each member can be trained and developed to the fullest extent of the individual's strengths. And because the members do not have to adjust to anybody else on the team, every position can be staffed with a "star," no matter how temperamental, jealous or limelight-hogging each of them might be.

But the baseball team is inflexible. It works well when the game has been played many times and when the sequence of its actions is thoroughly understood by everyone. That is what made this kind of team right for Detroit in the past.

As recently as 20 years ago, to be fast and flexible in automotive design was the last thing Detroit needed or wanted. Traditional mass production required long runs with minimum changes. And since the resale value of the "good used car"–one less than three years old–was a key factor for the new-car buyer, it was a serious mistake to bring out a new design (which would depreciate the old car) more than every five years. Sales and market share took a dip on several occasions when Chrysler prematurely introduced a new, brilliant design.

The Japanese did not invent "flexible mass production"; IBM was probably the first to use it, around 1960. But when the Japanese auto industry adopted it, it made possible the introduction of a new car model in parallel with a successful old one. And then the baseball team did indeed become the wrong team for Detroit, and for mass-production industry as a whole. The design process then had to be restructured as a football team.

The football team does have the flexibility Detroit now needs. But it has far more stringent requirements than the baseball team. It needs a "score"–whether it's the play the coach signals to the huddle on the field or the Mozart symphony everyone in the orchestra puts on his music stand. The specifications with which the Japanese begin their design of a new car model–or a new consumer-electronics product–are far more stringent and detailed than anything Detroit is used to in respect to style, technology, performance, weight, price and so on. And they are far more closely adhered to. In the traditional "baseball" design team every position–engineering, manufacturing, marketing–does its job its own way.

In the football team or the symphony orchestra, there is no such permissiveness. The word of the coach or the conductor is law. Players are beholden to this one boss alone for their orders, their rewards, their appraisals, their promotions.

The individual engineer on the Japanese design team is a member of his company's engineering department. But he is on the design team because the team's leader has asked for him -- not because the chief engineer sent him there. He can consult engineering and get advice. But his orders come from the design-team chief, who also appraises his performance. If there are stars on these teams, they are featured only if the score calls for a solo. Otherwise they subordinate themselves to the team.

Even more stringent are the requirements of the doubles team–the kind that GM's Saturn Division hoped to develop in its "flexible-manufacturing" plant, and that any such plant does indeed need. This team must be quite small, with five to seven members at most. The members have to be trained together and must work together for quite some time before they fully function as a team. There must be one clear goal for the entire team and yet considerable flexibility with respect to the individual member's work and performance. And in this kind of team only the team "performs"; individual members "contribute."

All three of these kinds of teams are true teams. But they are so different–in the behavior they require, in what they do best, and in what they cannot do at all that they cannot be hybrids. One kind of team can play only one way. And it is very difficult to change from one kind of team to another....

Teams, in other words, are tools. As such, each team design has its own uses, its own characteristics, its own requirements, its own limitations. Team work is neither "good" nor "desirable" -- it is a fact. Wherever people work together or play together they do so as a team. Which team to use for what purpose is a crucial, difficult, and risky decision that is even harder to unmake. Managements have yet to learn how to make it.

Wall Street Journal, Feb. 11, 1992.

For many reasons, Drucker's discussion and analysis are an excellent framework to evaluate the organizational culture in the cross-border hazmat projects and perhaps in many intercultural organizational contexts. First, the models are intuitively known to many readers, so the structure, interactions, and assumptions are easily understood and applied. Second, the simple models capture the overall breadth, but also complexity of organizational culture. And third, the models are as perhaps as close as we can get to a universal framework for comparing organizations. In other words, although these sports are a western product, they are still a useful, etic way of comparing the organizational cultures in intercultural contexts.

Table 1 summarizes these models in terms of organizational structure and task division; integration of roles and interaction; communication needs; time considerations; types of leadership; risk and trust; flexibility; procedural, affective, and substantive conflicts; and strengths and weaknesses. The following section then explores these issues in prose. The third section connects these models to the eight value sets.

Organizational Structure and Knowledge and Division of Task

One of the key differences in these three models centers on how they structure the performance of work. The baseball model assumes a high level of structure and specification, that is, each person

Table 1. Summary of team models

	Baseball	Football/Soccer	Tennis doubles
Knowledge of Task	Good for tasks that need little exploration, have a clear path, and need careful realization.	Good for tasks that are basically understood but path is not very clear.	Good for exploring ill-defined tasks. Path is not the issue.
Dividing & Sharing Tasks	Clear-cut, easy divisions with little sharing of responsibilities.	Some shared tasks and some individual tasks.	One general goal with completely shareable tasks.
Roles	Highly specialized roles	• Somewhat specialized roles but can be interchangeable. • Specialized teams.	Little specialization and continuous role backup.
Levels of Interaction & integration	• Little interaction and influence on others. • Complex integration	• Some interaction and mutual influence • General areas of integration	High levels of interaction and complete integration
Commun-ication needs	Clarity of task division and of integration.	Clarity of individual versus team responsibilities.	Clarity of interpersonal intelligence and involvement.
Time Considerations	• Some upfront time for task division. • A lot of finishing time to ensure full integration	• Mixture of upfront planning and finishing time. • Lots of separation and integration time.	• Lots of upfront time. • Very little finishing time. • Quickest if group understands each other well.
Types of leadership	Behind the scene leader who can organize division and integration.	Strong leader who can organize individual and team responsibilities and synergies.	• No leader—all lead together. • Good for those on equal playing field.
Risk/Trust	• A lot of trust that individual players will come through. • High risk. • Trusts needs to be developed over long period.	• Trust needed for general task areas; more trust needed for effective integration and backup. • Moderate risk.	• Built-in quality check even if others have to make up performance gap. • Risk based on the ability to work together.
Procedural Conflicts	• Dividing the task could take more time than really needed. • Disagreements about skills and task division could cause problems.	• Assigning the precise points of interactions for the general areas is difficult. • Effective procedural communication is a must.	• All have to be together to do the work→possibly massive amounts of discussion about procedures and points that don't matter that much.
Affective Conflicts	Good model for avoiding obvious personal conflicts.	Allows for mutual backup in case of affective problems.	Personalities can either make or break the project.
Substantive Conflicts	Weak at synergy because task division is usually not the most fruitful area.	Good at synergy.	Best model for ensuring substantial synergy for the project.
Strengths	• Good for clearly definable and divisible tasks. • Good for those with exceptional specialized skills.	• Allows for some separation and some mutual influence. • Flexible and structured.	• Built-in quality check, • Great for brainstorming. • Great for integrating styles and voices.
Weaknesses	• Difficult to integrate styles and voices well. • Quality check is often at the end when it is too late. • Complex structuring needed.	• Deciding boundaries and responsibilities is difficult, as well as assessing responsibility. • Fall through the cracks.	• Upfront time for meshing as a team could take more time than was anticipated. • Personalities can either make or break the project.
Suggestions	Good for those who cannot meet together but understand each other's strengths and can divide the project well.	Good for groups who can go in various general directions but who can communicate and assess accurately each member's responsibility.	Good for those who know each other well, have similar schedules, and can meet together more frequently.

is responsible for a very specific knowledge and task area, with very little overlap. In other words, in baseball, very rarely does a pitcher, catcher, or shortstop play other positions. They have highly specialized, unique roles. The baseball model is, therefore, very structured but not necessarily hierarchical. It is perhaps rather independent because it relies on clear separation of duties. This model is effective for tasks that need little help or synergy from other people, have a clear delineation of responsibilities, processes, and paths, and are best at very systematized realization of work, much like the Model T assembly line.

The tennis double models is just the opposite: there is little if no specialization of roles, for both players have to carry out all roles, such as serving, returning serve, volleying, passing, etc. Some players might have a better backhand or forehand, so some specialization is possible at unique moments, but the assumption is totally shared knowledge and performance of the task. The structure of the tennis organization is similarly flat, with no real hierarchy of roles. The tennis model is, therefore, is best suited to tasks that require a lot of interaction among members to produce synergy for the group. Synergy means the sum is greater than the whole, such as 2X2=6. There is little or no delineation of responsibilities; the processes are worked out through the group decision-making, and the paths are highly unique. Tennis doubles seems designed best for exploratory work.

The football model is situated between baseball and tennis doubles; it is flexibly structured with overlapping knowledge and tasks. In football, much like a hospital emergency room, there is some specialization of roles, but the team needs to approach the task as a team that is integrated but specialized. In other words, football has an offensive and defensive team, and in the offense, for example, there is a division between the line, running backs, receivers, and the quarterback, with each group having vaguely defined different tasks for each play, but the overall task is the play at hand. The hospital emergency room is similar because there are different kinds of doctors on hand (surgeons, anesthesiologists), accompanied by nurses, and other staff. Each sub-group has some defined responsibilities, but there is great interaction with the overall shared task of treating the patient. The football model is, therefore, the most complicated of the three models to actually carry out; and as Drucker explains, it is very important to keep the idea of "score" very clearly in mind. This is because the team members need to merge themselves with other team members at time, taking on different roles, while at the same time, carrying out specific functions without the help or perhaps even backup of other plays. For example, the quarterback in football is almost always the player throwing the ball, but he sometimes runs the ball, and sometimes other players can throw it. This tension between group and individual responsibility leaves room for ambiguity in terms of the task. For example, how much should the nurse know about anesthesia? Probably enough to alert the M.D. if there is a problem but not so much that the nurse can actually concoct the highly complicated cocktail of drugs that are given during a surgery.

Thus, the football model seems best suited to tasks that require some interaction among members to produce synergy for the group but also require specialization at very precise moments and knowledge areas. This is a complex structuring. The football model is actually a more powerful model, generally, as explained by Drucker, but it is more difficult to synchronize and then carry out.

It seems clear then that the three models have different assumptions about dividing and sharing the task. The baseball model is well suited to tasks that are clearly delineated and easily assigned to specific people with little sharing of responsibilities. Thus, this model favors exceptional talent. The football model is best for tasks that require some specialization and some group work, and favors an overall group effort with some specialization but lots of group work. The tennis doubles model seems suited to one general goal with no division of tasks.

Roles and Levels of Interaction and Integration

The three models assume very different roles and levels of interaction and integration. Baseball has highly specialized roles with clear-cut titles but very intricate and subtle connections between roles. For example, serious teams often study the batting patterns of key hitters, so pitchers know exactly where to pitch the ball, and the infield and outfield can vary their positioning ever so slightly to this knowledge. However, this change in positioning does not mean a change in roles; just the opposite: the roles become even more important because the pitcher needs to deliver the ball in the correct place for each key hitter so that the fielders can guess with better accuracy where the hit will go. Consequently, as compared to tennis doubles or football, there are relatively small levels of interaction and influence on others, but there is a very complex integration of roles to produce the right outcome. In other words, the baseball coach is a scientist or architect who studies the very complex performance of his team in their specific roles and matches that performance to the specialized roles of the players from the other team.

The tennis doubles assumes very little if no specialization of roles. In other words, each member can take on the role of the other member, and the nature of a good tennis doubles team is that ever-present approach of two players becoming one, a complete integration. The football model has somewhat specialized roles, but these roles can be interchangeable. There are specialized teams but roles are vague and integration is present at some moments but not at others.

General Communication Needs

The three models have different types of communication needs. The baseball models needs very clear communication of how the tasks are divided and the individual responsibilities of the team members. Break downs in communication and work occur when an individual does not understand or complete his or her specific task. A metaphor for this communication is an engineering specification sheet that delineates the precise features and functions of a technology. The tennis double model requires communications that clearly layout the methods of complete integration and involvement of the players. These communications assess the interpersonal, social, and emotional intelligence of the players as a method to best match players on each team. This approach also emphasizes the non-verbal and contextual cues that are so important to positioning on the court. The football model requires, perhaps, the most complex communications and training, for it must delineate individual versus group roles and responsibilities and always emphasize the goal is of the group. This delineation allows much space for things to fall through the crack. For example, when a football play fails, was it because the offensive line did not block, or the individual tailback ran the wrong way, or the quarterback and fullback did not sweep with them? Or can the quarterback call the team a success if his passing ratio is excellent but the team loses the game? Similarly, if someone dies in a hospital was it because the anesthesiologist gave the wrong mixture of medicines or the cleaning crew left areas infested with germs or the nurses were overwhelmed with other work and forgot to check on the patient? Or does it matter if someone died as long as the individual crew members made their money? Because of the ever-present tension of individual versus group responsibility, the football model requires well developed but flexible communications.

Time Considerations

The three models have different assumptions about how time is used. The baseball model requires much upfront or beginning time to correctly program the strict division of tasks, but once the game is in motion, it goes very quickly with little interruption. However, the baseball model also assumes lots of finishing time to integrate the different players together. Perhaps a writing metaphor could help here. Following a baseball model, an organization that is writing a grant proposal would have each of the writers write different sections of the grant, based on their individual expertise. The accountant would write the budget; the human resource person would write the section on collaboration; the engineer would write the technical specifications; and the project manager would write the time line. These different sections are easy to write individually, but someone has to integrate them into a coherent whole, which means a lot of finishing time. The baseball model works well for people who are not really familiar with each other but can come together at moments to work together.

Time for the football model is different. This model assumes a mixture of upfront planning and finishing time, but much time must be spent on both separating and integrating the roles and responsibilities of tasks. As a consequence, football also seems to be the most process-based or explicitly process orientation, with plays being drawn, analyzed, and evaluated. Following the writing metaphor, the football model would assume all of the writers for the grant project would gather to discuss individual and group responsibilities; some writers would compose specific parts but then get feedback from other members of the group; and then the group would gather together and as a group review the entire proposal but review it perhaps alone or in small groups. This model works well for people who can work individually and as a group.

The tennis doubles model requires much upfront time to get the players coordinated or synchronized; but once synchronized, the project can be finished very quickly. This model works well with people who understand each other extremely well can the very time-consuming if the players cannot synchronize or harmonize their relations.

Types of Leadership

Each model assumes a different kind of leadership. The effective baseball leader is the behinds-the-scenes leader who can organize the division of labor and individually motivate each player to do his or her best at their specific responsibilities. There is little need for public or overall group leadership. The football model requires a dynamic, perhaps stronger and more flexible leader. This leader needs to assign individual roles carefully but also explain how, when, and why the individuals need to work together or separately. This requires strong one-on-one leadership, tactical leadership, and public or group leadership. Then tennis double requires no leadership because each player shoulders the responsibilities equally.

Risk and Trust

Each model presents different issues related to risk and trust. Baseball players require a lot of trust that individual players will perform as expected because there is little backup for poor performance. For example, a pitcher can perform wonderfully but if his infield or outfield does not perform well, he will not have a good game. The same can be said of manufacturing automobiles–the person connecting the motor to the transmission cannot check the assembly of the motor itself and must assume that the motor assembling was carried about appropriately. In this model, trust needs to be developed, often over a long period of time. This is actually the highest risk model of teamwork because the low levels of interaction prohibit the checking of performance by team members. Using the grant writing metaphor, each member of the team needs to trust that the other person did the work correctly.

The tennis model has complete integration of roles and tasks; thus, it has a built-in quality check even if others have to make up performance gap. This risk is based more on the ability to work together rather on individual performance. Using the car manufacturing context, the person connecting the motor to the transmission knows the motor was assembled well because he actually took part in that assembly. Or the grant writer working on the grant budget knows the technical specifications are correct because she was working alongside the engineer who developed and wrote those specifications.

The football model needs some trust for general task areas; but more trust is needed for effective integration and backup. In other words, a quarterback needs to count on his entire line to protect him generally, but he might have to trust one specific lineman to block a highly talented defensive player. And the line needs to have confidence that the quarterback can complete the plays. From the automobile context, the person connecting the motor to the transmission trusts that the motor is assembled well, not because he participated in the actually assembling but because he understands what a correctly assembled motor looks like. He will also count on an overall leader that checked that motor assembly before it arrived at his station. This model has to trust that people will perform a team or individual function appropriately. There is moderate risk for the football model.

Flexibility and Adaptability

The three models have different levels of flexibility and adaptability. In many ways, the baseball model is perhaps the least flexible because the roles are so specialized and integration takes so long that adapting to change is very difficult. This is what Drucker meant by inflexibility of the baseball model. However, the baseball model has the advantage of specialized roles and careful integration, so if a role is changed and rationalized well into the process, the team can adapt and change. The tennis doubles model seems very adaptable, and its strength resides in its ability to adapt almost seamlessly to the ever-changing situation on the court. However, this adaptation is based on the re-occurring features of the everyday tennis game and court. It would be interesting to see if tennis doubles players could have the same level of adaptability when they play another sport because their adaptability was based on the specific context of tennis, with its implicit cues for behavior and action. The football model is a mixture. Because it has some group elements, much like the tennis doubles, it has adaptability built into the system. However, one of its major problems for adaptation is the need to spell out roles and responsibilities, for it often requires thoroughly analyzing the new process with careful attention to points where interactions might allow for problems in assessing performance and responsibility.

Procedural, Affective, and Substantive Conflicts[1]

Each model of team presents different problems of procedures, of the process of doing the work. Often the baseball model suffers from conflicts of dividing the task because the players and leader can disagree about defining the skills and tasks and assigning them to individual players. This task division and integration can take a long time. The football model often suffers from problems of assigning the precise points of interactions for individual versus group work. For example, sometimes, two members will block for one play, while at other times, a player is on his own. Because this model is so process-centered, it is critical to develop explicit procedural communications. In the tennis doubles model, all the team players have to be together to do the work. This can possibly lead to massive amounts of discussion about procedures and points that don't matter that much. For example, when writing a grant using the tennis doubles models, all members of the team would be present for all of the work. This has great potential for wasting time.

The three models differ in their handling of personality, emotional, and interpersonal issues. Because it so carefully divides roles, and the levels of integration and interaction are low, the baseball model is best for bad personalities or avoiding obvious personal conflicts. The players can simply avoid each other and do their jobs. The football model allows for mutual backup in case of affective problems, but it can produce affective conflicts when the ambiguity of individual-group responsibilities can damage performance. The tennis doubles model can be a disaster or scintillating success because personalities can either make or break the project. There is no cushion or room for problem people.

Substantive conflicts simply means disagreements over the content or performance of the group. Substantive conflicts can actually be productive because they are often the means, if handled correctly, of producing great synergy. The baseball model is the worst at substantive conflicts because the high levels of task division mean that people will not interact productively over disagreements. There is simply not enough shared knowledge. The tennis doubles model is best at ensuring substantial synergy for the project because the team members constantly work together and feed off each other. The football model is good at synergy at times, but it's weak in substantive conflicts because of the ambiguity of responsibility.

Strengths, Weaknesses, and Suggestions

The baseball model is good for clearly definable and divisible tasks and great for those teams that have exceptionally specialized skills that can be fine tuned for specific tasks. But in the baseball model, it is difficult to integrate different performance styles well. The quality check is often at the end when it is too late, and it needs very complex structuring. This is why many organizations have moved away from the baseball model.

The tennis doubles model has a built-in quality check, is great for synergy, and great at integrating performance styles. But it is also most prone to absolute failure because of personality conflicts and requires much upfront time for meshing the players. This model has been difficult to develop in the United States and other countries with high levels of individualism.

The football model has great flexibility, allowing for some separation and some mutual influence. It is structured, but not overly so, allowing for some quality checks on performance. However, in the football model, deciding the boundaries and responsibilities of individual versus group responsibilities is difficult. Things simply fall through the cracks. It probably requires the most explicit communications. As Drucker explains, this is the most used team model around the world.

The baseball model is generally good for teams who, for a variety of reasons, cannot meet together but understand each other's strengths and can divide the project well. The tennis doubles is good for teams who know each other well, have similar schedules, and can meet together more frequently. The football model is good for groups who can go in various general directions but who can communicate and assess accurately each member's responsibility.

As exemplified in many chapters in this book, this section will now describe the instructional design of the four manuals based on the eight intercultural values sets.

CONNECTING TEAMS MODELS TO INTERCULTURAL VALUES SETS AND CROSS-BORDER HAZMAT CASE

This section uses the discussion of the team models to evaluate the connection between culture, professional communication, and organization with the case of the cross-border hazmat. This connection explains clearly how professional communication across organizations needs to be grounded specifically in both the values sets of that target culture and their connections to the team models.

I/Other

This value set obviously correlates very strongly with the team models. Baseball exemplifies the rationalized independence of individualistic cultures, while tennis doubles exemplifies the implicit but strong mutual dependence in collective cultures. The football model ranks in the middle.

This correlation is fairly strong throughout the research and literature in cross-cultural organizational behavior (see, for example, House, et.al, 2005). This was precisely the point that Drucker was making—forcing a tennis doubles team model onto U.S. organizations was not going to produce the same outcome as the tennis doubles in Japanese cultures, which generally has high levels of collectivism.

The cross-border hazmat project was not an exception to this correlation. For example, the Mexican organizations were much more interdependent and centrally organized than the U.S. organizations. When we were carrying out the test, we planned to carry eight 55 gallon drums of water (to represent chemicals) and eight cubic yard boxes filled with newspapers (to represent solid wastes–we could not carry rags or dirt across the border). Thus, we had to obtain import permits for this cargo from both the United States and Mexico to do the test; the process for obtaining these permits was very different, showing overt differences in organizational culture and team functioning.

About two months before the test started, at a joint U.S.-Mexico Port of Entry Advisory Meeting, I meet with the directors of the Santa Teresa, New Mexico Port and the Jeronimo, Chihuahua Port to talk about the need for these permits. I also met with the Aduanas Director for the Ciudad Juárez area. All three said "no problem." When the time came to get the permits and conduct the tests, I walked into the CPB Office at Santa Teresa and notified them of the test that was going to take place in three days. They actually told me I did not need to fill out the import manifest for the RFID test; all I needed to do was identify the driver and trucking company, and they would inspect the cargo normally, but there was no need for documenting the cargo itself. This seemed much like the baseball model because they divided this task very simply and rationally with little thought about how the test would influence other members of the border community. This decision was made at the Santa Teresa Office, the smallest office in the El Paso Region, without consulting the region's CPB director, although she knew of the test and had signed off on the test plan.

The Mexican side was very different. The Jeronimo Port director, who worked for the Mexican Aduanas, was very easy to work with, but she officially asked permission from the area Aduanas director about documenting the cargo. Although he was aware of the test, had also signed off on the test plan, and was acquainted with test team, he said that documentation was necessary. He was worried about reconciling the data for the port: allowing the truck to pass without documentation would end up as a discrepancy between the number of trucks passing through and the documentation numbers; and his superiors would want an explanation of this discrepancy. This was frustrating for us, but we played by the rules, so we submitted the documentation for the cargo manifests. However, it became even more complicated because we had to submit the request through a private vendor who then forwarded the request to the centralized Aduanas Office in Mexico City for final approval. They, of course, had no knowledge of our project, so they were suspicious. They talked over the phone to the private vendor who was facilitating the process and then to the Cd. Juárez Aduanas Director. The Aduanas personnel in Mexico City decided to take a few days to think about their decision and actually called the private vendor to talk about the project. Meanwhile, we had to begin the test. We then put some pressure on the Aduanas, having his U.S. counterpart talk to him, but he simply shut down the test and refused to let any of it happen on the Mexican side.

When that happened, we did two things: we made a list of all of the people who had flown in from Washington D.C. and Columbus, Ohio and who were waiting on the project to start; and we listed all of the Mexican agencies, both state and federal, who had approved the project and who would be upset by his canceling it. We then sent the Aduanas area director the list, and my EPA colleague (a Mexican national) and I made an appointment to see him. Both of us traveled to his Juárez office where we eventually won his approval, but only after we decided not to let the trucks run through Juárez, where the Federal Police might stop them and then inquire about who gave the truck permission to conduct the test. We decided to run it outside the city limits and only through the countryside where the military was in charge. At this time, Juárez was witnessing extreme narco-violence with 10 murders a day. We then submitted the import documentation, which was approved in Mexico City only because the Cd. Juárez Aduanas director authorized it.

The major difference in the U.S. and Mexican organizational culture for this project was one of independence and dependence. Despite what many think about U.S. Federal bureaucracies, the CPB office was independent enough to make the decision not to require cargo documentation. They were much like the baseball manager who could rationally divide up the tasks assuming an independence among people involved. On the other hand, the Mexican organizations are much like the tennis doubles because each move on the part of one organization was assumed to immediately affect the other organizations, and all the organizations needed to be synchronized in order for the project to be carried out. This collective approach was due to the many, many levels of collective, dependent bureaucracy in Mexico: the port director had to ask for permission from area director; we had to obtain the import documentation from a centralized office in Mexico City; we could not drive through Cd. Juárez for fear of having the Aduanas director looking strange to the Federal Police; we used social pressure, showing how he would look bad in front of all these people who had traveled all that distance; and it took a personal visit from two well-know acquaintances of the Aduanas director to persuade him to allow the test.

The more collective approach of the Mexican organizations and the more independent or individualistic approach of the US organization have significant ramifications for professional communication, for knowledge management, and for organizational flexibility and adaptability. The first significant communication difference is that of formality and protocol. I obtained approval from the US CBP organization through an informal, oral form. On the other hand, we had to fill out numerous formal written documents from the Mexican side in order to obtain approval. Consequently, following the baseball model, the US organizations were able to focus on policies and procedures regardless of the leadership or people involved in the situation. In other words, the policies and procedures were developed and enacted to be free of the social influence. On the other hand, following the tennis doubles model, the Mexican organizations had to work in tandem with each other, meaning that the project had to map on to the existing social hierarchy in order for it to take place. As explained in the next section, these differences influence the adaptability of the organizations.

Rules Orientation and Status

The cross-border hazmat project demonstrated rather dramatically some of the conventions and contradictions between universal and particular values in organizations. As described more thoroughly in Chapter Two and exemplified throughout this book, one of the seeming contradictions in this value set is that universal cultures tend to have fewer laws, which are loosely defined and are based mostly on precedence but are to be applied forcefully and equally across the groups. These laws are usually explicitly written and publicized. On the other hand, particular cultures have many more rules because the rules vary according to relations, ascribed values, and context, but these laws are usually implicit, and their enforcement is based on the discretion of the authorities. From this view, the tennis doubles seems much more like the particular and ascriptive culture because it is flexible and based on the evolving context and relations; and baseball seems to be universal because the roles are rationalized and players are evaluated on their performance for their specific responsibility, regardless of the social context.

However, in the case of the hazmat project, the U.S. organization was more flexible and the Mexican organization was more rigid in some things, and in other ways the reverse was true. Perhaps the reader thinks this difference is simply because the project was based out of the United States. There might be some truth to that fact, but it truly was a joint project, fully supported by both U.S. and Mexican personnel; and we had almost an equal number of Mexican nationals on the team. In fact, the transportation company was Mexican and the largest, most well known, and most respected company in Cd. Juárez.

The difference in flexibility, however, points to interesting contradictions in the particular and universal orientations and shows a strong weakness in the baseball and tennis doubles models. As described in many chapters of this book, universalism usually means rationalizing, making visible, and emphasizing the process, a strategy that strongly correlates with achievement orientation, which is a process-heavy value. These processes are universalized so as to avoid human influence, which is anathema to achievement oriented cultures but the core of ascriptive cultures. Particularism usually means emphasizing the power relations, which are rarely explicit but always functioning. Further, particularism often emphasizes understanding and orchestrating the implicit ascribed relations that need to come together to bring about the realization of the goal. Most frequently, these relations downplay the mechanical or material conditions that are used in the processes, or they connect these conditions to the social relations. In ascriptive cultures, the process is not highlighted or made transparent because the process transparency is not nearly as important or relevant to the transaction because the transaction depends much more on the power players in the process itself. This is mostly because the power players are the process, that is, the person develops the process his or her own way, yielding an uniqueness and artistry that is very common in particular cultures.

This was precisely the distinction between the U.S. and Mexican organizational approach to the problem of import documentation. The U.S. officials did not really care much about my social relations; they knew me and that I was a professor at NMSU, and they knew other members of the team. They looked more carefully at the material process–how risky was it to not document the importing of water and newspapers? In the end, they deemed it not that risky, so permission was given rather quickly. On the other hand, this project was caught between the power players from the Mexican organizations. It did not matter that the Port Director at Jeronimo knew us and had worked with members of the project team for more than a year. She was not as important as the central Aduanas office in Mexico City and the Federal Police and Army patrolling Cd. Juárez. Thus, the project was finally accomplished because we allowed the Aduanas director to customize the actual material process so that it matched the ascribed power of the Mexican organizations. Once this match was in place, we had our permission, a perfect example of particular orientation.

This also shows the inflexibility of the more tennis model and flexibility of the baseball model. This project was truly unique–nothing like it had ever been done. From this angle, it was "outside the box" for both U.S. and Mexican organizations. However, in this case, the U.S. organization adapted more quickly, while the Mexican organization adapted very slowly and painfully. This difference had much to do with the different rules orientation: the U.S. evaluated the project based on their systematized rules and procedures for processing cargo through the ports, while the

Mexican officials evaluated the project based on how it matched their power positions; and because it was unique, it took some time to situate it correctly.

However as described later, once the Mexican organizations had fine tuned this project within their existing social structure, the process went very quickly, much like the tennis doubles team. Once we had attained their permission, they only minimally inspected us at their ports, while the US officials rigorously inspected our driver and his cargo 16 times, reflecting more of the baseball model's inflexibility in its systematized approach to the task.

The more particular-ascriptive approach of the Mexican organizations and the more universal-achievement approach of the US organization have significant ramifications for professional communication, for knowledge management, and for organizational flexibility and adaptability. First, professional communicators working in Mexico must understand the communication approaches that correspond to the particular-ascriptive elements of Mexican organizational culture. This approach centers on adapting the project to the specific circumstances and social relations of the Mexican organizations. To accomplish this, professional communicators must understand the ascriptive powers of the people involved and leverage those powers appropriately. This matching a project to social powers will take considerable time much like the time it takes for tennis doubles teammates to learn to work with each other. As will be summarized in most of these sections, knowledge management in the particular-ascriptive organization depends intimately on the implicit policies and procedures that are based on how the power structures have set them up to manage their relations. However, in the end, the particular-ascriptive organization was more flexible than the universal-achievement organization.

Professional communicators working in the United States must understand the communication approaches that correspond to the universal-achievement elements of U.S. organizational culture. This approach centers on having the project adhere to specific policies and procedures, regardless of the social relations and circumstances. Professional communicators must understand the universal logic of the policies and procedures themselves and work their project into them. This matching a project to universalized policies and procedures will usually be easy in the beginning, perhaps because of the connection between universal and specific values. But like the baseball model, there is usually much finishing time to make sure the project works well with the in-place policies and procedures. Knowledge management in the more universal-achievement organization is based on policies and procedures that are well publicized, are the standard criteria for evaluating performance, and are integrated into everyday activities regardless of the leadership or social relations. This approach makes for upfront flexibility in gaining access to organization, but significant difficulty in changing how the rationalized policies and procedures are working.

Public/Private Trust and Degree of Involvement

This value set assess the degree of involvement across different spheres of life, usually involving a public/private divide and trust. As shown by the circles in Chapter Two, the specific orientation is characterized by the ease in which a person can enter the relationship from a public sphere, which is shown by the dashed line, but once in, that relationship is usually sphere based and rarely crosses over. For example, in the specific model, friends made at school do not have automatic access to your fridge or to your friendships in other places. Further, it is very difficult to enter the small, private world signaled by the small center circle.

The diffuse circle shows that it is very difficult to pass from the public into a relationship, signaled by the thick line of the outer circle. And there is a small public/private mixture area between the two circles, but once inside the larger private sphere (signaled by dashed smaller circle), the relationship crosses boundaries, and there is no distinguishable private self. Diffuse communication patterns emphasize approaches that address the whole person in all aspects and dimensions, including social hierarchies. As a result, persuasion does not require salesmanship, but rather a long-term establishment of interconnected, interpersonal values. Consequently, diffuse patterns seem (to specific people) very indirect and to circle around the point, because diffuse communicators need to understand the whole person before getting to the point. Specific communication patterns easily section off people into different groups: students, faculty, staff, alumni, parents, and so on. Specific communications are also direct and inductive, stating the main point quickly and then supporting it.

Thus, specific orientation is atomistic or partial, only seeing one aspect of a person's life. And these relations do not cross boundaries, but are clearly separated. I have played much tennis doubles, both in high school and college. And I learned that it takes a long time to trust your tennis doubles partner, and there is great fear in changing partners. The same could be said of any team that is more collective such as basketball. There is great fear of outsiders, and trust only develops slowly and in diffuse ways–through holistic knowledge.

On the other hand, the levels of independence and rationalized roles and relations of the baseball model permit a much quicker movement of players. And players are not viewed holistically, that is, from all their character attributes; rather, they are viewed very specifically on how they can carry out their specific responsibility such as pitching, catching, hitting, etc. Thus, even though there is more risk in having the baseball team fail, there is much more trust in welcoming new players. On the other hand, collective and particular teams such as tennis doubles very carefully select teammates because they have to trust each member of that team extensively. But once those team members are selected, there is an extreme amount of trust in each other.

This was perhaps one of the most significant organizational differences for the cross-border project, with most of the problems occurring because of trust issues. One of the major differences was the strong lack of public trust that the Mexican officials had of people not directly involved in their organization; and at times, a strong mistrust in their own agencies. This has connections to corruption as well, which happens obviously on both sides of border. The Mexican Aduanas officials were so worried that their Port of Entry customs agents would succumb to corruption that they only hired people from outside the area to work at the ports, and then they would rotate these people to another assignment very quickly, generally every six months or at most a year. They theorized that people from the outside would not have the intimate social connections, and therefore be less prone to corruption. For example, when we finally got funding to do the project, we immediately begin working with the Jeronimo and Santa Teresa port authorities. However, the Jeronimo port authorities graciously explained that if the project were to take place six months later, they would probably be working at another port. They would "tell the next director about their approval of the project." But they also mentioned that their approval would have "little relevance." Thus, we actually started with one port director, then a second came in, and we finally worked with a third director, all within the space of a year. This director was from the southern states of Mexico who actually had little knowledge of the border but was an excellent learner. The constant rotation of personnel made it very difficult to keep the work going.

On the other hand, the port director at Santa Teresa, New Mexico was the same throughout the project, but that did not really matter, because the policies and procedures were so routinized–rationalized, made visible, and evaluated–that the director did not really matter. In other words, their systems were so well developed that corruption would become visible in the processes and then corrective action could be taken.

The issue of trust was key in the project. When the area Aduanas director decided to shut down the project, it purportedly was because he did not trust us. He asked: "How do I know that you will not be hiding drugs in the drums or cardboard boxes? How do I know that you are not working for the cartels?" When he asked me this, I was a bit dumbfounded, but I did respond that I was an NMSU professor working with an EPA project, and that we had high-level approval from Mexican authorities. This did not placate him much, so he asked us to explain again why and how the project was going to take place. He learned from our very detailed test plan, integration of the border stakeholders, and our trying to follow all his rules that he could trust us. But it was a real stretch for him.

On the other hand, when I received permission from the Santa Teresa CPB office to do the test without import documentation, I did not even talk to the port director that day. I talked to the person at the desk who was handling routine affairs. He went back and received permission from the director, whom I knew, but the director trusted him to tell me, and the director trusted me. However, even though we had been permission to not have documentation, the U.S. CPB personnel rigorously inspected our truck driver in his 16 entrances to the United States over a period of three days, while the Mexican Aduanas director authorizing a simple "hand waving" when our known truck driver passes through, both of which perfectly exemplify differences in specific and diffuse conceptions of trust.

Another problem related to the diffuse orientation was the duplication of efforts as a way to ensure trust and reliability. Another surprise came at the Mexican customs area when the truck was entering Mexico from the United States. In an effort to curb corruption, the Mexican Aduanas actually had two inspection stations in place: one was staffed by Mexican Aduanas personnel, but another one, duplicating the exact inspection policy and procedures as the first, was in place. This second one was a private vendor contracted by the Central Aduanas Office in Mexico City, and they reconciled their inspection data regularly to look for discrepancies. When we tried to enter Mexico with the truck for the first time, we passed easily through the Aduanas inspection, for the Port Director waived the driver through easily. However, the port director had not told the private vendor about the test or us. Thus, she had to rush down to the end of the inspection facilities to relay that information to them. The private inspection company inspected all of the cargo, just as it would with any other border crossing. It then took us about a ½ an hour to figure out how to document the discrepancy between the Vendor's inspection data, which included our test truck, and the Aduanas inspection data, which did not. The Jeronimo Port Director decided that she could annotate the books to justify the discrepancy and acknowledged she was taking a risk in doing so, but because she wanted the test to be carried out without further problem, she was willing to take that risk. On the other hand, the U.S. CPB personnel had one station because they were comfortable with the policies and procedures.

Finally, there was duplication in hazmat laws and compliance, which I have explained before. First, hazmat laws and compliance is split among four agencies in Mexico: SERMANAT, which sets policies; PROFEPA, which is the prosecutorial arm; Aduanas, which carries out the inspections but has no power to prosecute or arrest; and the Federal Police, who have power to detain and arrest. On the U.S. Side, the EPA sets laws and can prosecute offenders but cannot detain or arrest. CPB, which inspects, can detain and arrest, according to EPA and FMCSA/U.S. DOT laws. The EPA can use Federal Marshalls, the FBI, state police, or city or sheriff's departments.

Another interesting difference connected to issues of trust in specific and diffuse cultures is the handling of money. When carrying out an official government transaction in Mexico, the money for the transaction is usually paid to a national or licensed bank that has nothing to do with the government organization. The bank usually has a branch in the building as immigration or customs, but it is fully a separate entity. For example, when we paid for the import documentation for the drums and boxes, I wired money to the private Mexican important vendor, who wired it to a national bank, which sent the receipt to the customs official in Mexico City who then gave final approval for the documentation. In order to combat corruption, this separation of money and regulatory officials is very common in Mexico. When transacting business at the U.S. Ports, I simply pay the CPB person who is handling the transaction.

These are two huge differences in organizational culture as it relates to trust. Following the baseball model, U.S. organizations trusted their systems and processes, while following the tennis doubles model, the Mexican organization trusted very diffuse knowledge of the people and situations. These differences have important ramifications for communication patterns, knowledge management, and the learning and adaptability of the organizations. The U.S. organizations are very sphere and process-oriented, trusting their specific processes to carry out the work without discrepancies but only in their rationalized contexts of activity. Thus, following their specific value orientation, communications for these U.S. organization were direct and focused on the very specific context of the activity. Managing knowledge seemed very easy in the U.S. organization if the new knowledge fits their existing framework of policies and procedures. And if it doesn't fit, you can re-analyze and refit, regardless of who is running the organization.

On the other hand, the Mexican organizations seem to value the diffuse approach, that is, they needed to ground the test and our test team holistically, understanding who we were, what our specific plans were, and why we were doing it. Like the tennis doubles model, this took a lot of upfront time to accomplish, but once it was synchronized, things flowed very smoothly. Thus, following their diffuse orientation, the Mexican personnel required diffuse communications, which seemed out of focus or even unnecessary for many of the US on the team. The concept of knowledge is very interesting in a diffuse organization, for knowledge is so intimately wrapped up with the people who run the organization, that managing knowledge actually means managing the social relations across the organizations. Consequently, the Mexican organizations seemed really onerous in their flexibility at first, because of the difficulty of managing the social relations of the test itself. Following the tennis doubles models, once the team and the test were synchronized into the system, it became very flexible and easy to work with.

Power Distance

As explained in many Chapters in this book, Power Distance measures how inequality is handled in communications. In high power distances cultures, there is unequal, centralized distribution of power, acceptance of authority, high levels of overseeing, and top-down communication styles. Low power distance cultures expect more mutual interdependence between subordinate and authority. Communications between superior and subordinate tend to be more consultative, with the superior acting as perhaps someone with more knowledge, but not in reality being in a higher position. Authority is something to be used only as more of a last resort rather than the explicit framework for the communication situation. Subordinates are not afraid to disagree with superiors; in fact subordinates are often a source of good feedback for decisions is that the superiors need to take. In low power distance cultures, communicators tend to make the communications less formal as a way to ease the feelings of inequality in the communication situation.

As explained in the previous three sections, the Mexican organizations tended to have very high levels of power distance. This was evident in the centralized organizational structure of government agencies, with most of them having to go to the federal headquarters in Mexico City for final decision-making. In addition, as explained in the previous three sections, the Mexican personnel were very careful about lines of authority and power relations. On the other hand, the US personnel seemed grounded in a lower power distance value set, for they treated us as equals and did not need to go to their authorities for many decisions. However, there are interesting contradictions in this value set, which I think are important to point out.

When my EPA colleague and I visited the area Aduanas director in Ciudad Juárez, we entered a very large building and had to talk to the secretary who was behind a glass wall much like you see in banks and currency exchanges. This was definitely a symbol of authority. When we were invited in to see the director, we walked on marble floors and elegant woodworked walls. His office was just as luxurious as the hallways. Once we sat down and respectfully addressed him as the authority of the project, all of his high power distance strategies disappeared. He addressed us as equals and friends. Both my EPA colleague and I had doctorates and respected positions in the community. However, although clearly he was the authority in this situation, he treated us as equals and asked for our opinions, explaining the nature of his dilemma, of having the federal police in the streets and his worry about this truck being stopped by the police without proper documentation. He then simply asked us if it were possible to carry out the test outside the city limits of Ciudad Juárez. (I was guessing that a lot of the social pressures we had exerted on him previously were indeed working.) We said yes. Thus, although it was clear throughout this study that the lines of authority are very important for the Mexican organizations, once I showed respect and then connected well with the authority, the high power distance structure seemed to melt into low power distance.

The opposite seemed to happen with the US authorities. For example, although the US authorities said that are truck driver and his tractor-trailer needed no import documentation for the simulated hazmat cargo, they rigorously inspected the driver and cargo when officially entering the United States. And they rigorously inspected that driver the next 15 times as he entered the United States for the test, which took on average 90 minutes for each inspection. On the other hand, after receiving the very difficult approval of the Mexican Aduanas director, he instructed his personnel to not inspect the driver and his truck during the test, and that driver easily went through the check points the next 15 times.

Consequently, it seemed that the high and low power distance values reversed themselves for this test. Although the US personnel quickly gave us permission to conduct the test without documentation, they rigorously inspected our driver, while the Mexican personnel rigorously interrogated our test our procedures but then allowed for simple passing after that. This case helps develop perhaps a more etic approach to power distance: perhaps the better question is when and how authority is either emphasized or downplayed depending on the circumstances.

The reversing roles of power distance in both the Mexican and U.S. organizations have significant ramifications for professional communication, for knowledge management, and for organizational learning and adaptability. Communicators working with these US federal organizations need to be prepared to respect the systematic design of the policies and procedures, and even though the CBP personnel are most likely to be friendly and open, the system itself has incredible power that is often beyond the personnel involved. This simply means that changing personnel is easy, but changing the policies and procedures is very difficult, and thus, these types of organization will probably show corresponding inflexibility in their policies and procedures. Managing knowledge is most likely divorced from people, and new knowledge is most likely evaluated in light of current policies and procedures.

Communicators working with these Mexican organizations need to be prepared to respect the implicit but deeply rooted power structures, that Mexican personnel are most likely to be very attuned to these structures, and the power of the social structures often trump the policies and procedures of the organization. This simply means that changing policies and procedures is easy, but changing the power structures is very difficult, and thus, these types of organization will probably show corresponding inflexibility in their social hierarchies. Managing knowledge is most likely intimately connected with people, and new knowledge is most likely evaluated in light of personnel and the social hierarchies.

Context in Communication, Sources of Virtue and Guidance, and Time

This section combines the value sets of context in communication with the sources of virtue and time. First, perhaps the reason why the power distance values reversed themselves in my cross-border case is because of the high context communication values of the Mexican personnel and the low context communication values of the US personnel. As explained throughout this book, high and low context assesses the role of the context in the communicative interaction. Low context means that the meaning of the communication resides primarily in the explicitly coded part of the communication, not in the surrounding context. Thus, there is great focus on the accuracy of the explicitly coded text. There is a high attention to detail and low attention to intention. On the other end, high context communication assumes a strong reliance on the contextual and visual cues for the meanings of communications. There is low attention to detail and high attention to intention.

In the case of the cross-border hazmat study, the most important unit of analysis is attention to intention or attention to details. It seemed clear that once the Mexican Aduanas director noticed that our intentions for the test were real and sincere, and that we were working with him, he paid little attention to the details of rigorously inspecting the trucks as they left the United States for Mexico. On the other hand, the US personnel did not seem to worry about our intentions, for they trusted us initially, but once our test truck entered their inspection stations, all of our discussions and prior relations were out the door, and they inspected our test truck just as they would any other truck coming to United States from Mexico. From this perspective, it seems apparent that the U.S. personnel were using low context values from the start. In previous meetings, we had detailed the test plan, and these personnel also were intimately involved with reviewing the written test plan; therefore, since they had all of the details, they were willing to allow the truck to enter without import documentation. However, they were not flexible enough to allow the truck to bypass their usual inspection received as it entered the port. In other words, the context did not change the way they did their inspections, which shows the strong connection between low context communications and universalism. The Mexican Aduanas director seemed much more high context because he needed all of the contextual details up front, but once he had those details and had assessed the sincerity of our intentions, he allowed the little details of the inspection to be removed from the process. In other words, the context significantly influenced his decision making.

This difference probably correlates with the difference between inner and outer direction. As explained throughout this book, this value assesses the source of direction of the person, whether it comes from a mechanism from within (inner) that gives the person the drive or whether the person seeks to draw guidance from the outside forces (outer), often as a corollary, harmonizing with nature. Consequently, inner-directed cultures place the individual as the center and cause of activity, while in outer-directed cultures, the human is not directing or causing the activity but seeking to be aligned with the forces around the activity.

The CPB personnel seemed much more inner-directed because they closely followed the linear and rationalized inspection procedures that are central to their work, while the Mexican Aduanas director was much more interested in harmonizing the whole system, that is, of making sure that our test was properly situated with his organization in Ciudad Juárez, with the federal army, with the Jeronimo port, and with the central Aduanas office in Mexico City.

These two differences in context and sources of guidance also correlate with time orientations. Polychronic or synchronous time frames mean simultaneity, multiple tasks managed the same time, and apparent disorganization, focusing on the importance of place, and involvement of people rather than adherence to present schedules. On the other hand, monochronic or sequential time frames mean linked linear structures of cause and effect with an organized flow of events (Hall, 1976, 1983).

For the cross-border study, this difference centered mostly on the word "yes." In short, the CPB simply said "yes" to the study and then they followed their approval with their appropriate inspection procedures. On the other hand, the Aduanas director said "yes," but this was not a final and definitive "yes;" rather it was a "yes" to get the process going. After this initial "yes" from the Mexican Aduanas, we had to get the approval of the Aduanas office in Mexico City, which gave us a simple "yes" from the start which got the process going, but we never got final approval (in the form of the import documentation) until we have heard about 15 different versions of "yes," each one building up the final approval. For example, we had to get a "yes" for the type of truck, the trucking company, the containers, what was in the containers, who packed the containers, who was going to ride with the truck driver, what was the exact route, and what kind of technologies was going to be installed on the truck, and were these technologies going to be dumped off in Ciudad Juárez as a sort of illegal importation of technology. And each "yes" in the process further strengthened our mutual understanding of each other and the test plan itself. At about the 12th yes, which put the process forward but did not give us final approval, the team from Columbus, Ohio pretty much broke down and began to wonder about the meaning of "yes" in Mexico.

This example of yes correlate strongly with time frames (and high power distance values) because the initial yes was always in place as a kind of preliminary approval, and each additional yes seem to happen in a circular and simultaneous fashion, with each one building up to final approval. In addition, the 18 "yeses" helped harmonize the relations among all the Mexican agencies and helped contextualize and make more diffuse our relations.

These differences have important ramifications for communication patterns, knowledge management, and the learning and adaptability of the organizations. First, it demonstrates the need to see the Mexican "yes" in light of the immediate and specific context and as a part of a broader relationship building process that will be repeated in often a multitude of simultaneous events, closely following the tennis doubles model. The Mexican "yes" was also the process of building harmony among the involved organizations. The U.S. "yes" meant entrance into the specific sphere of activity where rigorous policies and procedures were to be carried out regardless of context, time, and people involved, closely following the baseball model. From this perspective, knowledge management again seems to be a US conception because it seemingly divorces knowledge from people and context and puts it into a linear and rationalized process. Knowledge management from the Mexican organization is managing people, events, and tasks at hand.

As mentioned earlier in previous sections, these models have different areas of flexibility and adaptability. The baseball model of the US organization has flexibility in how it rationalizes and integrates new policies and procedures without the influence of context, time, and human or social influences. The inflexibility comes in the procedures themselves, and when the procedures need to be altered because of current circumstances. The tennis doubles model of the Mexican organization proved to be onerous in its multiplicity of time frames, acute sensitivity to the context, and need to harmonize with the other organizations. However, once it was synchronized, it became very flexible in its policies and procedures.

In conclusion, it is interesting to hypothesize as to why either US or Mexican organizations did not appear to use the football model. I am certain that both organizations used the football model, and a more in-depth study of them would show that model can work. However, in the broad, cross-border comparative framework, the baseball model seem to correlate strongly with the values of US organization and the tennis doubles model with the values of the Mexican organization, with all their accompanying strengths and weaknesses.

THE ROLES OF TECHNOLOGY IN ORGANIZATIONAL CULTURES

One of the central questions of organizational theory is the role of technology in changing organizational culture, especially in international contexts. First, Chapters Four and Five discuss technology and cultural change, which can easily be applied to this chapter, so this point is not worth repeating here. However, the cross-border hazmat project exemplifies precisely some of the challenges and potential of new communication technologies for intercultural work across organizations. First, the premise of the test was to see whether RFID technologies would help monitor cross-border hazmat flow. The results of that test were overwhelmingly positive; we easily tracked the movement of the containers and drums in their cross-border hazmat route. The use of this information, however, needs to be integrated into policies and procedures of the U.S. and Mexican agencies, and political work that clears the way for procedural change is much, much harder than technological work. The technology was simply much further ahead than the actual policies and procedures of the government agencies. For example, the director of the Chihuahuan office of PROFEPA, who was responsible for hazmat compliance, watched on the computer screen as we tracked the movement of the truck between the turnaround point in Mexico and the disposal station in the United States. He loved this data, but his first and most scintillating question was how do we share this data across the border? Because of Mexican policies, he could not share his data officially or electronically, but only under-the-table and in paper format.

As much research has demonstrated, the problem of data sharing is acute among government agencies the United States. And across the border, data sharing is difficult at best. For example, at the Jeronimo and Santa Teresa ports of entry, the Mexican port director and a state of New Mexico customs facilitator used handheld walkie-talkies to talk to each other. They could not use cell phones, which were against regulations, nor were they allowed to use land lines, which were too expensive. They were able to purchase the walkie-talkies through NM state funds but with some difficulty. In addition, as explained elsewhere, there was a significant amount of cross-border communication but rarely was any of it official; rather, it was "a good neighbor talking to another good neighbor" about the very important common interests. Consequently, even though the RFID project showed great promise, developing a system that would be accessible and secure for both governments is the next step in the project, and it is a major step that is likely to drive the development of new policies and procedures on information sharing.

Despite these problems of information sharing, the United States government is currently developing two systems related to cross-border hazmat flow: ACE and the Hazardous Materials-Automated Cargo Communications for Efficient and Safe Shipments (HM-ACCESS).

The ACE system, which is a "commercial trade processing system designed to automate border processing, to enhance border security and foster our Nation's economic security through lawful international trade and travel" (cbp.gov/xp/cgov/trade/automated/modernization/). Its main component is the e-manifest, which are submitted electronically by carriers, enabling the CBP to prescreen the crew, conveyance, equipment and shipment information before the truck arrives at the border. The electronic manifest system allows for greater efficiency in data recording by eliminating redundancy. In addition, ACE's transponder or readers can identify trucks/drivers from a distance and activate the retrieval of manifest and entry data for CBP Officers. The goals of ACE are ambitious and include:

- Provide an information-sharing platform for trade data throughout government agencies
- Expedite legitimate trade by providing CBP with tools to efficiently process imports/exports and move goods quickly across the border;
- Improve communication, collaboration and compliance efforts between CBP and the trade community;
- Reduce processing times at ports and increase likelihood that trucks will be released at primary booth;
- Track the status of crew, conveyances, equipment and shipments, i.e. note they have arrived, are being held or have been released;
- Link a driver's account information to their truck carrier account thereby eliminating the need to create a duplicate record of the driver's account information in each carrier account;
- Create customizable reports to evaluate and identify compliance issues and risks.

At the time of the study (2008), ACE had not been fully implemented, but the RFID technologies used in the study were designed to be seamlessly integrated into the ACE system. Further, at the time of writing this book (late 2010), ACE was being pilot tested at various ports of entry with plans for nationwide implementation.

As a second component, the HM-ACCESS initiative is being developed by the U.S. Department of Transportation and "aims to identify and eliminate barriers to the use of paperless hazard communications technologies, thereby (1) improving the availability and accuracy of hazard information thus enhancing safety and reducing transportation risk; (2) improving the speed by which information is available to emergency responders when incidents occur; (3) and allowing U.S. companies to compete more effectively in the global economy by using the best tools available"(hazmat.dot.gov/HM-ACCESS/index.html). It is in the beginning of development and design stages, but two crucial pieces to it are missing: its connection to ACE and its ability to share data across the border with Mexico. It appears the developers in Washington DC have not thought about the cross-border issues.

Thus, both the ACE and HM-ACCESS systems are focused on sharing data among U.S. Federal and perhaps state agencies, with little to no planning to share with Mexico.

Mexico's use of communication and information technology is being developed at an astounding rate and might have significant benefits for streamlining and making visible transactions in Mexico. For example, because of Mexico's fears of corruption, they often duplicate transactions and then compare the transaction details, such as the port of entry. Current communication and information technologies can rapidly complete these tasks. Further, recent legislation has required transparency in all public transactions and institutions, which is having some tangible effects. Finally, cell phone technologies and internet capacity are rapidly increasing in Mexico, often surpassing many areas of the United States. Thus, the capacity is there and policies and procedures are changing.

However, I am going to end this chapter with a poignant narrative about my meeting in Ciudad Juárez with the area Aduanas Director. As my EPA colleague and I left his office, rather excited about his permission to carry out the test in Mexico, we both commented rather dryly: despite the great technological advances of information and communication technologies, Mexico is still an "interpersonal" culture, and we had to finalize the deal in person, the way it has been done since the beginning of time. Neither of us could anticipate when this would actually change in Mexico due to technological innovation.

CONCLUSION

I would like to have written a chapter that reviews the research and literature on communication across multiple international organizations, showing how the differences and problems reside, among many things, the cultural and rhetorical patterns. Unfortunately, this literature is not developed well. Instead, to demonstrate the same thing, I presented a case study, drawing on basic organizational models. This model should be sufficient, however, to demonstrate the complexities of communication across organizations.

REFERENCES

Adler, N. (2008). *International dimensions of organizational behavior*. Thomson Learning Center.

Drucker, P. (1992).There's three kind of teams. *Wall Street Journal*, Feb. 11.

Hall, E. T. (1976). *Beyond culture*. New York, NY: Doubleday.

Hall, E. T. (1981). *The silent language*. New York, NY: Doubleday.

Hall, E. T. (1983). *The dance of life*. New York, NY: Doubleday.

Hampden-Turner, C., & Trompenaars, A. (2000). *Building cross-cultural competence*. Wiley.

Hofstede, G. (2010). *Cultures and organizations, software of the mind* (3rd ed.). New York, NY: McGraw Hill.

House, R. J., Hanges, P. J., Javidan, M., Dorfman, P. R., & Gupta, V. (Eds.). (2005). *Culture, leadership, and organizations: The GLOBE study of 62 societies*. Thousand Oaks, CA: Sage.

Thatcher, B. L. (2010a). Introduction. *Rhetoric, Professional Communication, and Globalization*, *1*, 1–34.

Weick, K. with Sutcilffe, K. (2001). *Managing the unexpected: Assuring high performance in an age of complexity*. Jossey-Bass

ENDNOTE

1 Burnett, 1993, originally developed these useful terms of substantive, procedural, and affective conflicts for collaborative writing, which I adapt to the sports models.

Chapter 7
Distance Education and E-Learning across Cultures

ABSTRACT

This chapter examines distance education and e-learning across cultures. It first reviews the standards of distance education from five countries, UNESCO, and industry. Next, it shows how the curriculum in distance education must match the cultural and rhetorical traditions of the target culture. It prepares curriculum writers to understand how to adapt and develop distance education courses to the appropriate rhetoric and cultural expectations of the target audience.

INTRODUCTION

This chapter lays out a broad framework for developing distance and e-learning across cultures, showing how to internationalize the distance education curricular models for academia and industry. Currently, there is a massive amount of research concerning the development and delivery of distance education with an important area being the global and intercultural context (see, for example, *Globalized E-Learning,* Andrea Edmundson; 2007; *Global perspectives on e-learning,* Alison A. Carr-Chellman, 2005). Likewise, e-learning has become a key mechanism for training in the multinational organization (Fee, 2009). Although some of the research contextualizes e-learning from intercultural perspectives (Edmundson, 2007; Carr-Chellman, 2005), the vast majority ignores the intercultural context, especially when connecting culture to more than superficial taboos and Do's and Don'ts across culture. For example, Carr-Chellman's 2005 collection does a nice job of contextualizing e-learning across a variety of cultures in Asia and Europe, but the collection minimally connects the curricular and program design of e-learning to these specific cultural contexts. Edmundson's 2007 collection is better at connecting cultural values to curricular design, but these connections do not ground the curriculum holistically in a universal framework, drawing on the multitude of value sets that impact curriculum design.

Further, in rhetoric and professional communication, much has been written about distance education, especially in light of professional communication, including some work about the international elements of distance education (Starke-Meyerring, 2008; St. Amant, 2007a). However, much like many other areas of professional communication, little of this work in rhetoric

DOI: 10.4018/978-1-61350-450-5.ch007

and professional communication systematically evaluates e-learning curriculum and programs from an intercultural perspective. For example, much work in rhetoric and professional communication examines the communications developed in collaborative classes across cultures, focusing mostly on issues of student-student and student-teacher interactions across universities in online classes (Starke-Meyerring, 2008). This collection also theorizes globalization from an academic perspective and explores issues of global communication technologies and professional communication. However, this collection does not develop and then operationalize a theory of intercultural rhetoric and professional communication and only minimally grounds the work in distance education. Likewise, the work of St. Amant (2007a) looks at some features of intercultural education but does not focus on some of the deep structural issues related to curriculum development and the value sets. Thus, we do not understand adequately how the intercultural rhetoric is influencing the design and delivery of distance education and e-learning.

Consequently, intercultural professional communication educators and trainers working in distance or e-learning settings have little guidance for developing programs, courses, and training materials. For example, how do instructional designs for technical information across cultures differ according to the etic borders or other key indicators? How are problems of space, personal presence, motivation, and communication mediated by e-learning technologies? How much does the communication technology of e-learning influence learning and classroom management? How does technology transfer relate to curriculum design for implementing new manufacturing procedures across cultures? And how is knowledge managed across different countries and organizations?

Answering these questions fully would require a book-length approach; however, this chapter seeks to sketch a broad evaluative and planning framework for intercultural professional communicators working in distance education. This chapter presents seven major guidelines for evaluating the effective of distance education and course development. As it presents these seven sections, it simultaneously grounds the design of distance education curriculum using accreditation guidelines from five countries, UNESCO, and prevailing e-learning designs in industry. It also shows how the elements of curricular design vary according to the intercultural etic borders. And it explores a tentative framework for developing intercultural distance education curriculum.

DISTANCE EDUCATION ACCREDITATION MODELS AND INDUSTRY EXAMPLES AS A FRAMEWORK FOR DEVELOPING CURRICULUM

In response to the great amount of research and practice in distance education around the world, many countries have developed evaluation or accreditation criteria for distance education programs, which generally represent the best models and practices for each country. Accordingly, this Chapter compares the distance education accreditation models and guidelines in five countries (United States, the UK, Canada, Mexico, and India), from UNESCO's teaching training, and some of the leading industry e-learning models and evaluate these models from intercultural perspective, drawing on the value sets and other intercultural indicators.

For the United States, this Chapter presents the accreditation model from the Council for Higher Education Accreditation (CHEA; www.chea.org). This is the most widely used and recognized model for evaluating distance education at US universities. For the UK and Canada, this Chapter presents the evaluation criteria for distance education from The Quality Assurance Agency for Higher Education (QAA; www.qaa.ac.uk) and the Canadian Association of Community Education (CACE; http://cauce-aepuc.ca/), which are also nongovernmental associations that independently accredits university programs. Likewise, Mexico's La Federación de Instituciones Mexicanas Particulares de Educación Superior (FIMPES; www.fimpes.org.mx) is an independent association that has developed accreditation criteria for distance education. Unlike these non-governmental institutions, India has a federal accreditation system for distance education programs.

Next, UNESCO (The United Nations Educational, Scientific and Cultural Organization) has developed an extensive evaluation model for distance education teacher training. It was developed by a large, multinational team and is based on distance education case studies undertaken in Brazil, Burkina Faso, Chile, China, India, Mongolia, Nigeria, South Africa and United Kingdom. This model reflects the varied "individual national infrastructures and a wide complex of educational, social, cultural and economic issues, including the willingness and capacities of teachers themselves to become engaged in these modes in their various learning institutions and communities" (*Teacher Education Guidelines: Using Open and Distance Learning*, p. preface). Finally, this Chapter will present the course design model from Rossett's *ASTD E-Learning Handbook* (2001), one of the leaders in distance education evaluation and several other key books.

The six curricular models and industry samples are not meant to be exhaustive, critical reviews; rather, they are a representative framework of critical issues, which allow us to focus on internationalizing distance education and e-learning, the main purpose of this chapter. Further, in these discussions, I have not deemed it important to flesh out distinctions between distance education and e-learning, a topic that is often controversial, nor do I address differences between total e-learning and blended and hybrid systems. Fee (2009) for example presents five models of distance or e-learning, ranging from totally online, blended, and integrated performance systems (p. 24). My only purpose is examining learning that takes places outside of presence-based contexts, where students and teachers do not meet physically as the default means of instruction. Course designers can then create their own e-learning models based on their content, technologies, and instructional objectives.

Guideline 1: Institutional and Organizational Context

One of the most important guidelines for distance education is to situate the program within an integrated, fully developed and fully functional academic organization. The CHEA guideline from the United States explains "electronically offered programs both support and extend the roles of educational institutions. Increasingly they are integral to academic organization, with growing implications for institutional infrastructure" (Criterion 1). UNESCO underscores this institutional context by emphasizing the national context as well, stating that "the history of distance education is littered with projects that looked good initially but could not be sustained as they were not built into national educational systems" (p. 27). Thus, the quality of the distance education program is in direct relation to the quality of the physical institution and national standards. India even goes further to mandate that distance education programs can only take place within the state where a physical learning institute is located, which also must have a full functional learning center to supplement the distance education. Mexico's first criteria is similar in that the distance education program should "guarantee that all of its academic program impart the same values, ideals, principles and personal and institutional standards, regardless of the form of delivery" (Criterion 11.1). The UK presents this criterion more generally, stating: "Institutions offering distance learning programs should design and manage operations in a way that applies the principles generally relevant to higher education" (Guideline 1), while Canada does not present criteria connecting distance education to existing academic facilities.

The e-learning approaches in many non-academic settings are similar. For example, Rossett's *ASTD E-Learning handbook* (2001) states that e-learning makes senses but only "as one component in a larger, integrated performance system" (p.11). In addition to many of the reasons cited previously in academic contexts, the *ASTD Handbook* also argues that the great availability of information can actually overwhelm employees unless that information is integrated carefully and effectively into an existing training framework. Additional reasons for requiring e-learning to be housed in an integrated framework include these seven (pp. 11-12).

- Concerns about online classroom effectiveness, which can be alleviated by a comprehensive instructional approach, including e-learning.
- The easy trap of disseminating disparate or non-integrated information as a substitute for effective teaching and curriculum models.
- That e-learning is often carried out by outside vendors who do not have the holistic picture of teaching outcomes needed by the organization.
- That e-learning might foster a quick-fix mentality, rather than a slow, but more fully integrated and analyzed learning.
- That students or corporate leadership often have difficulty assessing the true expertise and capacity of instructors in the online environment.
- That online instruction often does not involve the actual experts in the field who are doing the work the students are receiving training for.
- An inability to integrate e-learning into existing management structures, which allows for access to resources and decision-makers.

For these reasons, the ATSD Handbook similarly recommends situating online learning within a viable curriculum framework. Interestingly, Fee (2009) never discusses this guideline for industry, instead arguing for designing appropriately the courses or programs.

Distance Education is Grounded in Local Cultures and Corresponding Institutional Capacity and Development

Much research helps ground distance education in the local institutions and culture. For example, the online journal *The International Review of Research in Open and Distance Learning* (IRRODL) consistently reports on area and country research from around the world, all of which concludes that the local contexts are the most important variable for developing distance education; however, very few of these studies actually show how to adapt a distance education to a local culture. On the other hand, the UNESCO research, which has significant experience with educational policy around the world, discusses international, national and organizational policy. For the international and national context, UNESCO suggests the following:

> *The international issues arise in part because the forces of globalisation are affecting the content and practices of education, in part because new policy issues arise when education is no longer confined within national frontiers. Programme planners are thus increasingly exposed to innovations in teacher education and need to make judgments about the desirability, feasibility and acceptability of these internationalised ideas within their country and programme.*
>
> *Changes to more practice-based teaching education, for example, have been encouraged internationally and become part of the common discourse about education. As we see in chapter 7, this has major implications for the local planning,*

implementation and management of programmes for teachers. International conventions on the role and status of teachers as agents of change naturally affect national policy. At the same time, educational cooperation across borders, and cross border enrolment, put on to the decision-maker's agenda jurisdictional questions about cross-cultural transference and language and about the control of crossborder enrolment and its accreditation or recognition (p. 26).

In addition to these general considerations, the UNESCO research suggests assessing the following specific national policy situations:

- Distance education in light of national communication policy;
- Political, economic, technical and regulatory issues especially as they concern the respective roles of the private and public sector; educational institutions.
- Investment policy, in relation both to the public sector and to the encouragement of particular areas of private-sector investment;
- Policy on tariffs and on any common carrier requirements; and government purchasing policy, and policy for the use of communication technologies for government's internal communication.
- Technical standards including frequency allocation, systems reliability;
- The national development of national capacity and expertise
- Scheduling, influence, control over content and intellectual property
- Issues of equity and access.

In addition to these national issues, UNESCO also provides criteria for the institutional contexts:

- Allocation and balancing of resources, fee policies, and the recognition of qualifications.
- The most appropriate contribution open and distance learning can make to different levels and types of education;
- Teachers' associations and unions will, for example, be interested in the conditions of service for teachers working in a new role;
- The systematic planning of policies to manage institutional change effectively. This is likely to include new faculty policies; student policy; and legal policy (intellectual property including ownership of materials, copyright, and faculty, student and institutional liability) (pp. 26-27).

Local Culture of Organization

In addition to the international, national, and institutional context, professional communicators need to assess the cultural, educational, and organizational nature of the institution or organization that will receive the distance education. For example, in Chapter Five of this book, the analysis of university websites in the United States, India, and Mexico demonstrate distinct cultural orientations. Thus, a distance educator developer from the United States will most likely assume U.S. cultural values for the educational context, including individualism, universalism, specific orientation, achievement orientation, inner-direction, low context communication, monochronic time frames, and low power distance. And as discussed in Chapter Six, these value orientations significantly influence organizational behavior and function, exemplified in the team models.

Surprisingly, although this is starting criterion for developing effective e-learning, it has received very little attention in the research and practice in cross-cultural contexts. It is very complex as well, but the use of the value sets and models developed throughout this book can be used for this assessment. For example, the following questions could be articulated about organizational culture:

- What kind of assumptions about the dependence or independence of people is assumed by the organization? In other words, as demonstrated in many Chapters of this book, does the organization assume distance education groups will function more like baseball, football, or tennis doubles teams (Chapter Six) and thus cohere differently into more dependent units; or is it given to provide the independence and personal space needed for individualism?
- What assumptions about rules and policies does the organization presume? Do they assume universal adherence or do the program the flexibility of contextual and relational factors?
- How holistic and interrelated (diffuse) or focused and isolated (specific) are the relations between students and faculty and among the students themselves?
- What are the overall guiding structures to the organizational culture: process and performance based (achievement and inner direction) or value assimilation, using deductive and often natural analogies and metaphors (ascriptive and outer directed)?
- What time frames are used to structure organizational activities (polychronic or monochronic)?
- How much does the organizational context influence the distance education programs?
- What are the power distance assumptions in the organizational cultures, that is, does the structure assume one or two way communications and what is the role or relevance of feedback loop from subordinates to superiors?

Obviously, much research is needed to assess the connections between organizational culture and distance education.

Guideline 2: Technology Commitment and Development

One of the key guidelines of most models requires that the institution has in place sufficient technology to effectively carry out the distance education modes of delivery. The CHEA criteria from the United States are the most comprehensive. It requires the following:

- The institution assures adequacy of technical and physical plant facilities including appropriate staffing and technical assistance, to support its electronically offered programs.
- The institution strives to assure a consistent and coherent technical framework for students and faculty. When a change in technologies is necessary, it is introduced in a way that minimizes the impact on students and faculty.
- The institution provides students with reasonable technical support for each educational technology hardware, software, and delivery system required in a program.
- The selection of technologies is based on appropriateness for the students and the curriculum. It is recognized that availability, cost, and other issues are often involved, but program documentation should include specific consideration of the match between technology and program (Guidelines 1d-1i)

India follows this model, but more generally, explaining that not only should the institution have the appropriate technology, but that this technology should be sufficient for student and faculty needs. UNESCO explains how critical it is for distance education institutions to have the technologies that are effective pedagogically and economically, given the technological infrastructure of the different countries. It then explains in detail (discussed next) the pros and cons of different technology such as radio, TV, internet, and others. The UK model does not address technology specifically, only that "prior to offering programs at a distance, an institution should explicitly design and test its systems for administering and teaching students, and should plan for contingencies in order to meet stated aims in academic quality standards" (Guideline 1.3). The Canadian and Mexican models do not specify the design of the educational technologies but require them to be effective for instruction.

E-learning in corporations have similar concerns about technology, but perhaps less so as the

Table 1. Selections from UNESCO Technology Discussion

Function in teacher education and development	Strengths	Limitations and requirements
Audio Cassettes Provides illustrations through sound. Can give examples of concepts and theory. Can provide discussion in a more natural way than through text. Can provide detailed instructions (e.g. in using a computer or manipulating equipment). Can be used as a teachers' 'talking newsletter'. Can provide models of pronunciation. Can act as a 'voice in the ear', to guide teachers through processes (e.g. learning to use a computer or observation tasks)	Offers a permanent resource for individuals or groups. Is relatively portable and are often widely accessible by teachers Can be re-played, stopped and started at will by learner. Combines effectively with print, and can extend the use of radio programmes through recording for re-play. Is low cost to develop and duplicate. Can be a more intimate or motivating medium than print, if not presented as a single-voice long lecture. Teachers can contribute to tapes or make them. Can be used by tutors to give feedback to students.	Audio-cassettes can deteriorate over time. Sound quality can be poor if a chain of recordings are made or if the equipment is poor. Cassettes need good management (e.g. accurate labeling, storing, mechanisms for circulating among teachers). Can fail to stimulate active learning if used just to deliver lectures. Tape-editing time often underestimated. Needs skilled integration with print or other media. Content often needs designing differently from radio programmes. A one-way medium.
Television Can reach a mass audience of teachers and the community. Can raise awareness in the community at large about educational issues and teaching. Shows processes in real-time or slowed down or in close-up. Shows a variety of school and classroom contexts and teachers in action Gives teachers comparisons and benchmarks. Can show specialists at work.	Can demonstrate real contexts and provide rich visual content. Can capture classroom realities. Can combine a variety of content (e.g. site visits to schools; interviews, dynamic simulations, and examples of teachers' work). Can be combined with other media. Can provide topical content.	High development costs and may be high transmission costs. Not always accessible to all teachers. Inadequate technical support Often inappropriate transmission times. Sometimes replicates traditional lecture formats which fail to make effective use of the medium's capabilities. One-way medium may foster passive viewing. Filming in schools requires considerable specialist skills and resources. Filming in studio classrooms is often easier but can lack authenticity.
Computer Communication Enables teachers to participate in larger professional communities, beyond their local ones. Provides access to databases, either on a local area network provided by the education authorities, or the Internet. Enables teachers to follow professional development programmes provided by remote institutions.	Can provide a wide range of multimedia materials, if the infrastructure (and bandwidth) permit. Supports a range of interaction, from formal to informal of varying group size. Can archive discussions for later use by other teachers. Allows teachers to participate widely and to exchange experience and materials in peer groups. Provides access to more sources of information and assistance, on topics from the specific ('How do I teach the new curriculum on environmental studies to Grade 3 children?) to more general educational topics.	Problems of access and cost in some countries. Requires an adequate infrastructure (electricity, telecommunications), affordable prices, supportive policy framework and investment of resources. Requires a change in perceptions and practices in teaching and learning. If lengthy print materials are produced through downloading, this may increase costs per copy over those of centralised print production and shift costs to the teacher, school or district. Requires training for effective use (often neglected). Requires considerable technical support.

technologies required for effectively conducting business in our global context are often the same technologies that can be used for distance education and e-learning. Further, one of the goals of e-learning instructional designers is to design the technology to match the task to be learned so seamlessly that the learner does without knowing he or she is learning. For example, in the *ATSD Handbook*, Gery (2001) argues that instead of thinking of the technology commitment as an afterthought to learning, that technology should be part of an "Electronic Performance Support System" (EPSS) (p.26), a concept that Gery helped develop in 1991 but one that is slowly catching on in e-learning. Thus, instead of an employee learning how to do a task, that employ would have a technology system, much like an installation wizard, that would guide that employee through the process, while at the same time reinforcing learning. This is much like a robust, learning-enhanced task wizard, which is supposed to integrate technology, learning, and business processes and tasks. EPSS includes six elements: Task, Structuring Support, Knowledge, Data, Tools, and Communications/Collaboration. As much research has demonstrated, this concept built in early 1990s, has evolved significantly in the last 20 years with the development of information and communication technologies. Information is much more available and layered strategically; elements of artificial intelligence can facilitate many processes; newer media are more usable and integrated; and support tools are more sophisticated.

Assessing Technology for Intercultural Development

Intercultural professional communicators working on distance education training must assess technology infrastructure and strategic use of existing technologies that are viable options for local populations or organizations. UNESCO's research is particularly relevant here because they discuss the pros and cons of all types of distance learning technology, including radio and television for different countries, especially those in development. Table 1 is an excerpt from UNESCO's research evaluating audio cassettes, computers, and television (p. 42):

In addition to these three technologies, UNESCO evaluates videos, video conferencing, computer to computer, and CD-Roms. Olaniran (2007) similarly argues for this kind of technology assessment in Africa. Further, Chapter Four in this book explores the relations of each of the eight cultural values to orality, writing, email, web, and social media, showing issues of cultural fit and reciprocity. Instead of copying Table 1 and reposting it here, I invite the reader to explore very carefully how the technology matches the target culture. Much research has shown that these technologies influence interactions in the intercultural e-learning classroom, a point to be fully developed later under the later section of this chapter, "Student Support."

Guideline 3: Curriculum Development and Instructional Design

In addition to the institution, all of the models emphasize the need to develop effective curriculum first, regardless of the technology design. The CHEA from the United States says the following:

Methods change, but standards of quality endure. The important issues are not technical but curriculum-driven and pedagogical. Decisions about such matters are made by qualified professionals and focus on learning outcomes for an increasingly diverse student population.... Academically qualified persons participate fully in the decisions concerning program curricula and program oversight" (Guideline 2).

The UK model offers a similar guideline, explaining that "institutions offering programs at a distance are responsible for ensuring that the academic standards of awards will be demonstrably comparable with awards delivered in other ways, and consistent with benchmarks recognized our own in the UK" (Guideline 2.6). Likewise, the Mexican model states: "The institution that provides distance education should (11-2) have a pedagogical model in which is established the appropriate theoretical guidelines and technological frameworks according to the educational offering" (Guideline 11.2). The India policy states that "the parent institution shall ensure that there is laid down mechanism for curriculum development and its approval by the statutory authorities of the parent institution, preparation of material in self-instructional format and proper policy for admission of students." The Canadian model does not address this criterion.

The UNESCO model focuses distance education on the instructional purposes that are most relevant to teacher training, generally explaining the need to develop the programs using traditionally qualified faculty and staff, and the most successful programs usually originate in already successful traditional programs. It explains:

Identifying the educational purpose is all-important. If the purpose and audience lend themselves to open and distance learning, then it makes sense to explore the nonconventional options open to the manager alongside the conventional approaches of teacher education. The point of these guidelines is not to argue for the application of open and distance learning to every problem in teacher education but to suggest where and how it can be used. The most successful programmes are those where open and distance learning is closely integrated with other approaches to education and professional development (p.27).

For e-learning in industry, curriculum development or *instructional design* has many of the same challenges as academia, but much like the example of Electronic Performance Support Systems, industry is more interested in integration and strategic use of information in meaningful ways, not relying on course and discipline divisions. For example, the *ASTD E-Learning Handbook* explains the importance of one core component of curriculum development: learning objects.

Learning objects, according to Wiley (2000), are usually small instructional components that can be used across a number of learning environments. Further, these objects can easily be delivered over the internet where people can use them in a variety of ways. Learning objects can be developed in collaboration by new wiki technologies and easily integrated at remote sites for different users and purposes. The *ASTD Handbook* explains that "objects come in many forms, from finished learning modules to the raw materials used to build them, such as text, photographs, job aids, tests, and video presentations, digitized and ready to be combined in new forms" (handbook website). For developing curriculum, these learning objects are powerful components of instructional design because they give the designer the flexibility to adapt curriculum to specific audiences and personalities; in addition, the objects are portable and easily shared. With these tools, the designers can focus more energy on delivering–rather than developing–the content. Further, these objects are often integrated with current management structures and corporate objectives, a sharing that can reduce organizational costs.

GROUNDING CURRICULUM DESIGN IN LOCAL CULTURES

A growing body of research is connecting local cultures to distance education curriculum design. To review an effective summary of this research, please see Uzuner, (2009) and McLoughlin (2007), but, keeping with the overall design of this book, I will summarize the research according to the value sets. This section assesses curriculum design with the first four of the eight value sets.

I/Other

As discussed in Chapter Two, people in individualistic cultures tend to be more self-reliant, competitive, and act in their own self interest for personal growth (Hampden-Turner & Trompenaars, 2000). In collective societies, individuals are integrated into strong, cohesive in-groups, with which they are loyal (Hofstede, 2005). This value set strongly influence many aspects of curricular design because it essentially grounds the relations between students and teachers and among the students themselves. As most intercultural research documents (see Hofstede, 2010, for example), teachers in collective cultures fill roles high in social hierarchy and are not to be questioned; they are generally the absolute authorities. On the other hand, teachers in individualistic cultures are more like consultants.

Much research in intercultural e-learning reflects this difference. For example, as summarized by Uzuner (2009), Thompson and Ku (2005) report that Chinese participants were less critical and opinionated in online discussions than their U.S. peers. Thompson and Ku attributed this finding to Hofstede's view that "Chinese culture is highly collective and feminine and tends to value group effort, harmony, affection, compassion and emotionality" (p. 43). Also as summarized in Uzuner (2009), Anakwe & Christensen (1999) and Tapanes, Smith, & White (2009) found that distance learning to be more compatible with individualists' rather than collectivists' motives and ways of interacting. Similarly, Lim (2004) used surveys to compare online learning motivation in Korea and the United States, finding that American students "prefer voicing personal opinions during class, enjoy learning and enroll in classes to obtain a sense of belonging," while Korean students expressed their tendency to "avoid voicing their opinions and keep passive and quiet during class as they are influenced by the authoritarian classroom context of Asian culture" (pp.169-170).

This research on individual-collective was also summarized by Uzuner (2009) as the anxiety about nail sticking out, reflecting a common proverb in Japan that if a nail sticks up, one must pound it in. Uzuner (2009) states the following recommendation:

Influenced by cultural traditions that discourage the "nail that sticks up," some students tend to show passive presence in ALNs. For example, Taiwanese participants in Chen, Hsu, and Caropreso's (2006) study "appeared to be passive toward interacting with group members, while U.S. students appeared actively engaged and energetic" (p. 23). Similarly, Zhao and McDougall (2008) found that some of the Chinese learners participating in their study "hesitated to ask questions and some even gave up on a discussion or contributed fewer messages when their opinions conflicted with those of other participants" (p. 72). Last but not least, Liang and McQueen's (2000) study demonstrated that Asian students "tend to hold back their thoughts when they perceive the teacher or majority of the learning peers will not favorably receive messages that are contrary to what they want to hear" (p. 28). These findings indicate that in distance learning contexts (such as the North American distance learning contexts) where active participation in discussions is highly valued, instructors should make specific efforts to promote critique and divergence and encourage students to create a safe space where opinions, experiences, beliefs, and knowledge can be shared (Uzuner, 2009).

As stated later in Inner and Outer Direction, perhaps another reason for this lack of aggressiveness in Asian students is founded on their desire to harmonize relations.

Rules Orientation

As described in Chapter Two, rules orientation in cultures seems to revolve around either the particular or universal orientation. In universalist cultures, laws are generally developed but enforced equally, creating the desire level playing field. In particularist cultures, the default approach is to apply rules and decisions depending on relations and context. Instead of "the level playing field," the particularist playing field is overtly structured, and thus, there is a specifically tailored set of rules for each social relationship. Surprisingly, very little if no research on rules orientation is available.

However, a small body of research assesses Hofstede's Uncertainty Avoidance, which ended up having applications to rules orientation. Uzuner (2009) summarizes his recommendation for this value as follows:

Some studies (e.g., Al-Harthi, 2005; Bing & Ai-Ping, 2008; Smith et al., 2005; Smith & Smith, 1999; Wang, 2007) showed that learners from strong uncertainty avoidance cultures are threatened by learning situations that are unstructured and unclear. They expect formal rules to guide their behavior. For example, Smith and Smith (1999) found that Chinese students display a strong need for "structured programs of instruction where the logic of that structure is transparent to the student" (p. 77). In a similar vein, when discussing the factors impacting Korean and Chinese students" participation in ALNs, Wang wrote: "the rules for online participation were unclear. Both Chinese and Korean students, who rarely spoke in traditional classrooms, felt lost when they were expected to speak online. They wondered if there were any rules and rituals for them to follow" (p. 304). To alleviate such student anxieties, online instructors should make their course structure transparent by setting clear expectations for participation, assignments, learning activities, team work, grading, submission dates, and assessment (Uzuner, 2009).

For rules orientation, this recommendation is difficult to apply, however, because, as I explain in Chapter Two, both particular and universalist cultures have rules; and often particular cultures have even more rules because they vary according to context and social situation. Universalist cultures, however, like publicized and evenly enforced rules while particular culture has rules that are implicit because they are grounded in contexts and relationships.

Thus, Uzuner's (2009) application and recommendation might be misguided. What is perhaps more likely is that in the new situation, the more particular students from Asian cultures were used to highly develop rules of engagement, causing them much anxiety because they could not infer these relations from the new context and relationship. On the other hand, students coming from more universal cultures did not need the additional rules because they were working off universal rules guiding education contexts in general. As I explain in Chapter Two, Hofstede's uncertainty avoidance value is flawed because it seems that all cultures are anxious about situations where their cultural values are in direct conflict.

Public/Private and Degree of Involvement

This value set assesses the degree of involvement across different spheres of life, usually involving a public/private divide and trust. Diffuse cultures are usually collective, particular, and outer-directed; thus, involvement in friendships, social relations, and work environments often crosses boundaries, thus sharing the relationship across these spheres. On the other hand, specific cultures are based on the ease and public trust that individualism and universalism give people in separate spheres of life, with friendship belonging to one or two spheres only, with little or no cross-over of authority. Specific orientation also relies on the reliable social structure of the level playing field, which allows them to quickly work or make friends with people in all kinds of spheres. Consequently, the specific orientation favors more public collaboration, something that is much more difficult in diffuse cultures. This value set has critical connections to intercultural e-learning.

As already mentioned in the section describing uncertainty avoidance, cultures from Asia that are traditionally more diffuse find this new, and often frighteningly public medium, very disconcerting. But the relevance to curriculum design goes well beyond this public and private divide. As explained throughout this chapter, diffuse professional communications are much more holistic, valuing comprehensive approaches to topics, while specific orientation is much more focused. This directly relates to curriculum design and in how specific or diffuse the curriculum should be. For example, diffuse curriculum will favor breadth or coverage, versus depth of inquiry, which is a manifestation of specific orientation.

In addition, as explained in Chapter Five Website Designs, many people from diffuse cultures are very reticent opening themselves up in public forums such as those on websites and computers, preferring instead to reveal their more private selves in more contained contexts. For example, many of the social sharing sites in Japan have very few pictures of people that own them; rather, these users prefer to place icons, drawings, or small pets. On the other hand, most of the social sites in the United States and other more specific countries have very open views of some of the most private parts of the users' lives. The research is silent on this value set, only arguing for a match between culture and curriculum design, which is not helpful for designers and planners.

Sources of Virtue and Guidance

The fourth value focuses on the source or origin of virtue, guidance, or method of aligning oneself rightly. Hampden-Turner and Trompenaars (2000) explained that there are generally two sources of virtue: the inner-directed source that "conceives of virtue as inside each of us--in our souls, wills, convictions, principles," or believes--in the triumph of conscious purpose. Outer direction conceives of virtue as our site each of us in natural rhythms, in the beauties and powers of nature, in aesthetic environments and relationships" (p.234).

Much like rules orientation, very little research has specifically address inner and outer direction, but much research has addressed the need for many Asian and Latin cultures to develop harmonious relations in online situations. For example, Catterick (2007) argues that to engage Chinese learners actively, the curriculum must be structured around relationships, defense mechanisms, harmony, and maintaining face. Likewise, Uzuner (2009) also summarizes the research detailing the differences between group harmony:

Anakwe and Christensen (1999) found that "relationship building is foremost" for students from collectivist cultures (p. 240). This finding has significant implications for online instructors who emphasize collaborative work in their courses. One implication is that online instructors should allow sufficient time to develop relationships prior to engaging learners in collaborative activities (Liang & McQueen, 2000). In addition, they should allow learners to work in small groups, encourage diversity in those groups (Thompson & Ku, 2005; Wang & Reeves, 2007), and always monitor the nature and scope of team work (Wang, 2007).

Uzuner (2009) also cites research that as compared to their American peers, Mexican students showed higher tendencies for affection, compassion, and emotion in online group processes, a finding that reflects the importance of care and affection in Mexican culture. Thus, an important component of curriculum design focuses on whether students will want to follow their own voice, so to speak, or seek to harmonize relations among each other, both used as vehicles for education.

Further, this research might be evidence for the Social Identity model of Deindividuation Effects (see Chapter Four). Deindividuation theory suggests that people in crowds become uninhibited and behave antisocially because of their reduced sense of self and lack of accountability. Online environments are simply like crowds where users experience the same lack of self awareness and accountability. The SIDE model, however, rejects the theory that lack of self awareness and anonymity encourage antisocial behavior. Instead it argues that online environments produce an enhanced ability to connect to the user's in-group and to segment off the out-group. This process produces a depersonalization of the user himself and his or her audience, connecting the user more closely to his or her in-group and stereotyping more the out-group. Consequently, the user's self perception changes, from more individualistic to more interchangeable with the in-group. Likewise, individual norms are transformed into group norms; and as opposed to Deindividuation, depersonalization does not imply irrational or disinhibited behavior; rather, the individual behaves rationally because he regulates behavior according to in-group standards.

Despite some of these connections to harmonious relations, the relevance of inner and outer also influences curriculum in many other ways. As shown in Chapter Five Website Designs, Visvra Bharati University's educational philosophy grounded itself explicitly in how effectively it could harmonize itself with its local context, India as a whole, and the history of great figures from the university. Further, as McCool has shown (2007), Mexican websites tend to use larger, over-arching nature metaphors to organize their websites. And as reviewed in Chapter Two and discussed by Hampden-Turner and Trompenaars (2000), this value set also gets at valuing innovation and invention (inner) versus refinement and adaptation of existing thinking to specific contexts (outer). These are serious differences when engaging with problem-based inquiry, which is often a specific view of the world (Stewart & Bennett, 1991); developing research topics that are either based narrowing down the topic until a specific problem is addressed or looking at a problem with a holistic, wide perspective; and understanding the interdisciplinarity of the work existing work in one's field. Much research needs to be done to appropriately assess this value set.

The final four value sets (status, time, power distance, context in communication) are also integral parts of curriculum development, but for the sake of space, I have saved this discussion for the next sections, which are more appropriate for these last values. However, key questions for these value sets remain and are as follows:

- What are the overall guiding structures to the curriculum: process and performance based (achievement) or value assimilation, using deductive and often natural analogies and metaphors (ascriptive). McCarty (2007) similarly argues that constructivism favors western, achievement based cultures.
- What time frames are used to structure the curriculum (polychronic or monochronic)?
- What role does contextual information play in curriculum design? Little (low context)? Or Much (high context)?

- What are the power distance assumptions in the curriculum design, that is, does the structure assume one or two way communications and what is the role or relevance of feedback loop from subordinates to superiors?

Obviously, much research is needed to assess these connections between curriculum design and distance education.

Guideline 4: Delivery of Courses and Knowledge Management

A vast majority of the criteria from all the models examined focus on the delivery approaches through distance education technology. The following three guidelines from the UK establish the basic parameters of delivery:

- Institutions are responsible for managing the delivery of each distance learning program of study in a manner that safeguards the academic standards of the award.
- Institutions are responsible for ensuring that each program is delivered in a manner that provides, in practice, a learning opportunity that gives students a fair and reasonable chance of achieving the academic standards required for successful completion.
- Learning should be treated as an activity involving all participants in the system, in which monitoring, review, and feedback to those who manage programs of study are used regularly to enhance all components of teaching, learning, and system delivery (Guidelines 12-14).

The Canadian model is generally more specific than the UK model, and most of its criteria focus on delivering instructional approaches that are effective. It requires that:

- Individuals are made to feel like valued customers.
- Scheduling of when to register, learn, and be assessed is flexible.
- Materials are interesting and motivating.
- Approaches and materials are free of cultural, racial, class, age, and gender bias.
- Students are given opportunities to demonstrate current skills and knowledge for advanced credit or a shortened program.
- The program provides a statement of acquired skills and knowledge, not just a completion certificate.
- Various approaches are offered to appeal to different learning styles (Guidelines 1-7).

Mexico's and India's models are very general, with the criteria discussed in the previous sections being the only ones to focus on pedagogical effectiveness. In addition, both India and Mexico stress the need to make available all of the resources for teaching such as library and research opportunities. UNESCO does not offer this criterion explicitly; yet it emphasizes developing the distance education model to fit local circumstances and student needs.

The U.S. model, under CHEA, is very specific and comprehensive regarding pedagogical effectiveness. It explains the institution has a contract with the student in which (1) all the necessary courses needed for the distance education program will be available; (2) that all supporting elements of the program are effectively designed and are available for students; (3) course management and delivery are effective and appropriate; (4) appropriate resources such as libraries and other sources of research and information are available; (5) and the model provides for appropriate interactions between students and teachers.

As explained previously, e-learning in industry is very focused on effective delivery of distance education courses, and in addition to the designs of EPSS and learning objects, the industry is now exploring three key elements of delivery (Jacobs & Dempsey, 2001): (1) developing and strategically distributing object-oriented learning environments. Objects permit the reuse of code and materials, saving time and resources needed by programmers, and expanding compatibility with Internet applications. (2) The development and integration of artificial intelligence that will permit control over instructional environments and activities and improving course management, a key aspect of instructional design. (3) Advances Cognitive science and neuroscience will encourage more accurate monitoring of brain activity and the targeting of experiences based on individual activity.

A key feature of this delivery is Knowledge Management, which is "delivering the right knowledge to the right people at the right time" (Rossett, 2001). Industry efforts emphasize the following: strategic development of knowledge pieces in the context of learning objects; continuous updating of objects and information; multi-layered distribution; and integrating knowledge so as to strategically facilitate work and social processes of all stakeholders, including management, leadership, customers, and vendors. Knowledge management is such a key component of instructional designer that it has become itself a full developed area of inquiry, and thus, a topic well beyond the scope of this Chapter. However, relatively very little has been developed on this key feature for distance education or e-learning, with almost all of the "culture" research connecting knowledge management to corporate culture.

Connecting Course Delivery to Value Sets

Since knowledge management critically lacks an intercultural component, this section first articulates key research questions in this area based on all eight value sets. Next, this section articulates unanswered questions for research for the first four value sets that are discussed previously, but the Chapter will discuss in detail the connection of delivery to the value sets of Status, Context, Time, and Power distance

The following are key questions for knowledge management across cultures:

- What kind of assumptions about the dependence or independence of people is assumed by the structures and applications of the knowledge? In other words, as demonstrated in many Chapters of this book, is knowledge shared as a way to make groups cohere into more dependent units; or is it given to provide the independence and personal space needed for individualism?
- What assumptions about rules and policies do the knowledge structures and applications presume? Do they assume universal adherence or do the program the flexibility of contextual and relational factors?
- How holistic and interrelated (diffuse) or focused and isolated (specific) is the knowledge?
- What are the overall guiding structures to organizing knowledge: process and performance based (achievement and inner direction) or value assimilation, using deductive and often natural analogies and metaphors (ascriptive and outer directed).
- What time frames are used to structure and distribute knowledge (polychronic or monochronic)?
- How much context and what are the roles of contextual knowledge in the knowledge and its structures and applications? How much visual versus verbal frames are used to structure and deliver knowledge? How in tune are the knowledge objects to the contextual needs of its users?
- What are the power distance assumptions in the knowledge management, that is, does the structure assume one or two way

communications and what is the role or relevance of feedback loop from subordinates to superiors?

Obviously, much research is needed to assess the connections between knowledge management across cultures.

In addition to these knowledge management questions, distance education need to assess the following four value sets in delivery:

- How much dependence or independence does the delivery assume between teacher and students and among students themselves? For example, does the delivery assume students will work together to solve problems, strongly relying on the distance educator as a guide? Or does the delivery assume independent, isolated students working alone?
- How adaptable or universal is the delivery based on the particular context of the student learning, institution, and course?
- Is the delivery of the materials integrated into the process much like the learning wizard, which is more of a diffuse approach? Or is the delivery a specific transmission of information that students must learn to integrate on their own?
- Is the delivery method internally driven by the user (inner direction)? Or is it organized around values and organizing schema (outer direction)?

In addition to these four critical questions, this next section describes delivery in the context of Status, Time, and Context.

Status

The next value set assesses how status can influence distance education. The two most common approaches are ascription and achievement. Ascriptive-oriented cultures derive status from their social group, race, gender, age, ethnicity, and language. These variables provide the communicator with the power to get things done in complicated social structures. In achievement-oriented cultures, it does not matter where you come from, who your family is, your age, language, etc, as long as you can achieve your goals.

This value set has not been specifically assessed across cultures for e-learning delivery, but its relevance could be very fascinating. For example, McCarty (2007) argues that the process heavy educational philosophies of much western education, which emphasizes Socratic dialogue, is difficult to import to non-western countries. As mentioned throughout this book, achievement orientation strongly emphasizes process, while ascription emphasizes power players.

In addition, distance education has status problems in all cultures, but much research shows that in traditionally ascriptive oriented cultures, distance learning suffers, even more, perhaps much more, with its status than in achievement orientated cultures. For example, in my research for this chapter, the lack of status in distance education in achievement cultures such as the United States, Canada, and Australia, seemed omnipresent but in the end, not that important because this status problem was never researched nor detailed. However, the status in traditionally ascriptive countries in Asian, former communist countries, Africa, and Mexico and Central America and many South American countries undergoes severe and detailed critique. Thus, professional communicators working in ascriptive cultures might face an even more difficult challenge assuring the quality of their distance education efforts.

Context

This value set assesses the role of the context in distance education. All cultures communicate in contexts, but how they rely on these contexts for the meaning of their communications differs. Low context means that the meaning of the communication resides primarily in the explicitly coded part of the communication, not in the surrounding context. Thus, there is great focus on the accuracy of the explicitly coded text. Low context communicators strongly adhere to and require clearly written protocols. There is a high attention to detail and low attention to intention. In addition, low context communicators try to program into the communication all of the verbal signs and cues to carefully guide the reader through the message, meaning that there is an overt emphasis on organizational and transitional strategies to guide readers through the writing.

On the other end, high context communication assumes a strong reliance on the contextual and social cues for the meanings of communications. Here, good writing focuses on how information elucidates the influence of the social context on meaning of the communications. High context communicator's generally focus on adhering to interpersonal relationships instead of fixed guidelines. There is low attention to detail and high attention to intention. Instead of parallelism high context communicators prefer novelty so as to match the uniqueness of the evolving relationship in the specific context. Parallelism is boring and artificial.

In the intercultural e-learning research, high and low context receives a little attention because e-learning is such a different context. For example, Morse (2003 as explained by Uzuner, 2009) compared students from low context countries (US, the UK, Australia, and New Zealand) to a high context group (Pakistan, China, Singapore, Sri Lanka, and Thailand). Morse found that students from high context cultures viewed the lack of face-to-face contact with faculty and peers as a challenge to their ability to learn and form social relationships, whereas low context participants did not believe that the lack of face-to-face contact impacted their learning abilities positively or negatively. Many more questions, however, remain. For example, because the e-learning context is so new, how much contextual information do high context learners need and why? How quickly can high context learners contextualize their learning situations and why? On the other hand, how much do low context learners need policies and procedures spelled out in great verbal detail, and why?

Monochronic and Polychronic Time

As described in Chapter Two, cultures view and use time differently, especially in communications. Polychronic or synchronous time frames mean simultaneity, multiple tasks managed at the same time, and apparent disorganization, focusing on the importance of place, and involvement of people rather than adherence to present schedules. On the other hand, monochronic or sequential time frames mean linked linear structures of cause and effect with an organized flow of events (Hall, 1976, 1983). Polychronic time frames enhance the relationships of a variety of people in rich contextual detail.

Surprisingly, very little research has assessed the role of time frames in intercultural distance education. As articulated in Chapter Four, most of the new technologies such as the internet and social networking actually favor polychronic time frames. Thus, one important line of research might focus on the effects of e-learning on traditionally monochronic cultures and organizations.

Guideline 5: Faculty and Trainer Support and Development

This guideline is only mentioned with the U.S., Indian, Mexican, and industry models. The U.S. CHEA argues that institutions should provide (1) an ongoing program of appropriate technical, design, and production support for participating faculty members; (2) training for distance education developers to help them become proficient in the uses of the program's technologies, including potential changes in course design and management; and (3) training for those responsible for working directly with students the orientation and training to help them become proficient in the uses of the technologies for these purposes, including strategies for effective interaction (Guideline 3). Mexico requires three criteria: (1) that instructors have the same preparation as non-distance education instructors; (2) that instructors have technological and pedagogical capacity to teach via distance education; and (3) that instructors in distance education have the same status, salary, and benefits as other instructors (Guidelines 11.12-11.14). For India, one criterion is to have a permanent staff dedicated to offering and overseeing distance education programs, and the other is that "the parent institution should arrange facilities for organizing training/ workshops for academic counselors, study centre coordinators and others." The Canadian and UK model do not address the issue of faculty support.

For industry, much research, theory, and practice have focused extensively on the role of transforming traditional classroom trainers into e-trainers. Many of the instructional design principles discussed throughout this section have been subjects of research and development for e-trainers. Further, many practitioners and researchers argue that "the work of the training professional will be devoted to managing knowledge, even more than delivering it" (Rossett, 2001). Thus, trainers do not focus just on students and courses; instead, they help develop and integrate information into the actual business processes and systems, much like the EPSS or Electronic Performance Support Systems. Thus, trainers can "maximize the 'smarts' that exist within people and organizations" (Rossett, 2001). Consequently, trainers are to understand relevant knowledge, nurture it, make it accessible, encourage conversations about it, and update it (Rossett, 2001).

Connecting Faculty and Teacher Training to Cultural Values

As mentioned earlier, all of the value sets influence teaching training, but perhaps one of the most important is power distance, the last of the eight value sets.

Power Distance

Power Distance is Hofstede's (2010) concept, and it measures how inequality is handled in communications. In high power distances cultures, there is unequal, centralized distribution of power, acceptance of authority, high levels of overseeing, and top-down communication styles. Further, in high power distance cultures, subordinates are afraid to just disagree with their superiors; further, there is a high level of overseeing of subordinate activities. Low power distance cultures use communications to downplay inequalities among people. As Hofstede (2004) explains, low power distance cultures expect more mutual interdependence between subordinate and authority. Communications between superior and subordinate tend to be more consultative, with the superior acting as perhaps someone with more knowledge, but not in reality being in a higher position. Authority is something to be used only as more of a last resort rather than the explicit framework for the communication situation. Subordinates are not afraid to disagree with superiors; in fact subordinates are often a source of good feedback for decisions is that the superiors need to take.

Some intercultural e-learning research has addressed power distance. Wang (2007) attributed Korean and Chinese students preference for asynchronous communication to an Asian cultural trait, "think more, talk less, and think it through before speaking" (p. 303). Although all three cultural groups found individual work boring and challenging, mixed results were found regarding their perceptions of online team work. Among the three groups, Korean students were found to be the least comfortable with online collaborative work. The study also showed that American students tended to communicate more with their instructors because they perceived them as equals, whereas Korean and Chinese students reported low levels of comfort in approaching their instructors. Wang (2007) attributed this finding to Asian culture's embodiment of power distance.

Guideline 6: Student Support and Facilitating Student Learning

All of the distance education models emphasize student support and designs to facilitate student learning. The UK model is perhaps the most comprehensive, and it argues for fully supporting student learning. It requires that

- Institutions should give attention to supporting and promoting autonomous learning and enabling learners to take personal control over their own development.
- Institutions should meet the needs of the students studying at a distance for full and clear information about the nature and expectations of the program of study, the relationship between achievement and assessment, academic progress and the accumulation of credit, and the characteristics of the distance learning system and how students interact with it. The information provided should be conveyed in a way that enables students to make informed decisions about their own education, and to monitor their progress against clear expectations of achievement.
- Institutions should monitor the effectiveness of information provided to students, and in response to their findings, take steps to enhance its provision.
- Institutions should take steps to determine what means of student representation are appropriate and realistic for students in a distance learning program, and provide those students with accurate information about them (Guidelines 15-18).

The CHEA is equally comprehensive explaining that: (1) students need to be qualified both academically and technologically to enroll in the programs; (2) that the institution needs to inform the students of all of the resources available for the program; (3) the institution needs to prepare the student to understand the nature of learning via distance education; and (4) the institution needs to develop a learning community, in conjunction with the distance education courses and programs to facilitate student development.

The Canadian model is focused even more specifically on student needs, requiring distance educators to assess these 15 student needs:

- What are the intended learning outcomes, and what entry level knowledge or skill is necessary for a reasonable chance of success?
- What recognition will be awarded upon successful completion (e.g., transferable credits, degree, professional designation, etc.)?
- What are the necessary learning skills needed for success (e.g., the ability to write, to manage time, to take examinations, etc.)?
- What types of material are to be covered, and what are the sources and the relevance of this content?
- What is the format for instruction and assignments (i.e., group or individual)?
- Who will be teaching and assessing the students?
- What is the nature of the assessments, and what are the criteria for success?

- How long can the course be expected to take, including mandatory or flexible timelines?
- What are the minimum computer and operation system requirements, and what options exist, if any?
- What technical skills will be required to access the course materials?
- What are the total costs, including tuition, books and materials, equipment, and other fees?
- How credible is the product? What are the qualifications of the design and delivery personnel, and how objective are the evaluation reports?
- How does one get started? What are the complete registration procedures and services?
- How does one get help? Who does one contact for technical assistance and content expertise?
- What are the policies for withdrawal and refunds? (Guidelines 1-15 in Basic Information Needs).

This list is exhaustive and detailed. Unlike this detailed list of student needs, the UNESCO model focuses on integrating distance education into national standards and current traditions and infrastructures as a way to facilitate and validate learning. This is not surprising because these criteria are meant to operate around the world. The Mexican model requires the institution to be registered with the government so that the degree is legally recognized; and that admission requirements and standards are clearly determined and applied. The Indian model only requires that "the number of students admitted for the programme(s) of study under the Distance Education programme shall not exceed the limits prescribed by the Distance Education Council, from time to time." India also requires the infrastructure and adequate instructors are available, but it does not explicitly discuss student support.

Industry has also focused exhaustively on student needs, following many of the guidelines already articulated with the academic models. In addition, much industry research has developed specific applications of many of these student issues. Clark & Mayer (2003) explore critical instructional design principles for effective student learning: (1) effectively integrating all types of media: written, audio, visual, graphical, video, etc; (2) maintaining coherency so as to facilitate focus and concentration; (3) using personalized, more informal style with coaches or tutors; (4) effectively structuring components into integrated wholes; (5) leveraging examples; and (6) practice.

Connecting Student Learning to Cultural Values

Since many of the value sets that affect student learning have already been discussed thoroughly in previous sections, I will use this section to focus on key influences of the communication technologies on potential student behavior in intercultural e-learning contexts. Much of the structure and theory of this section is derived from Chapter Four where the reader can go for more specific grounding. This section simply summarizes–and calls for–more research and theory about e-learning, communication technologies, and students.

Individual-Collective and Students' E-Learning

As explained in Chapter Four, orality strongly reinforces collectivity while writing seems to correlate very strongly with individualistic cultures; and hypertext and Web 2.0 might be encouraging new types of collectivity. This difference is mostly due to the availability of social presence in orality, and its lack in writing. And social presence most likely can be developed in the online environments. This simply means that students in collective cultures will most likely be stressed (at first) without the personal presence and intimacy cues that orality provides in traditional presence-based course, while students in individualistic cultures might enjoy the additional personal space and freedom. However, Social Information Processing (SIP) Theory (Walther, 1992) theorizes that electronic and online relations probably need more time to develop than face to face relations, but once established, these online relations maintained the same characteristics and relations as face-to-face communications. In addition, online media might facilitate interpersonal relations that were not possible with face-to-face, due to physical distance or social hierarchy or identity issues. Thus, since hypertext and Web 2.0 technologies are very rich media, they can allow for more ways to enhance the personal presence and intimacy cues associated with traditional collectivity in the e-learning context.

Certainly, since other types of communication technologies such as cell phones and texting are omnipresent, many students in collective cultures will be used to distance technologies but just not in instructional contexts. Perhaps this is a good example of adaptations according to Channel Expansion theory, which argues that the richness of the communication media depends on the uses and experience of the groups using it (Carlson & Zmud, 1999). Experience of communicators with the media allow communicators to "develop associated knowledge bases that may be used to more effectively both encode and decode rich messages on a channel" (p. 155). As communicators adapt to the media, they can encode and decode messages better, a process that seems to make the media richer than it at first appears to be. Carlson & Zmud (1999) identify four media richness building experiences: familiarity with the media; familiarity with the topic of discussion; knowledge of the communication or organizational context; and experience with the other people involved with the communication. Because media richness is produced or structured by the social context, its richness will vary according to the local cultural values.

Thus, curriculum developers and researchers might pay attention to how these newer technologies relate to the collective and individualistic needs and assumptions of their students. For example, distance educators might consider explicit mapping and signposting (concepts defined in Chapter Four) for collective and individualistic cultures. *Mapping* means the visual design of the digital space such as sitemaps, and ***Signposting*** refers to helping users understand where they are in the context of the entire digital space. Explicit mapping and signposting of the virtual space using oral metaphors or analogies would help orient collective students and instructors, while mapping and signposting of explicit guidelines of independence might help those from collective cultures.

Universal-Particular and Students' E-Learning

The relation of universalism and particularism to student learning in distance education is a particularly important variable. Writing has strong connections to universalism in organizational settings, while orality has strong connections to particularism. Since writing is so closely related to universalist, precedence-setting values and orality to particular, case-by-case norms, distance education instructors need to carefully consider the influence of the electronic media, which tend to be situated theoretically between writing and orality (Moran and Hawisher 1998; Kress 1999). Does the email have the force of a written or oral guideline? In the context of the interactive Web 2.0 technologies, the interactive elements probably encourage very particular relations and circumstances; however, the ability to store and retrieve information correlates with universalism.

Among many of the design features, this value set probably influences levels of *Homogeneity and Heterogeneity* (discussed in Chapter Four) the most in curricular design. As shown in Chapter Five Website Designs, universalist cultures strongly template their website designs, showing great levels of homogeneity across the pages and sections. Thus, interactions across the electronic course space should be highly regulated and templated in universalist cultures. On the other hand, particular cultures show a strong preference for heterogeneity in their websites, including many uses of art and other. Thus, interactions across the electronic course space should allow for the more oral like spontaneity and unique relations that are so common in particular cultures. In addition, Universal cultures using overt mapping (templating) and overt signposting, which increases uniformity across information designs, as an aid to users. On the other hand, particular cultures strongly focus on change, uniqueness, and novelty as motivation for reading information.

Universal and particular also address *Metadata/Taxonomy*, which refers to the need to label information, and *Pattern language*, which refers to the use of official language structures, policies, and codes for hypertext and Web 2.0 technologies. These two components vary significantly across for universal and particular cultures. Universal cultures have a strong tendency to categorize and label information verbally and uniformly across websites (Thatcher, 2009). This is often due to the "dumbing down" of websites for the universal reader. Particular cultures are much more sensitive to the levels of audience knowledge and will categorize or label information only when necessary and will often use non-verbal or visual labels instead. Universal cultures also strongly emphasize the development and dissemination of official language structures, policies, and codes for hypertext and Web 2.0 technologies, while particular cultures assume this development and dissemination is part of the institutional power structure and is not developed nor disseminated explicitly.

Specific and Diffuse and Students' E-Learning

This value set correlates strongly with the richness media studies. Specific cultures usually connect very favorably to writing, while diffuse cultures strongly correlate with orality. This is because as media, orality is more diffuse and writing is more specific. In comparison, email has less context and is much poorer in social information and social presence as compared to orality, but email can provide a certain online context, much like a hyperpersonal presence, which might encourage an online version of diffuse orientation. Hypertext is a much richer medium than email and thus can correlate to diffuse much better than email and writing. Web 2.0 can facilitate both, depending on the boundaries and mechanisms of online relations (see Chapter Four for more details).

These technology-culture relations influence a variety of information design principles. First is the design principle of ***Granularity***, which refers to the size or level of information, starting from large websites, to documents, and to bits of information. As explained in many chapters of this book, diffuse information is usually more detailed but also comes in a more holistic, larger, and more analogical and complicated chunk. On the other hand, universal information has been regularized so as to be presented in parallel fashion to a much more general audience. Thus, students coming from diffuse cultures will most likely prefer a larger over-riding structure of the information but inside that larger structure is a more complexly related combination of diffuse details. On the other hand, students from universal cultures will prefer overt parallel, often pyramid-like, structures where each section is linked analytically.

A key connection of specific and diffuse is the concept of mindfulness versus mindlessness, which is discussed more fully in Chapter Four. As Langer (1997) explains, mindfulness means (a) openness to novelty; (b) alertness to distinction; (c) sensitivity to different contexts; (d) implicit, if not explicit, awareness of multiple perspectives; and (e) orientation in the present. In other words, mindfulness is the ability to continually see something as new or novel, something like a beginner's mind, which encourages a continual and active quest for novelty. Mindfulness is also closely connected to play. On the other hand, mindlessness is the tendency to operate on autopilot, either through sheer boredom and roteness or simply not paying attention. Instead of play, mindlessness is connected to work. As Langer explains, mindlessness often results from three types of thinking; categorical or stereotypical; acting from a single perspective; and repetition. Based on much of my research involving instructional materials in Ecuadorian (2000) and Mexican (2006), I learned that the more diffuse Ecuadorian and Mexican personnel would quickly be bored with universalized training materials; and preferred, instead, the uniqueness of particular training materials. They associated mindfulness with diffuse and mindlessness with specific, while the Americans usually preferred the universalized rhetoric.

Ascription-Achievement and Students' E-Learning

This value set significantly influences the motivation for students doing the work, but as explained in Chapter Four, this value set probably does not correlate as well with the media as the previous three value sets. For example, the personal presence and context of orality probably allows the ascriptive variables to be acknowledged, but these same variables can be communicated through writing. Orality is also a very "active" medium because its performance is live and can be documented. This active orientation correlates with achievement orientation. In addition, many of the achievements that are communicated as data, results, and concrete accomplishments are perhaps best documented in writing.

Email, hypertext, and Web 2.0 also correlate with both ascription and achievement. As shown in Chapter Five, Hypertext is also quite adept at communicating ascriptive values such as graphics of coat of arms and traditional ascriptive icons. Because Web 2.0 has the same rich communicative potential and storage and retrieval abilities of both email and hypertext, it can also easily communicate ascriptive values. However, the interactive elements of Web 2.0, especially among relative strangers, probably encourage an approach that is less focused on ascriptive values of the participants and more on their actual performance or behavior, an achievement orientation.

For this value set, the most relevant design principles are probably mapping and sign posting. As explained in Chapter Ten Instructions and Chapter Six Organizational Behavior, the idea of process is very significant for achievement oriented cultures, and the idea of authority or decision-makers is very important in ascriptive cultures. Thus, educators designing online curriculum would be well served to map out and overtly sign the curriculum based on the learning processes or projects for the achievement oriented students; and map out and overtly sign the decision-makers for the ascriptive oriented students.

Inner and Outer Orientation and Students' E-Learning

Like many of the other value sets, orality and writing strongly correlate with inner and outer directed. Orality exemplifies an outer orientation because it is highly contextual and focuses on managing the relations in this context. On the other hand, writing strongly correlates with inner directed. Like writing, email probably is more comfortable with inner directed cultures where authors or audience can detach themselves from the communication context and ignore, fight, or accept the outside, contextual forces.

Hypertext and Web 2.0, unlike email, probably fit better outer direction. In fact, the web is a good metaphor for outer direction because its shows how all links and parts are harmonized into one whole. Even though the web is outer directed, much website design, especially in inner directed cultures such as the United States, focuses on the user's ability to create his or her own unique paths or control his path and processes. This is an outer-directed medium being designed for inner-directed users. The interactive features of Web 2.0 probably fit inner directed better than outer directed, unless those features significantly control the interactions, which is an outer-directed mentality.

This culture/technology connection is perhaps best addressed with information design principle of ***Ambience***, which refers to how the design of the communication technology allows the human agent to interact with it. Inner cultures assume human agency derives from the inner will, and thus, is in constantly battle with outside forces to impose that will on them. Outer cultures assume human agency needs to be reconciled and harmonized with outside forces. Thus, information designs in inner-directed cultures strongly emphasize the need to allow the user to impose an infinite variety of paths, while outer-directed cultures make that path more rigid, forcing users to follow much more rigid structures (Thatcher, 2009). These are general design principles for meeting students' needs in either inner or outer directed cultures.

High and Low Context and Students' E-Learning

High context communication correlates very closely with orality because orality is a much richer medium. On the other hand, low context communication correlates closely with writing (see Victor 1992) because it does not provide the rich contextual details that orality can. E-mail is a decontextualized medium, maybe more so than written communications; therefore, many e-mail communicators have developed the use of emoticons, graphically codified symbols to represent emotions and context, a logical approach in a medium that is too decontextual for the communicators' needs. Further, hypertext incorporates audio-visual features such as color, photographs, graphics, voices, and sounds, which perhaps invoke the context better—and in different ways—than writing and orality. The interactions of Web 2.0 technologies can be very low context as well, perhaps lower than hypertext because they usually have just verbal interactions, but Web 2.0 can incorporate all of the audio, visual, and perhaps even tactile features of hypertext.

High and low context correlates to four important information design principles. First, mapping and signposting can either take place through verbal means, connecting to low context, or visual or metaphoric means, which are more high context. For example, in low context (and monochronic) cultures, websites are designed in a very linear, box-like fashion, with many drop-down menus using verbal information and signposting. In high context (and polychronic cultures), narratives and visual images are used much more. In fact, in many high context cultures, instead of linear, drop-down menus as the predominant page design, pictures are used as visual analogies of the website design, with links coded into different parts of the picture.

The design principles of *Metadata/Taxonomy* and *Pattern language* are connected to high and low context. For example, low-context cultures have a strong tendency to categorize and label information verbally and uniformly across websites (Thatcher, 2009). This is often due to the "dumbing down" of websites for the universal reader. High-context cultures are much more sensitive to the levels of audience knowledge and will categorize or label information only when necessary and will often use non-verbal or visual labels instead. Low context cultures will most likely code the official language structures, policies, and codes into their information technology pages, while high-context cultures will assume that organizational structures and policies outside the electronic page are the appropriate places for this information.

Time and Students' E-Learning

Time orientation has an obvious correlation to student learning in distance education. Orality has built in polychronic time, that is, the simultaneity and flux. Writing, on the other hand, has a significant monochronic effect (see Kaufer & Carley, 1993). Email has elements of both oral and written rhetoric in its time orientation. It has a strong simultaneity as multiple authors can be discussing the same issue at the same time. However, email also has storage ability of writing, which can encourage a linear analysis of the happenings. Hypertext and Web 2.0 correlate with and can accommodate both monochronic and polychronic time frames. However, these two media also fit very nicely with polychronic time frames. Web 2.0 can also significantly encourage simultaneous interactions, especially with the instant public technologies such as twitter.

Time frames connect to one information design principle, mapping. The information design can rely on monochronic or polychronic mapping, that is a sequential (asynchronous) or synchronous general design. This has significant ramifications for all kinds of communication such as teacher-student and student-student, as well as students accessing information, and assessing performance. The second design principle is

Power Distance and Students' E-Learning

One of the traditional characteristics of high power distance communication is orality. Because orality provides the richest social presence and context, it is the best at communicating and maintaining authority. Writing also obviously occurs in high power distance cultures, but once something has been written down and separated from that author, this is a loss of power, especially if that information is disseminated widely or democratically. As a medium, email correlates rather oddly with power distance. Certainly, high power distance cultures can communicate their power symbols and control their power through email, but email has the dissemination, storage, retrievability, and thus, analyzability of writing, all of which probably encourages a more low power distance approach to communication. Hypertext has much more social and contextual richness of orality, which probably predisposes it to be a better medium for high power distance. Like hypertext, Web 2.0 probably favors lower power distance especially because the interactions are usually not based on existing power structures in society. However, it is entirely possible for Web 2.0 creators to develop rigid power structures into the interactive interface, thus exemplifying perfectly high power distance relations.

Power distance most directly affects ***Ambience***. In low power distance cultures, electronic information is like consultative peers, there to help in a more egalitarian manner, while in high power distance cultures, information pages have a strong authority, often mandating its use.

Guideline 7: Evaluation and Assessment

All of the evaluate models stress evaluation and assessment as critical factors in distance education. The CHEA model from the United State is the most explicit and detailed. It introduces assessment in the following way:

> *Both the assessment of student achievement and evaluation of the overall program take on added importance as new techniques evolve. For example, in asynchronous programs the element of*

seat time is essentially removed from the equation. For these reasons, the institution conducts sustained, evidence-based and participatory inquiry as to whether distance learning programs are achieving objectives. The results of such inquiry are used to guide curriculum design and delivery, pedagogy, and educational processes, and may affect future policy and budgets and perhaps have implications for the institution's roles and mission (Guideline 5).

To carry out this assessment, the CHEA recommends five approaches:

- That documented assessment of student achievement is conducted in each course and at the completion of the program, by comparing student performance to the intended learning outcomes.
- When examinations are employed, they take place in circumstances that include firm student identification. The institution otherwise seeks to assure the integrity of student work.
- Overall program effectiveness is determined by such measures as:
    - The extent to which student learning matches intended outcomes
    - The extent to which student intent is met.
    - Student retention rates, including variations over time.
    - Student satisfaction, as measured by regular surveys.
    - Faculty satisfaction, as measured by regular surveys and peer review processes.
    - The extent to which access is provided to students not previously served.
    - The extent to which library and learning resources are used appropriately by the program's students.
    - Measures of student competence in fundamental skills such as communication, comprehension, and analysis.
    - Cost effectiveness of the program to its students, as compared to campus-based alternatives.
- The institution conducts a program of continual self-evaluation directed toward program improvement, targeting more effective uses of technology to improve pedagogy, advances in student achievement of intended outcomes, improved retention rates, effective use of resources, and demonstrated improvements in the institution's service to its internal and external constituencies. The program and its results are reflected in the institution's ongoing self-evaluation process and are used to inform the further plans of the institution and those responsible for its academic programs.
- Institutional evaluation of electronically offered programs takes place in the context of the regular evaluation of all academic programs (Guideline 5).

The other models requirement assessment but not with the specificity of the U.S. model. For example, the UK has five assessment criteria:

- Institutions should be able to demonstrate that all summative assessment procedures used are appropriate for the mode of study, and that in all respects assessment procedures accord with the requirements to safeguard academic standards.
- Institutions should be able to demonstrate that the summative assessment of a module, or a program as a whole, assesses students' achievement of stated learning outcomes.
- Institutions should have direct control of the summative assessment process and of the determination of results.

- Formative assessments should be used as part of the design of distance learning programs.
- Institutions should monitor the soundness of their assessment practices and amend them in response to feedback (Guidelines 19-23).

The Mexican model is similar to the UK model. It requires seven assessment methods:

- The institution must have a continuous and systematic mechanism for assessing the quality of distance educational programs.
- The institution must develop, disseminate and implement an evaluation system for distance education teachers.
- The institution must develop, disseminate and implement an evaluation system for distance learning.
- The institution must carry out studies that allow identify the rates of retention and student satisfaction regarding these programs.
- The institution must collect and use the opinions of its faculty, alumni and the community to support the design, review or updating of distance educational programs.
- The institution must ensure that mechanisms to evaluate the academic performance of students be equivalent to those used by other institutions for the evaluation of these materials, whether in a classroom or at a distance.
- The institution must extend to students and graduates of distance education programs the same rights, qualifications, awards and treatment of any student receive any other type of education (Guidelines 11.18-11.24)

The Canadian model does not have a specific assessment category, although many of its questions relate to assessing overall performance of distance education. The India law simply states that "the parent institution should clearly spell out the evaluation mechanism and procedure duly approved by the statutory bodies of the universities and make available staff qualified for the purpose."

When comparing academia and industry, this is perhaps the first guideline where academia is more comprehensive. For example, Fee (2009) argues for five types of assessment:

1. Kirkpatrick's four levels: reactions, learning, behavior, results
2. Return on investment: total benefits of the education versus its costs.
3. Return of expectation: measures perceived needed value to mastered value
4. Sixth Sigma: measures the value of the e-learning by reduction of errors and defects in workprocesses and products.
5. Total value added: measures ideas, general knowledge, intellectual capital, improved processes, and creativity.

In assessing these objectives, Fee (2009) explains how objectives 1, 2, and 4 are easy to measure while 3 and 5 are very difficult. Not surprisingly, industry is better at assessing the effect on productivity and not as adept at values and more qualitative measures such as intellectual capital. The *ATSD Handbook* (2001) similarly presents assessment as (1) return on investment and (2) as a cost-benefit analysis. These measures are best at measuring specific learner objectives, but they do not get at some of the larger curriculum issues

Grounded in Local Cultures

Since assessment is a comprehensive process involving all of the guidelines, distance education designers must simply assess how well the curriculum meets the needs of the students, based on the projected cultural values of the student population. This is simple in principle; extremely difficult in practice; most intercultural research in organizational behavior has been trying to do that, with rather limited effectiveness.

It is important to point out, however, that assessment as an activity and process is generally more closely aligned with the following set of cultural values:

- Individualistic cultures because assessing group work in distance learning is difficult because many students are not working in groups;
- Universalist cultures because assessment usually sets up universal criteria for evaluating the curriculum; and assessing particular relations developed or strengthened are almost never part of the assessment methodology.
- Specific orientation because objectives and parts of curriculum need to be sectioned off the greater whole in order to measure performance; diffuse qualities like values are much more difficult to measure.
- Achievement orientation because intangible, ascriptive variables are often difficult to measure;
- Inner direction because of the assumption of aligning learning with specific proposed outcomes, not general deductive criteria such as harmony building;
- Low context because assessing the contextual influence of the e-learning and user contexts on learning is difficult.
- Monochronic because it is difficult to assess and instruct at the same time; and assessment is heavily process based.
- Low power distanced because students, not the authorities, have a significant voice in the quality of courses.

As it should be obvious, these values correspond mainly to western, developed nations. Thus, much research is needed to understand how assessment can work as effectively in cultures that do not exhibit these particular values.

CONCLUSION

In the final chapter of her edited collection, Edmundson (2007) provides a curricular development that merits summary here. It is essentially a 5x5 curricular table with the following curricular development steps on the left column and levels of culture going across the top row. The curricular development five parts are: content, pedagogy, media, values sets (much like this chapter), and adaptation. The row starts at basic information, moves to some fairly concrete cognitive attributes and ends at soft skills. This is a fairly comprehensive model, but it does not connect the value sets across the different layers of curriculum as the framework for using the seven guidelines does. This chapter has demonstrated that the guidelines from five countries, UNESCO, and industry are fairly similar in design and purpose but each guideline needs to be analyzed from an intercultural perspective. And each of the value sets influences all parts of the curriculum, including organizational culture, technology, instructional design, faculty support, delivery, student learning, and assessment. Thus, this chapter becomes a useful model for educators working on distance learning across cultures.

REFERENCES

Adler, N. (2008). *International dimensions of organizational behavior*. New York, NY: Thomson Learning Center.

Carr-Chellman, A. A. (2004). *Global perspectives on e-learning*. Newbury Park, CA: Sage Publications.

Catterick, D. (2007). Do the philosophical foundations of online learning disadvantage nonwestern students. In Edmunson, A. (Ed.), *Globalized e-learning cultural challenge* (pp. 116–129). Hershey, PA: IGI Global.

Clark, R., & Mayer, R. E. (2003). *E-learning and the science of instruction: proven guidelines for consumers*. New York, NY: Jossey-Bass.

Edmundson, A. (Ed.). (2007). *Globalized e-learning cultural challenges*. Hershey, PA: IGI Global.

Fee, K. (2009). *Delivering e-learning*. London, UK: Kogan Page.

Hofstede, G. (2010). *Cultures and organizations, software of the mind* (3rd ed.). New York, NY: McGraw Hill.

House, R. J., Hanges, P. J., Javidan, M., Dorfman, P. R., & Gupta, V. (Eds.). (2005). *Culture, leadership, and organizations: The GLOBE study of 62 societies*. Newbury Park, CA: Sage Publications.

Jacobs, J., & Dempsey, J. (2001). Emerging instructional technologies: The near future. In Rossett, A. (Ed.), *ASTD e-learning handbook* (pp. 322–337). New York, NY: McGraw-Hill.

McCarty, S. (2007). Theorizing and realizing the global classroom. In Edmunson, A. (Ed.), *Globalized e-learning cultural challenge* (pp. 90–115). Hershey, PA: IGI Global.

McCool, M. (2007). *Reaching a global online audience*. Cambridge, MA: Oreilly Media, Inc.

McLoughlin, C. (2007). Adapting e-learning across cultural boundaries: A framework for quality learning, pedagogy, and interaction. In Edmunson, A. (Ed.), *Globalized e-learning cultural challenge* (pp. 223–238). Hershey, PA: IGI Global.

Olaniran, B. (2007). Culture and communication challenges in virtual workspaces. In St.Amant, K. (Ed.), *Linguistic and cultural online communication issues in the global age* (pp. 75–91). Hershey, PA: Idea Group. doi:10.4018/978-1-59904-213-8.ch006

Rossett, A. (Ed.). (2001). *ASTD e-learning handbook*. New York, NY: McGraw-Hill.

St.Amant, K. (2007a). Online education in an age of globalization: Foundational perspectives and practices for technical communication instructors and trainers. *Technical Communication Quarterly*, *16*, 13–30.

St.Amant, K. (Ed.). (2007b). *Linguistic and cultural online communication issues in the global age*. Hershey, PA: IGI Global. doi:10.4018/978-1-59904-213-8

Starke-Meyerring, D., & Wilson, M. (Eds.). (2008). *Designing globally networked learning environments: Visionary partnerships, policies, and pedagogies*. Rotterdam, The Netherlands: Sense Publishers.

Stewart, E., & Bennett, M. (1991). *American cultural patterns: A cross-cultural perspective* (Rev. ed.). Yarmouth, ME: Intercultural Press, Inc.

Sullivan, P., & Porter, J. E. (1998). *Opening spaces: writing technologies and critical research practices*. Greenwich, CT: Ablex.

Thatcher, B. L. (2009). Understanding digital literacy across cultures. In Spilka, R. (Ed.), *Digital literacy for technical communication: 21st Century theory and practice* (pp. 169–198). London: Routledge.

UNESCO. (2002). *Using open and distance learning: Technology, curriculum, cost, and evaluation*. Paris, France: Higher Education Division, Teacher Education Section.

Uzuner, S. (2009). Questions of culture in distance learning: A research review. *International Review of Research in Open and Distance Learning, 10*(3), 1–17.

Victor, D. (1992). *International business communication*. New York, NY: HarperCollins Publishers.

Walther, J. B. (1992). Interpersonal effects in computer-mediated interaction: A relational perspective. *Communication Research, 19*, 52–90. doi:10.1177/009365092019001003

Walther, J. B. (1996). Computer-mediated communication: Impersonal, interpersonal, and hyperpersonal interaction. *Communication Research, 23*, 3–43. doi:10.1177/009365096023001001

Wang, M. (2007). Designing online courses that effectively engage learners from diverse cultural backgrounds. *British Journal of Educational Technology, 38*(2), 294–311. doi:10.1111/j.1467-8535.2006.00626.x

Wiley, D. A. (2000). Connecting learning objects to instructional design theory: A definition, a metaphor, and a taxonomy. In D. A. Wiley (Ed.), *The instructional use of learning objects: Online Version*. Retrieved from http://www.reusability.org read/chapters/wiley.doc

Chapter 8
Legal Traditions, the Universal Declaration of Human Rights, and Intercultural Professional Communication

ABSTRACT

This chapter examines the relations between rhetoric and law across cultures, grounding the discussion in U.S. common law, Latin American Civil law, and Asian law. It also explores the writing of the Universal Declaration of Human Rights as a model of developing "international" or "universal" approaches to law and human rights. It concludes by discussing recent events of international law involving intellectual property and global communications.

INTRODUCTION

More than 40 years ago, Octavio Paz, the great Mexican Nobel prize winner of literature, argued that to understand Mexican law is to understand Mexican culture and vice versa (1985). Guided by his own versions of Marxism, Paz continually emphasized the influence of Mexican law in structuring economic, social, and cultural institutions and practices in Mexico; and most often, his purpose for connecting law and culture was to compare U.S. and Mexican cultures as a way for those from the United States to better understand Mexico. Many other scholars have similarly argued for the extensive and comprehensive influence of law on Mexican culture, with some focusing on the era of colonialization (Kellogg, 2005) and current U.S.-Mexico relations (Castaneda, 1995). Kellogg's work (2005), for example, is useful for rhetoric and professional communication scholars because she shows how attorneys, Mexican law, and legal discourse were all key mechanisms for structuring colonialization and subsequent economic and social relations in Mexico.

Much like Paz and Kellog, the U.S. scholar James White (1985) argues for the intimate connections between law and culture, but White goes even further, claiming that the connection between these two is accomplished through rhetoric. In 1985, White argues that Law is most usefully seen not, as it usually is by academic and philosophers, "as a system of rules, but as a branch of rhetoric; and that the kind of rhetoric of which law is the species. It is most usefully seen not, as rhetoric

DOI: 10.4018/978-1-61350-450-5.ch008

usually is, either as a failed science or the ignoble art of persuasion, but as the central art by which community and culture are established, maintained, and transformed. So regarded, rhetoric is continuous with law, and like it, has justice as its ultimate subject" (p. 684).

White continued his inquiry into law and rhetoric for more than 20 years, always arguing for the connection between law and culture, with rhetoric as the mediator and justice as its end or purpose. In this work, White does not clearly lay out his theory of rhetoric, but he does argue for the use of language systems for structuring and encouraging legal systems, institutions, and education. Similarly from the UK, Neil McCormick's *Rhetoric and the Rule of Law* (2005) examines the rhetorical structures of legal reasoning and law, arguing "the whole enterprise of explicating and expounding criteria and forms of good legal reasoning has to be in the context of fundamental values that we impute to legal order" (p.1). Following a traditional view of rhetoric, such as the one articulated by Perelman (1982), McCormick examines the following rhetorical devices in legal reasoning: syllogisms, deductivism, universals-particulars, judging by consequences, analogies, narratives, and using precedents, among others.

The works of Paz, White, and McCormick are important for rhetorical scholars because they connect the formation of law and corresponding legal institutions, education, and practice with rhetoric and culture. Further, these works argue that rhetoric and law are connected to justice, that is, a sense of fairness, ethics, and rule of law, over rule of will (Tamanaha, 2006). McCormick (2005) explains that despite the current skepticism of values in the postmodern world, "that some arguments are genuinely better than others" (p.2). He centers this discussion of "better" in terms of argumentation (rhetoric) and grounds them in universal applications In a more developed way, Twining, in his critical work *Globalisation and Legal Theory* (2000), argues that the emic-like features assumed by postmodern law cannot provide the foundation for law in the age of globalization, a point more thoroughly discussed in the next section. McCormick's work is rich in rhetorical inquiry, but often controversial because it places rhetoric at the center of law making and justice, a sort of relativism that worries many legal scholars that are unfamiliar with rhetorical inquiry, but as explained later, is the kind of rhetorical ethics that are critical to law in a globalized world (Twining, 2000). Despite these rich rhetorical inquiries into law, McCormick's work is directed to the law field, not to professional communication; thus, applying his work to intercultural professional communication is difficult. Further, White's work predates most postmodernism, so he never directly refutes this epistemology or connects it to cross-cultural work. Neither scholar provides enough rhetorical or cultural theory to systematically compare law and rhetoric across cultures, the topic of this chapter.

Despite these groundbreaking inquiries by Paz, White, McCormick, and others, there is relatively little discussion of rhetoric, culture, and law in professional communication. There is some work with ethics and professional communication (Porter, 1998; Dombroski, 1999), but these works examine the relation of ethics and rhetoric through critical, postmodern theories, not grounding the connections to U.S. legal systems and culture, even though both works are based in the United States. In short, they are not useful for connecting law and rhetoric across cultures. Most current work in professional communication that addresses intercultural legal issues focuses on copyright and intellectual property, loosely linking the values of property and authorship of one culture (often China) with another culture (often the United States). (See, for example, St. Amant, 2007a). This important, but relatively narrow, view of law is critical for intercultural work, but it does not give a sufficient foundation for comparing the influence of law on rhetorical patterns across cultures. Further, the work in ethics and copyright has not systematically connected law and rhetoric in a way that provides for an effective, universal framework, much like that discussed in Chapters One and Two.

And despite the growing body of research connecting law and rhetoric, little research connects international law to rhetoric, let alone professional communication. For example, the newly created *Intercultural Human Rights Law Review* (St. Thomas University) is fairly typical in its discussion of law and culture as it presents compelling reviews of international law as connected to human rights. A large number of articles in this review evaluate the human rights effects of the U.S. embargo against Cuban, a topic very appropriate for this Miami-based journal. This is just a sample of a huge body of work connecting international law to human rights. However, this research rarely systematically explores the cultural nature of the legal systems, connecting this nature to rhetoric and professional communication patterns. Instead, as explained later, it discusses the nature of culture, rights, and values, especially in light of current postmodern, postcolonial, and globalization research.

Consequently, the current state of scholarship in law, culture, and professional communication leave many questions unanswered, especially the questions articulated by Paz connecting law, culture, and communication. For example, how do different legal systems influence professional communication patterns in predominant genres such as policies and procedures documents, technical specifications, copyright/intellectual property, and joint business ventures? And how can scholars and practitioners be assured that their communication approaches adhere to the rhetorical assumptions related to these patterns practices? And how do different legal traditions structure the rhetorical approaches to very critical global discussions of human rights, health, energy, economic development, environment, immigration, privacy and others? Do rhetorical and cultural differences influence the development and application of law in these areas, and if so, how do the global and local approaches compare?

This chapter seeks to develop such a framework and explore some of these questions. The first part integrates rhetoric, law, justice, and culture in an intercultural rhetorical model. The second part exemplifies how that theory of intercultural rhetoric and law is exemplified in the writing and application of the *Universal Declaration of Human Rights* (*UDHR*), especially in the contexts of human rights. The third part of this chapter applies the intercultural legal model to current issues facing intercultural professional communicators, articulating key questions for research and theory development.

CONNECTIONS AMONG RHETORIC, LAW, AND ETHICS FOR INTERCULTURAL PROFESSIONAL COMMUNICATION

Although the connections among rhetoric, law, and ethics might seem overly intimidating and complex, in reality, they are fairly simple for two reasons: because of the power of the intercultural rhetoric model developed in Chapters One and Two easily connects culture and law; and second, the need to compare law across cultures requires a simplified version of law. First, as explained in these chapters, the relation of rhetoric and culture is based on the four-part onion model from Chapter One, as pasted next, for the reader's convenience.

As shown Figure 1, the center of intercultural rhetorical theory is the definition itself. The second layer moving outward is the epistemology; the third layer is the ideology; and the fourth layer is the rhetorical patterns. Only the outer two layers are empirically observable while the other two layers are implicit. In addition, each inner layer structures the outer layers, while the outer layers continuously restructure the inner layers in a mutually constructive process. In other words, the same logic appears in all four layers but manifests itself differently. In short, we can observe the social behaviors or ideologies and the rhetorical patterns, and from most patterns we can infer the epistemologies and definitions of the self.

This model clearly connects culture and rhetoric, as exemplified in every chapter in this book. This model, however, does not overtly link rhetoric and law, but that connection is also simple. As shown in Figure 2, from Chapter One, the rhetoric portion of the culture-rhetoric model details the relationships among four key components: the author or originator of the message; the audience or the recipient; the medium such as the book, the e-mail, or the oral conversation; and the reality/topic of the conversation or message. The three sides of the triangle are mediated by the medium such as e-mail.

This rhetorical triangle has explicit connections to law, justice or ethics (as Bakhtin, 1990; 1993 or Burke, 1968 would say) because the rhetoric defines both the elements of the rhetorical triangle as well as the relationships among the four elements. In other words, this defining of people and their relations in a rhetorical context inherently involves ethics or justice (Bakhtin, 1993). For example, in my rhetorical situation at New Mexico State University, often my graduate students have difficulty in deciding which term to use when they address me. Some prefer "Dr. Thatcher" and others prefer "Professor Thatcher," while many simply call me "Barry." Eventually, each student decides, based on our evolving relations. Some of my Latin American students end up calling me "Dr. T," because "Barry" is too informal for our relation, but "Dr. Thatcher" is too distant for it as well. Regardless, each of these terms instantiates different definitions and relations among the four elements of the rhetorical triangle. The term "Dr. Thatcher" defines me more as a superior and the students more as subordinates; and thus, our relations is marked more by the hierarchy of power. The term also highlights my relation to the topic or reality (the course) as opposed to the students. The term "Barry" instantiates different definitions and relations, for with this term, I am more of an

Figure 1. Onion Model

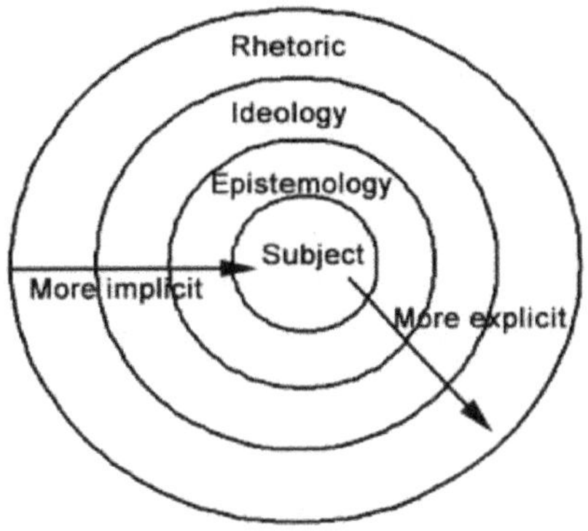

equal with my students; the topic is more as one to be explored by a group of researchers; and our relations is more like collaborators. My favorite term is "Dr. T" because it shows a more familial or intimate connection that is also simultaneously marked by respect for my title and authority.

Because the rhetorical act of students addressing me at New Mexico State University instantiates definitions and relations among me (audience), students (author), topic (class topic), and medium (oral or written conversation), the rhetorical act inherently involves ethics. And when these rhetorical acts become so common as to develop into genres, much like scripts for a play (Burke, 1968), the rhetorical genre or system becomes an ethical script or narrative. Burke (1968) does not overtly connect discourse to law, and the previous legal scholars (White, 1985 and McCormick, 2005) provide a model of rhetoric and law that favors legal researchers, so this section articulates a rhetorical view of law, first by connecting rhetoric to ethics, and then ethics to law.

As Bakhtin (1990; 1993) so carefully argues, ethics has to consider the relations of author, audiences, context, and topic as they develop through discourse. Chapter One addresses this concept more fully in relation to agency and ethics, but this section reviews the concepts as a way to connect ethics to law. Bakhtin rejects both the idea of a universal sense of ethics or right/wrong and what we might now call the moral relativism of poststructuralism. Both extremes work against the "answerability" of a person in a specific context (see, for e.g. Bakhtin's "Art," 1990; "Content," 1990). Instead, Bakhtin argues that "answerability" and verbal art (rhetoric) take place in three related dimensions: the material/physical, cognitive/ethical, and emotional/volitional. As explained in Chapter One, the material/physical dimension comprises the material and economic conditions that surround the rhetorical context. These physical and material conditions structure the cognitive/ethical possibilities. For Bakhtin, cognitive simply means decision-making and ethics means how people relate to each other. These previous two dimensions—physical/material and cognitive/ethical—provide certain rhetorical spaces and structures for the third dimension, the emotional-volitional. In this dimension, rhetors can understand the structures and space for their own agency and answerability.

Like McCormick (2005) and White (1985), Bakhtin argues that discourse plays an important role in all three dimensions. He argues that discourse structures thinking processes, mirrors corresponding cultural patterns, and provides space for agency and expression (Bakhtin, "Content" 1990). Thus, a group of people that shares certain discourses also shares the cultural patterns of those discourses, despite their other differences. According to Bakhtin, this sharing of discourse features creates a rhythm or unity, a dialogized configuration of agreed-upon cognitive processes and accompanying ethical actions (see "Content" 1990c). And only through this dialogized unity can people meaningfully participate in and be answerable for the events in their lives (Bakhtin, 1990: "Art;" "Content;" "Author"). As explained in Chapter One, this dialogized, ever-changing, and culturally produced unity is the ethical system that can be compared to the "unity" of another culture.

Consequently, the rhetorical triangle is also an ethical triangle, and since ethics is constructed through these rhetorical processes, much as White (1985) and McCormick (2005) articulate, we can use this comparative framework to examine ethics across cultures. As explained in Chapters One and Two, it is critical that any kind of comparative framework should be subject to critical scrutinizing of its physical, material, cognitive, ethical, emotional, and volitional structures. However, the fact that a comparative framework can be criticized does not mean that comparison should not be done (Twining, 2000). This is precisely the argument in international human rights discussions. Here, scholars have **not** been able to use difference-based discourse to argue against female circumcision or authoritative regimes because the supposed human rights violators argue that the "violation" is just a "cultural difference" in the myriad of different cultures; thus, no argument can be made against it (Higgins, 1999; Glendon, 1999; Twining, 2000). Consequently, even the most thoroughly postmodern human rights scholars and activists are now openly constructing what they believe all humanity should share, regardless of the cultural differences (Higgins, 1999). These constructed universals then become the benchmark for evaluating local human rights violations, such as the case of the United Nation's *Universal Declaration of Human Rights*, a point discussed next.

This rhetorical ethics does not rely on the postmodern foundation articulated by Porter (1998), Dombroski (1999), and Kirsch and Mortensen (1996) who try to tease out ethics in the context of the infinite indeterminacy of meaning and nihilism of values, and perhaps by necessity, reduce ethics to a personal matter of judgment or performance. As will be detailed next (and throughout this book), this reduction to the individual has severe limitations across cultures. Instead, the ethics needed for cross-cultural work is rhetorical, as articulated by Bakhtin (1990). And as White (1985) and McCormick (2005) argue, this rhetorical ethics can very easily be connected to law.

For those outside the law field, it might seem like a stretch to connect ethics to law, because ethics in professional communication is usually just a loose, abstract set of guidelines with very little or no ability to influence practice. However, law, generally defined, simply means regulating the relations of people, topics, and contexts, precisely what the Bakhtinian theory of ethics does. For example, the comparative law scholars Mark Van Hoecke & Mark Warrington (1998) argue that for too long, comparative legal scholars have focused on "laws as rules," but instead they should compare "the legal discourse, the way lawyers work with the law and reason about it" (p. 495), focusing on how reason and argumentation adjudicate people, events, and contexts in different legal systems.

Similarly, in his book *Comparative law in a global context: the legal systems of Asia and Africa* (2006), Menski strongly criticizes the approach of comparing law based on existing laws and institutions because this focus privileges western cultures that have these institutions and masks the implicit, yet very real, power of societies to regulate the behavior of their people (pp. 27-33). Instead, Menski argues for a context-specific plurality that explores how the process of legal development and regulation takes place. In addition, Menski (2006) urges legal scholars to appreciate the emic-like characteristics of law, but also at the same time "to search for uniformity" (p. 42) and to use comparative law as "a harmonizing handmaiden" (p. 45), an approach that closely resembles the argument in Chapter One of reconciling difference with commonality.

As a further development, Twining (2000) explicitly argues that despite the great evidence of local and emic-like laws, the "general jurisprudence" approach to law is the most effective in our context of globalization. His conception of general jurisprudence is not the universal or global one; rather, following closely the theoretical framework of this book, he explains that general jurisprudence addresses issues that "are not confined to or derived from a single legal system and they can be asked of many, if not all, legal systems" (p.39). Consequently, Twining's general jurisprudence attempts "to analyze societies at their most general (like the attempt to analyze human nature) and identify those features common to all social organizations which might lead to the need for similar institutions and practices" (p. 38). Thus, Twining argues for a legal theory that "it is not tied to any particular legal system or legal culture, but seeks to give an explanatory and clarifying account of law as a complex social and political institution with a rule governed (and in that sense "normative') aspect" (p. 38).

From Twining's (2000) perspective, "general jurisprudence" is "thinner" than comparative or international law because it does not include specific legal institutions and international laws (pp.41-43); however, "general jurisprudence is broader and more intellectually ambitious" than globalization and law because it "includes all the intermediate stages between two or more legal orders, traditions, or cultures, viewing law in the whole world and beyond" (p.254). Thus, for Twining (2000), an appropriate approach to global law means examining various levels in which law functions in our global context, including global (such as environment), international (nation state relations), regional, transnational (multi-national organizations), inter-communal, territorial state, sub-state, and non-state (p.139). This framework of using a general, but universal, approach across various levels mirrors precisely the etic border model developed in Chapters One and Two, both showing apparent simplicity but also the necessary complexity to account for very complicated cultural and rhetorical relations. Thus, as exemplified in the later section of this chapter that describes common law, civil law, and Asian law, the only commonality among these systems is that they regulate people, topics, and contexts. Although this connection between law and ethics might be too simple for many readers, it is the best way to compare how different systems regulate people, topics, and contexts, as shown next in the discussion of the *Universal Declaration*.

DEVELOPMENT AND APPLICATION OF *THE UNIVERSAL DECLARATION OF HUMAN RIGHTS*

This section analyzes the writing and application of the United Nation's *Universal Declaration of Human Rights* (*UDHR*) as a model of intercultural law and rhetoric. Most chapters in this book compare similarities and differences across cultures, but rarely do the chapters provide models for bridging differences. Similarly, one of the weaknesses in the current state of intercultural research is the lack of viable models of effective intercultural bridges, that is, of intercultural theory and practice that work effectively across cultures. This chapter tries to accomplish just that.

The United Nations *Universal Declaration of Human Rights* (UDHR) provides a model–albeit imperfect one– for addressing human rights across cultures. It was written more than 60 years ago shortly after World War II. More than 20 U.N. members from 18 nations participated in the *Declaration's* primary composing processes, and an additional 30 nations offered substantial input into its form and content (Morsink, 1999; Glendon, 1999). This extraordinary intercultural process was specifically designed to transcend cultural norms and create a "universal" declaration of humanity that would combat abuses of human rights that were witnessed during World War II (Humphrey, 1984). By most accounts, the document has been enormously successful, providing a powerful mechanism for human rights discussion (Glendon, 1999). Much of this discussion has focused on the question of universality and culture, the conception of the subject and political effectiveness, and the declaration's rhetoric (Higgins, 1999; Rosenfeld, 2000), all of which are central to this inquiry into intercultural rhetoric.

This section explores the history of the composition, debates, and uses of the *Universal Declaration of Human Rights*. First, it explores the universality of the UDHR in light of the Sapir-Whorf hypothesis, three predominant legal traditions and systems (U.S. Common law, civil law, and Asian law), and four value sets (individual-collective, universal-particular, ascription-achievement, and power distance). Finally, it unpacks the results of this inquiry exploring the issues of universality, influence of rhetorical variables, and the need for intercultural rhetorical theories in international law. This section then lays the foundation for the final section of the chapter, which explores legal issues in professional communication across cultures.

Writing the Universal Declaration

The *Universal Declaration* was developed shortly after World War II to combat the gross violations of human rights that occurred during the war. In this context, the recently formed United Nations was under "tremendous pressure…to include an international bill of rights in the Charter" (Morsink, 1999, p. 1). Among a variety of groups, this pressure came from the U.S. President Franklin Roosevelt's state of the Union speech, a coalition of Jews, Catholics, and Protestants, and a mandate from the Inter-American Conference on War and Peace held in Mexico City in 1945 (Morsink, 1999 p. 2). Since the original Charter of the United Nations already contained many of the fundamental ideas about human rights, inherent dignity of the person, and equality of races and gender, the Secretary of the United Nations agreed to develop a specific bill of human rights. The U.N. quickly formed the Human Rights Commission, which set as its first task the writing of the Universal Declaration.

Eleanor Roosevelt, the wife of the recently deceased Franklin Roosevelt, was chosen by the U.N.'s nuclear council to chair the committee. The U.N. nuclear council then explicitly used a geographic criterion (Morsink, 1999 p. 4) to select committee members from a total of 18 countries: Australia, Belgium, Byelorussia Soviet Socialist Republic, Canada, Chile, China, Egypt, France, India, Iran, Lebanon, Panama, Philippine Republic, United Kingdom, United States of America, Union of Soviet Socialist Republics, Uruguay, and Yugoslavia. The United Kingdom and the USSR had two delegates on the composing committee, while the rest of the nations had one, totaling 20 original members of the composing committee.

The drafting of the Universal Declaration took two years, and in addition to the input offered by these 20 committee delegates, more than 30 other members of the UN were able to offer substantive input (Glendon, 1999; Morsink, 1999). Under the direction of the committee, the first draft of the Declaration was developed by a Canadian lawyer, John Humphrey who was the newly appointed Director of the Human Rights Commission. Humphrey was a native speaker of English who later learned French as a second language. At this time, a number of western and non-western nations had already developed their own human rights bills, laws, and ideals on which Humphrey was able to draw. Thus, Humphrey's first drafting was more of a creative assembling of many of the existing thoughts about human rights from a variety of worldwide sources, including official state constitutions, but also from legal, philosophical, religious, political, and literary sources. According to Humphrey's own account, almost all the documents he originally worked from were either written or translated into English (Humphrey, 1984 p. 31). Humphrey drafted the outline in English, but as is customary at the U.N., all discourse is translated into either English or French.

Based on Humphrey's first draft, the *Universal Declaration* committee met and decided to form a sub-committee to develop Humphrey's "outline" into a polished prose document. Cassin from France headed this subcommittee, with one delegate from the United Kingdom and another from Lebanon. Led by Cassin, these three delegates composed the prose version and submitted it to the committee (Morsink, 1999). The committee, composed of 20 members from 18 countries, then carefully reviewed the draft and then asked for input from a wide variety of non-governmental groups and organizations, including world labor groups, trade unions, religious groups, International Committee of Red Cross, International Council of Women, and other non-governmental groups concerned about the social, cultural, religious, and economic issues of the Declaration (Morsink, 1999). This inclusion of non-governmental groups was an added attempt to broaden the universality of the document.

With the input of these groups and further debate by the Declaration's Committee, the Committee then submitted the draft to delegates of the United Nations as a whole, inviting them to submit their own drafts and revisions on at least four occasions (Morsink, 1999 p. 10). The following countries did offer substantial revisions in the first two opportunities: China, the United Kingdom, France, Chile, Ecuador, Cuba, Panama, India, and the United States. Later, fourteen other nations responded with minor revisions: Egypt, Norway, South Africa, Pakistan, Canada, the Netherlands, Australia, the United States, New Zealand, India, Sweden, Brazil, France, and Mexico (Morsink 1999 p. 10). After the input from all these delegates from outside the original composing committee, the committee further scrutinized the Declaration in preparation for the debate of the plenary session of the third General Assembly of the United Nations.

In the plenary session held in December of 1948, the delegates from the entire U.N. focused essentially on one issue: the universality of the declaration. Many of the members praised the composing process and final product as being extraordinarily conclusive of all cultures. However, coming from the Communist-Socialist perspectives, the delegates from Yugoslavia, Byelorussia, and the USSR argued that the Declaration represented a traditional, individualistic view of humanity because it posited the individual as the center or unit of discussion. They argued for inclusion of the concept or words representing the political "state" as part of the locus of discussion of human rights. This division was highly charged because the Cold War was beginning to be remarkably present, and even though Cold War conflicts were essentially disengaged throughout most of the composing processes (Morsink, 1999), at this plenary session, they surfaced at this moment.

In the final vote, however, 40 nations voted to approve the Declarations; eight nations abstained, and no nation rejected the Declaration. Six communist nations abstained from the vote because of their critique of individualism; Saudi Arabia abstained because they disagreed about the right to equality in marriages and to change religions (Articles 16 and 18); and South Africa abstained, presumably, because the U.N. could use the declaration to condemn South African racial policies. From most scholars' perspectives, the approval of the Declaration was a strong mandate, for even the obvious abstentions were not rejections, just abstentions (Morsink, 1999; Glendon, 1999). It seemed to represent the best efforts to develop a "universal" and therefore, non-culturally biased mechanism for human rights discussion and development.

50 Years later, during the anniversary of the acceptance of the Universal Declaration, scholars disagree about whether the document is truly universal, but an overwhelming majority agree that it has been the best mechanism for fostering a culture of human rights discussion (Brown, 2000; Glendon, 2000). It is the most translated document in history; and it has become the centerpiece for human rights discussion throughout the world. During the 1998, 50-year anniversary celebration, 180 nations officially re-certified the document as the foundation for discussing human rights in intercultural contexts.

Denaturalizing the Universal Declaration

As exemplified in the development, passing, and application of the *Universal Declaration*, two things are critical for a viable intercultural rhetorical act: 1) that the team that creates it be as universal as possible; and 2) that its form and content reflect as much universality as possible. The evidence of the *Universal Declaration* being developed by a universal team is overwhelming; however, the question of its universality remains. First, what is significant about the *Universal Declaration* being composed primarily in English and how might the rhetoric of that declaration be different if Chinese, for example, had been the composing medium? English has been described as encouraging agented, active, and constructivist rhetoric, so rhetorical patterns that emphasize agency, clear action, and constructive processes are naturally going to be deemed more effective than other patterns. Many U.S. rhetorical theories similarly presume values of agency, clear actions, and "constructivist" rhetorics (see Williams, 2009).

Second, how did the rhetorical features of the composers' common and civil law legal traditions influence the rhetoric of the *Universal Declaration* and what other rhetorical features might have been encouraged with Chthonic, Islamic or Asian legal traditions? As I have argued elsewhere (Thatcher, 2000), much of the precedence-setting and interpretive logic of U.S. professional communication and rhetorical theories is based on common-law rhetorical assumptions. However, many Asian legal traditions are based on Buddhist principles of persuasion and Confucian models of appropriate behavior, both of which assume strikingly different approaches to rhetoric and professional communication.

Third, what assumptions about politics, interpersonal relationships, and group behavior (mostly Western) are implicit in the *Universal Declaration* and how might other traditions be affected by these assumptions? Central to the *Universal Declaration* is the autonomous subject of enlightenment thinking (Higgins, 1999). Obviously, this autonomous subject and its corresponding politics have been severely criticized in many current U.S. professional communication and rhetorical theories. However, many of the assumptions about appropriate group behavior, which are based on this subjectivity, are still implicit in many U.S. theories of rhetoric and professional communication (see Thatcher, 2006, for my critique of technology and professional communication). The implicit subjectivity in many U.S. theories emphasizes the empowerment of the individual through "democratizing" and hierarchy-leveling processes (Hawisher & Selfe, 2000; Kirsch and Mortensen, 1996; Sullivan & Porter, 1997), which is a U.S. style of democracy, strongly linked to U.S. individualism (Hofstede, 2010; Stewart & Bennett, 1991; Hampden-Turner & Trompenaars, 2000). Other democracies such as in Africa and South America seek empowerment through community or group processes.

In this chapter, space limitations have allowed for a comparison of only these three variables, but many other intercultural variables such as the other five etic borders as well as the rhetorics of science and technology, religion, political systems, masculinity and femininity, education, geography, and others all influence differently rhetorical assumptions in intercultural rhetorical contexts. The discussion of these three variables should be sufficient to demonstrate, however, that U.S. professional communicators cannot bring their naturalized assumptions about rhetoric and to intercultural contexts.

Linguistic Relativity and Intercultural Rhetoric

Chapter Three carefully lays out the Sapir-Whorf hypothesis, the concept that language predisposes thought, reasoning, and cultural patterns. Thus, a language such as English, Spanish or Chinese is, in many ways, a rhetoric and therefore, corresponds to distinct conceptions of the self, thinking patterns, and ideologies. As a result, a central question to any intercultural inquiry is how important is the composing language in encouraging certain rhetorical features (see Lucy, 1996)? Consequently, since the *Universal Declaration* was written primarily in English and from English sources (Humphrey, 1984 p. 32), it might not be surprising to detect English-like rhetorical features in it. The following section builds on Chapter Three and overviews the research concerning some of the most predominant social and rhetorical patterns that English, as a communication medium, might encourage.

Individualism, Agency, and Causality

According to a variety of linguistic and cultural scholars, one of the strongest rhetorical patterns deriving from English syntax is the subject-predicate relationship (Stewart & Bennett, 1991). In this relationship, there is a strong syntactical tendency to place the subject first in the sentence and not subsume the subject in a conjugated verb such as the case of Spanish. This placement also tends to link the subject directly to the verb, all of which strongly encourages a focus on the subject as an agent who is responsible for the action (Li, 1999), thereby "constantly represent[ing] causality" (Li 77) in more of an individualistic or agented perspective (Li, 1999; Stewart & Bennett, 1999). Further, when there is no apparent agent, English syntax has to invent one using the word it, such as "it is raining." Thus, speakers of English "are habitually concerned about who the predicate is meaningful to" (Li, 1999 p. 81). It is interesting to note that Joseph Williams (2010) labels this clarity of agent and action as the fundamental marker of clear English composition style. Chinese, for example, has more of a topic/comment syntax rather than subject predicate syntax (Li, 1999). Li, in fact, argues "Chinese grammarians have been debating for decades as to what exactly the subject of a Chinese sentence is" (p. 78). As a result, it is extremely difficult to analyze Chinese from the English "actor-doing-being relationship" (Li, 1999 p. 79).

This predominant syntax of agency and individual causality likely corresponds to or encourages distinct rhetorical and cultural patterns. The first rhetorical conception is that humans are "agentful" and the center of causality (Li, 1999; Stewart and Bennett, 1991). This orientation, according to Li, is more concerned with "the entities that initiate, perform, or are otherwise affected by the action described in the predicate" (Li, 1999 p. 81), becoming what Li calls a participant-centered rhetoric or Fisher calls the "actor-action-result model" (p. 120). Stewart and Bennett and Li link this subject-predicate rhetoric to U.S. individualism, which places the individual at the center and cause of activity and thinking. Li links the topic/comment syntax in Chinese to their collectivism and focus on process rather than causality.

English and Social Status

Perhaps related to the subject-predicate rhetoric is English's relatively small range of syntactical strategies for designating social status. As Stewart and Bennett (1991) explain, "Thai, Japanese, and some other Asian languages have elaborate systems of second-person singular (you) words that indicate the status of the speaker relative to the listener" (P. 49). Practically speaking, English provides only one form, *you*, while many European languages such as Spanish provide two such as *usted* and *tu*. In addition to status markers, English is much more relatively weak in describing kinship terms. For example, Russian has a possible 300 kinship terms (Stewart and Bennett, 1999, P. 49). This difference makes it very difficult to read English-translated Russian novels such as those from Tolstoy or Dostoyevski because English lacks the lexical and syntactic precision of the original Russian kinship markers.

Relevance of English as the Composing Medium of the Universal Declaration

Given these rhetorical features that English as a composing medium might encourage, the critical question for the *Universal Declaration* and any other international document is how important was the native language in influencing the final rhetoric of that document? First, it is essential to point out the words *encourage* or *predispose*. The fact that the composing language is just one of many intercultural variables that most likely influences the *Universal Declaration* and other intercultural documents denies the determinism of what many scholars have labeled as the strong version of the Sapir-Whorf hypothesis (Lucy, 1996). Yet, there is enough evidence to show interesting correspondences between languages and cultural patterns to warrant such an inquiry.

One of the most damaging critiques of the *Universal Declaration* is that it has posited the individual as the reference point for all human rights discussions. This seems to correspond closely not only to the subject-predicate element of English, but also the rhetoric of causality and even lack of social markers. Interestingly, when Humphrey began composing the *Universal Declaration*, Chang, the Chinese member of the composing committee, was worried that the "individual" was going to take precedence over "process". Thus, Chang personally recommended that Humphrey and a number of other western delegates go to China to study Chinese philosophy (Humphrey, 1984). Humphrey did not have the time to do so, but Chang consistently brought in his Confucian and other Chinese cultural values into the collaborative efforts (Humphrey, 1984; Morsink, 1999). Furthermore, as mentioned earlier, the Soviet block countries abstained from voting in favor of the *Universal Declaration* because it posited the individual, not the state as the reference point for human rights discussions. Later, the question of the individualism of the *Universal Declaration* has been the lightening rod for critiques of its supposed universality, especially for Asian cultures (see for example, Engle, 2000).

What is interesting, however, is that despite this critique of individualism, most human rights scholars argue that this "essentialized" (Higgins, 1999) approach of the individual as the reference point is the most politically and rhetorically effective for the human rights agenda. Brown calls this "an attempt to create an artificial foundation for moral debate within and between societies by building upon the idea of a consensus constructed under ideal conditions" (2000, p. 44). Although some legal scholars (Rosenfeld, 2000) argue for using both the group and the individual as the reference point for human rights discussion, most worry that positing the state or group as the reference point will leave human rights activists unable to critique activities that they deem as unethical but which the groups deem as part of their cultural heritage, such as the circumcision of young women in some parts of Africa (Higgins, 1999). In other words, positing the group as the reference point means that what the group deems as ethical is essentially what is ethical for the individuals in the group, regardless of what outside observers think, a point that I develop in my critique of postmodern ethics earlier in Chapter One and later here. Humphrey and many of the other framers of the Declaration understood this point only too well, given the context of Hitler's organic cultural approach (Morsink, 1999; Glendon, 1999). Many human rights activists are unwilling to take this group or communal position (Glendon, 1999; Higgins, 1999). Even most Asian scholars who recognize the westernized individualism in the Declaration still argue that this essentialized approach can be applied better to their situations than any other approaches as yet developed (Hussein, 2000; Muntarbhorn, 2000). They consistently insist, however, in the need to contextualize and emphasize particular parts of this individualistic approach to their nations (Hussein, 2000) without western imperial pressures.

This essentializing of the individual as the reference point for human rights discussion is profoundly interesting for intercultural rhetors and law. What is the reference point for evaluating intercultural rhetorics in relation to law? Williams' *Style* (2010) clearly labels agency and action as the center of his style system for English composition, but how ethical and effective is the English-centered approach for intercultural rhetorics in a variety of academic, government, technological, and industrial contexts? In academic contexts, this U.S., English-centered approach has clearly been critiqued as the "universal" criterion for evaluating written compositions, not only in English, but also in other languages (see Connor, 1996, for example). As explored throughout this book, many "rhetorics" other than the agent-action rhetoric are effective in other cultures.

Constructing a Common Threshold for uses of Language

A common approach for constructing a "practical universality" among human rights activists is openly debating and agreeing upon the values so constructed (see Otto, 1997). For example, for many activists, the open debate about what the "inherent dignity of the individual" means (a central value in the *Universal Declaration*) has permitted them to construct a rather loose, but operable definition that seems applicable in most scenarios. However, constructing a common ground for language is perhaps one of the most difficult intercultural objectives to carry out for very practical reasons. Ideally, any document developed in an intercultural context needs to be composed and reviewed in all the languages of that context, ensuring that the "meaning" of the document is—depending on how you look at it—free from the rhetorical influences of the composing languages or at least has been denaturalized. However, getting qualified, bilingual or trilingual individuals to carry out this multilingual composition is difficult, for few exist especially in specific contexts. For example, ideally, the *Universal Declaration* should have been composed simultaneously in English, French, German, and China, and a multitude of other languages. This joint composition would have forced a denaturalizing of the rhetorical influences of English, but how possible is this process? It was impossible in the *Universal Declaration's* composing context because the committee only shared English or French as the common language.

The next best approach is effective translation that takes the English rhetorical influences out of the original *Universal Declaration*, for example, and substitutes in their place the rhetorical patterns of the target language. Translation theory is addressing these issues (see Connor, 1996). The translated document is, however, almost always seen in the light of the original document, much like comparing apples to oranges using an apple as the original template. For example, from my analysis, the translation of the *Universal Declaration* into Spanish seemed to not reduce the rhetoric of agency, individuality, and causality, even though Spanish does encourage these rhetorical patterns. This has been my experience with all of the translated software manuals that are in use in Latin America (Thatcher, 1997). "Real" translation might better be stated as a complete rewrite based on what some intercultural technical communicators call core knowledge (see the Conclusion to this book). Much more research and theory need to address these issues of translation and multilingual composition.

Legal Traditions and Rhetoric

This section explores how the legal traditions of the authors and collaborators of the *Universal Declaration* might have influenced its original rhetoric and how this rhetoric currently gets applied in a variety of global contexts. This type of denaturalizing of legal traditions then becomes a good model for scholars of rhetoric and professional communication. The *Declaration* was first composed by the Canadian attorney Humphrey and letter revised under the direction of the French attorney Cassin, both of whom were obviously influenced by the two prevailing legal systems in Europe and North America: civil and common law. Comparative legal scholars argue that these two legal systems and corresponding institutions have profoundly influenced the prevailing cultural and rhetorical patterns in Western Europe, Latin America, and the United States, while in China and other Asian countries, legal traditions have not been as influential as other cultural factors such as Confucianism and Buddhism (Lubman, 1999 pp. 13-32). This section overviews the civil and common law systems of Europe and the Americas and the general approaches in Asian law, focusing on how these legal systems might structure rhetorical assumptions in intercultural contexts. At least five other major legal traditions—Chthonic, Judaic, African, Islamic, and Hindu—could be similarly compared and explored as to their potential rhetorical influence in both the composition and application of the *Universal Declaration*. Again, space limitations prohibit this more extensive analysis.

Civil and Common Law Traditions

In the United States, Latin America, and Western Europe, two remarkable distinctions in the legal systems create different rhetorical assumptions in professional, governmental, and even academic contexts. The civil law is the basic legal system in all the countries in Latin America, and most of Europe (except for the United Kingdom). The civil law is based on a long tradition that dates back at least until the Roman Empire when Justinian developed a remarkable set of codes (Rosenn, 1988; Eder, 1950). The civil law was developed from emerging "Chthonic" or "natural," or community relational law and was used by the Romans as a way to allow some function of community law in the areas conquered but also provide for some stability and consistency (Glenn, 2000). Later, during the enlightenment era, these codes became more rigorously humanistic and rational, focused "on the centrality of the person and the growth of democracy" (Glenn, 2000 p. 129). Coming out of the enlightenment era, this approach to law was based on a Judeo-Christian ethic that humanity was created in the image of God and therefore, merited certain rights that could bring "about the conditions of basic human dignity" (Glenn, 2000, p 131). The generation of civil law, was, therefore, linked to humanist and enlightenment scholarship. As a result, "questions are more important that answers (which may change), understanding is more important than coherence; social contact more important than concision" (Glenn, 2000 p. 128). Writing was a heuristic for inquiry into the humanistic and enlightenment aspects of law.

The United States and the United Kingdom (and their former colonies) rely on a common law tradition that was developed in England and begun as unwritten assumptions about appropriate conventions and behaviors. In distinction to the growth of the civil law under Roman rule, in England there was little loyal community and little chthonic (indigenous) doctrine of law. There was also less of a religious source (Glenn, 2000) for law when compared to Islamic, Talmudic (Jewish) or philosophic-governmental (Confucianism) traditions. Thus, the royal monarchs of England developed a corps of trusted judges or adjudicators (Glenn, 2000 p. 207) who could work in a controlled and efficient manner. Since these judges had few source for their laws, they relied on the "local circumstances" and "intelligent local response" (Glenn, 2000 p. 207). From these local circumstances, the judges then developed a "writ" or writing about what was commonly judged to be law, or common law. Thus, the generation of the common law tradition was based on a judge's writing of a law in a local circumstance, based on what was commonly accepted behavior. The corpus of writs then became the precedents for future decisions. Writing was, therefore, both a generative and archival force in the development of common law.

As these two legal traditions continue to develop, they have integrated elements from each other, somewhat blurring their distinctions. For example, many common law traditions have developed statutory laws in various areas such as environmental or workplace codes. These statutes are like civil-law codes. Also, many civil law traditions look to legal precedent for guiding current interpretations. However, legal precedent and judicial decision are still the final or ultimate law-making mechanism in most common law traditions, and the generation of codes for civil law traditions.

Thus, even though the two traditions do share some feature, their significant differences correspond to different rhetorical assumptions about reading and interpreting texts. The civil-law tradition relies on the legislature for creating comprehensive and deductive legal frameworks or codes that are to be applied by judges to each case at hand, independent of previous cases. This approach emphasizes a correct understanding of the particularities of the comprehensive deductive frame to ensure correct interpretations. In fact, the original purpose of this system was designed to be judgeproof. As Eder (1950) has explained, "Latin America inherited from Spain a lack of confidence in the judiciary. It is for that reason that its hands are tied. .. by the rigid formalism of the Codes of Procedure" (p. 145). Thus, judges in Latin America have historically been subordinated to the legislature in creating laws (Rosenn, 1988). On the other hand, the common-law tradition is an inductive system based on case or common-law precedents. Legal interpretations are based on previous cases of similar situations, or what was commonly accepted as proper or legal conduct. Judges tend to have significant creative power in linking the case at hand with previous precedents, thereby continuously extending and refining the law, case by case. Thus, the inductive approach assumes more time and creativity in extrapolating the law from the basic precedents than in understanding the complex intricacies of the precedent itself.

These different legal approaches imply different expectations about certainty and ambiguity. One principal purpose of the civil law is to obtain certainty in judicial decisions. Merryman (1969) explains that "there is a great emphasis in the literature of the civil law tradition on the importance of certainty in the law.. . it has come to be a kind of supreme value, an unquestioned dogma, a fundamental goal" (p. 50). In this search for certainty, then, the codes or legal frameworks developed for judges in the civil-law systems have become exceedingly complex and ostensibly comprehensive, trying to cover as many contingencies as possible (Rosenn, 1988). They are also unwieldy and difficult to adapt to new situations. In contrast, the US legal tradition is best characterized as a loose framework of principles and guidelines. Ambiguity can be good because it can invite effective interpretation and application of laws (Glenn, 2000).

Asian Legal Traditions

The Asian legal tradition is not as developed in the formal sense because Asia has traditionally "refused to root normativity in formal structures and sanctions" (Glenn, 2000 p. 280), elements of law that are commonly associated with the civil and common law legal traditions. Instead Asian legal approaches are based mostly on Confucianism with some Buddhist traditions that seek "primarily to persuade and not oblige" (Glenn, 2000 p. 280). In China, for example, the tension between formal legal structures and sanctions, known as FA, and the informal, persuasive tradition, known as LI, was commonly understood, and only during a brief span of 15 years did the FA, or formal legal traditions dominate (starting in 221 BC), but its effects were so disastrous that LI has dominated ever since (Glenn, 2000 pp. 282-285). Thus, China's legal tradition is based on the "relational principles of Confucian society [that become] integrated into legalist statements of positive law" (Glenn, 2000 p. 285).

Rather than the precedents of the common law system or the codes of the civil law, this Confucian approach to law centers mostly on roles and their relationships. Thus, harmony in society is preserved and reinforced through mutual reinforcement of the norms of these roles, a positive process that re-makes the old traditions new and relevant to current situations. In this sense, the law is seen as an instrument of aspiration, a mechanism for constant renewal of relationships in personalized, contextualized, and particularized situations (Glenn, 2000 p. 289). Thus, "law must speak to individuals in the relationship in which they find themselves, in sufficient detail for them to recognize the information needed for guidance" (Glenn, 2000 p. 294). This approach rejects the universalism that is the center of common law approaches and the positivism of human behavior of the civil law approach. Instead, it is a "morality articulated through analogy with particular historical examples" (Glenn, 2000 p. 295).

Although Buddhism and Confucianism have long been at odds with each other, some Buddhist influences seem to correlate rather well and reinforce this relational approach to law. First is the Buddhist doctrine of interdependence, that is, the world is composed of interdependent relationships, and achieving enlightenment means understanding how this interdependence works. Second is the Buddhist denial of formal structures and constraints; and third is the art of compromise, the middle-way or socially constructed consensus.

Within the different countries that makeup the Asian legal traditions, there is clearly some variation. All Asian countries have integrated elements of Common, Civil, and Islamic legal traditions, but in varying degrees. Japan, for example, succeeded in integrating elements of German civil law. And Korean has been described as the most Americanized legal system (Shi, 2010). Much of South-Eastern Asian has integrated many parts of Islamic legal traditions (Glenn, 2000); and Singapore and Hong Kong have developed many common law approaches (Glenn, 2000). However, according to most legal scholars (Lubman, 1999; Glenn, 2000), Asia still retains the Confucian-based approach that emphasizes relations and informal, persuasive approach to legal situations. Further, it must be noted that Chinese legal traditions are changing rapidly, and in many ways, are taking on characteristics of western common and civil law (Peerenboom, 2002), especially in the areas of commerce and manufacturing; but despite these changes, the essential foundation of Chinese law are the same, a point discussed more thoroughly in the last section of this chapter.

Influence of Legal Traditions on Universal Declaration

Analyzing how the *Universal Declaration* has been influenced by legal traditions is very fruitful because it focuses on methods—of applying and enforcing values in public spheres, a very traditional realm of rhetoric. At first, the drafters of the *Universal Declaration* worried a great deal about enforcement, with the horrors of World War II fresh in their minds, and thus, they explored mechanisms of application (Humphrey, 1984). For example, Chang, the representative from China, originally proposed composing a three-part declaration: the articles, commentary on the articles, and proposals for their implementation (Humphrey, 1984 p. 40). When the "proposals for implementation" proved too unwieldy in the world legal context, the committee changed them to "measures of implementation," (Humphrey, 1984 p. 40) which focused on how well the values were being implement, not on how (methods or mechanisms) they were implemented. This change was a reluctant and significant one for many, given the post WWII context and its glaring lack of viable human rights mechanisms (Morsink, 1999). However, the great logistical, cultural, and institutional variety in the world prohibited any concrete discussion of method. Even Humphrey's initial proposal to include methods of petition to the United Nations (Humphrey, 1984 pp. 32-33) was eliminated from the final document. Thus, the final document exhibits qualitative measurements of implementation, that is, descriptions of qualities of human rights that all nations should endeavor to achieve.

Predictably, without mechanisms of implementation, enforcing the values of the *Universal Declaration* corresponds closely to the legal traditions of the specific countries and cultures. Consequently, many debates between western and Asian scholars rest on these different legal foundations, exemplifying how intercultural discussion cannot begin to bear fruit unless the rhetorical assumptions are denaturalized or unmasked. Furthermore, many feminist, Marxist, and postcolonial scholars critically examines methods of application, further challenging—but maybe in the end, re-affirming—many of the universal aspirations of the *Universal Declaration.*

Following closely the rhetorical assumptions of common law, many U.S. activists and policy makers assume that the *Universal Declaration* is much like the U.S. constitution (Higgins, 1999) in that it provides a universal or precedence-setting base (Engle, 2000) upon which appropriate values and behaviors can be extrapolated. And not surprisingly, the values that seem most important to U.S. scholars are the "civil and political rights" (Hussein, 2000 p. 78), which are closely linked to liberal individualism and universalism. Likewise, many European and Latin American scholars seek to apply the *Universal Declaration* assuming civil law hermeneutics; that is, drawing on the positivistic and humanistic values that are central to the *Declaration* and applying them deductively to human rights situations. For example, a significant influence on the *Universal Declaration* was the language of many recently emerging Latin American constitutions (Morsink, 1999; Humphrey, 1984). This wording of the *Declaration* emphasizes "positive rights," liberal democracy, and the enlightenment subject. Further, "the first sentence of Article 1 of the Universal Declaration is a virtual rewrite of the first article of the French Declaration" [of 1789] (Morsink, 1999 p. 281).

As explained earlier, many U.S. theories of rhetoric and professional communication seem to assume common-law reading and writing strategies. Thus, scholars and rhetorical theorists might question how much their theories rely on common law values to describe the purposes of writing in all types of organizations. First is the assumption that writing is a normalizing or universalizing mechanism. Winsor, for example, argues that writing tends to construct "a shared vision of order" (1996, p. 69) that each person can agree to accept. Klein & McKenna argue that the policy document "serves as a measure or standard against which actions can be judged" (1997, p.149). Second is the assumption that readers are to extrapolate, much like U.S. judges, the general relevance of the single case to their situations. The discussions in workplace literacy seem to assume that readers can construct applicable knowledge of basic written texts. Certainly, the comprehensive coding and narrating that is assumed in the civil tradition could be offensive and detracting to U.S. readers, as I document in a South American study (1999). Thus, as Klein & McKenna argue, writing should provide "the logical basis from which employees can extrapolate new procedures to deal with novel situations" (Klein and McKenna, 1997 p. 149). The key word here is *extrapolate*, an interpretive tradition based on an inductive approach that trusts the readers to make the correct application.

These common and civil law hermeneutics are not as easily applied in other contexts, especially in human rights. According to Hussein (2000), a Malaysian human rights scholar, Muntarbhorn (2000), a Thai scholar, and many other Asian scholars (see Engle, 2000), the U.S. and other northern countries view the *Universal Declaration* as founding U.S. and western approaches to freedoms and equalities: free speech, free association, freedom of religion, freedom from discrimination, and "democratic system[s] based on the right to self determination" (Muntarbhorn, 2000 p. 82). According to many Asian scholars, these common and civil law lenses ignore or sideline the "economic, social and development rights" (Hussein, 2000 p. 79) that more closely correspond to other cultural and legal traditions. These assumptions have become so naturalized for U.S. policy makers that legal scholars from other cultures and traditions have to continually remind their U.S. colleagues that the rest of the world has not naturalized their approach with U.S. common law approaches (Rosenfield, 2000).

True to their legal traditions based on Confucianism and Buddhism, Asian legal scholars tend to use the *Universal Declaration* as a model of appropriate human relationships (Engle, 1999) and seek to enforce these models of human relationships as the mechanism for carrying out human rights improvements (Muntarbhorn, 2000; Hussein, 2000). The purpose of these approaches tend to focus much more on economic, social, and literacy development; and even though the models of human relationships used as mechanisms to promote these rights are often sexist, hierarchical, and authoritarian—values antithetical to common law and U.S. styles of democracy—many Asian countries prefer the "rice before rights" (Muntarbhorn, 2000 p. 84) approach to human rights.

As could be expected, the intercultural communication among these three camps (Common law, civil law, and Asian law) breaks down into misunderstanding because of the legal assumptions that structure their rhetorical approaches. The U.S. activists and policy makers accuse the Asian and many Latin American activists as relativistic because they are unwilling to lay down universal standards of behaviors or precedence (Engle, 1999), which get fleshed out into individual rights (Hussein, 2000). For many U.S. activists and policy makers, relativism is antithetical to the *Universal Declaration*. Coming from their particularist and human relations models, Asian scholars accuse the U.S. scholars of monoculturalism—of not anticipating how other cultures work out the *Universal Declaration* in specific cultural sites (Engle, 1999; Higgins, 1999; Otto, 1997).

Tensions also exist between common law and civil law arguments. Some Latin American activists argue that U.S. methods are often fleshed out into negative rights—mechanisms for punishing or circumventing negative behavior rather than influencing positive obtainments.

Many feminist, Marxist, and postcolonial scholars critically examines the approaches of activists and policy makers of all three legal traditions—common law, civil law, and Asian law—linking all three to dominance of women, workers, and emerging nations and former colonies. For example, many of these scholars argue that Asian models of human relations that are used for economic and social development are based on class, gendered, and ethnic categories that only improve the economic conditions of the ruling elite (Engle, 1999; Brown, 2000). Further, some postcolonial scholars have argued that the *Universal Declaration* is itself a type of imperialism, because of its links to western liberal enlightenment ideologies (Brown, 2000 pp. 33-35). Feminist scholars have continually stressed that "all the rights talk" has only marginally improved the rights of many women (Engle, 1999; Higgins, 1999; Otto, 1997). The "freedom rights" that are so emphasized from the U.S. and western approaches to the *Universal Declaration* have not undone the masculine structures that oppress women; in fact, they might have just made the structures freer to do so (Engle, 1999; Otto, 1997). The more positive rights approaches in civil law cultures and the almost corresponding human relations models in Asian cultures similarly maintain status quo masculine social, culture, and economic structures. It is interesting to note, however, that these three U.S. feminist scholars also argue that the *Universal Declaration*, if contextualized and applied critically, is still the best mechanism to date for improving the rights of women (Engle, 1999; Otto, 1997; Higgins, 1999).

Constructing a Common Threshold for Law-making

As in all constructions of common ground, the first step has already been accomplished—the denaturalizing of legal traditions and their influence on rhetorical traditions. Next, the intercultural rhetoricians must openly debate their sources of law and how they can come up with their laws. What is the law based on? All these different legal traditions have some sort of foundation—humanism, precedents, religion, and cultural values. These different foundations also imply corresponding rhetorical and cultural patterns as well. Thus, the process of selecting the source of the law implies selecting—or privileging—a rhetorical and cultural pattern. Once this selection process is agreed upon in open, critical dialogue, the intercultural rhetoricians need to construction the mechanisms of enforcement, which too have clear rhetorical and cultural correspondences.

This universalizing process can become more effective and transforming if the cultural differences are seen in relative light. As explained in Chapter Eleven, Stewart & Bennett argue "each culture possesses integrity and, generally speaking, is neither inferior nor superior to any other culture. But in a structured situation and for a specific purpose, one cultural system may in fact work better than another" (1991, p.175). In other words, cultural differences can be discussed in synergistic terms if the dialogue is open and constructive. Thus, intercultural rhetoricians can choose among the many alternative legal approaches, denaturalizing them in every aspect, but also openly selecting those approaches and corresponding rhetorical patterns that best fit the situation. For example, maybe in some contexts, the Asian system that encourages model behavior as the motivation is the best mechanism, whereas negative case study from the common law is better in others. And during this processes, the intercultural rhetorician learns even more about the strengths and weaknesses of each system.

Leadership/Authority, Group Behavior, and Rhetorical Interactions

As the final variable for analysis, this section explores how a variety of social, cultural, and political values construct distinct expectations about interpersonal relationships, leadership, and group behavior, drawing on a number of the value sets explained in Chapter Two and exemplified throughout the book. Thus, cultures will tend to interpret and apply—and expect others to apply—the values of the *Universal Declaration* according to their cultural values. Similarly, as I have carefully explored throughout this book, many U.S. theories of rhetoric and professional communication assume U.S. values of leadership, authority, and group behavior. In both cases, this ethnocentrism consistently causes intercultural conflicts and miscommunication. Thus, intercultural scholars need to denaturalize expectations about group behavior in order to develop valid intercultural inquiries.

In short, U.S. values of interpersonal behavior, which are founded mostly on equality, empowerment, and individual agency, are not readily shared in other cultures. For example, as explained in Chapter Two, Hofstede's concept of "power distance" is used to measure differences in equality and agency in group relationships. Power distance measures "the interpersonal power or influence between B and S as perceived by the least powerful of the two, S" (Hofstede, 2010 p. 71). In other words, power distance measures the ability for two people of different power and authority to influence each other. In Hofstede's surveys of 44 nations, the United States scored 40, a mid to low range score. Austria, Israel, and Denmark scored the lowest. Hampden-Turner &Trompenaars (2000), other organizational researchers, similarly concluded that in the U.S., there are strong values of equality and personal agency that undergird achievement, versus ascriptivc, means of motivation. They connect this achievement orientation with the Protestant work ethic, thus demonstrating why low-power distance is more prominent in Protestant cultures. Stewart and Bennett (1991) argue that U.S. Americans clearly "function most effectively on an interpersonal level of equality. They are often confused when confronted with persons of a different status—particularly when that status has been achieved through a legacy of special privileges" (1991, p. 91).

Some Western European countries, Canada, and Australia share similar values of equality with the United States, but most other countries radically differ, demonstrating why U.S. rhetorical theories that are based on equality, empowerment, and individual agency will not work there. In Hofstede's discussion of power distance, most of the scores of Latin American countries sharply contrast with the scores of the US. Mexico and Venezuela tied for the second highest score of 81, second only to the Philippines, an original Spanish Colony. Colombia scored 67, Peru 64, and Chile 63. Other high power-distance countries include India, Singapore, and France. These scores strongly suggest a significant difference in the power relationships: obedience to authority starts in the home and continues in the work place; a high value on conformity; authoritarian attitudes are the social norm; both subordinates and superiors prefer superiors to make decisions autocratically and paternalistically; very close supervision of work; employees fear to disagree with the boss; and employees reluctant to trust each other (Hofstede, 2010). Hofstede also argues that in high-score cultures, there is a strong push for theoretical models of participation but much more resistance against de facto participation.

Likewise, Hampden-Turner &Trompenaars (2000) argue that in cultures with predominantly Catholic, Buddhist, and Hindu populations, ascriptive models based on social, educational, and professional differences tend to regulate relationships and motivate the realization of organizational goals. In China, for example, the purpose of the hierarchical order, under Confucianism, "was to preserve natural harmony through the promotion of ethical behavior....conducted by men who behaved like the ancient sages and set high moral examples for their subjects to follow" (Lubman, 2000 p. 13-14).

Although it may seem counter-intuitive to many U.S. researchers, both the ascriptive/high-power distance and achievement/low-power distance models can effectively motivate participation and regulate behavior, but the assumptions about how to do so are diametrically opposed (Hampden-Turner &Trompenaars, 2000). Low-power distance models assume that people will participate when barriers are broken down, when there is an equal opportunity for achievement, when participation is more democratic, and when the achievement of results is the focus of both the evaluation criteria and the process itself. High-power distance or ascriptive models assume that people will participate when lines of authority are clear, when the structure of the situation and work process are explicitly outlined and supervised, and when the work itself correlates with and reinforces the status markers of the participants.

It is not surprising, therefore, that the policy makers and others who debate the applications of the *Universal Declaration's* values draw on their own naturalized assumptions about leadership and group/individual behavior. Obviously, this ethnocentric approach causes conflict and miscommunication. For example, many U.S. activists and policy makers consistently criticize the power structures that inhibit the development of personal freedoms, individual accountability, and self-realization in Asian countries such as China. However, many Asian activists and scholars counter that this U.S. individual-rights approach is focused so exclusively on the "liberation" of the individual from dehumanizing power structures that it has blinded U.S. policy-makers to a number of other critical values in the *Universal Declaration*. Hussein, for example, argues that the U.S. individual, liberatory approach blinds them to the values of "human duties and obligations....the overall prosperity of the nation...[and] the economic, social, and development rights" (2000 p. 76-79). As mentioned, this debate is often labeled as "rice before rights" (Muntarbhorn, 2000 p. 84), which means many Asian countries focus on the overall development of the group as the mechanism of individual liberation, rather than the liberation of the individual first. Often, the development of the group requires temporary "sacrifices" of individual rights for the eventual improvement of all. Interestingly, the close relations between rights and individualism has prompted the construction of a complementary approach named the *Universal Declaration of Human Responsibilities,* which has not received the backing of the original *Universal Declaration*, but which seems to counter for many cultures the individualism of the original declaration.

Thus, people in other cultures might not want—or be capable of participating in—the empowering mechanisms described by many U.S. rhetoric and professional communication theories if these theories are based on the achievement, low power-distance model, or individual-rights model, as many U.S. rhetorical theories are. Kirsch & Mortensen (1996), for example, argue that recognizing the hierarchies of power and authority in group situations is critical. This recognition could easily represent both the ascriptive or achievement model, but in the case of Kirsch and Mortensen, its purpose seems to be for the equalization of power or "equity" (p. xxii), and almost every interpersonal mechanism for achieving this equity assumes low power distance or achievement logic. In addition, as I argue elsewhere (2001), many current theories of participatory research in rhetoric and professional communication assume low power-distance mechanisms for individual liberation. Thus, valorizing a U.S. conception of equality seems to have been so naturalized in the field of rhetoric and composition that thinking otherwise is perhaps anathema. Ironically, however, the very emancipatory approaches that are valued by U.S. scholars might in fact be a method of Americanizing people from more high-power distance cultures. A more critical view might argue that this model reinforces US individualism, a value strongly correlated with low-power distance, equality, and emancipatory social processes. Obviously, the ethics of this Americanization have to be debated.

It is interesting to note, however, that some rhetoric and professional communication scholars are problematizing these U.S. liberatory approaches. Porter, et al, (2000) argue that the localized acts of critique and resistance that are focused on individual student agency have done little to change institutional structure. They focus their work on institutional critique—that is, understanding and re-arranging larger political powers in organizations so that the situations of individuals can be improved. Their work has yet to fully articulate group and individual relationships in light of organizational values and material and economic contexts, but this kind of work has good potential in intercultural situations because of its complex view of social and individual relationships; and if worked out fully, might be a useful model for intercultural interaction.

Constructing Common Ground for Individual/Group Behavior

Constructing a common ground for analyzing group and individual relationships first needs to denaturalize the predominant group/individual relationships and their methods of motivation and leadership. As in all the other constructions, the next step then is to form a dialogue that clearly articulates group and individual responsibilities and freedoms; group and individual forms of motivations and leadership; and group and individual sources of identity and power. Further, as explored in the legal section, rather than seeing these differences as destabilizing, we can see them as synergistic, tapping into the strengths and weaknesses of the different cultural constructions and taking advantage of them to carry out more effective and ethical relationships. For example, the rights versus responsibilities debate might look at the positive values or more effective attributes of both concepts and draw on the more effective values at the right time, evoking the original Greek term Kairos. This approach then becomes what Otto (1997) and others call a "transformative universality," one openly constructed that yields more than the debilitating sums of the two separate parts. Obviously, the discussion of "better" for each situation is critical, but if denaturalized, this discussion of the "better" has a much better chance of actually happening.

Conclusion to Universal Declaration and Intercultural Law and Rhetoric

This section has explored only three intercultural variables: language, law, and group/individual behavior as applied to international law in the *Universal Declaration*. As mentioned, many other variables such as time, gender, religion, geography, economics, and history similarly influence rhetorical assumptions and need to be denaturalized for valid and ethical intercultural inquiry. Just denaturalizing these three variables, however, among a host of other potential variables demonstrates the remarkable difficulty and complexity of intercultural inquiry into law. Consequently, some U.S. scholars might feel the difficulty of the task is so great that it becomes easier to slide back into U.S. ethnocentrism and ignore the ethical and practical needs for intercultural legal inquiry. This is one potential cause of U.S. ethnocentrism.

Another potential cause is the almost hegemonic focus on difference in many current theories in rhetoric and professional communication, which might predispose many to feel that intercultural inquiry is misguided or even dangerous. It is interesting to note that many U.S. human rights scholars and activists have embraced—but then rejected—the difference lens because it does not provide valid, ethical, and practical approaches for working through international human rights issues (Menski, 2006). This intense focus on difference also has a paradoxical but strong correlation with U.S. individualism because it ignores how individuals do share some cultural and rhetorical patterns (Thatcher, 2001). Thus, in its very disavowal of intercultural inquiry, the difference lens might be showing a U.S. cultural bias, further reinforcing a U.S. ethnocentrism.

Finally, some scholars have combined this focus on difference with critical inquiry to denounce any type of analysis of a second culture as imperialistic, hegemonic, dangerous, and selfish, among many other epithets. Fear seems to rule in this camp—fear that any type of cultural analysis will be seen as an imperializing mechanism. Thus, because of fear, scholars slide back into U.S. ethnocentrism. Great care, respect, diligence, and competence should guide intercultural inquiry, not fear. Again, many of the most thoroughly postmodern human rights scholars (Higgins, 1999; Otto, 1997; Engle, 2000) clearly understand the dangers of intercultural comparison, but for them—and me—this great fear of engaging in intercultural analysis is far outweighed by the great need to construct what Higgins calls "a shared discourse of rights [that] may bridge cultural differences and build community" (1999, p. 226). By denaturalizing the rhetorics and accompanying cultural patterns and then openly constructing practical and transformative universal rhetorics, scholars in rhetoric and professional communication can build ways for cultures to interact ethically and effectively.

ANALYZING LEGAL ISSUES AROUND THE WORLD

Analyzing the *Universal Declaration* provides a viable model for evaluating the legal issues in many global contexts that professional communicators might encounter. These contexts are many, including intellectual property, environment, immigration, health, energy, technology transfer, economic development, human rights, privacy, organizational policies and procedures, dual manufacturing, organizational training, and others. However, since a thorough review of each one of these issues is well beyond the scope of this Chapter, I will explore four general legal issues as they are related to the eight etic borders. These include intellectual property, policies and procedures, privacy and information technologies, and legal procedures.

Intellectual Property in Light of Individual-Collective and Power Distance

One key variable in developing laws across culture is the level of dependence or independence assumed by the law. As shown by the analysis of the *Universal Declaration*, most individualistic cultures assume the individual as the point of reference, while collective cultures assume a group orientation. In addition, coming from business, Hampden-Turner and Trompenaars (2000) use the example of employee evaluation to demonstrate this difference in collective and individualism. In collective cultures, the group tends to accept blame for a workplace problem, while in individualistic cultures, there is a strong tendency to blame one person. Further, since most individualistic cultures area also low power distance, while many collective cultures are high power distance, the collective and high power distance cultures create very different assumptions about how laws regulate power among people with relatively different traditional power relations.

A simple example of this individual-collective includes inheritance laws. For example, as Nazarri (1995) explains, during colonialization, the UK's inheritance laws use the single male as the point of reference with very limited power of the wife or daughters to contest the decision. On the other hand, Brazilian inheritance laws were based on the community. Thus, the wives, children, and even the larger community in Brazil had claim to inheritance and were capable for arguing for their share of the inheritance, showing a more low power distance. On the other hand, only male children have claim with UK laws. Currently, most laws in Latin America use the family or community as the reference points for inheritance (Rosenn, 1988). The United States is similarly wrestling with this concept concerning immigration laws: how much should the family and group be considered when making immigration decisions?

This collective-individual and high and low power distance directly relates to different assumptions about intellectual property and copyright, especially in China, which has a different history of copyright as compared to the United States. When the People's Republic of China (PRC) was established in 1949, the regime tried to purge the prevailing legal traditions and systems (Shi, 2010). Consequently, "China experienced a lengthy period of "legislative vacuum" and had no legal system in the modern sense…And disputes between enterprises and individuals were normally resolved via administrative channels, as an integral part of the national planning system" (Shi, 2010, p. 498). Starting in the 1970, China undertook an ambitious program of reform, including law, which was seen as a foundation of stability and harmony (Shi, 2010, p. 499), but intellectual property was a radically new concept because it was mostly antithetical to communist ideology and Confucian-based relations. But in an effort to modernize and attract investment from the west, China begin to lay the foundation of intellectual property, including the Trademark Law (1982), the Patent Law (1984), and the Copyright Law (1990), representing "the backbone legislation governing IPR [intellectual property]" (Shi, 2010, p. 502). In addition, China developed an entire chapter of intellectual property under its civil law code (1986), which recognized proprietary rights involving intangible properties and equitable remedies for infringement (Shi, p. 503). China continued to develop its intellectual property structure with seven new laws from 1992 to 2001, most of them focused on modernizing its legal system as a way to work more effectively with western countries. In 2001, as a way to settle intellectual property law suits, China's Supreme Court issued specific judicial interpretations, further strengthening intellectual property laws (Shi, 2010). All of these efforts enabled China to be in compliance with the World Trade Organization's global standards of intellectual property.

However, as in most cases, the law precedes the practice, and China continues to work at implementing these laws. As Shi explains (2010), "China has made arduous efforts toward gaining admittance into the international IPR community and has transplanted an elaborate IPR regime that turns out to be "a castle in the air"--the harmonized legal system has been built without a political and social foundation to strengthen its adequate enforcement" (p. 502). Consequently, from a practical point of view, explains Shi (2010), "any approach to effectively analyzing and clarifying IPR problems in China must rest on a delicate interplay of political and cultural fundamentals" (p. 502). Peerenboom (2002) similarly argues that in China's quest for obtaining the rule of law, they have developed a significant legal structure, but often this quest is softened or hampered by local customs and relations.

Consequently, the key element of this cultural approach to intellectual property is still Confucianism (Shi, 2010; Glenn, 2000; Peerenboom, 2002; Heath, 2005), although other factors such as high power distance might have a role. As Hampden-Turner & Trompenaars (2000) explain, the idea of ownership is an individualistic concept because collective cultures tend to a community-generated ownership or the idea that it is impossible for one person or company to own something like an idea. Confucianism might inspire some in China to consistently "ignore" some intellectual property issues because of the potential of the intellectual property to achieve a greater communal good, for China as opposed to the ownership claims by a specific individual, corporation or country (Heath, 2005). This point is more thoroughly discussed in the latter section called "Ascription-Achievement."

Similarly, China has traditionally highly regulated Internet usage, allegedly denying individual rights in favor of a greater good of the community (see Amnesty International for updates on internet censorship in China). In other words, the collective rights of China trump the rights of individuals, who are not in a position to argue against the superior in the high power distance context.

Consequently, professional communicators who come from individualistic cultures such as the United States must be very careful about assuming the individual as the unit of reference in communications that regulate the behavior of people, especially when they assume the right of the individual to make relatively independent decisions. Instead, these communicators must understand that the group is often the reference point in collective cultures. This difference strongly influences communications such as policies and procedures, evaluation of performance, and designating innovations or ownership of ideas.

Policies and Procedures in Light of Universal-Particular and High and Low Context

These two value sets profoundly influences–or correlates strongly with–legal traditions, and is grounded concretely in organizational policies and procedures, the topic of this section. First, the common law legal tradition closely aligns with universalism and low context communications because it emphasizes developing broad and loose guidelines to be applied universally across all people. Similarly, the civil law has strong connects to particularism and high context communications because civil law provides comprehensive frameworks that are used to judge specific situations. In fact, as I explain more fully elsewhere (Thatcher, 2000), the common law, universalistic and low context assumptions of North Americans strongly encouraged their approaches to one organization's policies and procedures, while the South Americans working in this organization, seemed closely aligned with their particularism, high context communication, and civil law assumptions.

In the United States, policies and procedures documents have been described as one of the central mechanisms for developing, organizing, and maintaining a "consistent quality of interaction in organizations" (Klein & McKenna, 1997 p. 147). The U.S. scholar Dorothy Winsor (1996) explains that these documents are critical because they either make visible already agreed-upon organizational assumptions and practices, or they—through the writing process—create the assumptions and practices themselves. These constructive roles of writing are not new in rhetoric and professional communication; in fact, they are perhaps some of the most important principles or theories in the field. However, implicit in U.S. approaches to writing (especially in policies and procedures) is a U.S. cultural and rhetorical tradition that has historically valorized writing as a constructive and regulating mechanism of social interactions. This tradition draws on a variety of cultural values, including the common law legal heritage of the United States, which emphasizes a universalist, precedent-setting approach to the production of texts, and a flexible, creative, and productive interpretation and application of the texts. In other rhetorical and cultural traditions, however, writing may not carry out the same roles.

In my research at an organization in Ecuador (2000), many South American personnel seem predisposed to think of personal interactions and specific contexts as a mechanism of regulating behavior. Thus, orality tended to be the primary reference point for understanding appropriate organizational behavior and only in specific contexts. When dealing with written policies and procedures documents, the South American personnel also drew on a civil law hermeneutic. They expected very specific and comprehensive guidelines to ensure correct application and gave themselves little or no room for personal interpretation (Thatcher, 2000). Thus, in South America, the cultural values of particularism and collective-hierarchy, and the rhetorical traditions of orality and high context communication correspond to different roles of writing in policies and procedures (Thatcher, 2000). Writing has historically been associated with the original colonialization, unwieldy legal processes, or bureaucracies. As a result, orality and personal relations tend to be the main mechanisms (Thatcher, 2000) for regulating and constructing organizational behavior.

Professional communicators who come from universalist cultures will most naturally assume that writing is a precedent-setting act, one that becomes the guide for subsequent behavior. Consequently, documents that reflect this legal approach will not work the same way in particular and high context cultures.

Specific-Diffuse in Light of Privacy and Information Technologies

This value set has the best application to privacy laws, at all levels. As an example, perhaps I can narrate a personal experience. While we were living in Ecuador, my wife gave birth to our son, a truly intercultural experience, with many differences centering on privacy in public and private settings. It was a normal, unproblematic birth, much like the birth of our two daughters in the United States. However, upon being admitted to the hospital, my wife and I had to undergo strict admission scrutiny, including an examination of our clothing and belongings, and I was required to put on hospital clothes and thoroughly wash my hands and place special hospital slippers over my shoes. In addition, any of our friends who tried to visit us had to undergo the same strict scrutiny. All of these efforts were justified by the hospital personnel as a way to protect against infections, which I agreed with. When we were required to undergo this scrutiny, I simply assumed that my wife's room would be similarly protected. However, the opposite was true. The after-birth room was wide open to anybody who cared to walk by, including the many Ecuadorian strangers who wanted to take a friendly look at a fat, bald, blue-eyed gringo baby. The assumption seemed that because of the strict scrutiny used upon entrance, there was no need for protection inside the hospital, a perfect example of diffuseness. In contrast, in the U.S. hospitals where our girls were born, there was much less initial scrutiny upon entrance, but much tighter controls within the private room.

Our hospital experience demonstrate different attitudes toward privacy in public versus private contexts, which significantly influences privacy laws and policies at all levels, including organizational, national, and regional. This difference also influences current issues of privacy and evolving internet technologies. For example, it is interesting to note the intercultural influence of laws concerning Google's Street View and popular social sites such as FaceBook and MySpace. Street View photographs over 600 streets in North America, Western Europe, Japan, Korea, Taiwan, and Australia (as of December, 2010). They have high resolution cameras mounted on cars that can capture people, events, and contexts, including people inside their homes and other private contexts. Current privacy laws in the United States do not prevent Google or other companies from doing this, and on October 28, 2010, the U.S. Federal Trade Commission cleared Google for continuing their work in the United States because they had sufficient security controls to protect the information that was obtained. Following the same pattern, Australia was initially concerned and then placed–but quickly lifted–a temporary ban on Street View (*The Australian*, June 4, 2010). Australia was most concerned about the security of the private information, once it was obtained; but no discussions of the private images in public appeared in the discussions. Similarly, Canada has proposed–but failed to enact–a ban on Street View but insisted on strong security measures with the data obtained. These approaches seem eerily similar to our U.S. hospital experience and the Customs and Border, as explained in Chapter Six: provide for loose public guidelines for entrance, but strict controls once inside. In other words, the concrete details of the Street View images were less of a concern than how the personal information was eventually controlled, a perfect analogy of specific orientation.

However, like the hospital in Ecuador, other countries want to provide much stricter control of the up-front, public spaces and less on the use of the data after it is obtained, a perfect example of diffuse orientation. Currently, legislation against Street View is pending in other countries, specifically those with different views of public and private boundaries. For example, in September 2010, the Czech Republic banned Google because it violates people's privacy with its detailed public pictures (*The Mirror*, September 15, 2010). Likewise, Switzerland has banned Street View because "it fails to sufficiently blur faces and license plates" (*TechWeb*, August 24, 2009). Greece also banned Google Street until it could provide adequate up-front privacy measures. Japan is allowing Street View in three major cities (November, 2010), but only after its government required Google to abide by its "disclosure of information and personal information protection," which forced Google to "reshoot all of the footage for its online photo map service, using less intrusive camera angles" (*Daily Mail*, London, May 14, 2009). Likewise, the UK evaluated Google Street View after privacy concerns. Specifically, a women "filed for divorce after her husband's car was pictured outside another woman's house" (*Daily Mail*, London, May 14, 2009). However, the United Kingdom has yet to ban or require modifications to Street View, which, coincidentally exemplifies their mixed values of specific and diffuse.

Germany is also a country that has mixed specific and diffuse views (Hampden-Turner, 200), and it has also allowed Street View, but only after very strict controls were put into place on the concreteness of the photographs and a ban on obtaining information from WiFis (*The International Herald Tribune*, October 21, 2010). France and Italy are similarly investigating the public images as privacy issues associated with Street View.

Mirroring the indices of specific and diffuse orientations, those countries with more diffuse orientations are much more concerned about the concreteness of images for public display (Japan, Czech Republic, Greece, Switzerland), while the specific countries (U.S., Canada, and Australia) are much more concerned about what will happen with the data once it is obtained but not that concerned about the concreteness of public images. Likewise, U.S. and Canadian federal regulators are most concerned about the personal information that Facebook and MySpace acquire and share with advertisers, rather than the concrete public images that these two social sites make available across the internet.

These connections between specific-diffuse orientations and Google Street View are extremely broad, but at the same time, follow closely the value sets and are, therefore, valid on the one hand, but need much more research. Thus, critical questions facing legal systems are the types of privacy controls to enact: specific or diffuse? The diffuse approach emphasizes careful protection of people in public venues but less care once the information is obtained. The specific approach emphasizes less interest in the public space, but much care in how personal information is protected.

Legal Procedures and Achievement-Ascription, Inner and Outer directed, and Time Frames

These three value sets closely parallel the development of process-based or role based legal procedures, a difference that is critical in legal theory and development. One of the hallmarks of the U.S. common law legal systems is the concept of "due process," which means that the courts and legal systems faithfully followed the law through the legal processes (Glenn, 2000). A key component of due process is the explicit guarantee of *procedural rights* to the individual, the idea that the accused has specific and explicit rights with the procedures. The most common example of a procedural right is the Miranda warning, which states that the one best arrested "has the right to remain silent." In other words, in the United States, criminal prosecutions and civil cases are generally governed by explicit guarantees of procedural rights under the Bill of Rights; and it is usually up to the judge to ensure this process. Thus, in addition to "due process," the legal concept of "procedural due process" is now commonly used, with a key emphasis on judicial control of the legal processes. As explained in Chapter Six Organizational Behavior and Chapter Ten Instructions, U.S.-based achievement orientation strongly favors explicit, measured, and controlled processes as a way to enforce policies and instructions and improve organizational performance. And this process clearly delineates the linear, monochronic time frames. In addition, since the individual is the key reference point for most U.S.-based legal contexts, the due process also assumes an inner-directed person. The U.S.-based common law legal system strongly correlates to achievement, inner-directed orientation, and monochronic time frames through the key concept of procedural due process.

Other legal systems emphasize roles and harmonious relations as key mechanism of judicial control (rather than due process), a pattern that is common in ascriptive and outer-directed cultures. As explained in Chapter Two and throughout this book, ascriptive oriented cultures provide power through people and through the roles these people carry out. In other words, ascriptive cultures ascribe power to get things done, not through process, but through people. Further, outer-directed cultures emphasize the modeling of successful harmonious relations through looking to nature or great models of wisdom from the past, models that emphasize synchronous or polychronic time frames. Civil law explicitly and carefully spells out roles and responsibilities of judges, attorneys, and the accused, all with the assumptions that when these roles are clearly laid out and followed, justice will be carried out. This difference seems subtle but it has significant ramifications for legal issues.

Here is a concrete example of the achievement-ascriptive difference in professional communication: I frequently traveled into Mexico (before the start of the 2009 narco violence). To travel into the interior of Mexico, I need to obtain a temporary vehicle permit, which I must surrender on my last exit from Mexico. One time, however, I forget to surrender the permit, so I was required to carry out various transactions in Ciudad Juárez, Chihuahua to remedy my mistake. I asked for help at the Mexican Vehicle Import Office, and these were my instructions given by the staff: "Go to the Chihuahuan State building and find this specific agency and talk to the people there about obtaining a waiver for the surrender of the permit." However, when I arrived at the state building, the person I needed to talk to was out for lunch; and nobody else could help. After he returned, I was asked to return to New Mexico (twice) to obtain some specific paperwork on my vehicle, a part of the process that I was not aware of until I had waited for two hours and was mostly through the transaction. At that point, I realized that I was expecting to be guided using the monochronic, achievement-oriented process, which detailed every linear step and every component needed, rather than who I needed to talk to.

On the other hand, the staff who gave me directions simply ascribed to those people the roles and power to carry out my transaction, and these relations were not modeled after my monochronic time. Many, many of the transactions in Latin America are based on people or authority first, and process second, a strong connection between culture and civil law. In addition to these minor legal transactions, this process- or people-based difference profoundly affects law around the world. For example, the Letter O in Chapter One demonstrates very clearly that the issue of car registration is not a process problem, but an authority problem. Thus, clarifying who is responsible is the major way to improve the transaction.

Asian law, which is similarly grounded in ascriptive cultures, posits strong powers to government, community, and business leaders to carry out specific procedures and transactions, based on the long tradition of Confucius (Glenn, 2000). From this ascriptive, outer-directed, and polychronic base, formal laws are not needed; instead, roles and relations are concretely laid out and ritualized, and the goal is harmony. Interestingly, as Hahm (2009) argues, much of the work of making constitutional law pre-modern east Asia (China and Korea) is through Confucian rituals, which demonstrate the roles and relations that need to be mapped or modeled upon existing relations. For example, explains Hahm (2009),

Confucians of Choson Korea would not have comprehended how violation of ritual could be a lesser offence than violation of law. Ritual for them was not merely about ceremony and politesse, but rather was heavily imbued with normative power. In the political context, observance of ritual was integrally connected with the issue of the ruler's (and dynasty's) legitimacy. A ruler who failed to comport with the requirements of proper ritual was not qualified to be a ruler. With such an elevated notion of ritual, it is then hardly surprising that, in a society where Confucian values formed the basis of political morality, ritual could become the basic term of political discourse. Political actors utilized the language of ritual in debating political issues and in their criticism of government policy. Scholarly learning on ritual matters became directly relevant for political disputations regarding the legitimacy of the ruler. In other words, constitutional discourse on the proper roles of the throne and the bureaucracy, and by implication on the limits of state power, was conducted through the discourse on ritual (pp. 139-141).

This argument powerfully represents the idea that roles and relations as organized through formal ritual is the main law-making mechanism. This is a perfect example of ascriptive, outer-directed, and polychronic culture. It is also interesting to note that many of the misunderstandings between the United States and China (especially concerning copyright and intellectual property, as discussed earlier) are connected to this difference between process and roles/people. Glenn (2000) explains that China conventionally thinks of international law in terms of the logic or model of the relations between the countries or relations between officials of the same government, while the United States specifically focuses on processes and milestones. This difference has profoundly influence the discussion of intellectual property and copyright, with China arguing that the United States, in its role as the first-world developer, should be able to apply the standards differently to China, which is still under development (see Natividad, 2008).

Professional communicators who come from common law, achievement oriented, and monochronic cultures will most like create procedures based on these values, that is, process-based, monochronic, and with little reference to the people/agents who are needed to carry out the transaction. They will need to adapt their procedural communications to reflect the power of the people or agents to carry out these transactions.

CONCLUSION

As this Chapter has shown, law, rhetoric, and culture are closely combined, even though only a handful of scholars are making these connections. Thus, as rhetoricians in global contexts, we have much work to do examining, describing, and then reconciling differences as a way to improve professional communications across cultures.

REFERENCES

Adler, N. (2008). *International dimensions of organizational behavior*. New York, NY: Thomson Learning Center.

Alcalde, J. (1991). Differential impact of American political and economic institutions on Latin America. In Thompson, K. W. (Ed.), *The U.S. Constitution and the constitutions of Latin America* (pp. 97–126).

Bakhtin, M. M. (1990). *Art and answerability* (Holquist, M., & Liapunov, V., Eds.). (Liapunov, V., Trans.). Austin, TX: University of Texas Press.

Bakhtin, M. M. (1993). *Toward a philosophy of the act* (Holquist, M., & Liapunov, V., Eds.). (Liapunov, V., Trans.). Austin, TX: University of Texas Press.

Bourdieu, P. (1999). *Language and symbolic power*. Boston, MA: Harvard University Press.

Brown, C. (2000). An analysis of the 'human rights-culture' and its critics. In Patman, R. (Ed.), *Universal human rights?* (pp. 31–49). New York, NY: St. Martin's Press.

Burke, K. (1968). *Language as symbolic action. Essays on life, literature, and method.* Berkeley, CA: University of California Press.

Castañeda, J. G. (1995). *The Mexican shock: Its meaning for the U.S.* New York, NY: The New Press.

Dombrowski, P. (2000). *Ethics in technical communication*. Boston, MA: Allyn & Bacon.

Donnelly, J. (2003). *Universal human rights in theory and practice*. Ithaca, NY: Cornell University Press.

Eder, P. J. (1950). *A comparative survey of Anglo-American and Latin-American law*. New York, NY: New York University Press.

Engle, K. (2000). Culture and human rights: The Asian values debate in context. *New York University Journal of International Law & Politics. New York University. International Law Society, 32*, 291–323.

Glendon, M. A. (1999). Foundations of human rights: The unfinished business. *The American Journal of Jurisprudence, 44*, 1–14.

Glenn, H. P. (2000). *Legal traditions of the world: Sustainable diversity in law*. Oxford, UK: Oxford University Press.

Hahm, C. (2009). Ritual and constitutionalism: Disputing the ruler's legitimacy in a Confucian polity. *The American Journal of Comparative Law, 57*, 135–203. doi:10.5131/ajcl.2008.0005

Higgins, T. E. (1999). Regarding rights: An essay honoring the Fiftieth Anniversary of the *Universal Declaration of Human Rights*. *Columbia Human Rights Law Review, 30*, 225–247.

Hofstede, G. (2010). *Cultures and organizations, software of the mind* (3rd ed.). New York, NY: McGraw Hill.

Humphrey, J. P. (1984). *Human rights and the United Nations: A great adventure*. Dobbs Ferry, NY: Transnational Publishers.

Hussein, T. H. (2000). Human rights—The Asian perspective. In Patman, R. (Ed.), *Universal human rights?* (pp. 75–80). New York, NY: St. Martin's Press.

Ishii, S. (2006). Complementing contemporary intercultural communication research with East Asian sociocultural perspectives and practices. *China Media Research, 2*(1), 13–20.

Kellog, S. (1995). *Law and the transformation of Aztec culture, 1500-1700*. Norman, OK: University of Oklahoma Press.

Kirsch, G., & Mortensen, P. (Eds.). (1996). *Ethics and representation in qualitative studies of literacy*. Urbana, IL: National Council of Teachers of English.

Klein, W. D., & McKenna, B. (1997). Policies and procedures. *Journal of Technical Writing and Communication*, *27*(2), 147–161.

Leon-Portilla, M. (1996). *El destino de la palabra. De la oralidad y los códices mesoamericanos a la escritura alfabética*. México City, Mexico: El Colegio Nacional Fondo de Cultura Económica.

Lubman, S. (1999). *Bird in a cage: Legal reform in China after Mao*. Stanford, CA: Stanford University Press.

Lucy, J. (1996). The scope of linguistic relativity: An analysis and review of empirical research. In Gumperz, J. J., & Levinson, S. C. (Eds.), *Rethinking linguistic relativity* (pp. 37–69). Cambridge, UK: Cambridge University Press.

McCormick, N. (2009). *Rhetoric and the rule of law: A theory of legal reasoning*. Oxford, UK: Oxford University Press.

Menski, W. (2006). *Comparative law in a global context: The legal systems of Asia and Africa*. Cambridge, UK: Cambridge University Press. doi:10.1017/CBO9780511606687

Merryman, J. H. (1969). *The civil law tradition: An introduction to the legal systems of western Europe and Latin America*. Stanford, CA: Stanford University Press.

Morsink, J. (1999). *The Universal Declaration of Human Rights: Origins, drafting, and intent*. Philadelphia, PA: University of Pennsylvania Press.

Muntarbhorn, V. (2000). Asia and human rights at the crossroads of the new millennium: Between the Universalist and the Particularist? In Patman, R. (Ed.), *Universal human rights?* (pp. 81–95). New York, NY: St. Martin's Press.

Natividad, K. (2008). Stepping it up and taking it to the streets: Changing civil & criminal copyright enforcement tactics. *Berkeley Technology Law Journal Annual Review*, *23*, 469–501.

Nazzari, M. (1995). Widows as obstacles to business: British objections to Brazilian marriage and inheritance laws. *Comparative Studies in Society and History*, *37*, 781–802. doi:10.1017/S0010417500019952

Otto, D. (1997). Rethinking the 'universality' of human rights. *Columbia Human Rights Law Review*, *29*, 1–46.

Participants, S. (2000). Responding to the legal obstacles to electronic commerce in Latin America: General questionnaire. *Arizona Journal of International and Comparative Law*, *17*, 1–66.

Paz, O. (1985). *Labyrinth of solitude* (Kemp, L., Trans.). New York, NY: Grove Press.

Peerenboom, R. P. (2002). *China's long march toward rule of law*. Cambridge, UK: Cambridge University Press. doi:10.1017/CBO9780511493737

Perelman, C. (1982). *The realm of rhetoric*. Notre Dame, IN: University of Notre Dame Press.

Porter, J., Sullivan, P., Blythe, S., Grabil, J. T., & Miles, L. (2000). Institutional critique: A rhetorical methodology for change. *College Composition and Communication*, *51*(4), 610–642. doi:10.2307/358914

Porter, J. E. (1998). *Rhetorical ethics and internetworked writing*. Greenwich, CT: Ablex Publishing.

Rosenfeld, M. (2000). Human rights, nationalism, and multiculturalism in rhetoric, ethics, and politics: A pluralist critique. *Cardozo Law Review, 21*, 1225–1241.

Rosenn, K. (1988). A comparison of Latin American and North American legal traditions. In Tavis, L. (Ed.), *Multinational managers and host government interactions* (pp. 127–152). South Bend, IN: University of Notre Dame Press.

Shi, W. (2010). Globalization and indigenization: Legal transplant of a universal TRIPS regime in a multicultural world. *American Business Law Journal, 47*, 455–506. doi:10.1111/j.1744-1714.2010.01101.x

Stewart, E., & Bennett, M. (1991). *American cultural patterns: A cross-cultural perspective* (Rev. ed.). Yarmouth, ME: Intercultural Press, Inc.

Sullivan, P., & Porter, J. E. (1998). *Opening spaces: Writing technologies and critical research practices*. Greenwich, CT: Ablex.

Sutch, P. (2001). *Ethics, justice, and international relations: Constructing an international community*. New York, NY: Routledge.

Tamanaha, B. Z. (2006). *Law as a means to an end: threat to the rule of law*. Cambridge, UK: Cambridge University Press. doi:10.1017/CBO9780511511073

Thatcher, B. (1997). *Orality and writing in Latin American and USA professional communication.* Unpublished doctoral dissertation, Purdue University.

Thatcher, B. L. (2000). Writing policies and procedures in a U.S. and South American context. *Technical Communication Quarterly, 94*, 365–400. doi:10.1080/10572250009364706

Thatcher, B. L. (2001). Issues of validity in intercultural professional communication research. *Journal of Business and Technical Communication, 15*(4), 458–489. doi:10.1177/105065190101500403

Thatcher, B. L. (2006). Intercultural rhetoric, technology, and writing in Mexican maquilas. *Special Technology Transfer Edition of Technical Communication Quarterly, 15*(3), 383–405.

Twining, W. (2000). *Globalisation and legal theory*. Cambridge, UK: Cambridge University Press.

Van Hoecke, M., & Warrington, M. (1998). Legal cultures, legal paradigms and legal doctrine: Towards a new model for comparative law. Cambridge University Press.. *The International and Comparative Law Quarterly, 47*, 495–536. doi:10.1017/S0020589300062163

White, J. (1985). *The legal imagination*. University of Chicago Press.

Williams, J. (2009). *Style: Basics of clarity and grace* (3rd ed.). New York, NY: Pearson Longmann.

Winsor, D. (1996). *Writing like an engineer: A rhetorical education*. Mahwah, NJ: Lawrence Erlbaum Associates.

Chapter 9
Intercultural Rhetorical Dimensions of Health Literacy and Medicine

ABSTRACT

This chapter examines the relations between health/medicine and rhetoric across cultures, demonstrating the need to have culturally and linguistically appropriate health care communications. It compares the rhetorical strategies of two heart health manuals and informed consent, showing how culture is embedded in these documents and how to adapt them to target cultures.

INTRODUCTION

Now, it is widely recognized that medicine, health care and health communications are not universal but are intimately connected to local cultures and medical traditions (Purnell, 2009). Consequently, health and medical services are best delivered using the cultural and communication patterns of the patients (see, for example, Purnell, 2009; Tseng & Streltzer, 2008). The intercultural dimensions of health and medical treatment have undergone extensive research and practice, not only in the United States, but all around the world. Not surprisingly, much research has focused on improving health disparities or differences in health behaviors, based on cultural and ethnic groups, using culturally competent health care. This is especially true with Latinos or Hispanics (hablamosjuntos.org), which make up the largest U.S. minority. For example, new critical research has focused on the roles of Spanish translators and new multimedia forms to bridge cultural and linguistic differences for Hispanic populations (Angelelli & Jacobson, 2009).

This move towards "culturally competent health care" is so critical to reducing health disparities in the United States that it is mandated at the federal and many state levels (hrsa.gov/culturalcompetence). For example, the U.S. government has developed (and mandated) 14 dimensions of "culturally competent health care" for the four major U.S. minority groups (www.hrsa.gov/culturalcompetence). These 14 dimensions are titled *National Standards on Culturally and Linguistically Appropriate Services* and are listed in Table 1.

DOI: 10.4018/978-1-61350-450-5.ch009

Table 1. The Nation Standards on Culturally and Linguistically Appropriate Services

Standard 1	Health care organizations should ensure that patients/consumers receive from all staff member's effective, understandable, and respectful care that is provided in a manner compatible with their cultural health beliefs and practices and preferred language.
Standard 2	Health care organizations should implement strategies to recruit, retain, and promote at all levels of the organization a diverse staff and leadership that are representative of the demographic characteristics of the service area.
Standard 3	Health care organizations should ensure that staff at all levels and across all disciplines receive ongoing education and training in culturally and linguistically appropriate service delivery.
Standard 4	Health care organizations must offer and provide language assistance services, including bilingual staff and interpreter services, at no cost to each patient/consumer with limited English proficiency at all points of contact, in a timely manner during all hours of operation.
Standard 5	Health care organizations must provide to patients/consumers in their preferred language both verbal offers and written notices informing them of their right to receive language assistance services.
Standard 6	Health care organizations must assure the competence of language assistance provided to limited English proficient patients/consumers by interpreters and bilingual staff. Family and friends should not be used to provide interpretation services (except on request by the patient/consumer).
Standard 7	Health care organizations must make available easily understood patient-related materials and post signage in the languages of the commonly encountered groups and/or groups represented in the service area.
Standard 8	Health care organizations should develop, implement, and promote a written strategic plan that outlines clear goals, policies, operational plans, and management accountability/oversight mechanisms to provide culturally and linguistically appropriate services.
Standard 9	Health care organizations should conduct initial and ongoing organizational self-assessments of CLAS-related activities and are encouraged to integrate cultural and linguistic competence-related measures into their internal audits, performance improvement programs, patient satisfaction assessments, and outcomes-based evaluations.
Standard 10	Health care organizations should ensure that data on the individual patient's/consumer's race, ethnicity, and spoken and written language are collected in health records, integrated into the organization's management information systems, and periodically updated.
Standard 11	Health care organizations should maintain a current demographic, cultural, and epidemiological profile of the community as well as a needs assessment to accurately plan for and implement services that respond to the cultural and linguistic characteristics of the service area.
Standard 12	Health care organizations should develop participatory, collaborative partnerships with communities and utilize a variety of formal and informal mechanisms to facilitate community and patient/consumer involvement in designing and implementing CLAS-related activities.
Standard 13	Health care organizations should ensure that conflict and grievance resolution processes are culturally and linguistically sensitive and capable of identifying, preventing, and resolving cross-cultural conflicts or complaints by patients/consumers.
Standard 14	Health care organizations are encouraged to regularly make available to the public information about their progress and successful innovations in implementing the CLAS standards and to provide public notice in their communities about the availability of this information.

The 14 standards are organized by themes: Culturally Competent Care (Standards 1-3), Language Access Services (Standards 4-7), and Organizational Supports for Cultural Competence (Standards 8-14). These 14 standards present a comprehensive approach to the cultural competence, but in practice, much of cultural competence is reduced to translation and understanding the medical traditions of the patients' cultures, two critical components indeed, but far from true intercultural competence. Thus, the purpose of this chapter is not to review the body of literature and research on culturally competent health care; rather, this chapter demonstrates how to develop culturally competent health communications with each of the 14 standards. In addition, this chapter severely critiques many of the assumptions of these standards, including their definitions of

Figure 1. Fotonovela of Heart Health for Latino Community

culture, culturally appropriate communications, relations between group behavior and demographics, and translation.

To explore this critique and develop better intercultural health communications, this chapter first presents a comparative analysis of health care instructions and communication concerning cardiovascular health. Next, it analyzes the use of pre-operative consent forms, which it contextualizes along the U.S.-Mexico border, demonstrating the different connections associated with writing, orality, and legal and medical practices. Finally, the chapter connects the other aspects of the 14 standards to different chapters in this book, showing the breadth of what culturally competent health care is.

GROUNDING HEALTH LITERACY MATERIALS IN INTERCULTURAL RHETORIC

To demonstrate how health literacy materials need to be grounded in intercultural rhetoric, I present two pamphlets that are focused on cholesterol and heart health. Both were produced by the National Institute of Health (NIH; http://www.nhlbi.nih.gov/health/public/heart/index.htm). The first example is a *Fotonovela,* a pamphlet that was developed by Latino and Mexican health experts from the NIH for the Latino community in the United States. Figure 1 is a selection of six pages from the 24-page English version, which demonstrates a culturally sensitive approach for the Latino community. In other words, this document draws on the predominant cultural values of Latino and Mexican communities.

In English, *Fotonovela* means a photo soap opera or photo drama, and as a genre, the fotonovela has been a critical component of health instruction for Latino communities, not only in the United States, but around Latin America (see hablamosjuntos.org). This particular fotonovela has been very successful in the United States.

Figure 2 shows a pamphlet with the same content but delivered for a non-Latino audience. It exemplifies many of the cultural values of Anglo-Americans in the United States or the predominant values of the United States as described by many intercultural researchers and reviewed in Chapter Two.

The following discussion briefly grounds the discussion of the intercultural values and then it shows how each pamphlet carefully meets the cultural and rhetorical values of Latin America or the United States, following the eight values sets or common human thresholds that are described in Chapter Two.

I/Other

As discussed in Chapter Two, people in individualistic cultures tend to be more self-reliant, competitive, and act in their own self interest for personal growth (Hampden-Turner & Trompenaars, 2000). In collective societies, individuals tend to be integrated into strong, cohesive in-groups, with which they are loyal (Hofstede, 2010, as cited in Meeuwesen et al., 2009[1]). The Meeuwesen et al. (2009) study found that in individualistic nations–usually more wealthy countries–patients had more autonomy, flexible social roles, longer consultations, and more discussion of psychosocial issues. Physicians asked fewer questions, gave more information, and did less counseling. More often, patients reported that their expectations were not met (an indication, according to the authors, of less fixed physician and patient roles.)

In the U.S., which is more individualistic, all patients are required to receive full information enabling them to freely make decisions about their own health care (Ulrey & Amason, 2001). In some cultures, it is preferred that the patient's family be advised of a negative prognosis first. This is done so families can decide if they should inform the patient of any bad news, which may lead the patient to become upset, hopeless, and thus self-fulfill the poor prognosis. In this scenario,

Figure 2. Generic approach to health communications in the United States

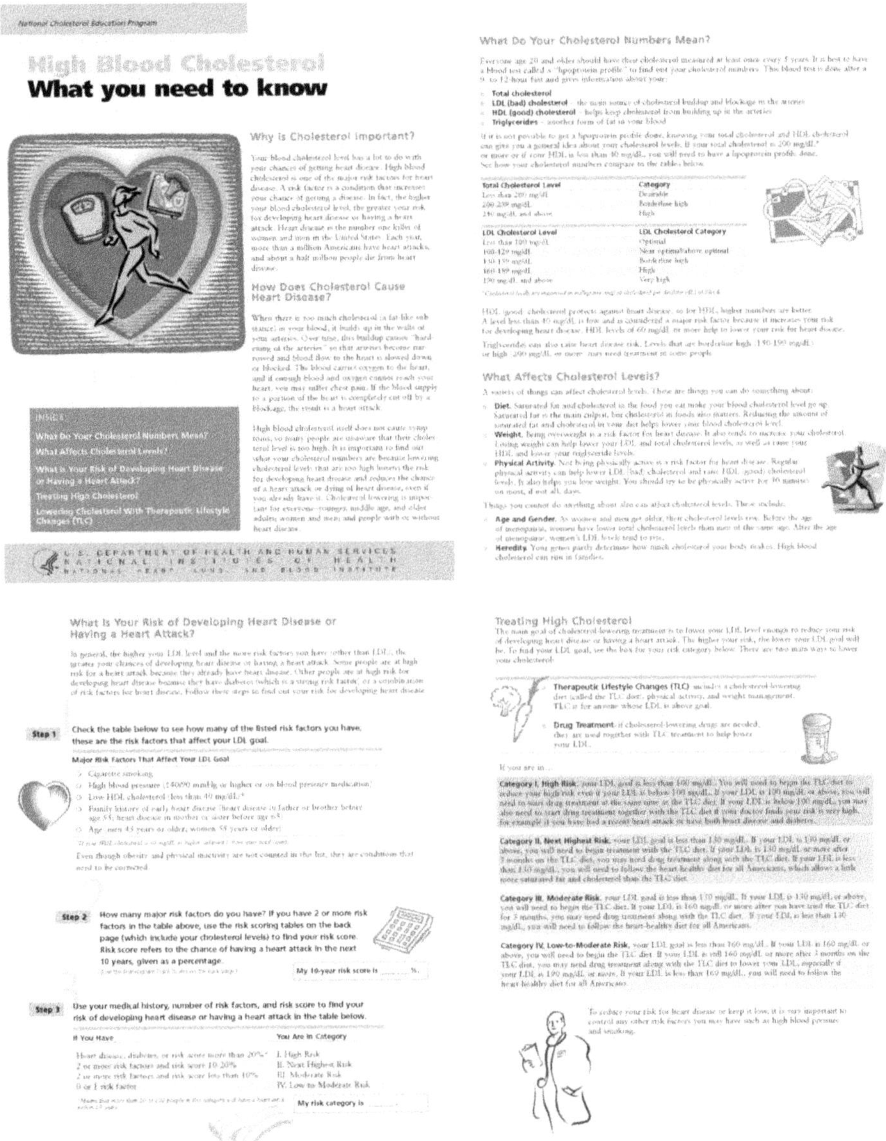

it is recommended that physicians explain that in the U.S. it is standard practice to inform the patient, then ask the patient which approach they prefer (Juckett, 2005; Galanti, 2000). In a study of end-of-life care, African American patients were more inclusive in selecting friends and family in discussions, whereas non-Hispanic white patients chose "closest" family and not friends (Shrank, 2005). This correlates with a more collective value, because it involves a more inclusive approach.

It is quite obvious from Figure 1 or the *fotonovela*, that there is a strong collective orientation, which meets the predominant values sets of most Latin American countries, including Mexico. The entire health scenario is grounded in the Ramirez family, including the specific roles of grandmother, father, mother, and the two children. The first page of this pamphlet does not define cardiovascular health; rather the first page lays out the family as the context for this discussion. And members of this family are not seen as independent equals, a characteristic of individualistic cultures; rather each member of the family is seen in a specific, traditional role with their corresponding hierarchies, further reinforcing the collective orientation of the pamphlet.

Not only is it the scenario grounded in the family, the discussions surrounding health is highly dependent upon each member of the family. The issue of health is not a question of one person such as a father and his high blood pressure; rather the father's health is connected to the mother's cooking and the daughter's new boyfriend. As described in Chapter Two, this approach emphasizes the interpersonal relationships among the family members and the social hierarchy involving the grandmother, father, mother, and children. It also emphasizes the close personal space and intimate family identity among the Ramirezes. Also, the collective communication patterns in this fotonovela do not bifurcate personal and objective strategies because they see the person in light of their social context, effectively combining the personal and social. Thus, instead of resorting to the uniqueness of the individual such as the father's high blood pressure, this pamphlet shows collective communicators resolving the potential conflicts through their respective collective roles.

On the other hand, Figure 2 shows strong patterns of individualism. The first page of the pamphlet shows a lone individual isolated from social context. There is no grounding in a specific time, place, context or social relations; rather, there is a strong emphasis of an objective analysis of cholesterol levels, divorcing these levels from anything other than the individual uniqueness. In addition, the figure of the lone person running in light of the heart and the checklist emphasize personal achievement and self-creation. Further, as will be described next, there is a friendlier document design pattern, which allows individuals to quickly locate desired information. On the other hand, the document design of the fotonovela is not as reader friendly, from U.S. cultural standpoint, because it is designed around the social interaction, not the information that needs to be presented to the user.

Rules Orientation

As described in Chapter Two, rules orientation in cultures seems to revolve around either the particular or universal orientation. In particularist cultures, the default approach is to apply rules and decisions depending on relations and context. Instead of "the level playing field," the particularist playing field is overtly structured, and thus, there is a specifically tailored set of rules for each social relationship. Hispanic mothers stated in one study (Cooper, Beach, Johnson & Inui, 2006) that providers did not recognize their children's unique strengths and abilities, which they considered essential for establishing a good relationship. They were exhibiting particularism, whereas U.S. trained providers may have been taught to be universalistic by treating all patients as homogenous (Bustillos, 2005). Cultural competency in relationship-centered care has been based on the notion that each person should be viewed as "a unique human being" (Cooper et al., 2006). This idea of a unique human being is more of a particular value, which is the opposite of universal value of the U.S. health care system, where care is standardized and patients are typically thought of as part of a disease-centered population and not as unique individuals (Bustillos, 2005).

Both pamphlets exhibit universal and particular traits, but in each one, one value orientation greatly predominates. In the fotonovela, particularist communications predominate. First, there is an uniqueness in the page design, for each page has a different layout based on the particular visual and verbal information needs. Second, there is no parallel information or lists. Third, and most importantly, the rules or subject of cardiovascular health are discussed in light of the specific relations and context of the Ramirez family. And the rules change according to the circumstances because the arrival of the boyfriend raises the blood pressure of the father, a classic particularist approach to rules. Thus, the fotonovela argues for improving the cardiovascular health for the benefit of the whole family. The fotonovela does give universal numbers for understanding levels of cholesterol, but these numbers are personalized for the one person filling out form or box. In addition, the colors used in the fotonovela are much more vibrant and contrastive, emphasizing the dynamic nature of particular cultures. As most intercultural researchers have argued and which is described more thoroughly in Chapters Two and Five, particularist cultures tend to favor more dynamic colors and more artistic patterns in their visual communications. Finally, this pamphlet generally hides or downplays the scientific "process" of determining appropriate cholesterol levels in the Ramirez family context and their social relations.

The second pamphlet demonstrates strong universalist tendencies. First, it focuses on defining cholesterol levels for everyone, notwithstanding their social or personal situations. In addition, this pamphlet presents objective information, which emphasizes the scientific and universal nature of health and cholesterol. Third, this pamphlet presents much of the information in the form of lists, a universalist strategy that emphasizes the parallelism and readability needed for universalist readers. And there is a general layout that carries throughout the whole pamphlet. Fourth, this pamphlet has much more muted or less dynamic colors. Finally, this pamphlet presents the process of determining appropriate cholesterol levels very differently than the fotonovela. In this manual, the process is overt, shown by the calculator and the tables used to calculate the different levels of cholesterol. This overt process further reinforces the universal approach.

Sources of Virtue and Guidance

The third value focuses on the source or origin of virtue, guidance, or method of aligning oneself rightly. In other words, all cultures look to different sources to understand if they are heading in the right direction, so to speak. Hampden-Turner and Trompenaars (2000) explained that there are generally two sources of virtue: the inner-directed source that "conceives of virtue as inside each of us--in our souls, wills, convictions, principles," or believes--in the triumph of conscious purpose. Not surprisingly, inner-directed cultures are mostly Protestant and believe that inside of each person is a spirit or conscience that tells the person the path to truth or virtuous behavior. Outer direction conceives of virtue as our site each of us in natural rhythms, in the beauties and powers of nature, in aesthetic environments and relationships" (p. 234). For example, hot and cold balances are prevalent within Asian and Latin cultures, which are typically outer directed. In both cultures, hot conditions should be managed with cold therapies and vice versa, and any hot-cold imbalance is thought to foster disease. For example, a mother might stop giving her child vitamins (a hot treatment) if the child gets a rash (a hot condition) (Juckett, 2005). Illnesses, practices, food and medications can all have hot and cold elements (Masi, 1988). Some patients on liquid diets may refuse cold fruit juices but, instead, accept hot bouillon, or vice versa (Masi, 1988).

Many Native Canadian cultures believe health can be maintained by respecting nature, such as following pork taboos, which were to reduce parasitic infections (Masi, 1988). African American patients may accept witchcraft and "fixing" as spells that cause illness and use "root doctors" to lift hexes through incantation to heal the mind and body (Juckett, 2005). Many cultures believe drafts can cause illness. A study by Mikhail (1994, as cited by Flores, 2000) showed conjunctivitis was more commonly believed to be caused by drafts and wind than by infectious agents by Hispanic mothers. Some cultures fear losing one's spirit through a current of air. In many cultures there is a basic energy of the universe: ch'i in Chinese philosophy, and prana in Indian teachings, which can be facilitated to move freely through Yoga. Life force can also be lost, according to some cultures, by the removal of blood (Masi, 1988).

In end of life care, African American patients tend to value protection of life at all costs, so as to allow a miracle to happen (Shrank, 2005; Koenig & Gates-Williams, 1995). They typically request life-sustaining therapy, spiritually-focused information, and the involvement of a religious leader in the decision process (Shrank, 2005). Hispanic and Korean patients in the Koenig and Gates-Williams study (1995) were also more likely to request life-sustaining machines at all costs in case of a miracle. Shrank found that non-Hispanic white groups expressed more concern with quality of life, and pragmatic issues such as cost of care and legal information.

The above examples of nature and spiritual forces affecting disease or disharmony in the body are examples of outer directed beliefs[2], while the U.S. tends to be more inner directed (Hampden-Turner & Trompenaars, 2000). Beliefs of outer directed cultures may seem odd to an inner directed health care provider, but if they do not interfere with the physician's suggested therapy, it is recommended that they be incorporated into the health plan, as ridiculing a custom is likely to jeopardize the patient's confidence or trust in the physician (Masi, 1988; Tate, 2003; Bussey-Jones, 2003).

As described in Chapter Two, this values sets of inner and outer direction correlate strongly with ethos, logos, and pathos. Ethos has a dual meaning, focusing on both the credibility and morality of the speaker or author as critical to believing in the communication. Logos, as the name implies, focuses on the logic or reason of the communication. Pathos basically means emotions. As Aristotle explains, all three are commonly used to convince an audience of one's communication purposes or objectives. Each of the strategies differs significantly depending on whether the culture is inner or outer direct.

The logos of the fotonovela is outer-directed because its reason or logic for controlling cholesterol and improving heart health is not analytical or vertical, universally breaking down the parts into its whole. Rather it is what Stewart and Bennett (1991) label as horizontal and relational, focusing on the context or the *what* and its relations rather than the *why*. This outer-directed approach connects the health of each of the family members together in their home with the father as the head. These horizontal connections have less to do with the actual cholesterol levels of each of the persons and more to do with the combination of what they eat and how they relate to each other in this specific context. Thus, exemplifying the outer-directed logos, the fotonovela focuses on the pattern-like correlations between one behavior and a natural setting. From this perspective, one looks to harmonize himself or herself with the world. This harmonizing logic is very powerful and often uses analogies and metaphors of the natural world as logical patterns to replicate. Thus, it is not surprising that the fotonovela uses a crossword puzzle as one of its contexts.

On the other hand, logos and inner directed culture focuses on the vertical *why*, which is often analytical and universal which is strongly reflected in the second pamphlet. This pamphlet emphasizes the analytical and cause and effect connections between cholesterol level and health. Because bad health is connected to high cholesterol, if a person eats foods lowering cholesterol and then measures his or her cholesterol, that person can control his cholesterol, which in the end will improve his or her health. This rational and universal approach assumes a person who has an inner will or conscience that can control what enters his or her body so as to improve health of the body. This reflects the analogy of deep or vertical thinking, which is an important characteristic of inner direction (Stewart and Bennett, 1991).

Ethos is defined and operationalized differently for each pamphlet. The credibility and morality of the fotonovela is grounded in the morally sound relations among the members of the Ramirez family. They treat each other kindly and based on their roles with good intentions. Thus, there is a moral connection between the family and healthy lifestyles. This is a profoundly effective ethical strategy for outer-directed cultures because the soundness or harmony of the relations is the pattern that healthy behavior should map on. In other words, the harmonious family relations are the guide or analogy for healthy bodies. By the way, this approach has much more in common with the holistic movements in medicine, that is understanding disease in light of the greater context and circumstances of the person.

In the second pamphlet, there are no social relations or harmonious contexts that become models or analogies for good health. Rather, the credibility of this pamphlet seems to rest on it scientific objectivity. Further, this pamphlet emphasizes scientific language and jargon as well as highlighting the US federal organization that produced this manual, two strategies that are based on scientific objectivity of inter-directed cultures, that is, cultures that see disease as a foreign object that enters and disrupts the internal health of a person.

Pathos also differs significantly between the two manuals. There are strong emotional elements in the fotonovela, including the loving family relations, the care for a father who might have high cholesterol, and the arrival of the boyfriend which invokes strong feelings in the family. These strong emotions are further reinforced by the contrastive colors and the vibrant dialogue and dynamic relations among the family members. This outer-directed approach connects all of the family members together in one united effort to improve health. On the other hand, there is very little pathos in the second pamphlet perhaps because emotions have very little to do with cholesterol. Rather, health is defined objectively in terms of cholesterol numbers.

Public/Private and Degree of Involvement

This value set assesses the degree of involvement across different spheres of life, usually involving a public/private divide and trust. Diffuse cultures are usually collective, particular, and outer-directed; thus, involvement in friendships, social relations, and work environments often crosses boundaries, thus sharing the relationship across these spheres. On the other hand, specific cultures are based on the ease and public trust that individualism and universalism give people in separate spheres of life, with friendship belonging to one or two spheres only, with little or no cross-over of authority. Specific orientation also relies on the reliable social structure of the level playing field, which allows them to quickly work or make friends with people in all kinds of spheres. Consequently, the specific orientation favors more public collaboration, something that is much more difficult in diffuse cultures.

In a large study, patients' perception that their physician 'knows them as a person' was more highly correlated with patient adherence to medical treatment than any other dimension of care measured (Cooper, 2006). In diffuse cultures, relationships lead to trust (Hampden-Turner & Trompenaars, 2000) and trust in one's physician has been linked to satisfaction, adherence to recommended treatment, use of preventive services, continuity of care, and self-rated health (Cooper, 2006). Hispanic patients may be seeking this kind of rapport since they have been shown to be less comfortable disclosing personal information due to modesty (Ulrey & Amason, 2001). For these patients, small talk is recommended (confianza in Spanish) to establish trust. Rapidly getting to the point is considered to be brash, uneducated, or rude among Hispanic populations, whereas in other cultures, it is inconsiderate to "beat around the bush" (Tate, 2003). In one study, Hispanic and Asian patients reported more often than other groups that they did not understand everything the doctor had to say and that the doctor did not listen to them completely; they also felt the doctor didn't involve them in decision-making or spend as much time with them as they wanted (Johnson, 2004). Overall, minorities are more likely to perceive bias and a lack of cultural competence in the health system than whites (Johnson et al., 2004).

The same may be true for African American patients, who have been shown to ask physicians fewer questions, respond to questions with less information, and exhibit less positive emotional tone in their visits with physicians than Non-Hispanic white patients (Cooper et al., 2006). In the same encounters, physicians have been shown to exhibit less nonverbal attention, empathy, courtesy, and information giving, to discuss more biomedical issues and less time chatting, answering questions and providing health education (Cooper et al., 2006).

The two pamphlets reflect these differences in specific and diffuse communications. As exemplified in the fotonovela, diffuse communication patterns demonstrate that any topic of discussion must situate the whole person in all his or her aspects and dimensions, including social hierarchies and context. Thus, the first thing that is introduced in this fotonovela is not a definition of good cardiovascular health; rather the first thing that is discussed is the family and their names and their roles. Consequently, the health of the family is holistically grounded in their relations, their diet, and their home. This multidimensional, but indirect, approach shows that persuasion does not require salesmanship, but rather a long-term establishment of interconnected, interpersonal values. Thus, as shown in this pamphlet, the diffuse patterns about cardiovascular health seem (to specific people) to be hidden in the drama of the family, circling around the point of cholesterol, because diffuse communicators need to understand the whole person before getting to the point. Finally, the Ramirez family is shown in somewhat of a private view and many aspects of their lives are shown at once. This represents the multidimensional and holistic nature of the private realm of diffuse lives. In other words, we see everything, or most everything about this family.

On the other hand, health for the second pamphlet is broken up into very specific topics and people, such as doctors, prescription drugs, age, gender, and other concrete components of the person, but never are these concrete or specific topics or issues brought together into a whole; rather they are discussed individually. In addition, instead of showing a concrete person or family with names and the context, the second pamphlet shows an icon of a person. Thus, this is not a person they are talking about, but this is a part of a person that is seen only in its relation to cardiovascular health, a perhaps extreme example of a specific communication strategy. The second pamphlet also gets at the topic very quickly, with a bulleted introduction as a caption in the left hand corner and then announcing the topic directly in the first line. Almost all of the paragraphs have a direct topic sentence that orients the reader to the specific topic of the paragraph, and rarely does a paragraph wander from that topic. Further, the layout of the second pamphlet is more specific, or as a diffuse person might say, it seems spotty and chaotic, with topics and pictures and information seemingly scattered all over the place without coherent connection. Finally, there is no distinction between public and private in the second pamphlet. In fact, the objective approach seems to demonstrate that this distinction is irrelevant.

Status

The next value set assesses how status is grounded and communicated. The two most common approaches are ascription and achievement. Ascriptive-oriented cultures derive status from their social group, race, gender, age, ethnicity, and language. These variables provide the communicator with the power to get things done in complicated social structures. In achievement-oriented cultures, it does not matter where you come from, who your family is, your age, language, etc, as long as you can achieve your goals.

The fotonovela emphasizes ascriptive variables on the first page, listing the people in the Ramirez family according to their ascriptive hierarchy. The father is first, then mother, grandmother, and children. In addition, the development of health is not carried out through an objective doctor and overt processes; rather the development of health is carried out through the ascriptive roles and familial processes of the father, the mother, a grandmother, and the children. Each one has a role in this process. Thus, the familial roles and processes handle the health issue. This is very similar to the family-run business, which is very common in ascriptive cultures because it takes ascriptive power to get things done. On the other hand, the second pamphlet carries out the development of health through quantifiable data and overt medical processes, emphasizing tangible markers or milestones of good health. From this perspective, developing good health is like running a business based on equal opportunity employment guidelines; that is, the roles and processes are based on verifiable, visible, and rationalized roles and processes that do not depend on ascriptive (illegal) variables.

Context

This value set assesses the role of the context in the communicative interaction. All cultures communicate in contexts, but how they rely on these contexts for the meaning of their communications differs. Low context means that the meaning of the communication resides primarily in the explicitly coded part of the communication, not in the surrounding context. Thus, there is great focus on the accuracy of the explicitly coded text. Low context communicators strongly adhere to and require clearly written protocols. There is a high attention to detail and low attention to intention. In addition, low context communicators try to program into the communication all of the verbal signs and cues to carefully guide the reader through the message, meaning that there is an overt emphasis on organizational and transitional strategies to guide readers through the writing. From this view, good writing is focused on the accuracy and interpretation of the explicitly coded text. Connor (1996) and Hinds (1987) label this type of writing as "reader friendly," writing that assumes a reduced reliance on the reader to bring in contextual cues and create transitions to understand the writing.

On the other end, high context communication assumes a strong reliance on the contextual and social cues for the meanings of communications. Here, good writing focuses on how information elucidates the influence of the social context on meaning of the communications. High context communicator's generally focus on adhering to interpersonal relationships instead of fixed guidelines. There is low attention to detail and high attention to intention. Instead of parallelism high context communicators prefer novelty so as to match the uniqueness of the evolving relationship in the specific context. Parallelism is boring and artificial. Connor (1996) and Hinds (1987) label this type of writing as a "reader-responsible" (Connor 1996, p. 42) or writing in which the reader is expected to fill in the information and create the transitions. In high context communications, there also tends to be more non-verbal, indirect forms of communication and complex overtures and concrete sensory stimuli to evoke the physical, social, and interpersonal contexts that add meaning to the discourse.

These two pamphlets exemplify low and high context communication strategies. For example, the second pamphlet is very low context in many ways. First, it is dumbed-down to the point that most any reader could understand it based on how concretely it codes the message into the language itself. Thus, there is little or no reliance on the context to understand what this message means in the lives of the readers. Secondly, there are many visual and verbal strategies that serve as signposts to guide the reader through the text. These include lists, boxes, small graphics and icons, lines across the page, and other ways to carefully guide how the reader processes the information. In addition, there is very specific text that can be used to accurately quantify levels of cholesterol risk, an approach that is highlighted by using the calculator icon. There is also attention to detail, including the different types of cholesterol, the different risk rates, and other concrete, and decontextual information. There are also many lists and much parallelism.

On the other hand, the fotonovela is classically high context. It communicates the message of improving cardiovascular health through the context, not through the actual codified text. Thus, the reader is supposed to infer the message of improving cardiovascular health through the family's discussion of the topic. Great attention is given to the intentions of the people, specifically the mother in wanting what is best for her family, the father in wanting what is best for him as the father in the family, the grandmother in her role, and the children in their roles. These intentions are highlighted by the perpetual smiles on the characters' faces and the positive language of the captions. In addition, the general outline or organizational patterns of the pamphlet is not topics based, but rather contextual or narrative, using the story to signpost the major sections of the pamphlet. In addition to these organizing strategies, much more detail is given to the context of where this happens, such as the house, the actual food being prepared, the details of the names of the people, and the events surrounding the topic. There is much less technical detail in the fotonovela because these details, in the appropriate context, will be worked out.

Monochronic and Polychronic Time

As described in Chapter Two, cultures view and use time differently, especially in communications. Hall (1976; 1983) first articulated a very useful distinction between linear and nonlinear time, defining linear time as monochronic and nonlinear time as polychronic. Hampden-Turner and Trompenaars (2000) offer similar definitions of synchronous (polychronic) and sequential (monochronic). Polychronic or synchronous time frames mean simultaneity, multiple tasks managed at the same time, and apparent disorganization, focusing on the importance of place, and involvement of people rather than adherence to present schedules. On the other hand, monochronic or sequential time frames mean linked linear structures of cause and effect with an organized flow of events (Hall, 1976, 1983). Polychronic time frames enhance the relationships of a variety of people in rich contextual detail. Written discourse in monochronic cultures emphasize linear structures of topics, a direct topic sentence to situate discourse, and given/new discourse structure. On the other hand, polychronic communicators favor the article orchestration of events, people, places, and issues in discourse. Often, writing in polychronic cultures exemplifies complex syntax and paragraph structures, with many narrative structures in polychronic or multiple timeframes.

Some cultures such as Hispanic and African American, may have a relaxed sense of time and value personal relationships more than schedules. If a patient is late, providers should explain the importance of being on time in the U.S. medical setting (Tate, 2003). According to Tate, most Hispanic groups view life as being lived for the present and as governed by fate. Nurses might label a patient noncompliant for missing an appointment, without investigating the client's approach to time. Providers should explain, however, the consequences for not meeting deadlines, and should be very specific about what time deadlines are, allowing, even then, some time for tardiness. (Tate, 2003).

The two pamphlets exemplify the differences in monochronic and polychronic time frames. Because the fotonovela uses the narrative or story to make its point, it manages to (1) tell the story while at the same time (2) describing high cholesterol, (3) the dietetic connection to high cholesterol, (4) the role of stress and high cholesterol, (5) the connections between age and gender for high cholesterol, and (6) how to reduce high cholesterol to improve health. This is a complex, polychronic orchestration of health, cholesterol, and the Ramirez family. In addition, as explained in the Rules Orientation section, the layout of the fotonovela is particular in that each page has its own page design showing the captions, which reflects the multitasking or simultaneity of the Ramirez family, further emphasizing the polychronic or simultaneity of the pamphlet.

The second pamphlet is much more linear. It has a listed introduction on the first page, and this introduction lays out the exact order of the pamphlet's organization. There are clear distinctions between each section, often highlighted by different colors or a line across the page. There are caption boxes to explain different sections, thus highlighting the different time frames. Each unit of information and is clearly differentiated either visually or verbally. And, as explained in the discussion of logos, the second pamphlet highlights the linear cause and effect of cholesterol intake relating to cholesterol indices, both of which directly lead to health indicators.

Power Distance

Power Distance is Hofstede's (2010) concept, and it measures how inequality is handled in communications. In high power distances cultures, there is unequal, centralized distribution of power, acceptance of authority, high levels of overseeing, and top-down communication styles. Further, in high power distance cultures, subordinates are afraid to just disagree with their superiors; further, there is a high level of overseeing of subordinate activities. In short, high power distance cultures use communications to reinforce and exemplify the hierarchy. The communication patterns connected to high power distance include top-down communication patterns, strict lines of authority and subordination, and formalities and titles that show social hierarchy; in addition, high power distance communicators are very careful with lines of authority, showing respect and deference.

Low power distance cultures use communications to downplay inequalities among people. As Hofstede (2004) explains, low power distance cultures expect more mutual interdependence between subordinate and authority. Communications between superior and subordinate tend to be more consultative, with the superior acting as perhaps someone with more knowledge, but not in reality being in a higher position. Authority is something to be used only as more of a last resort rather than the explicit framework for the communication situation. Subordinates are not afraid to disagree with superiors; in fact subordinates are often a source of good feedback for decisions is that the superiors need to take. In low power distance cultures, communicators tend to make the communications less formal as a way to ease the feelings of inequality in the communication situation.

Out of respect, some patients from Asian or Hispanic cultures will avoid eye contact at their visits, especially if they are of a different gender or social status. Maintaining direct eye contact is considered arrogant or confrontational unless used with one's peers or gender (Tate, 2003). Nodding in what seems to be agreement does not mean a patient actually understands (Masi, 1989). They may be embarrassed or aim to show respect by not asking questions. East Asians often find it culturally difficult to refuse a request directly, and their smile may mean they are embarrassed, instead of amused (Masi, 1989). It is therefore recommended that providers use the patient's formal name if they are unsure how to address the patient (Tate, 2003) as those who value high power distance see this as a sign of respect.

In a rare study of national cultural dimensions in medical communication, Meeuwesen et al. (2009) found that high power distance cultures correlated with shorter consultations where patients spoke less and doctors relayed less information. The patient/doctor roles were fixed in these situations, and there were more uniform expectations from patients. During the visits, there was less eye contact, more social talk, less shared decision-making, less unexpected information exchange. In countries where the power distance is larger, patients reported that psychosocial expectations were closely met. A patient's national culture was shown to affect their expectation of the health care provider.

The power distance is evident in both pamphlets, but perhaps in a more implicit or underlying way. First, the fotonovela clearly shows the power channels of communication. The grandmother, affectionately called Doña Fela, is the matriarch and an important leader of the Ramirez family. *Doña* is an honorific or dignified title, with no English equivalent, but it roughly means a dignified madam. As the mother of the father in the family, Doña Fela has strong authority in this family, especially over her son, the next in line in authority for the family context, although her authority is masked by the motherly or Virgin-Mary like strategies that are so common in Mexican households. These strategies include self effacement but also great care for the general welfare of others. Mariano, the father is the benevolent leader, and his wife, Virginia, speak to him in loving but very respectful and careful ways. The children are careful never to disrespect their parents or their grandmother. Thus, the lines of authority in the communication are not broken. There is no authoritarianism in the fotonovela, which can happen in less benevolent social situations.

The second pamphlet shows no authority among people. Rather it explains the information to readers who seem like intelligent, but uninformed equals in terms of authority. This low power distance approach is carried out through the other intercultural strategies such as low context communication, universalism, and achievement orientation. In addition, these four cultural values–low context, universalism, achievement, and low power distance–help the second pamphlet achieve this strategy of a user manual, one that gives the readers independence for themselves in understanding their specific heart help situation and empowering them to make their calculations of their health risk and corresponding corrective behavior that the readers can carry out independent of the manual itself. This independence is not evident in the fotonovela and demonstrates the strong connection between manuals and the four corresponding value sets. Thus, it is not surprising that instructional manuals originated–and are very common–in cultures that are low context, universalist, achievement oriented and low power distance.

This value set can be described as the difference between valuing a report (specific value) and a rapport (diffuse value). The U.S. is a more specific, evidence-based, bottom-line, differentiation-prone culture, whereas cultures such as Asian and Latin countries lean toward more diffuse, relationship-building, and tendencies of integration (Hampden-Turner & Trompenaars, 2000). These values can be seen in studies showing patients' lack of trust and the feeling that physicians do not get to know them.

In conclusion, these two pamphlets match the predominant cultural values of Latin America and the United States across all eight value sets, and as a result, that matching gives health providers concrete examples of how to operationalize the value sets in specific intercultural health communication contexts. This section will be combined with the next section to show how to operationalize these values sets in all 14 of the culturally appropriate standards laid out in the introduction of this chapter.

CONSENT FORMS: THE MEETING POINT OF MEDICAL, HEALTH, AND RHETORICAL TRADITIONS

The previous section demonstrates very clearly the connection between intercultural rhetoric and health literacy materials. This section grounds those connections even more deeply, showing how the differences originate in larger medical, health, and literacy traditions, including the history and use of writing versus orality. This section uses a case study of preoperative consent forms used in a hospital in the U.S.-Mexico border region where there is a high population of recent Mexican and Spanish speaking immigrants and a consent form developed by Cuban medical researchers and doctors. The rest of the chapter explores the social,

Figure 3. Pre-operative Consent form for Southern New Mexico Hospital

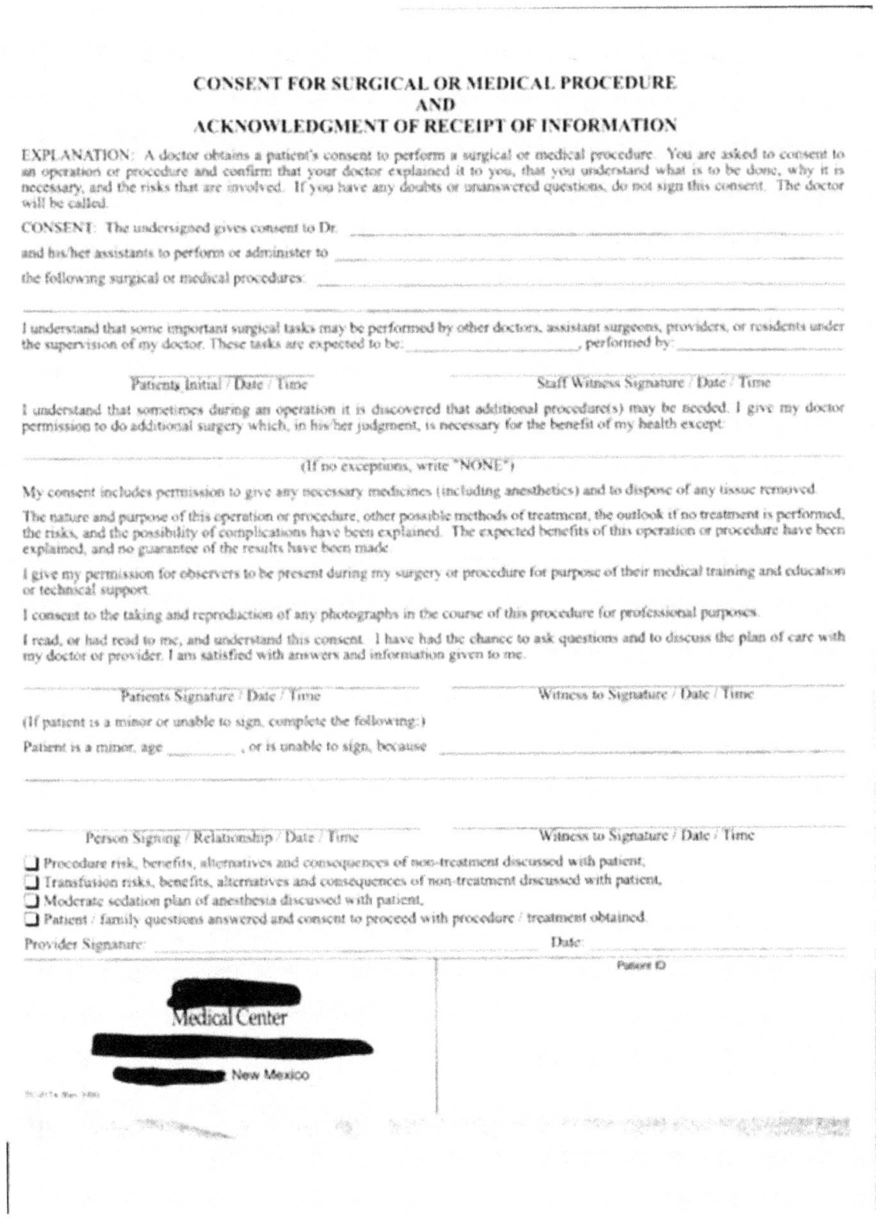

CONSENT FOR SURGICAL OR MEDICAL PROCEDURE
AND
ACKNOWLEDGMENT OF RECEIPT OF INFORMATION

EXPLANATION: A doctor obtains a patient's consent to perform a surgical or medical procedure. You are asked to consent to an operation or procedure and confirm that your doctor explained it to you, that you understand what is to be done, why it is necessary, and the risks that are involved. If you have any doubts or unanswered questions, do not sign this consent. The doctor will be called.

CONSENT: The undersigned gives consent to Dr. ____________

and his/her assistants to perform or administer to ____________

the following surgical or medical procedures: ____________

I understand that some important surgical tasks may be performed by other doctors, assistant surgeons, providers, or residents under the supervision of my doctor. These tasks are expected to be: ____________, performed by: ____________

Patients Initial / Date / Time — Staff Witness Signature / Date / Time

I understand that sometimes during an operation it is discovered that additional procedure(s) may be needed. I give my doctor permission to do additional surgery which, in his/her judgment, is necessary for the benefit of my health except:

(If no exceptions, write "NONE")

My consent includes permission to give any necessary medicines (including anesthetics) and to dispose of any tissue removed.

The nature and purpose of this operation or procedure, other possible methods of treatment, the outlook if no treatment is performed, the risks, and the possibility of complications have been explained. The expected benefits of this operation or procedure have been explained, and no guarantee of the results have been made.

I give my permission for observers to be present during my surgery or procedure for purpose of their medical training and education or technical support.

I consent to the taking and reproduction of any photographs in the course of this procedure for professional purposes.

I read, or had read to me, and understand this consent. I have had the chance to ask questions and to discuss the plan of care with my doctor or provider. I am satisfied with answers and information given to me.

Patients Signature / Date / Time — Witness to Signature / Date / Time

(If patient is a minor or unable to sign, complete the following:)

Patient is a minor, age ______, or is unable to sign, because ____________

Person Signing / Relationship / Date / Time — Witness to Signature / Date / Time

- ☐ Procedure risk, benefits, alternatives and consequences of non-treatment discussed with patient,
- ☐ Transfusion risks, benefits, alternatives and consequences of non-treatment discussed with patient,
- ☐ Moderate sedation plan of anesthesia discussed with patient,
- ☐ Patient / family questions answered and consent to proceed with procedure / treatment obtained.

Provider Signature: ____________ Date: ____________

Patient ID

Medical Center

New Mexico

Figure 4. Consent form developed by Cuban medical researchers and doctors

Consent Form for the performance of general surgical operations

- Identification
- Technical name of the intervention to carry out ______

Type of anesthesia ______

B. Patient Declaration ______

1. I have been satisfactorily explained the nature and purpose of this operation. I was also told the potential risks and complications, as well as alternative treatments. In addition, I have been explained the possible risks of the anesthesia that will be applied. I am aware that there are no absolute guarantees that the result of the operation will be the most satisfactory. I fully understand that the operation will consist of more or less the following: (Description of the operation in simple language) ______ and the most important potential risks ______ and that it will be performed by Dr. ______ or under his/her direction and responsibility.

2. I give my consent to have performed on me the operation described above and additional operations that are necessary or convenient during this surgery, according to the judgment of the professionals that are performing it.

3. I consent to be administered the anesthesia indicated above, as well as additional measures as deemed appropriate.

4. I give my consent for medical students or doctors in training to participate as aides or assistants in the surgery.

5. That photographs or film footage can be taken of the operation, which can later be viewed by trainees of this or another hospital. I consent to having these photographs or videos taken. I also give consent for authorized personnel to attend the operation as observers. But it must be that: a) the patient's name or that of his family not be used or identified by the photos or videos; b) its use is limited to teaching or research purposes.

- In any case, I want the following conditions respected (if there are none, write "none." If some of the other points are not accepted, please indicate) ______

______

Patient Signature

C. Declarations and Signatures:

- Surgeon in charge: I have informed this patient of the purpose and nature of the operation described above, its alternatives, potential risks, and expected outcomes.

______

Signature of Surgeon in charge

- Guardian or family member: I know that the patient ______ Has been for now considered to be incapable of making the decision by him or herself to accept or reject the surgery described above, or has been deemed incompetent.

The doctor has satisfactorily explained what the operation is, how it is carried out, and for what reason. I also have been explained its risks and complications. I understand all this perfectly and therefore I am ______ with CI ______, as ______ to give my consent so that Dr. ______ and the support staff that he/she deems necessary can perform this operation. I can withdraw this consent when, for the good of the patient, I deem it appropriate. ______

Guardian or family member signature

Relation of family member: husband, children, parents, siblings, other

______

D. Place and date

______

Patient Identification

1. Name ______
2. Age ______
3. HC ______
4. Service ______ Bed ______

medical, cultural, and rhetorical reasons why the consent forms are so difficult in the border region.

Pre-Operative Consent Form

Figure 3 is the English version of the pre-operative consent form used in a major Southern New Mexico hospital where a large majority of the patients are Spanish-speaking with strong roots in the Mexican cultural, medical, and rhetorical traditions. The English version has a closely translated Spanish version, retaining all of the formatting and rhetorical approaches, and although the Spanish version is used with many patients, it is not presented here.

Figure 4 is a consent form developed by Cuban medical researchers and doctors (Reyes Lopez, et al, 2006) to be a model for their country and for Latin America, generally.

This consent form is my close English translation of the Spanish original. I have tried to keep the wording, style, and format as close to original as possible. As is evident in the rest of this chapter, consent forms are "in development" in almost all of Latin America for many reasons, most of which is that they do not fit well their cultural and rhetorical traditions (Gonzalez Gonzales, et al, 2005). Thus, Latin American medical scholars and practitioners draw most of their models from Spain, the rest of Europe, Japan, and the United States (Reyes Lopez, 2006), and the use of pre-operative consent forms or consent forms in general is much lower in Latin America than in the United States, Canada, or western Europe.

Consequently, despite all of the new developments in research and theory, delivering culturally competent health communications (Purnell, 2009) is still fraught with many problems, especially in instructional and legal contexts such as informed consents. Informed consent forms are complex documents with multiple communication purposes such as explaining surgery procedures, outlining risks and benefits, and authorizing legal relations between doctors and patients. However, despite these multiple purposes, most informed consent forms in the U.S. are designed mostly for legal purposes. Not surprisingly, patients widely misunderstand informed consent in the U.S. and around the world, (Falagas, et, al, 2009).

The problem of informed consent is especially acute in the U.S.-Mexico border region where immigrant populations are very high and health disparities are significant and well documented (see borderhealth.org). Unfortunately, little is known about the comprehension or usability of consent forms for border populations, but the collective experience of the Chief Medical Office and practicing anesthesiologist at this hospital is that consent forms are a significant cause of Hispanic patients' misunderstanding many health care issues, including the risks of surgery and the responsibilities of patients and hospital and post-surgical recovery. This misunderstanding is likely linked to accusations of malpractice and corresponding litigation.

As research has documented (Granero-Molina, et, al, 2009), the poor comprehension of informed consent has many causes, including different languages, cultural clashes, asymmetry of communication between professionals and patients, assignment of rights on the part of patients, and overprotection of professionals and institutions. For this chapter, one key variable is the cultural clash, because the document design and language used in U.S. informed consents are most likely based on U.S. cultural, legal, and medical systems. As a result, translating the forms into Spanish simply transfers the U.S. patterns into Spanish; and thus, the forms not only fail to meet the cultural expectations but often feel strange or bizarre to Spanish-speakers because the U.S. cultural forms are presented to them in their native language (Thatcher, 1999; 2006). These U.S. cultural patterns most likely originate from the eight values sets discussed earlier in this chapter; and the U.S. common law legal system (Thatcher, 2006); U.S. and western concepts of evidence-based medicine (Thatcher & Urbina, 2010); and different assumptions about writing and orality in professional contexts (Thatcher, 1999; 2000; 2006). For example, the fotonovela must feel very strange to English speakers who have no experience in Latin America.

Another key cause of miscommunication most likely includes the literacy levels in general, and the health literacy levels in specific, a fact that is well documented among Latino/Hispanic populations (see borderhealth.org). For example, the 2003 National Assessment of Adult Literacy confirmed that Hispanics present lower levels of health literacy in comparison to other population groups. The lack of culturally competent health care for Latino populations is generally widespread but most acute in areas that do not have Latino traditions because the health care systems there are not equipped to deal with the communication and cultural problems, especially with informed consent (see borderhealth.org).

The questions for this section interrogate the nature of the problems of consent forms for this intercultural context. Are the problems related to orality and literacy? Or different medical traditions? Or different assumptions about uses of forms? Or is the form itself so entrenched in U.S. rhetorical values that it is mostly incomprehensible to Spanish speakers? To answer these questions, the next section analyzes the actual rhetorical and cultural patterns of two consent forms. This analysis will then become part of the ongoing discussion of how well the consent form used in Southern New Mexico actually fits the Mexican-American patients that use it. The second section contextualizes the US-Mexico border and health context; the third section highlights the different literacy traditions in Mexico and the United States; the fourth section analyzes the effectiveness of the preoperative consent form for a multicultural, border population, articulating questions about its purpose, readers, information, organization, and style.

Rhetorical and Cultural Analysis of the Consent Form

This section briefly analyzes the cultural and rhetorical values of the two consent forms, following the same eight values sets in order that were used previously to analyze the two pamphlets.

I/Other

Both consent forms rely on the same rights-based philosophy that underlies many individualistic and universalist cultures (Reyes Lopez, 2006). This includes the inherit dignity of the person who has the unfettered right and capability of making decisions that affect his or her life; the right to information about the processes in sufficient quantity and quality; and the right to connect that decision to realistic risks or vulnerabilities and to the opportunity for improvement through the surgery (Reyes Lopez, 2006). Consequently, both consent forms assume a lot of independence in the patient, a key indicator of individualism. The Cuba consent form does assume the presence of husband, children, parents, siblings, and other family members in the case of minors, but it generally assumes a very individualistic person making the choice. It is interesting to note, however, that the scholars developing this consent form strongly urge the doctor to talk to the patient with family members present.

The New Mexico Consent Form is strongly individualistic, assuming that the patient is a lone person responsible for all of the questions and information on the form, with the only qualification that perhaps the consent form will be read to the patient. There is no discussion of family members, unless it is a minor. It perfectly matches the independence of the US cultural value of individualism. The individualism of both consent forms probably does not fit many of these assumptions of more collective cultures such as Mexico or even Cuba.

Rules Orientation

As mentioned earlier, the philosophy behind consent forms is to ensure universal, therefore, ethical treatment of all patients. Thus, both consent forms present the policies and rules in a universalist way, that is, they are presented as though there were few or no exceptions, contingencies, or extenuating circumstances. The Cuba consent form, however, makes it more explicit that the doctors or the patients can change the circumstances if they judge the changes to be more appropriate to the situation. In the New Mexico consent form, the only qualifications are the additional procedures that may be necessary if a doctor discovers that necessity during the surgery. In addition, the New Mexico form asks the patient to articulate questions or doubts, but there is no discussion of the unique circumstances of the person, surgery, or doctors. It is as if all people were equal, all surgeries were equal, and all doctors will go about the surgery the same way. The Cuba form does not assume the same standardizing. In fact, one of the differences between Latin American and U.S. consent forms is that the Latin Americans tend to particularize the forms much more than the Americans, that is, to develop one form for each kind of surgery or medical procedure. One thing that is somewhat contradictory, however, is that the layout or format of the Cuba consent form is more consistent or parallel, representing a more universalist approach than the format of the New Mexico form. Again, one of the difficulties of informed consent in particulars cultures such as Mexico and Latin America is that the consent forms are strongly universal in most ways.

Sources of Virtue and Guidance

Consistent with the rights-based approach, both consent forms assume an inner-directed person, one that consults himself or herself to make the decision. The Cuban form has more discussion of other people, and of the actual person making decisions, which demonstrates that decisions are not made in a vacuum. However, both forms reveal nothing about harmonizing with other people, nature, or outside forces or patterns that might impinge upon the procedure or influence the patient or the surgeon. The New Mexico form is almost totally devoid of emotions or pathos, while the Cuban form uses more adjectives and adverbs throughout, particularly the word satisfactorily. This gives the Cuban form more pathos and ethos than the New Mexican. The Cuban form also talks about "the good of the patient," a connection to ethics and morality, whereas the New Mexican form has no discussion of ethical, moral, or credible behavior; rather, the form is almost exclusively logos based, although this logos seems both inner- and outer-directed because it presumes a focus on *what* will happen and *why* or reason for the form. The Cuban form similarly talks about what the operation is, how it is carried out, and for what reason, which are both inner and outer directed logos strategies. Consequently, both forms assume a more inner directed cultural value, demonstrating one of the difficulties that more outer directed cultures might face when filling out this form.

Public/Private and Degree of Involvement

Both consent forms show many signs of specificity, while the Cuban form shows some diffuseness. As explained earlier in this chapter and Chapter Two, the specific orientation allows for easy entry into one sphere of life but crossing over from one sphere to another sphere is quite difficult. The diffuse orientation allows for easy crossover from one sphere to another, that is, the sharing of authority across spheres of activity. The New Mexican form actually requires a signature for a doctor to crossover from one planned surgery to another, or for allowing people other than the surgeon him or herself to view the surgery. This great care for crossing over from a simple plan surgery to other areas exemplifies the difficulty of the specific orientation to cross spheres of activity. A more diffuse approach, such as the one demonstrated in the Cuban form, would assume that if a person is willing to receive the surgery, that person is also willing to receive additional or other kinds of surgical treatment that the surgeon deems necessary at that time, or that a large variety of people will be involved with the surgery not just the surgeon him or herself. In addition, both consent forms assume a specific-like entry into the surgical relation, that is, that the form does not ground or contextualize the patient and surgeon in more diffuse or holistic ways; rather, it only discusses surgery, and not other related, but nonsurgical issues. In conclusion, both forms are mostly specific, even though the Cuban form has some diffuse elements. It is interesting to note, however, that the Cuban researchers specifically call for contextualizing the patient and surgery in very holistic ways, information that cannot be put into the forms but should be gathered orally (Reyes Lopez, 2006).

Status and High Power Distance

These two value sets are discussed together because together they talk about the power relations between patients and doctors. It is interesting to note that the Cuban consent form is much more personal than that New Mexican form, using many more I's and you's. In addition, the Cuban form very carefully articulates egalitarian relations between the doctor and patient, and the Cuban scholars very specifically encourage the rejection of what they call paternalistic relations or high power relations because of the ascribed power of the doctor. The New Mexican form is not interpersonal at all, but it is egalitarian. Thus, both consent forms assume an achievement orientation and low-power distance relations, two values predominate in Anglo-American culture. The patient is placed in mostly an equal position of power in relation to the doctor and the hospital. It is the patient that can sign; it is the patient that can refuse additional treatment or the presence of non-surgical people. No ascriptive values are given to the doctor, who in ascriptive and high-power distance cultures would make this decision himself or herself, without consulting the patient, because the doctor is ascribed this power and role. Consequently, these consent forms will not fit those doctors or patients who are used to ascription and high-power distance cultures, for in these cultures the doctors have more power in what to say and in what they can order the patients to do.

Context

Both consent forms are low context, but the Cuban form has more context generally. In the New Mexican form, the only contextual information allowed or called for is the date, signature, and witness which do give some context; however; there are no discussions of the context in which the surgery will take place nor any other contextual information. In addition, in the New Mexican form, there are many general terms that are left undefined or undetailed, which in a high context culture would not be appropriate, because high context cultures are much more sensitive to what the audience needs to know, rather than a generic form. As explained in Chapter Two, the New Mexican form is dumbed-down to a low reading level, with little elaboration or explanations for this reading level. In addition to be a universalist strategy, this dumbing down is a low context strategy because it assumes that all of the meaning is there in the language, and nothing else needs to be explained. High context cultures would assume either that the person in authority would explain his information more fully or the text would give more information generally. The Cuban form has more information throughout, it relates to the reader in more interpersonal ways such as using many more I's and you's, and it prompts a readers to ask more questions or to get more information, all of which exemplify a higher context approach. Generally, however, both forms are low context, meaning that doctors or the medical staff will most likely have to add or contextualize information more consistently with those patients who come from high context cultures such as Mexico.

Monochronic and Polychronic Time

Both consent forms are mostly monochronic, but the New Mexican form is probably more monochronic or linear. First, the New Mexican form has an introduction, which sets the stage for the rest of the form, and the different sections of the

Figure 5. Border 2012 map

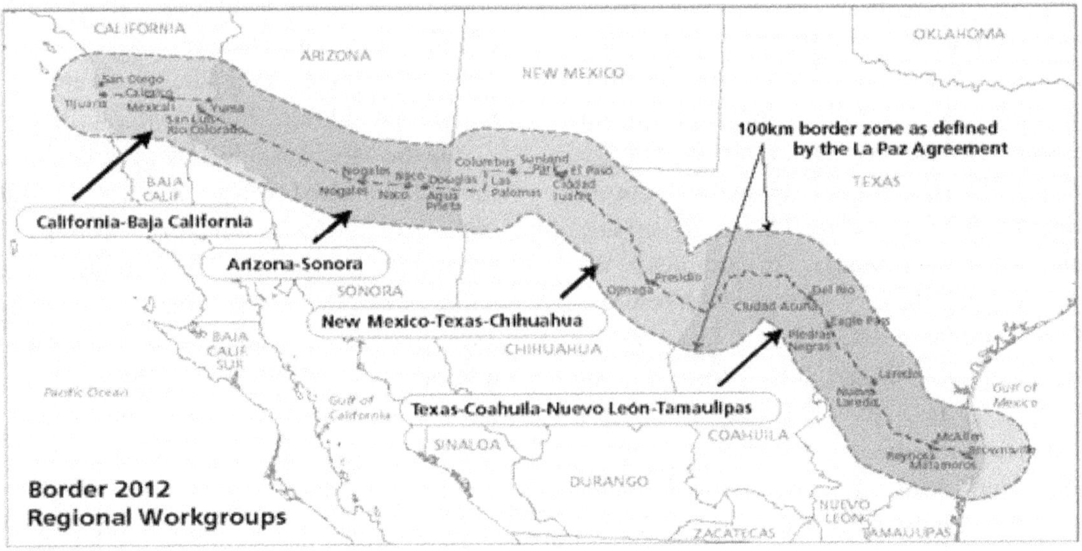

form are not based on the timing or sequence of the surgery; rather, these sections are topical: consent is first; additional procedures are next; permission for observers follows; and acknowledgment of understanding the form itself. The Cuban form is a bit more polychronic because it has more of narrative organizational pattern, storyboarding what will happen and simultaneously asking for all of these things throughout the story. However, the New Mexican consent form is rather chaotically organized, in that, the visual design does not present distinct linear steps; instead, it appears to be a polychronic or chaotic design. As a result, both consent forms fit better the cultural rhetorical patterns of monochronic than polychronic cultures.

In conclusion, both consent forms generally follow all of the eight predominant cultural values of United States, even though the Cuban form is developed in Cuba by Cuban scholars. Therefore, it is not surprising that people who come from other cultural and rhetorical traditions find the form itself strange and have a hard time processing it, and is not surprising that consent forms are not used more in Latin America or other countries or cultures whose values differ from those of the United States and Western Europe. Furthermore, as will be explained next, not only are the rhetorical features of this form strongly connected to US cultural and rhetorical values, the use of the form itself draws on U.S. traditions of literacy, organizational and legal behavior, and medical traditions. This combination of U.S. rhetorical forms and U.S assumptions about literacy, organizational and legal behavior, and medical traditions probably make either consent form doubly difficult to process for patients coming from Mexican traditions.

U.S.-Mexico Border Health Context

The New Mexican consent form is being used in an area that once was Mexico but is now the United States, in the U.S.-Mexico border region. As designated by both Mexico and the United States in the La Paz Treaty, the border region is a legally defined area that runs roughly 100 km north or south of the common border. The following map, developed by the joint US-Mexico Border 2012 Program, shows this legally defined area:

Not surprisingly, this region of both the U.S. and Mexican sides of the border share many cultural and linguistic traditions, environmental health issues, and educational levels (*Healthy Border,* 2010*)*. As a corollary, both sides of the border share elevated levels of diabetes, obesity, respiratory diseases, environmental health problems, among others (*Healthy Border 2010*, p vii). These socio-economic and health variables on the border also correlate very strongly with low levels of literacy in general, and even lower levels of English literacy, in particular (Rosal, Goins, Carbone, & Cortes, 2004). In other words, the U.S.-Mexico border population has two mutually reinforcing health problems: at-risk socio-economic data combined with low literacy levels, producing a double jeopardy effect on overall health. Not surprisingly, current research addresses health and literacy among border populations in the United States, with most focusing on diabetes (Rosal, Goins, Carbone, & Cortes, 2004), cardiovascular health (Elder, et al, 1998), and nutrition (Fidalgo & Chapman-Novakofski, 2001). However, very little has focused on consent forms.

Another important characteristic of border health communication is immigration and corresponding issues of assimilation. Most immigration patterns flow from Mexico to the United States with the exceptions being the bilingual, bicultural, and binational population; but the predominant populations for the U.S. side of border health literacy research are Mexican or Latino immigrants, and the predominant populations for research on the Mexican side are Mexican nationals. Thus, immigrants in the United States face specific assimilation problems with health literacy, including English as the second language, and different cultural, rhetorical, and medical traditions.

However, despite these similarities, there are some differences among border populations. In the U.S. side of the border area, education and income levels are some of the lowest in the United States (*Healthy Border 2010*). Not surprisingly, the U.S. border population has some of the highest rates of diabetes and obesity, lowest rates of access to health care, health insurance, and lowest quality of infant and maternal care. Further, U.S. border populations have some of the lowest literacy levels in the United States (Freeman, 2002).

On the Mexican side, however, health, education, and income levels are some of the highest in Mexico (*Healthy Border 2010*, 2003, p. 11). For example, while literacy levels in the U.S. border region are some of the lowest in the country at 28%, on the Mexican side, border cities report illiteracy rates of only 5.3%. The same is true for income and health care, with the highest levels of income and best health coverage in Mexico occurring in the northern, industrialized areas of Mexico, near the U.S. border. In addition, the usual research of Hispanic health and literacy does not consider the fact that the populations on both sides of the border area are usually either relatively affluent or poor, not reflecting the larger middle class percentages of either Mexico or the United States (*Healthy Border 2010*, 2003, p. 12).

Despite the great commonality among the border residents, research continually notes that the "medical profession has for decades been dominated by White, upper and middle class heterosexual males," and problems are heavily attributable to the need to alternate and change the "medical curriculum, how [the medical curriculum] is delivered, or the internship or residency experience" (Howard, Andrade, & Byrd, 2001). The disconnect between patient and physician occurs when there is an adherence on behalf of physicians to believe that "there are no alternative forms of healing; there are no other healers. A large portion of North American health-care providers have been socialized to believe that modern medicine as taught and practiced in Western civilization is the answer to *all* of humankind's needs" (Specter, 1996). There's a vast incongruence between the manner in which illnesses are addressed, termed, described and understood by practitioners of Western medicine and patients from border cultures. If the language of medicine and medical care differ on both sides of the border, borderland health consumers will seek out the service and institution that will "anchor [the communication] within the individual's and family's cultural reality" (Howard, Andrade, & Byrd, 2000).

The research continually reiterates that a large percentage (33% reported in 2001) of Latino Americans "with high proportion of Mexicans... have problems understanding or communicating with their doctor, with greater difficulty reported by those who primarily speak Spanish" (Rivers & Patino, 2006). The problem is nationwide and there are millions of Latinos of Mexican descent who struggle with today's health care system; "69.9% of the [Mexican] population is concentrated in two areas- California/Baja California and El Paso, Tx/Ciudad Juárez, Chihuauha" (Loustaunau & Sanchez Bane, 1999).

One of the major reasons that is continually cited as the primary cause driving borderland residents to travel across the border for medical care is that services and medication in Mexico are much more affordable; "health care costs in Mexico are 70-90 percent lower than in the United States" (Bustamante, Ojeda & Castaneda, 2008). A study which questioned 79 outpatients in the Internal Medicine Clinic at the Texas Tech University Health Sciences Center in El Paso, TX reported that 22% of the studies participants stated that they visited a private physician on a regular basis, 81% had purchased medication in Mexico, 75% purchased medication without a prescription, 49% reported they did so because medication was more affordable and 20% because they felt they did not need a prescription, and 29% of the respondent group reported being prompted by a family member or friend to buy medication across the border. This leads us to a very critical point that addresses the algorithmic process practiced by many Hispanics and Mexicans along the border. Although cost of goods is reported as a critical driving force behind the obtainment of medical care across the border, research also shows that a lot of border health consumers are much more comfortable maneuvering within a health system that literally speaks their language and culturally meets their expectations.

In Mexico (and Latin America, for that matter), there are fully developed health research initiatives and public institutions, but most health literacy research has been carried out under the term of "health education" and not health literacy. This difference is perhaps because the English term "literacy" has no actual equivalent in Spanish, with "educación" or "alfabetización" being the closest two. Secondly, written, how-to instructions are not common in Mexico and Latin America, not fitting their cultural and rhetorical traditions, an issue described next.

ORALITY AND LITERACY TRADITIONS IN MEXICO AND UNITED STATES

Mexico and the United States have different histories and approaches with written materials used for legal issues, governance, and self-instruction, critical variables for border health communication, including informed consent. The mechanisms for founding U.S. and Latin American societies perhaps illustrate these different reasons. In Latin America, the most important cultural and social mechanism of Spanish colonialization was the encomienda, or labor grant. A Spanish soldier or colonist was granted a certain track of land or village together with its native inhabitants. The Spaniards routinely set up a strict hierarchy over the land and its inhabitants, effectively creating an intricate caste system. An important part of this intricate caste system was intermarrying between races and social classes, effectively creating innumerable levels of social hierarchy. The encomienda also allowed for the establishment of the Catholic Church, which tended to dominate and structure education and social life.

The result of this foundation is a collective, yet highly stratified culture. Two critical patterns result from this collective-hierarchy: one is inequality and the other is particularism. Many scholars maintain that Latin Americans believe the societal norm is *inequality*: "there should be an order of inequality in this world in which everyone has his or her rightful place; high and low are protected by this order" (Hofstede, 2010, p. 94). This high collective-hierarchy corresponds to particularism, meaning that laws, policies, and procedures are applied differently to everyone, depending on that person's social standing. Both Hofstede and Fons Trompenaars argue that Latin American countries are consistently the most particular cultures in the world. This creates in Latin America was legal and social scholars label as a "dual morality." Glen Dealy (1992) argues the dual code in Latin America seems to turn a blind eye to the general public realm as a whole, lacking social concern for others, a sense of community, honest, frugality, and tolerance for those in the general public (p.11). "Inside the home, or between friends," however, explains Dealy, "one encounters qualities of rectitude and caring in abundance…The Latin American extended family is characteristically knit together by bonds of love and fraternity to a degree unrealized, and unrealizable, with the prototypical Anglo-American nuclear family" (p. 11).

On the other hand, the United States had a remarkably different formation and corresponding cultural values. Many of the original colonies were settled by religious dissidents escaping persecution in Europe and had little desire to return there. Unlike the situation in Latin America, these religious dissidents were automatically skeptical of authority, especially traditional religious authority mixed with state government. They tended to set up small, highly independent communities of like-minded individuals. Significantly, the U.S. colonizers did not intermarry with the indigenous populations; they just exterminated them. The U.S. colonizers had much weaker ties to their mother countries than did their Latin American counterparts, U.S. independence was much shorter and easier to carry out, and breaking with the cultural, religious, and social order of the mother countries was relatively easy and abrupt.

In this context, when colonizing Mexico, the Spaniards conveniently drew upon the literacy traditions of the native populations (Maya, Aztec, Mixtec, and Zapotec) for their colonizing purposes (see Marcus, 1992). All four indigenous populations themselves used writing as a colonizing tool: they re-wrote history for the benefit of their group, developed propaganda in their own interest, instilled myths appropriate to their positions of power, and established class markers. When the Spaniards arrived in Mexico, it was easy to use writing and written discourse the same way, and many researchers have argued that they did (see, León-Portilla, 1996). For example, Kellog (1995) explains that the Spanish used the legal system and legal documents "as a powerful tool of acculturation, profoundly altering Mexico and Nahua conceptions of family, property, and gender. And it played a critical role in establishing and maintaining Spanish cultural hegemony" (p. xxix). As a result, writing and literacy became associated with colonialization, serving what Kellog (1995) calls notary-like functions.

This connection of writing to the government or colonialization is also strongly rooted in the other parts of Latin America. The Peruvian scholar, Antonio Cornejo Polar argues that this paradigm actually started in 1532 at Cajamarca, Peru when the Archbishop of Cuzco, Vicente Valverde, and the Incan leader, Atahualpa met to discuss the fate of the two nations and cultures. In one of the first intercultural communication scenarios in the New World, these two leaders failed to reach an agreement because their assumptions about orality and writing corresponded to mutually unintelligible communication patterns. After Atahualpa refused to pay homage to the King of Spain, Valverde brought him the bible and asked him to pay homage to Christ. After turning a few pages, Atahualpa "became disillusioned with the book and angry at the strangeness of what Valverde was saying, certainly foreign, unintelligible, and heretical for his consciousness" (Cornejo Polar, 1994, p. 37). Coming from a completely oral cultural, Atahualpa exclaimed that since he couldn't "listen to the book," or "the book didn't speak to him," he threw it down (Cornejo Polar, 1994, p. 38). For Valverde, Atahuallpa's refusal to pay homage to the "written word" did not signify a confused attempt to understand a foreign communication medium; rather it signified his rejection of the King of Spain and Christianity and eventually unleashed the war and downfall of the Incan Empire. As many Latin American scholars have argued, this critical incidence at Cajamarca eventually became a cultural and rhetorical paradigm of native populations who developed their own oral dramatizations of it to continue to resist Spanish religious and governmental domination.

These assumptions about writing that developed from the colonizing and notary-like mechanism of Mexico or incident at Cajamarca contrast remarkably with the U.S. traditions that valorize constructive and precedence-setting functions such as the signing of the U.S. Declaration of Independence or many of the assumptions in informed consent. According to many comparative legal scholars (Rosenn, 1988; Alcalde, 1991), the signers of the Declaration and U.S. Constitution were able to rely on a cultural and rhetorical context that enabled such a use of written communication. This is why these documents have worked so well in the U.S, but comparable documents have had significantly less influence on Latin American countries (Alcalde, 1991). In the U.S., writing reflects and reinforces traditions of individuality, universalism, equality, and common law reasoning (Thatcher, 2006). On the other hand, the Mexican rhetorical traditions reflect and reinforce an in- and out-group orientation that is common in collective cultures, hierarchical social organizations, and particular or relational thinking patterns (Thatcher, 2006).

This different foundation has yielded strikingly contrastive cultural patterns in the U.S. In the United States, there has been historically a fusion of the public and private realm into one moral system that is ideally applicable to all. This emphasis of applicability stresses due process, adherence to standards, and impersonal routinization of policies, procedures, and standards of conduct. All of these characteristics of U.S. culture and rhetorical patterns precisely fit the goals of informed consent, whereas the patterns of Mexico do not fit the goals of informed consent.

Consequently, written instructions such as health materials in informed consent will mostly likely be perceived differently in the U.S. and Mexico. Recent Mexican immigrants to the United States will most likely approach written health materials with ambivalence: more suspicion of its origins and purpose yet more deference to its authority; and less practice in using written materials for self instruction yet a greater need to do so in the foreign health context.

An important ramification of these different histories of writing relates to economics. Per capita, Mexico has much less print materials (newspapers, magazines, textbooks, books in general) than the United States (Kloss, 2001). It is simply cheaper and more effective (by cultural standards) to hire and maintain health or social workers than it is to develop effective health literacy documentation. In fact, much of the health literacy work in all of Latin America and Mexico is carried about by grass-roots community organizations guided by health volunteers known as *promotoras*. These volunteers know the community well, have developed close interpersonal relations with it, and know how to educate and persuade to action. Writing simply does not have this history in Mexico and Latin America.

Finally, Mexico and the United States exhibit different preferences for how written instructions and policies are organized and explained, as described in the first section of this chapter and throughout this book, especially Chapter

Ten, Instructions Across Cultures. Understanding these cultural and communicative differences—especially as related to written instructions and informed consent s—is critical for developing effective health communications in border populations. U.S. health communications will most likely exemplify U.S. rhetorical traditions, including what the materials are used for, how one learns from them, and what they actually empower the reader to do in a specific context. Those not familiar with these U.S. traditions will probably not understand, learn from, or be capable of doing what the U.S. authors intend.

United States and Mexican Educational and Medical Systems

These different literacy contexts are compounded by distinct education and medical systems. Educational traditions in Mexico—both in the classroom (Kras, 1991) and business organizations –usually favor more rote, hierarchical, and theoretical approaches, while U.S. educational approaches have been described as more pragmatic, universal, and process-oriented. Although the U.S.-Mexico border area is dynamic and mutually influential, these assumptions about education routinely surface in U.S.-Mexican literacy contexts (see Thatcher, 2006).

The United States and Mexico also have distinct medical traditions, systems, and infrastructures, creating problems not only in cultural and literacy expectations, but also in managing two medical systems and traditions, a complex combination. One critical example is that many of the older generation in Mexico still believe in *curandero* traditions and might not seek medical attention from traditional westernized sources (Barbassa, 2005). "The US and Mexican health care systems respond to different societal values. In Mexico, as in many other countries, health care is based on solidarity; that is, on the principle of a national health system. In the United States the organization of health care responds to a principle of individualism" (Homedes & Ugalde, 2003). Another differences it that many Mexicans are used to treating themselves because prescription drugs are readily available with a written prescription from licensed doctors. In addition, Mexicans and other Latin Americans often draw on alternative methods of health care, such as *curanderismo*, which is "a type of medical practice that utilizes spiritual healers and traditional remedies to cure illnesses of physical and spiritual natures" (Lopiccolo, 1990). The body is comprehended in terms of the hot and cold dichotomy and relates back to Hippocratic notions of the four humors, blood, phlegm, yellow bile (choler) and black bile (melancholy), in the diagnoses and treatment of illnesses. Blood and yellow bile were considered hot humors, and phlegm and black bile were considered cold humors. The equal distribution of these four humors throughout the body yielded forth a healthy individual. An imbalance of the humors would result in sickness and was treated by balancing out the hot or cold humors. *Curanderismo* adopts the same notions of hot and cold. Diseases are classified as either hot or cold and foods are also believed to be innately hot or cold (Lopiccolo, 1990; Rose, 1978). A hot disease can be ameliorated or cured through a cold food or medicine and vice-versa. Maladies can afflict the individual when the body reaches a state of disequilibrium. This imbalance can be caused by both biological and social factors.

In contrast, Western medicine is grounded in the germ theory in which illness and diseases are caused by germs, and what is treated is the disease and not the mind and spirit. "Empiricism and strict modes of reasoning are essential to the mental processes that make clinical medicine... the correlation of cause and effect, especially of pathogen to disease in the case of infectious diseases" guide the practice of mainstream medicine. This is where much of the dissonance between western medicine and folk medicine stems from for Latino Americans. Differences in notions of effective health care are also dependant on social factors. The social dynamics between physician and patient are also determinants in how patients will perceive and understand their health care provider and setting, and whether or not the patient's welfare is met and secured through culturally appropriate approaches. Resistance by practitioners of Western medicine to embrace holistic medical approaches to treating patients leads to persistence by individuals to seek health aid through nontraditional means that acknowledge and speak to their value system (Kiev, 1968).

Besides the difference in medical approaches, it is critical to understand that the interpersonal, high power distance, diffuse, and collective values often encourage different approaches to the interaction between patient and doctor. Patient compliance can also be directly correlated to this patient experience. The Mexican culture places high value on establishing personal relationships with their health care provider. "Non verbal as well as verbal expressions of personal warmth (smiles, handshakes, and sometimes hugs) on the part of health care provider are important" (Bigby, 2003). It is possible that it take more than just one meeting with the patient to develop rapport, but once a foundation of trust is laid out they will feel at ease and talk more freely. Physicians of a Western orientation are both "time-conscious" and "deal-focused" (Gesteland, 2005), and doctor interviews conducted under the premise that such ideas are true for all individuals of a different culture will then proceed to interact with the patient through rhetorical traditions and cultural behaviors incompatible with those of individuals who inhabit the border region. The health care provider must acknowledge the generally diffuse relationships between Mexican patients and their close network made up of family and friends. Western medical practices protect patient's right to privacy, which is characteristic of U.S. individualistic culture, and Mexican cultures generally extend private matters and decisions to include family members. "To the Western man, illness is an impersonal event brought about by neutral, nonemotional, natural agents, such as germs, while for the Mexican-American, illness relates to an individual's life, his community, [and] his interpersonal relationships" (Kiev, 1968).

The propensity to engage in matters in a more collective fashion is also reflected in the manner in which borderland populations influenced by Mexican traditions resort to healing sources. It begins by first "exhausting the resources and knowledge at home, within the extended family, and the older members of the community" (Lopiccolo, 1990). Medical attention is initially sought out first through more familiar means and relationships such as through the mother, grandmother, or neighbor who would offer home remedies, and, if illness persists, the *senoria,* "a woman who is especially knowledgeable about the causes and treatment of illnesses"(Spector, 1996) or *yerbero* is sought out. In the case where further treatments is needed, *curanderos* are called forth to treat the illness on a more spiritual level because it is believed that they possess a *don* or the gift to cure (Lopiccolo, 1990; Spector, 1996). Professional health providers are usually resorted to last if the malady was not cured through the effort of traditional care, but patients who do so are reported to continue to refer to a healer during and after having sought out biomedical treatment (Bigby, 2003).

Why then is *curanderismo* given preference over mainstream medicine by a number of Mexican and Mexican-American individuals? *Curanderos* reside within the same community, both geographically and culturally. It is not so much a convenience factor as it is a comfort component that provides patients with a setting that is familiar and a context and environment that is "financially, logistically and culturally" comprehensible (Lopiccolo, 1990). Being part of the same community means that there is a higher likelihood that world views, beliefs, and values about what is considered proper, adequate, and effective health care will be very similar. The *curandero* has the ability to understand the factors causing illness not rooted in the physical body alone. Because the lifestyles between healer and patient are shared, the *curandero* will acknowledge other causes of illness such as supernatural forces as valid causal agents of sickness (Spector, 1996).

Physicians have their own views of illnesses and health, which for the most part are based on a modern scientific medical paradigm that was developed and nurtured in medical school. Modern medicine emphasizes the biological and clinical aspects of illness and health, and defines them through objective observation, measurement, and clinical quantification. But lay people have their own ways of describing these things and may even use definitions...that differ considerably from those used by medical experts (Molina & Aguirre- Molina, 1994).

How individuals understand the illness and what they believe are the causal factors of illness shape how the illness is verbally expressed. For example, in the case of *mal de ojo*, a doctor who does not discuss the nature of folk illnesses will quickly dismiss it as superstition. Conversely, doctors who discuss with a patient his condition through technical and medical terms risks not having the individual understand concepts that are culturally bound (Molina & Molina-Aguirre). Furthermore, *Curanderos* often offer their services without requiring any monetary or material reward because the gift they have been endowed with is to be used to heal and aid and not for personal gain. What the *curandero* receives depends on what the individual is able to provide, and from this practice stems yet another reason for why many border land individuals are wary of Western practitioners and institutions who are believed to be much too expensive and put forth a very complex financial language towards healthcare. Accustomed to a health care provider that sees the financial aspect of curing as secondary to the process of healing, individuals who practice *Curanderismo* or similar non Western forms of medical assistance believe that health care institutions are unfairly demanding too much.

Communication and person-to-person interaction along the border is influenced, hindered, and propelled by several factors–a major cause being the unique dynamics that result from cities located on opposite sides of the international border. Entering an unregulated health market for many border region inhabitants is enticing not only because it may be much more affordable, but because it is delivered within a system that grants the health consumer access to a medical discourse that makes sense to them. Research has yet to further develop knowledge on the health repercussions that may emerge as a result of this, and, equally important, probe deeper into the forms of communication that takes place between health consumer and prescription and non prescription medication providers and pharmacist across the border.

CONSENT FORMS, HEALTH LITERACY, AND PRIOS

This discussion of consent forms, first in the context of the eight value sets and then in the literacy context of the United States and Latin America, exemplifies what culturally appropriate health materials means. In other words, cultural appropriate means 1) the communication patterns match the eight value sets of the group, and 2) the communication itself fits the rhetorical assumptions of the communication context. These assumptions are traditionally broken down into five categories, and as discussed in Chapter One, these five categories are purpose–what the communication is supposed to achieve for its outcomes; reader-author relations–what relations are assumed between these two; information–what types of information are needed; organization–what organizational strategies are most appropriate; and style–what tone, posture, or rhetorical stance is most appropriate. These five categories make up the acronym PRIOS and are used to assess rhetorical appropriateness. The next section summarizes the appropriateness of preoperative consent forms, generally, and that New Mexican consent form specifically, for patients rooted in the Mexican cultural and rhetorical traditions.

Purpose

What is most evident in the previous discussion is that the consent form exhibits most strongly the cultural values of United States, not Mexico. As Reyes Lopez (2006) explains, this mismatch between Latin American culture and the consent form is difficult, but not impossible, to overcome. Their solution is to ground the written consent form in much oral conversation to explain the purposes of the consent form in ways that are culturally appropriate. Thus, it is important that healthcare workers grounded in the US cultural and rhetorical systems understand that the consent form will not achieve its Universalist purpose for patients coming from the Mexican or more particularist traditions in the same way as patients grounded in the U.S. tradition. Health care workers need to understand that patients coming from more particular cultures will not assume the same Universalist purposes and will want to particularize the rules, that is, understand how their unique situation will call for bending or situating in the rules more carefully. Furthermore, it is important for healthcare workers understand that put simply Mexican patients are much less used to using forms in their everyday behavior. Written forms are connected to colonial, notary-lie, and legalistic situations, which are to be avoided or resisted.

As a result, a significant difference might exist in the actual power or relevance of the form and the corresponding signature of the patient and doctor. Much like Atahualpa in the Cajamarca incident, many patients coming from Mexican or Latin American cultures, whose reality is grounded in a more oral and particular culture, might simply assume that the signature and document have little meaning and will "throw away" the document much as Atahualpa threw down the Bible in front of the conquistadores. In Latin American and Mexican cultures, as explained earlier, much more attention is given to perceived intentions of the healthcare staff, and not the low-context details on the form. Health care workers might consider carefully explaining the power of the consent form and signature in the context of the US legal and cultural systems.

Reader-Author Relations

As explained earlier, both the New Mexican and Cuban consent forms assumed more objective, and therefore, more individualistic, specific, achieved, and low-power distance relations between the hospital or doctor as author and the patient as the reader. The Cuban consent form reduces this objective feeling somewhat in its interpersonal and more collective, diffuse, and ascriptive approaches. However, both consent forms create reader-author relations that are not nearly as common in Mexican and other collective, diffuse, ascriptive, and high-power distance cultures. Consequently, health care workers would be well served by understanding how difficult it is for patients coming from these other traditions to process or even understand the kinds of relations assumed in these consent forms. As explained earlier, health care workers should emphasize the interpersonal relations between the worker and the patient, emphasizing the unique nature of the patient and forcing (ethically) a more egalitarian relationship so that the patient understands that he or she is expected to ask questions, to reflect upon the advice or direction given by the doctor, not simply to accept it. In addition, health care workers should understand when a patient has to rely on members of his or her collective group.

Information

Both consent forms emphasize information that is specific to the topic at hand and did not ask for more diffuse information. Further, both consent forms require little contextual information, nor ask for ascriptive markers or other symbols of power and authority. Finally, both consent forms communicate rules and policies as if they were non-negotiable, and assume little need for the patient to consult someone besides him or herself. Emphasizing the specific information and leaving out all of this other information is going to present problems for patients coming from other cultural traditions such as Mexico. First, these patients are going to feel the need to fill in the information gaps of context, diffuse relations, and authority structures. However, the need to fill in and understanding of the authority structures might not be present if the patient falls back on the customary high power-distance communication patterns in which the patient is supposed to simply listen to the higher power doctor or healthcare worker. Further, if the patient is willing to ask questions, often the patient will need to fill in the particular information gaps, which means how well the situation is adapted to the unique circumstances of the patient and this situation.

Organization of the Consent Form Document

As explained earlier, the consent form as a genre or document style follows a similar organizational plan because it is based on a fairly singular rights-based theory. Consequently, the consent form has a universal, monochronic, inner-directed, and specific organizational pattern. Thus, it is direct, with an introduction to the whole document and topic sentences for each paragraph; it is coherent in a monochronic and specific way, with each paragraph or unit of information discussing one topic only; it emphasizes parallelism and uniformity throughout; it is linear in its developmental fashion; and as a whole, because it leaves out the collective, particular, and outer-directed organizational information, it is more analytical than narrative, and more focused on cause and effect relations rather than horizontal or holistic relations. For those coming from particular, outer directed, and diffuse cultures, this organizational pattern will seem boring, unattractive, artificially parallel, and sterile or inhumane because of its assumed objectivity. In reality, there is not much that health care workers can do to change to standardize format or organizational patterns of the consent forms. However, as discussed earlier in reader-author relations, health care workers can do much to mitigate against these perceptions or misunderstanding of the organizational patterns of the consent forms. This probably includes re-stating the "content" in the forms of stories much like the fotonovela discussed in the first part of the chapter. This dramatizing of the consent form brings out many of the alternative cultural patterns much like fotonovela.

Style

The predominant style of the consent form is objective, scientific, and, therefore, detached from interpersonal human realities. The Cuban consent form is a little more interpersonal, but both consent forms are genuinely objective in their style. This objectivity presents a unique ambiguity to those coming from Mexican and Latin American cultures. As explained earlier, this objectivity was one of the major forces in the brutal colonizing of Latin America. Furthermore, scientific objectivity has been a major rhetorical ploy in maintaining the oligarchic power relations in Latin America (Osland, de Franco, S. & Osland, A., 1999). Furthermore, Osland, J., de Franco, S. & Osland, A. (1999) argues that despite great penchant for harmonious interpersonal relationships in Latin America, power trumps interpersonal relations; that is, a person in power does not have to show this strong interpersonal orientation to a subordinate. Consequently, a patient coming from the Latin American culture might expect the objective treatment in a perceived high power distance relation. However, if the Mexican or Latin American patient perceives the power relations to be fairly equal, that patient will most likely expect a much more interpersonal approach to the relation than

Table 2.Constructions of culture and cultural competence

Standard 1.	Health care organizations should ensure that patients/consumers receive from all staff members effective, understandable, and respectful care that is provided in a manner compatible with their cultural health beliefs and practices and preferred language.
Standard 3.	Health care organizations should ensure that staff at all levels and across all disciplines receive ongoing education and training in culturally and linguistically appropriate service delivery.
Standard 7.	Health care organizations must make available easily understood patient-related materials and post signage in the languages of the commonly encountered groups and/or groups represented in the service area.
Standard 12.	Health care organizations should develop participatory, collaborative partnerships with communities and utilize a variety of formal and informal mechanisms to facilitate community and patient/consumer involvement in designing and implementing CLAS-related activities.
Standard 13.	Health care organizations should ensure that conflict and grievance resolution processes are culturally and linguistically sensitive and capable of identifying, preventing, and resolving cross-cultural conflicts or complaints by patients/consumers

what is seen in both of these consent forms. As many theorists explain (Kras, 1991; Osland, J., de Franco, S. & Osland, A., 1999), it is very important to take an interpersonal relation with Latin American clients. Thus, health care workers should mitigate against the objective tone or style of these consent forms, much as Reyes Lopez (2006) explain in their research article.

CONNECTING THE PAMPHLETS AND CONSENT FORMS TO THE *NATIONAL STANDARDS ON CULTURALLY AND LINGUISTICALLY APPROPRIATE SERVICES*

As a conclusion, this section demonstrates the connections between cultural values and definitions and practices of literacy to the 14 standards of culturally competent care. It groups the 14 standards into three thematic areas: (1) constructions of culture and cultural competence (Table 2); (2) demographics, cultural behavior,

Table 3. Demographics, cultural behavior, and organizational behavior

Standard 2.	Health care organizations should implement strategies to recruit, retain, and promote at all levels of the organization a diverse staff and leadership that are representative of the demographic characteristics of the service area.
Standard 8.	Health care organizations should develop, implement, and promote a written strategic plan that outlines clear goals, policies, operational plans, and management accountability/oversight mechanisms to provide culturally and linguistically appropriate services.
Standard 9.	Health care organizations should conduct initial and ongoing organizational self-assessments of CLAS-related activities and are encouraged to integrate cultural and linguistic competence-related measures into their internal audits, performance improvement programs, patient satisfaction assessments, and outcomes-based evaluations.
Standard 10.	Health care organizations should ensure that data on the individual patient's/consumer's race, ethnicity, and spoken and written language are collected in health records, integrated into the organization's management information systems, and periodically updated.
Standard 11.	Health care organizations should maintain a current demographic, cultural, and epidemiological profile of the community as well as a needs assessment to accurately plan for and implement services that respond to the cultural and linguistic characteristics of the service area.
Standard 14.	Health care organizations are encouraged to regularly make available to the public information about their progress and successful innovations in implementing the CLAS standards and to provide public notice in their communities about the availability of this information.

Table 4. Translation

Standard 4.	Health care organizations must offer and provide language assistance services, including bilingual staff and interpreter services, at no cost to each patient/consumer with limited English proficiency at all points of contact, in a timely manner during all hours of operation.
Standard 5.	Health care organizations must provide to patients/consumers in their preferred language both verbal offers and written notices informing them of their right to receive language assistance services.
Standard 6.	Health care organizations must assure the competence of language assistance provided to limited English proficient patients/consumers by interpreters and bilingual staff. Family and friends should not be used to provide interpretation services (except on request by the patient/consumer).

and organizational behavior (Table 3); and (3) translation (Table 4).

Constructions of Culture and Cultural Competence

This chapter explains much more clearly the connections between cultural health beliefs and effective, understandable, and respectful care. One of the strongest critiques I have of the research in culturally competent care (which is beyond the scope of this chapter) is that culture is defined and operationalized in a haphazard way, often becoming inconsistent combinations of anecdotes, taboos, unique or interesting practices, or romantic forays into the strange behaviors of others. This inconsistent use makes developing culturally appropriate communications difficult. First, since culture is ill-defined, culture's connections to communication are ill-defined as well. Thus, creating communications that are culturally appropriate is almost impossible. And what usually happens is that an organization simply publicizes a few taboos or anecdotes and labels that as culturally competent care.

As this chapter (and book) exemplifies, culture and communication can be defined, operationalized, and connected systematically, thus creating clear connections between a cultural value and a communication pattern. Because culture and communications are defined and clearly connected, this chapter demonstrates what it means to be understandable, effective, and respectful—communicate using the cultural/communication patterns that correspond to the group addressed. This does not mean stereotyping the group—assuming no variation; rather, it means attempting to connect to the group in culturally meaningful ways. As a result, training can be systematic, effective, and empowering, both for the staff who receive the training and for the patients who benefit from it.

In addition, developing partnerships with communities is much easier because the health organization has systematic and effective ways for understanding the cultural and communicative behavior of the community groups. Finally, grievance problems and counseling must be grounded in the intercultural values of the groups involved. Much intercultural research demonstrates (Hampden-Turner & Trompenaars, 2000) that what some organizations have defined as interpersonal problems, which cause serious workplace issues, are in reality intercultural problems; and that once an intercultural competence is developed among the personnel, the amount and severity of official complaints and grievances is usually greatly reduced.

DEMOGRAPHICS, CULTURAL BEHAVIOR, AND ORGANIZATIONAL BEHAVIOR

These six standards essentially assess the relation between the organizational culture of the medical practice and the culture of the target group. Although organizational culture is discussed more thoroughly in Chapter Six, this chapter and the book teach us two critical thinks about these standards: First, one of the most interesting issues in intercultural research is assimilation and enculturation, two topics that are well beyond the scope of this chapter but are discussed in Chapter Two. As explained there, a person can have all the demographics of one culture but being culturally connected to another. For example, in my U.S.-Mexico border region, a person can be Hispanic or Mexican and speak Spanish, but those two characteristics might have little to do with the actual preferred cultural behavior. It is much more accurate and important to identify where each person's own values align with the predominant values of the groups that self-identifies with. For example, Chapter Three discusses the dilemma of Generation 1.5 English as Second Language students. These students are usually second generation Americans but learn their first language at home and English at school. They are bilingual but often not bicultural because their cultural values often quickly—but in hybrid fashion–align with their American context. They identify with some cultural values of their parents and home country but assimilate many other American values.

Thus, just bringing in health care staff who have the same demographics of the patients does not necessarily mean cultural competence. As explained in Chapter Six, the organizational culture of the health care center must understand and accommodate the cultural values of the group they want to recruit and promote or train. Also connected to assimilation, this aspect shows that even though an organization might hire a culturally representative person, if that organization does not support that person's cultural orientation, that person will either assimilate/change or leave. This book and chapter provide systematic approaches for developing the organization to be sensitive to other cultural systems.

TRANSLATION

Finally, this chapter explains very clearly what good translation is: Although the pamphlets or consent forms are translated into a target language, if they retain the cultural patterns from the original language and culture, the translation will be foreign or unnatural and will need lots of explanation and discussion to help the patients or audience process the information. Thus, it is appropriate to use the term "rhetorical translation," which is parallel to linguistic translation: it simply means explaining the same content but using the rhetorical or communicative patterns that correspond to the cultural values of the target group.

REFERENCES

Adler, N. (2008). *International dimensions of organizational behavior*. New York, NY: Thomson Learning Center.

Angelelli, C. V., & Jacobson, H. (2009). *Testing and assessment in translation and interpreting studies*. Philadelphia, PA: John Benjamins.

Barbassa, J. (2005). *Immigrants mix traditional medicine with advice from doctors*. Retrieved from www.fiob.org/centro.html

Bigby, J. (Ed.). (2003). *Cross-cultural medicine*. Philadelphia, PA: Versa Press.

Bussey-Jones, J., & Genao, I. (2003). Impact of culture on health care. *Journal of the National Medical Association*, *95*(8), 732–735.

Bustamante, A., Ojeda, G., & Castaneda, X. (2008). Willingness to pay for cross-border health insurance between the United States and Mexico. *Health Affairs*, *27*(1), 169–178. doi:10.1377/hlthaff.27.1.169

Bustillos, D. (2005, August 31). *States begin requiring cultural competency training for doctors*. Perspectives University of Houston Law Center. Retrieved November 12, 2009, from http://www.law.uh.edu/Healthlaw/perspectives/August2005/%28DB%29CulturalCompetency.pdf

Commission to End Health Care Disparities. (2007). *Addressing health care disparities: Recommended goal, guiding principles, and key strategies for comprehensive policies.* Retrieved December 1, 2009, from http://www.ama-assn.org/ama1 /pub/upload/mm/ 433/commission_pres_07.pdf

Connor, U. (1996). *Contrastive rhetoric: Cross-cultural aspects of second-language writing.* Cambridge, UK: Cambridge University Press.

Cooper, L. A., Beach, M. C., Johnson, R. L., & Inui, T. S. (2006). Delving below the surface: Understanding how race and ethnicity influence relationships in health care. *Journal of General Internal Medicine, 21*, S21–S27. doi:10.1111/j.1525-1497.2006.00305.x

Cornejo-Polar, A. (1994). *Escribir en el aire: Ensayo sobre la heterogeneidad socio-cultural en las literaturas Andinas* [*Writing in the Air: Essay about the socio-cultural heterogeneity in the Andean* Literatures]. Lima, Peru: Editorial Horizonte.

Dealy, G. (1992). *The Latin Americans: Spirit and ethos*. Boulder, CO: Westview Press.

Elder, J., Candelaria, J., Woodruff, S., Criqui, M., Talavera, G., & Rupp, J. (2000). Results of language for health: Cardiovascular disease nutrition education for Latino English-as-a-second-language studies students. *Health Education & Behavior, 27*, 50–63. doi:10.1177/109019810002700106

Falagas, M., Korbila, I., Giannopoulou, K. P., Kondilis, B. K., & Peppas, G. (2009). Informed consent: How much and what do patients understand? *American Journal of Surgery, 198*(3), 420–435. doi:10.1016/j.amjsurg.2009.02.010

Fidalgo, G., & Chapman-Novakofski, K. (2001). Teaching nutrition to Hispanics at an English as a second language (ESL) center: Overcoming barriers. *Journal of Extension, 39*. Retrieved from http://www.joe.org/joe/2001december/a3.html.

Flores, G. (2000). Culture and the patient-physician relationship: Achieving cultural competency in healthcare. *Journal of Pediatrics, 136*(1). Retrieved November 29, 2009, from http://download.journals.elsevierhealth.com/pdfs/journals/0022-3476/ PIIS0022347 60090043X. pdf

Galanti, G. (2000). An introduction to cultural differences. *The Western Journal of Medicine, 172*, 335–336. doi:10.1136/ewjm.172.5.335

Gonzalez Gonzalez, D., Rodríguez Almada, H., & Guido Berro, R. (2005). Consentimiento informado: Análisis crítico de su aplicación en un servicio quirúrgico. *Revista Médica de Uruguay, 21*(4), 291–297.

Granero-Molina, J., Fernández-Sola, C., & Aguilera-Manrique, G. (2009). Applying a socio-linguistic model to the analysis of informed consent documents. *Nursing Ethics, 16*(6), 797–812. doi:10.1177/0969733009341908

Hall, E. T. (1976). *Beyond culture*. New York, NY: Doubleday.

Hall, E. T. (1983). *The dance of life*. New York, NY: Doubleday.

Hampden-Turner, C., & Trompenaars, A. (2000). *Building cross-cultural competence*. New York, NY: Wiley.

Healthy Border 2010. (2003). *U.S.-Mexico Border Health Commission*. Retrieved from http://www.borderhealth.org/

Hinds, J. (1987). Reader versus writer responsibility: A new typology. In Connor, U., & Kaplan, R. (Eds.), *Writing across languages: Analysis of L2 text* (pp. 141–152). Reading, MA: Addison-Wesley.

Hobbs, W. (2009). Culture and medicine. In *Introduction to Human Behavior* (vol. 12, pp. 147-153).

Hofstede, G. (2010). *Cultures and organizations, software of the mind* (3rd ed.). New York, NY: McGraw Hill.

Homedes, N., & Ugalde, A. (2003). *Globalization and health at the United States-Mexico border.*

House, R. J., Hanges, P. J., Javidan, M., Dorfman, P. R., & Gupta, V. (Eds.). (2005). *Culture, leadership, and organizations: The GLOBE study of 62 societies*. Newbury Park, CA: Sage Publications.

Howard, C. A., Andrade, S., & Bird, T. (2001). The ethical dimensions of cultural competence in border health care settings. *Family & Community Health*, *4*, 36–49.

Johnson, R. L., Saha, S., Arbelaez, J. J., Beach, M. C., & Cooper, L. A. (2004). Racial and Ethnic differences in patient perceptions of bias and cultural competence in health care. *Journal of General Internal Medicine*, *19*, 101–110. doi:10.1111/j.1525-1497.2004.30262.x

Juckett, G. (2005). Cross-cultural medicine. *American Family Physician, 72*, 2267-2274. American Academy of Family Physicians. Retrieved October 12, 2009, from http://www.aafp.org/afp/2005/1201/p2267.html

Kellog, S. (1995). *Law and the transformation of Aztec culture, 1500-1700*. Norman, OK: University of Oklahoma Press.

Kiev, A. (1968). *Curanderismo: Mexican-American folk psychiatry*. New York, NY: Collier Macmillan Publishing Company.

Koenig, B. A., & Gates-Williams, J. (1995). Understanding cultural difference in caring for dying patients. *The Western Journal of Medicine*, *163*, 244–249. Retrieved from http://ethnomed.org/clinical/end-of-life/koenig.pdf/view.

Kras, E. (1991). *Management in two cultures*. Minneapolis, MN: Intercultural Press, Inc.

Leon-Portilla, M. (1996). *El destino de la palabra. De la oralidad y los códices mesoamericanos a la escritura alfabética*. México City, Mexico: El Colegio Nacional Fondo de Cultura Económica.

Lopiccolo, P. (1990). *Curanderismo in the El Paso, Las Cruces, Ciudad Juárez area*. Unpublished Master's thesis, New Mexico State University.

Loustaunau, M. O., & Bane, M. J. (1999). *Life, death, and in-between on the U.S.-Mexico border: Así es la vida*. West Port, CT Bergin & Garvey.

Marcus, J. (1992). *Mesoamerican writing systems: Propaganda, myth, and history in four ancient civilizations*. Princeton, NJ: Princeton University Press.

Masi, R. (1989). Multiculturalism, medicine, and health part IV: Individual considerations. *Canadian Family Physician Medecin de Famille Canadien*, *35*, 69–73.

Meeuwesen, L., Brink-Muinen, A. V., & Hofstede, G. (2009). Can dimensions of national culture predict cross-national differences in medical communication? *Patient Education and Counseling*, *75*, 58–66. doi:10.1016/j.pec.2008.09.015

Osland, J. S., De Franco, S., & Osland, A. (1999). Organizational implications of Latin American culture. *Journal of Management Inquiry*, *8*(2), 219–234. doi:10.1177/105649269982018

Pappen, U. (2009). Literacy, learning and health – A social practices view of health literacy. *Literacy and Numeracy Studies*, *16*(2), 19–34.

Purnell, L., & Paulanka, B. (2008). *Guide to culturally competent health care* (2nd ed.). F.A. Davis Company.

Retrieved November 21, 2009, from http://www.ncbi.nlm.nih. gov/pmc/ articles/ PMC1070887/

Retrieved October 26, 2009, from http://www.med-ed.virginia.edu/ public/ CourseSitesDocs/ IntrotoHumanBehavior/ coursedocs/unrestricted/ pdf/CULTRELA. W2009.print. pdf

Reyes Lopez, M., & Aquila, L. (2006). Consentimiento informado en pacientes sometidos a cirugía por mínimo acceso. *Revista Cubana de Enfermeria, 22*(4).

Rivers, P. A., & Patino, F. G. (2006). Barriers to health care access for Latino immigrants in the USA. *International Journal of Social Economics, 33*(3), 207–220. doi:10.1108/03068290610646234

Rosa, M., Goins, K., Carbone, E., & Cortes, D. (2004). Views and preferences of low-literate Hispanics regarding diabetes education: Results of formative research. *Health Education & Behavior, 31*, 388–405. doi:10.1177/1090198104263360

Rose, L. C. (1978). *Disease beliefs in Mexican-American communities*. California: R & E Research Associates, Inc.

Shohet, L. (2004). Health and literacy: Perspectives. *Literacy and Numeracy Studies, 13*(1), 65–84.

Shrank, W. H., Kutner, J. S., Richardson, T., Mularski, R. A., Fischer, S., & Kagawa-Singer, M. (2005). Focus group findings about the influence of culture on communication preferences in end-of-life care. *Journal of General Internal Medicine, 20*(8), 703–709. Retrieved November 13, 2009. doi:10.1111/j.1525-1497.2005.0151.x

Specter, R. E. (1996). *Cultural diversity in health and illness*. Stamford, CT: Appleton & Lange.

Stewart, E., & Bennett, M. (1991). *American cultural patterns: A cross-cultural perspective* (Rev. ed.). Yarmouth, ME: Intercultural Press, Inc.

Tate, D. M. (2003). Cultural awareness: Bridging the gap between caregivers and Hispanic patients. *Journal of Continuing Education in Nursing, 34*(5), 213–217. Retrieved from http://www.jcenonline.com/view.asp?rID=4526.

Thatcher, B. with Urbina, N. (2010). Comunicación médica y de salud en la región fronteriza de México y Los Estados Unidos. In V. Garza Almanza & B. Thatcher (Eds.), *Comunicación médica y científica en Mexico*. Casa Editorial de El Colegio de Chihuahua: Ciudad Juárez, Chihuahua, Mexico.

Thatcher, B. L. (1999). Cultural and rhetorical adaptations for South American audiences. *Technical Communication: Global issues, local concerns, 46*(2), 177-195.

Thatcher, B. L. (2006). Intercultural rhetoric, technology, and writing in Mexican maquilas. *Special Technology Transfer Edition of Technical Communication Quarterly, 15*(3), 383–405.

Thatcher, B. L. (2009). Understanding digital literacy across cultures. In Spilka, R. (Ed.), *Digital literacy for technical communication: 21st Century theory and practice* (pp. 169–198). Routledge.

Tseng, W. S., & Streltzer, J. (2008). *Cultural competence in health care*. Springer. doi:10.1007/978-0-387-72171-2

Ulrey, K. L., & Amason, P. (2001). Intercultural communication between patients and health care providers: An exploration of intercultural communication effectiveness, cultural sensitivity, stress, and anxiety. *Health Communication, 13*(4), 449–463. doi:10.1207/S15327027HC1304_06

ENDNOTES

1. I am thankful to Rebecca Berkson for gathering much of this initial intercultural research on medicine and health care.
2. Again, thanks to Rebecca Berkson for this initial research.

Chapter 10
Writing Instructions and How-to-do Manuals across Cultures

ABSTRACT

This chapter demonstrates how culture structures and is embedded in instructional manuals around the world. It examines two car repair instructions from Japan and the United States and two charcoal grill assembly instructions. It provides key units of analysis for professional communicators writing instructional materials for intercultural contexts.

INTRODUCTION

Despite the relevance of instructional design for intercultural organizational training, outsourced manufacturing, health care, and distance education, little work has been carried out in writing instructions across cultures. The work that exists includes Honold (1999) who compares Chinese and German cell phone manuals and argues that Chinese cell phone manuals were often a very terse in explaining many of the functions, because they assumed or even asked the users to seek help from their friends. On the other hand, the German manual tried to create an independent cell phone user because the quality of the German manual rested on its ability to independently provide all of the necessary information. Dong (2007) compared Chinese and U.S. heater manuals, positively correlating the cultural values of China and the United States to the different instructional designs.

DOI: 10.4018/978-1-61350-450-5.ch010

However, despite this minimal work, we have not systematically assessed elements of instructional design for cross-cultural contexts. For example, I recently started a project to educate residents of U.S.-Mexico border *colonias* in water sanitation and appropriate septic system use. Colonias are undeveloped, poor, and often rural communities that generally lack water and sewer infrastructure, and as a correlation, have higher incidences of infectious and gastro-intestinal diseases.

Much work has focused on colonia health with many instructional materials developed to educate colonias residents. Figure 1 shows two pages of a fotonovela (drama-pamphlet) developed by the University of Texas-El Paso's Center for Environmental Resource Management (http://research.utep.edu/Default.aspx?alias=research.utep.edu/cerm). This Center develops and distributes this and many other educational documents for distribution to colonias.

The left page shows how to sanitize water, and the right page discusses water safety and sewer (which I probably did not need to translate because the pictures are highly illustrative). Much as described in Chapter Nine, this instructional pamphlet follows many of the cultural patterns of Mexico, including its collective, high context, polychronic, and relations-based discussions (see Thatcher, 2006). It is also more visual than verbal, meeting the needs of a semi-literate population. The fotonovela is a very standardized approach in the border area for instructional contexts.

The instructional design, however, has many potential problems. First, it makes the mistake of treating the semi-literature adult population like children, not adults. This is like teaching adults a second language using the same methods as with children. Much research in adult education and second language studies severely critiques this approach. Second, and perhaps just as important, the instructional design does not counter-act some of the problems with the cultural design. As Stewart & Bennett argue (1991), "Each culture possesses integrity, and generally speaking, is neither inferior nor superior to any other culture. But in a structured situation and for a specific purpose, one cultural system may in fact work better than another" (p. 175). In other words, cultural values have pros and cons in specific structured situation. And in this situation, some of the cons of Mexican culture are apparent in the instructional design.

First, the narrative, drama-like approaches are very effective for demonstrating a problem, but often very weak at solving it, especially in situations that are minimally different, often inspiring an "exceptions to rules" mentality (Thatcher, 2000). Second, the relations-based approach is effective at modeling responsibilities and tasks, but when these exact relations models are not in place, users are resistant to perform work based on different models because they feel un-empowered to do so. Third, and similarly, when high-context approaches are used (showing specific contextual details), transferring the instructions from one context to another is difficult (see Thatcher, 2001; Thatcher, 2006). What we don't know, however, is

Figure 1. UTEP pamphlet on Water and Sewer Sanitation

how to develop alternative instructional designs for this context, which is the purpose of this project.

As is evident, we have much work to do for intercultural instructional design, including internationalizing many design components such as curricular assumptions, user-author (or student-teacher) interactions, assumptions about technology, layout, language, flow, feedback, and assessment, all of which are significantly connected to cultural values. Further, how do instructional designs across cultures differ according to the value sets or other key indicators? How do these differences affect dual manufacturing or outsourcing? How are instructional materials related to international certifications of management and environment and how can these certifications assure culturally sensitive approaches? How does technology transfer relate to curriculum design for implementing new manufacturing procedures across cultures?

This chapter examines how instructional manuals vary across cultures. The first part of this chapter presents four sets of manuals, two for assembling charcoal grills and two for replacing a water pump in vehicles. This section then describes how the instructional design of each of the four manuals corresponds to the eight value sets or etic borders used throughout this book. The second part of this chapter contextualizes the different instructional design with the prevailing rhetorical traditions around the world. This latter section draws on previous research (Thatcher, 2006) showing how instructional manuals were used in an outsourced manufacturing setting in northern Mexico. These two sections ground not only the design, but the use of intercultural instructional manuals.

Figure 2. Instructions for Grill manufactured by Guangzhou Hungkay Co., Ltd in China

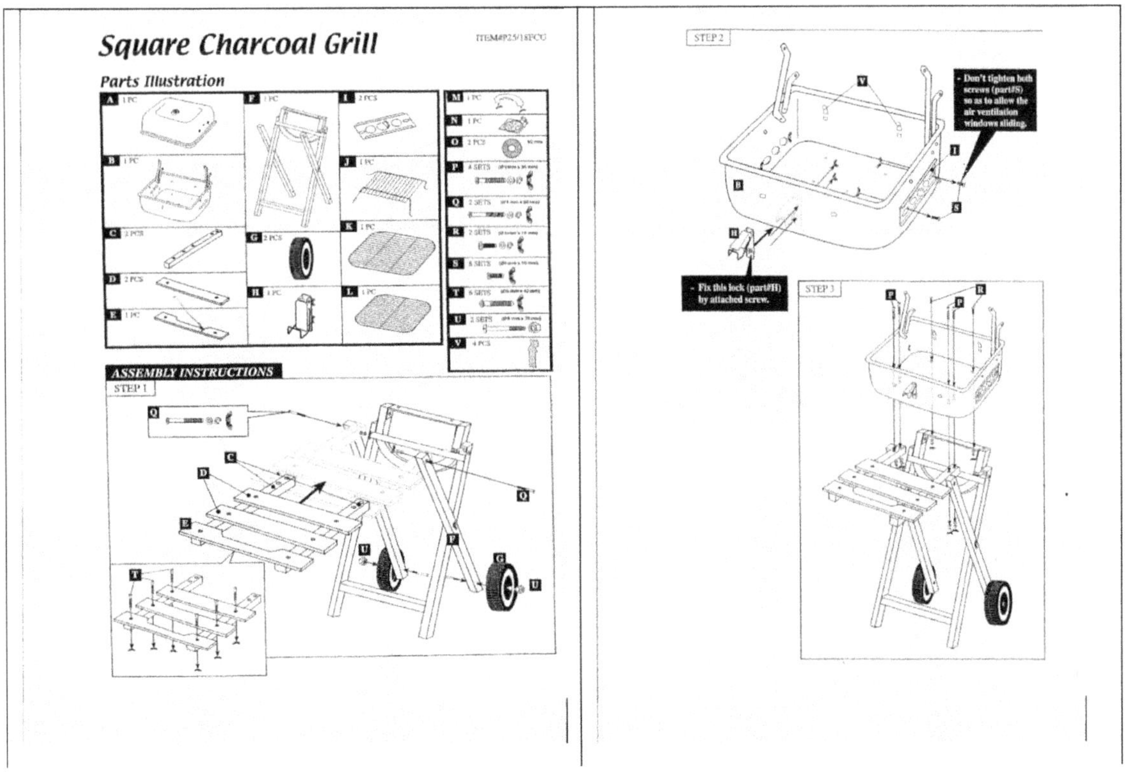

MANUAL DESIGN AND INTERCULTURAL VALUE SETS

Following the comparative framework articulated in Chapter Two, this section compares manuals that are written to accomplish the same thing in a similar context but from different cultures. The first set of manuals describes how to put together a simple charcoal grill. Figure 2 shows the first two of three pages of a manual that comes with a charcoal grill that was sold as a no-name brand in large retail chains across the United States. This grill and manual were manufactured by Guangzhou Hungkay Co., Ltd from China. The third page of this manual has the same instructional design as a second page.

Figure 3 shows four pages of instructions for the Gourmet Grill, which was manufactured by D&K Houseware Co. of China. Unlike the square charcoal grill, the Gourmet Grill was manufactured to be sold under the brand name of two U.S. corporations and: Academy Sports and Charbroil Grills. This specific manual was sold at Academy sports under their Gourmet Grill product line. It

Figure 3. Instructions for Grill manufactured by D&K Houseware Co., Limited, in China

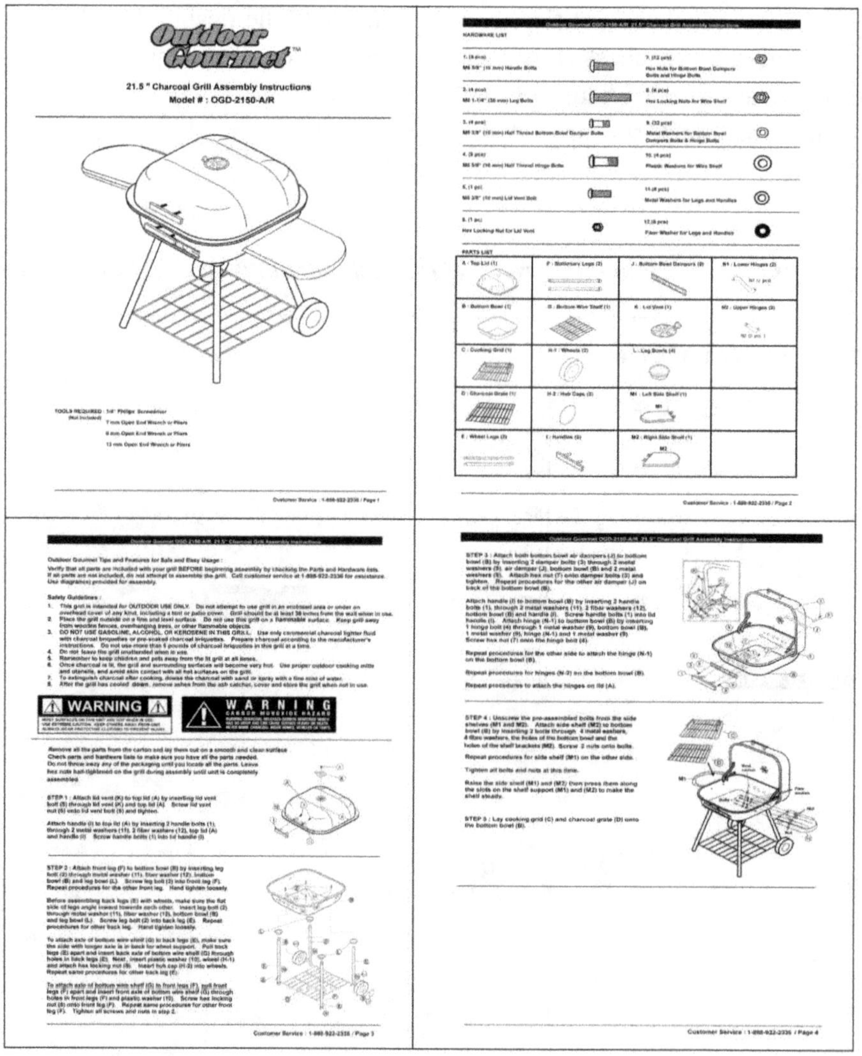

was impossible to contact the manufacturers of these two sets of instructions to determine whether they were written by U.S. or Chinese authors. In many ways, this determination does not matter, for our purpose in this part of the chapter is to simply describe the cultural values that are implicit in the manual designs.

The next sets of instructions show how to change the water pump in two sport utility vehicles. Figure 4 is for a 1997 Mitsubishi Montero, written in Japan, and Figure 5 is for 2002 GMC Yukon, written in the United States. Both are factory service and repair manuals. The Montero manual has only two pages, even though changing the water pump in the Montero is actually much more complicated than the Yukon, for it involves changing the timing belt. The Yukon manual selection displays four of a total of 10 pages for changing the water pump, but pages 5 through 10 exhibit the exact instructional design as the previous pages, so their display is not necessary. The Yukon water pump replacement is a relatively simple procedure compared to the Montero. I own both of these vehicles and factory manuals and have carried out these repairs in both.

As exemplified in many chapters in this book, this section will now describe the instructional design of the four manuals based on the eight intercultural etic borders.

I/Other

Unlike websites or health literacy materials, most manuals do not overtly show their individual or collective orientations such as pictures of groups or individuals. However, when this value set is connected to the particular-universal value set, we can see collective or individual orientations in subtle but consequential ways. The unit of analysis for the individual or collective value in manuals centers on the assumptions about writer- or reader-friendly rhetorical strategies. As explained in Chapter Two, the communication patterns of individualism (and universalism)

Figure 4. Instructions from 1997 Mitsubishi Montero Factory Manual

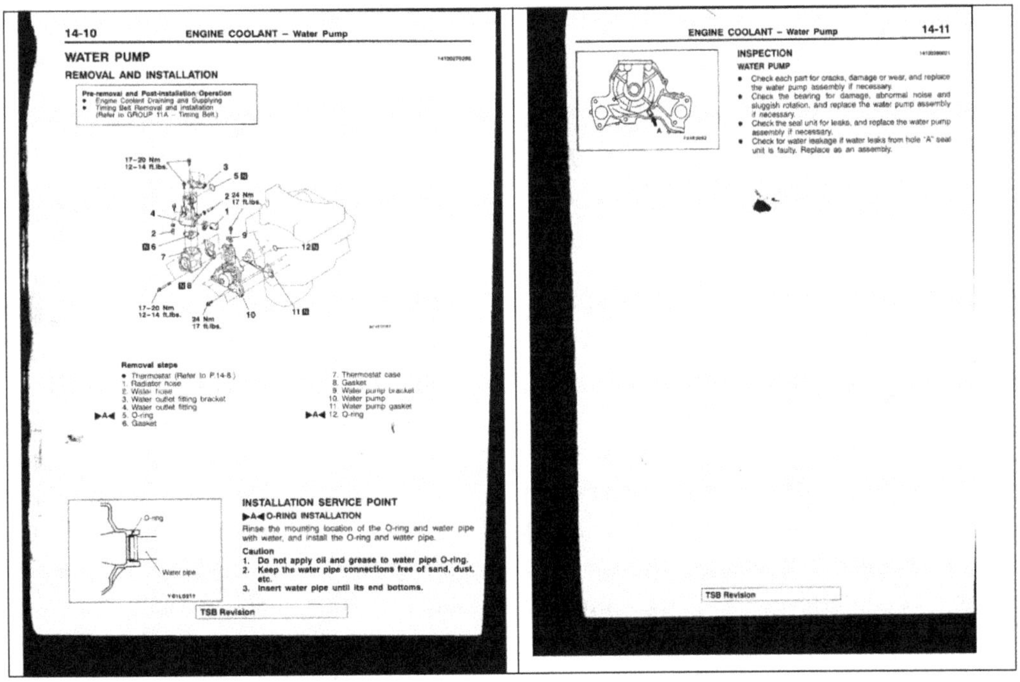

14-10 ENGINE COOLANT – Water Pump

WATER PUMP

REMOVAL AND INSTALLATION

Pre-removal and Post-installation Operation
- Engine Coolant Draining and Supplying
- Timing Belt Removal and Installation (Refer to GROUP 11A – Timing Belt.)

Removal steps
- Thermostat (Refer to P.14-8.)
1. Radiator hose
2. Water hose
3. Water outlet fitting bracket
4. Water outlet fitting
5. O-ring ▶A◀
6. Gasket
7. Thermostat case
8. Gasket
9. Water pump bracket
10. Water pump
11. Water pump gasket
12. O-ring ▶A◀

INSTALLATION SERVICE POINT

▶A◀ O-RING INSTALLATION

Rinse the mounting location of the O-ring and water pipe with water, and install the O-ring and water pipe.

Caution
1. Do not apply oil and grease to water pipe O-ring.
2. Keep the water pipe connections free of sand, dust, etc.
3. Insert water pipe until its end bottoms.

TSB Revision

ENGINE COOLANT – Water Pump 14-11

INSPECTION

WATER PUMP
- Check each part for cracks, damage or wear, and replace the water pump assembly if necessary.
- Check the bearing for damage, abnormal noise and sluggish rotation, and replace the water pump assembly if necessary.
- Check the seal unit for leaks, and replace the water pump assembly if necessary.
- Check for water leakage if water leaks from hole "A" seal unit is faulty. Replace as an assembly.

TSB Revision

Figure 5. Instructions from GMC Yukon Factory Manual

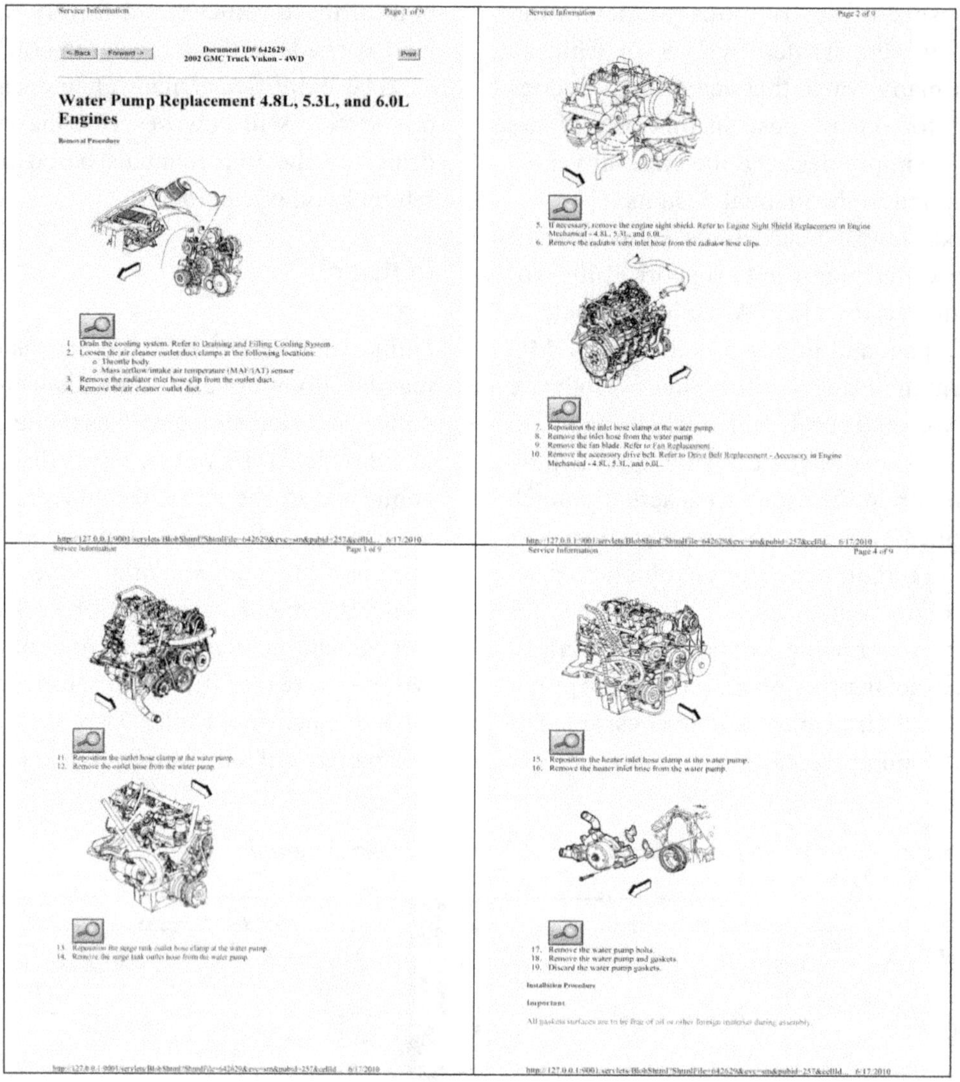

include "reader friendly designs" (Hinds, 1987), which often try to typify the audience at the lowest reading level (dumb-down), creating a more universal audience. In addition, reader friendly approaches rely on overt visual designs such as headings, hanging indents, concise introductions and conclusions, lists, and other formatting devices that signal the content of instructions through the visual design (see Anderson, 2011, for examples of the "reader-centered approach"). Although reader-friendly or reader-centered strategies such as those articulated by Anderson (2011) and explained in Chapter Twelve do not assume a universal audience; instead, Anderson teaches concrete audience knowledge. However, these reader-friendly strategies are strongly connected to universalism, low power distance, and specific orientation, because the purpose of their design strategies is to down play differences in social standing, technical knowledge, and performative capacity and bring this diversity together in public forums or contexts.

Although never stated this way, one consequence of these reader-friendly approaches is to carefully guide (or baby) the universal reader individually and independently through the reading processes, creating independence between author and audience. The results or consequences of this independence are profound. This connection might be difficult to understand, so perhaps an analogy can be drawn here. Reader-friendly designs have perhaps the same purposes and mechanisms as many initiatives in human rights and transparency ranking organizations (www.transparency.org) whose goal is to reduce or eliminate the corruption or abuses facilitated by particular, collective, and diffuse relations through universal and transparent mechanisms. For example, one tools of Transparency International (www.transparency.org/regional_pages/americas/crinis) is to make visible the financing of politics in developing nations such as Latin America, and in so doing, they can separate the particular, collective, and diffuse connections between money and political power. And to make these connections visible, Transparency International must set, be able to communicate, and operationalize universal criteria for a wide variety of people and cultures. Similarly, the goal of reader-friendly designs is not to connect the reader to a specific collective or particular orientation; rather the goal, much like Transparency International and other community organizations in individualistic, specific, and universal cultures, is to provide a stable and transparent platform from which readers can make independent, but informed decisions, without particular or collective influences.

On the other hand, writer-friendly patterns, according to Hinds (1987), reflect the complexity of the author's thoughts with little effort to revise the writing or design the document to accommodate different levels of audience knowledge and attitudes. In other words, writer-friendly designs assume an in-group connection to a precise audience knowledge base and place in the social hierarchy, much like a non-transparent interaction between two people from the same in-group. This writer-friendly design draws on the same tacit knowledge, non-verbal and contextual cues, and other rhetorical strategies and processes known only by the in-group. This non-transparent interaction assumes a significant level of insider knowledge, strongly fostering mutual dependence. It is also holistic (diffuse), therefore rapid comprehension and readability is not an issue. This difference was exemplified in Honold's (1999) comparison of Chinese and German cell phone manuals. Among the many conclusions, Honold argued that Chinese cell phone manuals were often a very terse in explaining many of the functions, because they assumed or even asked the users to seek help from their friends. On the other hand, the German manual tried to create an independent cell phone user because the quality of the German manual rested on its ability to independently provide all of the necessary information.

In general, Gourmet Grill and Yukon manuals are more reader-friendly, while the square charcoal grill and Montero manuals are more writer-friendly. First, the Yukon manual takes 10 pages to explain the procedures for changing the water pump, while the Montero manual takes only one and 1/4 pages, even though the Yukon procedure is much simpler. The Yukon manual follows an instructional design strategy much as Anderson (2011) argues for in his reader-centered approach. There is strong parallelism, effective use of white space, distinction between steps and other information, visual correlations between the text and graphics, and sufficient information to accomplish all that is necessary, not all that is possible. In addition, the reading level is more general. For example, the first page of the Yukon manual presents four steps and two substeps, five of which are used just to take off the air duct. The rest of the steps in the manual's 10 pages are similarly designed for much more universal or novice audience. Thus, it seems to baby the reader through each individual step, giving more details and more instructions, reflecting the more universal roles of readers assumed in individualistic cultures. The Gourmet Grill manual similarly babies the reader through most of the processes, assuming a lower level of readership or more generalized population. Figure 6 demonstrates a very low technical and reading level.

Although this manual does not have this many of the reader-center strategies that Anderson (2011), it does carefully guide the reader through the entire process.

On the other hand, much like the discussion of eBay advertisements in India and China described in Chapter Five, the Montero manual defines the audience much more particularly, with clearly defined mechanical knowledge and capacity. For example, while the Yukon manual takes five steps to explain how to disconnect and air duct, the Montero manual simply shows an arrow, indicating developed levels of knowledge that are brought to bear on the specific situation. While the Yukon manual takes three written steps demonstrating how to take the bolts off, then the water pump, and discarding of the gasket, the Montero manual has an arrow. In addition, the Yukon manual gives no technical descriptions of information that an expert GMC mechanic would need to know, such as how to inspect the water pump, or the torque specifications when reassembling the engine. Showing more sensitivity to what should and should not be said, the Montero manual clearly and comprehensively provides this information. The Yukon manual seems comprehensive, but that sense is because of the detail for a more general audience. The Montero manual reflects the understanding that collective and particular cultures have of the very specific roles, knowledge, and responsibilities of each person in the collective unit. The square charcoal grill manual strongly resembles the Montero manual from this point of view, for it is similarly terse, assuming a much writer-friendly approach.

Rules Orientation and Status

Rules orientation and status combine nicely for this discussion of the manual design. In addition to reader-friendly approaches described earlier, universalism usually means emphasizing the process, a strategy that strongly correlates with achievement orientation. Particularism usually means emphasizing the power relations and roles, which are rarely explicit but always functioning. This strategy is very common in ascriptive cultures. Much like the discussion of human rights and transparency initiatives, universal communication patterns emphasize making visible or explicit the tangible and analytical processes of the situation to enhance the rationalization, measurement, and

Figure 6. Step four of Gourmet Grill

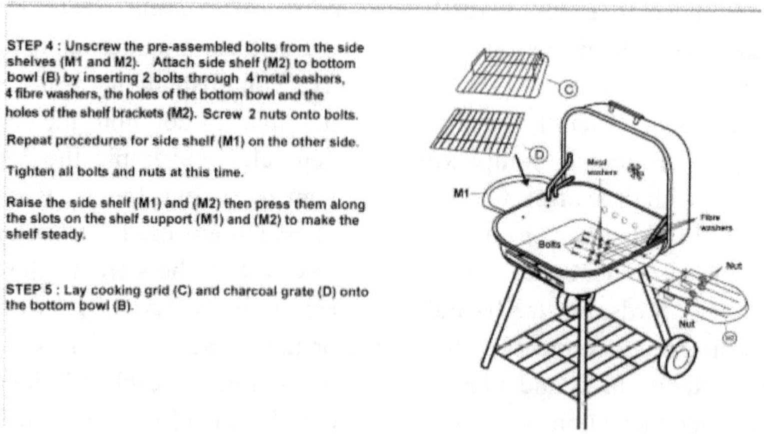

universalism of the processes. This universal process provides the level playing field for achievement oriented cultures to carry out their activities. In addition, these processes are universalized so as to avoid human influence, which is anathema to achievement oriented cultures but the core of ascriptive cultures, a process described in Chapter Six. In distinction, particularism often emphasizes understanding and orchestrating the implicit ascribed relations that need to come together to bring about the realization of the goal. Most frequently, these relations downplay the mechanical or material conditions used in the processes, or they connect these conditions to the social relations. In ascriptive cultures, the process is not highlighted or made transparent because the process transparency is not nearly as important or relevant to the transaction because the transaction depends much more on the power players in the process itself. This is mostly because the power players are the process, that is, the person develops the process his or her own way, yielding an uniqueness and artistry that is very common in particular cultures. This distinction was seen in the websites described in Chapter Five where universalist cultures tend to have heavy heavily templated websites where uniformity and consistency are key components, while particular cultures emphasize the uniqueness in their websites.

Consequently, universalist communication patterns tend to use parallelism, templating, and repetition in structuring their procedures as a way emphasize the standardized and rational elements of these processes. These universal approaches focus specifically on achieving a definite outcome, regardless of the ascribed status of the people involved. This approach is very similar to, if not the origin for, many of the ISO Total Quality Management certification processes in management and manufacturing. These standards were designed to objectively analyze management or manufacturing processes, strictly forbidding the influence of ascribed variables that could make the process very. For example, in the ISO 14,000 certifications, one of the major tasks is to make visible the handling and use of hazardous materials, often described as "from cradle to grave" as a way to standardize the processes in the most effective environmental way. This includes the transportation and handling routes, its containers, and how the materials are physically handled by human beings or used in the manufacturing processes and then recovered for disposal. Thus, it will not matter who carries the materials, or who manages the task; it only matters the process. To achieve this task, the process is broken down analytically, looking at each movement, milestone, connection, or separation, and the whole sum is brought back together to look at the process from a universalist and parallel fashion. As explained in Chapter Eight, this approach is very similar to the US concept of due process in the US legal system. Explained generally, due process means that the process was rationalized and legitimized according to preset standards and without considering ascribed status of the parties involved (blind justice), so that the judgment reached must be validated if the process was followed.

On the other hand, particularist communication patterns emphasize the dynamic and complex nature of the power relations that are responsible for the specific procedure or transaction. From this perspective, effective communication means understanding and managing the relations of the people or systems that are responsible for the transaction. Thus, it is very important to understand these ascribed status of people involved so that the transaction can be carried out, as shown in Chapter Eight when I describe the process for obtaining vehicle permits in Mexico. Instead of laying out the entire process of what would happen and what I needed, I was only told where to go and which authority to talk to. I was told only to talk to certain people in ascribed positions of power. I did not know that I needed verification of a sale of the previous vehicle registered or other specific documentation. It took me several trips to carry out this transaction because I was told only with whom I must talk, not what I must have for the process. From a U.S., universalist perspective, I was expecting a rationalized and transparent process that didn't depend on ascribed authority; rather, the process should have been laid out regardless of the authority such that I could carry out the process based on the specific information. However, the particular perspective from Mexico emphasized my need to work within the power relations who, by default, would tell me what I need to facilitate my transactions. I then had to follow their specific instructions.

The two charcoal grill manuals are perhaps best at exemplifying these differences in universalist and particular values. The most apparent difference is in the manuals' layouts, or in how the two manuals explain the parts needed for assembling the grill and the actual steps. In the square charcoal grill manual, the little boxes or spaces used to house the part vary in its size according to the size of the part that it houses, while the Gourmet Grill manual has the same size of box used to house each component, regardless of the size of the component house within the box. Uniformity in the size of the box, regardless of the size of the graphic that fits in a box, seems like a forced universalism (at least to me, someone who has been steeped in the particularism of Latin American cultures for many years). In addition, the space and location of the steps vary on each page of the square charcoal grill, precisely fitting the need for space for the graphics or steps, while the Gourmet Grill has overtly uniform spacing for the graphics and instructions. From this perspective, the square charcoal grill changes the size of the box according to the component or step housed within the box, a perfect example of a particular strategy of communication. On the other hand, the uniformity of the boxes or space in the Gourmet Grill manual, regardless of the size of the component or step housed within the box or space, perfectly exemplifies the uniformity desired in universalist cultures.

Like the square charcoal grill, the Montero manual also assumes that by understanding the relations of the parts to the whole, the mechanic will be able to carry out the procedure, and its page design is based on what needs to be laid out on the page. Because of space limitations, I could not show more pages from the Montero manual, which has over 500 pages, but none of 400+ pages that describe mechanical procedures or processes are similar; they all have unique layouts with some graphics being large or small depending on the need to see detail; text sections occupy an infinite variety of locations on the page; and the size of graphic depicting the engine, chassis, or other large part greatly varies, depending on which procedure is being described. The only thing that is similar across the procedural pages in the Montero manual is the listing of torque specifications next to the bolts. This is a uniqueness deeply entrenched in making the page fit the circumstances.

In addition to their layouts, the square charcoal grill does not emphasize the linear processes that are so apparent in the Gourmet Grill manual. As will be explained later in this chapter under "Time," the square charcoal grill emphasizes the relations of the parts to each other and the parts to the whole, and assumes that with this understanding, the user will be able to assemble the grill. This is much like my experience in Mexico where the authorities told me the ascribed power relations, assuming that I would be able to carry out the a transaction when I understood these relations, and I wanted, instead, a step-by-step process on what to.

The Gourmet Grill breaks the process down much more concretely and in a more parallel fashion as it lays out the process across the four pages, with the text on the left and the picture on the right. In addition, even though the text does not have visual design components such as bulleted lists and indented, the paragraphs feel very uniform because they follow so closely the graphics, listing the part number that corresponds to the graphic consistently in the text. Likewise, the Yukon manual breaks the process down in a much more linear, step-by-step format, which emphasizes the parallelism, repetition, and emphasis of due process that are so common in universalist cultures. The Yukon manual uses overt parallelism in the layout of the steps, using much uniform white space and repeating the same picture of the engine with minor variations showing how each part fits the engine. It is interesting to note that both the Yukon and Gourmet Grill manual use numbers to outline the order of the steps, while the Montero and square charcoal grill manual use little or no numbers to the order of the steps.

The Montero manual basically is not process oriented. It has large procedures listed by number chapters, and the number resides at the top of the page, as shown by the chapter and page number 14-11 and 14-12 in the displayed Montero pages. But because there is no uniformity across the pages, there is no explicit sense of process. Each section is unique and each page is unique.

Sources of Virtue and Guidance

This value assesses the source of direction or moral guidance of the person, whether it comes from a mechanism from within (inner) that gives the person the drive or whether the person seeks to draw guidance from the outside forces (outer), often as a corollary, harmonizing with nature. Consequently, inner-directed cultures place the individual as the center and cause of activity, while in outer-directed cultures, the human is not directing or causing the activity but seeking to be aligned with the forces around the activity.

All four manuals have elements of both inner and outer directed values, but one side usually predominates. In manuals, this value set is operationalized most easily in the implicit or explicit role of a human being in the process of putting together or fixing the object and how that human being relates to this process. The square charcoal grill is a splendid example of outer directed values because it shows all of the pieces coming together almost as if by themselves, with no human causality. In addition, everything starts from the outside and points in. The Montero manual is very similar, but not as extreme. It also shows all of the outside pieces coming together as if they happened by themselves without human causality, but there are descriptions, in the second page, where the user is commanded in the imperative form to check specific things about the water pump. This assumes a human is intervening in this precise process or procedure.

The Yukon and Gourmet Grill manuals are almost entirely inner-directed because nearly every prose description is telling the user how to intervene in the process and what that intervention should accomplish. Every step in these manuals uses an imperative verb form such as change, tighten, or loosen. This is a simple cause and effect reality with the user in total control of his or her destiny, without a need to align him or herself with the outside forces. The Yukon manual has only one description where it states that "All gaskets surfaces are to be free of oil or other foreign material during assembly" that assumes a user reacting to what he or she sees from the process; the rest of the manual is a user acting upon the environment. Likewise, Gourmet Grill manual only has one statement, where it tells the user to make sure that the flat side of the bottom legs angle toward each other. Otherwise the Gourmet Grill assumes this inner directed person is totally in charge of his or her destiny.

In addition to this clear causality, the Gourmet Grill is full of warnings, a feature common in inner directed cultures because of their more Protestant and, as explained in Chapter Eight, common law legal traditions. Both the Protestant and common-law traditions emphasize the application and integration of specific rules into direct cause and effect logic: if you do this, that will happen. Again, this approach emphasizes that the individual user is in charge of his or her destiny.

Public/Private and Degree of Involvement

This value set assesses the degree and process of involvement across different spheres of life, usually involving a public/private divide and trust. Diffuse cultures are usually collective, particular, and outer-directed; thus, involvement must be holistic (involving all aspects) and relations cross boundaries and are drawn together to form a whole. On the other hand, specific cultures are based on the ease and public trust that individualism and universalism give people in separate spheres of life, with friendship belonging to one or two spheres only, with little or no cross-over of authority. Thus, specific orientation is atomistic or partial, only seeing one aspect of a person's life. And these relations do not cross boundaries, but are clearly separated.

All four manuals have specific and diffuse elements, but one value dominates. First, it is obvious the square charcoal grill manual is diffuse because it shows the whole picture of everything coming together at once. There are three basic steps, which are universal because they have to follow that order, but these three steps are as holistic as possible, showing how all things work together to make the final whole. The Montero manual is similarly holistic in that it shows the whole thing coming together, but it does focus attention on the actual parts surrounding the water pump, and its picture of the engine itself is very general, not showing the details that are not involved with the water pump. This places the Montero as mostly diffuse but having more specific focus than the square charcoal grill.

The Yukon manual shows the entire picture of the engine in all its detail, which is a holistic view, but the reason for showing the entire picture is to show how the specific part relates to the whole. This manual also repeats the detailed picture of the engine throughout most steps, showing how one part relates to the engine for each step, but the repeating of the same graphic and detail (most of it extraneous) seems to imply consistency, connecting this specific orientation to its universalism. What is clearly specific in the Yukon manual is that it concretely breaks down each step, showing specific details of how the parts fit together and what the mechanic must do to make this work. Thus, almost each graphic or step highlights a definite part of the whole, exemplifying a strong specific orientation. The Gourmet Grill shows almost a divided approach to the specific and diffuse orientations. It has a more holistic views of the entire process, which are seen in the Montero and square charcoal grill manual, but it also breaks down the steps much more concretely, exemplifying more of the Yukon's approach to the specific steps and graphics.

Context

The four manuals differ significantly with this value set, showing perhaps that context is one of the most important areas of misunderstanding for instructions across cultures. High and low context assesses the role of the context in the communicative interaction. Low context means that the meaning of the communication resides primarily in the explicitly coded part of the communication, not in the surrounding context. Thus, there is great focus on the accuracy of the explicitly coded text. Low context communicators strongly adhere to and require clearly written protocols. There is a high attention to detail and low attention to intention. In addition, low context communicators try to program into the communication all of the verbal signs and cues to carefully guide the reader through the message, meaning that there is an overt emphasis on organizational and transitional strategies guide readers through the writing. From this view, good writing is focused on controlling for the accuracy and interpretation of the explicitly coded text.

On the other end, high context communication assumes a strong reliance on the contextual and visual cues for the meanings of communications when those cues are available for the reader or audience. There is low attention to detail and high attention to intention. Instead of parallelism high context communicators prefer novelty so as to match the uniqueness of the evolving relationship in the specific context. Parallelism is boring and artificial. It is important to note, however, that when high context communicators are in unfamiliar contexts or they cannot assume that the audience knows the nonverbal cues, they have to code those nonverbal cues in the language itself, becoming more low context in their reliance on the text, but this text is usually highly contextualized. As explained in Chapters Two and Chapters Five, high context, diffuse, and outer-directed cultures use more artistic and metaphoric communications, which draw on natural analogies or systems that the reader can easily connect to.

There are significant differences in the high and low context of these manuals. First, the Montero manual is perfectly, splendidly high context. As you will notice in Figure 5 and below in Figure 7, the Montero manual relies almost entirely on visual communications, which is best at communicating the diffuse and outer-directed relations. The only words used in almost all of these explanations are to identify the different pieces that are part of the process or the torque specifications for the bolts. In addition, in this holistic diffuse approach, the graphic does not present details of the engine that are not involved with the actual process or procedure, but it does show the whole engine. This is a very careful construction of the visual communication, presenting relevant details and hiding the relevant ones. A close-up version of the graphic is shown in Figure 7.

In addition to the torque settings, the last page shows a four bulleted list of things to check, which is a lot of verbal communication, but this verbal information–like the torque settings–is something the authors could not assume the readers would understand from the visual communications and was difficult to present visually. Thus, they had to verbally code it into the manual.

Consequently, a mechanic could follow almost all of the procedures in the Montero manual by simply looking at the graphic and then noting the careful details in the verbal information. Personally, I remember using this manual for the first time and noting how difficult it was for me to

Figure 7. Close up of engine and water pump graphic

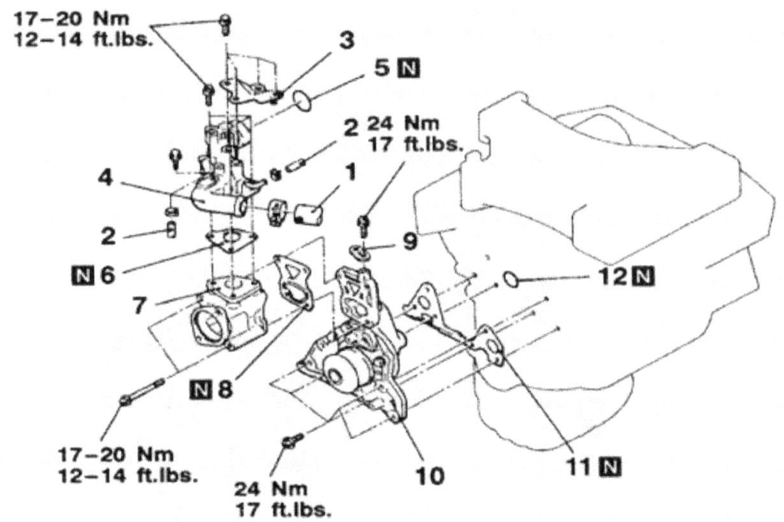

visually follow the process, rather than verbally, which was part of my low context tradition. I also remember that I had to focus very carefully on the details of the visual communication. I also remember, however, that once I was used to following the visual process, I thought it was okay to ignore the verbal information, an error that cost me many hours of work. Now that I am used to the Montero manual, I focus most of my attention on the overall visual process, noting where there are and are not details in the visual information, but I am very aware of the verbal information as well. Very little if nothing in this manual is extraneous or unneeded. The square charcoal grill manual is very much like the Montero manual because it relies mostly on visual communication, but it also uses critical verbal communication when it cannot assume that the author can infer information from the visual picture.

The Yukon manual is mostly low context for two reasons: first, the visuals are loaded with information that is not part of the specific procedure taking place, which means it doesn't have the audience sensitivity that is predominant in high context cultures. Second, it relies mostly on verbal information to understand the procedures. As shown in Figure-5, the Yukon manual presents a detailed picture of the engine throughout the 10 pages, and only a few of the details from this graphic are used in each step. For example, on the first page, the manual presents this image, seen in Figure 8.

The verbal information for this step, which corresponds to this graphic, are listed next:

1. Drain the cooling system. Refer to Draining and Filling Cooling System .
2. Loosen the air cleaner outlet duct clamps at the following locations:
   A. Throttle body
   B. Mass airflow/intake air temperature (MAF/IAT) sensor
3. Remove the radiator inlet hose clip from the outlet duct.
4. Remove the air cleaner outlet duct.

The graphic for this step only explains Substep 4: Remove the air cleaner outlet duct, but it explains it rather poorly, only showing where the air duct is. The rest of the details of the graphic are mostly wasted from a high context perspective because they do not contain any necessary information. This extraneous information would most likely confuse high context reader who

Figure 8. Graphic from step one of Yukon manual

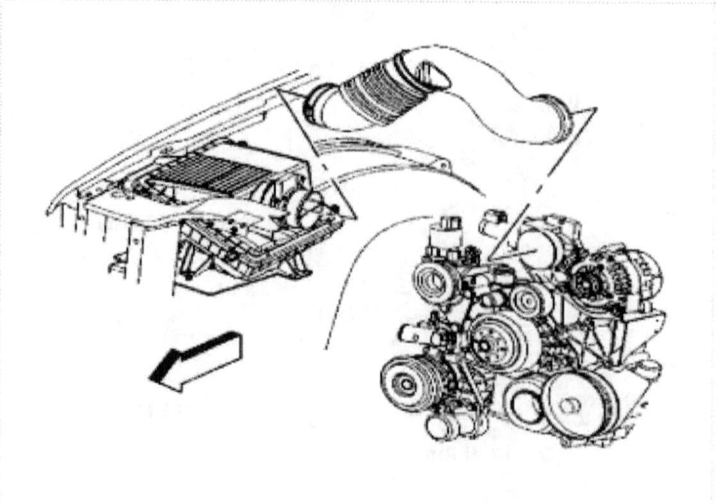

would erroneously focus their attention on the details of the graphics. In addition, if someone tried to follow these procedures using only the graphics, they would fail. The mechanic has to follow the verbal information. Thus, this manual is low context because the graphics are so poor at communicating what is going on, and the reader has to follow the verbal, not the visual information. Or stated differently, the manual is low context because the verbal information is primary and the visual is secondary.

The Gourmet Grill manual is very interesting in the light of a low-context Yukon manual in a high-context Montero manual because it is actually a mix of both values. Figure 9 is closeup of the second page, which illustrates the high and low context approaches.

The left side of this graphic is a low context because the amount of detail and focus of the procedures are in the verbal information. The right side is high context because it shows the pieces going together visually, the only verbal information being the letters that correspond to the different pieces, which were explained earlier. In other words, the right side resembles the Montero manual, and the left side resembles the Yukon manual. If I were to hazard a guess about the development of this manual, I would guess that the Chinese manufacturer developed the right side of the manual, much like the original square charcoal grill manual, but that the U.S. manufacturer demanded or contracted a writer to put the high context, visual information into verbal information, making it lower context. I would further guess that the verbal information on the left probably originates from China because, even though it is verbal, it is written in a narrative form. This narrative form corresponds to more diffuse, outer-directed, collective, and high context cultural values. In other words, the verbal information does not have a document design to it, those strategies such as bulleted lists, indentation, and other formatting devices that greatly aid in taking the reader through the strategies. It is interesting to note the numerous typos and misspelled words in the verbal information, a strong connection to both English as a second language writers and high context cultures, which I articulate in a variety of publications (Thatcher, 1999; 2006). In conclusion, although the Gourmet Grill has low context elements, its narrative format and reliance upon visual communication, making it predominately high context.

Monochronic and Polychronic Time

As described in Chapter Two, cultures view and use time differently, especially in communications. Polychronic or synchronous time frames mean simultaneity, multiple tasks managed at the same

Figure 9. Close up view of Gourmet Grill Instructions

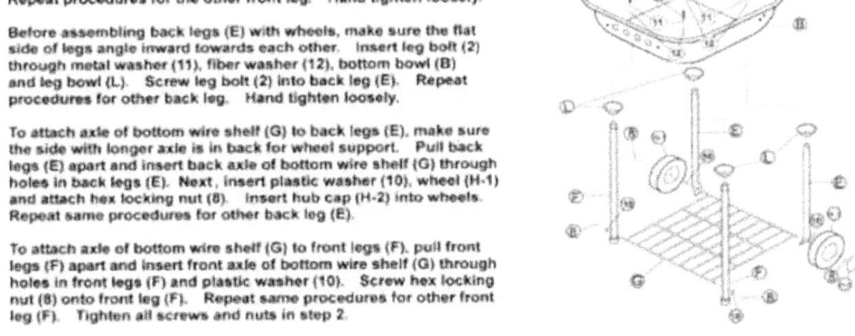

STEP 2 : Attach front leg (F) to bottom bowl (B) by inserting leg bolt (2) through metal washer (11), fiber washer (12), bottom bowl (B) and leg bowl (L). Screw leg bolt (2) into front leg (F). Repeat procedures for the other front leg. Hand tighten loosely.

Before assembling back legs (E) with wheels, make sure the flat side of legs angle inward towards each other. Insert leg bolt (2) through metal washer (11), fiber washer (12), bottom bowl (B) and leg bowl (L). Screw leg bolt (2) into back leg (E). Repeat procedures for other back leg. Hand tighten loosely.

To attach axle of bottom wire shelf (G) to back legs (E), make sure the side with longer axle is in back for wheel support. Pull back legs (E) apart and insert back axle of bottom wire shelf (G) through holes in back legs (E). Next, insert plastic washer (10), wheel (H-1) and attach hex locking nut (8). Insert hub cap (H-2) into wheels. Repeat same procedures for other back leg (E).

To attach axle of bottom wire shelf (G) to front legs (F), pull front legs (F) apart and insert front axle of bottom wire shelf (G) through holes in front legs (F) and plastic washer (10). Screw hex locking nut (8) onto front leg (F). Repeat same procedures for other front leg (F). Tighten all screws and nuts in step 2.

time, and apparent disorganization, focusing on the importance of place, and involvement of people rather than adherence to present schedules. On the other hand, monochronic or sequential time frames mean linked linear structures of cause and effect with an organized flow of events (Hall, 1976, 1983). Polychronic time frames enhance the relationships of a variety of people in rich contextual detail. Written discourse in monochronic cultures emphasize linear structures of topics, a direct topic sentence to situate discourse, and given/new discourse structure. On the other hand, polychronic communicators favor the article orchestration of events, people, places, and issues in discourse. Often, writing in polychronic cultures exemplifies complex syntax and paragraph structures, with many narrative structures in polychronic or multiple timeframes.

Much like the high and low context value set, polychronic and monochronic time frames are very evident in these manuals. First, the Montero and square charcoal grill manuals are polychronic, meaning that there is a very limited order in which these procedures have to take place; rather, the order can vary according to the mechanic's preference or circumstances. A close-up picture of the charcoal grill, as shown in Figure 10, shows the great variety of the ordering of the steps:

In this step one, the person assembling the base and the wooden table can assemble it in pretty much any order he/she wants. There are very few if no universal steps or order here. In not ordering the steps, the manual presents the information in a simultaneous fashion, in other words, in a polychronic fashion. This polychronic approach naturally correlates with the diffuse, high context, outer-directed, and particularist values. In other words, it is difficult to present steps in a linear fashion if you also want to show the context and how all of the individual parts come together to make the whole thing.

The Montero manual is similarly polychronic because it presents the information as a whole, and the mechanic has the option of disassembling or assembling in almost any order possible. There is some ordering here, because the mechanic has to drain the radiator fluid and take of the timing belt before he or she starts this step, but once that step has occurred, the mechanic has a wide variety of ways of carrying out the water pump replacement. This ordering and simultaneity exemplifies a universal, that is, all cultures have to

Figure 10. Close up of square charcoal grill

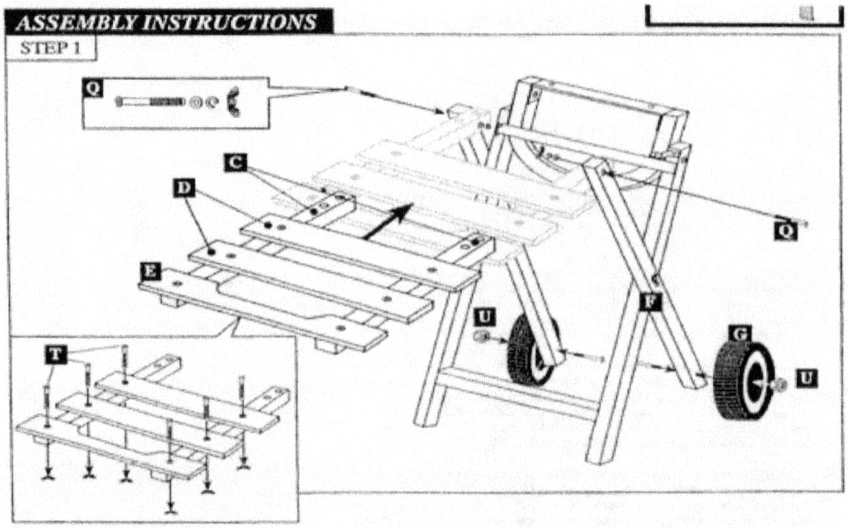

drain the radiator fluid intake of the timing belt before replacing the water pump, but the concrete processes of the water pump can greatly vary.

In distinction to the polychronic time frame of the square charcoal grill and Montero manuals, the Yukon manual is mostly monochronic. Its steps are ordered, and each one of the sub steps is ordered, and when the order is not necessary, there is a bullet rather than a number used. For example, as shown earlier, removing the air duct involves four steps in a hierarchical or linear fashion, that is, step one has to take place before step two, step three, etc. However, when unfastening the air duct it does not matter whether the mechanic starts with the throttle body or mass air flow sensor. Much like the visual precision in the Montero manual, the Yukon manual presents great precision in its monochronic time frame. Everything is in its order, and exceptions to this order are noted, both visually and verbally.

Much like the high and low context value, the Gourmet Grill manual presents information in both polychronic and monochronic fashion. As shown in Figure 9, the visual information implies that this step can be carried out in almost whatever order or fashion assembler wants. This highly polychronic approach is then put in a more strict monochronic fashion with the narrative verbal information on the left side of the page. It is interesting to note that the narrative format encourages a strong ordering of the processes, with little or no room for deviance or simultaneity.

Power Distance

Power Distance measures how inequality is handled in communications. In high power distances cultures, there is unequal, centralized distribution of power, acceptance of authority, high levels of overseeing, and top-down communication styles. Further, in high power distance cultures, subordinates are afraid to disagree with their superiors; further, there is a high level of overseeing of subordinate activities. In short, high power distance cultures use communications to reinforce and exemplify the hierarchy. Low power distance cultures use communications to downplay inequalities among people. As Hofstede (2010) explains, low power distance cultures expect more mutual interdependence between subordinate and authority. Communications between superior and subordinate tend to be more consultative, with the superior acting as perhaps someone with more knowledge, but not in reality being in a higher position. Authority is something to be used only as more of a last resort rather than the explicit framework for the communication situation. Subordinates are not afraid to disagree with superiors; in fact subordinates are often a source of good feedback for decisions is that the superiors need to take. In low power distance cultures, communicators tend to make the communications less formal as a way to ease the feelings of inequality in the communication situation.

The power distance levels in the four manuals seem somewhat contradictory and paradoxical, much like the seeming contradiction that individualism means uniqueness, which it does not, and collectivism means uniformity, which it does not. But in the end, this discussion of power distance helps us to contextualize how power is used in professional communication, especially instructions. In short, the exercise of power and authority must be contextualized in the system to understand how it works, much like the discussion in Chapter Three, which shows that the linearity or circularity of an argument is based on the rhetorical cultural tradition; what seems linear and one culture is circular in another and vice versa. Here, in this chapter, what seems authoritative or high power distance to one culture is probably just the opposite in another culture and vice versa.

To ground of this discussion, I'm going to present side-by-side one page each from the Montero and Yukon manuals, as shown in the following Figure 11.

Figure 11. Pages from Montero and Yukon manuals

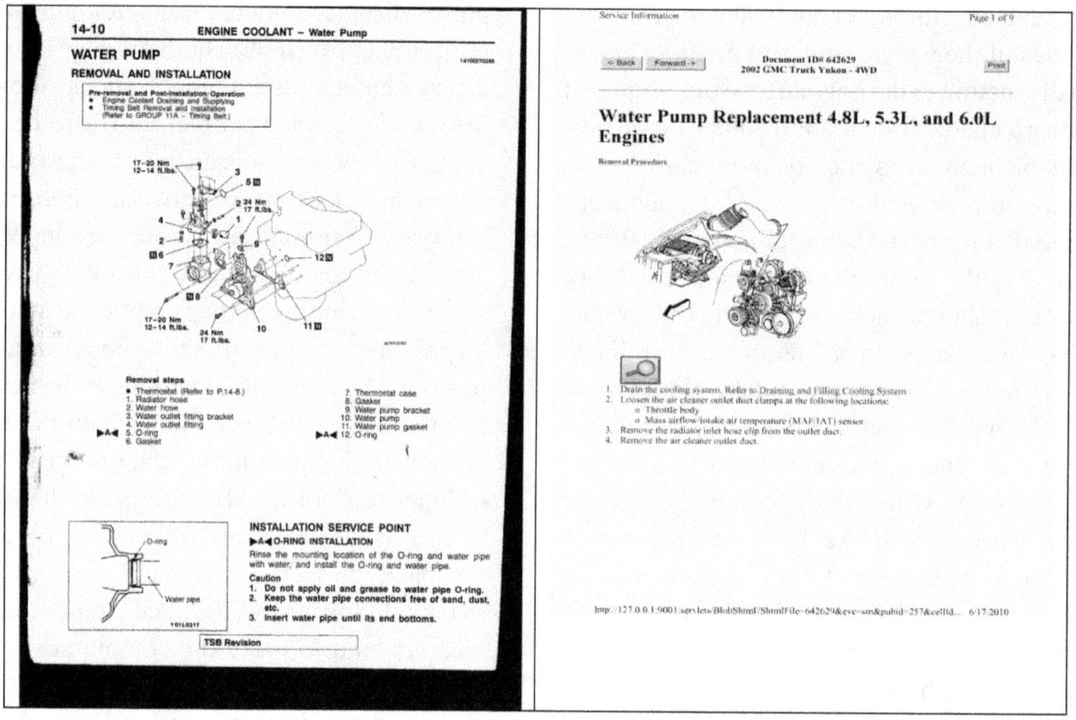

14-10 ENGINE COOLANT – Water Pump

WATER PUMP

REMOVAL AND INSTALLATION

Pre-removal and Post-installation Operation
- Engine Coolant Draining and Supplying
- Timing Belt Removal and Installation (Refer to GROUP 11A – Timing Belt.)

Removal steps
- Thermostat (Refer to P.14-8.)
1. Radiator hose
2. Water hose
3. Water outlet fitting bracket
4. Water outlet fitting
5. O-ring
6. Gasket
7. Thermostat case
8. Gasket
9. Water pump bracket
10. Water pump
11. Water pump gasket
12. O-ring

INSTALLATION SERVICE POINT

▶A◀ O-RING INSTALLATION

Rinse the mounting location of the O-ring and water pipe with water, and install the O-ring and water pipe.

Caution
1. Do not apply oil and grease to water pipe O-ring.
2. Keep the water pipe connections free of sand, dust, etc.
3. Insert water pipe until its end bottoms.

TSB Revision

Service Information Page 1 of 9

Document ID# 642629
2002 GMC Truck Yukon - 4WD

Water Pump Replacement 4.8L, 5.3L, and 6.0L Engines

Removal Procedure

1. Drain the cooling system. Refer to Draining and Filling Cooling System.
2. Loosen the air cleaner outlet duct clamps at the following locations:
   - Throttle body
   - Mass airflow/intake air temperature (MAF/IAT) sensor
3. Remove the radiator inlet hose clip from the outlet duct.
4. Remove the air cleaner outlet duct.

Theoretically, in high power distance cultures, there is little chance for negotiating, rejecting, or adapting communications given from a higher authority, whereas in low power distance culture, communications are sent to subordinates with the expectation that the subordinates will adapt, negotiate, or reject according to the more consultative relation between the superior and subordinate.

The units of analysis for power distance in these pages focus on the degree of variability or potential for negotiating the information or steps. From first glance, it seems that both of these manuals are high power distance because the instructions are given clearly, and there is no room for negotiation. However, both manuals exhibit space for variability, that is, an ability for the reader to adapt or negotiate the actual instructions. But the space for variability that the authors intended is most likely only evident for readers that fit the cultural expectation of the readers for both manuals. Readers from different cultures most likely will perceive a different ability or the length or potential for negotiating procedures with perhaps many unintended consequences.

This is a complicated but very important point. To further explain this, I'm going to show a data set that I use in Chapter Eight to discuss policies and procedures. I was researching (Thatcher, 1999) the training of Latin American accountants by U.S. personnel in a U.S. organization in Quito, Ecuador. I quickly learned that instructional materials that were developed by U.S. personnel did not work well for the Latin American accountants who preferred a different type of detail in the instructions. Figure 12, presents three ways of explaining how to document an inter-or intra-company transaction.

The first instruction is the original approach developed by the U.S. accountants and translated into Spanish; the second was a highly abstract, hierarchical, and direct U.S. rhetoric that I developed to test the situation; and the third was a narrative, detailed, and drama-like rhetoric that I

Figure 12. Alternative methods for explaining accounting transaction

Instruction 1--Inter/Intra Company Transactions	**Instruction 2--Inter/Intra Company Transactions**	**Instruction 3--Inter/Intra Company Transactions**
Provide a list of **Inter/Intra Company transactions and balances** with international offices, other Church departments or Church affiliates (see appendix C for a list of the affiliates of the church). This would include all transactions with entries to both an expense and an income account (e.g. debit your expense account and credit another department's revenue account). Do not include transactions that were recorded using expense accounts only (e.g. debit to your office expense account and credit to other international office or Church headquarters department's expense account). Do not include asset transfers in this schedule. The list of intercompany and intracompany transactions should be summarized by entity rather than including each transaction with each entity. For example, Asia North area should include as a single line item, all transactions with the Missionary department.	Provide a list of **Inter/Intra Company transactions and balances** with international offices, other church departments or affiliates (see appendix C for a list of the affiliates of the church). • Include all transactions with entries to both expense and income accounts. • Exclude the transactions that are recorded using expense accounts. • Exclude asset transfers • Summarize by entity instead of transaction the list of Inter/Intra Company transactions and balances.	Provide a list of **Inter/Intra Company transactions and balances** with international offices, other Church departments or Church affiliates (see appendix C for a list of the affiliates of the church), carrying out the following steps: 1. Make a list from the RLS and revise the movement between credit and debit distribution accounts. This includes all of the transactions with entries in expense as well as income (for example, debit from your expense account y credit the income account from the other department). This would include all transactions with entries to both an expense and an income account (e.g. debit your expense account and credit another department's revenue account). Do not include transactions that were recorded using expense accounts only (e.g. debit to your office expense account and credit to other international office or Church headquarters department's expense account). Do not include asset transfers in this schedule. 2. Review each transaction from the 1601 inventory account (focus on the transactions that are from clearinghouse). 3. Review all of the distribution sales using receipts that finance receives as supporting material. The Box Summary of CIF indicates by entity and to whom and to what account the sale was made. 4. Make a list of transactions that apply by entity (region, Missionary Department, Distribution Center SLC, Family History, each mission in your region, etc.). The list of intercompany and intracompany transactions should be summarized by entity rather than including each transaction with each entity. For example, Asia North area should include as a single line item, all transactions with the Missionary department. 5. Make backup copies of all listed transactions 6. Fill out the report and send with appropriate supporting documents to the Area Office.

developed according to my perceived needs of the Latin American accountants, based on their cultural expectations. I then developed a survey and asked the accountants which form of instruction they preferred and why. On the survey, every South American (15) except one wrote that they preferred the narrative and detailed writing of #3 for two sets of instructions and one definition. In contrast, both U.S. accountants preferred the more U.S.-like rhetoric of #2 in every case. Thus, the more narrative, detailed rhetoric was an important preference for almost all the South American accountants, but the more abstract rhetoric was preferred by the American accountants.

The South American personnel not only seemed to prefer the narrative structures in procedural writing, but their evaluation of non-procedural information (concepts/principles) was also based on their time-based relationship to it. Figure 13 displays the comments from the regional accountants about their preference for the three rhetorics of the *definition* of accrual.

These comments suggest that the South Americans preferred their instructional design based on their experience with the principle or idea being discussed—a sequenced or time-based preference that seems rooted in orality and particularism. Eduardo T. and Hermán P. filled out this survey after they had received the GAAP instructions but before they had started the actual work. And they preferred rhetoric #3, the narrative, drama-like rhetoric. On the other hand, Angel Aristo, Daniel P., and Victor B. took the survey one month after they had completed the work, and they preferred rhetorics 1 and 2 (early February). I actually sat down with Daniel when he filled out the survey, and he asked me: "how do you want me to fill it out—based on what I know now or based on what I knew when I first received the instructions?" Daniel explicitly expressed that his preference had changed because "he already had the experience." This greater variability echoes Hall's (1976) argument that high-context communicators need more contextual information in unfamiliar situations than low-context communicators, but much *less* detail when in familiar situations. Low-context communicators do not exhibit this variability. Daniel explicitly stated that the U.S. personnel's inability to sense their greater changing needs for in-

Figure 13. Accountant evaluations of the contrastive survey of accrual; my translation

Definition Accrual	
Which of the three forms do you prefer and explain why.	Eduardo T: Bolivia: Definition 3 because it clarifies the concepts and definitions that one needs to carry out, citing examples. Hermán P: Peru-Definition 3. It is a better developed definition. Angel A: Ecuador-definition 2. Guillermo A:Venezuela-#1 it gives a better explanation of what is accumulation. Daniel P: Ecuador: I prefer the #1; it is sufficiently clear. Vicente B:Ecuador: the definition 1 because it uses general instructions and can be applied to our accounting system.

formation was a sign that the U.S. personnel were not adept at handling the needs of the South American people.

Not surprisingly, this more pronounced changing need for information often perplexed the U.S. personnel. When I discussed this point with the American accountants, they remarked that it was depressing to know that after finally learning appropriate business writing in English, they had to learn it all over again for Spanish, and it wasn't an issue of translation. In other words, they had learned the forms of business writing in English and thought they were transferable or at least translatable. They did not perceive the U.S. forms of writing as originating from standardized audience expectations based on cultural values. When they realized that South Americans preferred different forms, based on different audience expectations and cultural values, they finally grasped the concept of the cultural content of writing, a major milestone in adapting their writing for the South American audiences.

This discussion of the South American accountants demonstrates an important point for high power distance communication. First, readers who come from high power distance cultures and are in a subordinate position expect the superior to provide a significant amount of detail in telling them exactly what to do, what I label as overseeing management styles (Thatcher, 1999). Both American accountants expected to give general details and let their South American accountants work out the particulars based on each accountant's judgment and professionalism. It was clear, however, that the South American accountants were not comfortable with the general details. They wanted more details, and they wanted the details to be put more in a narrative fashion, such as a story or timeline that strictly narrates exactly what they're supposed to do at that specific moment of time, a perfect example of particularism and high context communication. The U.S. accountants quickly learned that if they did not provide such a detailed narrative for the accounting procedures, the South American accountants would provide a wild variety of approaches to the procedures (Thatcher, 1999).

Thus, it is highly likely that readers who are conditioned by the cultural values of Latin America, such as particularism, collectivism, high context communication, and polychronic time frames, see a lot of space or variability in the Yukon manual because it only gives general details, and in this high power distance relation between superior (author) and subordinate (mechanic), these readers expect much more precision in the procedures; and if they don't get this precision, they have the right to deviate enormously according to their particular, high context, and polychronic situations.

The Montero manual might seem just as–or even more–general than the Yukon manual, especially for people like the South American accountants in Quito. However, in reality, the authority of the Montero manual is clear to those who hold to particular, diffuse, outer-directed, polychronic, and high context cultures. First, particular cultures often defiantly resist the general applications of rules to their situation, and instead argue for their unique situation. The Montero manual not only allows for, but encourages, unique approach to the situation because it does not define the order or general methods of the water pump procedure; rather it leaves this up to the judgment of the mechanic. This particularism, however, is greatly tempered by the diffuse and outer directed nature of the Montero manual, which provides an over arching analogy or logic of how they should carry out the procedure. Thus armed with a holistic understanding of the overall procedure, the reader can carry out the manual based on his or her own judgment. This allows for variance according to the context, time of the mechanic, and particular situation.

As explained Chapter Eight, this rhetorical approach is most likely encouraged by the deductive nature of civil law in Latin America and some Asian countries such as Japan. Civil law provides an over arching, deductive framework that is supposed to frame the application of the case at hand. Common law, which is the legal system in the United States, provides an inductive precedence from which the reader is supposed to build applications or interpretations in a range of constructive behavior that is appropriate for the reader in the context. The U.S. accountants in Quito were following the common law approach when they laid out a general inductive precedence and expected their South American accountants to extrapolate from this inductive precedence to carry out their accounting work. Similarly, McCool (2009) found that Mexican nationals used more metaphors in their online descriptions of environmental issues than their American counterparts on the US-Mexico border, which is an outer-directed approach the environment. The Americans, on the other hand, used much more specific language and more detail. McCool (2009) found that the Mexican sought their metaphors would provide an overall logic for understanding environmental issues, but also flexibility in its approach, while the Americans didn't understand how this holistic or deductive rhetorical strategies worked and wanted specific details.

Readers that hold to individualism, universalism, low context communication, specific orientation, and monochronic time frames will understand clearly the authority of the Yukon manual. As expected, this manual has parallel formats developed in a fairly rigid linear logic with a specific focus on a concrete procedure without extraneous information present in the verbal information. In addition, this manual expects readers to focus their attention on the verbal information generally with the visual information as a subordinate help. Readers from these cultural values will then be able to extrapolate within a reasonable range the variance in their approaches to the procedures, but the precedent has been set, and this extrapolation is limited. Consequently, the authority of the Yukon manual is clear to readers that hold to individualism, universalism, low context communication, specific orientation, and monochronic time frames because these readers expect a reasonable amount of adjustment for negotiation on their part, representing a more low context approach.

For the same readers, however, the Montero page is difficult to process. It is unique, rather than parallel; it is polychronic, rather than monochronic; it is holistic rather than specific; and it presents most of the information visually. This disconnect between the expected communicative patterns almost always presents misunderstanding, but in this specific case, the misunderstanding can lead to more freedom than what the authors anticipated. Since there is no verbal information explaining the actual steps, readers coming from a low context and monochronic culture might expect a wider latitude in how they put this water pump together than was expected by the authors. This is mostly because the authors expect the readers to possess a deductive or analogical framework from which they can govern the latitude, but readers from individualistic, universal, and low context cultures look at things much more specifically than diffusely. Thus, there are likely to have errors in judgment because of this lack of a holistic view of the process.

I see precisely the same behavior in many Americans when they are traveling in Mexico or Latin America. I have lived in South America for four years and have lived 30 miles from Mexico on the border for ten years. In these 14 years, I have never bribed an official, and that's not because I'm extremely honest; I just rarely run into situations where bribes are critical. However, many Americans when they see the polychronic traffic, or the particular legal system, or the collective and diffuse organizational culture, they believe that because it is not ordered in a linear fashion, nor universal, nor explicit in low context ways, then anything goes, which means that they can break the simple laws of traffic or they can bribe their way out of any situation. This is simply not true. First of all, to carry out a bribe in Latin America requires understanding very clearly the social hierarchy, who has power to bend the rules, and how much power that bending will cost. Despite my deep knowledge of Latin America, I am not confident of my understanding. There is clearly a logic to collective, particular, and polychronic cultures, and this logic, because it is not the same as the American logic, is seen as chaos by many Americans; therefore, they interpret it as anything goes. These Americans fail miserably in negotiating Latin American culture.

In summary, the authority of the instruction is present when the cultural values that underlie the instruction reflected the cultural values of the readers of those instructions. When the cultural values of instruction contradict the values of the readers, the readers can likely overestimate the space or latitude they have in the negotiating or changing instructions themselves.

CONTEXTUALIZING INSTRUCTIONS IN CONCRETE RHETORICAL AND CULTURAL TRADITIONS

In addition to the cultural component of instructional design, instructions are also connected to the larger rhetorical and cultural as well as local organizational context. In other words, just as I explain in Chapter Four about information technologies and in Chapter Five about websites, instructions are not used for the same purposes, do not imply the same author audience relations, nor do they require the same information, or organizational patterns, or stylistic preferences. Thus, meeting the cultural expectations of a cross-cultural audience needs not only to design, but the purpose, reader-author relations, information, organization, and style must meet the target audience. To demonstrate this difference, I will summarize the different literacy and rhetorical traditions of Mexico and the United States, which I explain more fully in Chapter Nine of this book; next I will explain the modular situation; and finally I will report on research conducted about technical writing in three maquiladoras in Mexico, which I report more fully elsewhere in previous publications (Thatcher, 2006).

RHETORICAL AND LITERACY TRADITIONS IN MEXICO AND UNITED STATES

As explained more fully Chapter 9, Mexico and the United States have different histories and approaches with written materials used for legal issues, governance, and self-instruction. These differences derive from very different foundations of the countries and roles of written communications for law and regulating behavior. Mexico's tradition emphasized the colonizing and notary-like mechanism of writing, which contrasts remarkably with the U.S. traditions that valorize constructive and precedence-setting functions such as the signing of the U.S. Declaration of Independence or many of the assumptions in informed consent. This is why these documents have worked so well in the U.S, but comparable documents have had significantly less influence on Latin American countries (Alcalde, 1991). In the U.S., writing reflects and reinforces traditions of individuality, universalism, equality, and common law reasoning (Thatcher, 2006).

On the other hand, the Mexican rhetorical traditions reflect and reinforce an in- and out-group orientation that is common in collective cultures, hierarchical social organizations, and particular or relational thinking patterns (Thatcher, 2006). Consequently, written instructions s will mostly likely be perceived differently in the U.S. and Mexico. An important ramification of these different histories of writing relates to economics. Per capita, Mexico has much less print materials (newspapers, magazines, textbooks, books in general) than the United States (Kloss, 2001). It is simply cheaper and more effective (by cultural standards) to hire and maintain workers than it is to develop effective documentation. Finally, Mexico and the United States exhibit different preferences for how written instructions and policies are organized and explained, as described in the first section of this Chapter 9.

Maquila Situation

The roles of instructional manuals in Mexico also need to be situated in U.S.-Mexican history of relations and the maquila situation (see Victoriano Garza-Almanza, 1999). Maquilas are manufacturing plants that are located in Mexican cities that border the U.S. During World War II, when almost all available U.S. labor was used for war-associated manufacturing, the U.S. government agreed with Mexico to allow Mexican nationals to work in the United States legally in non-war related areas such as agriculture. As many as five million Mexican "braceros" worked in the U.S. during this time (Garza-Almanza 1999). Many braceros stayed, but under the agreement, many returned to Mexico. Abruptly, in 1961, the U.S. ended this agreement, leaving many Mexicans either stranded in the U.S. or in northern Mexican border cities.

The large number of stranded Mexicans in northern border cities prompted the Mexican government to study the feasibility of a free trade zone to take advantage of its location to the U.S. and a surplus of inexpensive labor. The result of this research led to the development of the manufacturing industry of exportation, better known as "maquiladora," which began in 1966. The maquila industry has since flourished since its initial operations. There are more than 3,800 manufacturing plants along the U.S.-Mexico border, employing more than 500,000 people (Garza-Almanza, 1999). Materials are imported into Mexico where low-wage Mexican maquila workers typically perform the assembly portion of the manufacturing process. The finished products are then returned to the U.S. or other countries.

Since maquilas have more than 40 years of history in Mexico, many border areas are accustomed to U.S. rhetorical and cultural patterns. Almost 90% of the maquilas are U.S.-owned and many are U.S.-managed. Crucial questions for intercultural research focus on the hybridity of the maquila. What kinds of rhetorical traditions exist in the maquila situation? What elements of Mexican and U.S. rhetorical traditions thrive in this border environment? What elements are lost? How does this border situation influence the transfer of new technologies and what documentation and training strategies best serve this unique intercultural situation? Finally, how do these results explain the rules of instructional manuals in cross-cultural settings?

RESEARCH DESIGN

Qualitative Approach and Multiple Case Studies

To answer these questions, this study used a qualitative research design that was semi-exploratory, capable of assessing and designing communication and training materials in a cross-cultural situation. A multiple case study design is best suited for this context (Thatcher, 2000). First, since there was existing knowledge of maquila cultures, the study did not need the exploratory nature of an ethnography of a single site. Also, since the study sought to develop methods and materials that were applicable beyond one site, the study needed to assess training in new technologies at more than one site. Thus, a focused exploration of how multiple organizations in the border area have effectively developed new training systems for new technologies was the most appropriate design. Since the research design needed to be qualitative in order to assess cultural and communicative training needs, the number of research sites had to be limited. As detailed in other intercultural research on training in new policies and procedures (Thatcher 2000), four sites was an effective balance between the need for generalization and the complex management of qualitative data gathering and analysis

Research Sites

The first site is a U.S.-owned maquila in Chihuahua City, Mexico (250 miles south of El Paso, Texas). This maquila manufactures cruise controls for a major U.S. automobile manufacturer. The managers invited me to research their training processes because they hoped to improve these processes in order to obtain International Organization for Standardization (ISO) certifications. Although this maquila is U.S.-owned, all its management and personnel are Mexicans, mostly from northern Mexico. This maquila had about 200 employees at the time of the study; a small to mid-sized maquila. It has been in operation since 1991. The subject of the case study for this site was the communication processes used to train line personnel in new manufacturing procedures.

The focus of study for sites two through four was the training requirements for ISO 14000 Environmental Certifications for these Juárez maquilas. This research was funded by an EPA grant, which enabled me to collaborate with a Mexican university professor. The second site is a U.S.-owned maquila in Ciudad Juárez (border with El Paso, Texas) that builds complex electronic sensors for U.S.-armed forces. Its headquarters is in the northeastern United States. This site also has all Mexican management and personnel with about 500 employees. The third site is a U.S.-owned maquila in Ciudad Juárez that builds smoke detectors for the U.S. and global market. This site was a small maquila of about 100 employees with all Mexican management. The fourth site was a large international U.S.- and Dutch-owned conglomerate where consumer electronics—mostly televisions— are manufactured. This maquila is large, with about 4,000 employees. All managers and personnel are Mexican.

The units of analysis for all four cases focused on the relationships of U.S. and Mexican rhetorical traditions, border maquila situations, and training in new technologies.

Data Gathering and Analysis

Data gathering took place in two phases: The first stage, completed in less than a year, exclusively focuses on the training patterns of the first maquila. At its completion, the next stage, which lasted two years, tested the series of hypothesis and theories (Flick, 2002) developed from the first site. At all four sites, this study utilized a variety of data collection methods, which is the strength of the case study design (Flick, 2002). The data collection followed three basic stages common to qualitative research: ethnographic exploration, examination of the four cases, and the post study.

Stage One

At all four sites, this study used five ethnographic explorations of the culture and discourse of the two organizations: (1) analysis of the physical and social setting to understand broad communication and document cycling patterns. (2) Analysis of managerial procedures, policy, and company information to see how the corporate culture fits the contrasting cultural and social values. (3) Formal and informal interviews about the corporate culture and discourse patterns. (4) Exploratory observations of social interactions and management procedures. (5) Collection of, and interviews about, previous discourse to note genres and discourse conventions.

Before we began formal data gathering of sites two through four, we held a roundtable meeting with 15 environmental engineers from major maquilas in Juárez. The meeting was held at La Autonomous University of Ciudad Juárez (UACJ). In the meeting, a UACJ M.S. student and researcher for this grant guided the group through a 21-question discussion of ISO 14000 implementation in Juárez maquilas. This M.S. student and my co-principal investigator for the study, Garza-Almanza (UACJ professor of environmental engineering), created this diagnostic questionnaire as a way to assess their level of ISO 14000 implementation.

Stage Two

The second stage used six interactionist and ethnomethodological designs to examine the interactions of the four cases (Thatcher, 2001): (1) Collection of all key documents in the discourse project. (2) Observations and logs of social interactions such as formal and informal meetings, negotiations, and reviews among authors/writers, reviewers, and readers. (3) Discourse analysis of all key documents (Flicke, 2002); (4) Process- and discourse-based interviews of authors/writers, reviewers, and readers about their key processes and products of the discourse project. (5) Discourse-based preference surveys) asking informants to choose between different rhetorics (Thatcher, 1999). (6) Qualitative and quantitative surveys. I used thematic coding to study sites two through four (Flick, 2002) and evaluated the data in light of what I observed in site 1, researched in South America (Thatcher, 1999), and read in existing literature. I also used theoretical coding or grounded theory (Flick, 2002) to build a new and dynamic theoretical framework for the data.

Stage Three

The third stage was post-study research to check my findings with the participants, verify my information, and explore the typicality of this research situation. I carried out retrospective, formal, and informal interviews of authors/writers, audiences, and reviewers.

RESEARCH RESULTS

The results of this study show that instructional manuals in U.S.-owned—but Mexican managed—maquilas needs to address the complex border situation, comprising elements of both Mexican and U.S. rhetorical and cultural traditions. The results also show that U.S. researchers and technical communicators cannot assume the same relation of technology and documentation in other cultures, and they need to denaturalize their assumptions about these relationships to understand them even better in U.S. cultural contexts. This result sections first narrates the complete picture of technology transfer in the Chihuahuan maquila, which serves as a nice introduction to specific issues that will be explored in the subsequent four sections.

Technology Transfer in Chihuahua Maquila

The Chihuahuan maquila site, which was recently put into operation, allowed me to interview those who were still familiar with integrating the new technologies sent from the home factory in Ohio. The head manufacturing engineer, Eduardo (pseudonym) related the process of instructing his Mexican counterparts in the new manufacturing processes during our interview. He explained that the home office in Ohio sent a U.S.-American to Chihuahua as a head engineer to oversee plant development–four additional U.S.-Americans were sent throughout the process. The head engineer, John McGregor (pseudonym) remained four years in Chihuahua. He received specific instructions from the home office in Ohio and was responsible for relaying those instructions to the Mexican engineers. During the first four years, approximately 15 Mexican engineers were hired to get the plant up and running.

The following transcription of our interview explains that the critical part the Mexican engineers in this integration process was as their roles of "translating" the new technology for the Mexican line workers (my English translation followed by Spanish original):

Barry: *Tell me about the development of the maquila and your work with those from the United States. (Cuéntame del desarrollo de la planta y del trabajo con los de los estados unidos).*

Eduardo: *Ah, when it was decided to start up the plant here, uh, the first thing that was done after building the building was to bring here three or four engineers. One of them.. .was the plant manager for various years, uh, the engineering manager, Mr. John McGregor; he was the one that gave instructions about how the machinery should be setup. (Ah:: cuando se decidió que se arrancara aquí la planta, eh::: lo primero que hicieron la parte después de construir el edificio fue traerse aproximadamente tres o cuatro ingenieros, uno de ellos::: eh, le emplearon número uno que fue gerente de planta durante varios años; ah::, un gerente de ingeniería, el señor John McGregor, que fue el que dio instrucciones de cómo debía hacer la maquinaria).*

Barry: *U hum=*

Eduardo: *Ah:, what was done at that time was that the engineering personnel from the United States in collaboration with John McGregor saw what had to be done and told the contracted engineers. (lo que hacían en aquel entonces era el personal de ingeniería de estados unidos en colaboración con el señor Joe Gregory veían que era lo que se tenían que hacer y les decían a los ingenieros que han sido contratados)*

Barry: *=in Chihuahua?==¿en Chihuahua?=*

Eduardo: *In Chihuahua—what it was that they had to do; and they were in charge of telling the operators [line workers] how to carry out their operations (=en Chihuahua—que es lo que se tenía que hacer; y ya ellos encargaban de decirles a los operadores cómo realizar las operaciones).*

Barry: *Thus, since the beginning, the engineers have been the translators, so to speak. (Entonces, desde el principio los ingenieros han sido los traductores, digamos=*

Eduardo: *=That, exactly (=Eso, exactamente).*

Later, I asked Eduardo about why the engineers had to be the translators of the technology transfer and how they ended up doing that job decided upon the best means of technology integration. Eduardo said that the original U.S. "instructions were very vague," and that the Mexican engineers could not figure out what to do with them. Finally, as their frustration grew, so did the necessity to understand fully the operation of the Equipment. So they ignored the manuals and tried to understand the machinery in their own way:

Eduardo: *Once we got rid of our fear and begin to see how they functioned, we begin to take them apart and begin to understand all of the black magic. Thus, this was when we were finally able to really improve many, many, many processes. It was like EVERYTHING depended on ALL the instructions given by the American engineers; and the people in the United States did not touch anything. Yes, faithfully, we followed the orders until the moment arrived that we begin to have initiative, thus, we begin to see the problems and begin to propose solutions (Y una vez que nos quitamos el miedo con trabajar con las máquinas, este, empezamos ya a ver cómo funcionaban, empezamos a desarmarlas y empezamos a entender todo esa magia negra. Entonces, fue cuando ya realmente pudimos mejorar muchos, muchos, muchos procesos... Este::, en un principio, es como TODO depende de TODAS las instrucciones que tenían dados por los ingenieros americanos; y gente que está en estados unidos no se tocaba nada. Sí fielmente seguíamos las órdenes hasta que llegó un momento en la que empezó a tener iniciativa, entonces, empezaban a ver los problemas y se empezaban a proponer soluciones).*

After understanding the machinery from their own perspective, Mexican manufacturing engineers were able to improve several processes. ("many, many, many processes.") Later, Eduardo then detailed how the Mexican manufacturing engineers—armed with their own experience with the machinery—wrote their own machinery specifications which eventually become the base for the written instructions for the work processes at this maquila.

As the next four sections explain, developing an appropriate design for instructional manuals at the four maquilas has four components: 1) situating the roles of written documentation in Mexican organizational culture; 2) documentation, hierarchy, and information control; 3) understanding the high turnover rate as it relates to problem-solving and documentation requirements; 4) understanding the profiles of technical communicators and documentation.

Writing and Technology in Mexican Organizational Culture

One major obstacle in U.S-Mexican transferring US technologies through manuals is the different expectations in management styles. Much like the South American accountants in Quito, Mexico's high-power distance modes of management correlate strongly with linear technology transfer; that is, superiors are followed with little questioning, including the integration and uses of technology. U.S. Conversely, U.S. managers assume that subordinates will ask many questions and function in a partner-like manner during technology transfer.

In the Chihuahuan maquila, Eduardo and the other Mexican engineers were working in the high-power distance model until they saw it failing; the Mexican engineers were afraid to disregard the specific instructions from the American engineers. However, the Mexican engineers' initiative was *not* punished; and when they exhibited initiative, the plant flourished. It was impossible to interview the U.S.-American plant manager who left six years earlier, but it seems possible—based on my experience in similar U.S.-Latin American interactions (Thatcher, 1999)—that the U.S. engineers expected the Mexicans to take the initiative and learn the engineering processes for themselves. However, the Mexican engineers who were used to high power distance management were nervous about doing so.

Documentation, Hierarchy, and Information Control

This high power distance management mode re-situates the roles of instructional manuals and information control in the organizational hierarchy, becoming almost a complete reversal of many U.S.American approaches to technical communication. In addition to the Chihuahuan maquila, a difference in assumptions about power played an important role in the training for ISO 14000 certifications in cases two through four. The interview was structured around a 21-question assessment of the different parts of the ISO 14000 process, including the role of documentation and manuals in this process. Each of the 21 questions had a 1 (weakest) through 5 (strongest) range of possible answers. The following question assessed the roles of manuals and documentation in the environmental management processes (my English translation):

Concerning formal environmental documents and procedures manuals, the maquila

1. Has nothing.
2. Local administration prepares manuals and documentation when necessary, sends copies, and whoever needs them takes a copy.
3. Manuals and documentation are available for the majority of activities that have significant impact on the environment, and copies are sent and are available for those who need them.
4. Manuals and documentation are comprehensive, referencing all activities with significant environmental impact and are distributed according to agreed upon circulation lists.
5. Manuals and documentation are comprehensive and are revised periodically, their distribution is authorized by proper authorities, are distributed according to agreed upon circulation lists, are available in all facilities where they are needed, and are removed when obsolete.

The average score for all 15 environmental engineers representing a range of maquilas in Juárez was 2.6; which is a weak score. More importantly, these questions invoked a "strong" debate (*polémica*) in the group interview about the roles and types of instructional manuals needed in the organization. Some environmental engineers did not want to document their work procedures because they believed oral training was best. However, oral training had many drawbacks, including the problems of hierarchical management systems and the need for constant re-training due to high turnover rates. Some environmental engineers also understood that reliance on oral training fostered an inability to solve problems and a shirking of responsibilities. Other engineers maintained that traditional lines of authority and decision-making needed to be in place to effectively manage personnel. A few engineers strongly asserted their right to limit the amount of instructional manuals so as to maintain their control of the manufacturing processes.

Victoriano Garza-Almanza, my Mexican colleague in this EPA-sponsored study, had written the 21-question assessment and, knowing my approach to the problem, listened to the debate and then asked my opinion. I told him that I believe that the issues of high turnover rates and low problem solving skills (to be discussed later) could be addressed by better-written instructional manuals. Two engineers vehemently disagreed with me, never linking problem-solving and effective training to written manuals. From their perspective, the best training was to have the on-site engineer on site to oversee all functions at all times. They feared that written manuals brought line worker independence, which could introduce errors into the manufacturing process.

Another maquila "environmental engineer" who was an M.D. serving as the health and environmental specialist for the smoke-detector maquila immediately saw the link between high-power distance modes of management and problem solving skills at her maquila. She quickly challenged the two engineers about their high-power distance methods. Garza-Almanza then explored his general frustration that hierarchical management styles promote passivity in Mexican line workers, a passivity that he sees in Mexican culture in general, regarding instruction in new technologies. From his perspective, there is great resistance to empowering employees to solve problems or influence policy, procedures, or workplace practices. This high- powered distance relationship was not isolated to this group interview. Lines of authority in all four maquilas were very clear. Rarely were subordinates in positions to influence training, and authority figures were very system to writing instructional manuals because they felt they would lose power.

Turnover, Problem-Solving, and Documentation

This high-power organizational culture combined with a high turnover rate for employees worked against a culture of effective training. Since managers or superiors at all four maquilas insisted on maintaining control through interpersonal power relations, this type of training methods takes much time to develop so that it functions well (see Victor, 1992, on this point). However, the maquila industry is consistently plagued by high turnover rates and limited training budgets. In good economic times with plenty of job opportunities, many employees job hop—that is, move from job to job looking for the best wages and situations. However, in the maquila industry during the study (August 2003-December 2004), a large number of maquilas laid off employees because a sizable number of maquilas moved their operations to Asia where production costs are lower. As a result, most maquilas had even tighter than normal operating budgets. Personnel at all four maquilas noted that training was the first budget item to be eliminated. For example, in the large Dutch maquila almost all surveyed employees expressed a desire and need for more training. They were hungry for training.

As Kras (1991) explains, management in high-power distance and high- context cultures require a capable person at the top to orchestrate all relationships. When this person is capable and functions as expected, the organization runs well. However, there is considerable lag time when personnel change (pp. 138-158). This finding correlates with the four maquilas studied. Despite the desire of some engineers to tightly control operations on an oral basis, many Mexican personnel saw a need to change the organizational culture through more instructional manuals and documentation. This desire was sparked by what Mexican management perceived as a lack of initiative and problem solving at the line worker level. Eduardo, the head manufacturing engineer at the Chihuahuan maquila linked "effective" written manuals to initiative and problem solving. When I asked Eduardo what kind of documentation would he recommend that the home base, in the U.S. send to a maquila in Mexico, he answered:

Eduardo: *First, the most basic, that those responsible understood first how things work, the machinery as well as the product—so that they would be able to base their information on what to do. One thing we had here when the planted started with was the contracted people that normally felt uneasy about working and taking initiative ...if it's something new, with initiative to responsibility [is needed] because initiative without responsibility causes, can created many, many problems that can be worse. What's better—the key word—the "WHY" of the things (Lo básico primero sería, este, que los responsables entendiesen primero cómo funcionan las cosas, tanto la máquina como el producto—ya para poderlos basar, para hacer información sobre qué hacer.*

> *Una cosa que tuvimos aquí cuando inició la planta era la gente que era contratada, era normalmente gente que sentía inquietud para trabajar y tener iniciativa.. .. si es algo o un proceso totalmente nuevo, con iniciativa a responsabilidad, porque iniciativa sin responsabilidad causa, se pueden crear muchísimos problemas que puedan ser peores... Eso mejor—es la palabra clave—el PORQUE de las cosas.*

According to Eduardo, the strict oral and hierarchical management mode produced workers that did not have initiative or responsibility. Thus, they were not valued as much as those who used combined initiative and responsibility. When I asked Eduardo how can workers combine initiative and responsibility to understand maquila operations, he commented that fostering a problem solving ability, based on good documentation, was key. In an interesting move, he argued that this combination of initiative, responsibility, and problem solving was precisely what the ISO 9000 certifications produced when their maquila obtained it a few years earlier.

From a similar perspective, in the Dutch maquila, line workers were surveyed about the kind of training they liked most: oral, written, or a combination both. In 30 surveys, only 3 preferred oral training; 13 preferred written training; and 14 preferred a combination. Many of those who argued for the written training wanted the "independence and time that written documentation affords when learning new procedures. None of the respondents linked written documentation to initiative, responsibility, and problem solving. This is not surprising given the lack of operational perspective exhibited by line workers. However, in addition to Eduardo (the head manufacturing engineer at the Chihuahuan maquila), the head plant manager at the Chihuahuan maquila, the M.D. health employee at the smoke-detector maquila and Victoriano Garza-Almanza, all made the connections between well-written user manuals and problem solving—and argued for the necessity of doing it in Mexico.

One of the difficulties, however, in implementing written documentation in Mexico is the strongly correlated cultural values of "personalismo," orality, writing, relatively low salaries and the high-power distances modes of management Perhaps the economic variable is most illuminating. Most environmental engineers at these maquilas made between $600 and $1,500 U.S. dollars a month –a salary well above Mexico's minimum wage but well below U.S. averages. This is an important factor because developing effective user manuals is actually more expensive than simply hiring another engineer to explain the processes that the manuals would have explained in a U.S. context, for example. In addition, Mexico has been described as having a strong interpersonal orientation (Kras, 1989; Osland, et al, 1999) associated with collective cultures and maintained by a strong preference for oral rather than written communication (for a better explanation, see Leon-Portilla, 1996). Written communications, as mentioned earlier Andean Chapter 9, are, at times, strongly associated with official and legalistic communication purposes. Thus, these three variables (interpersonal orientation, dislike of writing, and greater cost of developing written documentation) strongly encourage an oral and high power distance approach to training in new technologies. Consequently, using writing in Mexican maquilas as a medium of training faces significant obstacles that require, perhaps, key changes in predominant cultural values. Until there is a change in the predominating cultural values, obstacles exist that cannot be overcome via written communication.

One force for change, however, seems to be the desire to obtain ISO certifications, which require standardized and written documentations of work processes. As mentioned, the ISO 9000 Management Certification forced the Chihuahuan maquila managers to rethink their views of written documentation and user manuals. And in the three Juárez maquilas that were studied undergoing ISO 14000 Environmental Certification, the need for written documentation seemed to foster some openness and desire for change in traditional Mexican cultural and rhetorical traditions. It seems, however, that without these kinds of "outside forces," many Mexican maquilas will continue with high power distance culture and oral methods of training their personnel in new technologies.

Profiles of Technical Communicators in a Mexican Maquila

None of the four maquilas studied had a position labeled as a technical communicator; following what Garza-Almanza writes (2004): "in distinction to our country [Mexico], in the United States, science writing or scientific dissemination has obtained a social importance to the point that many universities have professionalized its duties. That is, have formally instituted the career path of a science writer" (p. 4). My work with other universities throughout Mexico confirms what Garza-Almanza said: technical and scientific writing exists on a limited basis in Mexico for a variety of social, economic, and cultural reasons.

Although technical and scientific writing is uncommon in Mexico, there were written training manuals in all four maquilas. Who was doing the technical writing? How was it being done? and what was it like? In short, mostly engineers did the writing when they had the time and felt the necessity. Technical documentation development procedures at the Chihuahuan maquila is perhaps most revelatory in situating the profiles and roles of technical communication in Mexican maquilas. At this maquila, there were three employees who did the technical writing, specifically, the instructional manuals for manufacturing cruise controls. These three writers were not called writers; rather, they were trainers in the human resource department; and as a way to improve their training effectiveness, they worked with the manufacturing engineers to create short manuals delineating the line operations. All three trainers had much in common: they were young female workers from the surrounding area with no formal technical writing training. However, all three developed written technical documents to enhance their training programs.

The profiles of the three writers are as follows:

Ana Maria (pseudonym) had worked for this maquila for four and one half years, three of which she functioned as an instructor/trainer and two and one half years she wrote technical manuals. Like all the other personnel in the human resource department, Ana Maria began working as a line worker but was promoted by HR to be a technical trainer because she demonstrated an ability to master the line operations quickly and was able to teach others effectively. Ana Maria was about 25 years old at the time of the interview, was from Chihuahua, and finished only her secondary (middle school) education. She remembers receiving some instruction in her schooling on orthography (grammar/syntax) but no formal writing instruction. She became a writer because she really liked to write.

Lourdes (pseudonym) was the second technical manual writer at this maquila. She was born in a small pueblo in the state of Chihuahua, just south of Chihuahua City. Lourdes was forced to quit school after the fourth grade and work. She had worked at this maquila for eight years, and before that had worked at another U.S.-owned maquila in Chihuahua for three years. Like Ana Maria, Lourdes was also in her mid 20s. She was hired as one of the first line workers at this maquila and had been there "since the beginning." She was also one of the first to create (generar) the job of writer/trainer at this maquila. She liked to write and enjoyed her job.

The third writer was Belen (pseudonym) who had recently graduated from a local university as an industrial engineer. She was in her mid 20s and had worked at this maquila for six years while completing her college degree. Belen was also from Chihuahua City, and like Ana Maria, was one of the first to develop the role as a technical writer. Belen was looking to continue her studies and obtain a MS in Manufacturing Engineering. She liked to write, but her heart was in engineering and was also looking for a job as an engineer that designed and managed engineering manufacturing, rather than as a trainer and writer.

Development and Roles of the Written Documentation

Like the profiles of these three writers, the roles of written documentation at this maquila reflect the cultural and rhetorical traditions of Mexico and maquila workers. When I asked the writers about the purposes of the manuals, they strongly argued for their great necessity and important functions that they filled. My conversation with Ana Mara is representative:

Barry: *What purpose do the manuals have? (¿Qué propósito tienen los manuales?).*

Ana Maria: *What purpose? That the people know with what materials they are working so that each one works well with the parts with which they are working. This and analysis of materials, that they know how to handle the material (¿Qué propósito? Es que la gente sepa con qué materiales está trabajando para que sirva cada una de las partes con las que estamos trabajando. Este, y análisis de material, que lo sepan manejar el material.)*

Barry: *Ok, and about training. Are the manuals an important part, of little importance or very important? (Ok. En cuanto a la capacitación, ¿son los manuales una parte importante, poco importante, muy importante?=).*

Ana Maria: *I believe they are a very important part because if they do not know something, they would be failing on the floor. And if they don't know what each one of the parts does, it's likely they do not know an adequate handling of the material. (Yo creo que es una parte muy importante, porque, si no saben esto, estaría faltando ya en el piso. Y si no saben para que sirva cada una de las partes, y a lo mejor no saben el adecuado manejo de material.).*

Both Lourdes and Belen similarly agreed with the importance Ana Maria placed on the manuals. However, Belen connected the use of written manuals to a theoretical—not practical and rote—understanding of the manufacturing process and accompanying problem-solving skills. Belen argued that the initial training and accompanying manuals were provided for information transfer–to transmit information from one generation to another (era de transmitir conocimiento en generación entre generación). However, the introduction of written manuals forced a focus on "criteria for judging engineering acceptability" and "reason" in the manufacturing process, something far beyond information transfer.

This difference between information transfer and criteria highlights the different approaches to manual development. Ana Maria and Lourdes essentially saw themselves in notary-like functions in service of the engineers. They took the technical specification sheets from the engineers and put those sheets together, with minimal additions, to develop their manuals. However, every change—deletion or insertion—had to be certified by the engineers. Thus, it was not surprising that when I asked them if they liked being technical writers, they were a bit puzzled at the question. They did not consider themselves technical writers, but trainers/instructors that took engineering specifications and bound them in a usable format for the readers.

On the other hand, when I asked Belen if she liked writing manuals, she said:

Yes, it like to because it's a part of design. I don't know if you realized or saw, for example, that each person has her own method of designing the manuals, of structuring them. I like the design and development of manuals. (Sí, me gusta porque es parte de diseño. No sé si usted logró captar o ver que por ejemplo cada área, cada persona tiene su manera de diseñar los manuales, de estructurarlos. Me gusta el diseño y la formación del manual.).

In fact, I had noticed Ana Maria and Lourdes sensed that their manuals were different, but they never used the terms "design" or "development.," They just referred to their manuals as being different.

After commenting on that point—that Belen considered manual writing as a part of design, I asked Belen how she learned to do that kind of design. She laughed and said: by myself (Sóla). When I pressed her a bit more, she reasoned that perhaps because of her own gregarious and interpersonal personality, she was able to tell what audiences needed in the manuals and was able to design for them based on trial and error. Part of this ability was in visual rather than verbal thinking, for Belen had integrated the most visual elements in the manuals. In fact, I was surprised manual design followed many of the design principles that I teach at New Mexico State University in my technical writing classes using Anderson's (1999)*Technical Communication*. These principles include: effective relationship of graphics and visuals, warning and troubleshooting, introduction, and theory of operation. I later presented Belen with a copy of this text, and she was delighted to see some theoretical discussion of what she had tried to with her own technical manuals.

Ana Maria's and Lourdes' manuals were 95% text and contained very few visuals. Most of their manuals were formatted according to the technical specifications of the engineers, not the manufacturing processes of the line workers. Belen had not linked her design approach to to her BS in Industrial Engineering. But when I pointed out the possible connection, she agreed that maybe there was a connection.

In light of these descriptions of developing procedures manuals, I was actually surprised about the roles that the manuals actually played in the manufacturing process. In order for a worker to do a job, on a specific line or post, the worker had to be certified to do that job. Certification required that they pass a written exam, and then pass an on-site exam, demonstrating correct handling of the manufacturing process. When I heard about this certification process, I automatically assumed (from a typical U.S. individual and universal approach) that the written manuals would be available to the employees to study by themselves at their own pace. However, I was wrong. In this training process, the trainers/instructors orally read the manuals to the trainees to orient or familiarize them to the process, and then the instructors took the trainees to the actual line and demonstrated the process itself. Then the trainees were given the technical specification sheets to study. Finally, the trainees took the written exam, which did not really test their knowledge of the procedures. Rather, the exam tested knowledge of rote technical specifications. The technical manuals were only used to introduce—and as I later hypothesized—to legitimize the process. The technical manuals were not an integral part of the hands-on learning that seemed so critical to the manufacturing process. To me, the manuals served much like the notary-like functions of writing that Kellog (1995) argues are still predominant in Mexico because of their legal heritage and institutions. When I asked Belen about this seemingly unproductive role of her manuals, she commented that the line workers did not want to use her manuals for anything more than an introduction to the general process of their line.

The surprising use of manuals in this Chihuahuan maquila brings the discussion full circle, in a way, when understood in the light of predominant Mexican rhetorical traditions. Even though Belen's manuals seemed entirely adequate for self-teaching, of the process, which need not involve anybody else, these maquila personnel saw the manuals as fulfilling a very specific role—of verifying and legitimizing a process that would be taught through oral and hierarchical methods. In this Chihuahuan maquila, I also surveyed a significant portion of the lineworkers, asking them what kinds of training media they preferred. Almost all preferred an oral medium rather than a written medium. Thus, it was quite surprising to me to see in the large Dutch maquila an expressed desire by line workers for written documentation.

Answering the Research Questions and Recommendations for Further Research

The introduction and literature review setup the possibility of hybridity, a mixing of Mexican and U.S. cultural traditions in the Mexican-border maquilas. Did I see hybridity? Perhaps I did witness hybridity, but it was much less than what might be assumed with many border and postcolonial theories. Even though these maquilas were headquartered in the United States, which presumably brought their own corporate culture to Mexico, the traditional Mexican cultural and rhetorical traditions were clearly predominant in all four maquilas. More U.S.-like purposes for writing seemed to surface but not take root, as exemplified by the notary-like functions of writing in the Chihuahuan maquilas. Thus, the border seemed to have little influence on the relations of rhetoric and technology, at least at these four maquilas.

Based on the little blending of rhetorical traditions, it is interesting to hypothesize about how much U.S. technical communication theory and practice is based on the assumption that people use writing to learn new technologies, rather than to legitimize the technology so that oral methods of training can be effective. The lone technology user sitting at his/her desk with a pile of documentation trying to understand the technology is a U.S. vision of documentation, which probably rarely happens in Mexico.

In addition to these findings, this study helps articulate some interesting questions about the relationship of technology transfer and rhetoric. It seems that written documentation was linked to problem solving and corresponding responsibility: a link that Ong and other scholars have argued for (see Kaufer & Carley, 1993, on this debate). Thus, despite the different purposes or uses of writing in the U.S. and Mexico, it seems as though users from both cultures agree with this one function of written documentation. Another important variable in this picture is the growing globalization of economies and corresponding drive for ISO certifications. These ISO certifications require written documentation of work processes. Thus, are these ISO requirements forcing a U.S. or European written rhetorical tradition on cultures that more comfortably work with more oral traditions? What might be the cultural ramifications of this written requirement?

CONCLUSION

This chapter situates instructional materials and manuals, both in their instructional design, based on the eight etic borders and the literacy and writing contexts. Much research needs to be carried out in instructional designs, perhaps specifically linking this area with distance education, the topic of Chapter Seven.

REFERENCES

Adler, N. (2008). *International dimensions of organizational behavior*. New York, NY: Thomson Learning Center.

Alcalde, J. (1991). Differential impact of American political and economic institutions on Latin America. In Thompson, K. W. (Ed.), *The U.S. Constitution and the constitutions of Latin America* (pp. 97–126).

Anderson, P. (1999). *Technical communication: A reader-centered approach* (4th ed.). Fort Worth, TX: Harcourt Brace College Publishers.

Anderson, P. (2011). *Technical communication: A reader-centered approach* (7th ed.). Florence, KY: Wadsworth Cengage Learning.

Dong, Q. (2007). Cross-cultural considerations in instructional documentation: Contrasting Chinese and U.S. home heater manuals. *SIGDOC, 2007*, 221–228. doi:10.1145/1297144.1297192

Flicke, U. (2002). *An introduction to qualitative research*. Thousand Oaks, CA: Sage Publications.

Garza-Almanza, V. (1999). Comercios regionales y ambiente: Integración del desarrollo y el ambiente en el tratado de libre comercio de América del Norte. *Ambiente Sin Fronteras, 2*, 6–7.

Garza-Almanza, V. (2004). La divulgación de la ciencia en México. *Cultura Científica y Tecnológica, 1*(5), 3–16.

Hall, E. T. (1976). *Beyond culture*. New York, NY: Doubleday.

Hall, E. T. (1983). *The dance of life*. New York, NY: Doubleday.

Hinds, J. (1987). Reader versus writer responsibility: A new typology. In (eds.) U. Connor & R. Kaplan, *Writing across languages: Analysis of L2 text* (pp. 141-152). Reading, MA: Addison-Wesley.

Hofstede, G. (2010). *Cultures and organizations, software of the mind* (3rd ed.). New York, NY: McGraw Hill.

Honold, P. (1999). Learning how to use a cellular phone: Comparison between German and Chinese users. *Technical Communication, 46*(2), 196–205.

House, R. J., Hanges, P. J., Javidan, M., Dorfman, P. R., & Gupta, V. (Eds.). (2005). *Culture, leadership, and organizations: The GLOBE study of 62 societies*. Newbury Park, CA: Sage Publications.

Kellog, S. (1995). *Law and the transformation of Aztec culture, 1500-1700*. Norman, OK: University of Oklahoma Press.

Kras, E. (1991). *Management in two cultures*. Minneapolis, MN: Intercultural Press, Inc.

Leon-Portilla, M. (1996). *El destino de la palabra. De la oralidad y los códices mesoamericanos a la escritura alfabética*. México City: El Colegio Nacional Fondo de Cultura Económica.

Osland, J. S., De Franco, S., & Osland, A. (1999). Organizational implications of Latin. American culture. *Journal of Management Inquiry, 8*(2), 219–234. doi:10.1177/105649269982018

Thatcher, B. with Urbina, N. (2010). Comunicación médica y de salud en la región fronteriza de México y Los Estados Unidos. In V. Garza Almanza & B. Thatcher (Eds.), *Comunicación médica y científica en México*. Casa Editorial de El Colegio de Chihuahua: Ciudad Juárez, Chihuahua, México.

Thatcher, B. L. (1999). Cultural and rhetorical adaptations for South American audiences. *Technical Communication, 46*(2), 177–195.

Thatcher, B. L. (2000). Writing policies and procedures in a U.S. and South American context. *Technical Communication Quarterly, 94*, 365–400. doi:10.1080/10572250009364706

Thatcher, B. L. (2001). Issues of validity in intercultural professional communication research. *Journal of Business and Technical Communication, 15*(4), 458–489. doi:10.1177/105065190101500403

Thatcher, B. L. (2006). Intercultural rhetoric, technology, and writing in Mexican maquilas. *Special Technology Transfer Edition of Technical Communication Quarterly, 15*(3), 383–405.

Thatcher, B. L. (2009). Understanding digital literacy across cultures. In Spilka, R. (Ed.), *Digital literacy for technical communication: 21st Century theory and practice* (pp. 169–198). London, UK: Routledge.

Victor, D. (1992). *International business communication*. New York, NY: HarperCollins Publishers.

Chapter 11
Core Competencies in Intercultural Teaching and Research

ABSTRACT

This chapter summarizes much of the previous chapters into a set of five core competencies, including assessment criteria for those seeking to do research or teach across cultures.

INTRODUCTION

This chapter addresses two related and significant parts of intercultural professional communication: teaching and research. Although these areas seem broadly unrelated, both can be assessed the same way with the goal of making the curriculum effective and the research valid. It seems surprising that despite the growing body of literature that addresses the practices of intercultural professional communication and establishes the need to teach and research it, very little research and theory actually explore teaching methods and assessment. Recently, I developed with Kirk St. Amant a book on teaching intercultural professional communication, but this textbook focuses more on how it is taught around the world with little discussion of assessment and curriculum design (Thatcher & St.Amant, 2010). Further, a number of textbooks on intercultural professional communication have been developed (Bosley 2001; Andrews 2000; Varner & Beamer 2004), but sufficient research and theory are not available to guide and evaluate their use.

Further, as I explain more than a decade ago (Thatcher, 2000), very few scholars are addressing research issues in intercultural rhetoric and professional communication. At first thought, overlooking intercultural empirical methods might not seem that problematic because many research methods now assess US multiculturalism and the various social and cultural constructions of power in the workplace, all of which seem easily adaptable to intercultural situations. As explained in Chapters One and Two, however, these research methods are not designed to assess cross-cultural contexts, variables that move far beyond a US multiculturalism. Further, these methods seem derived from and designed for predominant US cultural and rhetorical values, especially those associated with US equality and individualism. Thus, these methods need to be critically adapted for intercultural studies.

DOI: 10.4018/978-1-61350-450-5.ch011

This lack of assessment tools for evaluating teaching and research leaves us with a number of critical questions inadequately explored:

- How do we know that our teaching and research of intercultural professional is communication is not ethnocentric, using U.S. or western research values?
- How do we know that our research designs of intercultural professional communication are generally valid, that is, assessing what we plan to assess?
- How do we know that our conceptions of effective intercultural communication for a target culture are valid, ethical, and effective?

Obviously, these questions are comprehensive and adequately exploring all of them is beyond the scope of this chapter. However, this chapter sketches a broad framework of competencies and assessment questions that begin to address these problems of curriculum and research in intercultural professional communication. These core competencies are based on my 25 years of experience researching, teaching, and practicing intercultural professional communication as well as a strong body of literature available in general intercultural studies. I do not review theory, curriculum, and practice of teaching and research in rhetoric and professional communication, which I sketch out in Chapter Twelve; rather, I explore the core competencies that need to be added to an already effective curriculum or valid research designs.

This Chapter outlines five core competencies that are essential to good intercultural communicators and serve as criteria to assess curricula (programs, courses, and assignments) and empirical and theoretical research designs. The next Chapter Twelve exemplifies these competencies in an intercultural course I consistently teach at New Mexico State University.

The five core competencies discussed throughout this chapter are:

1. Accurately and ethically generalizing about other cultural and rhetorical traditions without falling into damaging stereotypes.
2. Connecting the common human threshold/value sets to rhetorical and literacy traditions.
3. Understanding the fit, reciprocity, and kairos of communication media and technologies to rhetorical and cultural traditions.
4. Connecting fit, reciprocity, and kairos to rhetorical purpose, audience-author relations, information needs, organizational strategies, and stylistic preferences.
5. Transforming "taboo" knowledge into effective and ethical rhetorical strategies

These core competencies become the reference points or criteria for assessing the other elements of intercultural curriculum and research. At the end of the Chapter, I describe a case study for modifying a website following these core competencies.

1. ABILITY TO GENERALIZE ACCURATELY WITHOUT FALLING INTO STEREOTYPES

One of the most difficult proficiencies for professional communicators is the ability to generalize accurately and ethically about other cultural and rhetorical traditions without falling into damaging stereotypes, a problem that I carefully outline in Chapters One, Two, and Three. This competency is particularly difficult for those from more individualistic and universalist cultures (like the United States) and for scholars who unreflexively embrace the prevailing approaches of critical cultural and post-colonial studies, poststructuralism, and New Literacy Studies. However, this proficiency is fundamental to all major theorists and researchers of intercultural communication. Milton Bennett, for example, explains that the world has a miserable history dealing with cultural difference and similarity, as evidenced by problems such as world wars and genocide to dealing with neighbors. Thus, according to Bennett, "the topic of difference—understanding it, appreciating it, respecting it—is central to all practical treatments of intercultural communications" (1998 p. 2). Hofstede (2010), Hampden-Turner and Trompenaars and (2000), Stewart and Bennett (1991), Adler (2008), and Kras (1991) similarly argue that the most important intercultural competency is effectively and ethically managing difference.

The obvious question, then, is how to best deal with difference? As Chapter One explains, the first answer is that intercultural communicators cannot fall into what Bennett calls a "naïve individualism, where we assume that every person is acting in some completely unique way" (1998, p. 6). As much of this book has demonstrated, this naïve individualism is especially predominant in the current methods of inquiry in rhetoric and culture, which have valorized the local and the supposed incomparability of people and cultures. This emic-only approach presents significant validity problems for intercultural research because rhetorical and cultural traditions (and the value sets that underlie them) are not only local. As explained in Chapter One, if we were to treat the two Ecuadorian transit commission letters as simply local practices, we would be dismissing the significant influence of: the civil law in Latin America; the encomienda colonialization processes and structures; the Spanish language; the government bureaucracy that Ecuador inherited from Spain but made it their own; the economic system in developing countries such as South America; the transportation systems in South America and much of the developing world, and the list could go on and on and on. These are just a large scale influences; we could also focus on the regional issues such as the coast versus the mountains of Ecuador, or the unique situation of a Transit Commission of the Guayas Province. Therefore, the hegemonic lens that privileges the emic-only autonomous model presents significant issues of validity for intercultural research and teaching.

Consequently, the ability to generalize without falling into stereotypes requires the following steps:

1. Selecting the aspects of culture that connect most clearly to rhetorical and professional communication patterns. As Chapter One explains, the aspects of culture that most clearly connect to rhetoric are the every day, sense making activities that structure human interactions. The least relevant aspects of culture are the unique, emic, and esoteric, but often most interesting, cultural patterns that seem to make one culture incomparable to another culture. The rhetorical model of the onion with the four layers, including subjectivity, epistemology, ideology, and rhetorical patterns help us ground the connections between culture and rhetoric. One important component of the value sets is to select those values that are most relevant to the intercultural situation. As Stewart & Bennett (1991) explain, it is difficult for intercultural researchers to select the most relevant cultural differences because of the great complexity and overwhelming us that a different culture can present. Thus, it is not only important to connect rhetoric and culture together, it is also important to select those values sets that are most relevant to the communication situation.
2. Setting up an etic-then-emic framework that looks at cultural differences as predominant responses to common human thresholds of activity and then grounds the emic details in this framework. Chapter Two explains eight common human thresholds that are effective for looking at predominant cultural differences. When setting up this framework, it is important to note that the framework is, as

Burke (1968) so careful explains, a terministic screen; that is, the framework will only get at the large and obvious behaviors, and will not assess the emic uniqueness in each person and culture. As explained in Chapter One, this etic framework is much like comparing the sports of basketball to soccer. While acknowledging that each game and player are highly unique, it is not the uniqueness that structures the differences between the games; rather, it is the field and habitus, as Bourdieu (1992; 1999) so aptly describes. Thus, there is an incredible amount of commonality that happens in all basketball and soccer games, despite the uniqueness of each game and player. It is this commonality that becomes the basis for cross-cultural cultural comparison. This approach obviously opens up room for critiques about overgeneralization and oversimplification, especially in light of the postmodern valorization of difference. Bennett similarly explains that "whenever the topic of cultural difference is discussed, the allegation of stereotyping usually is not far behind" (Bennett 1998, p. 5). Our experience, as intercultural researchers and teachers, is exactly that. Whenever we discuss cultural or rhetorical traditions across the globe, almost invariably someone in the audience will raise a hand and make, what we often call, the "exceptional argument;" that is, "I know a man or woman, or culture, or person, who is not that way at all." As a result, we have learned that just as there is a need to make cross-cultural generalizations there is a need to make the ever-present disclaimer or qualification on generalizations. As explained in Chapter Two, most intercultural researchers propose similar methods for balancing difference and generalization, usually relying on a bell-curve approach or assessments of preponderance of values (Kras 1991; Stewart and Bennett 1991).

3. After the cultures for comparison are set in a comparative etic frame, we need to compare cultures at a variety of levels using a bell curve, quantitative logic. As explained in Chapter One, the bell-curve logic only looks at predominant differences, and situates the individual within the predominant differences of the cultures analyzed. From these approaches, a cultural generalization takes on more of a deductive and statistical bell-curve logic. The perceiver believes that in the perceived culture there will be range of behavior, with the people in the culture exhibiting all possible beliefs and values. However, the culture maintains it difference and relative integrity by the central tendency or distribution of beliefs with the exceptions forming the lower numbers at the bottom of each side of the bell curve. For example, in my research (Thatcher 1999, 2000, 2001), I argue that the collective values of Ecuadorian professional communicators and the individualistic values of their U.S. counterparts dramatically influenced their choices of rhetorical strategies. This generalization was based on bell-curve or preponderance of values logic; that is, the majority of Ecuadorians would exhibit collective values, while the majority of U.S.-Americans would hold to individualistic values, but also noting relatively fewer exceptions to this distribution. This bell-curve approach also avoids the problems of stereotyping, as I explain in Chapters One and Two. It is important to point out one key component of this bell curve approach in the onion model is that the rhetorical patterns of culture almost always oversimplify the values of the culture. For example, Chapter Five presents different website designs across cultures and shows that university website designs in the United States display significant commonality despite the location or origin of the university. They are

strongly individualistic, universal, specific, achievement oriented, inner-directed, low context, monochronic, and lower power distance. However, although these rhetorical patterns are extremely consistent, that does not mean that the universities exhibit the same level or degree of commonality. There is a correspondence between the rhetorical patterns and the culture that makes these rhetorical patterns more general than the culture they come from; thus, the rhetorical patterns are much like a genre, which reflects the predominant values, thereby simplifying the complexities of the people and cultures. As much genre theory research has demonstrated (Berkonkotter & Huckin, 1995), rhetorical patterns are much like the agreed upon strategies for solving common human problems, reflecting a standardized approach.

4. Use the bell-curve generalizations, as opposed to race or other ethnic markers, to focus on where each individual fits the predominant values. As explained in Chapters One and Two, cultural behavior is not hardcoded into races or ethnicities. Rather, cultural behavior is learned in a specific context, and as such, we cannot assume behavior based on the genetic features of people. The bell curve generalization allows us to situate one person's behavior in light of the predominant behaviors of the group from which the person comes. Thus, predominant behaviors of a group of people becomes a working hypothesis or first best guess as to the possible behaviors of that person, but the intercultural researcher continually situates and revises his perception of the person or group under study, thus viewing people as situated and dynamic.

Questions for Assessing Ability to Generalize in Teaching and Research

- Are the students or researchers capable of characterizing cultures and rhetorics in terms of bell-curve values, or are they stuck in the naïve individualism of emic differences and local practices or in problematic deductive or inductive stereotypes?
- Are these cultural characterizations developed as a working hypothesis, one that is automatically open to change with each new experience or data set?
- Are rhetorical patterns understood as simplified representations that always have more complexity behind the people that create those patterns?
- Are ethnicity, race, and gender understood as having no correspondence to rhetorical and cultural patterns; rather, students, researchers, or communicators need to situate their analysis of people in the context of their predominant, and often contradictory, value sets, showing how people can be a complex hybrid of a variety of cultural groups.

2. CONNECTING COMMON HUMAN THRESHOLDS (ETIC BORDERS) TO RHETORICAL TRADITIONS

The second competence is the ability to connect knowledge of the etic borders or common human thresholds to rhetoric and intercultural professional communications. This knowledge must be built on the first competence—balancing the fact of difference with the need for generalization—and will serve as references points for cross-cultural comparison and then communication and research. This capability has three core components or strategies:

First, students, researchers, communicators must understand how the onion model of rhetoric and culture functions. As shown in Figure 1, the center of intercultural rhetorical theory is the definition itself, or subjectivity.

A culture's predominant conception of the subject implies a specific epistemology, both of which imply a certain ideology, and all three correspond to distinct rhetorical patterns. Thus, each of the four components shares a similar logic, but each component corresponds differently to the common thresholds or value sets. This distinction is very important because the logic or pattern crosses all four layers, making it easy for students or researchers to confuse a pattern concerning subjectivity as opposed to ideology. Consequently, students and researchers need the capacity to understand two things simultaneously: that the logic crosses over the layers, but that each of the value sets has a common human threshold with a corresponding unit of analysis. This capacity will help them to understand overall cultural patterns but also some interesting contradictions in the predominant patterns of some cultures, and consequently, as discussed later, will help them move beyond the taboo approach to culture.

Second, students and researchers must thoroughly understand the etic borders or common human thresholds, including the units of analysis for each threshold and how each one differs. Chapter Two explains thoroughly the eight thresholds and their specific units of analysis, so repeating that information is not needed here. The Table 1 in Chapter Two is especially helpful because it summarizes the eight etic borders, including specific units of analysis and connections to the four elements of the intercultural rhetorical model. The eight etic borders are obviously not the only value sets that can be used. However, after working with these issues, and assessing value sets from the major intercultural researchers, as explained throughout this book, these eight value sets most clearly connect to writing in professional communication patterns.

Figure 1. Model of Culture and Rhetoric

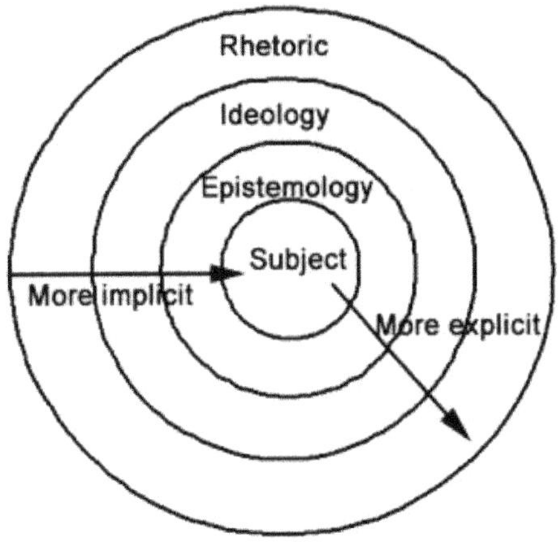

Table 1 helps researchers and students focus on the most valid units of analysis to assess a cultural and rhetorical pattern. For example, is a formal, hierarchical communication an example of collectivism, high power distance or diffuse orientation. It is probably all three, but to assess collectivism, the communicator or researcher needs to look at how the formality and hierarchy create interdependence; to assess high power distance, the communicator looks at the flow of communication and power relations; and to assess diffuseness, the communicator examines how authority crosses spheres of activity in public and private contexts. Thus, an example of communication can exhibit a great variety of values, but students, researchers, and communicators must focus on the actual units of analysis to make valid assessments.

Consequently, as the onion model of rhetoric and culture implies, there is much repetition of the logic or patterns across the eight value sets. For example a collective culture is most likely particular, diffuse, ascriptive, high context, polychronic, outer-directed, and high-power distance; and in individualistic culture is most likely the opposite. These correlations present two problems for students, researchers, and communicators: First, it is easy mix up the value sets, describing "a behavior" or rhetorical patterns as collective when in fact the researcher is analyzing public-private interactions, which is a unit of analysis for the specific and diffuse value set. This table shows how to operationalize the value sets very carefully without mixing them up.

Second, students, researchers, and communicators must be very careful not to correlate together too strongly the eight etic borders, as explained in Chapter Two. Third, it is important to note that that only the outer two layers are empirically observable while the other two layers are implicit. In other words, the same logic appears in all four layers but manifests itself differently. In short, we can observe the social behaviors and the rhetorical patterns, and from most patterns, we can infer the epistemologies and definitions of the self. Consequently, a very important capacity for intercultural communicators and researchers is to infer the implicit inside layers from the explicit outside layers of social behaviors and rhetorical patterns. For example, researchers can understand the conception of the self or epistemology based on the observable social or rhetorical behaviors. This inference, connecting the explicit to the implicit values, is critical in developing intercultural competence. However, as explained earlier, the rhetorical patterns are much like genres—oversimplified patterns that belie the complexity of the cultures that create them. Thus, researchers and students must not equate the generalized patterns with the behavior of the culture that is responsible for those patterns, a deductive stereotype.

Questions for Assessing Value Sets in Curricula and Research

- How well connected and operationalized are the conceptions of culture with rhetoric?
- How well can the researcher, communicator, or student understand the logic of the value sets as it crosses the four layers of the onion model, yet how capable are they of focusing on the specific units of analysis for each value set?
- How well understood are the possible contradictions among the value sets for a given culture and how do these contradictions surface in explicit or implicit uncertainty avoidance?
- How capable are the researchers, students, or communicators of inferring the implicit cultural values from the explicit social behaviors and rhetorical patterns? In other words, can they peel the layers of the onion, looking at the explicit behaviors as indicators of implicit values?

3. UNDERSTANDING THE FIT, RECIPROCITY, AND KAIROS OF COMMUNICATION MEDIA AND TECHNOLOGIES TO RHETORICAL AND CULTURAL TRADITIONS

As explained thoroughly in Chapter Four, communication media are not neutral devices that correspond equally and favorably to all rhetorical and cultural traditions. Instead, communication media restrain and reinforce certain communication possibilities and corresponding rhetorical and cultural patterns, thus developing complexly different relations to each cultural/rhetorical tradition across the globe. Consequently, each rhetorical tradition develops with each communication media a sense of timing or kairos, purpose, audience-author relations, information needs, organizational patterns, and stylistic preferences. Researchers, practitioners, and students of intercultural rhetoric and professional communication, therefore, need to understand how professional communication is situated with communication media and cultures across the globe; otherwise, they might use one of these media assuming a rhetorical purpose that is not suited to the cultural context.

This competency has significant ramifications for validity, for assessing what one intends to assess. As I explain more fully in Chapter Four, because many Western scholars have not understood the connection between culture and the media, they have assessed incorrectly how that media and culture functions together, thus misunderstanding rhetorical purpose and audience-other relations in intercultural professional communication. For example, as summarized in Chapter Four, I recently completed a U.S.-Mexico border environmental project. For this project, we used e-mail, FTP, and web/Internet technologies to communicate with stakeholders. The main deliverable for this project was a collaborative test plan that I initially composed but submitted for review to a multitude of U.S. and Mexican stakeholders, including the U.S. Environmental Protection Agency (EPA) and its Mexican counterpart SERMANAT. To help develop and review this test plan, the stakeholders needed to download the test plan document using FTP protocol over the internet, comment on it using Microsoft Word's review function, and send their comments back to our team via email. All of the stakeholders were required to be literate in these technologies, to have and appropriately use these media in order to participate in the design of the technology test plan. In addition, the test team needed to use the digital media in a cross-cultural situation, something that proved difficult for many to do.

This difficulty in cross-cultural communication occurred mostly because many of the Mexican and U.S. collaborators used the media according to ***their*** rhetorical and cultural traditions, not understanding how these traditions differed on the other side of the border, even though many have significant cross-border experience. Consequently, some collaborators used e-mail in situations or in certain stages of the document production that were appropriate for U.S. contexts but inappropriate for Mexican contexts and vice versa. As a researcher, it would have been easy to have misdiagnosed the mis-timing or miscommunication as resistance, or common misunderstanding, or other weaknesses or faults with the US or Mexican communicators. However, much of the difficulties centered on the fact that the EPA set up the document development cycle following U.S, not Mexican, cultural values. This cycle used e-mail and FTP for the initial planning stages, phone calls for the intermediate stages, and e-mail and FTP for the final stages of the document cycle. This review cycle timing works well in the United States because it corresponds perfectly with the values of specificity, individualism, universalism, and monochronic time orientation. This cycle, however, did not work well in Mexico, which has a diffuse orientation, requiring much upfront time between the parties to develop a holistic, and therefore, trusting view of each other; a more collective orientation, which requires more attention to authority and roles; and a more polychronic orientation, which assumes a more of a simultaneous, back and forth, process rather than the more linear process set up by the EPA. I continually tried to bridge that cultural problem but at times had limited success because of the rigidity of the timing cycles.

I was fortunate enough to have on my team a Mexican national who was working for the EPA in our border area. Both of us knew full well that in Mexico, setting up the test plan needed to be done initially in face to face meetings, then we could use e-mail and FTP to iron out the main differences, and finally a combination of face to face and email to finalize the details. However, the EPA guidelines for this contract would not allow us to conduct the face to face interviews until the test plan document was in good enough shape for review. I was strictly forbidden to carry out these interviews. We tried to work through these problems by "re-purposing" the emails. For example, when we were assigned to write the Spanish translation of the official email that explained and asked for participation in the review, we composed a very different email than the U.S. version. As shown in Figure 2, the original email was issued from the project leader in Ohio. It typified U.S. cultural and communicative practices: it is short, reader friendly, happy, and functional, based on what the single reader needed to do.

Both my Mexican EPA colleague and I knew the U.S. email version (even in Spanish) would not work in Mexican contexts, even though the audience in the United States was similar to that of Mexico. (By the way, most of us who work on the border are fully or bilingual; therefore, the language of the communication–Spanish or English–has less to do with its effectiveness than with a rhetorical approach.) When we communicated this concern to the EPA project team, I was asked by the EPA project leaders to develop a Spanish version that was based more on the needs of the Mexican audience. When I wrote it, I introduced myself (Mexican term for giving my name, title,

Figure 2. Original email letter to project stakeholders

ETV ESTE RFID Vendor participants,

Thank you for your interest in the ETV/ESTE Program Evaluation of RFID in Tracking Hazardous Waste Shipments across International Borders. A DRAFT test plan/Quality Assurance Project Plan (QAPP) was prepared for verification field testing and is now available for your review and comment. In addition to describing all the elements of this Verification Program, this document includes information that was submitted by each vendor participating in the program (Section 3).

At the beginning of Section 3 is a summary table that introduces each vendor and summarizes basic system operating information. Information presented in the subsections includes the system description (with schematic diagram or photograph, if desired) and a description of the system approach for tracking HAZMAT and operating instructions (with schematic diagram or photograph, if desired).

Vendors should review and submit corrections to the summary table, as well as any additional information for inclusion in the subsection that highlights the vendor system. Your comments and input are very important to us.

The ESTE Test Plan/QAPP can be downloaded for review at the following internet address:

ftp://ftp.xxyy.com/outgoing/DRAFT%20RFID%20Test%20Plan%20QAPP/

Comments and additional information for the document must be received by January 18, 2008. Questions and submittal information may be sent by email to xxxyy@xyy.com.

Happy New Year!

Jane Doe
Senior Program Manager
XXYY Research Group
1000 Anytown Road
Suite 190
Cincinnati, OH 45242
513/555-5555

occupation, and location), clarified my relation to the EPA and the project, spelled out the authority relations among the members of the project team, and used a more formal tone. I sent it to my Mexican EPA colleague who revised it even more in terms of tone, interpersonal relations, and authority, making it into what he thought was more appropriate for our Mexican audiences. We both agreed upon its approach and sent it to our Mexican colleagues. The translated version of our email revision appears in Figure 3.

As is evident, the two emails have distinct purposes: The U.S. email is to explain how the stakeholders can download the information, while the Mexican email re-introduces me and my EPA colleague, briefly describes how to review the document, and asks for continued collaboration. In essence, we tried to re-purpose the email and the development cycles of the project based on the Mexican communicative traditions.

However, although many of the EPA personnel and project team knew many of these Mexican colleagues, and they were aware of the project before they received this email, we still did not get an adequate level of participation and input from our Mexican colleagues. A month later, at a joint cross-border environmental forum, the EPA border director formally introduced me to the director of SERMNAT (Mexican equivalent of the EPA) for our border area. He had been put in charge of our RFID project from the Mexican side. In this oral context, the SERMANAT director laid out his review of the project, something he was unable or unwilling to do via email. For many reasons, in this face to face situation, he was able to accomplish his review. In other words, he was using his Mexican sense of kairos or timing. However, the EPA border director knew his SERMNAT colleague would not do the email review, so he set up the oral meeting at the forum. Based on my 20+ years of experience, I knew the whole communicative cycle and its use of communication technologies did not match the communicative cycles and rhetorical traditions in Mexico.

Unfortunately, this kind of ethnocentrism–of assuming another culture will simply use communication media the same way as your own, following the same process and document cycling—is actually quite common in much U.S. research and theory, a point I discuss more thoroughly in Chapter Four and elsewhere (Thatcher, 2006, 2010). To develop this effective cross-cultural communications, teachers, researchers, and communicators need four competencies: First, they need to understand the rhetorical characteristics of the digital medium itself and its fit and reciprocity with the value sets, a point that I thoroughly explain in Chapter Four and summarize in Table 4-1 of that Chapter. Second, they need to match those characteristics to the demands, constraints, purposes, and audience expectations of the situation in their culture, a point that I describe in the next section. Finally, communicators and researchers need to adapt their strategies to the different rhetorical expectations for the target culture, which is explained later as competency #5.

Questions for Assessing Communication Media across Cultures

- Are students, researchers, and communicators capable of comparing communication media to the different cultural values across the globe?
- Do they understand how the communication media is generally used in the target culture?
- How well can researchers and students match the kairos or communication development cycles with the cultural values of the intercultural context?
- Are students or communicators capable of "repurposing communications" to make the content of the media bridge conflicting uses of the media in cross-cultural situations?

Figure 3. Adapted Email for Mexican stakeholders

Esteemed Directors:

Please receive a warm hello from Las Cruces, New Mexico. I would like to introduce myself—I am Dr. Barry Thatcher, and I am working with the EPA on a pilot project using Radio Frequency Identification technologies to track the transportation of hazardous materials between the warehouses in the United States and the maquiladoras in the northern border areas of Mexico. You can read more about RFID in the following website: http://es.wikipedia.org/wiki/RFID

For the pilot project, we plan to place RFID readers in a few maquilas in Ciudad Juárez and at the inspection point at the Santa Teresa, New Mexico International Port of Entry and attach RFID tags to the barrels and cartons of hazmat materials that are transported in tractor trailers. All of us working on the project—my project team as well as the EPA—believe that a reader placed at the Geronimo, Mexico port of entry would give us many benefits.

Since we would like the full collaboration of our Mexican colleagues, we have archived a draft of the plan at the following web address: ftp://ftp.xxy.com/outgoing/RFID%20Revised%20Test%20Plan/

We would very much like to ask you to help us develop this plan. You can download the draft, review it, and send you comments to Ms. Jane Doe at the following email address: jane.doe@xxyy.com.

The pilot project will have no cost for you; you only need to provide a small amount of space at the Geronimo Port of Entry for the reader and help us install computer equipment inside the office at the Port. The private RFID vendors will provide all the necessary equipment for the project.

Dr. Juan Carlos, from the EPA, and I are ready to meet with you to discuss directly the plan and clarify what doubt or comment you may have. Please communicate directly with me.

I am at your orders.

Sincerely,

Dr. Barry L. Thatcher
bathatch@nmsu.edu

4. CONNECTING FIT AND RECIPROCITY TO RHETORICAL PURPOSE, AUDIENCE-AUTHOR RELATIONS, INFORMATION NEEDS, ORGANIZATIONAL STRATEGIES, AND STYLISTIC PREFERENCES

Once students, researchers, and communicators understand the fit, reciprocity, and kairos of media and the value sets, they are prepared to design communications for cross-cultural settings. This section first explains how to assess rhetorical purpose, author-audience relations, information needs, organizational strategies, and stylistic preferences for the communication media across culture. Then it demonstrates this process using a case study of modifying the Texas Tech University's website for a Latin American or Mexican audience.

Purpose

The first common strategy and analysis involves purpose, which simply means, what must the communication achieve without it failing? As shown in Table 2, Chapter Four, the purposes associated with different media differ markedly. When I was teaching in Ecuador, my first mistake was to assume a universalist, precedent-setting purpose for writing: that is, writing should be the norm to regulate and normalize behavior. I quickly learned that in Ecuador, orality served that regulating purpose more effectively than writing (Thatcher, 1999). Further, orality strengthened the default Ecuadorian collective, particular, and diffuse orientations, while writing worked against those traditions. Similarly, in four organizations in Mexico, I observed that writing tended to have more notary-like purposes, which served to legitimize the source of information; but orality had fit well the precedent setting purposes when explaining processes or how-to instructions (Thatcher, 2006).

As exemplified in the earlier EPA emails, email can have different purposes in non-U.S. contexts, something that technical communicators need to consider. First, the collective features of e-mail will map onto collective cultures more quickly and deeply than in individualistic cultures; and vice versa, the individualistic features of e-mail will be more awkward in collective cultures (Thatcher, 2006). Second, since writing is so closely related to univeralist, precedence-setting values and orality is related to particular, case-by-case norms, technical communicators need to consider carefully their purposes for using email, which tend to be situated theoretically between writing and orality (Moran and Hawisher 1998; Kress 1998). Finally, the lack of media richness in email will be more awkward for those in diffuse, rather than, specific cultures (Thatcher, 2006).

Hypertext relates to the cross-cultural values in different ways, further affecting communication purpose. First, hypertext has more media richness than writing and even email because of its ability to convey verbal, visual, and audio information. Thus, hypertext communications can easily reinforce collective as well as individualistic traditions. For example, in recent research (Thatcher, et.al. 2007), many traditional, collective elements of Chinese culture, including icons, colors, idioms, and paintings combined rather forcefully in three Chinese university website communications to contribute to collective, rather than individualistic, purposes for university websites. U.S. and Canadian websites, on the other hand, used the visual, verbal, and audio to highlight western individualism.

Audience

The broad communicative traditions encourage distinct assumptions about audiences for different digital media. First, in collective cultures, email and hypertext can have highly ambiguous relations to audience. They can be taken as encouraging the collective orientation because of their oral-like features, or reinforcing a more suspicious relation, based on their written-like connection to legal and particularist contexts or combinations of both. For example, in Mexico and many other parts of Latin America, civil law legal systems dominate. In perhaps paradoxical ways, civil law systems rely mostly on written evidence often matched to legal codes, with very little oral testimony, which is deemed too unreliable because of the highly particular relations. In common law systems such as that of the United States, oral testimony is an accepted method of discovery and adjudication perhaps because of universalism, while written precedence serves to guide all processes. As a result, in Mexico, writing has a strong colonial and legal purpose associated with it, so strong in fact, that some scholars argue that it was attorneys and their written rhetoric that conquered Mexico rather than the blood and warfare of the conquistadores (see, León-Portilla, 1996; Kellog, 1995). In addition, email and hypertext could encourage universal, level-playing field relations between author and audience, based on their written-like features, or they could encourage particularism, based on their connections to orality. Finally, email (not hypertext) does not have the holistic, nonverbal richness that is so necessary in building relationships in diffuse cultures and that is usually unnecessary in specific cultures. Thus, email is usually more of an effective means of initiating and building audience-author relations in specific cultures, and not as much so in diffuse cultures.

Hypertext, however, is characterized by distance and isolation, which work against collective, particular, and diffuse audience-author relations.

A key example of how these differences might play out across cultures is distance learning, the topic of Chapter Seven. Most U.S. distance learning approaches pre-suppose student-teacher relations based on U.S. values of individualism, universalism, and specific orientation. These values encourage a more level playing field between teacher and students, assuming that teachers are valued more as content experts rather than holistic mentors and that "distanced" interactions are possible because of the presupposed equality and specific nature of their relations. In cultures where collective, particular, and diffuse communications predominate, distance learning relations are different. The particular adaptations mean that online written materials are often viewed less like legal, precedent-setting guidelines and more like adaptable starting points that are continuously revised as the relationships evolve, including lessons and assignments. The diffuse approach relies on the richness of hypertext to highlight the holistic elements of both the students and teacher, bringing out non-instructional dimensions of life that are so critical to diffuse interactions. Finally, the common argument that hypertext will destabilize social hierarchies (Friedman 2006) does not work as well in collective cultures where social hierarchies and role relations are often strongly in place. Thus, on-line instructors working in collective cultures usually reinforce clearly and explicitly these roles and relationships.

Information Needs

Since purpose and audience vary according to the cultural approaches, the information needed in the communications in each media vary as well. For example, in more collective cultures, there is a greater need for role-based and group information in all communications (Thatcher, 2006). This role-based information usually includes formal titles and positions within the group or organization. Collective cultures also tend to emphasize solidarity in relations, common good of the group, and little need to focus on individuals. Thus, as reported in Chapter Five, this difference was seen very prominently in a recent study of 27 public university websites in 12 countries (Thatcher, et.al, 2007), the study of border universities, and eBay ads. First, in most collective university websites, pictures or photographs were rarely of one individual; usually, they depicted a group of people in a specific context in which the roles (such as teacher or student) were clearly communicated. The websites of Mexico, Costa Rica, Colombia, Chile, Nepal, and China generally portrayed students in tight-knit groups, working together to accomplish projects. The language in the collective websites rarely focused on one individual and his or her needs; rather, the most common terminology was either the "we" or group names and affiliations. In more individualistic cultures, there were frequently pictures of a single person, and that person took up most of the space in the picture. It is important to point out that this analysis focused on what was happening, not what was deemed best practices by university website developers or other university stakeholders

The kinds of information needed in email and hypertext communications also differ in universalist and particular cultures. For the more universalist cultures, websites and emails were often a vehicle for disseminating policies and procedures, while for the particularist cultures, websites were a vehicle for displaying specific relationships (Thatcher et al., 2007). Further, universalist websites always highlighted the diversity of their students and faculty so as to emphasize the level playing field. The pictures on each homepage often showed a group of students composed of many ethnicities, both male and female, and some age variation, a combination that in no way reflects the actual breakdown of students. This level playing field was also emphasized by the strong presence of policies and procedures manuals, which were usually one or two links away from the homepage, thus making them easily available for public use. And following closely universalism, these policies and procedures were based on equality, uniformity, and transparency. The uniformity, parallelism, and universal audience strategies allow for the widest readership possible, further emphasizing universalism.

On the other hand, countries that score high on diffuse values emphasize information that contextualizes the university in the community, including local news, impact of the university on the community, and relevance of the university's graduates to the overall well-being of the community (Thatcher, et al., 2007). This was most notable in the Chinese websites, which drew complexly on icons of Chinese heritage to display the significance of the collective whole. Not surprisingly, many of these contextual and interpersonal details get in the way of readers from more specific cultures who want information specific to their problem at hand. As another particularist impulse, the Latin American, Nepalese, and Chinese universities displayed policies and procedures that were not uniform across groups; in fact, they emphasized the differences between each group. Further, these universities did not display the diversity of their students. For example, Kathmandu University in Nepal has both male and female students from a variety of classes in Nepal, but the pictures only show males, and most often professors.

One interesting variable that emerged with the specific and diffuse threshold was the amount of pictures of people and their poses in the pictures. The Nepalese universities, for example, had very few pictures of people, because, according to Marohang Limbu, a graduate student researcher, this public space was not the appropriate medium for something as private as a picture. Likewise, the more diffuse websites had relatively few pictures, and in almost no picture were the people are smiling. On the other hand, the websites in the United States, Canada, Israel, and Ireland all had many pictures of people, and in most of the pictures, the people had big, bright, welcoming smiles.

Organizational Strategies

Different purposes, audiences, and information needs often encourage different approaches to organizational strategies for digital communications. As shown in Kaplan's doodles, Figure 3, Chapter Three, there is a great variety of prose organizational styles around the world, based on the eight etic borders as well as native language. Likewise, digital information organized differently according to cultural values. As shown in Chapter Four, Latin American, Chinese, and Nepalese websites preferred non-parallel or non-templated organizing strategies, while all the U.S. and Canadian websites studied strongly preferred the parallel, templated approach to website design (Thatcher, et.al, 2007). This strong universal impulse ensured the equality of different sections of the website across the sites, and uniformity of the total web itself. In addition, all U.S. and Canadian websites showed a strong preference for linear and parallel web pages across the sites, making for a uniform and simple navigation.

Instead of this templating, the universities in particular cultures tend to demonstrate a lot of uniqueness across each page in website designs. For example, as shown in Chapter Four, rarely did the pages from particular cultures mirror each other. Sometimes, the format was similar, but some aesthetic feature is either added or altered in some way to preserve uniqueness. The universities in Latin America, in particular, also emphasized more aesthetic elements in their display of uniqueness, using art, symbols, or collages of scenes. Most departments in Latin American websites had their own unique logo and own unique way of presenting their information, which is indicative of a particular environment. Uniqueness—rather than the consistency of templating—was a common feature in website from particular cultures.

Thus, all the advice given in U.S. website design textbooks that emphasize parallelism, uniformity, and consistency simply does not fit more particular cultures. McCool (2007) also found that contrary to much advice given in U.S. textbooks, using metaphors to organize websites can be effective in cross-cultural situations because analytical website organizations are actually more culturally specific than metaphors, especially natural metaphors such as animals or birds. In diffuse cultures, metaphors or other global organizing strategies were frequently employed so as to increase a diffuse understanding of the communication.

Stylistic Preferences

Style, or the communicative stance or posture of communications, varies according to different purposes, audiences, information, and organization. For example, in cultures where individualism predominates, there is a strong preference of personal expressions of individual beliefs; rarely are those beliefs tied to an overriding holistic philosophy; and they are simply reduced to the individual (Stewart and Bennett, 1991). Thus, expressions such as "I believe," or "I feel" or "my opinion is" occur very frequently. On the other hand, in collective cultures, style tends to be more formal, which addresses the roles in social hierarchy, and more group-oriented, stressing the "we" instead of the "I" orientation.

In universalist cultures, communicative styles tend to be less formal as an effort to downplay social hierarchies; in addition, they have more overt signposting of organizing strategies; and word choice and information structure are developed for the lowest common reading style ("fifth-grade reading level). For example, Chapter Five shows that the universal orientation of the U.S. and Canadian websites was also strongly encouraged by their universal audience strategies. The vocabulary choice and syntax, technical content, and assumptions of knowledge about the university were designed for the lowest common denominator so that as many kinds of people as possible could understand. This reduction of the reading level has the important purpose of granting almost universal access to the information. In contrast, in particular cultures, more attention is placed on the uniqueness and sophistication of the particular readers and context, rather than "dumbing down" the style so as to make it more universal.

Finally, in specific cultures, the style tends to be much more direct and focused on the issue at hand. This usually manifests itself as direct topic sentences and thesis statements, which orient the reader to what follows. It also includes a lot of metadiscourse (Williams, 2010), which breaks the information down into specific categories with the goal of helping the reader process the information carefully. On the other hand, diffuse styles are indirect because issues have to be understood holistically. Often, diffuse styles are much more artistic and unique, representing the uniqueness of the situation.

CASE STUDY OF ADAPTING TEXAS TECH UNIVERSITY'S WEBSITE TO THE MEXICAN CULTURAL TRADITION: GUIDELINES FOR U.S. WEB COMMUNICATORS

As a guide for professional communication, the following case illustrates many of the adaptations needed for effective cross-cultural communication in digital media, university websites. This case was first reported elsewhere (Thatcher, 2009), but I am integrating it into this chapter as an example of this competence. This case study is based on adapting Texas Tech's University website to meet the expectations of a Mexican communicative and cultural tradition. This section follows the same format of purpose, audiences, information, organization, and style.

Since much of the information will come from the home page, Figure 4 displays the Texas Tech website's homepage.

Purpose

As is evident, this homepage very closely reflects the cultural values of individualism, universalism, and specific orientation. This is evident by the single person alone sitting down, the use of links that separate people according to categories, and little overt mixing of people across spheres. Accordingly, one major purpose of this website is to direct an individual reader (student, parent, faculty, etc) rapidly and equally to the right navigational paths to obtain information specific to her problems and circumstances. If the reader is not able to access information quickly that is specific to her individual needs, this website has failed. In a Mexican communicative tradition, however, one major purpose of university websites is to encourage collective knowledge and community solidarity. Thus, adapting Texas Tech's homepage for the Mexican communicative tradition might include the following:

- **Individual→ Collective.** This adaptation requires much less focus on the individual reader wanting as fast access as possible to her immediate needs and more focus on the common knowledge needed by members of Texas Tech as a community to function effectively. This change would mean much more prominence of the history of the university, its foundation, and its role in current local, state, and national issues.
- **Universal→Particular.** Here, the website developer would downplay using the website as a vehicle for disseminating information so as to enhance universal application of policies and procedures and emphasize instead links to organizational structures, roles, and important relationships at the university. From this information, readers could understand how university relations work, such as student-teacher and administrator-faculty. In other words, instead of telling the reader how to do something, it

Figure 4. Texas Tech Homepage

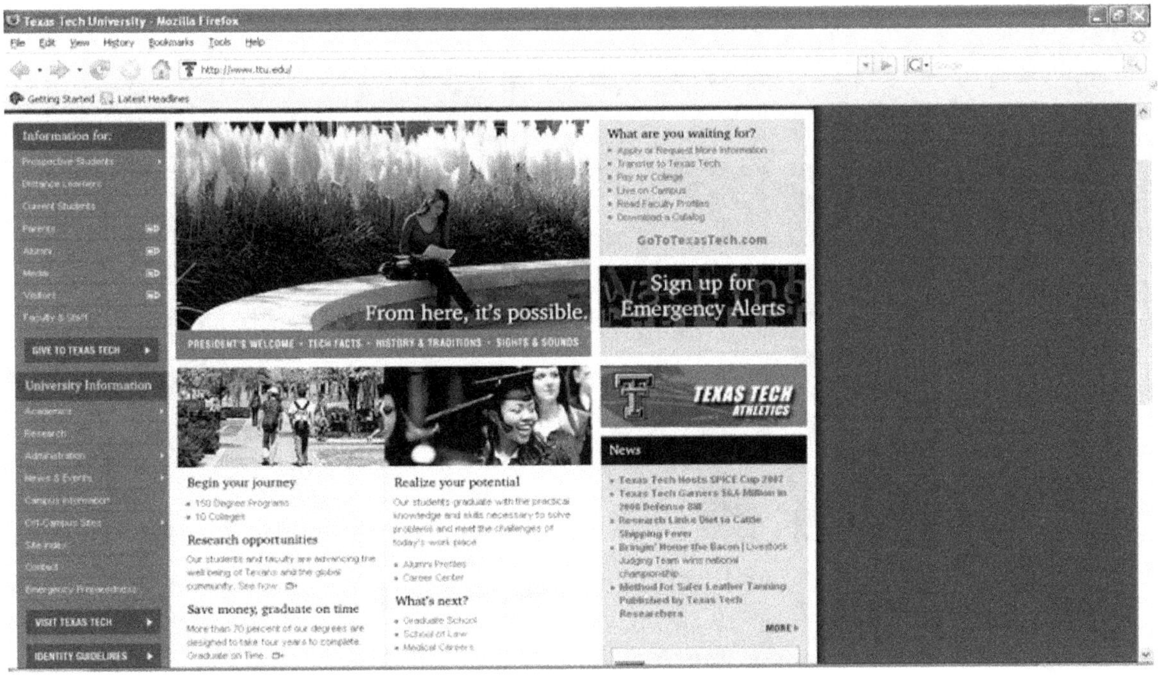

would direct readers to the right people through which they could accomplish their goals.

- **Specific→ Diffuse.** This adaptation requires redesigning the links topically instead of by specific type of person (such as student, faculty, community). These topics would include holistic views of the student body, the Texas Tech educational philosophy, Texas Tech campus, and Texas. Included in these links would be connections between the university and surrounding community and the role of education in the overall development of a person.

Audience

As designed, this home page assumes a reader very largely independent of—and equal to—the author, processing universalized information at will, and designed for his or her specific needs at the moment. Adapting these U.S. values to fit more the expectations of audiences will include the following:

- **Individual→ Collective.** Instead of the independence assumed by this website, the web communicator could assume a natural co-dependence based on concrete roles and relations. Thus, much of the language of "you can do it" needs to be changed to reflect a you and the university (through faculty, staff, and administrators) can do it together.
- **Universal→Particular.** The audience assumed in the Texas Tech website is one of a level playing field. Neither the author (university) or its readers is more important than the other. In fact, the student-center focus is an important hallmark of universalism, of treating everybody equally. Interestingly, the only role articulated on this home page is the president's link. Because this link is so compelling in its cultural context, it is pasted in Figure 5.

In a classic U.S. audience assumption, the photograph in this picture greatly downplays the distance between the president and his students

Figure 5. Texas Tech University's homepage of its President

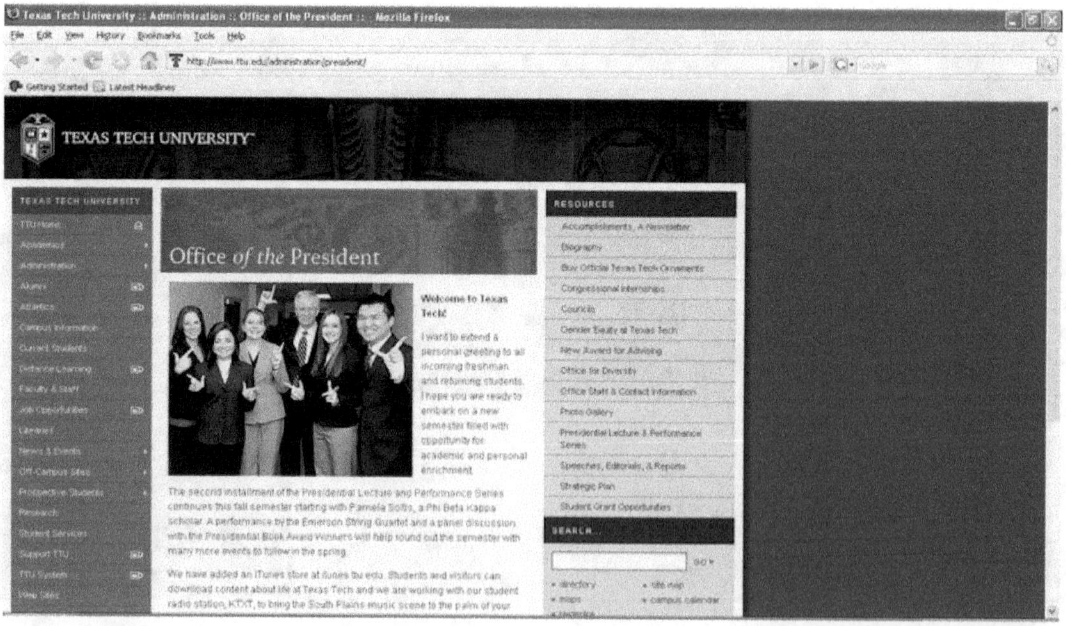

and staff. This happens to the point that we can hardly recognize who is the actual president. In particular cultures, the hierarchy is almost always exceedingly clear, whether in photos, language, or organizational charts. For the Mexican communicative tradition, the web designer would need to help readers understand clearly that they are to be treated according to their roles and relationships.

- **Specific→ Diffuse.** Because of the independence of the audience-author relations created by the individual and universal values, this website also creates specific orientation—that is, each person is put into a specific category with little carry over into other categories. Thus, there might be a picture or reference to a professor in his or her classroom working with students, but never does Texas Tech show a professor outside the classroom in a non-classroom setting mentoring students. The relations are based on their articulated specific relations. Adapting to the Mexican tradition would show teachers mentoring in non-classroom settings; further, it would show how the university and its graduate help the overall situation of the community.

Information

Not surprisingly, most of the information on the Texas Tech website closely reflects U.S. cultural values of individualism, universalism, and specific orientation. And much of this needs changing for the Mexican communicative tradition.

- **Individual→ Collective.** The verbal information that very frequently references the "you" as individual needs to be replaced with group information. The pictures of the lone individual or individuals with no apparent grouping need to be replaced with group shots that reflect social roles and hierarchy. The information on individual goals, objectives, and achievements needs to be replaced with how the university and its graduates are holistically influencing the groups around them. Individuals need to be seen in the light of the groups they are a part of
- **Universal→Particular.** The links need to portray organizational relationships, showing how the roles and relationships in the collective works. The pictures need to highlight the structure of the relationships, rather than downplaying it.
- **Specific→ Diffuse.** The information needs to be placed in better context generally, showing a more holistic view. For example, rather than the lone student sitting down, a larger more global picture showing this student in relation to a building, other students, and Texas Tech would provide a more diffuse approach, meeting better the expectations of a Mexican audience. Further, overt links and more information are needed about the history of Texas Tech and its role in the community.

Organization

As the purpose, audiences, and information changes for the Mexican communicative tradition, so does the organization of the communication. As is evident, the organization of the homepage very closely reflects the cultural values of individualism, universalism, and specific orientation. First, it is organized according to an individual's need to access as fast as possible information that is specific to his or her needs. Second, the organization is strongly templated; it uses the same color scheme and basic page design throughout the whole website. Third, the links slice up the human users into specific categories such as students, faculty, and visitors. Adapting Texas Tech's homepage for the Mexican communicative tradition would include the following:

- **Individual→ Collective.** Two intercultural researchers, Milton and Bennett (1991) explain rather clearly how most laws and institutions on the United States assume the unit of reference to be the individual, rather than the group. In addition, as explained in Chapter Eight, the U.S. common law legal tradition works much better if the focus at hand is the individual, instead of the group; thus, it is not surprising that the Texas Tech website's organization revolves around the individual, not the group. Instead of the individual reader (most frequently the student) being the overall organizing, the university should come first. This means that information about the University, its history, and its current status should be prominent in the web page's organization. Next, the web page would be organized around groups of students and their roles and relations. Finally, the overall achievement of the university would be figured prominently in the homepage, instead of the individual achievement and aspirations of the lone student.
- **Universal→Particular.** Following quite closely universalism, Texas Tech's website is strongly templated. This means that an overarching design and motif carry throughout the whole website. Thus, an important adaptation for Mexican would be in creating uniqueness, rather than consistency, across the websites. This uniqueness would draw on and reflect the local organization that is represented by the different pages.
- **Specific→ Diffuse.** The first key adaptation is to re-organize the pages according to topics such as academics, organization, instruction, etc instead of people in their different spheres. The second adaptation for moving from specific to diffuse means reducing the linear and listed information and making the web pages more artistic, nuanced, and holistic, effectively and artistically merging the verbal, visual, and audio together. Since the original Texas Tech webpage is templated so heavily, the visual template frequently does not correlate strong with the information. In addition, there are many lists and categorizations that heighten the specific rather than diffuse approach.

Style

The style needs to reflect the changes in purpose, audience, information, and organization. Thus, the following adaptations are recommended.

- **Individual→ Collective.** The style of the language and visuals needs to be more formal generally, which signals better the social relations in the hierarchy. For example, the picture of the president and students all doing the TTU symbol with their hands and smiling is highly informal. In addition, as explained next, the style needs to change the "I" focus to the "we" focus. Pictures need to show more group dynamics and relationships.
- **Universal→Particular.** One oxymoron of the individual-universal relation is that universalism provides the level playing field for individualism to flourish. However, as Stewart and Bennett explain (1991) individualism does not mean uniqueness. In other words, universal cultures tend to breed people who are individualistic in the same way, while particular cultures breed uniqueness that is derived from a common identity. Thus, a key adaptation for the Mexican communicative situation would be to reduce the equal treatment of individuals and focus instead on their great uniqueness and particular situations and

relationships of the students, groups, and organizations. Other adaptations include reducing the linearity and parallelism that reflects strong the universalist tendencies and instead focus on simultaneity and uniqueness.

- **Specific→ Diffuse.** This requires contextualizing people, the university, and its organizations in their complex wholes first and then getting to the point.

As should be evident by now, my approach for adapting the Texas Tech website for Mexico is a radical localization (see the Conclusion to this book) that assumes much more than translation alone. All five elements—purpose, reader, information, organization, and style—need to be adapted so as to be effective. Perhaps, as I have found in other cross-cultural contexts such as the U.S.-Mexico border (Thatcher, 2006), it would actually be easier to start over instead of redesign. However, adaptation is possible and necessary when working across cultures.

Questions for Connecting Fit and Reciprocity to Rhetorical Purpose, Audience-Author Relations, Information Needs, Organizational Strategies, and Stylistic Preferences

- How well can students and researchers assess rhetorical purpose, audience-author relations, organization, information, and style based on a culture' s value sets and their connections to the specific communication media?
- How well can students and researchers adapt their communications to fit rhetorical purpose, audience-author relations, organization, information, and style based on a culture' s value sets and their connections to the specific communication media?

5. MOVING BEYOND TABOOS: ETHICAL AND EFFECTIVE ADAPTATION OF COMMUNICATION PATTERNS

The last capability or proficiency is helping students, researchers, and communicators to move beyond cultural and rhetorical taboos to adapt their communication patterns for those of other cultures. One of the most damaging approaches to intercultural communication is the taboo approach—the listing of "do's" and "don'ts" for communicating with people of other cultures. First, the taboo approach essentializes the patterns of cultures and communication, directly contradicting the first capability of effectively generalizing with stereotyping. In other words, the taboo approach presents strategies that are not connected to the value sets, and therefore the researcher and communicator does not know whether the advice is appropriate. For example, most textbooks give the advice that Latin American cultures and people are affectionate and warm to each other. However, this strategy must be contextualized in the Latin American values of collectivism, diffuseness, high context communications, and high-power distance. Yes, Latin Americans tend to be affectionate, but usually only within their in-group (collectivism); and usually in private, not public contexts where they are at times anything but affectionate (diffuseness); and even in private contexts, the situation has to be right for affection (high context); and authority and power often trump affection (high power distance), meaning that a superior or authority does not need to be affectionate simply because of his or her authority, despite the fact it is an in-group, appropriate situation (Osland, et al, 1999). Consequently, a North American who follows advice of being affectionate with a Latin American often does so based on US values: with relatively loose social groups (individualism); in more public, not private contexts (specificity); with less regard to context (low context); and without distinguishing the power situation (mid- to low- power distance). I have witnessed many Americans following this advice, which has produced not only funny and awkward situations, but serious allegations of sexual harassment and aggression, which is the opposite purpose of the taboo advice.

Second, the taboo approach does not give students a range of knowledge of intercultural values, especially as that knowledge is tied to communication patterns. In other words, the taboo approach is stereotypical in two ways: first it is an inductive stereotype because it attributes cultural values based on incomplete or and accurate information, a pattern that Matveeva (2007) repeatedly argues as appearing in most U.S. professional communication textbooks. It also becomes a deductive stereotype because it does not supply a range of behavior, which is implicit in the bell curve approach. Thus, students and researchers do not approach people from a target culture expecting a predominant value with a range of behavior on both sides of the curve; rather, there is a monolithic expectation. For many reasons, this is obviously problematic. For example, it has always been fun (and interesting) for me to work in Latin America. Both sides of my family emigrated from England to the United States in the 17th and 19th centuries. I am as white or Anglo-Saxon as anyone; however, I speak Spanish with an academic and business fluency that surprises most of my Latin American colleagues. I am often their first exception to their stereotypes of Americans, most of the time being a good exception. As I break the stereotypes, it is interesting to note how many of my Latin American colleagues assess my non-stereotypical behavior. Many simply accept it, while others seem confused and resist. Perhaps the confusion or resistance stems from the taboo approach or advice to intercultural relations.

Finally, the taboo approach cannot help students situate a communication media such as orality or writing with a rhetorical approach. As explained earlier, to situate the media, a researcher or student must look at culture from a bell curve perspective, must situate behavior in that culture between the Ying/Yang nature of the value sets, and connect the media culture to a specific context. This is simply impossible with the taboo approach

Moving beyond Taboo

This anti-taboo or rhetorical capability has a developmental process, building off the previous four capabilities already discussed. When students or researchers are able to generalize effectively across cultures, then link the value sets to communication patterns, and finally correlate the cultural patterns and rhetorical strategies with the proper communication media, they are in a position to adapt their rhetorical patterns to a target culture. It is important to note that I am following Bennett's advice that distinguishes between adaptation and assimilation (1998, pp.24-25). Assimilation means replacing one's own cultural patterns with those of the target cultures. Bennett prefers adaptation because "it's additive, not substitutive" (p.25). In other words, students should not mimic or assimilate the rhetorical patterns of other cultures; rather, they should adapt their patterns to be more effective and ethical for those of the target cultures. The first step is developing a framework for understanding how to move from broad generalizations to local uses; the second step is showing goodwill and charity; and finally, the third step is looking for synergy among intercultural differences.

Moving from Broad Cultural Categories to Local Uses

To help students move beyond the taboo approach, it is essential that they distinguish—theoretically and practically—among at least four levels or kinds of intercultural rhetorical patterns: (1) rhetorical patterns that originate from the larger rhetorical tradition, (2) professional genres with specific rhetorical patterns, (3) organizational discourse, and (4) local and personal, audience-author patterns. This framework of four levels is, obviously, tentative, and for a fuller theoretical explanation see Thatcher 2000; 2001. However, at least proposing the four levels forces students to break out of the taboo mode of intercultural communication.

As mentioned earlier, the broad cultural patterns used in cross-cultural comparisons are useful because they tie rhetorical purpose to communication patterns. These broad patterns come from larger historical, economic, linguistic, and cultural factors and serve as foundations for what Berlin calls a rhetorical tradition (Berlin, 1987). Students, however, need to see these rhetorical patterns as rhetorical strategies that writers appropriate and individualize to make sense of every-day rhetorical situations (see, for example, Thatcher 2000). In other words, students need to understand that writers from a more collective culture, for example, will draw on—but not parrot—oral and high-context strategies to reinforce the in-group collectivity, but that these same writers might draw on other strategies to achieve the same purposes. If students see these patterns as internal to all writers of the target culture and not as strategies, they commit errors of deductive stereotyping. See Chapter One on agency and Chapter Two on stereotyping.

As explored by a variety of cultural and rhetorical theorists (see Bakhtin, 1990, for example) and in Chapter One, these patterns are the very content and material that writers use to express their own wills in concrete rhetorical situations (see Bakhtin, 1990; and Thatcher, 2001). Thus, writers subject, appropriate, reject, reconfigure and adapt these strategies for local purposes. Often, these strategies such as flexible organization or high contexting (see Victor 1992) become standardized in a particular way in an organizational culture, becoming genres of professional communication based on the organization or profession (See Berkenkotter & Huckin 1995). In addition, local organizational cultures similarly subject both the larger rhetorical patterns and the genres of professional communication for their own organizational purposes and cultures. And finally, authors subject these professional and organizational patterns to serve their own purposes, constantly revising them, so intercultural researchers need to assess how personal appropriations of the strategies are influencing the development of these broad or organizational patterns (see, for example, Thatcher 2000).

This four-level analysis could include many other variables and levels, such as writer development, influence of software and communications technology, and others; but in all my intercultural rhetoric courses, I have found it essential to use some kind of multi-level framework for all intercultural analysis. For example, in a recent graduate intercultural rhetoric course at New Mexico State University, a PhD student from Russia was comparing her university's website with the website of NMSU. The universities were comparable in size, purpose, and general website development. This student was able to quickly find rhetorical patterns from each website that corresponded very closely to broad historical and cultural patterns from each country. These included high and low context, high power distance, and collectivism-individualism. However, she argued that there was a difference, overall, in organizational cultures between the two universities that accounted for some rhetorical differences, despite the national cultures. Further, her Russian University had developed specific relations with certain U.S. universities that reflected distinct author-audience relations that NMSU website did not have. And finally, she explored how different web authoring tools corresponded to specific differences between the two websites. This distinction among the different levels of rhetorical patterns was essential for understanding what the authors of the two websites intended to do. Conflating the differences in any of these levels of analysis creates problems of stereotyping and intercultural misunderstanding.

Goodwill and Intercultural Synergy

Another problem with the taboo approach is that it most likely fosters a sense of suspicion and ill will when one is trying to avoid "inappropriate behavior" without knowing why. Thus, when looking at the various levels of rhetorical patterns, intercultural communicators also need to develop a sense of goodwill and openness about those of the other culture. In his introduction to intercultural communication, Chick (1990) likens communicators from similar cultures to "ballroom dancing partners of long standing, confident in the mutual knowledge of the basic sequence of dance steps and of the signals by which they inform one another of changes in direction or tempo" (p. 227). In distinction to this synchrony, Chick argues that interactions between persons from different cultures

may be marked by a series of uncomfortable, asynchronous moments...like ballroom dancers who are strangers to one another, they misinterpret one another's signals, struggle to develop a sequence or theme, or establish a rhythm...metaphorically speaking, trample one another's toes. (p. 227)

This metaphor of ballroom dancer's is a nice approach for the last intercultural competence: goodwill and intercultural synergy. Goodwill on part of the intercultural communicators is essential, because, otherwise, every misstep on the communication dance floor can easily be interpreted as ill will rather than simply a misstep. Drawing on Davidson's philosophy, Yuan (1997) argues that "charity" is the supreme example of goodwill for intercultural communications:

Most of all, the principle of charity is an extremely necessary idea to cross-cultural collaboration, not only because sincerity and trust are critical to successful collaboration, but also because respect for other's ways of thinking and doing things—and 'counting them right,' up to a point, as Davidson says, fosters a healthy collaborative relationship (p. 314).

The purpose of this goodwill or charity is to attribute integrity and rationality to other's ways of doing things, and as such, is an essential step.

Cultural Relevance, not Relativity

This goodwill does not imply cultural relativism, however, or what Bennett calls "giving up any set of ethical principles or moral guidelines" (1998 p. 30). In fact, Bennett (1998), Hampden-Turner & Trompenaars (2000), Stewart & Bennett (1991), House, et al (2005), and Hofstede (2010) all argue that coupled with this sense of goodwill and charity is cultural relevance, the idea that

Each culture possesses integrity, and generally speaking, is neither inferior nor superior to any other culture. But in a structured situation and for a specific purpose, one cultural system may in fact work better than another (Stewart & Bennett p. 175).

Bennett (1998) later expands on this idea, drawing on Perry's cognitive development scheme and argues for "ethnorelative ethics" (p. 30). Ethnorelative ethics is based on Perry's third developmental stage where intercultural rhetors can argue for what is ethical in a specific cultural situation and based on reasoned out positions. For example, in the area of international human rights, the founders of the *Universal Declaration of Human Rights* all agreed that many of the atrocities of World War II were in fact immoral. These writers, coming from a great variety of backgrounds, articulated their arguments of immorality based on their own cultural systems and applied to the specific case of World War II.

Later, the *Universal Declaration* has served as an example of intercultural relevance to argue against the community practices of female circumcision (see Glendon, 1999).

This idea of cultural relevance can be powerfully synergistic, if handled appropriately. Hampden-Turner & Trompenaars (2000) examine seven major intercultural variables in the workplace, exploring ways that international managers can take advantage of the strengths of major cultural differences. For example, when exploring particularism or universalism, they argue that in some situations the particular orientation is more effective, and in others, the universal. They explore the same synergistic reconciliation with individualism-universalism, achievement-ascription, specific-diffuse relations and others. An intercultural team that is aware of these differences can openly lay out these differences and plan strategies for exploiting their strengths, while minimizing the risks weaknesses. This requires openness, as already discussed, but it also requires an honest assessment of the pros and cons of cultural values. For Hampden-Turner & Trompenaars (2000), this synergistic reconciliation is the central strength—and challenge—of intercultural collaboration.

Questions for Moving beyond the Taboo Approach

- How well can students, researchers, and communicators to move beyond taboos and situate intercultural behavior and rhetoric in the appropriate value set contexts?
- How well does the student or researcher assess the varying levels of cultural and rhetorical influence on a specific intercultural situation, instead of relying on simplistic emic or monolithic attributions?
- How well can they exercise good will and charity in their intercultural efforts?
- How effectively can they evaluate the virtues and vices of the values in specific contexts?

CONCLUSION

One of the weaknesses of intercultural rhetoric and professional communication is the lack of research and teaching models, though teaching (Bracken Scott, 2010) has received a bit more attention; and I develop a concrete teaching approach in Chapter Twelve. For this chapter, I would have liked to have analyzed a variety of research designs and curricular models, but well developed models simply do not exist. Thus, I chose to approach teaching and research from competencies and assessment, which become the criteria for evaluating effective teaching and research regardless of the specific research methodology or curriculum. These criteria are essentially based on the framework of the entire book, serving as well as a nice summary of my overall approach.

REFERENCES

Adler, N. (2008). *International dimensions of organizational behavior*. New York, NY: Thomson Learning Center.

Bakhtin, M. M. (1990). *Art and answerability* (Holquist, M., & Liapunov, V., Eds.). (Liapunov, V., Trans.). Austin, TX: University of Texas Press.

Bennett, M. J. (Ed.). (1998). *Basic concepts of intercultural communication*. Yarmouth, ME: Intercultural Press.

Berkonkotter, C., & Huckin, T. (1995). *Genre knowledge in disciplinary communication: Cognition/ culture/ power*. Hillsdale, NJ: Lawrence Erlbaum.

Berlin, J. (1987). *Rhetoric and reality: Writing instruction in the American colleges, 1900-1985*. Carbondale, IL: Southern Illinois University Press.

Bracken Scott, J. (2010). Intercultural rhetoric in the technical communication curriculum: A review of the literature. *Rhetoric, Professional Communication. Globalization, 1*(1), 77–90.

Burke, K. (1968). *Language as symbolic action. Essays on life, literature, and method.* Berkeley, CA: University of California Press.

Chick, K. J. (1990). Reflections on language, interaction, and context. In Carbaugh, D. (Ed.), *Cultural communication and intercultural contact* (pp. 253–259). Hillsdale, NJ: Lawrence Erlbaum Associates.

Condon, J. C. (1997). *Communicating with the Mexicans* (2nd ed.). Yarmouth, ME: Intercultural Press, Inc.

Friedman, T. (2005). *The world is flat.* New York, NY: Farrar, Straus and Giroux.

Hofstede, G. (2010). *Cultures and organizations, software of the mind* (3rd ed.). New York, NY: McGraw Hill.

House, R. J., Hanges, P. J., Javidan, M., Dorfman, P. R., & Gupta, V. (Eds.). (2005). *Culture, leadership, and organizations: The GLOBE study of 62 societies.* Newbury Park, CA: Sage Publications.

Matveeva, N. (2007). The intercultural component in textbooks for teaching: A service technical writing course. *Journal of Technical Writing and Communication, 37*(2), 151–166. doi:10.2190/85J8-2P74-1378-2188

McCool, M. (2007). *Reaching a global online audience.* Oreilly Media, Inc.

Osland, J. S., De Franco, S., & Osland, A. (1999). Organizational implications of Latin. American culture. *Journal of Management Inquiry, 8*(2), 219–234. doi:10.1177/105649269982018

Stewart, E., & Bennett, M. (1991). *American cultural patterns: A cross-cultural perspective* (Rev. ed.). Yarmouth, ME: Intercultural Press, Inc.

Thatcher, B., Barrantes, E., Dalzell, A., Dong, Q., Ford, C., & Klein, S. … Ramirez, L. (2007). Website analysis across cultures. In K. St. Amant (Ed.), *Linguistic and cultural online communication issues in the global age* (pp.124-142). Hershey, PA: Idea Group.

Thatcher, B., & St.Amant, K. (Eds.). (2010). *Teaching intercultural rhetoric and technical communication: Theories, curriculum, pedagogies, and practices.* Baywood Publishing.

Thatcher, B. L. (2000). Writing policies and procedures in a U.S. and South American context. *Technical Communication Quarterly, 94,* 365–400. doi:10.1080/10572250009364706

Thatcher, B. L. (2001). Issues of validity in intercultural professional communication research. *Journal of Business and Technical Communication, 15*(4), 458–489. doi:10.1177/105065190101500403

Thatcher, B. L. (2006). Intercultural rhetoric, technology, and writing in Mexican maquilas. *Special Technology Transfer Edition of Technical Communication Quarterly, 15*(3), 383–405.

Thatcher, B. L. (2009). Understanding digital literacy across cultures. In Spilka, R. (Ed.), *Digital literacy for technical communication: 21st Century theory and practice* (pp. 169–198). Routledge.

Thatcher, B. L. (2010). Reading and writing new media across cultures: Issues of fit, reciprocity, and cultural change. In Kalmbach, J., & Ball, C. (Eds.), *Reading and writing new media.* Hampton Press Series New Dimensions in Computers and Composition.

Victor, D. (1992). *International business communication.* New York, NY: HarperCollins Publishers.

Williams, J. (2009). *Style: Basics of clarity and grace* (3rd ed.). New York, NY: Pearson Longmann.

Chapter 12
Teaching Intercultural Rhetoric and Professional Communication

ABSTRACT

This chapter first examines the cultural and rhetorical assumptions implicit in three popular U.S. rhetoric and writing textbooks, denaturalizing the U.S. foundation for these texts and showing how to adapt them to global and intercultural contexts. The second part describes an intercultural rhetoric and writing class that I have been teaching for 13 years, including syllabus, course goals, assignments, teaching strategies, and assessments. It provides the first comprehensive model of an intercultural rhetoric and writing class.

INTRODUCTION

As a U.S. intercultural researcher, teacher, and practitioner, one of the most interesting tensions or troubling contradictions that I face daily is to understand some of the deep diversity around the world, while I simultaneously witness constant references to U.S. diversity but sense that this U.S. diversity is perhaps quite shallow. For example, as I have shown in Chapter Five, university websites designs in the United States are strongly homogenized, closely following the cultural and rhetorical values attributed to the United States by intercultural researchers. And much of my field research points to homogenized U.S. professional communication patterns, as compared, for example, to the diversity that exists among Latin American countries (Thatcher, 1999; 2000; 2006; 2010). My perception about the lack of true global or intercultural diversity in the United States is shared by almost all U.S. intercultural researchers who have worked outside the United States (Bennett, 1998; Stewart & Bennett, 1991; Kras, 1991; Adler, 2008; Condon, 1997) as well as non-U.S. researchers who have worked in the United States (Castaneda, 1995). Most of these researchers argue that U.S. homogenization is largely historical and linguistic, based on U.S. isolation, individualism, and English as the de facto language. I think it also has much to do with U.S. education systems, which, though seemingly diverse, still draw on traditional U.S. cultural values. And I have felt that much of the intercultural professional communication research coming out of the United States is either focused on relatively surface features such as time, money denominations, and translation, or it is bound up in the local approach (Hunsinger, 2007), implicitly reinforcing U.S. cultural values.

DOI: 10.4018/978-1-61350-450-5.ch012

Aother troubling feeling I have of this diversity is that I have watched many non-U.S. students enroll in U.S. graduate programs in rhetoric and professional communication, and before too long, some either demonstrate strong values of individualism based and the local approach; strong denunciations of stereotypes, based on U.S.-like universalism; and many rhetorical patterns of specific and monochronic orientation, including directness, thesis statements, and linear development. Or others struggle through programs with faculty and committee advisors not understanding the difficulty in developing U.S. rhetorical competencies. Of course, many students might have been inclined for or against U.S.-like cultural and rhetorical patterns in the first place, and certainly they must be adept at handling them or they will not succeed, but I sincerely wonder about the effects of this enculturation.

In this context of shallow diversity, I become even more worried about the Anzaldúa-like diversity that I critique at the end of Chapter Two. There, I argue that U.S. diversity seems to mean bringing in other races, ethnicities, and other so called diverse traits, romanticizing the surface features of this diversity, and then integrating these people into U.S. cultural and rhetorical systems, masking the deep U.S. foundation for this integration, and calling it diversity. This critique is profoundly difficult for many Anzaldúa fans to understand because the great sophistication and complexity of Anzaldúa's derridian approach to language and identity are refreshing and seem to correspond to complex and deep-rooted diversity. However, when viewed from a global/intercultural context, this complexity is strongly based on U.S. assumptions about writing and corresponding foundations of individualism, universalism, specific orientation, achievement orientation, and low power distance communication styles. Consequently, this approach is simply masquerading as diversity, but it really is U.S. ethnocentrism. In other words, this "diversity" would be extremely difficult to carry out outside U.S. cultures. Not surprisingly, all of my Mexican colleagues who do research in rhetoric and culture have never even heard of Anzaldúa, and when they do read her, they very quickly situate her as a U.S. Tejana.

In this context of shallow diversity, I also have wondered about U.S. rhetoric and writing curriculum and associated textbooks: how truly diverse are they? Matveeva (2007) has shown that the global elements in most U.S. professional communication textbooks are based on anecdotal, taboo-based approaches, further emphasizing the naïve individualism I describe in Chapters Two and Eleven. And Bracken Scott (2010) discusses the dearth of valid and relevant work in intercultural teaching for rhetoric and professional communication. In Chapter Eleven, I address many of these program and curricular issues, focusing on the criteria for evaluating their intercultural effectiveness. But in this chapter, I am more interested in U.S. mainstream approaches to rhetoric and writing and the cultural and rhetorical assumptions in their approaches. How much do they base their approaches on naturalized U.S. cultural and rhetorical values? Or how open are they to global and intercultural diversity? And what kinds of cultural and rhetorical adaptations must non-U.S. students face, either implicitly or explicitly, when enrolling in U.S. university composition and professional communication classes?

This chapter seeks to explore these questions. The first section examines and denaturalizes the cultural and rhetorical values in three of the most popular writing and professional communication textbooks in the United States, demonstrating the kinds of adaptations that students from other cultures most likely have to carry out when using these textbooks. The second section describes an intercultural writing class that I have been teaching at New Mexico State University for ten years. Based on the core competencies of teaching and research described in Chapter Eleven, this section describes the goals, assignments, processes, and assessment criteria for the course. This kind of course presents a different approach to diversity, one I call global diversity, complete with a set of core competencies, knowledge areas, and writing activities.

EVALUATING THE CULTURAL AND RHETORICAL ASSUMPTIONS IN U.S. RHETORIC AND WRITING TEXTBOOKS

For this section, my goal is to evaluate typical approaches to teaching writing and professional communication in the United States. Thus, I chose three very popular textbooks: Lester Faigley and Jack Selzer's *Good Reasons* (2008); Joseph Williams' *Style: Basics of Clarity and Grace* (2009); and Paul Anderson's *Technical Communication* (2011). I chose these three because they are not only popular in the United States, but they approach different components or elements of writing. Faigley and Selzer's *Good Reasons* specifically focuses on arguments and persuasion, two areas that are deeply founded on cultural values but surface in a wide variety of academic and non-academic writing and communication situations. Anderson's *Technical Communication* has a more specific domain (professional communication) and lays out a much more specific pedagogy than *Good Reasons*. Williams' *Style* focuses on more surface writing issues such as sentence structure and paragraph organization, which are also founded on cultural values. Together, these three provide a window into the cultural values that probably underlie many approaches to teaching rhetoric and writing in the United States.

I chose not to evaluate dedicated ESL writing textbooks because most of these are designed for lower levels of English where linguistic concerns are more important than cultural patterns. In addition, most ESL students take dedicated ESL courses at the freshman and sophomore level but then are mainstreamed into non-ESL classrooms at the junior and senior level. It's at this intermediate level where the cultural concerns became critical, especially for intercultural rhetorical competencies; and it's at this level where I feel we need to denaturalize U.S. writing theory and pedagogy as a way of understanding how culture and rhetoric work around the world.

This section follows the common format in most chapters of this book, evaluating the three textbooks in light of the eight etic borders or common human thresholds. Within this framework, I also point out important connections to rhetorical purpose, audience-author relations, information, organization, and style. This section also demonstrates how important it is to see the etic borders in a ying/yang perspective, for no textbook manifests solely one side of the border; rather all are deeply connected and immersed in the etic tensions. Regardless, all three textbooks show strong bell-curve preferences for U.S. values, not surprisingly.

Individual-Collective and Communication Media

As explained in Chapter Two, the individual-collective etic frame assesses the levels of dependence or independence among people. For some cultures, the most likely approach to the "I" relating to the group is individualistic, while in others it is collective. The communication patterns of individualism include a focus on the "I" rather than the group, with the individual as the unit of analysis; a strong bifurcation between personal and objective communication strategies, which resolves interpersonal conflicts by going back to the uniqueness of the individual rather than to that person's political or social context (Stewart and Bennett, 1991); a dumbed-down readership level so as to uncomplicate the interpersonal dependence of communicators (Kras, 1991); and an emphasis of personal achievement, self-creation, and reader-friendly document design patterns (Hinds, 1987).

On the other hand, collectivism predominates when people view themselves as highly dependent upon others and define themselves, see the world, and negotiate life based on social or family groups. Collective communication patterns emphasize interpersonal relationships, social hierarchy, social leveraging, group identities, close personal space, and writer-friendly writing patterns (Hinds, 1987). Collective communication patterns do not have a strong bifurcation between personal and objective strategies because they see the person in light of their social context, effectively combining the personal and social political. Instead of a dumbed-down readership level, collective communicators tend to complicate their interpersonal dependence as a way of stating the purpose of the communication and their involvement; this creates writer-friendly document design patterns Hinds, 1987).

In light of this etic border, all three textbooks show a strong preference for the U.S. value of individualism, with some more than others; all three demonstrate a ying-yang tension for this value; and all three show strong uncertainty avoidance for the alternative value. First, individualism is the key foundation or unit of reference for *Good Reasons*. The language of this text not only consistently addresses the reader as "you," but a "you" that is independent and only situated rather abstractly in larger social groups and issues, and not intimately or deeply connected to specific in-groups, which are usually carefully demarcated in more collective cultures. In fact, the textbook is mostly issue based, with relatively little discussion of how different groups and classes of people approach these issues. Further, much like the assumptions of U.S. instructional materials (described in Chapter Ten), this text assumes that only one person will be writing the argument, even though collaboration is discussed. For example, page 16 discusses "the writer" defining the issues, taking a clear position, and making convincing arguments. Further, one key way to finding a good argument is "what interests you" (p. 34) and then "you" can argue by definition, value, or compare and contrast (p.45). In a really strong individualistic approach, the authors list of eight ways to put good reasons into action that all start with "you" (p.109).

Figure 1. Picture of lone person in Good Reasons

This individualism is also clearly seen in the photographs, which overwhelmingly show only one person, often in the context of a march or demonstration. For example, Figure 1 shows the picture of one lone person making an argument in a public context.

This picture, which is the introductory page to the first section of reading and discovering arguments, strongly highlights the U.S. value of individualism because it's one person, actively engaging in a public debate, complete with an open smile, writing, and the U.S. flag. Almost all other pictures in this text display one person, much like the individualistic websites described in Chapter Five.

In addition, although this text argues for understanding the audience, this audience approach is mostly individualistic because it assumes that "readers" are not group-oriented or role-based, the basic assumption in collective cultures. Rather, the audience strategies are to understand what the reader knows, understand the reader's attitudes towards "you" (the author), and understand the reader's attitude toward the subject, all of which is explained in about three pages. This approach is individualistic because it assumes readers that are independent enough from social groups to make personal (not group), and therefore, objective decisions; because it reduces audience-author relations to one of knowledge and attitude, rather than strong in- and out-group connections; and because it assumes the issue at hand can be encapsulated more on knowledge and attitudes than group affiliation. As shown in Letter O of the Transit Commission, a more collective approach would place up front the social group that is being written to, understanding very clearly—but treating indirectly—the political, economic, gender, class, and professional ramifications, relations, and roles of arguing this issue with the social groups.

Another interesting individualistic foundation in *Good Reasons* is its purposes and kairos for writing. As explained in Chapters Two and Four, writing is often initiated differently in collective and individual cultures, with writing in individualistic cultures starting early on to become the foundation for further negotiation and development. However, as shown in the EPA RFID project, writing in collective cultures usually starts later on, once orality has developed sufficiently the collective and diffuse relations. Put simply, *Good Reasons* presupposes the individualistic (and universal) foundation for writing. In *Good Reasons*, almost every example of an argument starts with the development of a good piece of writing that becomes the touchstone for influencing all that came after. This is probably difficult for those in collective cultures where shared traditions, relational solidarity, and maintaining face can be accomplished through writing, but the preferred—and the most effective medium—is still orality. As shown in the EPA example in Chapters Four and Eleven, the kairos and rhetorical processes in *Good Reasons* assume a U.S. base of individualism, among many other values.

In addition, Faigley and Selzer exemplify many of the argumentative strategies using the local approach, something strongly–but paradoxically–tied to individualism. First, the writing samples for the textbook are almost all from writers who explore in detail an issue based on that writer's local, interpersonal context; and almost all are written by creative/fiction writers such as columnists and editorialists. None of the writing samples are written by high level policy people in government, academia, or industry who oversee many of the issues being discussed. For example, Silko's "The Border Patrol State" explores the situation of driving on southern New Mexican and Arizonan roads, something that I am very familiar with. Almost every paragraph is devoted to Silko's concrete and local observation, including her conclusions and commentaries on these situations. But it is clear she has little experience with the Border Patrol beyond these encounters, only knows the superficial policies that affect her, does not understand their investigation protocols and the great complexities of their work, including the danger they face in their everyday job (this is in contradiction to how Faigley & Selzer characterize her, p. 73). She never discusses the role-based and perspectival approaches to an issue, the hallmarks of particularism. Silko's approach is not surprising, given that the text is exemplifying the "narrative argument," but Faigley & Selzer likewise use local approaches for definition (comic strip), causal arguments ("why should I be nice"), evaluation arguments ("Gangsta rap and American culture"), and rebuttal arguments ("Illegal immigrants"). Even the chapter on Global issues portrays a variety of editorial-like pieces on global issues, rarely connecting issues to other-than-local situations and rarely or never drawing on stakeholders in government, industry, or NGOs; overwhelming, the argument samples are simply localized, editorial-like pieces. This local approach strongly reinforces a local, individualized epistemology, despite the universal frames and classifications, and thus, it's much like the localized derridian performance epistemologies discussed in Chapters Three and Eight.

In addition to the local approach used for the sample argument essays and classification of arguments, the authors teach the students that the source of an argument is in that individual's specific context and should "think about what interests you" (pp. 35-37) and then list and analyze issues specific to that student's local, regional, national or world context. Based on this introspective, individual analysis, the student should then explore the arguments to make. This local approach, however, seems not to stick well with the students, for three of the four student writing samples use larger than local approaches. The evaluation argument of Giddens (pp. 169-174) explores the recruitment strategies of the U.S. armed forces, drawing on both local and larger approaches; Lee's proposal argument (p. 218-221) is a large-scale argument about the U.S. melting pot; and the free speech paper by Nguyen (pp. 129-133) discusses the broad cultural and legal issues of free speech with some local situation.

This disjuncture between what is being taught and what the students produce is actually quite interesting, perhaps reflecting the schizophrenia associated with the local approaches and ethics, as discussed in Chapter Eight. The textbook espouses broad universalism in its audience approaches, textual organizational strategies, and classifications of argument, but its samples are highly localized, exemplifying a broad gap or schism. Perhaps a better approach would have reconciled the broad universal and high localized approaches, which, for example, Hampden-Turner &Trompenaars (2000) demonstrate in their chapters on universalism and particularism. Much of this reconciliation focuses on the roles and responsibilities of concrete groups of people. For example, Silko could have introduced narratives from the Border Patrol, immigrants, local residents, and others to represent how the roles and responsibilities of these groups portray particular perspectives on the situation.

Anderson's *Technical Communication* likewise assumes the individual as the unit of reference. First, like *Good Reasons*, *Technical Communication* generally assumes the one-writer, "you" approach in almost all descriptions. Thus, the writer or "you" approaches the writing task usually alone, making decisions alone, but with some help of stakeholders. This one-person approach is seen throughout, especially in the latter chapters that explain major genres such as reports, proposals, and instructions.

However, despite assuming the individual as unit of reference, *Technical Communication* argues for thinking about the reader as the key rhetorical strategy of the book. In fact, the subtitle of the book is "a reader-centered approach" and "the main advice of this book is to think constantly about your readers" (p. 11). For example, the writer-audience dynamics include the readers constructing meaning, responding in situations, and reacting by the moment (p. 12). Further, as demonstrated in the chapter on writing resumes and cover letters, the reader-centered approach includes:

- Consider the audience's characteristics, goals, expectations, situations, and other factors.
- Concentrate on crafting a communication that will be persuasive and usable in your readers' eyes.
- Focus specifically on the ways your readers will respond, moment by moment, while they are reading your communication (p.27).

In addition, when researching and planning for the communication, the author needs to assess the reader in the following nine ways:

1. Create a mental movie of your reader in the act of reading.
2. Describe the task your communication will help your reader perform.
3. Describe the way you want your communication to alter your readers' attitudes.
4. Create a profile of the reader: professional specialty, organizational role, familiarity with topic, knowledge of your specialty,

relationship with you, personal preferences, and special considerations.

5. Global guideline: describe your readers' cultural characteristics.
6. Learn who all the readers will be.
7. Describe the context in which your reader will read.
8. Identify any constraints on the way you will write.
9. Ethics guidelines: Indentify your communication's stakeholders (pp. 68-94).

Thus, there is much more interdependence assumed between reader and writer in this text, as compared to *Good Reasons*.

Despite this enhanced attention to the reader, however, Anderson still assumes great levels of independence among the readers, author, and other social groups, which is not surprising, given his U.S. context. This individualism is framed mostly in how this reader-centered analysis is then transformed into writing strategies. The first strategy is to make sure the "information is complete, that it will include all the information your readers need in order to complete the task" (p. 101). The need for completeness assumes that readers will not want to be reliant upon the author for more information, a key approach in individualistic cultures. Second is to organize around the readers' tasks (p. 101). And third is to identify ways to help readers quickly find what they want (p. 102). These two assumptions also assume individualism, first because organizing around the reader makes the reader more independent from the writer; and also the quickness needed assumes a busy person uninterested in extraneous information. All of these characteristics assume a more or less independent reader, grounded in the level playing field of universalism.

Although these individualistic strategies seem minor in comparison to the large, comprehensive reader-centered approaches, the individualism still strongly undergirds most of the previously discussed reader-centered approaches. Perhaps the best way to demonstrate better why these approaches are individualistic is to recast them for more collective cultures. I have, in fact, used Anderson's textbook to teach professional communication in Ecuador (1997) and Mexico (2005), two countries with high and medium levels of collectivism. When I first began teaching professional communication in Ecuador in 1994, I was thoroughly schooled in audience-centered strategies, but when I first began to ground all communications in the audience, my Ecuadorian students moved quickly through the audience analysis process and were bored quickly (unlike my U.S. students). Focusing so extensively on the audience was something their collective cultures naturally taught them to do. This was my first indicators of high levels of uncertainty avoidance regarding audience analysis in U.S. textbooks. As explained in Chapter Two, uncertainty avoidance is a etic border or value set that Hofstede (2010) uses to ascertain the anxiety levels among cultures. I think uncertainty avoidance, however, is best understood in light of each etic border or value set. In essence, because of deep individualism in the United States, it is not surprising that many U.S. textbooks are anxious about students learning more collective strategies through comprehensive audience analysis strategies.

However, both my Ecuadorian and Mexican students were deeply anxious about other values more closely associated with their cultures. These included the difficulties of communicating in diffuse, particular, high power distance, ascriptive, and high context cultures. Thus, instead of spending time discussing audience analysis based on the independence of U.S. individualism, in both my Ecuadorian and Mexican contexts, we spent time analyzing in and out-group relations, as connected to issues of power and fairness through people, holistic views of people, and the great influence of context in communication. Consequently, I developed for my Ecuadorian

Figure 2. Audience analysis for Ecuadorian professional communication courses

Organizational Analysis	Audience Analysis
Organization's physical culture. • How does the physical layout of the organization's building influence communication patterns? • How does communication technology influence the types and patterns of communication? (e-mail, fax). • What are the common forms of communication for this type of company? (hi-tech=reliance on com tech; low tech=orality) • How will your proposal compare to these established forms of communication? What adaptation does this comparison imply? • What external factors affect the communication situation? Laws, competition, market? • What is the organization's corporate culture and how does it influence communication? • How has previous communication reflected, shaped, or changed the physical culture?	Audience's relation to physical culture. • How does the audience's office or place of reception influence communication patterns? • How does the audience's knowledge of and relationships to communication technology affect her communication patterns? • What forms of communication does the audience customarily use in this physical setting and with topics like your proposal? • What factors outside the audience's conscious control influence her writing? (Organizational circumstances; current business climate; financial stability; stability of audience's position within the organization; personal crises, dilemmas, events). • How does the audience fit the corporate culture and its established forms of communication? • How does the audience's relation to the physical culture affect the way you will write your proposal?
Organization's cognitive and ethical culture • How is an idea generated, presented, and deemed acceptable, and what are the ethics of this idea-constructing process? • What criteria does the organization have for evaluating your proposal? What are the ethics of these criteria? • What intellectual image does the organization hold to and what are the ethics of that image? • Who authorizes decisions and what are the ethical ramifications of this authorization process? • How is writing and communication involved in the decision-making and ethical functions of the organization? • Who makes ethical decisions? How can the ethics of the organization be reshaped, changed, rejected? • How could your proposal reshape the cognitive and ethical culture of the organization?	Audience's cognitive and ethical nature • How does the author generate, present, and accept an idea, and what are the ethics of her idea-constructing process? • What is the audience's role in generating ideas for the whole organization? • How does the audience hold to the intellectual image of the organization, and how does she perceive the ethics of this image? • How is the audience involved with authorizing decisions, and how does she acknowledge the ethics of this process? • How does the audience use writing to carry out the cognitive and ethical functions of the organization? • What are the audiences' ethical positions? How does she reshape the ethics of the organization? • How could your proposal reshape the cognitive-ethical nature of your audience?
Organization's emotional and individual culture. • How do the company's forms of communication utilize the writer's emotional and individual natures? • Are these forms conducive to individuality or teamwork? • What are the methods of finalizing writing? - How do the author and audience work together on writing projects? - Who has the final say on how the written proposal will eventually read? • How does an author feel he or she is actually creating her own writing? • How will your proposal compare to the emotional and individual culture of the organization?	Audience's emotional and volitional nature. • What would be the audience's likely emotional and individual response to your proposal? • What kind of individuality & emotion does the audience expect? • How will you finalize your writing? - How will you and the audience collaborate? - Who has the final say on the writing? • How might the audience appropriate your proposal as her own text for other audiences? • How might the audience use your proposal to change the cognitive and ethical culture of the organization? • How could your proposal reshape the emotional and individual nature of the organization?

students an organizational analysis sheet, based on Bakhtin's theories of situated agency, which I discuss in Chapter One. Figure 2 is an English translation of this "audience" analysis assignment. I would revise some elements now, given my much greater understanding of how the values or etic borders work, but this sheet will suffice for the demonstration.

Audience Memo

In a coherent memo to me, answer the following questions in paragraph form about the audience for your final project. If your audience is part of a larger organization, such as IBM, Coca Cola, or GM, answer the questions for the organizational analysis and then explain how your specific audience fits the organizational culture. If your audience *is* the organization, answer a combination of organization and audience analysis questions. Answer each question as best as possible.

This audience analysis sheet is based on Bakhtin's (1990: "Content") three related realms of discourse: physical, cognitive-ethical, and emotional-volitional (see Chapter One, under agency). The key to the worksheet is to situate the Ecuadorian professional communicators in a more collective, diffuse, outer-directed, high power distance, and ascriptive context, which it did very well. However, when I tried to carry it out in the United States (Ohio University), it was very difficult. Upon this re-entry to the United

States, I had to re-familiarize myself again to U.S cultural values and once again focus on concrete analysis strategies using Anderson's text.

Thus, if I were to revise Anderson's reader centered guidelines for more collective cultures, I would probably do the following:

1. Envision the entire organization context and its mutually dependent roles, including the decision makers, organizational communication patterns, and power relations (instead of "Create a mental movie of your reader in the act of reading").
2. Situate the communication task in the organizational processes (instead of "Describe the task your communication will help your reader perform").
3. Situate the readers' roles in the context and power relations, including in- and out-groups (instead of "Describe the way you want your communication to alter your readers' attitudes").
4. Create a profile of the entire organizational context (instead of "Create a profile of the reader").
5. Describe the cultural characteristics of your readers and its organization (instead of Global guideline: describe your readers' cultural characteristics).
6. Delete: Learn who all the readers will be.
7. Delete: Describe the context in which your reader will read.
8. Delete: Identify any constraints on the way you will write.
9. Delete: Ethics guidelines: Indentify your communication's stakeholders (pp. 68-94).

Among the many values, this approach assumes a writer more thoroughly dependent upon others (collectivism);the concrete nature of organizational decisions (particularism); the entire context (diffuseness); the decision-making power of roles (ascription); and how the situation calls for specific communication strategies (high context). Likewise, the writing strategies would be to develop an appropriate relation with stakeholders (instead of completeness); situate the writing in the organizational context and people who have power to get things done, instead of just the readers' tasks; and third, to quickly identify clearly the writer's roles and power in relation to context. All three emphasize more collective or dependent relations among the people involved in the rhetorical context.

Like *Good Reasons* and *Technical Communication*, Williams' *Style* similarly assumes a strongly independent reader. In fact, almost all of the strategies for improving the clarity of the writing are to have the reader process the writing as clearly as possible, which has the effect of reducing the readers' reliance on the writer. For example, it emphasizes clarity of agents and actions in a more simple cause and effect syntax, using the agent in the subject position and the more important action in the verb position. As shown in Chapter Three, this simple causality strongly correlates to the English language and the values of individualism, universalism, and specific orientation, which I discuss more extensively later.

As shown in these three texts, individualism still reigns in U.S. writing and professional communication textbooks, although not without a collective impulse shown in *Technical Communication*.

Universal-Particular and Communication Media

As discussed in Chapter Two, the Universal-Particular value set assesses the approaches to rules. In universalist cultures, the default approach is to establish rules that define what is good and right regardless of the social standing of the individual with the ideal of a "level playing field" as an apt analogy. Universalist communication patterns emphasize uniformity, parallelism, and templating. They also include strategies of fairness, justice, and equality. In particularist cultures, the default approach is to apply rules and decisions depending on relations and context. Instead of "the level playing field," the particularist playing field is overtly structured, and thus, there is a specifically tailored set of rules for each social relationship. Particular communication patterns include uniqueness in document design; emphasis of context and particular relationships; importance of exceptional circumstances; and consideration of social prestige and power relations.

In the context of universal and particular, the three textbooks are situated in complex ways, demonstrating some of the interesting dynamics of the etic borders. First, *Good Reasons* shows some general universal impulses with its views of audience analysis, which presuppose, among many things, almost a universal audience. However, it also shows some strong local approaches to logic and argumentation, which paradoxically seem like particularism but also draw on individualism. First, the reasons for thinking about readers (pp. 229-230) are so that the writer can signal the topic to the reader, make the organizational visible to the reader, and help the reader navigate the text, all of which are signs of universal writing designed for the widest audience possible. Further, Faigley and Selzer argue that arguments are based on the "because clause," which typically means cause and effect, which historically is a universal approach (Hampden-Turner & Trompenaars, 2000). In addition, these authors separate arguments from statement of facts (which they probably do not believe but use it for students), personal taste, and personal belief. As explained in Chapter Two, this separation or bifurcation is a hallmark of universal cultures, for particular cultures strongly connect facts, personal tastes, and belief to the in- or out-group. Further, Faigley and Selzer attempt to break down the types of arguments into classes, such as casual, evaluation, narrative, rebuttal, and proposal, classifications that also signal the more universal-like approaches to arguments. In addition, they talk about universal categories of logic and logical fallacies (pp. 27-28). Finally, the textbook argues for making a compelling introduction and title (p. 58) as a way to catch the attention of the reader, and the way to do this is to cast the widest net possible, trying to reel on the largest audience possible, a sign of universalism.

Much like its mixed individual-collective values, Anderson's *Technical Communication* displays much universalism in its strategies for structuring and making readable the text, but the text also needs to be situated in the prevailing genres of the context, a sign of particularism. For example, this textbook employs the same universal textual strategies as *Good Reasons*: clear, universal intro; signposting of document organization and readers' paths; and lots of emphasis of parallelism and effective document design as methods to ensure good readability. Further, the text lays out six professional communication superstructures, which are common genres for most situations. However, the text demonstrates how to conduct usability research on the develop document to make sure it works with the specific context. And this readability is focused on user's attitudes, needs, and specific context (pp. 120-140). The designed flexibility in *Technical Communication* makes for a more particular approach to rules orientation.

Williams' *Style* is almost completely universal. First, as explained earlier, its major goal is to write so clearly as to make the reader independent from the author. And the universal strategies for doing this include clarifying cause and effect, trimming unneeded words, developing a linear paragraph and sentence to sentence flow, and creating balance and symmetry in complex sentences. All of these are hallmark characteristics of universals.

Specific and Diffuse and Communication Media

This value set assesses the degree of involvement across different spheres of life, usually involving a public/private divide and trust. As shown by the circles in Chapter Two, the specific orientation is characterized by the ease in which a person can enter the relationship from a public sphere, which is shown by the dashed line, but once in, that relationship is usually sphere based and rarely crosses over. For example, in the specific model, friends made at school do not have automatic access to your fridge or to your friendships in other places. Further, it is very difficult to enter the small, private world signaled by the small center circle.

The diffuse circle shows that it is very difficult to pass from the public into a relationship, signaled by the thick line of the outer circle. And there is a small public/private mixture area between the two circles, but once inside the larger private sphere (signaled by dashed smaller circle), the relationship crosses boundaries, and there is no distinguishable private self. Diffuse communication patterns emphasize approaches that address the whole person in all aspects and dimensions, including social hierarchies. As a result, persuasion does not require salesmanship, but rather a long-term establishment of interconnected, interpersonal values. Consequently, diffuse patterns seem (to specific people) very indirect and to circle around the point, because diffuse communicators need to understand the whole person before getting to the point. Specific communication patterns easily section off people into different groups: students, faculty, staff, alumni, parents, and so on. Specific communications are also direct and inductive, stating the main point quickly and then supporting it.

Good Reasons is strongly specific, for many reasons. First, Faigley & Selzer provide the following list of components or strategies for arguments, almost all of which are specific in nature (p. 30): state explicit claims; support claims with reasons; base reasons on evidence; consider opposing positions; analyze with insight; investigate complexity; organize information clearly; signal relationship of parts; and document sources carefully. One of the hallmarks of specific orientation is to make explicit the claim or argument first, exemplifying the direct and easy approach into the relation. This explicit claim need not contextualize the people and issues; rather, it is stated up front. Next, the fact that claims can be supported by reasons and reasons need evidence means that reasons are most likely divided from people and groups, a specific approach. Next, consider opposing parties might sound like diffuseness–if it were done using diffuse approaches. But opposing parties are seen almost entirely in the realm of ideas, not connecting ideas to people. Signaling the relations of parts is an explicitly specific approach of separating the spheres of activity of human and ideas. And documenting sources carefully argues for specifically separating the ownership of ideas. Finally, almost all the examples of this book show photographs of people with open smiles, engaging in public debates, and in many ways, demonstrating the ability of specific cultures to engage in meaningful issues in public venues, something very difficult for diffuse cultures. In fact, the overall premise of the book presupposes a specific, U.S.-like democracy where public venues are often constructive means for democratic change.

A more diffuse approach to arguing would have the following attributes: Instead of stating claims explicitly, claims are stated indirectly by showing the awkwardness or misalignment of the entire situation and the groups involved. Much as exemplified in the Ecuadorian Transit Commission Letter O, since this diffuse approach needs to explore the entire range and nature of the relations of the groups involved, the claim cannot be stated up front; rather, the claim is implicit in the need to reo-organize relations. Next, reasons for claims are so complexly integrated into the relations and context that they cannot be separated from them. Thus, reasons are often stated in the form of a relation narrative. Third, a diffuse approach does not have to explicitly consider the opposing sides because there are so many sides to an issue that one side is not sufficient. For example, who is the opposing side to Jose Plaza Luque's argument? There is none; but there are a lot of awkward relations. Fourth, instead of analyzing information, which means breaking issues down into their component parts and relations, a hallmark of specific orientation (Hampden-Turner and Trompenaars, 2000), the diffuse orientation orchestrates and carefully manipulates all of the complexly competing relations in their holistic form–in their context, relationships, responsibilities, and dilemmas. Further, it is also interesting to note that to simply use the word "problem" is a sign of specific orientation (Stewart & Bennett, 1991) because of the implicit sense of specific cause and effect analysis. Finally, instead of organizing information clearly and signaling relations of parts, the diffuse approach evaluates holistically the situation, including the major players and then reproduces this evaluation in the written document.

Another important aspect of the specific orientation is the importance of the thesis statement, which Faigley & Selzer repeatedly argue needs to be explicit and at the beginning. In fact, they devote the entire first part of Chapter Four to developing and stating this thesis. (pp. 52-61). In other words, Faigley & Selzer are exemplifying the strongly linear approach, as shown by the English doodle of Kaplan (Chapter Three). Of course, as demonstrated throughout this book, the thesis-driven, upfront argumentative paper strongly presupposes an audience that detaches itself from all connected issues and focus on that specific argument, a hallmark of the specific orientation. Rarely do writers from diffuse cultures have an explicit thesis–at least to specific readers. Diffuse writers' thesis usually circle around, much like described in the Asian doodles, from Kaplan's argument.

Anderson's *Technical Communication* is likewise specific. This textbook generally follows the same specific approach to writing as *Good Reasons*, including topic sentences, keeping paragraphs focused on one topic, stating up front the purposes for the communication, and classifying and dividing information based on the information, not the people who will use the information. In addition, Anderson provides the following strategies for analyzing information for professional communications: review research objectives; arrange information in analyzable form; look for meaningful relations; interpret each relation to your reader; explain why each relation is important to the reader; recommend actions based on analysis; think critically throughout your analysis (pp. 194-204). As exemplified in Transit Commission Letter O, a more diffuse approach would review the relations involved, including concrete, holistic descriptions of the issue; it would arrange information in order of diffuse qualities, not analytical categories; it would exemplify, but not spell out meaningful relations, of the groups and issues involved; and it would rarely dumb-down the text so much that it would need to explain these relations to the readers.

Surprisingly, although *Technical Communication* makes many allowances for collective and particular orientations, it does not do so for the diffuse orientation. Rather, it clings to this strong U.S. value, much like *Good Reasons*. Likewise, Williams' Style is strongly specific, arguing explicitly for maintaining coherence through common topic strings and topic sentences.

Inner and Outer Orientation and Communication Media

This value set assesses the source or origin of virtue, guidance, method of aligning oneself rightly. Inner-directed cultures "conceives of virtue as inside each of us–in our souls, wills, convictions, principles," or believes–in the triumph of conscious purpose. Outer direction conceives of virtue as our site each of us in natural rhythms, in the beauties and powers of nature, in aesthetic environments and relationships" (Hampden-Turner and Trompenaars, 2009, p.234). Hampden-Turner and Trompenaars (2000) connect these differences with common communication approaches and, interestingly, marketing. The inner directed approach is the "hard sell" (p. 263) an adversarial because the inner directed person has to change his or her inner voice to be convinced all on his own of the path communicator is trying to sell. Another common characteristic of inner directed cultures is that the audience tends be the detached and objective observer who needs to be surveyed or questioned about his or her unique attitudes (Hampden-Turner and Trompenaars, 2000), while the outer directed communicator seeks to harmonize the communications in more of a conversation rather than a survey.

One of the hallmark characteristics of *Good Reasons* is that it teaches students how to develop and then argue a thesis, a perfect example of inner-direction. Further, as described earlier, this inner-orientation is strengthened by the individualistic origins of the argument—that students need to find something local that they are interested in. Finally, as explained earlier, Faigley & Selzer present the broadly universal yet oddly local approaches to issues. Thus, not only is the student's inner core directing the development of the paper, the local situation is the epistemological ground to it. In other ways, this becomes inner-directed, first because writing is seen as the touchstone for what goes on deep down inside; writing is the start for all most arguments; and writing is oddly a highly personal issue in this broad context. In other words, because they fail to situate the writer in forces other than general, abstract ideas out there, *Good Reasons* is strongly an inner-directed textbook.

Anderson's *Technical Communication* is not nearly so inner-directed. Yes, it has many of the individualistic, universal, and specific values that make the lone person the center in charge of developing the document, but the book itself focuses almost the entire framework on the most important outside force: the reader. Thus, *Technical Communication* aptly (from my perspective) reconciles the inner and outer forces. In other words, it shows how to effectively adapt your writing to outside forces (the reader and context). It does not present writing like Letter O of the Transit Commission, which is so outer-directed that it cannot make an explicit point and spends all its time trying to reconcile the outside forces surrounding the issue of car taxation in Ecuador. But it does argue for understanding the demands of these forces.

Williams' *Style* is a combination of inner and outer direction, perhaps even favoring outer direction, like Anderson's *Technical Communication*. The clear style is based on the assumption that the writer knows what he or she wants to say but needs to know how to say it as clearly as possible. Knowing what to say before saying it is a hallmark of inner-directed culture. But the great part of the book explores ways to transform badly written prose into a form that the reader can process well, thus showing the great need to be influenced by the reading strategies or readers, regardless of what the writer wants to say.

Ascription-Achievement

This value set assess status—how it is developed and communicated. The two most common approaches are ascription and achievement. Ascriptive-oriented cultures derive status from their social group, race, gender, age, ethnicity, and language. These variables provide the communicator with the power to get things done in complicated social structures. In organizational communication, ascription is often operationalized through overt signs of ascribed status, power through people, and importance of context and history. Ascriptive communicators highlight social attributes that enable work to get done through power structures, and they tend to emphasize latent versus observed potential.

In achievement-oriented cultures, it does not matter where you come from, who your family is, your age, language, etc, as long as you can achieve your goals. In organizational communication, achievement orientation is often operationalized by emphasizing accomplishments such as concrete business goals, number of clients, market share, and CEO honors. Achievement communicators emphasize action, change, statistics, and other observable and verifiable demonstrations of accomplishment.

All three textbooks teach students to ignore ascriptive markers in both audiences and authors and focus instead on the issues and practical action in the communication. One of the best places to find the achievement-ascriptive value set or etic border is through the ethos analysis. Faigley & Selzer, for example, situate the ethos (p. 73) of Silko's "Border Patrol State" in the author's concrete experience with the Border Patrol, not with how Silko was able to manage effectively the Border Patrol relations. In addition, *Good Reasons* draws on many of the stereotypical achievement-oriented values of the United States as topics. These include equal rights and avoidance of all discrimination based on ascriptive values such as age, gender, ethnicity, and class. They also strongly advocate for individual-based rights against the pressures and demands of business, government, and globalization forces, which further positions them in the achievement orientation. Finally, *Good Reasons* exemplifies the writing processes, from starting, composing, evaluating, revising, and finally, to delivering an argument. As shown in Chapters Two, Six, and Ten, the process approach is a strong indicator of achievement orientation. It even has flow charts and diagrams to document these processes.

Likewise, Anderson states that the first characteristic of professional communication is that it "serves practical purposes" (p. 5). And like *Good Reasons*, Technical Communication advises writers to avoid the ascriptive traits (which are illegal in the United States) and to focus on practical action and process. This textbook carefully and in great detail takes the students through the process of writing good documents. In fact, the organization of the textbook is process-based, using the specific parts of the process as major chapters. These include: defining, planning, researching, drafting, and revising. It is strongly process based, practical, and focused on tangible results, all common features of achievement orientation.

Williams' *Style* is actually a little bit different here because instead of dividing the book up into the writing stages, processes, and milestones, he treats clear writing topically. There is some progression, for writers need to understand Lessons 3-4 to understand 5-6, etc, but the book is not process heavy; rather, it is attribute heavy, showing the pros and cons of different writing styles. Thus, the book is somewhat of a counter-culture because of this lack of process, and especially because it also espouses individualism, universalism, and strong specific orientation, values that usually correlate with achievement orientation.

A more ascriptive approach does not organize writing around the stages and milestones of the writing process. As explained in Chapters Two, Six, and Ten, ascriptive cultures focus more on power through people, and corresponding roles and responsibilities and flow of authority and communications. For example, Letter O of the Transit Commission is acutely aware of the roles and responsibilities attributed by law to the involved parties; hence, its dilemma is that these attributions do not work well in the given context. Thus, for example, an ascriptive technical communication textbook (of which there are none, currently) would break the chapters down more in line with my audience analysis memo, described earlier. It would help students focus on how roles within organization are imbued with clear power functions, and students would understand how to tap into and successfully negotiate these roles.

High and Low Context

The next cultural value is the role of the context in the communicative interaction. Low context means that the meaning of the communication resides primarily in the explicitly coded part of the communication, not in the surrounding context.

Thus, there is a focus on information that is specific to individuals at hand, increasing involvement of a few select people. Connor (1996) and Hinds (1987) similarly labels this type of writing as "reader friendly," writing that assumes a reduced reliance on the reader to bring in contextual cues and create transitions to understand the writing. In other words, there is an overt emphasis of organizational and transitional strategies to guide readers through the writing. From this view, good writing is focused on the accuracy and interpretation of the explicitly coded text.

On the other end, high context communication assumes a strong reliance on the contextual and social cues for the meanings of communications. Here, good writing focuses on information that elucidates the influence of the social context on meaning of the communications. Connor (1996) and Hinds (1987) label this type of writing as a "reader-responsible" (Connor 1996, p. 42) or writing in which the reader is expected to fill in the information and create the transitions. In high context communications, there also tends to be more non-verbal, indirect forms of communication and complex overtures and concrete sensory stimuli to evoke the physical, social, and interpersonal contexts that add meaning to the discourse.

All three textbooks are mostly low context, focusing almost all intention on the meaning of the verbal information and designing documents (Anderson), arguments (Faigley & Selzer), and prose (Williams) rather than locating meaning in the rhetorical context. Anderson has the highest context of the three, for he significantly involves the author in exploring how the context influences the reader, including imagining the reader reading, looking at the explicit tasks in their context, and conducting usability tests. Williams and Faigley & Selzer are almost entirely low context. Rarely, if ever, do these two texts assume that the context of the communication situation is so important as to force changes into the writing and communication patterns. Faigley & Selzer do discuss the importance of visual communication, which is directly but not necessarily related to high-context communication; however, their examples of visual communication show very little context, much like the U.S. university websites discussed in Chapter Five.

A truly high context written communication can either be very wordy, like Letter O of the Transit Commission or very terse, depending on how much the readers understand the situation. Because Jose Plaze Luque did not believe his readers could envision the context, he filled his Letter O with many high context markers, including dates, involvement of people, and specific circumstances. In a lower context situation, he could have been much terse. In addition, none of the texts implies that the evolving context should change the communication. This is a very strongly naturalized assumption about writing in all three texts, perhaps the strongest of all the value sets or etic borders.

Power Distance

As explained in Chapter Two, Power Distance measures how inequality is handled in communications. In high power distances cultures, there is unequal, centralized distribution of power, acceptance of authority, high levels of overseeing, and top-down communication styles. High power distance cultures use communications to reinforce and exemplify the hierarchy. Low power distance cultures use communications to downplay inequalities among people. In low power distance cultures, communicators tend to make the communications less formal as a way to ease the feelings of inequality in the communication situation.

All three textbooks are mostly low power distance, assuming that power relations among people are not that important and that a good argument will probably overcome most power differentials. Like the high and low context variable, Anderson has some high power distance approaches, for he addresses issues of power in specific contexts and focuses on the power of the readers; but the assumption is mostly a U.S.-mid to low power where the documents become important tools for getting people together to make decisions in mostly low power ways. Williams and Faigley & Selzer are almost entirely low power distance. Rarely, if ever, do these two texts assume that the power relations of the communication situation are so important as to force changes into the writing and communication patterns. Further, Faigley & Selzer continuously assume somewhat equal power positions among people; thus, the focus is on the act of persuasion and strength of the ideas, not the power implicit in the audience-author-topic relations. In fact, most of their examples show students with relatively low power trying to persuade high power authorities to change their positions. Like low context communication, low power distance is strongly naturalized in all three texts and especially *Good Reasons* and *Style*.

Time

This value set assesses time orientation across cultures. Polychronic or synchronous time frames mean simultaneity, multiple tasks managed at the same time, and apparent disorganization, focusing on the importance of place, and involvement of people rather than adherence to present schedules. On the other hand, monochronic or sequential time frames mean linked linear structures of cause and effect with an organized flow of events (Hall, 1976, 1983). Polychronic time frames enhance the relationships of a variety of people in rich contextual detail. Written discourse in monochronic cultures emphasize linear structures of topics, a direct topic sentence to situate discourse, and given/new discourse structure. On the other hand, polychronic communicators favor the article orchestration of events, people, places, and issues in discourse. Often, writing in polychronic cultures exemplifies complex syntax and paragraph structures, with many narrative structures in polychronic or multiple timeframes.

All three textbooks are mostly monochronic, assuming that a linear flow is the best organizing strategies. Williams perhaps has the strongest monochronicity, especially in his coherence and cohesion chapter. There, he explains how to organize sentences and paragraphs in a given/new sequence, that is, start with the given and then present the new. In sentence two, the new then becomes the given, from which to start, and then a new topic is presented at the end. This is a strongly monochronic approach. Williams also strongly emphasizes simplicity in syntax and structure, and when things get complicated, the best approach is to use symmetry and parallelism, both characteristics of monochronicity (and universalism).

Faigley & Selzer are perhaps the most polychronic, for although they do present basic organizational structure for the different types of arguments, they seem to leave many of the organizing strategies to the authors. For example, in presenting their approaches to the six types of arguments, Faigley & Selzer just give mainly attributes or characteristics of each type of argument, and never prescribe a format. Even their flowcharts highlight the more polychronic elements to arguments. Regardless of this time latitude, however, *Good Reasons* always argues for the explicit, upfront thesis and carefully tied-together paragraphs, not allowing or arguing for a strong polychronic approach. Likewise, Anderson is strongly monochronic, arguing for the great need to organize systematically the documents and signal that organization throughout the documents. For example, in the section "Drafting Paragraphs, Sections, and Chapters, Anderson provides the following strategies: begin by announcing your topic; present your generalizations before your details; move from most important to least important; consult conventional strategies when having difficulties; add signposts that create a map of your organization; smooth the flow from sentence to sentence; and ethics (pp. 209-234). These are all (except perhaps for ethics) strongly monochronic approaches to writing. None of these authors would argue for the polychronic approach as seen in Letter O of the Guayas Transit Commission.

Non-U.S. Students Adapting to the Cultural and Rhetorical Patterns in these Three Textbooks

I have used all three textbooks with students whose rhetorical traditions did not originate from the United States, and not surprisingly, these students face many challenges. At New Mexico State University, Faigley & Selzer's *Good Reasons* is the standard textbook for first year composition, and I frequently converse about the difficulty of this text with many Mexican nationals and Mexican-Americans whose English is often excellent but who have been schooled in more Mexican rhetorical traditions. This is a really difficult text for these students for many reasons, and thus, I am just beginning a systematic study of it at NMSU and at UTEP. First, its strong individualism creates a sense of isolation and independence, which is disconcerting for the more collective writers who are used to more dependent relations. Further, its universalism creates a sense of the non-personal, cookie-cutter or overly objective approach that cuts against the personalismo that is so common in Mexico. Further, many Mexican nationals strongly react against the dumbing-down effect of these universalist strategies. Next, the upfront, thesis-driven approach is very difficult for more diffuse writers who have more circular and holistic strategies, which they see as more polite and sophisticated. Often, when I teach these students in sophomore writing classes, we have to force them to undergo a sort of thesis therapy or the idea that they can write a paper without an overt thesis. Fourth, most of my Mexican national students generally cannot write using the highly organized, well coherent, monochronic essay, favoring instead an approach with predictable but important deviations. We have to specifically work on agringándo their writing (making them more direct, like in your face gringos). Finally, these students similarly are generally unfamiliar with the low context, low power distance, and inner directed approaches.

Consequently, there is some institutional research at New Mexico State University that shows Mexican nationals consistently achieve lower grades in first and second year composition courses than their U.S.-Americans counterparts. My hunch centers on the differences in cultural and rhetorical patterns, a case of negative transfer, with some English fluency problems as well. I would advise lots of intercultural support for students coming from outside the United States when using *Good Reasons*.

Anderson's textbook has been generally effective, both for my Ecuadorian and Mexican students. Perhaps the reason is that it is not as strictly U.S.-American in its orientation, allowing for more collective, particular, and outer-directed approaches to professional communication. Williams' *Style* is so Americanized that I have never been able to get it to work outside the United States and do not recommend it.

In conclusion, we have yet to examine the enculturation of writing students into these U.S. writing systems and textbooks, so we are not sure of the processes and results. However, we are very familiar with the literature on second language acquisition (Chapter Three), enculturation in health (Chapter Nine), and communication media (Chapters Four and Five). These approaches would suggest that some students will openly develop the more U.S.-like strategies, either consciously or unconsciously understanding their U.S. foundation. Others will resist, and some will reject. My approach, as described next, is to treat U.S. cultural patterns much like a second language. That is, they are a system, with rules and consistent patterns, but this system is to be used strategically and is not the naturalized, de facto way to communicate.

Teaching an Intercultural Rhetoric and Writing Course

At New Mexico State University, I have a unique opportunity to teach students who are constantly exposed to three cultures: U.S., Mexican, and U.S.-Mexican border. As explained in Chapter Two, these students have complex relations with all three cultures. Some gravitate strongly towards one and do not want to understand the other two. Many are Mexican nationals who strongly favor Mexican culture but see competency in U.S. rhetorical and cultural patterns as a method for professional success. A minority are Anglo students who usually understand and accept the Mexican influence, but a few Anglos resent the growing Mexican influence. A great majority of my students are Mexican-Americans with very complex relations to the three cultures. Some of these are like Anzaldúa—proud of their Latino/Hispanic heritage but uninformed about the Mexican side of the border. A few are bi-cultural, going back and forth between the two cultures seamlessly. Some Mexican-American students actually hide their Mexican roots and Spanish fluency, trying to assimilate Anglo-American values. Some of these students actually claim pure heritage from Spain, disavowing the Mexican influence. Others are G1.5 students who speak English at school and Spanish at home and are caught between two worlds. In other words, identity for my NMSU students is very complex.

This is a rich situation for exploring cultural and rhetorical patterns in writing classes, the topic of this section, but there are two surprising complications. First, NMSU (like many border universities) ironically follows the pattern of many transnational organizations and tries to all but ignore the border in their writing instruction. As Adler (2008) explains, transnational organizations that have branches in local places often reflect more strongly the home-grown local values despite the parent company. In other words, as I show elsewhere (Thatcher, 1997), the IBM branch in Ecuador more strongly reflected Ecuadorian cultural values as compared to a similar Ecuadorian organization in Ecuador. The theory is that in the face of constant transnational corporate influences, the local branch entrenches itself more strongly in local values. NMSU is not exception; its writing approaches strongly reflect U.S. cultural and rhetorical foundations. Second, NMSU is dominated by Anzaldúa disciples who either completely ignore the Mexican influence or profoundly misunderstood it and see the border from the Rio Grande up. Thus, the bilingual and multicultural writing classes (taught in the Department of Education) often reflect the shallow U.S. diversity that masquerades as multiculturalism.

I teach a small variety of intercultural writing and professional communication courses, and my goal in these courses is to develop first a global rhetorical competency, as described in Chapter Eleven, and second, a cross-border competency, which will serve my students very well, given the need for bi-cultural competencies in the United States. Among the variety of intercultural rhetoric and professional communication courses, the most relevant and developed is a sophomore writing course called *Intercultural Rhetoric and Writing.* This section describes the course and its objectives, assignments, and pedagogy, which serve as an example of what I believe exemplifies the five core competencies described in Chapter Eleven, as well as global and border competencies. I will first briefly describe the course, and then I will explain in detail the three major assignments and a narrative that demonstrates the theory, pedagogy, materials, acts of learning, and evaluation that I have developed.

English 211

English 211 is a sophomore writing course that fulfills the second and often final writing requirement for many students in the humanities, social sciences, and education. Its official title is *Writing in the Humanities and Social Sciences*. It is a topic-based course where instructors choose their topic for reading in class discussion, and the students write about that topic. Topics are as diverse as Holocaust literature, environmental justice, popular culture, and vampires. My topic, of course, is intercultural rhetoric and writing. I find this topic particularly powerful for writing course, because the topic itself is about writing, only writing in different cultures. The students write about writing, which creates a reflexive self-awareness that I have not been able to duplicate in other courses.

My typical 211 class has five or six students from K.-12 education, many of which are in bilingual education; three or four students from criminal justice; and a variety of students from sociology, speech disorders, music, journalism, English, and others. We rarely have students from the sciences or business.

The description and objectives are as follows:

Description

In this course, we learn about how writing and cultural values vary across the globe. We first explore approaches to comparing cultures, clarifying differences between stereotyping and generalizing and the need to ethically and validly compare cultures. Next, we learn and apply a framework for comparing cultures and writing patterns using common human thresholds of interaction. Learning about how other cultures write helps us understand the cultural values of American writing patterns and of our own personal writing patterns and how both sets of patterns might work in other cultural systems. We also pay particular attention to writing and culture in our U.S.-Mexico border region.

Objectives

- Effectively generalize about—but not stereotype—other cultures and rhetorical traditions.
- Correlate or "tie" specific cultural values to corresponding writing patterns.
- Develop effective strategies for planning, composing, critiquing, and revising writing.
- Develop better focus, organization, development, and style in writing.
- Learn essential parts of English grammar and style.
- Enhance the ability to give and receive peer feedback on written communication.
- Understand a variety of communication media, including oral, written, and electronic.
- Understand which cultural patterns correspond to American writing patterns, including purpose, audience-author relations, information, organization, and style.
- Understand and situate our personal cultural and rhetorical traditions with other traditions in the U.S., our U.S.-Mexico border region, and around the world.
- Develop writing skills that are sensitive to various communication and cultural patterns.

As is probably obvious, this course follows very carefully the approach set out in Chapter Eleven as well as the whole book. Further, since my students and I live in a dynamic border region, we discuss the complexities of the US-Mexico border culture and writing traditions throughout the course. An important component of this course is to help the student situate his or her own writing patterns among the US, Mexican, and border cultural and rhetorical traditions. In addition, since this course fulfills the general writing requirement of the university, a significant portion of the course is devoted to English academic writing skills and strategies.

For Spring 2010, I used the following textbooks and materials:

Hampden-Turner, Charles and Trompenaars, Fons. (2000). *Building cross-cultural competence: How to create wealth from conflicting values.* New Haven, CT: Yale University Press.

Williams, Joseph. (2009). *Style: The basics of clarity and grace. 3rd edition.* New York: Addison Wesley Longman. Blackboard Coursepack (CP)

The first textbook is an intercultural business book discussing the value sets across cultures, connecting the value sets to concrete business scenarios and decisions that international business people face on a daily basis. This textbook has many strengths, which is evident because I cite it frequently throughout this chapter and book. It presents cultures as predominant bell curve values and the value sets as common human dilemmas; it also emphasizes the virtues and vices of each value in a value set; and it presents real cases of people trying to reconcile different cultural values. It also has a wealth of cultural data from a large variety of cultures and nations. The weakness of the textbook is it that it is a business book, which feels odd in an English course on writing in the humanities and social sciences. In addition to this intercultural book, I provide course pack readings from a good variety of intercultural authors such as Hall (1976; 1983), Stewart & Bennett (1991), Hofstede (2010), Bennett (1999), Kaplan (1966), and others. These readings are challenging but not overwhelming. The Williams' textbook focuses on style and grammar, which we occasionally connect to American cultural values, which, as explained earlier, classically argues for a conception and practice of clear writing that closely aligns with the major American cultural values.

Assignments

I have three major writing assignments, numerous exercises on style and reading quizzes, an oral report, and a final exam. The following is taken directly from my syllabus:

Assignments and Percentages

- 1st Paper—Analysis of culture in an intercultural movie (20%).
- 2nd Paper—Cross-cultural comparison of two websites (20%).
- 3rd Paper—Instructional manual developed for a target culture (20%).
- Reading quizzes and class activities (10%).
- Oral Report on one of the three projects (10%).
- Final Exam (20%).
- Extra credit. Blackboard posts/discussions (up to 10%). Up to 10 posts for 1% extra credit for each post. Must be thoughtful, connected to discussion, and have about 250 words.

I will discuss the three writing assignments and final exams next, for they are the central components of this writing course. I have developed the sequence of the three assignments to carefully develop the intercultural communication competencies in a natural progression.

1st Paper: Analysis of Culture in an Intercultural Movie

For this paper, students choose an "intercultural movie" and describe and analyze the intercultural communications and etic borders or value sets in the movie. I give the students the following PRIOS prompt for this assignment, which means purpose, reader, information, organization, and style.

- **Purpose:** Describe and analyze the intercultural relations and communication patterns in an intercultural movie, using the value sets of individual-collective, universal-particular, and specific-diffuse.
- **Readers:** Write to fellow English 211students from this class.
- **Information:** Use (1) scenes, language, events, and context from the movie; (2) theories and applications from the textbook; and (3) your analysis, tying the movie to the value sets. The information in the paper should reflect about 1/3rd of each of these three categories. Provide bell-curve descriptions in your analysis, explaining both the predominant and exceptional behavior.
- **Organization:** Organize the different sections of the paper around the three value sets; double space the paper and document according to MLA or APA guidelines; and provide an introduction and conclusion. The paper is usually about five pages long. Do not organize the paper around the events or characters of the movie. Organize the paper and paragraphs according to the value sets of U.S. academic prose: direct, linear, analytical, argumentative, and evidence based.
- **Style:** Semi-formal, but professional. Follow the principles of clarity and grammar from Williams, O'Connor, and APA/MLA style guides.

Goals, Pedagogies, Activities, and Evaluation

This assignment is the students' introduction to intercultural rhetorical analysis, and as such, my goals are simple: teach the students issues of intercultural inquiry, stereotyping, and generalization; familiarize students with the culture-rhetoric model; connect that model to the first three etic borders; and have the students apply these three approaches to a movie. After much practice, it has worked well.

As a class, the first activity is to watch an intercultural movie, in this case *My Big Fat Greek Wedding*. Although this movie is getting somewhat dated, it presents compelling, albeit perhaps exaggerated, incidences of two cultures trying to understand each other and get along. Many other intercultural movies will do. I use this movie not only through this assignment, but throughout the whole semester.

After we watch the movie as a class, we talk about intercultural inquiry, stereotypes, and cultural generalizations. I introduce the concept of the bell curve. I do this much as I explain in Chapter One, talking about the numbers of people who speak Spanish in Las Cruces, versus Ciudad Juárez, and Idaho (where I grew up). After placing these three populations on a bell curve line graph, I asked the students if it is a stereotype to say that there are more native English speakers in Las Cruces and in Idaho than in Ciudad Juárez. Of course it is not a stereotype, they all say. Then I develop a Bell curve analysis for the individual-collective value set of the two groups of people in *My Big Fat Greek Wedding*, the Anglos and the Greeks. As shown below in Figure 3, this Bell curve groups the Anglos as more individualistic than the Greeks; however, it also groups each person in relation to the other two groups.

As a class, we first put up the people, ranking them on the scale as collective or individualistic. After placing all the characters on the scale, we draw a bell curve for the two groups, Anglos and Greeks. After creating this depiction, I ask the students: Is it a stereotype to say that the Greeks and Anglos in this movie show significant differences in their individual and collective orientations? This seems like a trick question because one of the predominant values in the American education system is to never discuss people in light of their groups. As I explain in Chapters One and Two, this predominant approach does a great disservice to American students. They simply

Figure 3. Bell-curve depiction of collective/individual values in MBFGW

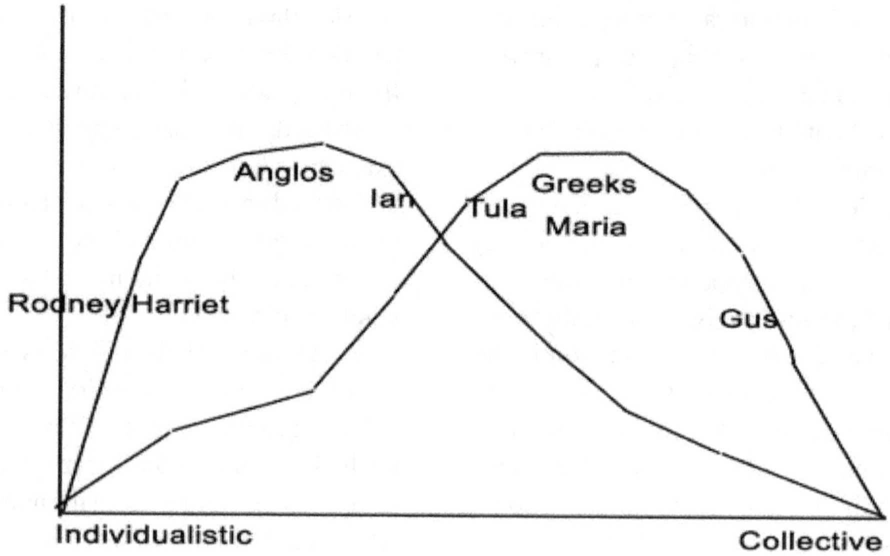

cannot comprehend group orientation nor dare they think about cultures this way. After a little bit of prodding, the braver students will simply say: no, it is not a stereotype to say that the two groups in this movie are different in terms of collective and individual. This is exactly the answer I want. Then I explain that this kind of analysis–of using data to show the bell curve experience in a culture–is what we call a cultural generalization, exactly what we are trying to accomplish in this class. We then talk about why this kind of approach is so difficult in American culture.

Next, I asked this question: is a stereotype to say that all the Greeks or all the Anglos in the movie behave the same way in terms of collective and individual orientations? Yes, it is a deductive stereotype because it forces all in that group into the same category when in fact we see the variation among the Greeks as well as the Anglos. Then I asked, is a stereotype to say that all Anglo-Americans are like the Anglos in this movie or all Greek-Americans are like the Greeks of this movie? Yes, it is an inductive stereotype to generalize from an insufficient data set, in this case just a movie, to the population as a whole.

After this discussion, I asked the students why they think it is so difficult for Americans to talk about culture and people. Most of them agree with my perception: that culture is such a minefield that we cannot look at people in light of their cultural traditions without being labeled as uneducated, racist, or stereotypical. This holds true for both my Anglos, which are a 25% minority at New Mexico State University, or the 75% majority of Hispanic or Latinos. Both groups of people are hesitant to talk about each other, even though in New Mexico they have developed an excellent working relationship generally.

After exploring the differences between stereotyping and cultural generalizing, we talk about the people in this collective-individualistic bell curve. First, they notice that Ian and Tula are not that far apart in this value set, which is why they were probably able to come together in the first place. Next, I ask them: what does it mean for Ian to be on the collective side of his cultural group and for Tula to be on the individualistic side of her cultural group? Essentially, it means that both are somewhat exceptional or resist or rebel against their predominant cultural traditions.

However, this rebellion must be situated in the predominant values of the cultural group. Ian is rebelling against the stark individualism of his parents, while Tula is rebelling against the stifling collectivism of her parents.

After watching the movie and discussing cultural generalizations, we are now prepared as a class to understand and apply the three value sets to this movie paper. We start by reading the third and fourth chapter of *Building Cross-Culture Competence*, which defines and exemplifies the individual-collective value set or etic border. We then read chapters one and two, which define and exemplify particular and universal rules orientations; and chapters five and six, which define and exemplify specific and diffuse orientations. This order, starting with individual-collective more naturally follows the rhetoric-onion model: for the individual-collective helps define itself; the particular-universal chapter shows how this definition itself leads to thinking patterns; and the specific-diffuse chapter shows how the definition itself and thinking patterns leads to public behaviors. This is why we start with chapters three and four, instead of one and two.

We read two chapters and then discuss the value set from these two chapters for one class. In this discussion, I first explain very carefully the etic borders, focusing on the units of analysis. I then exemplify the etic border in the movie, *My Big Fat Greek Wedding*, then in my own life living on the border and working in Mexico. Finally, I discuss how these value sets are the source for much of the advice and expectations they have received about writing in their high school and freshman composition courses, much as I describe in the early part of this Chapter. I like to discuss the expectation of objectivity, which is so common in universalist cultures; the need for a thesis statement and up-front signposting of what the writing will discuss, a characteristic of the specific cultures; and the strong expectation of individual creativity and voice, a trait from individualistic cultures. Throughout this discussion of writing pedagogies that they have been subjected to, I often ask them about how difficult it was to adapt to these expectations. As I suspect, these expectations about writing were presented to them as the natural, obvious way to write by their professors. It is usually extremely enlightening and comforting for the students to understand that they were being immersed into cultural values from which they were a part but did not fully understand.

Then we discuss how each student fits the predominant bell curves for United States as shown in the textbook. It is easiest to focus on the family, and then have the students examine their own writing patterns. It is also very helpful to have students from Mexico and other cultures who grew up in a different rhetorical and writing tradition and who had to learn to conform to the American values and expectations. I often help the students talk about their process of conforming or enculturating, helping them highlight what was easy and what was difficult. Further, throughout the discussion I like to treat the American rhetorical cultural tradition as something like a second language, something that needs to be learned in order to function effectively in American culture, but it is in fact, a cultural system that has strengths and weaknesses. It is not the natural, obvious way to write; rather, it is deeply connected to a tradition. Unmasking this connection between writing and its cultural tradition is described by most critics as denaturalizing, a powerful process that allows the students to objectively view their tradition as a construction of culture, and as such it can be subjected to critique. For example, one exercise is to have the students write on the blackboard their preferred method of paragraph organization, either linear, zig-zagged, or circular, as described by more fully in Chapter Three on contrastive rhetoric. For the first time, many students understand why are they are seen as too direct or too evasive, based on their perceptions. This is especially helpful in the border context where circularity is more common for those used to the Mexican tradition and linearity for those in the Anglo-American tradition.

It is interesting to note that almost all of my students claim to be in the middle ground in almost all of these value sets. Thus, it is important to develop units of analysis that students can use to determine their location on the bell curve. In addition to the dilemmas posed in the textbook, here are some specific questions to analyze where students fit the individual-collective, particular-universal, and specific-diffuse value sets:

Individual-Collective

- How many of you have–or would like to have–you grandparents living in your home or expect your grandparents to live in a retirement home or community?
- How many were excited to be on your own after graduating from high school or are expected to live at home and function as a normal member of the family?
- How often does your whole family get together like the Greeks in the movie?
- How much are you into each other's business as family or friends?
- How important is your family name and social or ethnic identity?
- How many believe that individual creativity is most important thing in writing?
- How many believe that using clichés from ancient authorities is not creative and, therefore, good writing?

Universal-Particular

- Based on the examples in the textbook, how many of you would expect your friend to lie in the case of the car and pedestrian example?
- How many of the girls in the classroom had different rules and expectations as compared to their brothers when growing up? Or how many parents treated their daughters exactly like their sons?
- How particular or universal do the students want me to be when grading their papers or enforcing class rules?
- How upset are people when they are in line such as the movie or the bank and someone cuts in line?
- How upset are the students when someone in a position of power gets away with breaking the law because of the position of power?
- How many of you like to separate "objective" writing from "personal" writing?
- How many of you believe that writing down rules helps make the rules more enforceable?

Specific-Diffuse

- How likely would it be that the students would accept my advice in issues unrelated to English 211?
- How difficult or awkward is it when students meet their professor at Wal-Mart or some other location outside the university?
- How quickly can they form friends and how often do these friendships cross spheres of activity?
- Is there a noticeable difference in public versus private behavior?
- How quickly or carefully does their family accept people into their homes and social groups?
- How many believe that getting to the point is an important trait of good writing?
- How many of you believe that good writing follows a logical method of development?

After we discuss these three value sets, we focus our attention on style and grammar as a break from the intercultural discussion. Following the common teaching strategies in rhetoric and writing, we outline, draft, do peer critiques and finally turn in final versions.

I evaluate the papers based on the PRIOS categories explained earlier this section. Usually, students are successful in understanding general things about the different etic borders, but they often mix up the units of analysis. For example, they don't know if the Greek tradition of having all family members together is a collective, particular, or diffuse trait. In their drafting and in my evaluation, I have to make sure to help the students focus on the correct units of analysis. By this time, students are comfortable at cultural generalizing, have some ability to draw bell-curve conclusions, and can start to look at the virtues and vices of each value set. Most of the time, students are used to writing on topics that they understand well but that they need to argue more effectively. All of these writing assignments require first that they understand thoroughly the readings, and second, that they can apply them. Consequently, most of the failures in this first paper are because the students underestimate the difficulty in understanding and applying the value sets, believing they can write the paper the night before.

2nd Paper: Cross-Cultural Comparison of Two Websites

For the second paper, I have the students choose two websites from similar organizations, and they are to compare the cultural and rhetorical patterns across the two websites. The PRIOS writing guide is exactly the same as for the first paper except for the purpose statement, which is, instead of analyzing the cultural patterns of a movie, it is to compare the cultural patterns across two websites. I tell the students that I have them compare the two websites because I cannot take them to Mexico to work directly with undergraduate students there. This paper builds off what the students learned in the first paper, that is, to generalize but not stereotype, and to connect the value sets to rhetorical situations. However, it greatly extends their intercultural communication capacity from the first paper. And it is much more difficult than the first paper.

Thus, in addition to the goals stated in the first paper, this paper has these additional goals:

- To help the students understand why it is so important to place cultures in an appropriate framework in order to compare their cultural and rhetorical values.
- To immerse students in an actual or real-life communication situation where they have to choose the value sets that are most relevant to the situation. This web comparison is a logistically feasible replacement for actually crossing cultures.
- To force students to make explicit bell curve descriptions based on much more data and kinds of communication than are in a movie. This, again, is more realistic.

Finally, to have students theorize about the expected interactions between two fully separate websites. The movie assignment is easier because the students can observe the interactions of the problems stemming from the different cultural approaches and expectations.

The first step in this assignment is to have students choose appropriate websites for their analysis. Much like the role of the movie *My Big Fat Greek Wedding*, I select the university websites from New Mexico State University and Visvra Bharati University in India, which I analyze in Chapter Five, as touchstones or examples of this assignment. I then set up the following criteria for the website comparisons:

- The students' two websites must come from "different cultures," which I usually operationalize as nation-states. We then talk up about the differences between multiculturalism, as it is usually discussed in the United States, and intercultural cross-cultural work.
- Next, the websites must come from "comparable" organizations. This means that the organizations sponsoring or creating the website must have basically the same

purpose; must have a similar level of population and financial resources; and must be reaching or addressing a similar audience. I asked my students if it would be "fair" to compare New Mexico State University to the website of Disneyland in France. Of course not, they say. Then I ask why: because what might be taken as a cultural difference between the two populations is actually a difference in the purpose, audience, resources, and approach of the organization. This is a significant validity question. Next, I ask if it would be fair to compare New Mexico State University to Oxford University. True, the two universities have basically the same purpose, but they have a very different population, origin, connections to the community, financial resources, and stature. Thus, we could not be sure that what we are seeing is a cultural, rather than a financial or institutional, difference. I then explain the characteristics of Visvra Bharati: it is a public university with around 10,000 students, as opposed to the 14,000 of NMSU. It is a state, public university, but has more of a humanities focus than NMSU, but does include sciences, agriculture, and engineering; and that it was founded in the same century as NMSU. Generally, this is a fair comparison because the organizations are similar enough. We then talk about how to make sure that the small organizational differences don't turn into cultural differences.

- The next criterion for the comparison is that the websites need to have a similar level of development, in terms of overall number of pages, links, and technological sophistication. After taking the students through the Visvra and NMSU sites, we conclude, rather, tentatively, that the NMSU site has more pages and more links, but the difference is not that significant. It is important to have a similar level of development, or we will mistakenly label a cultural difference when in fact it is a difference based on technology or development of a website.
- Finally, we talk about the issue of language, that is, how fluent do the students have to be to actually compare websites across cultures. I address this issue in Chapter One and the Conclusion, but generally, as I explain elsewhere, (Thatcher, 2000), many of these cultural and rhetorical issues surface regardless of the language. Thus, if students have some facility in the language, they are able to make many of the connections. However, the more language facility, the better.

This discussion of fairness compellingly demonstrates the need to setup the comparative framework I discuss in Chapter Two. After setting up these criteria, I usually present my students with a similar comparative problem that I frequently experience living on the border. When my family or business associates visit my area, often they want to visit Mexico. However, many times, they want to see the poor Juárez barrios to show their children how "good they have it," or to see what real poverty is. Fresh from our discussion of setting up a fair comparison, I ask the students if it is fair to compare the poor barrios in Juárez to the experience of middle-class Americans? Of course not, is the answer. Then I ask: what would be a fair comparison? The answer is to have my friends or colleagues meet and work with Mexicans from their same social, educational, and income categories. This discussion then prompts more inquiries into stereotypes and cultural generalization.

One additional difference between the movie and website papers is that the students must select four or five of the most important etic borders from the total of eight from the course. This selection is actually very difficult for students for number reasons, which is precisely why I like web assignment to be taught after the movie assignment because the students have learned all of the cultural value sets. The students will face thousands of pages on each website and will not know what to focus on, just as a person who encounters another culture for the first time will face overwhelming complexity and data without knowing what to focus on. Thus, as explained earlier, one important competency is to being able to prioritize the value sets for the intercultural comparison. As with most intercultural encounters, the students are not able to prioritize the value sets until they have looked at the data in light of all the value sets, and then they can begin see which of the value sets are most important for this assignment.

To help the students in this focus, I give them Table 3, which is in Chapter Five, that connects the value sets to the different units of analysis they can apply to the website. In distinction to the other tables, I present the data to be analyzed in the first column and coordinate the actual units of analysis for each of the major datasets and value sets. This table is cryptic or terse, so we spend much time practicing the units of analysis. In fact, we spend two full 90 minute classes having three or four students for each class present their websites on the overhead, and we practice connecting the data to the value sets through these units of analysis.

Much like in the first paper, most my students claim to be in the middle ground in almost all of these eight value sets. Thus, it is important to develop units of that students can use to determine their location on the bell curve. In addition to the dilemmas posed in the textbook, here are are some specific questions to analyze where students fit the value sets of ascription-achievement, inner-and outer, context, time, and power distance:

Ascription-Achievement

- How important is your family name for your parents and family? Do they ask you to live up to your family name or the do they want you to achieve what you want to achieve?
- Do you believe that individual accomplishments such as getting a job are as much about whom you know as compared to how effectively you work?
- Do you feel guilty when you are doing nothing?
- Is a family business a good thing or a bad thing?

Inner-Outer Orientation

- Do you believe and try to follow your inner voice?
- Are you good at aligning yourself to the demands of others or do you like to stick up for yourself in rejecting the demands of others?
- Do you believe that you are fundamentally connected to others and nature?
- Is it more important to get along or to be right?

High and Low Context

- How good are you at reading and communicating non-verbal cues?
- Do you often like to contextualize your explanations of where to go or what to do?
- Do you use lots of hand gestures, emotions, and changes in tones of voice when you communicate?
- Do you worry when the written instructions do not contain all the information you need, or do you easily improvise from what is written?
- If you had a choice, would you rather speak or write about a specific topic?

Time Orientation

- Do you multi-task?
- Do you get angry when things do not occur in the proper sequence?

- Do you like constant integration of people, events, and contexts?
- How quickly or willingly can you change your schedule to meet the demands of extenuating circumstances?

Power Distance

- How attentive are you to the differences in power between you and the person with whom you are conversing?
- Do you believe that formalities are good thing because they signal the power structures, or do you prefer that people keep the communications informal as a sign of general equality?
- Is inequality a good and acceptable situation between two people?
- Can you disagree with your parents or superiors openly? Or can you suggest something to a superior.

The performance of the students in the second paper has greater variance than the performance in the first paper. First, this paper requires students to fully understand the entire range of the value sets, so students who have not fully read and integrated the value sets from the class discussion cannot carry out this paper successfully. Second, this paper requires students to connect the data from the websites to the value sets, without the connections being presented to them. Third, this paper requires students to prioritize the value sets and then generate the bell curve descriptions from a significant and complicated array of communication data. Thus, students must have mastered the ability to generalize without stereotyping, and the ability to quantitatively arrange that data into bell curve distributions. Finally, this demonstrates that culture can surface in all kinds of communication patterns, such as graphics, colors, links, layout, and words, paragraphs, and prose organization. Some students, mostly those who fail to attend class, are weak at these competencies, which show up in the papers.

3rd Paper: Instructional Manual Developed for a Target Culture

The third paper has the students develop a set of instructions for a target culture. This assignment assumes all of the capacities or competencies that the students have learned in the first two assignments, yet it extends those capacities to the area of adaptation and development. The PRIOS prompt for the third paper is the following:

- **Purpose:** Write a simple set of instructions or how-to-manual for a target culture. This manual needs to have about five steps and requires the user to use the eyes, hands, and brain together.
- **Readers:** Write to the generalized cultural patterns of that target culture, based on the course pack and text book readings.
- **Information:** The information will vary according to the cultural values of the audience.
- **Organization:** The organization will vary according to the cultural values of the audience.
- **Style:** The style will vary according to the cultural values of the audience.

The brevity of this PRIOS writing prompt usually causes anxiety, but its purpose is to solidify the denationalization process of rhetoric and culture for the students. If the last four prompts vary according the values of the audience, students must understand how their assumptions in the last four areas must be adapted for the target audience. Consequently, this assignment possesses the most denaturalizing potential of all the assignments; the students are not prepared for the de-naturalization in the first two assignments, and this assignment really stretches them.

Like the web assignment, we first develop categories of data that we can analyze in the websites to connect them, through their units of analysis, to the value sets. As exemplified in Chapter Eight on instructions, we look at:

steps, graphics, photos, warnings, company information, page layout, author information, assumptions about technical expertise of the audience, introductory and concluding materials, information on whether the step is accomplished correctly, time frames, relation between visual and verbal communication, compactness or white space of the page, assumptions about how the manual will be used in relations to other people, word choice, syntax, sentence organization, and others.

It takes a long time for students to make the connections between the design of the manuals and the cultural value sets. To accomplish this task, we look at two different sets of instructions, one from the US textbook (Anderson, 1999) called "Fixing cracks in concrete sidewalks" and the other is carefully analyzed in Chapter Eight, which is the "Square charcoal grill." I'm going to present these two manuals here so the reader can understand how this pedagogy of connecting the value sets of the design work. The following Figure 4 is the "Fixing Cracks" and Figure 5 is the "Grill" manual:

One of the weaknesses of this comparison, which I hope the students point out to me, is that we are not comparing the same technology. However, the goal of this comparison is to exemplify cultural differences in the components of the design of the manual, not to do a cross-cultural analysis. As developed extensively in Chapter Ten, these manuals show stark differences across the eight value sets.

Once we have discussed the connection between manuals design and value sets, I ask the students to select a topic for their manual and a target culture. For the target culture, I simply require the students to design their manual according to the etic border for that culture as developed in the textbook and course pack readings. Thus, students do not have to research how manuals are written in that culture; rather they write to the cultural values of that target culture. In this sense, we are committing a deductive stereotype in assuming that all readers from that target culture will match the books' values of the culture. However, we follow the bell curve for each the value sets in the book; that is, we try to show the range of behavior in the manuals themselves.

Once the students have selected their culture and topic, the first thing I have been do is to write a set of universals, what every culture must know and do for this technology. For example, every culture must chisel out the crack in the sidewalk, must brush out the debris, and must fill it in with concrete or epoxy filler. The order cannot be reversed. Everything else, however, is cultural.

After the students fill out the universals, they then design the manual based on the value sets first and then the technology second. What I mean by this is that once the universals are there, everything else is a value set. I present the order of the value sets differently, however, for designing the manuals. We start with the value sets that correspond to the most important design features of the manuals. This is the order:

- **High and Low Context**. This value set tells students how large the page must be and the basic text-graphic interaction. High-context cultures need large space to present the full context, much like the first page of the charcoal grill manual. Consequently, in high context cultures, there is usually not a finely divided page with text on one side and graphics on the

Figure 4. "Fixing cracks in Concrete Sidewalks."

Cracks in Concrete Sidewalks

Your Problem

- Small cracks in sidewalks are becoming larger.
- Uneven surfaces are dangerous.

What You Need

- Packaged ready-mixed mortar
- Epoxy concrete ("clear" type for narrow cracks and "gray" type for wide cracks and concrete breaks)
- Wire brush
- Pointing trowel and wood float
- Heavy-duty paint brush

How-To: Repairing Cracks

1. Caution! Repair only when concrete is dry.
2. Chisel out the crack or hole wider under the surface (fig. 1).
3. Clean the concrete surface thoroughly with the wire brush (fig. 2).
4. Mix a batch of mortar according to the directions on the package. Mix in the epoxy concrete with the mortar according to the direction on the epoxy container.
5. Using the trowel, put mixture into the crack (fig. 3).
6. Using the wood float, smooth the mixture even with concrete surface (fig. 4).
7. Clean the tools immediately with paint thinner.
8. Note: Work fast! Most epoxies will harden in an hour. If the patch should harden before the operation is completed, apply a second coat and smooth the surface again.

For big cracks, spread the mixture over the full width of the crack until the level of mortar is slightly above the concrete surface. If repairing a full break in the concrete, use the trowel to force the mortar mixture to the bottom of the break (fig. 5).

Your Benefits

- A more attractive sidewalk
- Prevention of further damage
- A safer walking surface

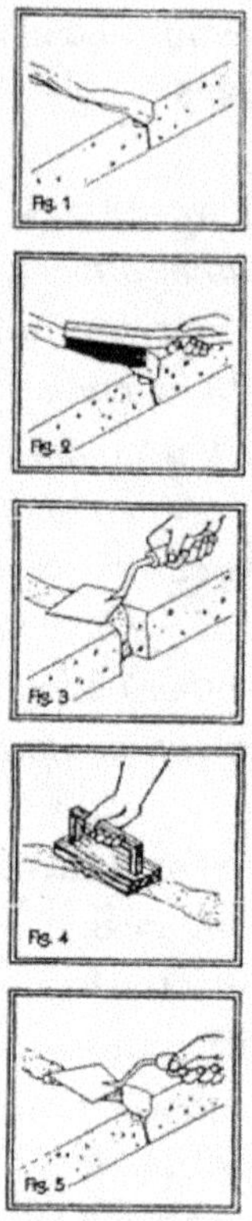

37

other. Rather, there is usually a large picture to show the technology in the context and words supplementing the picture as necessary. Low-context cultures are verbal or word heavy, and thus, they need a very clear document design to communicate the design of the verbal information very carefully, such as designating what is a step from a warning and other different types of verbal information (see Anderson's superstructure description).

- **Specific-Diffuse**. This value set correlates strongly with the high and low context value set. Low-context cultures are usually specific, and that means that the page must be broken up into more concrete parts, which allows a more specific focus on the individual step or verbal information. The "Fixing Cracks" sections off the steps in a specific manner. Likewise, high-context cultures want to see holistically the steps and the technology, just as we see the whole charcoal grill coming together. Part of a specific-diffuse value set is the role of humans in the manual. As mentioned in Chapter Ten, Asian cultures rarely have people in the manual, while Latin American cultures always have peo-

Figure 5.Square Charcoal Grill

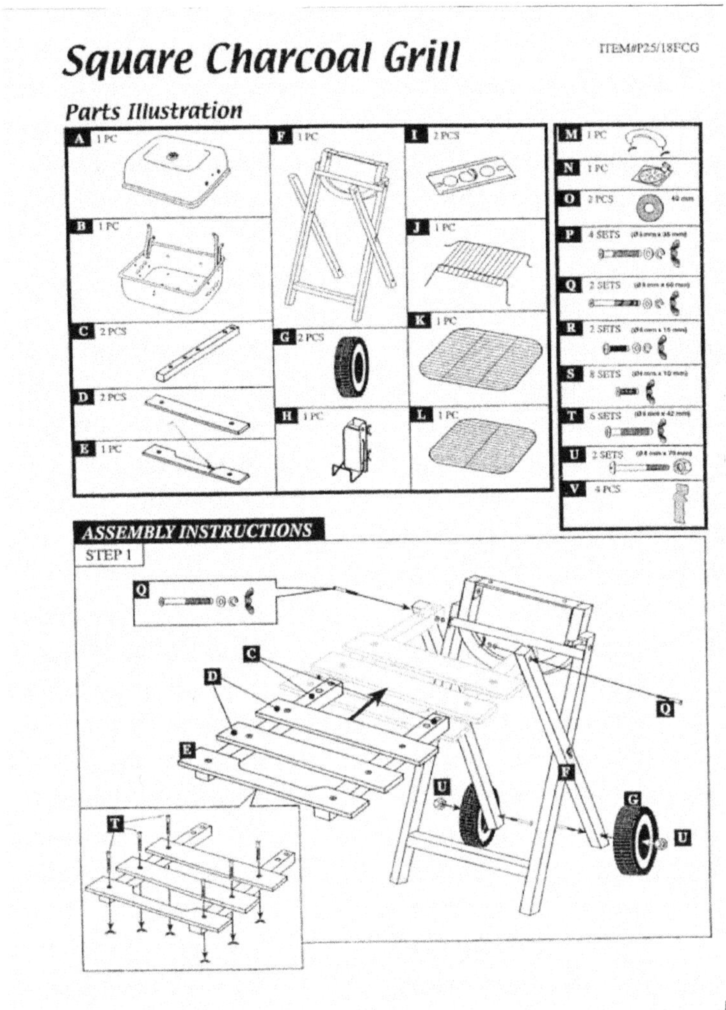

ple in a rich context doing something. This value set corresponds very closely to the inner-and outer value set with high context almost always being outer and low context almost always being inner.

This value set also explains the relative focus of the manual. As Dong (2007) explains, manuals in Chinese diffuse cultures often have advertising, company information, and other products explained—a more diffuse approach. Manuals in specific cultures teach how to do the exact step it is supposed to teach and little else.

- **Particular-Universal.** Once the students have the basic page layout based on the context and specific-diffuse value set, they move towards the particular and universal value sets. Here, the unit of analysis is how universal or particular is a step for the context. Particular cultures like to see the steps be designed to accommodate the unique situation of the culture, while universal cultures like to pretend that steps fit all situations. The "Fixing Cracks" manual is mostly universal because all cracks can be defined as either large or small. The "Grill" manual can be put together in most any fashion, regardless of the context, which, oddly, reflects the particular approach to situations.

- **Polychronic and Monochronic time**. This value set correlates the previous three value sets. High-context and diffuse cultures often present information in polychronic fashion, because they cannot divide up the steps or process specifically and universally. Thus, students need to integrate the high context and diffuse approach with the polychronic time frame, while students working with low context and specific approach will need to develop the monochronic time frame.
- **Ascription-Achievement**. This value set will tell the students how much to emphasize the process the (concrete steps) or the final product. The "Fixing Cracks" is a traditional US-based process-heavy manual, describing point by point how to carry out the process, while the "Grill" manual simply shows the product and components, and the process is implicit. In addition, this value set gets at how much information about the company and its products is present in the manual. In ascriptive cultures, manuals gain more credibility when the technology is linked to other products that have notoriety. In addition, ascriptive cultures emphasize the greatness of the company, its founders, and its history, as a way to strengthen the credibility of the manual, while achievement oriented cultures do not care about the company as long as the manual teaches them what to do. This value set also has relevance to the authors. When my students write manuals for ascriptive cultures, I encourage them to fictionalize ascriptive titles that will give them credibility in ascriptive cultures, such as Dr. or CEO or technical expert. Students who write for achievement oriented cultures do not even need to put their names on the manual.

One of the key connections between the value sets is that achievement and specific cultures break down the types of verbal information very carefully, and give all kinds of help to the reader. Achievement oriented cultures will supply notes, warnings, trouble shooting, and what will result from appropriate actions. All this verbal process-based information also presents a lower-context reality.

- **Power distance**. This value set assesses the tone and the authority of the communications. Low power-distance cultures present the information more as a suggestion, while high power-distance cultures presents the information as more of a command. Power distance also gets at the level of formality, with low power-distance cultures generally being much more informal, and high-power distance cultures generally being much more formal in the language, graphics, and photographs.
- **Individual-Collective.** This value set has very little relevance to manuals other than the level of expertise assumed by the manual. Individualistic cultures assume a more generalized audience, while collective cultures assume specific roles and technical knowledge. This difference is explained more fully in Chapter Eight.

This process of designing the according to the value sets or etic borders often becomes the first point of de-naturalization for the students because they automatically create the manual according to American value sets without realizing it. Thus, at this moment of the assignment, we present some of the manual designs on an overhead camera and look at how well the students designed their manuals according to the value sets. Most of the time, the students can connect to one or two of the value sets such as high context communication, but then they will put it in a linear, monochronic fashion. This process of designing for the value sets takes two or three classes of workshop to get

Figure 6. Student manual designed for China

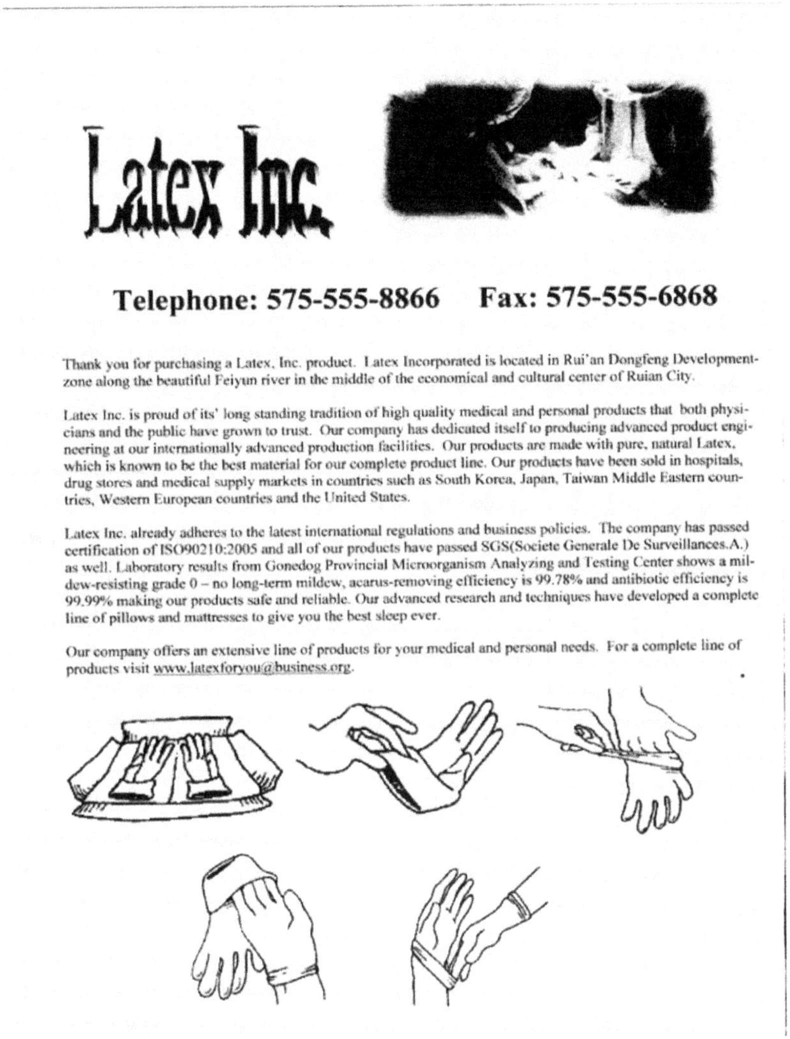

Latex Inc.

Telephone: 575-555-8866 Fax: 575-555-6868

Thank you for purchasing a Latex, Inc. product. Latex Incorporated is located in Rui'an Dongfeng Development-zone along the beautiful Feiyun river in the middle of the economical and cultural center of Ruian City.

Latex Inc. is proud of its' long standing tradition of high quality medical and personal products that both physicians and the public have grown to trust. Our company has dedicated itself to producing advanced product engineering at our internationally advanced production facilities. Our products are made with pure, natural Latex, which is known to be the best material for our complete product line. Our products have been sold in hospitals, drug stores and medical supply markets in countries such as South Korea, Japan, Taiwan Middle Eastern countries, Western European countries and the United States.

Latex Inc. already adheres to the latest international regulations and business policies. The company has passed certification of ISO90210:2005 and all of our products have passed SGS(Societe Generale De Surveillances.A.) as well. Laboratory results from Gonedog Provincial Microorganism Analyzing and Testing Center shows a mildew-resisting grade 0 – no long-term mildew, acarus-removing efficiency is 99.78% and antibiotic efficiency is 99.99% making our products safe and reliable. Our advanced research and techniques have developed a complete line of pillows and mattresses to give you the best sleep ever.

Our company offers an extensive line of products for your medical and personal needs. For a complete line of products visit www.latexforyou@business.org.

rid of the natural patterns and in their place develop the patterns for the target culture. Once, however, students understand that every part of the manual needs to connect to a cultural pattern, they begin to make the connections much more easily.

In the end, 70% or 80% of the students are able to make manuals that reflected very little if no US ethnocentrism and are appropriately designed for the value sets of the target culture. Figure 6 is a manual that two students designed for China. These students have no experience with China, but wrote this manual to the cultural values of China as described in the textbook.

Although the manual has some flaws like the opening thank you line, it follows generally the design decisions for China's cultural values. It shows the high-context, diffuse, particular, ascriptive, outer-directed, polychronic, and high power-distance values.

Final Exam

The students take a final exam at the end of the semester. The exam covers the reading materials in class discussion, but it mostly focuses on having the students synthesize the information that is, connect the value sets to writing patterns. The following is a representative exam, which gave in a summer class in 2008.

English 211, Final Exam, Summer 2008

In short paragraphs of 2-5 sentences, please respond to 20 of the following 25 questions (5 points each).

1. Why do diffuse writing patterns seem indirect to those from specific cultures?
2. Explore differences in null logic/negative reasoning between Letters O and R.
3. Why do high context communicators vary more than low context communicators in the amount of oral or written words they use to communicate?
4. What is the Sapir-Whorf hypothesis and how is it related to the approach in this class?
5. According to Williams, how are writing style and ethics related? Do you agree?
6. Compare the high and low context approaches in Letters O and R.
7. Compare the universalist and particularist writing patterns in Letters O and R.
8. Universalism and individualism are usually highly correlated (go together). Why is this correlation a paradox—seeming, but not truly, a contradiction?
9. What's the difference between stereotyping and cultural generalizing?
10. Explore differences in power distance between Letters O and R.
11. Compare the individual and collective writing patterns in Letters O and R.
12. Explore differences in achievement/ascription between Letters O and R.
13. What are nominalizations and why are they usually evidence of unclear writing?
14. What is metadiscourse and how can it impede clear writing?
15. Compare the time frames in Letters O and R.
16. Compare the ascriptive and achievement writing patterns in Letters O and R.
17. Why does moving from a nominalized writing style to an agented style often require using more conjunctions such as "however, although, because, and but?"
18. What are Williams' principles for ensuring coherence and cohesion?
19. Why does Williams argue that changing negative into positive syntax improves writing style?
20. Why do universalist cultures prefer parallelism and symmetry in writing?
21. What cultural values are usually associated with thesis driven and sales oriented writing?
22. Revise the following sentence according to Williams' principle of agented style: My suggestion is that our discussion of the issue be done with care.
23. Revise the following sentence according to Williams' principle of agented style: There has been a speculation by educators as to the positive effect of a good family environment on educational achievement.
24. Prune the redundancies from this sentence: Critics cannot avoid employing complex and abstract technical terms if they are to successfully analyze literary texts.
25. Prune the redundancy from this sentence: In regard to desirable employment in teaching positions, prospects for those engaged in studies at the graduate level are at best not certain.

Extra credit (10 points): In 4-5 sentences, explain how knowledge of the cultural values learned in this class has improved (or can eventually improve) your writing ability.

As you can see, the exam covers questions of style and grammar, but also focuses significantly on the intercultural writing component. The questions that involve Letter O and Letter R refer to the transit commission letters, as explained in Chapter One. I give these letters to them at the time of the final exam and get them the basic context of the letters.

This exam is considerably difficult for the students who have not been involved consistently throughout the semester. However, those students who have attended the class, taken good notes, and have synthesized information end up doing very well on the exam. The exam should be the capstone in developing all of the intercultural communication competencies discussed in this chapter.

CONCLUSION

Because of space limitations, I have not been able to address curricular designs for degrees, certificates, or even courses; nor have I been able to discuss collaboration across cultures or developing teaching materials. However, the critique of the three rhetoric and professional communication textbooks and descriptions of my class in intercultural writing demonstrates approaches that focus on global diversity and competencies, especially as they are explained in Chapters Two and Eleven in this book.

REFERENCES

Adler, N. (2008). *International dimensions of organizational behavior*. New York, NY: Thomson Learning Center.

Anderson, P. (1999). *Technical communication: A reader-centered approach* (4th ed.). Fort Worth, TX: Harcourt Brace College Publishers.

Anderson, P. (2011). *Technical communication: A reader-centered approach* (7th ed.). Wadsworth Cengage Learning.

Andrews, D. (2001). *Technical communication in the global community* (2nd ed.). New York, NY: Prentice Hall.

Anzaldua, G. (2007). *Borderlands/La Frontera, the new Mestiza* (3rd ed.). San Francisco, CA: Aunt Lute Books.

Bakhtin, M. M. (1990). *Art and answerability* (Holquist, M., & Liapunov, V., Eds.). (Liapunov, V., Trans.). Austin, TX: University of Texas Press.

Bennett, M. J. (Ed.). (1998). *Basic concepts of intercultural communication*. Yarmouth, ME: Intercultural Press.

Bracken Scott, J. (2010). Intercultural rhetoric in the technical communication curriculum: A review of the literature. *Rhetoric, Professional Communication. Globalization, 1*(1), 77–90.

Castañeda, J. G. (1995). *The Mexican shock: Its meaning for the U.S.* New York, NY: The New Press.

Condon, J. C. (1997). *Communicating with the Mexicans* (2nd ed.). Yarmouth, ME: Intercultural Press, Inc.

Connor, U. (1996). *Contrastive rhetoric: Cross-cultural aspects of second-language writing*. Cambridge, UK: Cambridge U Press.

Dong, Q. (2007). Cross-cultural considerations in instructional documentation: Contrasting Chinese and U.S. home heater manuals. *SIGDOC, 2007*, 221–228. doi:10.1145/1297144.1297192

Faigley, L., & Selzer, J. (2009). *Good reasons with contemporary arguments* (4th ed.). Pearson Longmann.

Hall, E. T. (1976). *Beyond culture*. New York, NY: Doubleday.

Hall, E. T. (1983). *The dance of life*. New York, NY: Doubleday.

Hinds, J. (1987). Reader versus writer responsibility: A new typology. In (eds.) U. Connor & R. Kaplan, *Writing across languages: Analysis of L2 text* (pp. 141-152). Reading, MA: Addison-Wesley.

Hofstede, G. (2010). *Cultures and organizations, software of the mind* (3rd ed.). New York, NY: McGraw Hill.

House, R. J., Hanges, P. J., Javidan, M., Dorfman, P. R., & Gupta, V. (Eds.). (2005). *Culture, leadership, and organizations: The GLOBE study of 62 societies*. Newbury Park, CA: Sage Publications.

Hunsinger, R. P. (2006). Culture and cultural identity in intercultural technical communication. *Technical Communication Quarterly*, *15*(1). Retrieved from Http://www.informaworld.com/smpp/content~content=a785834024~db=all. doi:10.1207/s15427625tcq1501_4

Kras, E. (1991). *Management in two cultures*. Minneapolis, MN: Intercultural Press, Inc.

Matveeva, N. (2007). The intercultural component in textbooks for teaching: A service technical writing course. *Journal of Technical Writing and Communication*, *37*(2), 151–166. doi:10.2190/85J8-2P74-1378-2188

My big fat greek wedding. (2002). Gold Circle Films, Home Box Office (HBO), MPH Entertainment Productions.

Osland, J. S., De Franco, S., & Osland, A. (1999). Organizational implications of Latin American culture. *Journal of Management Inquiry*, *8*(2), 219–234. doi:10.1177/105649269982018

Stewart, E., & Bennett, M. (1991). *American cultural patterns: A cross-cultural perspective* (Rev. ed.). Yarmouth, ME: Intercultural Press, Inc.

Thatcher, B., & St.Amant, K. (2010). (Eds). *Teaching intercultural rhetoric and technical communication: Theories, curriculum, pedagogies, and practices*. Baywood Publishing.

Thatcher, B. L. (1999). Cultural and rhetorical adaptations for South American audiences. *Technical Communication*, *46*(2), 177–195.

Thatcher, B. L. (2000). Writing policies and procedures in a U.S. and South American context. *Technical Communication Quarterly*, *94*, 365–400. doi:10.1080/10572250009364706

Thatcher, B. L. (2001). Issues of validity in intercultural professional communication research. *Journal of Business and Technical Communication*, *15*(4), 458–489. doi:10.1177/105065190101500403

Thatcher, B. L. (2006). Intercultural rhetoric, technology, and writing in Mexican maquilas. *Special Technology Transfer Edition of Technical Communication Quarterly*, *15*(3), 383–405.

Thatcher, B. L. (2009). Understanding digital literacy across cultures. In Spilka, R. (Ed.), *Digital literacy for technical communication: 21st Century theory and practice* (pp. 169–198). London: Routledge.

Varner, I., & Beamer, L. (2011). *Intercultural communication in the global workplace*. Richard D Irwin, Inc.

Victor, D. (1992). *International business communication*. New York, NY: HarperCollins Publishers.

Williams, J. (2009). *Style: Basics of clarity and grace* (3rd ed.). New York, NY: Pearson Longmann.

Conclusion

SO WHAT?

At the end of this book, perhaps the reader is asking "so what" or "what shall I do now?" I have argued across these twelve chapters that culture and rhetoric are strongly correlated around the world; and that often these cultural and rhetorical differences not only strongly correspond to a preference for communication styles, but perhaps, more importantly they connect to deep, implicit values such as sense of sense, thinking patterns, and appropriate social behavior. Thus, using a rhetorical pattern from one culture in another culture might strike a strong discordant chord with these deeper values. If the reader does not believe this, then I will refer him or her to the first reading of Letter O, from the Guayas Transit Commission. How easy was it to read that letter? Did it confuse, frustrate, or annoy you? Most likely yes. It is an extreme, perhaps uncommon rendition, of Ecuadorian cultural values, but it does resonate for many Ecuadorian readers. Interestingly, when I first read it 18 years ago, I could hardly process it, but after having lived in Ecuador for four years and on the U.S.-Mexico border for eleven years, Letter O is just as natural to me as Letter R, but I prefer to read Letter O in Spanish and Letter R in English. They seem more natural to me that way. That sense of naturalness for both Letters kind of un-nerves me on the one hand, but on the other, it shows that I can process each rhetorical and cultural system much like a language system.

When professional communicators are working in intercultural contexts such as Ecuador, do they need to culturally translate their equivalent of Letter R to be more like Letter O? This is a tough question because it essentially involves almost a total rewrite, drawing on each of the eight etic borders and using the appropriate medium at the writing document or communication cycling time. Translation theorists are trying to address these issues. James (2002) explains that the cultural implications for translation may take several forms ranging from lexical content and syntax to ideologies and ways of life in a given culture. The translator also has to decide on the importance given to certain cultural aspects and to what extent it is necessary or desirable to translate them into the TL (target language). (p.1)

James' definition is especially telling in the context of this book, and she gives a translation continuum, from more literal translation to a full cultural translation. The variables she uses for the more cultural translation include the material culture, gestures and habits, vocabulary (terminology), and cultural references or touchstones (using an appropriate reference to the Eifel tower, for French culture). This cultural approach gives a "dynamic translation" (James, 2002), but I am not sure that it meets the criteria for effectiveness in intercultural professional communication situations. In other words, how would she suggest translating Letter O?

Localization is a similar term used originally by the information products and software industry, but now is a common term for many global services and products. Localization means to develop or adapt products that are usable for local cultures. For example, the *Localization Industry Standards Association* (www.lisa.org) sets basic localization standards explaining that linguistic, physical, business, cultural, and technical issues all must be adapted to meet the needs of the local contexts. Further, in order to make this adaptation as efficient and effective as possible, industries must internationalize their products, enabling the product to be localized easily across multiple local cultures. "In other words, an internationalized product does not require remedial engineering or redesign at the time of localization. Instead, it has been designed and built to be easily adapted for a specific market after the engineering phase" (LISA, 2007, p. 17). In many ways, internationalization is like the learning objects discussed in Chapter Seven, Distance Education, because they are products that can easily be integrated into a variety of cultures by adapting them to that culture's local context.

Thus, all three terms–translation, localization, and internationalization–are key concepts for professional communicators working across cultures. And in many ways, this book has explored ways to do all three successfully, but I will leave it up to the reader, researcher, and practitioner to develop the level or depth of cultural adaptation. At least the book provides a comprehensive framework for doing it. However, I have some general recommendations: translation is minimal but most likely not adequate. Instead, I prefer to adapt the target communication to meet the etic borders or frameworks for the target culture. Just as I did for Letter R, professional communicators might have their target communication meet the sense of self, thinking patterns, and appropriate social relations of their target population, using the etic borders as a guide. This adaptation or meeting simply assumes the bell-curve values of the target culture, which in many ways is a deductive stereotype, but at least it will make the communication adapted. I prefer the approach of adapting, not imitation, a complex discussion well beyond this conclusion (see Stewart & Bennett, 1991). We have much research left to develop the most effective, ethical, and efficient methods for doing this cultural adaptation.

Effective Rhetoric-Culture Model for Translation, Localization, and Internationalization

In other words, the "so what" of this book is that it at least provides a framework for translating, localizing, and internationalizing communications and information products around the world. The book's approach or framework is theoretically integrated, but holistic and provides the analytical tools and methods for doing this important work. First, this book shows how to examine the relations between culture and rhetoric, understanding the deep cultural foundation of rhetorical patterns, an approach that provides a very powerful tool for understanding how a given reader, from a target culture, might have distinct rhetorical expectations. Using the onion model of rhetoric and culture shows why a definition of the self corresponds to thinking patterns, both of which correlate to appropriate social behaviors, and all three reinforce–and are reinforced by–rhetorical patterns. This model powerfully connects rhetorical patterns to sustained, long term cultural and social patterns, exemplifying why the local, postmodern approaches are not useful in a global context. Further, it shows, for example, in Chapter Eight how to develop a more "universal" approach to a situation, providing a process and product model for developing international initiatives.

Etic Borders with Operationalizable Approaches and Units of Analysis

Carefully tied to this rhetoric-culture model are the eight etic borders or value sets, which provide a useful heuristic or a powerful tool for ensuring the cultural adequacy of translation, localization, and internationalization. First, the etic-then-emic approach assures as little ethnocentrism as possible, balancing the approaches to cultures. Second, the etic frame as operationalized as a border shows the dynamic, virtue-vice or cultural relativity approaching showing how one system may work well in a cultural context, and not in another. This moves intercultural analysis away from the taboo approach and into connecting behavior to structured, cultural situations.

Third, the etic borders have clear units of analysis, which are powerful tools for analyzing cultures and communications. Thus, instead of vaguely defining culture as habits, gestures, or vocabulary (translation model) or language, culture, and business context (localization), intercultural professional communication have clearly defined, operationalizable, systematized, and validated units of analysis to conduct their work. The units of analysis are summarized as follows:

The I/Other border describes independence or dependence between one person and a group;
Rules orientation examines the development and application of rules;
Specific/diffuse looks at crossing public and private boundaries;
Inner/outer direction assesses sources of virtue and guidance;
Achievement/Ascription assesses performance and status in getting things done;
High and Low Context assesses role and relevance of context for communication;
Time assesses conception and operation of time, including past, present, and future, and monochronic and polychronic time.
Power Distance assesses the handling of interpersonal inequality in communications.

As demonstrated throughout this book, these etic borders have been studied consistently around the world and provide a useful starting point for researchers, practitioners, and teachers of intercultural rhetoric and professional communicators. The chapters in this book systematically connect these etic borders to concrete communication or rhetorical patterns, providing a useful model for intercultural professional communicators.

Chapters Devoted to Critical Areas of Inquiry and Intercultural Contexts

Once intercultural professional communicators understand the culture-rhetoric model and can integrate this model into the etic analysis of a target culture and corresponding rhetorical patterns, they can then draw on much of the research in this book to carry out their work. As explained in Chapters Three and Four, professional communicators can now understand how languages and technologies might encourage cultural and rhetorical patterns. Armed with this knowledge, communicators can assess how one language, such as Chinese, might predispose certain cultural patterns, as compared to English. Further, Chapter Four explains how communication media, such as orality, writing, email, hypertext, and Web 2.0 have strong correlations to the eight etic borders, reflecting relationships based on fit, reciprocity, and kairos. Thus, intercultural professional communicators can make sure that the medium they choose fits the rhetorical situation well, or they can adapt their communication to effectively re-purpose the communication to make up for the problem of fit. This knowledge also helps communicators understand the kairos of the different communication technologies, showing when each one of the technologies might best fit the different stages and purposes in the communication process. Chapters Three and Four also explore and predict the future of culture and communication patterns, based on the predominance, for example, of English and Chinese in the world, and the rapidly developing communication technologies, such as the internet and Web 2.0 technologies. All of this knowledge can help professional communicators internationalize and localize their products.

As examples of how to carry out this process of localization and internationalization, Chapters Five through Twelve explore specific contexts where intercultural professional communication is critical. Chapter Five shows that website designs strongly correlate to the local cultures, regardless of the forces of globalization. Thus, it provides specific units of analysis to tie website design to the etic borders, showing professional communicators how to both internationalize and localize websites. Chapter Six explores the relations between organizational structures and corresponding cultural and rhetorical patterns. Its baseball, football, and tennis doubles models provide specific analytical tools for assessing division of task, roles and relations, types of interaction, and corresponding communication patterns. Further, it demonstrates the great inter-organizational complexity of international business, showing the great need for effective communication across multiple federal, state, and local entities.

Chapter Seven, Distance Education, provides a comprehensive framework for developing and evaluating distance education and e-learning across cultures. This chapter is framed around seven distance education assessment criteria from five countries, UNESCO, and industry, showing how the eight etic borders influence the seven basic criteria or assessment guidelines. This includes understanding the local situation, including government policies, the curricular frame, and delivery to students, evaluation of student performance, and concrete issues such as student-teacher and student-student interactions. All of these capacities are helpful for both internationalizing and localizing e-learning projects.

Chapter Eight connects rhetoric and culture to law, providing intercultural professional communicators the ability to ground comparisons of law with the eight etic value sets. This connection is becoming critical for a variety of reasons, especially in the global context. First, it allows organizations to develop internal policies and procedures documents that are usable both across and for multiple local situations, that is, both international and local. Second, it provides a ground for understanding how cultural and rhetorical values, as exemplified in the eight etic borders, are the foundation for much law and legal processes around the world, which also demonstrates the great role of professional communication in these international legal situations. Third, this Chapter and the book grounds the discussion of privacy, intellectual property, and information and communication technologies in relevant legal and cultural foundations, showing professional communicators how to manage these complex relations and why certain cultures approach privacy and intellectual property differently. All these capacities are critical for both internationalizing and localizing communications, services, and products.

Chapter Nine, Health and Medical Traditions, illustrates the complex, but holistic connections between assumptions about medicine/health and health communications. This chapter greatly expands the definitions of culturally sensitive and appropriate health care communications, demonstrating why cultures need specific rhetorical approaches to their health communications, especially doctor-patient communications. It also greatly expands the definitions of health literacy, showing that different rhetorical traditions, literacy education, and assumptions about medicine and health treatment have long, historical, cultural, and economic structures and values. This is perhaps why many current forms of health communications, such as informed consent forms, are not effective for a large variety of intercultural or multicultural context. Professional communicators now are enabled to connect health and medical traditions to the eight etic borders, thus preparing them to develop effective communications for the local, target populations.

Chapter Ten, Instructions, shows how instructional designs vary around the world, and why different cultures approach the teaching or instructional situation differently. It provides in-depth analysis of four manuals, operationalizing the etic borders effectively. This knowledge provides critical tools for technical and professional communicators who write instructions for intercultural contexts, which, given our global situation, is an increasingly common situation. This Chapter also combines nicely with Chapter Seven, Distance Education, showing how to develop international modules or learning objects that can quickly and effectively be culturally adapted to the specific etic borders or value sets of the target population.

Chapters Eleven and Twelve discuss research, teaching, and curriculum for intercultural professional communication. Chapter Eleven provides very clear assessment criteria for evaluating the effectiveness of research and teaching approaches, in all their varieties, showing in many cases why the local, post-modern approaches are ill-suited for global contexts. Chapter Twelve evaluates the implicit curriculum in three popular U.S. rhetoric and professional communication textbooks, denaturalizing the implicit U.S. foundations, thereby, providing a scaffolding or framework for helping ESL and other students develop U.S. rhetorical capacities. Chapter Twelve also exemplifies an intercultural rhetoric and writing course that I routinely teach, modeling the process, competencies, activities, and projects that can enable intercultural and global competency in our student writers.

LIMITATIONS AND QUALIFICATIONS

Although these chapters provide a comprehensive look at theory, research, and practice of intercultural professional communication, it is just a start, and the book has some limitations, some of which are severe. First, most of the chapters could be a book, in and of themselves. Thus, my list of works cited is extremely long, demonstrating that I just scratched the surface with each chapter and that much more extensive, detailed work is needed for each area. This also means that I could not cite or explain in detail many of the views, resorting, instead to high-level analysis and framing. This was necessary and planned because the book is meant to frame the work for years to come. By the way, it also probably speaks to my becoming more Mexicanized (Kras, 1991), because I prefer larger, more diffuse or holistic approaches to issues. In this larger analysis, I had to generalize at a level that made me uncomfortable at times, but I hope I did justice with such a larger, interdisciplinary project. I am sure that experts in the rhetoric of law, technology, second language studies, organizational behavior, distance education, health/medicine, and instructional design will find some faults and errors in my approaches. That's ok; it was a lot of material to cover.

The second limitation or weakness is that this book obviously draws on my rich, lengthy, deep, and varied experience in Mexico and Latin America. Every chapter is grounded in either my previous research or professional experience in U.S.-Latin American contexts. Thus, I cannot do justice to the many other cultures around the world. But I am quite proud of the varied experiences I have in this context, as a professor, professional communicator, project administrator, researcher, expatriate, and resident in Ecuador and Mexico. But oh, that I had the time to develop the same capacity in Chinese-U.S. relations or German-U.S. relations! But I am still learning much about the U.S.-Latin American issues, and will probably spend the rest of my career doing so.

Most of the chapters also reflect the weaknesses in the body of intercultural research. Chapter Four does not integrate well the characteristics of online communication theory into intercultural contexts because that research simply does not exist. Chapter Five is mostly my work and analysis because not much research exists on intercultural website design, at least work that gets beyond superficial issues of translation. Chapter Six is notably weak because I chose not to integrate the work into existing organizational theory and information models, which I found to be particularly useless for intercultural inquiry. Chapter Seven powerfully assesses the assessment criteria from around the world, but I do not provide specific examples of intercultural distance education because I either did not have access to or have not experienced it. Regardless, it does draw on the growing body of literature discussing the intercultural elements of it. Chapter Eight provides a strong theoretical framework for intercultural rhetoric and law, but this connection is mostly mine; and much relevant research needs to take place. Chapter Nine points to great research and theory gaps in intercultural and multicultural health communications and practices; I just wish I could have analyzed better the significance of these gaps, especially as the U.S. Federal government approaches culturally appropriate care and service.

Chapter Ten is mostly my intercultural rhetorical analysis of four manuals with which I have lots of experience, pointing to the great dearth of research in this area. Chapters Eleven and Twelve show limited approaches to teaching and research. I found very little discussion of explicit intercultural research methods or teaching that I found valid and worth discussing. Thus, Chapter Eleven provides a broad assessment frame and Chapter Twelve critiques the curricular approach in three textbooks, both of which are quite inadequate; but they are both a good start and provide analytical and practical models for continuing the research.

Despite these efforts, though, I feel the book is comprehensive, yet integrated, theoretical, yet practical, draws on a large body of research, but is grounded in my experience, and addresses key issues with enough clarity to motivate further research, but provides enough answers to influence current practice.

REFERENCES

James, K. (2002). Cultural implications for translation. *Translation Journal, 6*(4). Retrieved from http://translationjournal.net/journal//22delight.htm.

Kras, E. (1991). *Management in two cultures*. Yarmouth, ME: Intercultural Press, Inc.

LISA. (2007). *LISA Globalization Industry Primer*. The Localization Industry Standards Association (www.lisa.org). Retrieved from http://www.lisa.org/Primers.600.0.html.

Stewart, E., & Bennett, M. (1991). *American cultural patterns: A cross-cultural perspective* (Rev. ed.). Yarmouth, ME: Intercultural Press, Inc.

Compilation of References

Adler, N. (2008). *International dimensions of organizational behavior*. New York, NY: Thomson Learning Center.

Alcalde, J. (1991). Differential impact of American political and economic institutions on Latin America. In Thompson, K. W. (Ed.), *The U.S. Constitution and the constitutions of Latin America* (pp. 97–126).

Anderson, P. (1999). *Technical communication: A reader-centered approach* (4th ed.). Fort Worth, TX: Harcourt Brace College Publishers.

Anderson, P. (2011). *Technical communication: A reader-centered approach* (7th ed.). Wadsworth Cengage Learning.

Andrews, D. (2001). *Technical communication in the global community* (2nd ed.). New York, NY: Prentice Hall.

Angelelli, C. V., & Jacobson, H. (2009). *Testing and assessment in translation and interpreting studies*. Philadelphia, PA: John Benjamins.

Anzaldua, G. (2007). *Borderlands/La Frontera, the new Mestiza* (3rd ed.). San Francisco, CA: Aunt Lute Books.

Badiou, A., & Feltham, O. (2007). *Being and event*. Continuum.

Bakhtin, M. M. (1990). Art and answerability. In Holquist, M., & Liapunov, V. (Eds.), *Art and answerability: Early philosophical essays* (Liapunov, V., Trans.). Austin, TX: University of Texas Press.

Bakhtin, M. M. (1993). *Toward a philosophy of the act* (Holquist, M., & Liapunov, V., Eds.). (Liapunov, V., Trans.). Austin, TX: University of Texas Press.

Ball, C., & Kalmbach, J. (2010). (Eds.) *Reading and writing new media*. Creskill, NJ: Hampton

Barbassa, J. (2005). *Immigrants mix traditional medicine with advice from doctors*. Retrieved from www.fiob.org/centro.html

Barthes, R. (1972). *Mythologies* (Lavers, A., Trans.). New York, NY: Noonday Press.

Baudrillard, J. (1983). *Simulations. Semiotext(e)*. Press.

Bennett, M. J. (Ed.). (1998). *Basic concepts of intercultural communication*. Yarmouth, ME: Intercultural Press.

Berkonkotter, C., & Huckin, T. (1995). *Genre knowledge in disciplinary communication: Cognition/culture/power*. Hillsdale, NJ: Lawrence Erlbaum.

Berlin, J. (1987). *Rhetoric and reality: Writing instruction in the American colleges, 1900-1985*. Carbondale, IL: Southern Illinois University Press.

Berlin, B., & Kay, P. (1969). *Basic color terms: Their universality and evolution*. Berkeley, CA: University of California Press.

Bhabha, H. (1994). *The location of culture*. Routledge.

Bhabha, H. (2003). Statement for the *Critical Inquiry* Board. *Critical Inquiry*, *30*(2). Retrieved from http://criticalinquiry.uchicago.edu/issues/v30/30n2.Bhabha.html.

Bhawuk, D., & Triandis, H. (1996). The role of culture theory in the study of culture and intercultural training. In Landis, D., & Bhagat, R. (Eds.), *Handbook of intercultural training* (2nd ed., pp. 17–34). Thousand Oaks, CA: Sage.

Bigby, J. (Ed.). (2003). *Cross-cultural medicine*. Philadelphia, PA: Versa Press.

Blyler, N., & Thralls, C. (Eds.). (1993). *Professional communication: The social perspective*. Newbury Park, CA: Sage Publications.

Bolter, J., & Grusin, R. (1999). *Remediation: Understanding new media*. Cambridge, MA: MIT Press.

Bosley, D. (2000). (Ed.) *Global documentation: Case studies in international technical communication*. Boston, MA: Allyn & Bacon.

Bourdieu, P., & Wacquant, L. (1992). *An invitation to reflexive sociology*. Chicago, IL: University of Chicago Press.

Bourdieu, P. (1999). *Language and symbolic power*. Boston, MA: Harvard University Press.

Bracken Scott, J. (2010). Intercultural rhetoric in the technical communication curriculum: A review of the literature. *Rhetoric, Professional Communication. Globalization, 1*(1), 77–90.

Brandt, D., & Clinton, K. (2002). Limits of the local: Expanding perspectives on literacy as a social practice. *Journal of Literacy Research, 34*(3), 337–356. doi:10.1207/s15548430jlr3403_4

Brown, C. (2000). An analysis of the 'human rights-culture' and its critics. In Patman, R. (Ed.), *Universal human rights?* (pp. 31–49). New York, NY: St. Martin's Press.

Burbach, K., Nunez, O., & Kagarlitsky, B. (1996). *Globalization and its discontents: The rise of postmodern socialisms*. Pluto Press.

Burke, K. (1968). *Language as symbolic action. Essays on life, literature, and method*. Berkeley, CA: University of California Press.

Buss, D. (Ed.). (2005). *Handbook of evolutionary psychology*. New York, NY: John Wiley & Sons.

Buss, D. (2005). (Ed.). *Handbook of evolutionary psychology*. New York, NY: John Wiley & Sons.

Bussey-Jones, J., & Genao, I. (2003). Impact of culture on health care. *Journal of the National Medical Association, 95*(8), 732–735.

Bustamante, A., Ojeda, G., & Castaneda, X. (2008). Willingness to pay for cross-border health insurance between the United States and Mexico. *Health Affairs, 27*(1), 169–178. doi:10.1377/hlthaff.27.1.169

Bustillos, D. (2005, August 31). *States begin requiring cultural competency training for doctors*. Perspectives University of Houston Law Center. Retrieved November 12, 2009, from http://www.law.uh.edu/Healthlaw/perspectives/August2005/%28DB%29CulturalCompetency.pdf

Butler, J. (2006). *Gender trouble: Feminism and the subversion of identity*. Routledge.

Carliner, S. (2009). Computers and technical communication in the 21st century. In Spilka, R. (Ed.), *Digital literacy for technical communication: 21st Century theory and practice* (pp. 21–50). London, UK: Routledge.

Carlson, J. R., & Zmud, R. W. (1999). Channel expansion theory and the experimental nature of media richness perceptions. *Academy of Management Journal, 42*, 153–170. doi:10.2307/257090

Carr-Chellman, A. A. (2004). *Global perspectives on e-learning*. Newbury Park, CA: Sage Publications.

Castañeda, J. G. (1995). *The Mexican shock: Its meaning for the U.S.* New York, NY: The New Press.

Catterick, D. (2007). Do the philosophical foundations of online learning disadvantage nonwestern students. In Edmunson, A. (Ed.), *Globalized e-learning cultural challenge* (pp. 116–129). Hershey, PA: IGI Global.

Charney, D. (1996). Empiricism is not a four-letter word. *College Composition and Communication, 47*(4), 567–593. doi:10.2307/358602

Chick, K. J. (1990). Reflections on language, interaction, and context. In Carbaugh, D. (Ed.), *Cultural communication and intercultural contact* (pp. 253–259). Hillsdale, NJ: Lawrence Erlbaum Associates.

Clark, R., & Mayer, R. E. (2003). *E-learning and the science of instruction: proven guidelines for consumers*. New York, NY: Jossey-Bass.

Clark, D. (2009). Shaped and shaping tools: The rhetorical nature of technical communication technologies. In Spilka, R. (Ed.), *Digital literacy for technical communication: 21st Century theory and practice* (pp. 85–102). London, UK: Routledge.

Commission to End Health Care Disparities. (2007). *Addressing health care disparities: Recommended goal, guiding principles, and key strategies for comprehensive policies.* Retrieved December 1, 2009, from http://www.ama-assn.org/ama1 /pub/upload/mm/ 433/commission_pres_07.pdf

Condon, J. C. (1997). *Communicating with the Mexicans* (2nd ed.). Yarmouth, ME: Intercultural Press, Inc.

Connor, U. (1996). *Contrastive rhetoric: Cross-cultural aspects of second-language writing*. Cambridge, UK: Cambridge U Press.

Connor, U., Nagelhout, E., & Rozycki, W. V. (Eds.). (2008). *Contrastive rhetoric: Reaching to intercultural rhetoric*. Amsterdam, The Netherlands: John Benjamins Publishing Company.

Cooper, L. A., Beach, M. C., Johnson, R. L., & Inui, T. S. (2006). Delving below the surface: Understanding how race and ethnicity influence relationships in health care. *Journal of General Internal Medicine*, *21*, S21–S27. doi:10.1111/j.1525-1497.2006.00305.x

Cornejo-Polar, A. (1994). *Escribir en el aire: Ensayo sobre la heterogeneidad socio-cultural en las literaturas Andinas* [*Writing in the Air: Essay about the socio-cultural heterogeneity in the Andean* Literatures]. Lima, Peru: Editorial Horizonte.

Daft, R. L., & Lengel, R. H. (1986). Organizational information requirements, media richness, and structural determinants. *Management Science*, *32*, 554–571. doi:10.1287/mnsc.32.5.554

De Groot, A. B. (2010). *Language and cognition in bilinguals and multilinguals: An introduction*. New York, NY: Taylor & Francis.

Deacon, T. W. (1998). *The symbolic species: The co-evolution of language and the brain*. New York: W.W. Norton and Company.

Dealy, G. (1992). *The Latin Americans: Spirit and ethos*. Boulder, CO: Westview Press.

Deleuze, G., & Guattari, F. (1987). *Thousand plateaus: Capitalism and schizophrenia*. Minneapolis, MN: University of Minnesota Press.

Denzin, N. K., Lincoln, Y. S., & Smith, L. T. (Eds.). (2008). *Handbook of critical and indigenous methodologies*. Thousand Oaks, CA: Sage Publications.

Derrida, J., & Spivak, G. (1998). *Of grammatology*. Baltimore, MD: The Johns Hopkins University Press.

Diamond, J. (2005). *Guns, germs, and steel: The fates of human societies*. New York, NY: W. W. Norton & Company.

Ding, H. (2007). *Rhetoric of a global epidemic: Intercultural and intracultural professional communication about SARS.* Unpublished Doctoral Dissertation, Purdue University.

Dombrowski, P. (2000). *Ethics in technical communication*. Boston, MA: Allyn & Bacon.

Dong, Q. (2007). Cross-cultural considerations in instructional documentation: Contrasting Chinese and U.S. home heater manuals. *SIGDOC*, *2007*, 221–228. doi:10.1145/1297144.1297192

Donnelly, J. (2003). *Universal human rights in theory and practice*. Ithaca, NY: Cornell University Press.

Drivonikou, G. V., Kay, T., Regier, R. B., Ivry, A. L., Gilbert, A. F., & Davies, I. R. L. (2007). Further evidence that Whorfian effects are stronger in the right visual field than the left. *Proceedings of the National Academy of Sciences of the United States of America*, *104*(3), 1097–1102. doi:10.1073/pnas.0610132104

Drucker, P. (1992). There's three kind of teams. *Wall Street Journal*, Feb. 11.

Durso, S. C. (2009). The past, present, and future of human communication and technology research: An introduction. *Journal of Computer-Mediated Communication*, *14*(3), 708–713. doi:10.1111/j.1083-6101.2009.01459.x

Eder, P. J. (1950). *A comparative survey of Anglo-American and Latin-American law*. New York, NY: New York University Press.

Edmundson, A. (Ed.). (2007). *Globalized e-learning cultural challenges*. Hershey, PA: IGI Global.

Elder, J., Candelaria, J., Woodruff, S., Criqui, M., Talavera, G., & Rupp, J. (2000). Results of language for health: Cardiovascular disease nutrition education for Latino English-as-a-second-language studies students. *Health Education & Behavior*, *27*, 50–63. doi:10.1177/109019810002700106

Engle, K. (2000). Culture and human rights: The Asian values debate in context. *New York University Journal of International Law & Politics. New York University. International Law Society*, *32*, 291–323.

Faigley, L. (1992). *Fragments of rationality: Postmodernity and the subject of composition*. Pittsburgh, PA: University of Pittsburgh Press.

Faigley, L., & Selzer, J. (2009). *Good reasons with contemporary arguments* (4th ed.). Pearson Longmann.

Falagas, M., Korbila, I., Giannopoulou, K. P., Kondilis, B. K., & Peppas, G. (2009). Informed consent: How much and what do patients understand? [Bottom of Form]. *American Journal of Surgery*, *198*(3), 420–435. doi:10.1016/j.amjsurg.2009.02.010

Fee, K. (2009). *Delivering e-learning*. London, UK: Kogan Page.

Flicke, U. (2002). *An introduction to qualitative research*. Thousand Oaks, CA: Sage Publications.

Flores, G. (2000). Culture and the patient-physician relationship: Achieving cultural competency in healthcare. *Journal of Pediatrics*, *136*(1). Retrieved November 29, 2009, from http://download.journals.elsevierhealth.com/pdfs/journals/0022-3476/ PIIS0022347 60090043X. pdf

Foucault, M. (1979). *Discipline and punish: The birth of a prison* (Sheridan Smith, A. M., Trans.). New York, NY: Vintage/Random House.

Foucault, M. (1972). *The archaeology of knowledge* (Sheridan Smith, A. M., Trans.). New York, NY: Harper Colophon.

Friedman, T. (2005). *The world is flat*. New York, NY: Farrar, Straus and Giroux.

Galanti, G. (2000). An introduction to cultural differences. *The Western Journal of Medicine*, *172*, 335–336. doi:10.1136/ewjm.172.5.335

García-Canclini, N. (1992). Cultural reconversion. In Yudice, G., France, J., & Flores, J. (Eds.), *On the edge: The crisis of contemporary Latin American culture* (pp. 29–44). Minneapolis, MN: University of Minnesota Press.

Garza-Almanza, V. (1999). Comercios regionales y ambiente: Integración del desarrollo y el ambiente en el tratado de libre comercio de América del Norte. [Ciudad Juárez, México: Universidad Autónoma de Ciudad Juárez.]. *Ambiente Sin Fronteras*, *2*, 6–7.

Garza-Almanza, V. (2004). La divulgación de la ciencia en México. [Ciudad Juárez, México: Universidad Autónoma de Ciudad Juárez.]. *Cultura Científica y Tecnológica*, *1*(5), 3–16.

Gentner, D., & Goldin-Meadow, S. (Eds.). (2003). *Language in mind: Advances in the study of language and thought*. Cambridge, MA: The MIT Press.

Ghemawat, P. (2007). Why the world isn't flat. *Foreign Policy.* Retrieved from www.Foreignpolicy.com.

Gilbert, A. L., Regier, T., Kay, P., & Ivry, R. B. (2008). Support for lateralization of the Whorf effect beyond the realm of color discrimination. *Brain and Language*, *105*(2), 91–98. doi:10.1016/j.bandl.2007.06.001

Glendon, M. A. (1999). Foundations of human rights: The unfinished business. *The American Journal of Jurisprudence*, *44*, 1–14.

Glenn, H. P. (2000). *Legal traditions of the world: Sustainable diversity in law*. Oxford, UK: Oxford University Press.

Gonzalez Gonzalez, D., Rodríguez Almada, H., & Guido Berro, R. (2005). Consentimiento informado: Análisis crítico de su aplicación en un servicio quirúrgico. *Revista Médica de Uruguay*, *21*(4), 291–297.

Granero-Molina, J., Fernández-Sola, C., & Aguilera-Manrique, G. (2009). Applying a sociolinguistic model to the analysis of informed consent documents. *Nursing Ethics*, *16*(6), 797 812. doi:10.1177/0969733009341908

Grewal, D. S. (2008). *Network power: The social dynamics of globalization*. New Haven, CT: Yale University Press.

Grosjean, F., Li, P., Munte, Th., & Rodriguez-Fornells, A. (2003). Imaging bilinguals: When the neurosciences meet the language sciences. *Bilingualism: Language and Cognition, 6*, 159–165. doi:10.1017/S136672890300110X

Grossberg, L. (1992). *We gotta get out of this place: Popular culture and postmodern culture*. New York, NY: Routledge.

Gumperz, J., & Levinson, S. (Eds.). (1996). *Rethinking linguistic relativity*. Cambridge, MA: Cambridge University Press.

Hahm, C. (2009). Ritual and constitutionalism: Disputing the ruler's legitimacy in a Confucian polity. *The American Journal of Comparative Law, 57*, 135–203. doi:10.5131/ajcl.2008.0005

Hall, S. (1997). *Representation: Cultural representations and signifying practices*. New York, NY: Sage.

Hall, E. T. (1981). *The silent language*. New York, NY: Doubleday.

Hall, E. T. (1976). *Beyond culture*. New York, NY: Doubleday.

Hall, E. T. (1981). *The silent language*. New York, NY: Doubleday.

Hall, E. T. (1983). *The dance of life*. New York, NY: Doubleday.

Hall, S. (1997). *Representation: Cultural representations and signifying practices*. New York, NY: Sage.

Hampden-Turner, C., & Trompenaars, A. (2000). *Building cross-cultural competence*. New York, NY: Wiley.

Harris, R. A. (2005). *Rhetoric and incommensurability*. West Lafayette, IN: Parlour Press.

Hawisher, G., & Selfe, C. (2000). *Global literacies and the world-wide web*. London, UK: Routledge.

Healthy Border 2010. (2003). *U.S.-Mexico Border Health Commission*. Retrieved from http://www.borderhealth.org/

Herndl, C., & Nahrwold, C. (2000). Research as social practice: A case study of research on technical and professional communication. *Written Communication, 17*(20), 258–296. doi:10.1177/0741088300017002004

Higgins, T. E. (1999). Regarding rights: An essay honoring the fiftieth anniversary of the *Universal Declaration of Human Rights. Columbia Human Rights Law Review, 30*, 225–247.

Hinds, J. (1987). Reader versus writer responsibility: A new typology. In Connor, U., & Kaplan, R. (Eds.), *Writing across languages: Analysis of L2 text* (pp. 141–152). Reading, MA: Addison-Wesley.

Hofstede, G. (2010). *Cultures and organizations, software of the mind* (3rd ed.). New York, NY: McGraw Hill.

Hoft, N. (1995). *International technical communication*. New York, NY: John Wiley & Sons.

Homedes, N., & Ugalde, A. (2003). *Globalization and health at the United States-Mexico border.*

Honold, P. (1999). Learning how to use a cellular phone: Comparison between German and Chinese users. *Technical Communication, 46*(2), 196–205.

House, R. J., Hanges, P. J., Javidan, M., Dorfman, P. R., & Gupta, V. (Eds.). (2005). *Culture, leadership, and organizations: The GLOBE study of 62 societies*. Newbury Park, CA: Sage Publications.

Howard, C. A., Andrade, S., & Bird, T. (2001). The ethical dimensions of cultural competence in border health care settings. *Family & Community Health, 4*, 36–49.

Humphrey, J. P. (1984). *Human rights and the United Nations: A great adventure*. Dobbs Ferry, NY: Transnational Publishers.

Hunsinger, R. P. (2006). Culture and cultural identity in intercultural technical communication. *Technical Communication Quarterly, 15*(1). Retrieved from Http://www.informaworld.com/smpp/content~content=a785834024~db=all. doi:10.1207/s15427625tcq1501_4

Hussein, T. H. (2000). Human rights—The Asian perspective. In Patman, R. (Ed.), *Universal human rights?* (pp. 75–80). New York, NY: St. Martin's Press.

Ishii, S. (2006). Complementing contemporary intercultural communication research with East Asian sociocultural perspectives and practices. *China Media Research, 2*(1), 13–20.

Jacobs, J., & Dempsey, J. (2001). Emerging instructional technologies: The near future. In Rossett, A. (Ed.), *ASTD e-learning handbook* (pp. 322–337). New York, NY: McGraw-Hill.

Jameson, F. (1990). *Postmodernism, or, the cultural logic of late capitalism*. Durham, NC: Duke University Press.

Jarvis, S., & Pavlenko, A. (2008). *Crosslinguistic influence in language and cognition*. New York, NY: Routledge.

Johnson, R. L., Saha, S., Arbelaez, J. J., Beach, M. C., & Cooper, L. A. (2004). Racial and Ethnic differences in patient perceptions of bias and cultural competence in health care. *Journal of General Internal Medicine, 19*, 101–110. doi:10.1111/j.1525-1497.2004.30262.x

Johnson-Eilola, J., & Selber, S. (Eds.). (2004). *Central works in technical communication*. Oxford, UK: Oxford University Press.

Juckett, G. (2005). Cross-cultural medicine. *American Family Physician, 72*, 2267-2274. American Academy of Family Physicians. Retrieved October 12, 2009, from http://www.aafp.org/afp/2005/1201/p2267.html

Kaplan, R. (1996). Cultural thought patterns in intercultural education. *Language Learning, 16*(1-2), 1–20. doi:10.1111/j.1467-1770.1966.tb00804.x

Kaufer, D. S., & Carley, K. M. (1993). *Communication at a distance: The influence of print on sociocultural organization and change*. Hillsdale, NJ: Lawrence Erlbaum.

Kellog, S. (1995). *Law and the transformation of Aztec culture, 1500-1700*. Norman, OK: University of Oklahoma Press.

Kiev, A. (1968). *Curanderismo: Mexican-American folk psychiatry*. New York, NY: Collier Macmillan Publishing Company.

Kirsch, G., & Mortensen, P. (Eds.). (1996). *Ethics and representation in qualitative studies of literacy*. Urbana, IL: National Council of Teachers of English.

Klein, W. D., & McKenna, B. (1997). Policies and procedures. *Journal of Technical Writing and Communication, 27*(2), 147–161.

Kock, N. (2005). Media richness or media naturalness? The evolution of our biological communication apparatus and its influence on our behavior toward E-communication tools. *IEEE Transactions on Professional Communication, 48*(2), 117–130. doi:10.1109/TPC.2005.849649

Koenig, B. A., & Gates-Williams, J. (1995). Understanding cultural difference in caring for dying patients. *The Western Journal of Medicine, 163*, 244–249. Retrieved from http://ethnomed.org/clinical/end-of-life/koenig.pdf/view.

Kras, E. (1991). *Management in two cultures*. Minneapolis, MN: Intercultural Press, Inc.

Kress, G. (1998). Visual and verbal modes of representation in electronically mediated communication: The potentials of new forms of text. In Snyder, I. (Ed.), *Page to screen: Taking literacy into the electronic era* (pp. 53–79). New York, NY: Routledge. doi:10.4324/9780203201220_chapter_3

Kubota, R. (1999). Japanese culture constructed by discourses: Implications for applied linguistics research and ELT. *TESOL Quarterly, 33*(1), 9–35. doi:10.2307/3588189

Langer, E. (1997). *The power of mindful learning*. Reading, MA: Addison Wesley Publishing Company, Inc.

Latour, B. (2003). Why has critique run out of steam? From matters of fact to matters of concern. *Critical Inquiry, 30*(2). Retrieved from http://criticalinquiry.uchicago.edu/issues/v30/30n2.Latour.html.

Leon-Portilla, M. (1996). *El destino de la palabra. De la oralidad y los códices mesoamericanos a la escritura alfabética*. México City: El Colegio Nacional Fondo de Cultura Económica.

Lett, J. (1996). Emic/Etic distinctions. In Levinson, D., & Ember, M. (Eds.), *Encyclopedia of cultural anthropology* (pp. 382–383). New York, NY: Henry Holt and Company.

Lett, J. (2010). *Emic/Etic distinctions*. Retrieved from http://faculty.ircc.cc.fl.us/faculty/jlett/Article%20on%20Emics%20and%20Etics.htm

Li, P. (2009). Lexical organization and competition in first and second languages: Computational and neural mechanisms. *Cognitive Science*, *33*, 629–664. doi:10.1111/j.1551-6709.2009.01028.x

Li, P., Jin, Z., & Tan, L. (2004b). Neural representations of nouns and verbs in Chinese: An fMRI study. *NeuroImage*, *21*, 1533–1541. doi:10.1016/j.neuroimage.2003.10.044

Li, A. (1999). Agency: A cultural perspective implicit in language use. In Chu, M. (Ed.), *Mapping the course of the Chinese language field* (*Vol. III*, pp. 71–101). Kalamazoo, MI: Chinese Language Teachers Association Monograph Series.

Lopiccolo, P. (1990). *Curanderismo in the El Paso, Las Cruces, Ciudad Juárez area*. Unpublished Master's thesis, New Mexico State University.

Loustaunau, M. O., & Bane, M. J. (1999). *Life, death, and in-between on the U.S.-Mexico border: Así es la vida*. West Port, CT Bergin & Garvey.

Lubman, S. (1999). *Bird in a cage: Legal reform in China after Mao*. Stanford, CA: Stanford University Press.

Lucy, J. (1996). The scope of linguistic relativity: An analysis and review of empirical research. In Gumperz, J. J., & Levinson, S. C. (Eds.), *Rethinking linguistic relativity* (pp. 37–69). Cambridge, UK: Cambridge University Press.

Lyotard, J. F. (1984). *The postmodern condition: A report on knowledge*. Minneapolis, MN: University of Minnesota Press.

Marcus, J. (1992). *Mesoamerican writing systems: Propaganda, myth, and history in four ancient civilizations*. Princeton, NJ: Princeton University Press.

Martín Barbero, J. (1988). Communication from culture: The crisis of the national and the emergence of the popular. (P. Schlesinger, Trans.). *Media Culture & Society*, *10*, 447–465. doi:10.1177/016344388010004004

Masi, R. (1989). Multiculturalism, medicine, and health part IV: Individual considerations. *Canadian Family Physician Medecin de Famille Canadien*, *35*, 69–73.

Matveeva, N. (2007). The intercultural component in textbooks for teaching: A service technical writing course. *Journal of Technical Writing and Communication*, *37*(2), 151–166. doi:10.2190/85J8-2P74-1378-2188

McCarty, S. (2007). Theorizing and realizing the global classroom. In Edmunson, A. (Ed.), *Globalized e-learning cultural challenge* (pp. 90–115). Hershey, PA: IGI Global.

McCool, M. (2007). *Reaching a global online audience*. Oreilly Media, Inc.

McCormick, N. (2009). *Rhetoric and the rule of law: A theory of legal reasoning*. Oxford, UK: Oxford University Press.

McLoughlin, C. (2007). Adapting e-learning across cultural boundaries: A framework for quality learning, pedagogy, and interaction. In Edmunson, A. (Ed.), *Globalized e-learning cultural challenge* (pp. 223–238). Hershey, PA: IGI Global.

McLuhan, M. (1967). *The medium is the message*. New York, NY: Bantam Books.

Meeuwesen, L., Brink-Muinen, A. V., & Hofstede, G. (2009). Can dimensions of national culture predict cross-national differences in medical communication? *Patient Education and Counseling*, *75*, 58–66. doi:10.1016/j.pec.2008.09.015

Melton, J. (2009). Going global: A case study of rhetorical invention, packaging, delivery, and feedback collection. *IEEE Transactions on Professional Communication*, *52*(3), 229–242. doi:10.1109/TPC.2009.2025305

Menski, W. (2006). *Comparative law in a global context: The legal systems of Asia and Africa*. Cambridge, UK: Cambridge University Press. doi:10.1017/CBO9780511606687

Merryman, J. H. (1969). *The civil law tradition: An introduction to the legal systems of western Europe and Latin America*. Stanford, CA: Stanford University Press.

Miller, C. R. (1993). Rhetoric and the community: The problem of the one and many. In Enos, T., & Brown, S. C. (Eds.), *Defining the new rhetorics* (pp. 79–94). Newbury Park, CA: Sage.

Moder, C. L., & Martinovic-Zic, A. (Eds.). (2004). *Discourse across languages and cultures*. Amsterdam, The Netherlands: John Benjamins Publishing Co.

Moran, C., & Hawisher, G. (1998). The rhetorics and languages of electronic mail. In Snyder, I. (Ed.), *Page to screen: Taking literacy into the electronic era* (pp. 80–101). New York, NY: Routledge. doi:10.4324/9780203201220_chapter_4

Morris, M., Leung, K., Ames, D., & Lickel, B. (1999). From inside and outside: Integrating emic and etic insights about culture and justice judgments. *Academy of Management Review*, *24*, 781–796.

Morsink, J. (1999). *The Universal Declaration of Human Rights: Origins, drafting, and intent*. Philadelphia, PA: University of Pennsylvania Press.

Muntarbhorn, V. (2000). Asia and human rights at the crossroads of the new millennium: Between the Universalist and the Particularist? In Patman, R. (Ed.), *Universal human rights?* (pp. 81–95). New York, NY: St. Martin's Press.

My big fat greek wedding. (2002). Gold Circle Films, Home Box Office (HBO), MPH Entertainment Productions.

Natividad, K. (2008). Stepping it up and taking it to the streets: Changing civil & criminal copyright enforcement tactics. *Berkeley Technology Law Journal Annual Review*, *23*, 469–501.

Nazzari, M. (1995). Widows as obstacles to business: British objections to Brazilian marriage and inheritance laws. [Cambridge, UK: Cambridge University Press.]. *Comparative Studies in Society and History*, *37*, 781–802. doi:10.1017/S0010417500019952

New London Group. (1996). A pedagogy of multiliteracies: Designing social futures. *Harvard Educational Review*, *66*(1), 60–92.

Olaniran, B. (2007). Culture and communication challenges in virtual workspaces. In St.Amant, K. (Ed.), *Linguistic and cultural online communication issues in the global age* (pp. 75–91). Hershey, PA: Idea Group. doi:10.4018/978-1-59904-213-8.ch006

Osland, J. S., De Franco, S., & Osland, A. (1999). Organizational implications of Latin American culture. *Journal of Management Inquiry*, *8*(2), 219–234. doi:10.1177/105649269982018

Otto, D. (1997). Rethinking the 'universality' of human rights. *Columbia Human Rights Law Review*, *29*, 1–46.

Panetta, C. G. (Ed.). (2000). *Contrastive rhetoric revisited and redefined*. New York, NY: Routledge.

Pappen, U. (2009). Literacy, learning and health – A social practices view of health literacy. *Literacy and Numeracy Studies*, *16*(2), 19–34.

Participants, S. (2000). Responding to the legal obstacles to electronic commerce in Latin America: General Questionnaire. *Arizona Journal of International and Comparative Law*, *17*, 1–66.

Paz, O. (1985). *Labyrinth of solitude* (Kemp, L., Trans.). New York, NY: Grove Press.

Peerenboom, R. P. (2002). *China's long march toward rule of law*. Cambridge, UK: Cambridge University Press. doi:10.1017/CBO9780511493737

Pennycook, A. (1999). *Development, culture and language: Ethical concerns in a postcolonial world*. Retrieved from http://www.languages.ait.ac.th/hanoi_proceedings/contents.htm

Perani, D., & Abutaleb, J. (2005). The neural basis of first and second language processing. *Current Opinion in Neurobiology*, *15*(2), 202–206. doi:10.1016/j.conb.2005.03.007

Perelman, C. (1982). *The realm of rhetoric*. Notre Dame, IN: University of Notre Dame Press.

Pike, K. (1967). *Language in relation to a unified theory of the structure of human behavior*. de Gruyter Mouton.

Pinaud, R., Tremere, L. A., & De Weerd, P. (Eds.). (2006). *Plasticity in the visual system: From genes to circuits*. New York, NY: Springer. doi:10.1007/0-387-28190-8

Pinker, S. (2003). *The blank slate*. New York, NY: Penguin Books.

Plato,. (1956). *Phaedrus*. New York, NY: Macmillan Publishing.

Porter, J. E. (1986). Intertextuality and the discourse community. *Rhetoric Review*, *5*, 34–47. doi:10.1080/07350198609359131

Porter, J. E. (1998). *Rhetorical ethics and internetworked writing*. Greenwich, CT: Ablex Publishing.

Porter, J., Sullivan, P., Blythe, S., Grabil, J. T., & Miles, L. (2000). Institutional critique: A rhetorical methodology for change. *College Composition and Communication*, *51*(4), 610–642. doi:10.2307/358914

Press Series, New Dimensions in Computers and Composition.

Purnell, L., & Paulanka, B. (2008). *Guide to culturally competent health care* (2nd ed.). F.A. Davis Company.

Pütz, M., & Verspoor, M. (Eds.). (2000). *Explorations in linguistic relativity*. Amsterdam, The Netherlands: John Benjamins Publishing Company.

Ramathan, V., & Atkinson, D. (1999). Individualism, academic writing, and ESL writers. *Journal of Second Language Writing*, *8*(1), 45–75. doi:10.1016/S1060-3743(99)80112-X

Reicher, S. D., Spears, R., & Postmes, T. T. (1995). A social identity model of deindividuation phenomena. *European Review of Social Psychology*, *6*(1), 161–198. doi:10.1080/14792779443000049

Reppen, R., Fitzmaurice, S. M., & Biber, D. (2002). *Using corpora to explore linguistic variation*. Philadelphia, PA: Johns Benjamin Publishing.

Retrieved November 21, 2009, from http://www. ncbi. nlm.nih. gov/pmc/ articles/ PMC1070887/

Retrieved October 26, 2009, from http://www.med-ed. virginia.edu/ public/ CourseSitesDocs/ IntrotoHuman-Behavior/ coursedocs/unrestricted/ pdf/CULTRELA. W2009.print. pdf

Reyes Lopez, M., & Aquila, L. (2006). Consentimiento informado en pacientes sometidos a cirugía por mínimo acceso. *Revista Cubana de Enfermeria*, *22*(4).

Rivers, P. A., & Patino, F. G. (2006). Barriers to health care access for Latino immigrants in the USA. *International Journal of Social Economics*, *33*(3), 207–220. doi:10.1108/03068290610646234

Rosa, M., Goins, K., Carbone, E., & Cortes, D. (2004). Views and preferences of low-literate Hispanics regarding diabetes education: Results of formative research. *Health Education & Behavior*, *31*, 388–405. doi:10.1177/1090198104263360

Rose, L. C. (1978). *Disease beliefs in Mexican-American communities*. California: R & E Research Associates, Inc.

Rosenfeld, M. (2000). Human rights, nationalism, and multiculturalism in rhetoric, ethics, and politics: A pluralist critique. *Cardozo Law Review*, *21*, 1225–1241.

Rosenn, K. (1988). A comparison of Latin American and North American legal traditions. In Tavis, L. (Ed.), *Multinational managers and host government interactions* (pp. 127–152). South Bend, IN: University of Notre Dame Press.

Rossett, A. (Ed.). (2001). *ASTD e-learning handbook*. New York, NY: McGraw-Hill.

Said, E. (1979). *Orientalism*. New York, NY: Vintage Books.

Salvo, M., & Rosinki, P. (2009). Information design: From authoring text to architecting virtual space. In Spilka, R. (Ed.), *Digital literacy for technical communication: 21st Century theory and practice* (pp. 103–127). London, UK: Routledge.

Scott, J. B., Longo, B., & Wills, K. V. (Eds.). (2006). *Critical power tools: Technical communication and cultural studies*. SUNY Series, Studies in Scientific and Technical Communication.

Shi, W. (2010). Globalization and indigenization: Legal transplant of a universal TRIPS regime in a multicultural world. *American Business Law Journal*, *47*, 455–506. doi:10.1111/j.1744-1714.2010.01101.x

Shohet, L. (2004). Health and literacy: Perspectives. *Literacy and Numeracy Studies*, *13*(1), 65–84.

Short, J., Williams, E., & Christie, B. (1976). *The social psychology of telecommunication*. London, UK: John Wiley.

Shrank, W. H., Kutner, J. S., Richardson, T., Mularski, R. A., Fischer, S., & Kagawa-Singer, M. (2005). Focus group findings about the influence of culture on communication preferences in end-of-life care. *Journal of General Internal Medicine*, *20*(8), 703–709. Retrieved November 13, 2009. doi:10.1111/j.1525-1497.2005.0151.x

Spack, R. (1997). The rhetorical construction of multilingual students. *TESOL Quarterly*, *31*(4), 765–774. doi:10.2307/3587759

Spears, R., & Lea, M. (1992). Social influence and the influence of the "social" in computer-mediated communication. In Lea, M. (Ed.), *Contexts of computer-mediated communication* (pp. 30–65). London, UK: Harvester-Wheatsheaf.

Specter, R. E. (1996). *Cultural diversity in health and illness*. Stamford, CT: Appleton & Lange.

Spilka, R. (Ed.). (2009). *Digital literacy for technical communication: 21st Century theory and practice*. London, UK: Routledge Press.

St.Amant, K. (Ed.). (2007). *Linguistic and cultural online communication issues in the global age*. Hershey, PA: IGI Global. doi:10.4018/978-1-59904-213-8

St.Amant, K. (2007a). Online education in an age of globalization: Foundational perspectives and practices for technical communication instructors and trainers. *Technical Communication Quarterly*, *16*, 13–30.

Starke-Meyerring, D., & Wilson, M. (Eds.). (2008). *Designing globally networked learning environments: Visionary partnerships, policies, and pedagogies*. Rotterdam, The Netherlands: Sense Publishers.

Stewart, E., & Bennett, M. (1991). *American cultural patterns: A cross-cultural perspective* (Rev. ed.). Yarmouth, ME: Intercultural Press, Inc.

Street, B. (Ed.). (2001). *Literacy and development: Ethnographic perspectives*. London, UK: Routledge. doi:10.4324/9780203468418

Sullivan, P., & Porter, J. E. (1998). *Opening spaces: Writing technologies and critical research practices*. Greenwich, CT: Ablex.

Sutch, P. (2001). *Ethics, justice, and international relations: Constructing an international community*. New York, NY: Routledge.

Swaak, M., de Jong, M., & de Vries, P. (2009). Effects of information usefulness, visual attractiveness, and usability on web visitors' trust and behavioral intentions. *IEEE International Professional Communication Conference*, (pp. 1-5).

Swales, J. (1997). English as Tyrannosaurus Rex. *World Englishes*, *16*, 373–382. doi:10.1111/1467-971X.00071

Tamanaha, B. Z. (2006). *Law as a means to an end: Threat to the rule of law*. Cambridge, UK: Cambridge University Press. doi:10.1017/CBO9780511511073

Tate, D. M. (2003). Cultural awareness: Bridging the gap between caregivers and Hispanic patients. *Journal of Continuing Education in Nursing*, *34*(5), 213–217. Retrieved from http://www.jcenonline.com/view.asp?rID=4526.

Thatcher, B. (1997). *Orality and writing in Latin American and USA professional communication.* Unpublished doctoral dissertation, Purdue University.

Thatcher, B. (2001). Issues of validity in intercultural professional communication research. *Journal of Business and Technical Communication*, *15*(4), 458–489. doi:10.1177/105065190101500403

Thatcher, B. (2006). Intercultural rhetoric, technology, and writing in Mexican maquilas. *Special Technology Transfer Edition of Technical Communication Quarterly*, *15*(3), 383–405.

Thatcher, B. (2007a). Online education in an age of globalization: Foundational perspectives and practices for technical communication instructors and trainers. *Technical Communication Quarterly*, *16*, 13–30.

Thatcher, B., Barrantes, E., Dalzell, A., Dong, Q., Ford, C., & Klein, S. … Ramirez, L. (2007). Website analysis across cultures. In K. St. Amant (Ed.), *Linguistic and cultural online communication issues in the global age* (pp.124-142). Hershey, PA: Idea Group.

Thatcher, B., & St.Amant, K. (Eds.). (2010). *Teaching intercultural rhetoric and technical communication: Theories, curriculum, pedagogies, and practices*. Baywood Publishing.

Thatcher, B. with Urbina, N. (2010). Comunicación médica y de salud en la región fronteriza de México y Los Estados Unidos. In V. Garza Almanza & B. Thatcher (Eds.), *Comunicación médica y científica en México*. Casa Editorial de El Colegio de Chihuahua: Ciudad Juárez, Chihuahua, México.

Thatcher, B. L. (1999). Cultural and rhetorical adaptations for South American audiences. *Technical Communication, 46*(2), 177–195.

Thatcher, B. L. (2000). Writing policies and procedures in a U.S. and South American context. *Technical Communication Quarterly, 94*, 365–400. doi:10.1080/10572250009364706

Thatcher, B. L. (2001). Issues of validity in intercultural professional communication research. *Journal of Business and Technical Communication, 15*(4), 458–489. doi:10.1177/105065190101500403

Thatcher, B. L. (2006). Intercultural rhetoric, technology, and writing in Mexican maquilas. *Special Technology Transfer Edition of Technical Communication Quarterly, 15*(3), 383–405.

Thatcher, B. L. (2009). Understanding digital literacy across cultures. In Spilka, R. (Ed.), *Digital literacy for technical communication: 21st Century theory and practice* (pp. 169–198). London: Routledge.

Thatcher, B. L. (2010). Reading and writing new media across cultures: Issues of fit, reciprocity, and cultural change. In Kalmbach, J., & Ball, C. (Eds.), *Reading and writing new media*. Hampton Press Series New Dimensions in Computers and Composition.

Thatcher, B. L. (2010a). Introduction. In *Rhetoric, Professional Communication, and Globalization, 1*, 1-34.

Timmerman, C. E. (2002). The moderating effect of mindlessness/mindfulness upon media richness and social influence explanations of organizational media use. *Communication Monographs, 69*, 111–131. doi:10.1080/714041708

Tokar, B. (2009). *Social ecology: Resistance and reconstruction.* Retrieved from http://news.infoshop.org/article.php?story=2009050612390170. December, 2010.

Triandis, H. C. (1995). *Individualism and collectivism*. Westview Press.

Trompenaars, F. (1994). *Riding the waves of culture: Understanding diversity in global business*. New York, NY: McGraw Hill.

Tseng, W. S., & Streltzer, J. (2008). *Cultural competence in health care*. Springer. doi:10.1007/978-0-387-72171-2

Twining, W. (2000). *Globalisation and legal theory*. Cambridge, UK: Cambridge University Press.

Ulrey, K. L., & Amason, P. (2001). Intercultural communication between patients and health care providers: An exploration of intercultural communication effectiveness, cultural sensitivity, stress, and anxiety. *Health Communication, 13*(4), 449–463. doi:10.1207/S15327027HC1304_06

UNESCO. (2002). *Using open and distance learning: Technology, curriculum, cost, and evaluation*. Paris, France: Higher Education Division, Teacher Education Section.

Uzuner, S. (2009). Questions of culture in distance learning: A research review. *International Review of Research in Open and Distance Learning, 10*(3), 1–17.

Van Hoecke, M., & Warrington, M. (1998). Legal cultures, legal paradigms and legal doctrine: Towards a new model for comparative law. Cambridge University Press.. *The International and Comparative Law Quarterly, 47*, 495–536. doi:10.1017/S0020589300062163

Varner, I., & Beamer, L. (2011). *Intercultural communication in the global workplace*. Richard D Irwin, Inc.

Verhulsdonck, G. (2010). *Virtual Chironomia: A multimodal study of verbal and non-verbal communications in a virtual world.* Unpublished dissertation, New Mexico State University.

Victor, D. (1992). *International business communication*. New York, NY: HarperCollins Publishers.

Vila, P. (2000). *Crossing borders, reinforcing borders: Social categories, metaphors and narrative identities on the U.S.-Mexico frontier*. Austin, TX: University of Texas Press.

Walther, J. B. (1992). Interpersonal effects in computer-mediated interaction: A relational perspective. *Communication Research, 19*, 52–90. doi:10.1177/009365092019001003

Walther, J. B. (1992). Interpersonal effects in computer-mediated interaction: A relational perspective. *Communication Research, 19*, 52–90. doi:10.1177/009365092019001003

Walther, J. B. (1996). Computer-mediated communication: Impersonal, interpersonal, and hyperpersonal interaction. *Communication Research, 23*, 3–43. doi:10.1177/009365096023001001

Wang, M. (2007). Designing online courses that effectively engage learners from diverse cultural backgrounds. *British Journal of Educational Technology, 38*(2), 294–311. doi:10.1111/j.1467-8535.2006.00626.x

Weick, K. with Sutcilffe, K. (2001). *Managing the unexpected: Assuring high performance in an age of complexity*. Jossey-Bass

White, J. (1985). *The legal imagination*. University of Chicago Press.

Whorf, B. L. (1956). The relation of habitual thought and behavior to language. In Carrol, J. B. (Ed.), *Language, thought, and reality: Selected writings of Benjamin Lee Whorf* (pp. 134–150). Cambridge, MA: Technology Press of Massachusetts Institute of Technology.

Wiley, D. A. (2000). Connecting learning objects to instructional design theory: A definition, a metaphor, and a taxonomy. In D. A. Wiley (Ed.), *The instructional use of learning objects: Online Version*. Retrieved from http://www.reusability.org read/chapters/wiley.doc

Williams, J. (2009). *Style: Basics of clarity and grace* (3rd ed.). New York, NY: Pearson Longmann.

Winsor, D. (1996). *Writing like an engineer: A rhetorical education*. Mahwah, NJ: Lawrence Erlbaum Associates.

Zhang, Y. (2008). Social science or social control: Qualitative researchers' dilemma in contrastive rhetoric. *Small Cities Imprint, 1*(1), 15–20.

Zizek, S., Laclau, E., & Butler, J. (2011). *Contingency, hegemony, and universality: Contemporary dialogues on the left* (2nd ed.). Verso.

About the Author

Barry Thatcher is an Associate Professor of Rhetoric and Professional Communication at New Mexico State University and "Profesor Asociado" at El Colegio de Chihuahua, Ciudad Juárez, Mexico. He is Founder and Editor-in-Chief of *The Journal of Rhetoric, Professional Communication, and Globalization* and Co-Editor of *La Revista Latinoamericana de Retorica*. He has published widely on the area of intercultural professional communication and rhetoric, rhetoric in Latin America, border literacy, and research methods. He has worked in a large variety of cross-border and globalization projects, including health, transportation, security, technology transfer, and education.

Index

F

G

H

I

L

M

N

O

P

Q

R

S

T

U

www.ingramcontent.com/pod-product-compliance
Lightning Source LLC
LaVergne TN
LVHW062140200926
848484LV00007B/1837